SOCIAL PSYCHOLOGY THROUGH SYMBOLIC INTERACTION

SOCIAL PSYCHOLOGY THROUGH SYMBOLIC INTERACTION

SECOND EDITION

GREGORY P. STONE
UNIVERSITY OF MINNESOTA

HARVEY A. FARBERMAN
STATE UNIVERSITY OF NEW YORK AT STONY BROOK

JOHN WILEY & SONS   NEW YORK   CHICHESTER   BRISBANE   TORONTO

Library of Congress Cataloging in Publication Data:

Stone, Gregory Prentice, 1921–   comp.
  Social psychology through symbolic interaction.

Includes bibliographical references and index.
    1.   Social psychology—Addresses, essays,
lectures.   2.   Social interaction—Addresses,
essays, lectures.   I.   Farberman, Harvey A.
II.   Title.
HM251.S818   1981   302   80-23770
ISBN 0-471-03029-5

Printed in the United States of America.

10 9 8 7 6 5 4 3 2 1

To Herbert Blumer, teacher and scholar, who has kept the perspective of symbolic interaction alive and lively in the continuing dialogue that we call social psychology

and

To Issei Misumi, who devoted an entire lifetime to distributing and cultivating the teachings of George Herbert Mead in the fertile intellectual soil of Japanese scholarship and who built and reinforced yet another bridge between the East and the West

PREFACE

The first edition of SOCIAL PSYCHOLOGY THROUGH SYMBOLIC INTERACTION sought to engage audiences at various levels of technical preparation including undergraduate students, graduate trainees, and professional practitioners. To do so, it included material at various levels of technical difficulty arranged in a fashion that displayed historical development, interdisciplinary relevance, and research innovation. The selections in this second edition were chosen with undergraduate students in mind and accordingly follow a pedagogical rather than an investigatory format. Whereas the first edition contained sixty-nine articles organized into ten parts, plus an extensive appendix, this edition contains forty articles organized into seven parts. Thirteen of these forty articles are new to this edition. We also have markedly reorganized the presentation in a way that (we hope) is both accessible to students *and* gives emphasis to areas of emerging concern within the field. This reorganization applies in equal measure to the sequencing of chapters, the content of chapters, and the interstitial material that introduces each of the chapters and the book as a whole.

In Part One, entitled Situations, Staging, and Awareness Contexts, we emphasize the uniquely human ability to construct reality through the proferring, arranging, and manipulating of "definitions of the situation." These definitions may be implemented through verbal, gestural, or physical means and may be executed overtly (or covertly), and honestly (or deceptively), in a manner that others may become aware of (or not). Part Two, Interaction, reinforces the idea that, symbol-using actors, far from reacting automatically to their surrounding environments, change those environments as they themselves are changed. This human transaction, moreover, is cross-cut by both cognitive and affectual dimensions which have great potency and impact; life is drenched with feelings and emotions that powerfully disrupt, integrate, include, and exclude people. Out of this already ongoing universe of interaction the self emerges. Part Three, devoted entirely to the Self, traces the development of a way of thinking about this crucial phenomenon. There we present the classic formulations of William James, Charles H. Cooley, George H. Mead, and Harry S. Sullivan. Gregory P. Stone's research seeks to bring these contributions into a single frame of reference, while the more recent contribution of Ralph H. Turner links the self to the larger social process.''

Part Four, Socialization as a Life Process, suggests how human actors—with selves—develop *and continue* to develop throughout the entire life cycle as they pass from childhood to adolescence to adulthood. Part Five, Motives, deals with how people ''explain'' to themselves, and others, why they are doing what they are doing; it shows how people keep each other in line or get away with stepping out of line. Part Six, The Politics of Reality, illustrates how those who depart from conventional expectations are thought to be ''sick'' and, as such, are kept under some state of surveillance. The point is that deviance is not contained in an act but in the judgments conferred upon the act. Part Seven, Developments and Debates, presents a review of the last decade and a half of the field of symbolic interaction, assesses developments in neighboring fields, and examines modes of logical inquiry used by interactionists. In all, we have attempted to provide students with access to the perspective of symbolic interaction without unduly compromising its depth, richness, and utility. Each part of this book is introduced with a section by the editors that seeks simultaneously to cast the ensuing readings in the larger perspective of symbolic interaction and to summarize the gist of those readings. We recommend that students read those introductions at least twice, both before and after completing the readings in each part of the book.

Finally, we wish to thank those students, friends, colleagues, and critics who, in various ways, have helped us in the preparation of this edition. If we have neglected some, we hope they will excuse that all too common, but unintended, flaw of human memory. Those who come most readily to mind are Howard Becker, Herbert Blumer, Carl Couch, David R. Crist, Norman K. Denzin, Dorothy J. Elrod, Judith Erickson, Nelson Foote, Frank P. Forwood, Charles E. Frazier, Elihu Gerson, William J. Gooder, Peter M. Hall, Richard Harman, Eileen Imaba, David R. Maines, Suzanne McMillan, Clark McPhail, Thomas J. Morrione, John W. Petras, R. S. Perinbanayagam, Raymond L. Schmitt, Robert Stewart, Gladys I. Stone, Richard V. Travisano, Charles W. Tucker, Ralph Turner, Allan Turowetz, and William C. Yoels.

GREGORY P. STONE
HARVEY A. FARBERMAN

CONTENTS

INTRODUCTION

A distinctive mark of all science is the persistence of problems and the obsolescence of theories.[1] Important problems persist; theories die. In fact, the history of any science can be looked upon as a graveyard of theories. In sociology, the paradox of society's persistence and the individual's uniqueness continues to mobilize scientific inquiry. Kant's formulation of man's "asocial sociability" captured this paradox, and theories of social psychology have long addressed themselves to this problem. How can we explain how men are held together and, at the same time, set apart? The science of social psychology can be viewed as a continuing disciplined dialogue focused upon this question. By and large, the dialogue has singled out either the bonds that tie people together or the variables that presumably account for individual differences. This book emphasizes that the very fact of man's sociability is a basis for his uniqueness and that his uniqueness is a basis for his sociability.

For us, the perduring question is: What is the meaning of the personal life? Observations of reflex (as opposed to reflective) behavior, conditioned (as opposed to interpretive) behavior, and bodies (as opposed to persons) simply have no general *relevance* for our conversation. Herbert Blumer made the point when he frequently raised this question in his lectures on social psychology: "What is the difference between the accounts of a physicist observing a falling object and those of a social psychologist observing two people falling in love?"[2] By raising this question, Blumer was suggesting that there is a multifaceted set of transactions established between the social psychological observer and the objects of his inquiry. This is fundamentally different from the interaction established between the physicist and his objects of inquiry. People think; particles don't. For us, six questions demarcate the field of social psychology from the standpoint of symbolic interaction:

1. What is meaning?

2. How does the personal life take on meaning?

[1]See the preliminary remarks of Dennis H. Wrong, "The Oversocialized Conception of Man in Modern Society," *American Sociological Review*, XXVI (April, 1961), pp. 183–193.

[2]The question obviously implies something other than the "principle of indeterminancy" in physics, something other than the fact that the measurement of an object in one dimension, for example, velocity, distorts measurements accomplished in another dimension, for example, location, and vice versa. Cf. R. Rosenthal, *Experimenter Effects in Behavioral Research* (New York: Appleton-Century-Crofts, 1966).

3. How does the meaning persist?

4. How is the meaning transformed?

5. How is the meaning lost?

6. How is the meaning regained?

In asking such questions, we eschew the notion that meaning is preeminently a philosophical or speculative matter. We shall regard meaning as objective or behavioral after the fashion of George H. Mead. Specifically, the problem of personal meaning lies in the forefront of our conversation and gives it its relevance. Meaning, however, can only be established in communication. Should the reader deny this, quite clearly we cannot discuss it!

OBJECTIVE MEANING AND THE ANALYSIS OF COMMUNICATION

Essentially two strains of development need to be distinguished in the analysis of meaning proposed by symbolic interaction. Over the history of pragmatism, the "philosophy" in which symbolic interaction finds its roots, a line of inquiry attends to the instrumental nature of meaning, culminating in the vastly simplified dictum: *the meaning of an object is in its use*. The profound implication is to place meaning in the act, the process, rather than the object, the thing. In George H. Mead's happy example,

> . . . one has a nail to drive, he reaches for a hammer and finds it gone, and does not stop to look for it, but reaches for something else he can use, a brick, a stone, anything having the necessary weight to give momentum to the blow. Anything he can get hold of that will serve the purpose of a hammer. The sort of response which involves the grasping of a heavy object is a universal.[3]

A chair, then, is something we sit on, and, as any child knows, a bat is anything we can hit a ball with. Mead goes on to say that such universals are also concepts (etymologically what we seize *together*) and are opposed to percepts. As such, they are found in language that makes it possible for *us* to hold on to them. This is a fundamental transition in the investigative focus of pragmatism. It moves from psychological concerns to a genuine "social pragmatism."[4] Meaning is placed *in* communication. It is this second contribution of pragmatism that has been picked up and nurtured by sociologists and social psychologists concerned with the frame of reference called symbolic interaction.

Language, a central concern of symbolic interaction, is preeminently social. Indeed, humanity has been conceived as *homo sapiens* (man the wise). It might better be described

---

[3]George H. Mead, *Mind, Self, and Society* (Chicago: University of Chicago Press, 1934), p. 83.

[4]For an elaboration of this point, see Gregory P. Stone and Harvey A. Farberman, "On the Edge of Rapprochement: Was Durkheim Moving Toward the Perspective of Symbolic Interaction?" *Sociological Quarterly*, VIII (Spring, 1967), pp. 149—164. Quite independently, H. S. Thayer has also comprehended Mead's perspective as "social pragmatism." See his *Meaning and Action* (Indianapolis: Bobbs-Merrill Co., Inc., 1973), a shortened version of his book first published in 1968. In the short version, the relevant pagination is pp. 206—210.

as man the languaged communicator, since people frequently do not display much wisdom in their communications. Yet, we are involved with language in many ways that extend beyond communication. It is always a collective *re*-presentation, as Emile Durkheim put it. It represents our membership in larger collectivities *to* ourselves and others—nations or areas within nations—states such as Arkansas, Hawaii, or Texas; even smaller social territories, like Flatbush or Beacon Hill. As a collective representation, language is often passionately embraced and imposed on those who may not speak it ''naturally'' but live in the space claimed for it.

In 1955, for example, the Charter of the French Language was adopted by the provincial legislature of Quebec, Canada, an area peopled by five million French Canadians and one million English-speaking residents. The bill has 232 sections, one of which makes a strong argument for sending all the children of newcomers to French schools, though ''loopholes'' were later provided to appease the highly embittered English-speaking minority and ease the recruitment problem of large corporations based in Montreal. Other sections of the charter make the knowledge of French mandatory for all professionals and the use of French mandatory on product labels and in official communications of larger businesses. Powerful minorities have also imposed their language on subordinate majorities or, as in South Africa, forbidden its use by such majorities. In the latter instance, the segregation of languages gave rise to open hostilities and bloodshed. Thus, the social nature of language is intricate and complex, and pervades many dimensions of the larger society.

In the final analysis, however, the meaning of language arises, is maintained, and changes in communication, in our view another term for symbolic interaction. We attempt here to develop a model for the analysis of this process from the standpoint of the one who initiates a communication eventuating in the establishment of meaningful discourse or conversation between two persons. Let us take a very simplified example—two persons in ''communication.'' Person A ''presents'' or ''gives off'' a spate of symbolism (S) to Person B, who ''responds'' (R). See Figure 1. The meaning of A's symbolism, then, is the response of the other, and this seems easy enough to grasp. Yet, there are great complexities even here, and they raise a range of questions for the symbolic interactionist.

Just what is symbolism? Certainly it includes not only language, as Freud, Jung, and Harry Stack Sullivan have told us, using psychoanalytic and psychiatric perspectives; or as Erving Goffman, Edward T. Hall, and Raymond Birdwhistell have emphasized, using sociological and anthropological perspectives. Symbols may include any aspect of human action—a change in ''gaze-line,'' a change in breathing tempo, a blush, a posturing of the body, clothing, makeup, hair sculpture or disarray, or, of course, a languaged statement. The list is almost endless.

You will also notice that we have used the terms *presents* and *gives off*. Here we wish to catch the setting forth of symbols within the limits of awareness of all the dimensions of this simplified version of communications—A and B, the symbolism, and B's ''response.'' When one is highly aware of himself and the other, his symbolism, and the other's response, we say that he is *aware*. In this sense, his symbolism is *presented*. At the other extreme, one may be totally unaware of most facets of his communication. Examples would include one's talk while sleeping when heard by a bed partner, or slips of

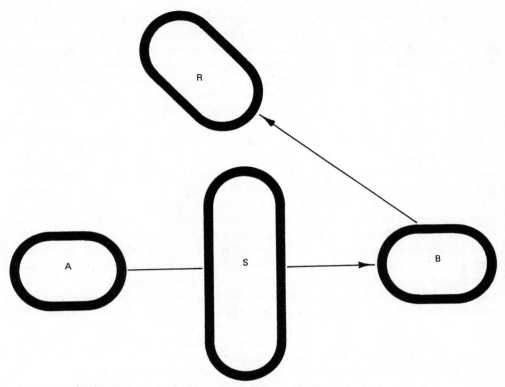

FIGURE 1.   The meaning of A's symbolism (S) as in B's response (R).

the tongue. Such communications, in our terms, are *given off*. These are obviously extreme examples, and it seems correct to assert that every communication must be examined in terms of both awareness and out-of-awareness contexts.

A further complication is provided by the fact that one can be aware of one's awareness, as is the case with sentries, military scouts, those on outpost in military combat, or anyone in a reconnaisance position—spies, hotel detectives, and double agents. Too, one may be aware that "something" lies outside one's awareness. One may have a vague feeling that something's wrong, but can't put a finger on it, or "something's going on here, but I can't figure out what."[5]

By *response,* we merely mean that B presents or gives off another spate of symbolism—not merely a change in "motor activity," as some psychologists define it, or a change in motion. Thus, the analysis of response carries with it all the complexity we have discussed with reference to symbolism. There is also the matter of determining just who these two persons, A and B, are, even in this elementary analytical model.

[5]This discussion owes much to the work of Herman Schmalenbach. See his *On Society and Experience,* edited, translated and with an introduction by Günther Lüschen and Gregory P. Stone (Chicago: University of Chicago Press, 1977), especially pp. 76–77 and p. 258, footnote 6.

However, the diagram is inadequate at the end. A lecturer lectures, that is, presents and gives off a spate of symbolism, to his students who fall asleep. If we used the model in Figure 1, the lecture would be interpreted as a lullaby, for its meaning is in the response of the students. Were we to inform the lecturer of our find, he would surely be appalled and would probably protest that a lullaby was not quite what he had in mind. In other words, the symbolic interactionist must take into account both the response of the other *and* the one presenting and giving off symbolism. Moreover, there must be some "overlap" or coincidence between the two responses, and it is in this "overlap" that "true" meaning, in the sense used in this book, is established.

How is such meaning established or guaranteed? In the simplest dimension, we can turn to an analysis of the "vocal gesture," a term employed by George H. Mead, for the analysis of rudimentary social meaning, for one's vocalizations come to one's own ears about the way they come to the ears of the other. Figure 2 captures the idea. This is the way early cybernetics or "feedback theory" conceptualized the act of communication, and such theory has since been considerably extended. Still, the conceptualization seems to us inadequate for the full-blown analysis of meaningful communication. How do the deaf learn to vocalize? To mention only one other shortcoming, it cannot, at this point, effectively handle the affective dimensions of communication or the establishment of moods as meaningful. How does one's hostility to another bring out hostility in others? How do two people "fall in love"? How can one's anxiety make the other anxious? How

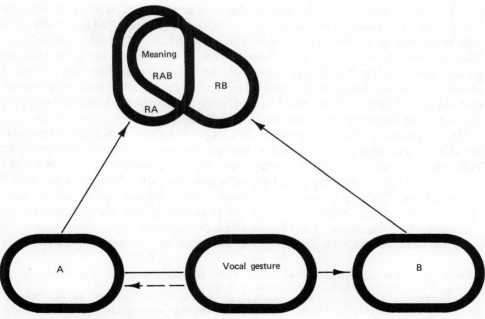

FIGURE 2.   The significant vocal gesture.

are fright and terror communicated? We could go on, and we invite the student to think it over and imagine further examples.

Above all, Figure 2 neglects the *re*-presentative nature of symbolism which is made possible, as Mead puts it, by placing one's self in the attitude (incipient act) of the other or by the more familiar phrase "role-taking." Through such processes, Mead points out, meaning is guaranteed in communication. One places one's self in the attitude of the other and, from that standpoint, directs symbols back to himself, calling out in himself the response of the other. The other employs the same techniques, calling out in himself the communicator's response to his own symbolism. To return to the lecture: in our sense, a meaningful lecture occurs when the lecturer speaks the students' words and the students write his. Of course, the overlap is never complete, for the lecture and note-taking are self-mediated, and selves always extend beyond single identities. The student is never merely a student, nor the lecturer merely a lecturer. Every communication includes more identities than bodies. Put in another way, we always carry a load of "identity freight" along with us. Thus, we always "play" and "take" more than one role at a time, and a role is best construed as those attitudes mobilized by an identity in a specified social situation.

However, we think the phrase "role-taking" is unnecessarily restrictive. True, we do place ourselves in the incipient act of the other, and this is a very concrete, physiologically grounded process, as may be seen when the listener blurts out the stutterer's word, in the contagion of the yawn, or when we call up in ourselves the sound of the other's voice in its absence. Indeed, a lecturer can often detect the voice of a respected teacher in his own voice. That such an assumption of the other's attitude is physiologically grounded may be seen in sport. Watching a high-jumper, the spectator may raise his own leg. At a boxing match or merely watching a film or televised production of a match, one may come away with biceps aching. The bowler may even "take the attitude" of the ball, attempting to affect its course down the alley with "body English." Who's to say that communication through ESP (if it, in fact, occurs) is not linked up to the process? Even some forms of cancer may be manifestations of "role-taking." Specifically, the death of a beloved husband or wife from cancer is often followed by the development of cancer in the spouse with a relative frequency, or probability, greater than "chance."[6]

The process often includes an affective dimension, "sympathy," which is not given its due share of consideration in the more cognitive treatment of meaning and communication by George H. Mead. Figure 3 presents this model of meaning and the essentials of Mead's behavioral analysis of meaning.[7] We have substituted the phrase "empathic processes" for "role-taking" because it seems more general, and it includes at least three dimensions of "taking the attitude of the other": (1) sheer physiological empathy (often out-of-awareness); (2) "role-taking"; and (3) the forms of sympathy.

Again, there are problems. First, how can we empathize with and, in particular, take

---

[6]We are indebted to our colleague, Robert Fulton, of the University of Minnesota, long a student of the sociology of death and bereavement, for documentation of this point.

[7]For an alternative, but more formal and more processual model, see H. S. Thayer, *ibid.*, pp. 190−200. The focus there is on a schematization of George H. Mead's view of gestures and significant symbols as their social use gives rise to the self—a place where we begin.

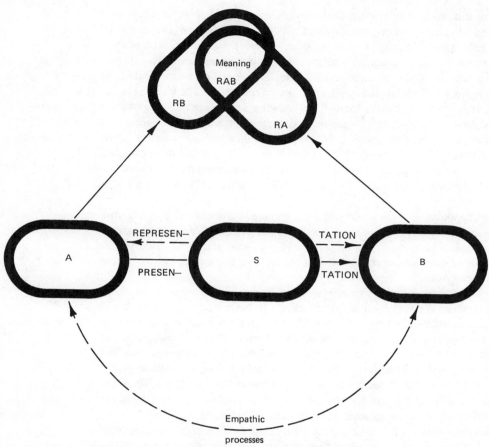

FIGURE 3. Meaningful communication from the standpoint of George H. Mead.

the role of the other without knowing who or what the other one is? Second, even knowing who or what the other one is, how can one anticipate the other's conduct without knowing what the situation is?

Appearance, Situation, and Circumstance Verbal communication is built upon at least three dimensions of silence which serve to let those who are in communication build images of (personify) one another and place those images in context so that reasonably accurate empathy can be accomplished. Of course, the silence may be broken at any time by direct questions—"Who do you think you are?" or, perhaps better, "Who do you think I am?" Ordinarily, however, such information is *presented* silently, as one dresses up, down, or out for an encounter, sculptures the hair, prepares the face, teeth, and hands; or is *given off*. When such information is given off, the one appearing (the apparition?) is unaware of the information conveyed. For example, the hotel detective, seeking to detect a known thief, discounts the face. That can always be altered. Instead, he pays careful attention to posture and gait, which are out of the awareness of most people (except very careful thieves and hustlers, models, and actors). Such symbolism we call *personal appearance,* and such appearances are "read" constantly during encounters with others.

However, situations are also "read," and they may also be *presented* or staged. Imagine two parties scheduled for the same social circle. The same bodies are invited. At the first party, the lights are dimmed. Bach or Corelli are on the stereo. The host(ess) seats the guests in the living room and asks them their drinking preference. The drinks are served on a tray. Coasters are provided. At the next party, the lights are a bit brighter (not too bright!). The host(ess) greets the guests in loose sports clothes and indicates that "The drinks are in the kitchen. Help yourselves!" The stereo spews disco, and the carpet has been rolled back. Quite obviously, the spirals of action and the attitudes mobilized are differentiated by the variation in staging. The two parties will have different careers. The bodies remain the same.

As is the case with appearance ("Who do you think you are?"), questions may interrupt such staging. One may well ask, "What's up?" or "What's going on?" In such cases, the definition of the situation becomes a matter of discourse or conversation. Usually such discursive definitions of situations occur, as W. I. Thomas said, in moments of crisis or at turning points in interaction.

Yet, situations themselves occur in contexts, often beyond the awareness of those caught up in encounters. We call such larger contexts *circumstances,* for they "stand around" situations. These are "taken-for-granted" aspects of interaction. Language is probably the most enveloping circumstance, and in encounters, we do take language for granted. We have already suggested the pervasive dimensions of language, of that circumstance. Sex, age, and status may also be circumstances for some, but situations for others—transsexuals, patients of plastic surgeons, or those who "pass." Circumstance is a highly important source of context for interaction, usually silently established, but always subject, less easily than appearance and situation, to question.

Meaningful Situated Conduct   We have attempted to diagram this highly complicated process in Figure 4. Figure 4 indicates to the student, first, how complicated the analysis of one person's (A's) meaningful conduct is; and, second, how far the analysis of meaningful conduct has proceeded since its earlier embodiment in sociality. Of course, a student cannot be expected to comprehend such complexity early on in a text. Consequently, we hope that our readers will return, from time to time, to this paradigm or model to assist their understanding of further materials.

Right now, we ask the reader to let his vision glide over the diagram to these places and in these directions. First, consider the oblong at the left of the diagram, called "A's Self." Second, consider the oblong at the right of the diagram, called "B's Self." Third, note that the relationship of A and B is "boxed in" by a kind of wall called "Situation." Fourth, note that, like all walls, the situation has at least an outside (Circumstances) and an inside. Fifth, consider the complexity of what is portrayed within the wall. Finally, attempt to follow the communicative process from bottom to top, that is, from "apparent symbolism" to "discursive meaning." We shall elaborate on these "places" and "pathways" in the diagram to assist an initial comprehension, or a grasping together by all of us of the object or model.

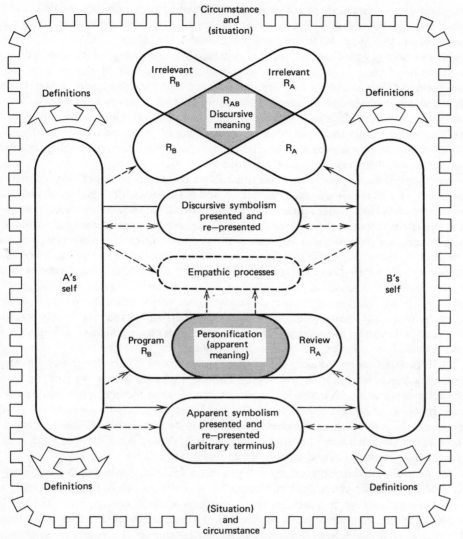

FIGURE 4. Model for the analysis of meaningful situated conduct from the standpoint of A.

First, the student should realize that the diagram, as complex as it seems, is an oversimplification. Moreover, it has been designed from the standpoint of A, for social psychology is interested in the personal life—acts or conduct. Thus, B need not be present for the analysis of A's meaningful act, though he/she/they must be taken into account. The symbolic interactionist begins his analysis on the assumption that one's act takes on meaning in the response of some other who may or may not be physically there; physically *re*-presented, as by a voice on a phone, a stationery letterhead, or a distinctive script; or imaginatively *re*-presented, *re*-constructed, or *re*-membered in or out of awareness at the time. Usually the other is not a single presence, *re*-presentation, memory, or *re*-construction. As Walt Whitman sang of himself, the other is large and contains multitudes; so it is with one's self (the self of which Whitman sang). It is easier to think of A as coming before B in a situation that each presumes will be the occasion for a conversation. The circumstance is such that each is clothed and physically poised (ready). Such nonverbal symbolisms enable a conversation that will employ a shared vocabulary. Often the shared circumstances within (or among) which definitions of the situation are made mean that single and separate selves are introduced. These selves are usually *given off,* especially among friends and familiar acquaintances, by the very clothing, postures, and gestures that are circumstantially provided.

Such nonverbal or apparent symbols are interpreted, and persons are built up more or less coherent with the situational definition. A and B are personified, that is, identities are announced and placed; values established for such identities, as value-symbols, are shown and appraised; moods are shared, as they are expressed and appreciated; and attitudes or incipient acts are proposed and anticipated, thereby activating the persons that have been constructed. From the standpoint of A, his personhood—identity, value, mood, and attitude—may be viewed as a program, the meaning of which is found in the review by B. A's program is, in a sense, an imagination of B's review, as B's review is an imagination of A's program. Thus, some consensual validation is established for the personification of A and B. When it is known who one another is in the defined situation, empathy is further facilitated. Obviously, the personification process cannot proceed without empathy, so we have arbitrarily terminated our analysis at that point.

Such personifications *always* transform the selves of those caught up in them. Following the personification, each may know a bit more surely who he is, or the interaction may take such a turn in this often silent phase of the interaction that each may find himself a person neither had intended to be. Some surprise or disappointment usually enters into the interaction at this phase. The point to be remembered is that appearances, like discussions, are always transforming of the self. At any point in time, none of us is ever precisely what he or she thought either was!

Knowing about who one another is, A presents a spate of words, but this is the way it seems. The symbolic interactionist observes that A places himself in the attitude of B, and from the standpoint of B represents those words to himself, calling out in himself B's response. In receiving those words, B proceeds in a reverse direction. Taking A's attitude, B *re*-presents A's words to himself, calling out in himself A's response. It is in the coincidence of these responses that A's words become meaningful or are understood. Obviously, there are areas of ambiguity, that is, where there is no overlap or coincidence. These areas may usually be traced to difficulties in the phases of appearance, empathy, or the intrusions of irrelevant identities from the "identity freight" of either A or B. But this discussion must seem very abstract to the student. Let us return to the example of the lecture. Students and the lecturer must personify one another as such. Staging and apparent symbolism make this possible. Given these personifications, each takes the other's role. The lecturer attempts to speak in the vocabulary of the student, and the student writes or summarizes the lecturer's words. When these symbolic responses coincide, the lecture will have been meaningful. Student and lecturer will have understood one another.

METAPHORS

Obviously, this model for the interpretation of the personal life presumes an image of man—a metaphor—and social psychology is replete with such images: *homo sapiens,* man as a member of a species; man as a machine, man as a computer; man as a goal-directed individual; man as a moving object. Our model presumes that man is a self-and-other designating agent who realizes a meaningful personal life in communication with present or absent others.

Underlying our emphasis is the matter of metaphors—images of man, society, communication, and their interrelations. For social psychology, the image of man is of crucial importance. Two fundamentally disparate images persist. First, man is conceived as a passive neutral agent buffeted about by stimuli that impinge upon his nerve endings. These stimuli may be external—reifications of society, culture, physical environment, or words and other symbols. They may also be internal—instincts, needs, or drives. Or they may be some combination of external and internal forces. Second, and in direct contrast, man is viewed as an active agent, selecting those stimuli or objects to which he shall respond, accomplishing his selections in the matrix of communication, and transforming his society or his social world in the process. Embracing one or the other of these metaphors, and we obviously embrace the latter, will determine the kind of questions the social psychologist raises about human conduct. *The question establishes the relevance of his observations.* Frequently, relevance has been confused with validity in social psychology.

RELEVANCE

An extreme example of this confusion may be found in an early effort by Floyd H. Allport to demonstrate that such concepts as "group" and "institution" did not permit explicit denotation.[8] In effect, Allport argued that if a physicist, a physiologist, and a behavioral psychologist were to come across a prostrate man during a nocturnal stroll, each would "stumble over," "see," and perhaps initiate a natural science investigation of the event. A sociologist, looking for a group, "would never encounter him at all."[9] Such a position incensed many sociologists. Louis Wirth, in his lectures at the University of Chicago, railed at Allport's contention, observing that only a sociologist would have made valid observations in the situation. Realizing that the prostrate man was preeminently a member

---

[8]Floyd H. Allport, " 'Group' and 'Institution' as Concepts in a Natural Science of Social Phenomena," in Ernest W. Burgess (ed.), *Personality and the Social Group* (Chicago: University of Chicago Press, 1929), pp. 162–180. Allport has since revised his argument, but the original statement carries with it the rhetorical advantage of clarifying the distinction between relevance and validity.

[9]*Ibid.,* p. 168. Allport presumed a "kickable" world. First, he missed the perspectival differences of physics, physiology, and behavioral psychology—the three people would ask different questions of the prostrate body. Second, and more important, he assumed that all objects are "kickable." On the fallacy of this point, see Simmons and McCall, "The Stolen Base as a Social Object," in Part One of this reader.

of social groups, Wirth argued that a sociologist would recognize immediately that the man carried a wallet containing a record of many of his group affiliations (identity freight), would notify those close to him of his condition, and, if necessary, would contact the appropriate religious representatives. In addition, the sociologist would know that groups existed precisely to cope with such emergencies. He would call the police, a hospital, or whatever agency was appropriate to the situation. (Undoubtedly, he would not call a specific individual policeman or doctor). In fact, Wirth defined sociology as the study of what is unique about man by virtue of the fact that everywhere and at all times he has lived in social groups. To be social is to be human, and this is the basic premise of sociology.

In such a way, psychologists and sociologists became polarized with regard to the place of social psychology in the social sciences, and the argument persists today. Note well that the argument centers not at all on the matter of validity, but on that of relevance. Neither Allport nor Wirth was correct, for the physicist, the physiologist, the behavioral psychologist, *and* the sociologist all would have been able to formulate statements about the prostrate figure. Each would have asked different questions. Talcott Parsons illustrated this nicely long ago:

> . . . the velocity of a man falling off a bridge, as he is about to strike the water is a physical fact. But if the person in question is a suicide it is certainly not proved by the statement of the fact that all the antecedents of which this velocity is a consequence can be explained in terms of the theory of mechanics. Similarly, if there has been a great rise in the price of wheat in the first few days of war, there is no proof that this fact . . . a fact relevant to the descriptive and analytic schemata of economics, can be satisfactorily explained in terms of the factors formulated in economic theory.[10]

Parsons' point was that any "piece of reality" is differentially relevant for different inquirers—a point reminiscent of the old tale about the encounter of blind men with an elephant. As Florian Znaniecki has written somewhere, concrete reality is inexhaustible. Indeed, our very formulated questions bring objects of inquiry into our disciplined conversation. It is simply not the other way around. Even in everyday conversation this is the case. Of course, the carrying on of a conversation requires that we know who one another is—a point not made in the tale of the elephant and the blind men.

Suppose a close friend were to call some Friday night and ask whether you were available for a blind date on the weekend. Some desperate readers might accept outright; others might be a bit more circumspect and ask who their friend had in mind. Suppose, then, the friend replied, "It's a member of the human species." Now, this statement conveys a fantastic amount of valid information (check any reference on human anatomy or physiology). Again, for some readers this amount of information may be adequate for arriving at their decision about the weekend; others may still insist on circumspection. Questions about age, education, occupation, and other characteristics of the species member undoubtedly would be raised during the telephone conversation. (Questions about sex are seldom asked!) The meaning of the potential blind date will be established only in the telephone conversation prior to the decision to accept or reject that particular future.

[10]Talcott Parsons, *The Structure of Social Action* (Glencoe, Ill.: The Free Press, 1949), p. 29.

Thereafter, the meaning may well be altered, but only in the communication that ensues with the blind date.

Or consider another apparently simple matter—the description of a room. Some time ago, one of us carried out a demonstration (by no means an experiment) of the point. At the outset of a course in social psychology, the students (about sixty) were asked to imagine that they were writing letters to friends and, for whatever reason, to list the three most important features of their classroom. Three weeks later, they were asked to imagine that they were social psychologists (admittedly difficult for some) and were writing letters to some other social psychologist. Here, again, for whatever reason, they were asked to list the three most important features of their classroom. Figure 5 presents the most outstanding differences in the listings. Clearly, the objects of observation changed emphatically in the three-week interim, although the room presumably remained much the same. The instructor and the students were regarded by some as features of the room at the outset, but their prominence had increased two- or threefold in the second trial. References to physical features, such as lights and windows, decreased by half over the time period. Mention of the blackboard (a means of communication as well as a "physical" object) decreased less in frequency. Most striking was that "behavior" was not considered part of the room by any student during the first trial, but was viewed in that manner by half the students in the second.[11]

In addition to the specific changes illustrated in Figure 5, the number of categories in terms of which the students' reports were classified decreased between the first and second

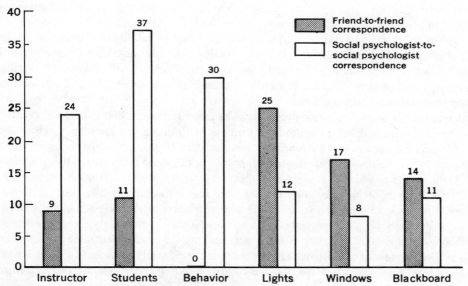

FIGURE 5. Perceptions of a room from different perspectives.

[11]This demonstration anticipates the importance of staging and defining situations. These things are taken up in more detail in Part One of this volume. This study was replicated in 1979, and essentially the same results were obtained.

trials. (In classifying the students' responses, an attempt was made to remain as true or close to their written materials as possible.) Features of the room listed by students writing to friends *as* friends generated forty descriptive categories. This number decreased to twenty-nine in the classification of descriptions made by students writing to social psychologists *as* social psychologists. Intimate communication undertaken on a first-name basis, as in the case of the communication between friends, in a sense expands the world of objects established by the communication. Less personal communication undertaken by those sharing the same titles or categories, as in the communication between social psychologists, constricts the world of objects established by the communication to the extent an analytical vocabulary is introduced that alters one's standpoint.

But to constrict the world of objects in communication enables a sharper focus, a deeper inquiry, and often a tighter analysis. In this respect, Veblen has spoken of the "trained incapacities" of those socialized into occupational identities and role performances ("seeing" is always simultaneously "not seeing"), while Dewey has conveyed the same notion with the phrase "occupational psychosis."

VALIDITY

Now the point is that observations may be relevant but not valid, or valid but not relevant, in addition to the other evident combinations of these distinctions. Our contention is that the argument between sociologists and psychologists about the proper place of social psychology has centered around two assertions: (1) that irrelevant observations are invalid; and (2) that valid observations are relevant. When we express our disagreement with such assertions, we must obviously turn to the matter of validity. This is the domain of method or, better, techniques of investigation. Criteria of validity lend discipline to the social psychological conversation about the meaning of the personal life. Three criteria of validity are conventionally proposed: universal applicability of statements, logical coherence of statements, and the consensus that such statements may be able to mobilize among competent observers.[12]

Universality   The criterion of universality asks that statements about whatever observation hold (established by replication), regardless of the time or the place in which the observation has been made. Presumably, then, in social psychology our statements about the meaning of the personal life ought to apply historically and cross-culturally. The latter stipulation seems rather easy to meet in these days of the Human Relations Area Files, Inc., but there are difficulties. First, as we have implied in our discussion of relevance, many of the cross-cultural studies that have been conducted ask questions that are, at best, only peripherally relevant to symbolic interaction. This is particularly the case because such questions about the meaning of the personal life have been generated by Freudian theory.[13] Our view of meaningful human conduct considerably transcends that of Freud. As we see it, Freud has made one seminal contribution to the study of meaningful human

[12]Lectures by Louis Wirth at the University of Chicago during the mid-1940s.

[13]See various studies of "personality and culture," for example, the work of Abraham Kardiner or Geoffrey Gorer. An earlier work remains relevant today. See Alfred R. Lindesmith and Anselm L. Strauss, "A Critique of Culture-Personality Writings," *American Sociological Review*, XV (October, 1950), pp. 587–600.

conduct: *Any instance of human conduct may be construed as symbolically significant*. If, as we shall see in this volume, the meaning of an object or an event is established in the mutual transactive responses of persons, then there is no call to single out sexual response as determinative of the meaning of the personal life.[14] Besides, the notion of mutual response or communication implies a universe of discourse—an ongoing relationship of common meanings or mutually adaptive responses. Freud, or more especially the Freudians, focus upon the family as a universe of discourse, particularly child-parent relations. Our view conceives the meaning of the personal life as established in any number of a wide variety of relationships that include the family but reach out into the world of work, politics, the peer group, the church, the circles of the elderly, the insane, and the whole variety of social worlds that, taken together, comprise what we so glibly call society. Because so many cross-cultural studies have been conducted within the more restrictive Freudian perspective, it is difficult at this time to test out our statements cross-culturally. Second, there is again the relation between the social psychological observer and the persons observed. Louis Wirth used to say sardonically in his lectures, that Margaret Mead had visited all the primitive societies and that they weren't primitive any more.

Nevertheless, while barriers to the universal applicability of statements in space might well be overcome (as social psychologists carry relevant questions to distant places and begin to solve the problem of the interaction between the social psychologist and his subject), the former stipulation, that our statements about human conduct apply historically, seems not at all capable of being met. There are at least two barriers in this regard that will probably never be overcome. First, the further we go back in history, the more specialized are the accounts of human conduct. This is the case simply because literacy was restricted to higher status segments of populations in past centuries, and the other artifacts and relics available to us from archaeology permit few inferences about social psychological problems. Second, and more important, the meaning of the personal life changes drastically from historical epoch to historical epoch. How, for example, can we arrive at historically universal generalizations about the socialization of children, when, in fact, there is evidence to indicate that the social identity ''child'' did not emerge in recent European history until the seventeenth century?[15] Are we not deluding ourselves when we draw upon twentieth-century vocabularies of motive to ''explain'' the conduct of a Moses or a Leonardo?[16]

That the criterion of universality will likely never be met does not mean that it ought to be dismissed out of hand. In our view, it is best maintained as an ideal toward which the serious social psychologist ought to strive, knowing that the ideal can never be achieved. Embracing such an ideal will encourage historical and cross-cultural study and, at least, enlarge the universe of human conduct within which our statements can apply. It will also encourage replication of observations, a most important content of the scientific dialogue.

[14]Freud's *Psychopathology of Everyday Life* goes beyond this limitation on the analysis of meaning and comes close to the perspective we have adopted. Freud, following the pattern of Marx, would probably have said, ''As for me, I am not a Freudian.''

[15]See Philippe Ariès, *Centuries of Childhood,* translated by Robert Baldick (New York: Alfred A. Knopf, Inc., 1962).

[16]See C. Wright Mills, ''Situated Actions and Vocabularies of Motive,'' reprinted in Part Five of this volume.

Logical Coherence   This criterion of validity rests upon a trust or faith in the rules of syntax or grammar. If statements do not contradict one another or if statements are "logically," that is, grammatically or syntactically, derivative from one another, then we may acknowledge their validity. It is from such notions that *truth tables* are built in conventional courses of logic. Yet, we know that this criterion is not often met in the physical sciences and very seldom met in the social sciences. Writers of texts in the social sciences have frequently grasped at this fact to excuse themselves from the disciplined requirements of science. They appeal to the criterion of eclecticism.

Eclecticism is defined in the dictionary as the use of a method that proceeds by:

> Selecting; choosing from various sources; not following any one system . . . but selecting and appropriating whatever is considered best in all systems; also, made up of what is selected from diverse sources; also, broad in acceptance of ideas, etc., from other sources.[17]

Those who adopt such a perspective adhere to the naive faith that the more diverse points of view presented in the examination of an event, the nearer to the whole truth the examination will arrive. Thus, textbook writers provide books written on the assumption that all points of view must be presented in their texts. In so doing, they neglect the problem of relevance and assume that "reality" is somehow all of one piece, so that, if we fit all the pieces together, we shall come eventually to understand the "laws" that govern, in this case, the matter of human conduct. Obviously, in this book of readings, we reject the approach of naive eclecticism. We agree that concrete reality is really inexhaustible; that the question is at the center of our inquiries; that different accounts of human conduct are generated by the different questions that are asked. We abjure naive eclecticism.

Scientists, however, must be reluctantly eclectic. At this writing, physicists have yet to decide whether wavular or particular models can answer the questions they are directing toward the "nature" of light. Right now, the evidence seems to favor the particular model, but some observations remain that can only be accounted for in terms of a wavular model. What is needed is some kind of crucial experiment. Physics has not yet been able to design such an experiment. Social psychology is in a much less desirable position—the crucial alternatives have not yet been specified. For example, most social psychologists assert that early childhood experiences have an extreme influence upon subsequent adult conduct. There is evidence that challenges that assertion.[18] However, for us, the evidence itself rests upon an unacceptable holistic view of both personality and early childhood experiences. In the face of such evidence, we cannot reject the original assertion out of hand. Our guess is that early childhood experience must be taken into account insofar as it is relevant to adult conduct. Sexuality and ethnicity, insofar as they remain problematic throughout the life cycle, must be considered. Until such crucial distinctions are made and incorporated into research designs, we can neither reject nor accept conventional social psychological hypotheses. In arriving at this position, we would say that we are reluctantly eclectic.

---

[17]*The New Century Dictionary* (New York: D. Appleton-Century Co., 1946).

[18]See, *inter alia*, William H. Sewell, "Infant Training and the Personality of the Child," *American Journal of Sociology*, LVIII (July, 1952—September, 1952), pp. 150—159.

Once having arrived at such a position, we must admit our misgivings about the fact that our very conceptions of logic are totally ethnocentric. Conventional logic (the logic that social psychologists know best) is merely a formalization of Greek grammar.[19] Why, then, should Greek grammar be accepted as a criterion of validity when there are so many other grammars at our disposal? Greek grammar breaks down the world as a number of objects acting upon other objects to bring about certain observed results or consequences. From our earliest childhood we are constrained to parse sentences in terms of subjects (active agents), predicates (processes exerted upon some object), and objects (the agents acted upon). We see the world as an outcome of things acting upon other things. Consequently, we look to things (independent variables) as acting upon other things (dependent variables) to bring about our observations (associations, correlations, and the like). We miss the processes that may well alter the very identity of things we have observed. In this presentation, we can only ask—supposing we were to adopt another grammar, let us say Turkish—and state: "I will go to Turkey." The student can parse the complete sentence for himself, but in Turkish the statement would read, *Türkiyeye, gideceğim*, literally "Turkey-to-my-going-in-the-future." In this case, the subject is conceived as literally caught up in the process of "going-to-Turkey," or "going-to-Turkey" is *his* process. Greek grammar emphasizes things; Turkish grammar, processes.

In social psychology, we are very much concerned with the matter of process, and the English language is ill-equipped to talk about it. Why, then, ought we to rely on a logical criterion of validity that contravenes the processes we are trying to discuss? Whether mathematical sociology can provide an escape is moot. To date, mathematical sociology explores trite problems couched in the grammar of the Greeks. Apparently, some mathematical sociologists are already disenchanted, and the criterion of logical coherence does not seem to be very compelling. This, of course, is not to say that social psychological statements ought to fly in the face of all logic!

Consensus of the Competent If, following Mannheim,[20] we adopt a relational, rather than an absolutistic or relativistic, conception of truth, the criterion of the consensus or agreement maintained by competent, that is, skilled and trained, observers with reference to the validity of our social psychological statements seems to be the most basic. In social psychology, however, there are various perspectives concerning how human conduct must be interpreted. Consequently, there is no overriding consensus among social psychologists about the validity of statements. Indeed, some pools of consensus, for example, those bounded by orthodox psychoanalysis, seem to be circumscribed by wishes, beliefs, and assertions that eschew the ideals of universality and logic in complete ignorance of the impress of history or the variety of syntax in the human world.

Those who find themselves swimming in such pools of consensus, if they are creative at all, are seldom content with agreements commonly held, and they intrude upon other areas of commonly held "knowledge" to inform and reshape their own notions about the

---

[19]See Benjamin Lee Whorf, *Language, Thought and Reality* (New York: John Wiley and Sons, Inc., 1956), pp. 207−219; and Chang Tung-Sun, "A Chinese Philosopher's Theory of Knowledge," *Etc.: A Review of General Semantics*, IX, No. 3 (1952), pp. 203−226.

[20]Cf. Karl Mannheim, *Ideology and Utopia* (New York and London: Harcourt, Brace, and World, Inc., and Routledge and Kegan Paul, Ltd., 1963), pp. 76−83.

validity of their statements concerning human conduct. George Herbert Mead was such a person, moving from a concern with physical science to a concern with the behavioral components of meaningful human conduct. Harry Stack Sullivan sought to throw off the constraints of psychoanalytic theory by investigating the promise of social science. We could name others—William I. Thomas, Ernest W. Burgess, Benjamin Whorf, Edward Sapir—each of whom penetrated beyond his own particular circle of consensus, his own particular universe of discourse, to call into question truths commonly held and maintained. This is the way science progresses. Consensus, then, is always a dynamic, shifting, never realizable agreement among those who are competent to pass judgment upon observations or statements.

Consensus is Always Emergent. It is Never Fixed   If this is the case, then there is a political dimension to truth. Consensus is something that must be, if only for the moment, won or lost. It is a consequence of struggle. One offers up his statements in the arena of the competent and waits on their decision. This fact has two implications. First, the arena of the competent is structured. Judgments of competence parallel the ranking of universities—a skilled and trained social psychologist, ensconced in a Harvard, Columbia, Chicago, or Berkeley chair, carries more weight in his judgment of the validity of a statement than a skilled and trained social psychologist at, let us say, Valley State Teachers College in North Dakota.[21] Second, the social psychologist is constrained to employ rhethoric[22] to have his statements heard in the arena of the competent, that is, to get published. The rhetoric employed may often belie his mode of data gathering and presentation, but it is nevertheless of predominant concern.[23] What is valid, then, depends upon the political structuring of the discipline, the willingness of scientists to challenge consensual conceptions of truth, and the effectiveness of the rhetoric they employ. All this goes on within the constraints of a larger society, but this point must be skirted in this book.

CONCLUSIONS

We have maintained in the preceding pages that questions of validity lead us into the realm of method and that rhetoric is an important method that has long been ignored in social psychology, above all in the sciences. The question of relevance seems to us to be the

[21]Although there is considerable documentation for this contention, see especially the work of William C. Yoels: "Destiny or Dynasty: Doctoral Origins and Appointment Patterns of Editors of the ASR: 1948–1968," *American Sociologist* (May, 1971), pp. 134–139; "On the Social Organization of American Sociology," *British Journal of Sociology* (Spring, 1974), pp. 150–161; and "The Structure of Scientific Fields and the Allocation of Editorships on Scientific Journals: Some Observations on the Politics of Knowledge," *Sociological Quarterly* (Spring, 1974), pp. 264–276.

[22]The term is used in the sense employed by Kenneth Burke: ". . . a symbolic means of inducing cooperation in beings that by nature respond to symbols." See his *Rhetoric of Motives* (New York: Prentice-Hall, Inc., 1950), p. 43.

[23]One of us submitted an article to the *Americal Sociological Review* some years ago. It was rejected because of a lack of "empirical" evidence. The author looked about and found a statistical table that had a very peripheral bearing upon the statements in question and inserted the table in a footnote. The article was then published. Both editors of this volume agree that rhetoric should be included as a basic area of methods. Then, however, a moral problem is raised: Shall the rhetoric be employed to further one's scientific reputation or further the science? We adopt the latter value-judgment without qualification.

more fundamental, establishing, as it does, the problems of a discipline. In reviews of the development of any scientific discipline, we find that problems live and theories die. The questions are important in that they mobilize and focus the continuing disciplined dialogue that we call science. Moreover, questions always imply metaphors, that is, ways of picturing objects of inquiry. In social psychology, as construed, we ask questions about the meaning of the personal life, and we assert that such meaning can never be established outside the matrix of communication. We think of any attempt to understand personal conduct outside such a matrix as a "psychologistic fallacy."

So, we turn to our attempt to carry out what this introduction implies. The first two parts of this book spell out the essentials of what we have called the "communicative matrix" of the personal life, by showing how others have viewed the circumstances and situations within which the interaction that lends meaning to the personal life is carried on. Details of the interaction process are sketched out. The next four parts focus more on the "content," "process," "directions," and "loss" of personal meaning—self, socialization, motives, and mental illness. In considering each contribution, the student is asked continually to raise questions of the universality, coherence, consensual validity, and method (including rhetoric) characterizing the propositions set forth.

SUGGESTED READINGS

Blumer, Herbert. *Symbolic Interactionism.* Englewood Cliffs, N.J.: Prentice-Hall, Inc., 1969.

Brittan, Arthur. *Meanings and Situations.* London: Routledge and Kegan Paul, Ltd., 1973.

Cardwell, Jerry D. *Social Psychology, A Symbolic Interaction Perspective.* Philadelphia: F. A. Davis Co., 1971.

Charon, Joel M. *Symbolic Interactionism.* Englewood Cliffs, N.J.: Prentice-Hall, Inc., 1979.

Hewitt, John P. *Self and Society: A Symbolic Interactionist Social Psychology.* 2d ed. Boston: Allyn and Bacon, Inc., 1979.

Kando, Thomas M. *Social Interaction.* St. Louis, Mo.: The C.V. Mosby Co., 1977.

Karp, David A., and William C. Yoels. *Symbols, Selves, and Society.* New York: J. B. Lippincott/Harper and Row, Publishers, 1979.

Lauer, Robert H., and Warren H. Handel. *Social Psychology, The Theory and Application of Symbolic Interactionism.* Boston: Houghton Mifflin Co., 1977.

Lindesmith, Alfred R., Anselm L. Strauss, and Norman K. Denzin. *Social Psychology.* 5th ed. New York: Holt, Rinehart and Winston, 1977.

Manis, Jerome G., and Bernard N. Meltzer. *Symbolic Interaction.* 2d ed. Boston: Allyn and Bacon, Inc., 1972.

Mead, George H. *Mind, Self, and Society.* Edited with an introduction by Charles W. Morris. Chicago: University of Chicago Press, 1934.

Rose, Arnold M. (ed.). *Human Behavior and Social Process.* Boston: Houghton Mifflin Co., 1962.

Thayer, H. S. *Meaning and Action.* Indianapolis: Bobbs-Merrill Co., Inc., 1973.

Vernon, Glenn M. *Symbolic Aspects of Interaction.* Washington, D.C.: University Press of America, Inc., 1978.

PART ONE

SITUATIONS, STAGING, AND AWARENESS CONTEXTS

The universe is inherently meaningless and totally indifferent to the existence of man. While it *conditions,* it does not determine. Indeed, the universe presents itself as an occasion for man's creative capacities. *It is there*. It awaits his investiture of identity, meaning, value, sentiments, and rules. It is a convertible commodity—a taken, not a given; a concept, not a datum. Witness the history of thought in Western civilization as its basic paradigm of natural order was transformed radically by the genius of Ptolemy, Copernicus, Newton, and Einstein. At this very writing some physicists are questioning even the Einsteinian conception. For better or worse, man is the locus of purpose and power. He is the reality maker and the reality breaker. He alone is engaged in the "politics of reality." Should it be asked: "Whose definition of reality shall prevail?" no easy answer can be given, except to say that it is a matter of "negotiation" that can range from arbitrary imposition through reasonable dialogue to uncritical acceptance. But no matter what, it will be man who creates, sustains, and changes meaning.

That man creates meaning is obvious. Consider the fact that a red, white, and blue cloth, which has no inherent meaning, takes on enormous meaning when arranged in a configuration of stars and stripes. Obviously, multicolored cloth can be transformed into a socially meaningful object that symbolically represents the United States of America. Although the decorated cloth is an arbitrary designation and might well have been substituted for by something else—say, a totem pole—we have endowed it with such value and sentiment that any desecration of the transformed cloth is interpreted as an assault upon the nation for which it stands.

While the relationship between an object and its representative designation is arbitrary, it is nevertheless established and maintained through consensus. The power of consensus is such that a man can transform the essence of that which exists, even at the expense of denying the obvious, such as labeling a white man nonwhite, depicted in the selection by Langston Hughes; or, he can bring into essence that which has no ''kickable'' existence, for example, Santa Claus, Easter bunnies, and, as McCall and Simmons suggest, ''stolen bases''; or, he can label things in such ways as to mobilize manifestly inappropriate responses, as in the example provided by Benjamin Lee Whorf—where highly ignitable fuel vapors are ignored because the drums that contain them are labeled ''empty.''

Lest the point be missed, the creation and alteration of meaning require the participation of all those concerned. It takes eleven men, all playing under a set of rules, to create such things as stolen bases. If the reader alone insisted that from October 22−28 since 1939 A.D., little green men have emerged from the depths of the earth to help in the celebration of damn-it-all-to-hell week, he would not be long deprived of more secluded surroundings.

Although the power of collective definition and meaning is enormous, let there be no confusion: no amount of collective definition or consensus can wish away the reality of a brick wall. As with all things that object, walls offer a resistance through which we may not walk. Just such resistance, however, offers up the occasion for the creation of meaning. The meaning of a wall would be quite different were we to play handball against it, or execute, by firing squad, someone standing in front of it. Using the wall as a means toward an end establishes or alters its meaning. The meaning of the wall is in the response made to it. As a mere datum, the wall awaits an action that will interpret it to mean one thing rather than another. And exactly what meaning we give to the wall, in large measure, derives from the overall situation in which the wall is included. A political situation will compel one line of meaning, whereas a recreational situation will compel another. Accordingly, the overall ·''definition of the situation'' is a crucial variable. Generally speaking, the definition of the situation is now regarded—at least, within sociology—to be a necessary condition of human conduct.

Yet, we should keep in mind that situations can be and usually are—staged. That is, the elements of a situation are typically assembled, arranged, manipulated, and controlled by human beings, so that the vast range of possibilities for human conduct is circumscribed. (All this is accomplished, of course, within the context of history, but this is one of the most difficult facts that situational analysts confront.) Willard Waller, so far as we know, was the first sociologist to make an analysis of this basic process of staging.[1] He investigated the classroom situation in detail and began his observations with the axiom *The definition of the situation is a process*. In proposing this axiom, and with no little difficulty, Waller removed the concept from its formulation as either culturally given or mentalistically adduced. *Man creates definitions of the situation*—''one person defines a situation for another.'' *This should not be taken to mean that each situation is defined de novo*. For many situations of human life are conventionally defined, as is their staging.

---

[1] Willard Waller, *The Sociology of Teaching* (New York: John Wiley and Sons, Inc., 1932).

The elements persist—Christmas trees, fireworks, Easter eggs, flags, altars, churches, courthouses, classrooms, and so on. Thus, there is a continuity of situational elements—collective representations—*and the mode of their arrangement may be thought of as a kind of grammar, a set of rules regulating how such elements should be assembled, arranged, manipulated, and controlled.*

Such a definition—and the variable capacity to implement it self-consciously—is illustrated in Stone's article ''The Circumstance and Situation of Social Status.'' Here clothing is worn strategically and appropriately relative to time and place, so as to exhibit the kind of image the wearer would like the audience to ''see.'' The ability to manipulate clothing, or an apparent symbolic representation, presupposes the economic resources to do so, but with those resources one may easily enlist clothing as an instrument to overcome, alter, or transform—at least, situationally—one's comparative status in life.

But clothing is just one element that is subject to artful manipulation. More comprehensively, staging the definition of a situation requires that at least five elements be assembled, arranged, manipulated, and controlled: (1) spaces; (2) props; (3) equipment; (4) clothing; and (5) bodies. This operation may be equally or more important than the employment of linguistic symbols, although it must ultimately be interpreted linguistically. What permits such staging to be carried off lies outside, beyond, or under the staging process. It is a matter of taken-for-granted rules—what Garfinkel calls ''routine grounds,''[2] Goffman, ''working consensus,''[3] and Gross and Stone, ''performance norms.'' Such common assumptions allow for flexibility in role performance and give the other fellow the benefit of the doubt. Again, these assumptions permit the distinctively human con, but, we must add, some delight and surprise in human encounters. When performance norms do not permit such flexibility, as in some bureaucracies, encounters may be fraught with disappointment.

Notwithstanding these assumptions, there is something about spaces, particularly enclosed spaces, that requires further investigation. The enclosure itself, modified by lighting, sound, color, odor, temperature, and humidity, affects the character of the interaction carried on inside. Variations in any or all of these elements can noticeably effect the mood of the interaction.

Mary K. Zimmerman provides interesting material on this matter in her comparative ethnographic analysis of two abortion clincs. Although hardly a decade ago abortionists were thought of as deviants who perpetrated immoral acts in sleezy back alley flats, today there are abortion clinics and abortion counselors, partly subsidized by public money. The changing moral attitude toward abortion has been reflected in the way abortion clinics are staged.

In the past, abortionists attempted to neutralize or offset the illicit nature of the process by normalizing it and making it look conventional. Thus, luxurious office settings with sunken waiting rooms, deep carpets, and hospital uniforms affected an air of a

[2]Harold Garfinkel, ''Studies of the Routine Grounds of Everyday Activities,'' *Social Problems,* XI (Winter, 1964), pp. 225–250.

[3]Erving Goffman, *The Presentation of Self in Everyday Life,* Monograph No. 2 (Edinburgh: University of Edinburgh Social Sciences Research Centre, 1956), pp. 4–5.

business-as-usual medical routine.[4] Today, however, presenting an exaggerated medical front is not of primary concern and has given way to an (ostensibly) personalized, nonhospital, human style. Exterior physical plant, interior decor, staff appearance, patient processing, and professional vocabulary all underplay the medical rhetoric. Note well, however, that even though the content of the rhetorical presentation has changed, the use of rhetorical presentation to establish and buttress current definitions remains.

Over and above the collectively constructed nature of meaning, and its codification in the various forms of rhetorical staging, there is the supervening matter of awareness contexts—those circumscribing, transcending, structural properties of social interaction, which condition it. Glaser and Strauss call attention to the fact that, regardless of the situation, the participants in an interaction sequence have more (or less) information about each other's identity, and this information serves as a context that can be manipulated strategically. There are four types of awareness contexts: an *open* as opposed to a *closed* context is one in which each participant is aware of the other's true identity, as well as his own identity from the other's point of view. A *suspicion* context prevails when one party suspects the identity of the other, and a *pretense* context occurs when both know each other's identity but pretend they do not. During the span of an interaction sequence, any context can be transformed into any other, depending on the information acquired.

In particular, Glaser and Strauss report on the manipulation of awareness contexts in the hospital situation. Patients for whom death is imminent may not be advised of the fact because the hospital staff may believe that the patient is thereby spared stressful emotional scenes with friends and relatives. Accordingly, the manipulation of contexts points towards a more general proposition: by offering up (or withholding) information concerning possible future identities, one gains control over present conduct. Deliberate manipulation of awareness contexts may be seen, therefore, as a desire for gaining control over interaction.

While Glaser and Strauss confine their discussion of awareness contexts to the domain of identity interaction, the idea may be broadened in two directions: first, to include what any interactant knows about any aspect of the *transcendent* features of his situation, and second, to encompass the possibility that some contexts are out of the interactants' awareness altogether. For example, Farberman's article entitled "A Criminogenic Market Structure: The Automobile Industry," describes how lower level (dependent) participants in the automobile industry cleave to an individualistic vocabulary of motives which explains their own plight in terms of the individual venality of business associates in a fashion that obscures the operation and impact of a transcending economic market structure. Put another way, the operation of the market constitutes an out-of-awareness context which, nevertheless, and precisely in virtue of its invisible, hidden operation, all the more shapes behavior.

In sum, interactionists should continue to build a more refined and comprehensive understanding of the systematic interrelationships among "meaning," "situations," "staging," and "awareness contexts." In the future, concerted effort should be given to

---

[4]See Donald W. Ball, "An Abortion Clinic Ethnography," *Social Problems,* No. 5, (Winter, 1967), pp. 293–301.

an understanding of the impact of "power" on meaning; the development of a general theory of situations that articulates the operation of situations within situations, the temporal-spatial boundaries of situations, their comparative pliability or rigidity, and their transformation. There should be empirical study of staging to uncover how the rhetorical manipulation of sites induces mood and affect, and, perhaps, more importantly, how it inhibits or shuts out certain lines of unacceptable behavior. (The impact of power on meaning may well be best studied in the arena of "staging.") Finally, awareness can be conceived of as a continuum running from "awareness-of-awareness" to "simple awareness" to out-of-awareness." Symbolic interaction may well widen its scope and unleash its emancipatory power, if it puts more focus on the conditions that impede or aid the heightening of awareness.

SUGGESTED READINGS

Balztell, Digby. *An American Business Aristocracy*. New York: Collier Books, 1962.

Becker, Ernest. *Denial of Death*. New York: The Free Press, 1973.

————. *The Birth and Death of Meaning*. New York: The Free Press of Glencoe, 1962.

————. *The Structure of Evil*. New York: The Free Press, 1968.

Berger, Peter L., and Thomas Luckman. *The Social Construction of Reality*. Garden City: Anchor Books, Doubleday, 1967.

Berreman, Gerald, D. *Behind Many Masks*. The Society for Applied Anthropology, Monograph No. 4, 1962.

Birdwhistell, Ray. *Kinesics and Context: Essays on Body Motion Communication*. Philadelphia: University of Pennsylvania Press, 1970.

Bourdieu, Pierre. *Outline of a Theory of Practice*. Cambridge: Cambridge University Press, 1977.

Brittan, Arthur. *Meanings and Situations*. London: Routledge & Kegan Paul, 1973.

Cassirer, Ernst. *An Essay on Man*. New Haven and London: Yale University Press, 1944.

Dewey, John. *Experience and Nature*. New York: W. W. Norton, 1925.

————, and Arthur F. Bentley. *Knowing and the Known*. Boston: Beacon Press, 1949.

Duncan, Hugh D. *Communication and the Social Order*. New York: Bedminster Press, 1962.

————. *Symbols in Society*. New York: Oxford University Press, 1968.

Irwin, John. *Scenes*. Beverly Hills: Sage Publications, 1977.

Firey, Walter. *Land Values in Central Boston*. Cambridge: Harvard University Press, 1945.

Gans, Herbert J. *The Urban Villagers*. New York: The Free Press, 1962.

Glazer, Nathan, and Daniel Patrick Moynihan. *Beyond the Melting Pot*. Cambridge: Harvard University Press, 1963.

Goffman, Erving. *Frame Analysis*. New York: Harper & Row, 1974.

————. *The Presentation of Self in Everyday Life*. Garden City: Doubleday, 1959.

————. *Behaviour in Public Places*. New York: The Free Press of Glencoe, 1963.

Hall, Edward T. *The Hidden Dimension*. Garden City: Doubleday, 1966.

————. *The Silent Language*. Greenwich, Conn.: Fawcett Publications, 1964.

Hoijer, Harry (ed.). *Language in Culture*. Chicago: University of Chicago Press, 1954.

Hooker, Evelyn. "The Homosexual Community," Proceedings of the XIVth International Congress of Applied Psychology. *Personality Research,* Vol. 2, Copenhagen, Munksgaard, 1962.

Hughes, Helen MacGill (ed.). *The Fantastic Lodge*. Boston: Houghton Mifflin Co., 1961.

Langer, Suzanne K. *Philosophy in a New Key*. New York: Penguin Books, Inc., 1948.

Lewis, Oscar. *La Vida*. New York: Vintage Books, 1968.

Liebow, Elliot. *Tally's Corner*. Boston, Toronto: Little, Brown and Co., 1967.

McHugh, Peter. *Definition of the Situation*. Indianapolis: Bobbs-Merrill, 1968.

Mead, George H. *Mind, Self, and Society*. Chicago: University of Chicago Press, 1934.

Merton, Robert K. "The Self-Fulfilling Prophecy," *Social Theory and Social Structure.* Glencoe, Ill.: The Free Press, Rev. ed., 1957, pp. 421−436.

Pirandello, Luigi. *Naked Masks*. Eric Bentley (ed.). New York: E. P. Dutton, 1952.

Polsky, Ned. *Hustlers, Beats, and Others*. Chicago: Aldine, 1968.

Riezler, Kurt. *Man: Mutable and Immutable*. Chicago: Regnery, 1950.

Sapir, Edward. *Language*. New York: Harcourt, Brace and Co., 1921.

Scheff, Thomas J. "Negotiating Reality: Notes on Power in the Assessment of responsibility," *Social Problems,* 16 (Summer, 1968), 3−17.

Shostak, Arthur B., and William Gomberg (eds.). *Blue Collar World*. Englewood Cliffs, N.J.: Prentice-Hall, Inc., 1964.

Stebbins, Robert A. "A Theory of the Definition of the Situation." *Canadian Review of Sociology and Anthropology,* 4 (August, 1967), 148−164.

Suttles, Gerald D. *The Social Order of the Slums*. Chicago: University of Chicago Press, 1968.

Whorf, Benjamin Lee. *Language, Thought, and Reality*. John B. Carroll, (ed.). Cambridge: Technology Press of Massachusetts Institute of Technology, 1956.

Wirth, Louis. *The Ghetto*. Chicago: Phoenix Books, 1956.

ONE

THAT POWERFUL DROP

LANGSTON HUGHES

Leaning on the lamp post in front of the barber shop, Simple was holding up a copy of the *Chicago Defender* and reading about how a man who looks white had just been declared officially colored by an Alabama court.

"It's powerful," he said.

"What?"

"That one drop of Negro blood—because just *one* drop of black blood makes a man colored. *One* drop—you are a Negro! Now, why is that? Why is Negro blood so much more powerful than any other kind of blood in the world? If a man has Irish blood in him, people will say, 'He's *part* Irish.' If he has a little Jewish blood, they'll say, 'He's *half* Jewish.' But if he has just a small bit of colored blood in him, BAM!—'*He's a Negro!*' Not, 'He's *part* Negro.' No, be it ever so little, if that blood is black, '*He's a Negro!*' Now, this is what I do not understand—why our *one* drop is so powerful. Take paint—white will not make black *white*. But black will make white *black*. One drop of black in white paint—and the white ain't white no more! Black is powerful. You can have ninety-nine drops of white blood in your veins down South—but if that other *one* drop is black, shame on you! Even if you look white, you're black. That drop is really powerful. Explain it to me. You're colleged."

"It has no basis in science," I said, "so there's no logical explanation." . . .

TWO

THE STOLEN BASE AS A SOCIAL OBJECT

GEORGE J. MC CALL AND J. L. SIMMONS

. . . Mead was perfectly aware that *things*—the bundles of stimuli the animal encounters—exist prior to and independent of the animal. Mead was simply drawing a distinction between such "things" and what he called *objects,* which exist only in relation to acts. In brief, "things" are converted to "objects" through acts.

Perhaps the best way to wrestle with this point is by example. What is the object of a given act? Let us take eating. The object of the act of eating is *nutrition*. Therefore, if one is hungry (has an impulse to eat), he seeks out stimuli that will release the act of eating. If, in this seeking, he comes across a tomato, he picks it up, puts it in his mouth, chews it, and swallows it. The object of this act is nutrition.

But if he has a different impulse—if he is angry at someone nearby—and he comes across that same tomato, he may suddenly snatch it up and throw it at his tormentor. And what is the object of that act? Expression of his anger.

Really to grasp Mead's concept of objects, we have to play on his *double-entendre*. Let us take our tomato, which is simply a red, leathery firmly soft, juicy spheroid with a mildly pungent smell and a slightly acid taste. This same bundle of stimuli, this one "thing," releases two very different acts (eating and throwing) with two very different objects (nutrition and expression of anger). Now, this tomato *serves* as both of these objects of acts. It is nutrition when eaten, and it is an expression of anger when hurled at someone. A thing thus *becomes* an object, through the completion of an act. The tomato is not nutrition until it is eaten, nor is it an expression of anger until it is thrown.

Thus, in Mead's theory, "things" are made to serve as various "objects" (in an enriched sense of that word), objects of acts—that is, the *consummations* of those acts.[1]

But this usage is somewhat confusing as long as

SOURCE: George J. McCall and J. L. Simmons, "Social Acts and Social Objects." Copyright by The Free Press, 1966, 1978. From George J. McCall and J. L. Simmons, *Identities and Interaction,* Revised Edition (New York: The Free Press, 1978), pp. 49–50. Reprinted by permission of The Free Press, A Division of Macmillan Publishing Company, Inc.

[1]Mead, *The Philosophy of the Present,* Chicago: Open Court, 1932, pp. 190 ff.

we confine ourselves to what we ordinarily think of as *physical* objects. The strength of Mead's notion is more apparent when we consider *social objects,* which are the objects of *social acts* (acts involving the coordinated activity of a plurality of persons).[2] Let us consider one admittedly bizarre act. A rather young man, in a park in the Bronx, is standing quietly but very alertly in the afternoon sun. Suddenly he tenses and scurries a few tentative steps to his right, still rather frozen, his gaze locked on a man only a few feet away. This other man makes a sudden movement with his right arm, and the first fellow breaks into sudden flight. Twenty or thirty yards away, still another fellow starts to run to cut him off, and the first man falls flat on his face, skidding and bouncing roughly along the ground for several feet as a result of his great momentum.

What object has this act created? What was the object of the act? Male readers, at least, may have recognized this common social object for what it is, a "stolen base." It has no physical structure but is simply a social object, a symbolic structure generated by a cooperative social act. A stolen base cannot be touched, smelled, or tasted, but it does exist, through the joint efforts of human actors. No one person can create a stolen base all by himself. It takes at least eleven men, laboring together under a common rule, to do so.

Such social objects are insubstantial, but they are extremely abundant and important. Most of the things we officially strive for—marriage, academic degrees, occupational positions, grades—do not exist in nature but are created jointly by the persons involved. Perhaps the reader has never pondered the metaphysical status of these social objects, but it is sobering to do so, and it raises profound theoretical questions as to why we should be so exclusively oriented to such "insubstantial" objects. . . .

[2] *Ibid.,* pp. 180, 185.

THREE

THE NAME OF THE SITUATION AS AFFECTING BEHAVIOR

BENJAMIN LEE WHORF

. . . In the course of my professional work for a fire insurance company, . . . I undertook the task of analyzing many hundreds of reports of circumstances surrounding the start of fires, and in some cases, of explosions. My analysis was directed toward purely physical conditions, such as defective wiring, presence or lack of air spaces between metal flues and woodwork, etc., and the results were presented in these terms. Indeed it was undertaken with no thought that any other significances would or could be revealed. But in due course it became evident that not only a physical situation *qua* physics, but the meaning of that situation to people, was sometimes a factor, through the behavior of the people, in the start of the fire. And this factor of meaning was clearest when it was a LINGUISTIC MEANING, residing in the name or the linguistic description commonly

SOURCE: Benjamin Lee Whorf. "The Name of the Situation as Affecting Behavior." Copyright by the Massachusetts Institute of Technology, 1956, Benjamin Lee Whorf, "The Name of the Situation as Affecting Behavior," in his *Language, Thought and Reality* (Cambridge, Massachusetts: M.I.T. Press, 1956), pp. 135–137. Reprinted by permission of the Massachusetts Institute of Technology.

applied to the situation. Thus, around a storage of what are called "gasoline drums," behavior will tend to a certain type, that is, great care will be exercised; while around a storage of what are called "empty gasoline drums," it will tend to be different—careless, with little repression of smoking or of tossing cigarette stubs about. Yet the "empty" drums are perhaps the more dangerous, since they contain explosive vapor. Physically the situation is hazardous, but the linguistic analysis according to regular analogy must employ the word "empty," which inevitably suggests lack of hazard. The word "empty" is used in two linguistic patterns: (1) as a virtual synonym for "null and void, negative, inert," (2) applied in analysis of physical situations without regard to, e.g., vapor, liquid vestiges, or stray rubbish, in the container. The situation is named in one pattern (2) and the name is then "acted out" or "lived up to" in another (1), this being a general formula for the linguistic conditioning of behavior into hazardous forms.

In a wood distillation plant the metal stills were insulated with a composition prepared from limestone and called at the plant "spun limestone." No attempt was made to protect this covering from excessive heat or the contact of flame. After a period of use, the fire below one of the stills spread to the "limestone," which to everyone's great surprise burned vigorously. Exposure to acetic acid fumes from the stills had converted part of the limestone (calcium carbonate) to calcium acetate. This when heated in a fire decomposes, forming inflammable acetone. Behavior that tolerated fire close to the covering was induced by use of the name "limestone," which because it ends in "-stone" implies noncombustibility.

A huge iron kettle of boiling varnish was observed to be overheated, nearing the temperature at which it would ignite. The operator moved it off the fire and ran it on its wheels to a distance, but did not cover it. In a minute or so the varnish ignited. Here the linguistic influence is more complex; it is due to the metaphorical objectifying . . . of "cause" as contact or the spatial juxtaposition of "things"—to analyzing the situation as "on" versus "off" the fire. In reality, the stage when the external fire was the main factor had passed; the overheating was now an internal process of convection in the varnish from the intensely heated kettle, and still continued when "off" the fire.

An electric glow heater on the wall was little used, and for one workman had the meaning of a convenient coathanger. At night a watchman entered and snapped a switch, which action he verbalized as "turning on the light." No light appeared, and this result he verbalized as "light is burned out." He could not see the glow of the heater because of the old coat hung on it. Soon the heater ignited the coat, which set fire to the building.

A tannery discharged waste water containing animal matter into an outdoor settling basin partly roofed with wood and partly open. This situation is one that ordinarily would be verbalized as "pool of water." A workman had occasion to light a blow-torch near by, and threw his match into the water. But the decomposing waste matter was evolving gas under the wood cover, so that the setup was the reverse of "watery." An instant flare of flame ignited the woodwork, and the fire quickly spread into the adjoining building.

A drying room for hides was arranged with a blower at one end to make a current of air along the room and thence outdoors through a vent at the other end. Fire started at a hot bearing on the blower, whch blew the flames directly into the hides and fanned them along the room, destroying the entire stock. This hazardous setup followed naturally from the term "blower" with its linguistic equivalence to "that which blows," implying that its function necessarily is to "blow." Also its function is verbalized as "blowing air for drying," overlooking that it can blow other things, e.g., flames and sparks. In reality, a blower simply makes a current of air and can exhaust as well as blow. It should have been installed at the vent end to DRAW the air over the hides, then through the hazard (its own casing and bearings), and thence outdoors.

Besides a coal-fired melting pot for lead reclaiming was dumped a pile of "scrap lead"—a misleading verbalization, for it consisted of the lead sheets of old radio condensers, which still had paraffin paper between them. Soon the paraffin blazed up and fired the roof, half of which was burned off.

Such examples, which could be greatly multiplied, will suffice to show how the cue to a certain line of behavior is often given by the analogies of the linguistic formula in which the situation is spoken of, and by which to some degree it is analyzed, classified, and allotted its place in that world which is "to a large extent unconsciously built up on the language habits of the group." And we always assume that the linguistic analysis made by our group reflects reality better than it does.

FOUR

THE CIRCUMSTANCE AND SITUATION OF SOCIAL STATUS

GREGORY P. STONE

A frequently echoed argument against generalizing about social stratification in the society at large from observations made in the context of local community organization asserts that the "upper class" person in the small town is not "upper class" in the large city. I must reject this line of reasoning. Status is a *circumstantial* fact for some people, a network of life fate, but, for others, status is a *situational* phenomenon, eminently capable of manipulation and established by one's self or one's social circle by the artful staging of appearance. To say that "upper class" people living in small towns are, *de facto,* not "upper class" in large cities is to emphasize the circumstantial aspects of status to the neglect of its situational character and to assume that one's personal horizons of experience are circumscribed by local community boundaries. However, not all the residents *in* local communities are *of* those communities, nor are all people whom the sociologist may place *in* status categories *of* those categories.

Some are. For such people, the manipulation of status is outside the realm of possibility. They are existentially committed to their status circumstances. Thus, when asked what kind of clothes should not be worn by persons in the respondent's social position, a truckdriver replied, "I wouldn't have any use for a tuxedo or things like that. . . . I'd just be out of my class wearing evening clothes and morning clothes." A part-time housewife, working in a local restaurant, replied, "Some of these nice, fancy, expensive furs. They wouldn't fit me—real expensive, kinda high-tone clothes. Them and I wouldn't mix. It would be someone tryin' to overdo, and make people think they're higher than they are."[1] The operator of a small body-repair shop echoed the same sentiments:

> Anyone who is in this category of business should not be outstanding. It looks like you're trying to step out of your class a little bit, go too far in your dress. You should be conservative.

SOURCE: Gregory P. Stone. "The Circumstance and Situation of Social Status." Original paper prepared especially for the first edition of this volume, 1970. Reprinted by permission of the author.

[1]Note the conception of *fit*.

Similar thoughts were provided in responses to other questions. For example, when a household domestic was asked whether or not she would like to dress like some of the better dressed people in town, she answered, "I couldn't afford to. If I could, I would be out of place."

This circumstantial quality of appearance—one dresses as he does, because he is what he is—does seem to be generally (but, as we shall see, not exclusively) typical of life in the lower ranges of socio-economic status. For one thing, of course, the range of apparent symbols is sharply restricted for these people. Apparent symbols cost money. Also contributing to the matter of "apparent circumstance" is the restricted exposure on the part of those in the lower socio-economic levels to the range of apparent symbols. Asked whether she could tell social differences among people by the clothes they wear, the wife of a core-maker in the local foundry said:

> You probably could. Now we don't go to the Country Club, 'cause we don't belong. They might dress better, but we don't see them, but when you go uptown, they are all dressed about the same.

Significantly, in an analysis of clothing shopping, questions asking the day of the week and the time of the day preferred for clothing shopping in town revealed that housewives at the extremes of the socio-economic scale could seldom, if ever, meet one another while shopping for clothing. Typically, higher status women shopped early in the day and lower status women shopped late in the week. The probability is that the people seen by the wife of the core-maker are dressed the same, because they are "the same" in status terms.[2]

On special occasions, the circumstances of appearance may cause minor discomfort and embar-

rassment, but lack of facility with impression management is only underscored. A carpenter's wife put it this way:

> Sometimes when you go to a party, you wish you'd worn a little better dress, after you see what they've got on. Sometimes I go to Bible Study in a cotton dress, and the others are more dressed up. Then, I'll go more dressed up, and all they'll have on is cotton dresses.

Or lack of facility with the staging of appearance may prevent the consolidation of social mobility. A former molder in a local foundry had managed to set enough aside to establish his own small aluminum foundry in partnership with another man. The small foundry was quite successful, but the former molder had not consolidated the "move" with the appropriate apparent symbolism. In fact, he *could not,* so immersed was he in the circumstances of his former status. A typical work day still sees him "in the shop" from 7:00 A.M. until 5:00 P.M. Under the protection of night, he goes to the office. When asked what kind of clothes he would suggest for his kind of work, he replied:

> You might say just for comfort—sport clothes, maybe—to meet the public. That doesn't go over too good sometimes. I've worked in the foundry all my life. I don't belong to the executive class; I'm not a white collar man.

Later, "I don't like office work. I'm not cut out for it. I liked molding, when I was able to do it." His response to this aspect of life is comprised by a fatalistic "philosophy" documented by legend:

> If you can put up a front, you can get by for a while, but eventually it seems to catch up with you. That reminds me of some boys I grew up with. Their father was a plain everyday man. He founded the business. When he'd go out of town on a business trip, he'd maybe go on some side street and get a good meal, but, when the boys went out, they had to stay at the best hotels and get expensive dinners. They were just putting up a front. It didn't mean

[2]Gregory P. Stone and William H. Form, *The Local Community Clothing Market: A Study of the Social and Social Psychological Contexts of Shopping* (East Lansing, Michigan: State University Agricultural Experiment Station Technical Bulletin 262, November, 1957), pp. 21–24. I might add, "It's *really* a small world!"

anything. They could go any place, and they were the life of the party. There were four of them—two younger than me and two older. They inherited a good business and, in a few years, went bankrupt. A man came in and straightened the business out from the creditors, and they got back on their feet. But the boys were very much putting up a front.

Yet, in the lower socio-economic levels, there are occasional signs of ambivalence leading to embryonic attempts to manipulate appearance. A shipping foreman in the stock room of a local manufacturing plant, for example, permitted himself the hope of mobility. He mentioned "businessmen" and "party-goers" as the best dressed people in town, and, asked whether he would like to dress as they do, he replied, "I have hopes of being able to." He has, in fact, attempted to manage his impressions. Thinking that clothing does influence one's chances on the job, he says, "I buy my clothes purposely for work." Yet, in conjunction with this question, the foreman observes, "Well, your dressing brings out your character." (The "character" is there to begin with!) Asked later what clothes should not be worn by those in his social position, the foreman responded:

> They shouldn't wear expensive or flashy clothes. [Interviewer: Why not?] Because they can't afford expensive clothes. [Interviewer: Why shouldn't they wear flashy clothes?] It builds bad character, because you're trying to attract attention by other than your social position. [Interviewer: Would you explain that a little more?] Well, if you can't have the friends or the attention of people by your social position, it seems false to get it by the clothes you wear.

The foreman, cautiously aspiring, may be moving out of the circumstance of the working class.

A freight hand and trucker's helper had also begun to question the fated character of his appearance. We can see this in his response to the question: "Do you think the way you dress on the job makes any difference in your job opportunities or advancement?"

Yes and no. It's possible that you could get a better job, if you dressed different, but I don't know. It's possible, but I wouldn't want to say either way. [Interviewer: How is it possible?] In contacting people—different stores and different customers. [Interviewer: Do you do anything about this in planning what you wear on the job?] I've thought some I'd change to a wool dress pant, but I like a good overall. It's comfortable. You're not all bundled up.

But the circumstances of work and the controls exerted by his social circle provide imposing obstacles to the manipulation of his appearance:

> The truckers dress like I do in the summer time. In the winter, they're inside and those truck heaters keep them warm. Me and the other fellows are outside most of the time.

Asked what should not be worn by people in his social position, the freight hand replied:

> You should wear clothing that fits the occasion. [Interviewer: Why?] Well, I could dress real fancy at some occasion, if I wanted to, but, where I am socially, my kind would start talking about you quite easily, and that's one thing I can't stand at all.

Moreover, one's dress may not gibe with his discursive appearance. As a doctor's wife put it:

> Some gals who make their own clothes and have little social prestige, you meet downtown, might fool you for a while. But I say it would be something they do or say that would give them away rather than clothes.

Although there are instances, here and there, of a manipulative or rhetorical orientation to the apparent representation of status by the selection of clothes among those in the lower ranges of socio-economic status, seldom are there instances of the use of dress to maintain and define situations which can parallel the case of a seventy-year-old wife of a retired cigar manufacturer. Her facility with dress is wonderfully exemplified in the following remark:

I knew I would look bigger in that coral suit, but . . . [it would] . . . bring out the color in my face. That would offset making my hips look larger.

The same acuity in contriving appearance is manifested in her comments on dressing up:

I never go out without dressing up. I don't feel right. I think there are certain kinds of clothes to be worn outside the home, a kind for inside the home on an afternoon, and a thing to scrub—when you wear any old thing. In Florida, at Gulfport, you'd never wear a formal. You never see a formal there. At the Moonlight Club, where we go every Wednesday night, you wouldn't think of going without a formal. You'd keep trying to pull your skirt down longer, if you did. Only people who are tourists—just there for a couple of weeks—could go like that. If they were just there for a couple of weeks and didn't bring many clothes, that would be all right. I'm not self-conscious. There are just standards that you should abide by.

Her staging of appearance at the Moonlight Club, however, is not simply a matter of immediate response to standards of propriety. Appearance is a product of collective staging undertaken jointly by herself and her husband:

When we're going to a dance, I ask what he's going to wear. Then, we dress in harmony so the colors won't clash. When he's going out, I ask what he's going to wear, so I'll know its suitable and wear the same thing.

This collective staging of appearance extends to her larger social circle and reflects the conscious maintenance of status enforced by informal controls. Asked what others in her social position should not wear, the lady replied:

You must dress well. [Interviewer: Why is that?] You're kinda looked at as an example or pattern, and, if you go around looking sloppy, you're taboo. [Interviewer: Who would you be a pattern to?] My associates—the same as I use them as a pattern—not that we keep up with the Joneses. They'd say, "See Patricia!! Can't imagine what's got into her. Never saw her look that way before."

Still, the circumstantial character of status does not exclusively typify the lower levels of socio-economic status. Interesting contrast is provided by the response of Mrs. Branchwood to the "invasion of the cosmopolitians,"[3] and the response of Mrs. Cavendish. Both belong to the "old families" of Vansburg, the first to an "old retailing family" and the second to a "local manufacturing family." Mrs. Branchwood, like members of many other old families, has "retired" from the competition for status:

I know, before the war, we used to dress up in formals for dinner parties and dances. Now we don't dress up. In fact, we don't have much in the social life way.

Mrs. Cavendish presented a "double face" to the world—one for the benefit of the local community audience, the other for the benefit of the world at large, represented locally by the "cosmopolite set."

A lot of people feel they have to have the latest style—a lot of older people especially. You have to grow old graciously. To me a mink coat is lovely no matter the style. The things can be changed a little. Once a year I get the fashions from Paris and look them over. The people in New York dress entirely different from the people in the Middle West. Everyone downtown will tell you that I don't care what I wear. But I was trained to teach art, and I'm always looking at design—not so much for the style. When I dress to go out, I dress. The dinner gowns I wear in New York are considered conservative there, but I wouldn't dare wear them here.

Asked whether she preferred to shop for clothes in chain stores or local independent stores, Mrs. Cavendish replied, "Well, we don't think the chain stores give to the community. I certainly give my home merchants the chance." In contrast: "I don't mind shopping in New York. They know me

[3]A point discussed extensively in William H. Form and Gregory P. Stone, "Instabilities in Status: The Problem of Hierarchy in the Community Study of Status Arrangements," *American Sociological Review*, XVIII (April, 1953), pp. 149–162.

and what I want. . . . I have ten or twelve pairs of kid gloves that I send to New York at one time to be cleaned.''

Such impression management requires extremely careful definitions of situations. Mrs. Cavendish was careful to note, ''Some people who have come from New York dress as though they are still there. They are overdressed.'' By artfully employing dress, however, she could adapt herself to varying status situation:

> Naturally I'd dress differently in the Chateau-Frontenac in Quebec or in the Ambassador Hotel in New York. . . . I do most of my buying in New York, and I dress differently when I am there. . . . When I'm around here, I dress differently from when I'm away. I'm apt to wear medium-priced garments so I won't be overdressed.

On the other hand, Mrs. Branchwood seemed unable to rise above the circumstances of status:

> When I was in Florida, I was invited to a luncheon. We didn't know what to wear—hats or gloves. When we got there, everyone else was wearing gloves and hats.

The two present an interesting contrast, indeed. Both were the same age (50 and 51 years old), both were members of ''old families'' in town, both were rated as ''upper class,'' but their status worlds were different. Mrs. Branchwood seemed somehow ensnared by the circumstances of her status; Mrs. Cavendish looked upon status as a situation to be defined and redefined by dress as she moved back and forth between town and metropolis.

Status, like age, presents a permeable world, but, in a sense, it is a less permeable world for some. Penetration of status barriers and the misrepresentation of the self require anonymity—the kind that is afforded by the metropolis and to residents of Vansburg whose visits away from town are frequent—but within the town itself, knowledge of one another, at times unexpectedly intimate, precludes extensive manipulations of the status world. If one stays *in* town and becomes *of* the town,

status is circumstantial, but frequent movement out of town loosens local status controls.

If we are to establish social stratification as a universe of appearance, we must first establish that people in different strata dress differently. Of course, the demonstration seems unnecessary, since all studies of dress show income and status differences, but the point may be emphasized by referring to a few selected interview materials. Listen to the spate of remarks volunteered to an interviewer by a local furniture salesman before the matter of status had been introduced in the interview:

> You'll find that, generally speaking, the crowd we run with are conservative. I travel with the conservative crowd. We don't try to outdo each other. Associations have some effect on everything you do. They have money, but it doesn't show much. They are all business and professional folks, but nobody can crap anybody. You can look 'em up in D and B. There is no object to foolin' around. [Interviewer: Who does ''fool around''?] The ''tin-horn millionaire'' crowd—they dress to beat hell. They owe about three-quarters of the amount for their clothes. They have everything but the money. They aren't crapping anyone but themselves and some half-ass people. A lot of 'em have minor administrative jobs in the plants. You don't find many professional people in that group. That crowd spends a lot of time at the Elks. They hate to go to the Chamber of Commerce, but they do. They do more partying; we spend more time at home. They go to the dance halls and taverns. Their organizations are the Elks, the Country Club, the Lions, and the Rotary. Ours are Kiwanis—there's not so much money there as in the Rotary, but they're all swell—the Masons rather than the Elks, because it's not a drinking crowd, and the Chamber of Commerce. Most of my gang are too old for the Junior Chamber of Commerce. Now we are in the Chamber of Commerce.
>
> It shows up in clothes and clubs. We go to good shows and good places to eat. They go to burlesques. There is no clash between the two, but they are two different types. I can figure a guy fairly good. You take solid people. They are straight down the line. . . . There have to be a few lines drawn. You can't help it. It's just normal that you have to associate

with people in your station. You don't go out and eat with them. You can call them by name, but you can go to associate with people you eat with.

Status was this man's circumstance:

> I remember the time I pulled into the Palmer House [in Chicago] with no coat. They asked me to leave. I was griped. I went down to Walgreens.

And the principal cleavage he perceived as differentiating the dress of people in different walks of life seems to have been the cleavages between those who dressed to meet their status and those who, from his standpoint, sought to have their status meet their dress.

Other respondents presented more conventional pictures of different dress in different statuses. An accountant at the State Training School, when asked to enumerate the "social classes" in Vansburg, said:

> You'll find three groups. There's not much difference in what they do, except that they do it by themselves. First, a low income group—$3,000 and less; second, the average—from $3000 to $6,000; and third, a small group above $6,000.[4] Then there are sub-groups. They are the first to adopt new fads. They gamble for higher stakes more flamboyantly. Finally, the element that's always being the newest thing. They will follow the trend of the above group, if they are buying something that's worth the money or the trouble.

Still, the cleavage between those who "dress in" and those who "dress out"—the conservatives and the Country Club group—persists. A radio repairman and bill collector missed the cleavage completely and commented upon the different dress of three strata:

> I wouldn't say that I dress any differently from other people, except maybe the foundry workers or the so-called 400's that are going out to the Country Club. In a small town, you dress more informally in

[4]Interview taken in the early '50's.

work clothes or business clothes and then change. And then there are those that stay continually dressed up. They don't work. They just change clothes several times a day.

Most respondents, however, observed differences in dress only among extreme groups. A funeral director's wife observed, "The *Gute Freunden* [a high status club] may look frumpy. The Grange group are lovely people, but they dress differently." A weighmaster singled out:

> The "codfish aristocracy"—they may be the luminaries of a lodge gathering who spend all their dough treating everybody and feeding the slot machines. They want to impress everybody that they have the dough.

His wife echoed his words: "The 'codfish aristocracy.' They have a different pair of shoes to go with every gown and a purse and all that." A carpenter and mason commented on the different dress of those in the lower reaches of socioeconomic status:

> Most of 'em all have pants and shirt alike, unless you get into dirty work; then they wear overalls. There's some don't dress as good as I do even when they're working. A lot of 'em drink it all up instead of puttin' clothes on their body. I know two or three guys who drink up their pay check as soon as they get it. Monday morning they're wearing the same old pants and shirt.

An osteopath, whose clientele are drawn from the lower socio-economic levels, observed:

> Well, you know, some of the people I visit—I wish you could go with me on my calls. There's one family. They sleep in an attic. They have to climb a ladder to get up. If you gave them my clothes or your clothes, in one week they'd be filthy and ragged. They just wouldn't know what to do with them.

The osteopath expounded at length on the importance of knowing how to wear clothes. Ambitious and aspiring, incidentally, he was caught in an interesting dilemma. To maintain his clientele (his source of wealth), he had to speak the language of his lower status patients. This adversely affected his own speech *vis à vis* his acceptance in the social circle to which he aspired.

Differences in dress among the different levels of socio-economic status are, of course, maintained by present-day counselors, not only of beauty, but of occupation. A sales manager for a local foundry talked at length upon the importance of matching occupation and clothing, concluding:

> I helped and made a fellow quite a success in Chicago in a clothes bureau. He charged ten dollars to interview people and tell them how to dress. First question he asked them was, "What is your position?" Then he asked them, "What is your work?"

Those in different status levels dress distinctively. The wife of the sales manager, just cited, observed:

> Clothes and speech. I can tell the minute a person comes through the door what kind of person they are and what their home surroundings are like. Speech is a very important factor. Those things tell class, too.

A hotel clerk assigned "social classes" on the basis of dress. Asked to enumerate the different social classes in Vansburg, she replied:

> Oh, I don't know. There would be the "butterfly type"—you know—just a bit on the overdressed order. Second, the conservative type. Then, the lower class, of course, who try, but get their clothing from Wards, Sears, or Spiegels, who get their clothing without trying it on to see if it suits their personality.

A nurse noted, "It's either the very wealthy or the lower class who get themselves decked out. You expect it with the wealthy." An oil salesman's wife said, "Millionaires dress better. There's no place in this town for that. That's why they look peculiar to us." The wife of an accounting supervisor asserted, "People of higher class wear clothes of better quality."

Interview excerpts also provide some evidence

for the contention that different dress, construed as a variable symbol of status, does in fact mobilize the responses of different people. Consider the remarks of Elmer Olds—one of the "dirty Oldses"—a conspicuous "lower-lower" family. Asked, "What happens to people around here when they don't dress right?" Elmer replied:

> I don't know. [Interviewer: Are there any people around here who don't dress right?] A lot of 'em don't. [Interviewer: Well, what happens?] They get in for vagrancy mostly. They think they're from out of town. There is a place for 'em, but I don't know what they do with 'em. Around here they don't bother 'em too much.

Now consider the remarks of a local policeman in response to the same question:

> Most of them are fellows that we have trouble with at the office. They wear anything that someone else throws away. [Interviewer: Why is that?] Mostly because they don't want to work.

I think these remarks can be construed as rather plausible evidence that the dress of those of very low status in Vansburg mobilized a particular response from a particular group—the police—that such dress is not calculated to arouse within the social circles of those manifesting very low status.

Sometimes one's dress culminates in a somewhat more subtle response than that of police arrest—social ostracism. Asked what might happen to her should she appear on the streets in a ragged and torn housedress, a carpenter's wife replied:

> They'd probably stick up their noses at you and say, "Funny she comes uptown dressed that way." [Interviewer: What people did you have in mind?] There are some people that go around with their noses up in the air. If you're all dressed up, they'll pass the time of day with you. If you're not, they won't speak to you. They're the snobbish people.

Others provided evidence of similar consequences for the person who does not keep up his appearance according to local standards. In response to the question: "What happens to people around here when they don't dress right?" a woman employed as an assembler at Amalgamated Chieftain, a national corporation which had recently established an assembly and packaging plant in Vansburg, replied:

> They're generally shoved off to the side. With me, I don't shove them off to the side. I can speak to someone in overalls as well as someone in furs. If we'd all dress in overalls, we'd be better off.

Yet, not everyone dresses in overalls, as a livestock broker observed, and these variations in dress mobilize different people as members of continuing social circles:

> I usually go with people according to the way they dress. Groups dress about the same. If they don't dress right, they'd probably go with another group of people.

His wife validates her husband's comments:

> Nothing happens to them. [Interviewer: You mean socially?] Yes. They wouldn't associate with them. [Interviewer: Who?] The people in their social class.

In a more direct manner, the differential mobilization of audience and dress was captured by the terse remark of an oil salesman: "Now, when you go to the Elks, you got to dress up, but not at the Eagles." Or, an iron molder, admitting that he is more careful with his clothes when he appears in some groups rather than others, explained:

> 'Cause I was going out, and, if somebody thought they was a little better than I was, I'd dress a little better. If I was among my friends, I wouldn't. [Interviewer: What do you mean—a little better than you?] There's a certain group in town. They don't make any more money than you do, but they think they're better—"nickel millionaires"—you know what I mean.

A local nurse, wife of a civil employee, explained her early wishes for clothing in much the same way:

> We were thrown together with a group of girls, various types, various classes: I wanted to be well dressed. In groups like that, there's a class distinction, and you want to be dressed nice.

This perceived relation between audience, symbol, and self facilitated for some a "full-blown" rhetoric:

> You can do well, if you're judicious and far-sighted, too. It pays to look smart and have a good appearance. When I was in school, my sister and I associated with people who had more money than we did, but nobody knew, because my mother planned well for me. I was afraid to join a sorority because many of the girls used to take thousand-dollar summer vacations and had plenty. I was afraid I couldn't keep up with the Joneses. But my mother said that, as long as I could pay the dues and not be any more shabbily dressed than the others, that I would make out all right.

Others somehow merely *experience* the audience response and never quite manage to anticipate it. For them, status is their circumstance. Asked to recall an early unpleasant experience with clothing, a carpenter's wife remembered:

> We was going to children's exercises, and we put on the best we had, and we went up there, and the woman who was in charge asked us if we were going home and change our dresses.

Such entrapment is frequently economic, as the wife of a weight-shifter in one of the foundries put it, when she was asked whether she would like to dress like some of the salesclerks she saw in the clothing stores:

> Yes. So I'd look nice on the street, and people wouldn't talk about you. I try to look as nice as I can, but, if you haven't got the money to buy the clothes, you have to do something else.

These data suggest that the situations and circumstances of social status are sharply distinguished by the residents of Vansburg. Perhaps for this reason, the universes of appearance mobilized around problems of status—its conferral, appropriation, and maintenance—are revealed more by the responses the residents of the town make to one another's clothed appearances, than in gross variations of meaning dress may be said to have for people of differing socio-economic ratings. The comprehension of one's status as a situation to be defined *for* as well as *by* others would, indeed, sensitize one to the status-meanings of dress. It is the very situational character that status has for some people that enables them to "escape" the limits of status "objectively" imposed upon them by their work by manipulating the apparent symbols available on the consumer market.

FIVE

THE ABORTION CLINIC: ANOTHER LOOK AT THE MANAGEMENT OF STIGMA

MARY K. ZIMMERMAN

Donald Ball's 1967 ethnographic analysis of an abortion clinic focused on how the clinic arranged and used symbols in an attempt to manipulate the meaning of the abortion situation. In Ball's words, his analysis was intended to "illuminate the presentational strategies employed by an habitually deviant establishment in its dealings with a situationally deviant clientele" (Ball, 1967, p. 293). The present analysis also focuses on the abortion clinic. This time the purpose is twofold: first, like Ball, I am concerned with presentational strategies—specifically, how societal changes after 1967 altered the clinics' presentational strategies; and second, I am interested in examining an aspect of the clinics' presentations which Ball neglected—namely, the success of the presentational strategies as viewed from the perspective of abortion clients.

SOURCE: Mary K. Zimmerman. "The Abortion Clinic: Another Look at the Management of Stigma." Original paper prepared especially for the 1980 edition of this volume. Reprinted by permission of the author.

Abortions in the United States were illegal in 1967, and, even though the abortions Ball studied were performed just on the other side of the California-Mexico border, the criminal or deviant implications for clients were undoubtedly intense. These implications could be expected to have had a particularly strong impact given the fact that most abortion clients were not accustomed to being classed as criminals. Most were otherwise law-abiding persons, caught temporarily with an unwanted pregnancy and only momentarily involved in a deviant act.

Under such circumstances, interaction between the "habitually deviant" staff members participating in abortion as a routine matter of career, and "situationally deviant" clients participating in abortion as an isolated, once-in-a-lifetime event, could likely result in disruption, hampering the smooth, efficient operation of the clinic. Thus, it would appear to be in the clinics' interest to try to minimize disruption. Apparently following this line of reasoning, Ball became interested in studying the ways by which the clinic went about managing impressions for its audience (clients)— the ways the clinic tried to transform a deviant situation into a normal one. Specifically, Ball said he wanted to "focus . . . upon techniques used by the clinic to key itself to the demands and expectations of a patronage drawn from the conventional culture" (Ball, 1967, p. 294).

By 1975, the legal status of abortion in the United States had changed. Abortions had become legal in every state. Yet, while the legal status of abortion had shifted dramatically, its moral status remained much the same. The most common abortion situations (where the woman could not afford a child, where the woman was unmarried, and where the woman was married but did not want a child) were still disapproved of by at least half the population (Arney and Trescher, 1976). For the abortion clients of the mid-1970s, this produced the paradoxical situation of participation in a legal but possibly immoral act. The implications of deviance had not disappeared.

It is at this point, a decade after Ball's observations and with abortion legal but with the implications of deviance still something clients must confront, that I return to take up his interest in how abortion clinics "present themselves" so as to meet the needs and expectations of their clients and, also, to pursue my own interest in how successful these presentations are in the view of clients.

ABORTION IN A MIDWESTERN CITY

Data for the following descriptions and analysis were obtained from (1) observations of the everyday routines of two abortion clinics, (2) informal interviews with administrative staff members in both clinics, and (3) guided, in-depth interviews with thirty-five systematically selected clients of the clinics. (A more detailed discussion of the methodology appears in Zimmerman, 1978.)

The two abortion clinics were located in dif-

ferent suburban areas of the same large Midwestern city. Both clinics obtained their clients in approximately the same ways, and both had approximately the same general organizational patterns and operating procedures. The following exemplifies a typical sequence of staff-client involvement.

A woman suspects that she is pregnant and contacts either her physician or a family planning clinic to arrange for a pregnancy test. The test confirms that she is, in fact, pregnant, so she asks about having an abortion and is referred to the abortion clinic. The referral is made directly from the family planning clinic to the abortion clinic; however, if a private physician is involved, he or she may either refer the woman to the abortion clinic or—and this is more likely—refer the woman to a family planning clinic which, in turn, refers her to the abortion clinic. Some women call the abortion clinic themselves without a referral agent. Once the initial call is made, an appointment for the abortion is arranged, generally just a few days in advance. The arrangements are made just as for any other medical procedure. The woman receives a written sheet of instructions which informs her of the cost of the abortion, the medical risks involved, and how she should prepare for the procedure. She is instructed to come to the clinic with another person so that she will not have to drive afterward.

On the day of the abortion, the woman and her companion (typically, either a parent or the male partner in the pregnancy) usually leave home early in the morning and drive to the clinic location. Most appointments are fairly early in the day. At both clinics, the average length of stay was six hours, so that a woman with a 9:00 A.M. appointment would typically remain at the clinic until midafternoon.

As has been indicated previously, both clinics followed approximately the same routine in handling each abortion case—checking in, paying, examinations, counseling, the abortion procedure, and recovery period. The following traces the route through one of the clinics. (The reader should keep in mind that the other clinic's routine was nearly identical.)

The client and her companion enter on the main floor where a receptionist refers them to the admissions office. There the fee is paid, a medical chart is made up, and the woman signs a general consent form. She and her companion then are sent to the second floor where she signs another consent form. At this point, the companion is taken to a visitor's waiting room where he or she remains until the client has completed the entire abortion and recovery sequence. Meanwhile, the client has blood and urine tests and a pelvic examination. After these tests, if the results reveal that her pregnancy is more advanced than previously indicated, she may have to pay an additional amount (the clinic incrementally increases the cost for pregnancies over twelve weeks). The next step is counseling, which consists of the woman being asked if she has any problems or questions about her abortion decision. If she does, these are discussed. If not, the counselor gives a detailed description of the abortion procedure and goes over the medical risks involved and the proper aftercare procedures. The counselor also talks to the woman about her future use of contraceptives. After counseling, the woman prepares for the abortion by putting on a gown and slippers. The procedure itself takes only a couple of minutes. Both clinics use the vacuum aspiration or suction technique. Afterward, the woman is taken to a recovery room where she relaxes. She is given crackers and a soft drink and a heating pad (to relieve pain from cramping) if she needs one. She stays in the recovery area for approximately an hour, then dresses and leaves the clinic.

With this background information about the clinics, some basic differences between them and the clinic Ball studied are apparent. First, in 1966 at Ball's clinic an average abortion cost $500. In 1975 at the two Midwestern clinics, an average abortion (performed through the twelfth week of pregnancy) cost $150. Because of the expense, Ball estimated that the clientele of his clinic was predominantly composed of middle- and upper middle-class persons. The clinics in this study were also frequented by the upper middle class, but the most common client was either middle or working class.

A second difference stems from the obvious fact that the clinic Ball studied was a clandestine, illegal establishment. As such, the location was not revealed to clients until the last minute, and even then, what was revealed was a "place of rendezvous" where the client was picked up by strangers and transported to the clinic building. In addition, the nature of Ball's clinic led him to suggest that the persons performing the abortions were less than certified physicians ("ostensibly physicians") and that the clinic's sanitary practices were questionable ("pseudo-sterility"). These features were absent in the 1975 clinics. These clinics were openly visible, legal, and regulated by the same professional standards as other established medical institutions.

ANALYSIS

Ball explained the presentational strategies of the abortion clinic with the term *rhetoric of legitimation:*

> Sociologically, a rhetoric is a vocabulary of limited purpose; that is . . . a set of symbols functioning to communicate a particular set of meanings, directed and organized toward the representation of a specific image or impression. Such vocabularies are not only verbal, but also include visual symbols such as objects, gestures, emblems, etc. (Ball, 1967, p. 296).

Because of the stigma associated with abortion, the clinic's "rhetoric" was one of legitimation—one that would "neutralize the context of deviance" and "generate a picture of legitimate activity" (Ball, 1967, p. 296).

To elaborate on his notion of "rhetoric," Ball drew on Goffman's (1959) concept of "front." Goffman used "front" to indicate a strategically organized presentation of self, composed of a person's particular "setting," "appearance," and "manner." Extending the meaning of "front" to include an organization's or establishment's presentation of self, Ball proceeded to analyze the abortion clinic in terms of each of Goffman's three components. From this analysis he concluded that the rhetorical theme of legitimation was one that stressed medical professionalism, buttressed by cost and luxury. Through displaying certain symbols of medical competence and cleanliness, the clinic tried to counter the stereotypic image of quack practitioners and shabby backrooms commonly evoked by the thought of abortion.

The present analysis finds a striking contrast in rhetorical theme to the "medical model" approach found by Ball. The two Midwestern clinics of a later decade, while making sure their clients were aware of the high medical standards of their facilities, nevertheless were primarily committed to the *deemphasis of the traditional medical model* of health care delivery. In other words, their approach was to avoid rather than to exaggerate the "hospital look." Such an approach stemmed from their belief that traditional medical practices are sterile, cold, and impersonal, and that they work against the best interests of clients by making them uneasy and afraid.

This contrast in rhetorical themes of legitimation will be seen more clearly as we compare the clinics of both decades in terms of Goffman's distinctions among "setting," "appearance," and "manner."

SETTING

The setting includes the clinics' physical and spatial characteristics. Since the entire setting produces the rhetorical effect for the client, both the exterior and interior setting must be considered.

At Ball's 1966 clinic, the character of the setting was established initially by the location of the clinic in a prestigious, residential neighborhood—prestigious presumably because persons tend to associate competent medical care with wealth. The fact remains, however, that the structure outwardly resembled a private home rather than a medical facility and, therefore, was not in keeping with the "medical model" stressed inside. The exterior settings of the two 1975 clinics were as different from each other as they were from the 1967 clinic. Both were housed in institutional as opposed to residential structures, but neither could be identified immediately as a medical facility.

One clinic was located in an older, three-story brick building that once had been a small community hospital. In 1975, a nursing home occupied the basement, and the abortion clinic was located on the upper two floors. The surrounding neighborhood, on the edge of the city, was low income and predominantly black. That, in addition to the simple landscaping and mud and gravel parking lot, gave the otherwise well-cared for building a stark and perhaps foreboding appearance.

The other clinic was located in a basement suite of a professional office building situated just off a major commercial street in a well-traveled, middle-class suburban area. This building was also brick; however, it was larger and relatively new, with such embellishments as wrought iron trim, professional landscaping, and a large, paved parking area. Other occupants of the building included a standard variety of business and professional firms.

According to Ball, presentational strategies are chosen so that audience impressions will conform to appropriate expectations. In his study, the assumption was (no data on expectations were presented) that "conventional" clients were expecting a "conventional" establishment. Moreover, with situations such as abortion, where there are also incipient deviant images to be countered, the problem of impression management is compounded. For success, the staff of the abortion clinic must be able accurately to "take the role of the other" and correctly assess just what clients' expectations are and how best to "present" the clinic.

The women clients of the two abortion clinics in this study were expecting a traditional hospital-type facility:

I was expecting like [my hometown] hospital or something like that. . . .

We were looking for this big hospital . . . I expected a big, white hospital with all these guys walking around in white suits, white overcoats and all. . . .

It didn't look anything like a hospital. . . .

With these expectations in mind, let us examine how the Midwestern abortion clients in this study began to define their situation upon first seeing the exterior of the clinic building. As might be expected, the clinic in the low-income setting was less successful in initially countering the deviant stereotypes of abortion. Its exterior produced definitions betraying fear laced with images of crime and unsanitary conditions—in fact, confirming the stigma of immorality still attached to abortion.

The clinic looked like a jail or something to me. It kind of scared me because . . . you see on all these movies how they did it in strange ways with knives and stuff and that's what it made me think of . . . something the law didn't know about . . . and you could get disease in about three seconds. . . .

To me it looked like a prison. It had bars on the windows and I didn't like it at all . . . I was thinking, "I wonder what kind of medical facilities they've got. Is it such a grubby place that all it is is a doctor who isn't even qualified?"

It was such an old, dilapidated building to me . . . and I was scared. Maybe I would go in there and there would be cockroaches running around . . . maybe I wasn't going to have the kind of care that I had thought I was going to have. . . . It made me think, "Well, abortions are something you don't talk

about, so maybe that's why they are sending me back here to this old, dilapidated building.

The more modern-appearing clinic in the office building was only mildly problematic, if at all. Typically, it was the accompanying person who was most concerned:

The [family planning] counselor said it was in the basement of the building and that sounded . . . well, I didn't want some place raunchy. . . . then, when we saw it, it didn't look like a medical building. My husband was very suspicious. He said if it was too bad, we'd leave.

. . . the outside of the place was like a motel or an apartment and [my boyfriend] goes, "I don't think we should go in there. I don't want you hurt.

Since most women were expecting a large, modern, hospital-like structure, the further away from that expected image their actual image was, the more troubled and suspicious they were, readily applying criminal abortion stereotypes.

Ball focused his analysis of "setting" on the clinic waiting room because, according to him, it gave clients their first impression of the clinic. As we have seen, however, the women's impressions began to form from the moment they saw the exterior and surroundings of the clinic.

Clients of the older-appearing clinic entered into a small reception lobby that was neat and clean but had sparse and simple furnishings. There the receptionist, a middle-aged black woman, directed them to the admitting room where they paid their fee and, along with their companion, were directed upstairs to the second floor. Clients of the more modern-apearing clinic entered into a more elegant setting, an open, carpeted central space with expensive lounge furniture. Various firms were identified on the series of doors that led off this space. A sign directed the client to the basement level where they entered the clinic's suite. Tnere they were met by one of the young white women who belonged to the clinic's staff. Just as in the older clinic, after the formalities of admission and fee-paying, accompanying persons were shown into a separate waiting room for the duration of the client's stay.

The rooms that housed the older clinic were relatively small. They had been recently redecorated in pastel shades (pink, lavender, blue, and yellow), with flowered curtains, colorful rugs and wall posters, and stick-on flowers scattered here and there. The ceilings had been inlaid with pieces of a glittering substance that sparkled when the light struck it. As in the downstairs lobby, the furniture tended to be plain and serviceable rather than stylish or elegant. The overall effect of the interior decor was attractive, but with an unsophisticated, do-it-yourself look that is probably more appealing to working-class than to upper middle-class tastes.

The rooms in the newer clinic's suite tended to be somewhat larger. They were thickly carpeted and professionally decorated. The emphasis was on bright colors, with casual, modern furniture and wall decorations. The overall effect of the decor was bright and cheerful in a sophisticated style appealing to middle- and upper middle-class tastes.

Ball's interest in the waiting room was noted previously. In the clinics of this study, the waiting rooms were less central in shaping the clients' impressions of the clinic. For one reason, they did not dominate the physical layout of the clinic. For another, there were several rather than just one waiting room. The waiting room in Ball's study was arranged into private areas, "structured so as to create withdrawal niches for each set of patrons" (Ball 1967, p. 297). Distances between groupings were maximized, according to Ball, so that clients did not have to direct visual contact with each other. Such attempts at intimacy and privacy were not found at the two Midwestern clinics. Clients were placed very close to each other, generally in chairs and couches placed along the walls, in an arrangement that offered no protection from interpersonal contact. In addition, clients were separated from their accompanying others, so

that, if there were conversation, it was necessarily among clients.

The rooms where the abortions were done were just large enough for one gynecological table, the suction machine, and either cabinets or small tables for other examining equipment. No superfluous equipment—such as the bottles, vials of pills and liquids, and stainless steel pans and trays found by Ball—were in evidence.

For most clients of both clinics, the interior settings were successful in countering the deviant stereotypes of abortion and in fostering an image of competent medical care. With a few exceptions, the success of the more modern, bourgeois clinic can be attributed to the same phenomena Ball's analysis suggests—that "elegance" and cost are symbolically associated with high-quality medical care. The older-appearing clinic, however, constitutes a slightly different set of circumstances. Its attempt to present an attractive, reassuring interior was generally working-class bound. It was effective because most of the clients referred there were also working class. Occasionally, however, a middle-class client would be referred there, and her impressions would be quite different. This is exemplified in the contrasting reactions below—the first by a working-class woman, the second by a middle-class woman:

It was a blooming riot of color. They've got this—on the doors they've got this stick-on—it looks like shelf paper. They got that cut-out in flower designs and stuff that matches the paint. It was great! The doors are all painted a different colored pastel than the walls and the woodwork is all different . . . and the carpet, it clashes, but it's real bright, cheery, riotous stuff. . . .

The whole atmosphere—well, just like the curtains: they have daisy curtains. It looked like an old school building and yet they have tried to dainty it up like a little girl's room. . . . I would much rather it had just been white walls and white light . . . because the whole thing—I don't know, maybe some girls feel relaxed in that area, but I didn't because it just came across as phony to me . . . I guess you'd say that it was shady, sneaky, sly—you know, dishonest.

Thus, the success of the clinics' interior settings in eliminating deviant suspicions was contingent upon class-based expectations of appropriate decor. This was not a problem with working-class women being referred to the bourgeois clinic, but it was with the middle-class women.

The older, less sophisticated appearing clinic also evoked more suspicion because of its problematic exterior. Doubts, once aroused, were difficult to eliminate. Women entering with the criminal abortion stereotype in mind interpreted other aspects of the clinic accordingly. For example, the clinic used colored lines painted on the hallway floors to designate traffic directions for the clients. For some women, these lines symbolized the "assembly line" approach of an abortion mill:

. . . they had all of these little arrows on the floor pointing which way to go . . . and it made it seem like they do this everyday . . . like they were packing us all in and standing in line and getting it done and then walking out. . . .

You are just following a bunch of lines . . . it was kind of like an assembly line. . . .

APPEARANCE AND MANNER

For Ball, appearance and manner referred to the clothing style and behavior, particularly verbal behavior, of staff members. For our purposes, appearance can also refer to physical characteristics such as age, sex, and race. In addition, while the discussion here is limited to staff appearance and manner, it should be noted that the clients were also observing and forming impressions of fellow clients.

In his 1966 analysis, Ball focused on the traditional medical attire—classic white gowns, tunics, and uniforms—worn by staff members, pointing out the impression of sterile, hygienic conditions suggested by this mode of dress. Staff manner or demeanor was also in keeping with the "medical model" front. Ball's analysis dealt primarily with the "professional" (medical) behavior of staff members, with verbal strategies cited as a case in point. According to Ball, the clinic vocabulary was "strictly medical, with no effort either made or implied to speak down to the less knowledgeable lay patron" (Ball, 1967, p. 298). Another interesting linguistic feature of the clinic's verbal presentation was that at no time during the clients' stay was the word "abortion" used. Instead, the abortion was called the "operation," "procedure," or "D and C."

In the two Midwestern clinics of 1975, staff dress and demeanor were also orchestrated; however, the thematic composition was substantially different. These clinics had a nontraditional medical model emphasizing "individualized" and "personalized" care. Thus, both dress modes and interaction patterns were less formal and less "medicalized." Staff members in both clinics tended to wear casual street clothes rather than uniforms. If uniforms were worn, they generally were in pastel tones rather than the traditional, stark white. A further contrast between the decades concerns the use of language. While Ball's clinic deliberately avoided using the word "abortion," just the opposite was the case in 1975. In fact, an explicit effort was made in the course of staff-client interaction to use the word naturally; all the technical details were explained in order to "normalize" the experience and to dispel any myths. Far from covering up abortion with another word, the clinics did everything they could to encourage their clients to discuss it openly. Ironically, while Ball's clinic chose the word "operation" as a substitute for "abortion," the 1975 clinics avoided "operation" deliberately. It was viewed as a symbol of the traditional medical model. Thus, in the interest of "demedicalizing" abortion, any reference to "operation," "surgery," or "operating room" was avoided. Instead, the 1975 clinics preferred to call the operation a ''procedure'' and the room where abortions were performed a ''procedure room.''

Another feature of clinic behavior that Ball noted was the attempt to imitate a teaching hospital by having an ''apprentice practitioner'' on hand during the performance of the abortion. According to Ball, ''the teaching aspects of the senior practitioner's role help to generate confidence in his skill'' (Ball, 1967, p. 298). Once again, the intended purpose was to ''medicalize'' the abortion experience as much as possible. In contrast, the clinics of 1975 included an additional person in the abortion procedure for the express purpose of *deinstitutionalizing* or demedicalizing the abortion; that is, the clinics routinely had the counselor who had explained the abortion procedure to the client earlier in the day, and who had presumably developed good rapport with her, come in to the procedure room in order to talk, comfort, and even hold the client's hand while the suction machine was in operation. Clearly, the emphasis here was on interpersonal support and individualized care rather than on following traditional medical practices.

As previously pointed out, Ball did not extend his analysis of appearance to include the physical characteristics of the staff other than their clothing. The 1975 study, however, revealed the importance of age, sex, and race characteristics in the clients' definitions of the situation. The modern-appearing clinic, for example, had only young, female staff members (including the physician). This was intended to enhance the possibilities for rapport between the staff and the relatively young, female clients, with the ultimate aim of increasing their confidence. The older-appearing clinic also had only young women on its counseling and administrative staff; however, the gynecologists were males. Further, the newer clinic had no blacks on staff. The older clinic, on the other hand, had a number of blacks. These racial characteristics were particularly important in the clients' initial impressions:

I walked in and all there were were black people—to me, I saw black people as meaning that they're doing it unlawfully. ''It's going to be a black doctor.'' That's the first thing that I thought—that this doctor is going to be a black doctor, I kept thinking about that. . . .

. . . when we came, all we could see outside, playing ball, everywhere, on the first floor, was just colored people . . . it kind of scared me to think I'm going to go in and there's going to be all these colored people. . . .

The first floor scared me because everybody I saw was colored. Everybody! I didn't see one white person except the girls that were waiting, too. Then, I got upstairs and I was so relieved . . . I got upstairs and saw some white people. . . .

Despite these problematic aspects of the clinics' presentations, the overall ''rhetoric of legitimation''—the portrayal of a casual and friendly rather than rigidly professional front—appears to have been successful. Summing up their reactions to the clinics, the clients seemed to have been most affected by the relaxed, interpersonal style of the staff:

I didn't know what it was going to be like . . . just that it would be a cold, technical-like place. And, they weren't. They were just real, warm, human people.

. . . the atmosphere was different. They weren't real uptight or anything . . . I expected it to be very clinical, *very* clinical . . . I didn't expect any personalization. I didn't expect the loose attitude about what you were doing . . . you didn't feel like you were doing something bad. . . .

. . . they were really friendly. They made, I think, everybody really feel just so much better because they were. They didn't run around in their white nurses uniforms. . . .

It should be observed, however, that presentations do not always strike members of an audience in the same way. While the clinics' presentations were successful for most clients, here is an example of one woman for whom the production was a failure:

> . . . it was an informal feeling. They didn't give a damn if you were going to have an abortion. You were just a nameless person—well, this is number so and so. Just like a prison . . . cold and unfeeling. . . .

DISCUSSION

The preceding analysis reveals considerable variation between the presentational strategies of abortion clinics of the mid-1960s and those of the mid-1970s—variation reflecting the dramatic societal changes in the status of abortion that occurred within that decade. Specifically, the shift from illegal to legal abortion has been accompanied by a shift in "rhetoric of legitimation" from one emphasizing medical professionalism to one that deemphasizes it, stressing instead "personalized," "individualized," nontraditional care.

In 1966, because of their illegal status, abortion clinics operated outside the control of established medical guidelines and inspection procedures. Some clinics and individual practitioners offered vastly inferior care, as a result of which thousands of women died. Out of this situation, helped along by vivid movie portrayals of abortion, came the criminal abortion stereotype—unqualified persons using crude instruments in dirty, sleazy settings. Abortion, in short, became associated with the idea of inferior medical care. Thus, a clinic such as the one Ball studied was primarily oriented to countering this stereotype by employing a powerful symbolic display of traditional, conventional medical practices. In order to legitimize the clinic, to protect it from the aura of "quack" medicine, the "medical model" became the key rhetorical theme.

By 1975, however, the societal scene had changed. Abortion clinics were legal and, accordingly, had been brought within the guidelines and control procedures of mainstream health care practice. To the staff of the mid-1970s clinics, therefore, presenting an exaggerated medical front was not of central concern. Clean, competent care was stressed but did not serve as the major rhetorical theme of the two clinics studied here. Instead, clinic staff attention was focused on public moral sentiment and the abortion controversy of which nearly all persons were aware. What they thought had to be countered by the clinics of the mid-1970s were the fear and condemnation of doing something immoral. In line with this belief, the clinics adopted a rhetoric of "personalized" nonhospital-like medical care. The aim was to relax the client, to give her the view of abortion as a normal, appropriate medical procedure, and to encourage her to "open up" her doubts and fears in a supportive atmosphere. Thus, rather than stressing the rigid, professional practices typically associated with medicine, the abortion clinics of 1975 stressed a more personal, "human" approach. Rather than a *medical* theme, the 1975 clinics chose a *moral* theme.

Through comparative analysis, we have demonstrated the relationship between the particular presentational strategies chosen and the social structural arrangements of the times. The success of presentational strategies, however, also depends on the presenting parties' ability to "take the role of the other"—to assess accurately audience demands and expectations. The present study showed that 1975 abortion clients were much more vulnerable to the illegal, criminal stereotypes than clinic staff may have anticipated. Hence, discrepancies in the clinics' presentations such as the exterior facade or certain aspects of decor were perceived with suspicion. Many clients came expecting more traditional care. In most cases, initial suspicions were quelled and the clinics redefined when the clients began to interact with staff members whose manner reassured them. In other cases, however, particularly when the rhetoric of the clinic was oriented toward working-class women and the client was middle class, the presentation remained a failure throughout the experience.

Ball, in his analysis, discussed "flaws" in the clinic's presentation—those that may have been recognized by clients as well as those that may not have been. A "flaw" is a discrepancy between a symbolic element and the overall rhetorical theme. In the present analysis, most of the flaws previously discussed have been those recognized and commented upon by clients. One that we have not yet considered is perhaps the most important discrepancy of all: the fact that, even though the clinics' rhetoric of legitimation stressed personal, individual care, the abortion experience as orchestrated by the clinics was far from private and personal. To the contrary, it was an experience shared with others from the beginning. While the vacuum aspiration was performed with only one client in the room at a time, the waiting, counseling, and recovery phases of the abortions (the events taking the major portion of the client's time) were conducted with several patients grouped together. Thus, the abortion was a group rather than an individual experience—in effect, a public rather than a private experience. It should be noted that Ball also commented on the lack of privacy for clients in his clinic; however, his clients did not sit in direct confrontation with each other in the waiting rooms, did not go into a group counseling session together, and apparently did not stay together in the recovery room. Hence, while the 1975 clinics stressed "individualized" and "personalized" care, they afforded clients the least privacy.

Earlier, it was suggested the clinics adopt a "rhetoric" or presentational strategy in order to smooth interaction where there is potential for disruption. While clients may arrive at the clinic with their own definitions of the situation—definitions that may be at odds with those of the staff—the clinic's rhetoric provides a mutual definition, one that not only promotes the smooth operation of clinic routine but also protects the possibly threatened identities of participants. For staff members, the rhetoric reinforces their self-image as professionals and, perhaps more important for the 1975 clinics because of their open portrayal of abortion, gives them the self-gratifying notion of contributing to a social "cause." For clients, the rhetoric protects them from doubt about the morality of what they are doing and validates their worth as persons. In the present study, in cases where the rhetoric was unsuccessful, it was the client, not the staff member, whose social world was disrupted—and, for whom it was particularly difficult to construct a nonproblematic, legitimate definition of abortion.

REFERENCES

Arney, William R. and William H. Trescher. "Trends in Attitudes Toward Abortion, 1972–1975," *Family Planning Perspectives* 8 (May/June, 1976): 117–24.

Ball, Donald. "An Abortion Clinic Ethnography," *Social Problems* 14 (Winter, 1967): 293–301.

Goffman, Erving. *The Presentation of Self in Everyday Life*. Garden City: Doubleday, 1959, p. 5.

Zimmerman, Mary K. *Passage Through Abortion: The Personal and Social Reality of Women's Experience*. New York: Praeger Publishers 1978.

SIX

AWARENESS CONTEXTS AND SOCIAL INTERACTION

BARNEY G. GLASER AND ANSELM L. STRAUSS

When men confront each other, each cannot always be certain—even when given seemingly trustworthy guarantees—that he knows either the other's identity or his own identity in the eyes of the other. An honest citizen may be taken in by a confidence man, a government official by a foreign spy passing as his secretary, or a dying patient by his doctor. But the confidence man's mark may actually be from the local detective squad; the official, suspecting undercover play, may be pretending innocence while spilling the secretary false documents; and the dying patient may suspect his true condition but not reveal his suspicion to the physician. Thus, who is really being "taken in" is a matter of the awareness of both parties to the situation.

The phenomenon of awareness—which is central to the study of interaction—can be quite complex for at least two reasons. First, interaction may involve not merely two persons, but a third or quite a few more. For instance, when a homosexual flashes cues to another homosexual in the presence of many straight people, some may not notice and others may misread the cues, while others may be aware of their intended meaning. The identity of the homosexual is, therefore, unknown or suspect to some straights and known to still others. Conversely, a homosexual cannot always be certain who suspects or who is not aware of his true identity. Second, each person involved may be the representative of a system with specific requirements for, and perhaps a high stake in, how the person manages his own and the other's identity. Spies and counterspies are linked to such systems as often as are doctors and nurses.

These considerations highlight important features of the relation between interaction and awareness. To establish our basic notions, however, we shall content ourselves in this paper with the least complex situation: two interactants (whether persons or groups) who face the dual problem of being certain about both their identity in the other's eyes and the other's identity.

SOURCE: Barney G. Glaser and Anselm L. Strauss. "Awareness Contexts and Social Interaction." Copyright by the American Sociological Association, 1967. Barney G. Glaser and Anselm L. Strauss, "Awareness Contexts and Social Interaction," *American Sociological Review*, XXIX (October, 1967), pp. 669–679. Reprinted by permission of the American Sociological Association.

CONTEXTS OF AWARENESS

By the term *awareness context* we mean the total combination of what each interactant in a situation knows about the identity of the other and his own identity in the eyes of the other.[1] This total awareness is the context within which are guided successive interactions between the two persons over periods of time—long or short. Empirically the question of true identity may focus only on that of one of the two persons (the dying patient) or on that of both persons (spy and counter-spy).

We have singled out four types of awareness context for special consideration since they have proved useful in accounting for different types of interaction. An *open* awareness context obtains when each interactant is aware of the other's true identity and his own identity in the eyes of the other. A *closed* awareness context obtains when one interactant does not know either the other's identity or the other's view of his identity. A *suspicion* awareness context is a modification of the closed one: one interactant suspects the true identity of the other or the other's view of his own identity, or both. A *pretense* awareness context is a modification of the open one: both interactants are fully aware but pretend not to be.

These types illustrate how the sociologist's total picture may differ from that held by each interactant, no matter how well informed or expert. For

[1]The concept of awareness context is a structural unit, not a property of one of the standard structural units such as group, organization community, role, position, etc. By "context" we mean it is a structural unit of an encompassing order larger than the other unit under focus: interaction. Thus, an awareness context surrounds and affects the interaction. Much as one might say that the interaction of staff with dying patients occurs within the context of a cancer ward or a veteran's hospital, one can also say that this interaction occurs within a type of awareness context. Note that ward or hospital are concrete, conventional social units, while awareness context is an analytic social unit, constructed to account for similarities in interaction in many diverse conventional units.

A more general definition of awareness context is the total combination of what specific people, groups, organizations, communities or nations know what about a specific issue. Thus, this structural concept can be used for the study of virtually any problem entailing awareness at any structural level of analysis.

example, a doctor may state that a patient does not yet know that he is dying (his identity in the eyes of the doctor) while the patient may very well suspect the physician's definition. Thus, the doctor believes that closed awareness obtains when actually there is a suspicion context within which the patient is testing his suspicions. If the doctor recognizes those suspicions, he may attempt to parry them. If the doctor believes himself successful, he may only report to the sociologist that as yet the patient is unaware, neglecting to mention the patient's suspicions. Therefore, delimiting an awareness context requires always that the sociologist ascertain independently the awareness of each interactant. The safest method is to obtain data, through observation or interview, from each interactant on his own state of awareness. To accept the word of only one informant is risky, even perhaps for the open awareness context.

The successive interactions occurring within each type of context tend to transform the context. As yet it is an empirical question as to the direction in which a change in one context will lead, or what are some patterns of successive transformations. Thus, a closed context can be shattered by arousing suspicions; but if suspicions are quelled, the closed context is reinstituted. If suspicions are validated, the context may change to either pretense or open awareness. With a change in identity of one interactant in the eyes of the other, an open context can easily become either closed or pretense. For instance, the government official who suspects that his secretary is a spy must now check his suspicions. If he discovers that she is a spy but does not reveal his knowledge, then she in turn misreads his view of her identity. Thus, a closed context now obtains! If she in turn surreptitiously learns of his new view of her but says nothing, the context is again closed. But if he unmasks her spying, then the context now becomes open, since each now fully acknowledges the other's true identity.

How long each context will last before it is transformed is also an empirical question. In the abstract none is inherently less stable than another;

although within a given substantive area, differential degrees of stability may become apparent. For dying patients, a suspicion context is probably the least stable, becoming resolved by successive interactions with staff which confirm the patient's suspicions.

A PARADIGM FOR THE STUDY OF AWARENESS CONTEXTS

To organize a study of interaction within different awareness contexts, we have developed a paradigm or set of directives. These directives focus on the study of developmental interaction process—interaction that changes as it continues—as distinct from the relatively static study of the rules that govern interaction.[2]

The component parts of the paradigm are as follows: (1) a description of the given type of awareness context; (2) the structural conditions under which the awareness context exists;[3] (3) the consequent interaction; (4) changes of interaction that occasion transformations of context, along with the structural conditions for the transformations; (5) the tactics of various interactants as they attempt to manage changes of awareness context; and (6) some consequences of the initial awareness context, its transformation and associated interactions—for interactants and for the organizations or institutions notably affected.

To illustrate the use of this paradigm, we briefly

[2]Cf. Erving Goffman, *Behavior in Public Places*, New York: Free Press of Glencoe, 1963.

[3]We use the phrase "structural conditions" to emphasize that the conditions are conceived of as properties of social structural units. These units may vary from the smallest (such as role, status, or relationship) to the largest (such as organization, community, nation or society) and may be either larger or smaller than the unit of discussion. Usually they are larger contextual units. Structural conditions tend to have a determining or guiding effect on the unit of discussion. Since structural conditions are the tools-in-trade of most sociologists, this footnote is not meant for them. The structural conditions under which interaction takes place, however, are not typically included in the work of social psychologists, especially those trained in departments of psychology.

sketch the closed awareness context surrounding dying patients.

(1) Hospitalized patients frequently do not recognize their impending death while staff does.[4] Thus interaction between staff and patient occurs within a closed awareness context about the patient's true identity.

(2) At least four major structural conditions determine this closed awareness context. First, most patients are not especially experienced at recognizing the signs of impending death. Second, the hospital is magnificently organized, both by accident and design, for hiding the medical truth from the patient. Records are kept out of reach. Staff is skilled at withholding information from him. Medical talk about him occurs generally in far-removed places. Also, the staff is trained or accustomed to act collusively around patients so as not to disclose medical secrets. Third, physicians are supported in their withholding of information by professional rationales: "Why deny them all hope by telling them they are dying?" Fourth, ordinarily the patient has no allies who can help him discover the staff's secret: even his family or other patients will withhold such information if privy to it.

(3) To prevent the patient's comprehension of the truth, the personnel utilize a number of "situation as normal" interaction tactics. They seek to act in his presence as if he were not dying but only ill. They talk to him as if he were going to live. They converse about his future, thus enhancing his belief that he will regain his health. They tell him stories about others (including themselves) who have recovered from similar or worse illnesses. By such indirect signaling they offer him a false biography. Of course, they may directly assure him that he will live, lying with a clear purpose.

To supplement these tactics the staff members use additional ones to guard against disclosure.

[4]We shall assume that the staff members all share the same awareness and that the staff's definition of a patient's identity (dying) is correct.

They carefully guard against the patient's over-hearing any conversation about his real condition. They engage also in careful management of expressions, controlling their facial and other gestures so as not to give the show away:[5] they must control the expression of any sadness they experience over the patient's approaching death. Almost inevitably they attempt, not always consciously, to reduce the number of potentially disclosing cues by reducing time spent with the patient or by restricting their conversations with him.

(4) In such collusive games, the teamwork can be phenomenal but the dangers of disclosure to the patient are very great. Unless the patient dies quickly or becomes permanently comatose, the patient tends to suspect or even clearly understand how others identify him. Patients do overhear occasional conversations about themselves. Personnel unwittingly may flash cues or make conversational errors, which arouse the patient's suspicions. Day and night staff may give him contradictory information or divergent clues. The frequent practice of rotating personnel through the hospital services, or adding new personnel, may add to the danger of disclosure. The patient himself may become more knowledgeable about what is going on around him after some days in the hospital, or after repeated hospitalizations. Eventually, he may also understand that the hospital is organized not to give him all the information about his condition but rather to withhold most information. He therefore takes what is told him with a grain of salt and some distrust of its accuracy. In short, the original structural conditions that sustain closed awareness begin to disappear, or are counteracted by new structural conditions that make for suspicion or open awareness. This is true even when the patient's symptoms do not badly worsen, but when he does turn worse this may cause him to ask new questions about his illness, which staff members

[5]Erving Goffman, *The Presentation of Self in Everyday Life,* Edinburgh, Scotland: University of Edinburgh, 1956; see also the Doubleday-Anchor Book edition.

need to handle cannily to keep from him their knowledge that he is dying.

(5) Some interactants may wish to move him along into other types of awareness context. If so, they can employ certain interactional tactics which are, for the most part, merely the opposites of the non-disclosure tactics. Intentionally, a staff member may give the show away wholly or partly, by improper management of face, by carefully oblique phrasing of words, by merely failing to reassure the patient sufficiently about a hopeful prognosis, by changing all talk about the future into concentration upon the present, or by increasing avoidance both of conversation and the patient himself. Of course, personnel occasionally may just plain tell him that he is dying.

(6) The closed awareness that "surrounds" the dying patient has many significant consequences for patient and staff. The patient, unaware of the other's view of his identity, cannot act as if he were aware of dying. Thus he cannot talk to close kin about his fate. He cannot assuage their grief. Nor can he act toward himself as if he were dying, by facing his expected death gracefully—or with panic and hysteria.

The kinsmen and hospital personnel are saved from certain stressful scenes that accompany open awareness about death, but they are also blocked from participating in various satisfying rituals of passage to death. Wives cannot openly take fare-wells of husbands; personnel cannot share the patient's sometimes ennobling acceptance of death. A profound consequence for the hospital itself, as well as for staff, of the closed awareness context is an interesting division of labor wherein nurses carry the brunt of stressful verbal interaction during which dying and death talk must be avoided. The physicians escape much of this stress since only brief visits are required for patients seemingly on the mend, hence talk is held to a minimum. Moreover, the climate of certain hospital services would be quite different (usually less oppressive) if closed awareness contexts were completely absent—as they are on certain special types of hospital wards.[6]

PREVIOUS ANALYSES OF INTERACTION

The notion of awareness context is useful for understanding other theoretical approaches to awareness as it relates to social interaction. Our paradigm for the study of interaction within awareness contexts may be used to locate, in a single scheme, the diverse aspects of awareness and social interaction attended to in sociological writings. To illustrate this application of both concept and paradigm, we shall discuss the theoretical work of George H. Mead and Erving Goffman as well as the researches of Donald Roy and Fred Davis. Rather than assess their work *per se,* we shall discuss the writings of these men as good examples of the current state of theory and research about social interaction.

GEORGE H. MEAD

Mead's concern with social interaction was secondary to a lifetime preoccupation with the problems of social order and its orderly change. We interpret his analysis of interaction—also his writing about communication and thought—as bearing principally on an open awareness context. In a well known passage he wrote that: "In short, the conscious or significant conversation of gestures is a much more adequate and effective mechanism of mutual adjustment within the social act—involving, as it does, the taking, by each of the individuals carrying it on, the attitudes of the others toward himself—than is the unconscious or non-significant conversation of gestures."[7] For Mead, "awareness" was essentially an *accurate* awareness of how one's own gesture (vocal or otherwise) was being defined by others, followed by further action based on that awareness. Thus: "That process . . . of responding to one's self as another responds to it, taking part in one's own conversations with others, being aware of what one is saying to determine what one is going to say thereafter—that is a process with which we are all familiar" (p. 217). This perceptive social philosopher gave his readers a rich but highly generalized analysis of that universal situation in which men genuinely and openly communicate.

Mead was not always consistently concerned with shared communication but—as the preceding quotations suggest—also with how one guesses the other's perception of his behavior so as further to direct that behavior oneself. Whether on the basis of these guesses one then misleads the other or plays the game honestly is left ambiguous. Presumably Mead meant the ensuing interaction to be genuinely open and cooperative.[8] The full force of our commentary on this aspect of his work is best demonstrated by an unusual passage wherein Mead raises and dismisses those aspects of interaction that do not involve shared symbolization. He remarks:

> There is, of course, a great deal in one's conversation with others that does not arouse in one's self the same response it arouses in others. That is particularly true in the case of emotional attitudes. One tries to bully somebody else; he is not trying to bully himself. . . . We do at times act and consider just what the effect of our attitude is going to be, and we may deliberately use a certain tone of voice to bring about a certain result. Such a tone arouses the same response in ourselves that we want to arouse in somebody else. But a very large part of what goes on in speech has not this . . . status.

[6]Cf. Renée Fox, *Experiment Perilous,* Glencoe, Ill.: The Free Press, 1959.

[7]Anselm Strauss (ed.), *The Social Psychology of George Herbert Mead,* Chicago: University of Chicago Press, 1956, p. 173. All references are to this volume.

[8]Herbert Blumer, in pointing to the great value of Mead's approach, has also emphasized concerted action, whether accomplished or developed. See Blumer's "Society as Symbolic Interaction" in Arnold Rose (ed.), *Human Behavior and Social Processes,* Boston: Houghton Mifflin, 1962, esp. pp. 187–188.

It is the task not only of the actor but of the artist as well to find the sort of expression that will arouse in others what is going on in himself . . . the stimulus calls out in the artist that which it calls out in the other, but this is not the natural function of language. . . . (pp. 224–226).

And what is the natural function of language? "What is essential to communication is that the symbol should arouse in one's self what it arouses in the other individual." Mead seems here to touch on interaction based on something different from open awareness and genuine communication. In deliberate bullying, for example one's activity may frighten the other but does not frighten oneself. In writing poetry, one finds the means to arouse responses in others what one finds in himself (and Mead remarks that Wordsworth took some years to turn those immediate responses into poetry). And in this same passage, Mead notes that "we do not assume that the person who is angry is calling out the fear in himself that he is calling out in someone else"; that is, in this spontaneous expression of feeling, actor and audience do not respond identically. We should not be surprised to find, sandwiched within this passage, Mead's laconic comment that though we can act—quite like the actor does—"It is not a natural situation; one is not an actor all of the time." Of course no one is! But what about the times when we do act?

Mead's analysis is especially pertinent to this paper because it emphasizes a property of interaction so often absent in other men's work: the developmental properties of interaction. In Mead's writing the concept of significant symbol not only underscores the consensual character of social order but also shows how social order is changed—how social objects are formed and transformed during the course of constructed acts. In current reading of Mead, this developmental aspect tends to be overlooked; so does his processual, rather than substantial, treatment of the self. The self as process insures that interaction is usually not static or merely repetitive. In Mead's world, acts are open-ended, frequently surprising to the

actors themselves. And in some of his finest writings Mead emphasizes how even past events are reconstructed, powerfully influencing the directions taken by present events. In short, interaction always tends to go somewhere, but exactly where is not always known for certain by the interactants.

ERVING GOFFMAN

Erving Goffman's work is probably the most influential among current theoretical analyses of interaction. If he does not stand at an opposite pole from Mead, he surely stands far removed—in style, temperament, theoretical perspective, and above all in his focus on the interplay of people. In his first book, *The Presentation of Self in Everyday Life*,[9] one can easily follow his detailed, central analysis of interaction.

From the beginning, Goffman emphasizes an audience's need to define an individual's identity. "When an individual enters the presence of others, they commonly seek to acquire information about him or to bring into play information about him already possessed" (p. 2). Whether or not an actor wishes, his actions yield impressions of him to his audiences. Therefore, people most frequently "devote their efforts to the creation of desired impressions" rather than act completely without guile or contrivance. "Engineering a convincing impression" is an inescapable fact (p. 162). It is a way for each interactant "to control the conduct of others" (p. 2).

Because of such impression management, "events may occur within the interaction which contradict, discredit, or otherwise throw doubt upon the actor's projection of himself." Much of Goffman's book turns around the confusion or embarrassment that occurs when interaction is thus disrupted. He analyzes extensively the "preventive practices" consequent upon disruptions: "defensively by the actor himself, and protectively when

[9]All references are to the original Edinburgh edition.

the audience strives to save the definition of the situation projected by another'' (p. 7).

In all of this, Goffman focuses on closed awareness. He has a section on "team collusion" (pp. 112–120), and another on the "maintenance of expressive control" (pp. 33–37). Second, he explicitly treats pretense awareness contexts. For instance, "each team tends to suppress its candid view of itself and of the other team, projecting a conception of self and a conception of other that is relatively acceptable to the other. And to insure that communication will follow established, narrow channels, each team is prepared to assist the other team, tacitly and tactfully, in maintaining the impression it is attempting to foster" (p. 107).[10] In general, Goffman, at least in this volume, is uninterested in open awareness contexts; and though he touches on contexts where audiences are suspicious of the actor's projected definition, he does not go into the ways in which the suspicion gradually grows and then is validated.

But whether pretense or closed awareness is at issue, Goffman's principal focus is on how the interaction is kept going, or if disrupted, how interactants manage to get it going again. He has little interest in awareness contexts that are transformed through the deliberate operations of the interactants or through the continued course of the interaction itself. Indeed, his analysis is geared to episodic or repeated interactions rather than to sustained interplay. Consistently with this nondevelopmental focus, his dramaturgical model refers to the *team* of stage actors who night after night seek to create an acceptable illusion, rather than to the *drama* itself, with its plot line and evolving, relatively unpredictable, sequence of transactions.[11] Particularly it is worth underscoring

that the identity of Goffman's actor is rarely problematical to himself, but only and always to his audience.[12]

In this book Goffman tends to leave implicit the structural conditions imposed by the larger social unit. Rather, he focuses mainly on situational conditions such as setting and front and back regions. Of course, most interaction in *The Presentation of Self* occurs in establishments containing service personnel and clients, insiders and outsiders; that is, persons who are either relatively unknown to each other or respectively withhold significant aspects of their private lives from each other. Goffman leaves to his readers the task of considering what kinds of structural conditions might lead to interactions quite different from those described. For example, his discussion of impression management might have been very different had he studied neighborhood blocks, small towns, or families, where participants are relatively well known to each other. Similarly, he is not much concerned with systematically tracing various consequences of the interaction (especially for large social units); although for interactants, of course, consequences are noted in terms of specific linkages with the disruption or smooth continuance of encounters.

Aside from its restricted range of awareness contexts, Goffman's world of interaction is nondevelopmental and rather static. In other writings, he is concerned with interaction of considerable duration, but characteristically his interest is in the rules that govern that interaction. Often interaction proceeds to its termination almost as inexorably as a Greek tragedy.[13] For these aspects, however, his analysis is a considerable advance beyond those of his predecessors.

Next we re-examine two useful papers, our aim being first, to locate the reported research within our awareness paradigm; second, to assess its

---

[10]This passage is a pretty fair description of the situation in which a dying patient and his nurses both engage in pretense by delicately avoiding talk about the patient's impending death.

[11]Many readers seemed to have missed this point. Cf. a similar comment in Sheldon Messinger, Harold Sampson, and Robert Towne, "Life as Theater: Some Notes on the Dramaturgic Approach to Social Reality," *Sociometry*, 25 (March, 1962), p. 108.

[12]To Goffman, surprise means potential disruption of interaction—as compared with Mead's notion of the creative and surprising impulsivity of the "I."

[13]Cf. Messinger, *et al., op. cit.*

contribution to interactional analysis; and third, to suggest what might be added to that analysis if one were now to undertake such research.

DONALD ROY

In his "Efficiency and 'The Fix': Informal Intergroup Relations in a Piecework Machine Shop,"[14] Roy is interested in demonstrating "that the interaction of two groups in an industrial organization takes place within and is conditioned by a larger intergroup network of reciprocal influences." The interaction is a contest between management and the workers. The latter adroitly scheme, connive and invent methods for attaining quotas set by management; while management attempts to minimize the success of these "black arts of 'making out.' " These arts "were not only responses to challenge from management but also stimulations, in circular interaction, to the development of more effective countermagic in the timing process" established by management's time-checkers. An important segment of Roy's discussion deals with "intergroup collusion" among workers from other departments, who become allies in this unending contest with management.

Where shall we locate Roy's research in our awareness context paradigm? From Roy's description, the awareness contexts are not entirely clear since we do not always know the extent to which management was aware of what was going on among the workers. But in general, workers' attempts to keep closed awareness about their specific collusive games seem to have alternated with management's periodic awareness of such games. Whether this periodic awareness of management transformed the closed context temporarily into pretense or open awareness is difficult to determine. Roy does, however, clearly give the structural conditions that permit both the closed awareness context and its periodic, temporary

[14]*American Journal of Sociology*, 60 (November, 1954), pp. 255–266.

transformation to pretense or open before the workers reinstitute the closed context with a new collusive game.

Roy describes in great detail the interactional tactics of both sets of players which maintain, transform and reinstitute closed awareness. Teamwork on the worker's side is exceptionally well sketched. Managerial tactics, however, are described principally from "below," for two reasons. First, Roy was doing field work as an industrial worker, and could scarcely be privy to management's specific perspectives and decisions. Second, he did not need to scrutinize management's views because his research was designed to explore how workers organized their work.

In spite of the fact that Roy describes the phases through which the contest, and hence the awareness context, oscillates, true temporal development is lacking. This is because he conceives of the interaction as unendingly the same. Apparently the limits of the interaction were set by the time period devoted to the research itself. As Roy himself notes in passing: "How far the beginning of the series [of new rules] antedated the writer's arrival is not known. Old-timers spoke of a 'Golden Age' enjoyed before the installation of the 'Booth System' of production control." An interest in interactional process must raise these questions: from what situation did the interaction phases develop, where did they end, and what happened if someone attempted to bring the collusive interaction out into the open?

The consequences of the interaction are noted sporadically—mainly in terms of work blockages and cumulative inefficiency—but again we might wish to know much more, especially about diverse consequences for the functioning of the organization at large.

FRED DAVIS

A very different presentation of interaction is Fred Davis' "Deviance Disavowal: The Management of Strained Interaction by the Visibly Handicapped.''[15] The sub-title accurately describes what this paper is all about. The visible stigma of the handicapped person presents a threat to sociability which ''is, at minimum, fourfold: its tendency to become an exclusive focal point of the interaction, its potential for inundating expressive boundaries, its discordance with other attributes of the person and, finally, its ambiguity as a predicator of joint activity.'' These are ''contextual emergents which, depending on the particular situation, serve singly or in combination to strain the framework of normative rules and assumptions in which sociability develops.''

After a discussion of these various emergents, which constitute a grave threat to interaction, we are shown ''how socially adept handicapped persons cope with it so as to either keep it at bay, dissipate it or lessen its impact upon the interaction.'' The analysis is aimed at delineating ''in transactional terms the stages through which a social relationship with a normal typically passes.'' The stages are: (1) fictional acceptance, (2) ''breaking through'' or facilitating normalized role-taking, and (3) institutionalization of the normalized relationship. From the viewpoint of the handicapped person, the ''unfolding'' of the stages represents deviance disavowal; from that of the normal person it is normalization. For each stage in the process, a certain number of interactional tactics are noted, though Davis is more interested in interactional stages than in the ''tremendous variety of specific approaches, ploys and stratagems that the visibly handicapped employ in social situations.''

This research deals with the transformation of pretense awareness (''fictional acceptance'') to open awareness (''institutionalization of the normalized relationship''), chiefly but not solely under the control of transforming operations by the handicapped. As Davis describes it, the handicapped person attempts first to keep interaction in the fictional mode (both interactants mutually aware of

[15]*Social Problems,* 9 (Winter, 1961), pp. 120–132.

his stigma but neither acting as though it existed); then, gradually, the handicapped person engineers matters to a final phase where it is openly ''fitting and safe to admit to certain incidental capacities, limits, and needs''—that is, where both parties may openly refer to the stigma of the handicapped person.

Davis' discussion is additionally rich because he makes some very explicit remarks about how difficult the open awareness (normalization) phase is for either party to maintain. For instance: ''to integrate effectively a major claim to 'normalcy' with numerous minor waivers of the same claim is a tricky feat and one which exposes the relationship to the many situational and psychic hazards of apparent duplicity. . . .'' By implication, this relationship between the two parties has a future: because it is difficult to maintain, it cannot remain at a standstill. We say ''by implication'' because Davis is content to carry the story only to where something like normal sociability can take place. Said another way, Davis actually is analyzing a developmental—not merely an engineered—interaction situation. ''As against the simplistic model of a compulsive deviant and a futile normalizer we would propose one in which it is postulated that both are likely to become engaged in making corrective interactional efforts toward healing the breach.'' Precisely because *both* are likely to make those correctional efforts, this is a developmental relationship. Our paradigm helps raise the questions of where the relationship is going and what further transformations, under what conditions, may occur.

Our paradigm also suggests focusing on both parties to the interplay even when it is relatively adeptly controlled by one, since our understanding of the relationship's developmental aspects necessarily requires knowledge of the actions and awareness of both parties. Thus, how does the normal interactant see the handicapped, and the interaction, at various phases of the interaction—and what is he doing, or deciding to do, about it? What will his tactics be, whether occasional or continual? Davis also assumes that the handicapped person has often been through this type of interaction—hence has evolved tactics for handling it—while the normal person is a novice. This may be so, but in actual life both players may have had similar experiences.

Lastly, Davis attempts to specify one class of structural conditions that permit the handicapped person to manage strained interaction. He begins his paper by referring to "that genre of everyday intercourse" which is characteristically face-to-face, not too prolonged but not too fleeting either, with a certain degree of intimacy, and "ritualized to the extent that all know in general what to expect but not so ritualized as to preclude spontaneity and the slightly novel turns of events." This explicit detailing is not a mere backdrop but an intrinsic part of the analysis of interaction in the presence of physical stigma. The consequences of interaction (e.g., the satisfaction of both parties and the possibility of a continuing relationship) are left mainly implicit.

GENERAL IMPLICATIONS OF PARADIGM

Our examination of these four writers indicates that future research and theory on interactional problems should encompass a far broader range of phenomena than heretofore. Of course, one need not do everything demanded by the paradigm. But it guides the researcher in exploring and perhaps extending the limits of his data, and in stating clearly what was done and left undone, perhaps adding why and why not. The paradigm helps the theorist achieve greater clarity, integration, and depth of analysis by encouraging reflection upon what he has chosen *not* to make explicit. It also raises questions about development and structure that a straight factor approach to the study of interaction typically does not:[16] how does one type

[16]The factor approach is a standard one in sociology: it is legitimated by the notion that one can only consider so much at one time with precision and clarity, and therefore boundaries must be chosen, usually according to one's interests, provided they are theoretically relevant. For a discussion of "simultaneous *versus* sequential" factor models, see Howard S. Becker, *Outsiders,* New York: The Free Press, 1963, pp. 22–25.

of context lead to another; what are the structural conditions—including rules—in the relevant institutions that facilitate or impede existence of a context, and changes in it; what are the effects of a changing awareness context on the identity of a participant; why does one party wish to change a context while another wishes to maintain it or reinstate it; what are the various interactional tactics used to maintain or reinstate change; and what are the consequences for each party, as well as for sustaining institutional conditions?

This developmental focus helps to eliminate the static quality and restricted boundaries for analysis that are characteristic of the factor approach. The factor approach is useful only when the analyst is conscious of the location of his conceptual boundaries within a larger developmental, substantive scheme, and can thereby explain their relevance to his readers, rather than implicitly declaring all other substantive factors out of bounds. Only then is it sensible to leave out so much that other sociologists, in the light of present theory and knowledge, recognize as relevant to the area under consideration.

The focus on structural conditions increases the likelihood that the microscopic analysis of interaction will take into account the nature of the larger social structure within which it occurs. The usual structural approach in sociology tends to neglect microscopic analysis of interaction and also inhibits attention to its developmental character. Our paradigm encompasses in one developmental scheme the twin, but often divorced, sociological concerns with social structure and social interaction. Neither need be slighted, or forgotten, for a focus on the other.

Our discussion has touched on only four possible types of awareness contexts: open, closed, pretense, and suspicion. These four types are generated by the substantively relevant combinations of four variables found in our study of the literature and in our data on awareness of identity and interaction. We have considered two variables as dichotomous—*two interactants; acknowledgement of awareness* (pretense or no pretense)—and two as trichotomous—*degree of awareness* (aware, suspicious, and unaware); and *identity* (other's identity, own identity, and own identity in the eyes of the other). Logical combination of these variables would yield 36 possible types, but to start research with all the logical combinations of these variables would be an unnecessarily complex task, considering that many or most types are empirically non-existent. Therefore, the procedure used to develop awareness context types related to interaction was first, to search data for relevant types; second, to logically substruct the variables involved; and third, on the basis of these variables to judge whether other possible types would be useful or necessary for handling the data.

Presumably, more empirically relevant types can be found by scrutinizing the sociological literature, one's own data, and one's own life.[17] Another implication of the present analysis is that increasingly complex types of awareness contexts and their distinctive consequences should be systematically sought. We recommend our procedure for evolving types, as opposed to starting out with the full set of logical combinations, each of which must then be screened for empirical relevance.

We suggested, at the beginning of the paper, two factors that further complicate awareness contexts: additional people, and people representing organized systems with a stake in certain types of awareness context. Certain types of social phenomena are probably strategic for extending our knowledge of awareness contexts: for example, research discoveries in science and in industry, spy systems, deviant communities whose actions may be visible to "squares," types of bargaining before audiences, such as occurs in diplomatic negotiations, and unofficial reward systems like those depicted by Melville Dalton and Alvin Gouldner.[18]

---

[17]We are working with the "unawareness" context, in which neither party knows the identity of the other or his identity in the other's eyes. This is illustrated by strangers meeting or passing each other on a dark street. If they stop to talk, the first task they are likely to engage in is to transform the "unawareness" context to facilitate interaction.

[18]*Men Who Manage,* New York: Wiley, 1959; and *Patterns of Industrial Bureaucracy,* Glencoe, Ill.: The Free Press, 1954, respectively.

SEVEN

A CRIMINOGENIC MARKET STRUCTURE: The Automobile Industry*

HARVEY A. FARBERMAN

Sociologists have come under attack for ignoring the role powerful elites play in controlling society's central master institutions by establishing political and economic policies which set the structural conditions that cause other (lower level) people to commit crimes[1] (Gouldner, 1968, 1970;

SOURCE: Harvey A. Farberman. "A Criminogenic Market Structure: The Automobile Industry." Copyright by The Sociological Quarterly, 1975. Harvey A. Farberman, "A Criminogenic Market Structure: The Automobile Industry," *The Sociological Quarterly,* XVI (Autumn, 1975), pp. 438–457. Reprinted by permission of The Sociological Quarterly.

*I presented working notes for this paper at the Minnesota Symposium on Symbolic Interaction in June, 1974, and at the annual meetings of the American Sociological Association in August, 1974. I wish to thank Herbert Blumer, Norman K. Denzin, Erich Goode, Peter M. Hall, David R. Maines, Carolyn and Martin Needleman, Harold Orbach, and Gregory P. Stone for helpful comments.

[1]Typical explanations for this neglect include the observation that sociologists of deviance often work out of a symbolic interactionist perspective, and that this perspective has an ideological theoretical bias which offers tacit support to power elites (Thio, 1973); that it has a philosophical-methodological bias which focuses attention on the passive, powerless individual and thus cannot conceptualize transcendent, unobservable, active groups. (Schervish, 1973); and, finally, that it tends toward a grounded-emergent rather than a logico-theoretic style of theory construction and thus is vulnerable to the unequal power distribution embodied in everday life and, consequently, has a conservative bias (Huber, 1973). For a reply to some of these points, see Stone et al. (1974).

Quinney, 1970; Liazos, 1972; Taylor et al., 1974). My aim here is to suggest how one elite, namely, automobile manufacturers, creates a "criminogenic market structure"[2] by imposing upon their new car dealers a pricing policy which requires high volume and low per unit profit. While this

[2]I borrow the term "criminogenic market" from Leonard and Weber (1970), who contend that the most useful conceptual approach to occupational crime is to see it as a *direct consequence of legally established market structure.* In the present study, by "criminogenic market structure," I mean the deliberate and lawful enactment of policies by those who manage economically concentrated and vertically integrated corporations and/or industries which coerce lower level (dependent) participants into unlawful acts. Those who set the conditions which cause others to commit unlawful acts remain non-culpable, while those who perform under these conditions remain eminently culpable. A micro illustration suggestive of this approach was played out in the heavy electric industry where the U.S. government was able to show that a cartel existed among corporations which resulted in a price-fixing conspiracy. Nevertheless, the actual corporate officials who were indicted and convicted came from the second and third echelon of the corporate hierarchy and, upon exposure, were legally and morally disavowed by the first level echelon. Division heads and vice-presidents were censured and repudiated by presidents and directors for contravening corporate policy. Those indicted and convicted, however, never for a moment thought of themselves as contravening corporate policy, nor of having done anything but what was expected of them—their jobs (Smith, 1961). Although this case describes activity *within* corporations, I wish to extrapolate it to an entire industry. Thus, at the pinnacle of the economically concen-

strategy gives the *manufacturer* increased total net aggregate profit (by achieving economies of scale and by minimizing direct competition among oligopolist ''rivals''), it places the new car dealer in a financial squeeze by forcing him to constantly free-up and continuously recycle capital into fixed margin new car inventory. This squeeze sets in motion a downward spiral of illegal activities which (1) inclines the new car dealer to engage in compensatory profit taking through fraudulent service operations, (2) under certain conditions, generates a ''kickback'' system which enables used car managers of new car dealerships to exact graft from independent used car wholesalers, and (3) forces the independent used car wholesaler into illegal ''short-sales'' in order to generate unrecorded cash for kickback payments. I shall present the evidence which provides the grounding for this model as I came upon it in the research process. What follows, then, is a natural history which reconstructs the stages of my investigation.[3]

THE BASE SITE

My principal research site was a medium-sized used car wholesale operation located in an eastern metropolitan area.[4] There are approximately forty

other wholesale operations in this area,[5] the top three of which sell between 6,000 and 8,000 cars per year.[6] My base operation, which sold 1,501 cars in 1971 and 2,124 in 1972,[7] carried a 125-car wholesale inventory and a repair shop at one location and a 25-car retail inventory at another location. There were 16 employees altogether, including three partners (an older one who runs the office and two younger ones who function as buyers), three additional buyers (who also sell wholesale when not on the road), a retail manager, a retail salesman, two shop workers, a bookkeeper, and two-to-five drivers. The firm also retains the services of a lawyer and an accountant.[8]

Entry into my principal research site and later into other operations was relatively easy, for during my high school and college days I had made pin money selling used cars on a lot owned by the older partner. Later, I came across two old ac-

---

trated auto industry sit four groups of manufacturers who control 92 percent of the new car market and who, on the distribution side of the industry alone, set economic conditions which control approximately 31,000 franchised new car dealers, approximately 4,000 used car wholesalers, and approximately 65,000 ''independent'' used car retailers. Despite the fact that those on the top cause the conditions which compel others into untoward patterns of action, they do not reap the public's wrath. At the same time that new car and used car dealers consistently trail far behind every other occupational grouping in terms of public esteem, there never has been a presidential administration—beginning with Franklin Roosevelt—without an automobile *manufacturing executive* in a cabinet or sub-cabinet position!

[3]For a discussion of this presentation format see H. Becker (1970:37).

[4]For a breezy journalistic description of the used car wholesaling scene see Levine (1968:26–29). For sociological insight into various levels of the auto industry see: Brown (1973) for independent used car retailing; Vanderwicken (1972), for franchised new car dealing; and Robbins (1971) for manufacturing.

[5]This figure derives from enumeration by wholesalers themselves. I was forced to rely on this source for three reasons. First, the appropriate State Departments of Motor Vehicles informed me that their statistical information does not distinguish between new and used and wholesale and retail dealers. Nevertheless, they intend to introduce such breakdowns within the next few years. Second, the *U.S. Bureau of the Census, County Business Patterns, 1970* places fundamentally different *kinds* of wholesale automobile establishments into the same reporting category. Thus, wholesale body and fender shops, junk yards, auction sales, freelance wholesalers, and regular wholesalers appear in the same category. Moreover, the census also includes businesses that are legally chartered in a state but not actually doing business there. Consequently, for my purposes the census was not helpful. Third, the various county *Yellow Pages* phone books in which used car wholesalers advertise did not allow me to distinguish ''cut-book'' wholesalers, who freelance and work out of their home addresses, from regular wholesalers, who have substantial business premises, a staff of employees, and sizeable inventories.

[6]This figure also comes from wholesalers themselves.

[7]I compiled these figures from the dealers' ''Police Book.'' For each car in stock, dealers must enter 23 items of descriptive information. Detectives from the Motor Vehicle squad routinely inspect this book.

[8]Subsequent to the completion of my study, three more operations were opened: a retail lot with a thirty-car capacity, a wholesale lot with a forty-car capacity, and a twelve-stall body and fender shop. Each of these operations was situated on land or in buildings purchased by the corporation. The staff also increased with the addition of three more buyers, two retail salesmen, seven body and fender men, one mechanic, and a pool of part-time drivers which fluctuates from three to ten on any given day.

quaintances from high school days who hustled cars when I did; one is now a new car agency general sales manager, and the other a partner in a "family-owned" new car dealership.

Although I was always more an observer than a participant, I increasingly was expected to answer phone calls, take messages, move cars around the wholesale lot, and deliver cars as part of a "caravan" with the regular drivers.[9] Eventually, I gained access to all files. At about the same time the firm offered me a gasoline credit card, reimbursement for my private telephone bill, maintenance work on my own car, and drivers to pick me up at the airport when I returned from out-of-town trips. I did not decline the maintenance work or the airport service,[10] however, I did break off field appearances—but maintained social contact— when the firm adopted one of my opinions as the basis for its expansion policy, and it became clear that my role as an investigator had somehow given way to that of an advisor or consultant.

From December 1971 to August 1973, I spent an average of one day a week including evenings and weekends at my principal site, on the road, and at the homes of or out socializing with various members of my base organization and their families. Sometimes, though, I would hang around the lot for two or three consecutive days in order to get some sense of the continuity and rhythm of the operation. I always carried a notebook and, when necessary, made entries in full view of all present.

[9]For a discussion of the ratio of observation to participation see Gold (1958:217—233).

[10]During one of these trips, I parked my car—a small 1965 Buick Special—on the wholesale lot. As a gag, and in addition to whatever prudential motives may have been involved, the firm sold my car and with the proceeds put me into a large 1970 Oldsmobile. The firm, at considerable expense to itself, and, in the words of one of the partners, "felt that a Professor, who you also call Doctor, should drive around in a better car." At one and the same time the "gag" shows deference to my status, takes liberty with my property, (albeit improves it) and coerces me into a more conventional status appearance. This gambit smacks of something approaching a hazing ritual. It is fun, yet it prepares the initiate for further entree into the club by manipulating him into club conventions. I imagine field workers often run this sort of gamut before they gain entrance into the secret place. Unhappily, these experiences usually remain unrecorded.

I also tape-recorded extensive in-depth interviews with the consent of participants, but only when I knew more or less what I wanted information about, thus not abusing the privilege. These "formal" interviews allowed me to nail down—for the record—what I had observed, participated in, or been told during the course of everyday activity or conversation over the course of nearly two years. The insight and information gleaned from these informal conversations were the basis for the "formal" interviews, the first of which I held during the sixth month of my field appearances.

SERENDIPITY

I should note here that I did not start out to study a criminogenic market structure. Rather, I wanted to follow up on a speculative hypothesis which grew out of some previous research on low income consumers (Farberman, 1968; Farberman and Weinstein, 1970). As a result of the latter study in particular, I had hypothesized that low income consumers strengthened their bargaining position *vis-á-vis* high status or expert sales or service people by changing the normative ground of the transaction from universalism to particularism, and thereby were able to coerce the expert other to respond as a concerned friend rather than as a mercenary stranger. Consequently, I began the present investigation to see if I could discover if people who bought used cars employed (wittingly or unwittingly) a set of bargaining tactics. I therefore observed over 50 transactions between retail customers and used car salesmen and, indeed, have been able to identify several bargaining tactics, associate them with distinct types of customers, and provide a theoretical interpretation.[11]

My interest in the systemic nature of occupational crime developed without my realizing it for sometimes, while I wrote up notes in the office after watching a sales transaction, I would vaguely overhear or observe the sales manager and cus-

[11]See my forthcoming article "Coming-To-Terms: The Reconciliation of Divergent Meanings and Values in the Sale of Used Cars."

tomer "write-up" the deal. I began to notice that occasionally the customer would make out a check *as well as* hand over some cash. This was accompanied by the customer's saying how "taxes were killing the little man" and "if you didn't watch out, the Governor would bleed you to death." Out of simple curiosity I began *deliberately to observe* the "write-ups"—something I had originally paid no attention to since I thought the transaction was actually over after the bargain had been made and the salesman had "closed" the deal. It was at the "write-up," however, that a new research problem emerged, because what I had witnessed—and what, in fact, led me off in a new direction—was an instance of "selling short," or "a short-sale," an illegal act which constitutes the first link in a chain of activity that goes back to Detroit.[12] In the section which follows, I will describe (a) what a "short sale" is; (b) how it benefits and costs both the retail customer and the dealer; and (c) why the dealer feels compelled to engage in it.

THE SHORT-SALE

A "short-sale" begins to develop when a retail customer observes the sales manager compute and add on to the selling price of the car the state sales tax—a hefty eight percent. Often, the customer expresses some resentment at the tax bite and asks if there is any way to eliminate or reduce it. The sales manager responds in a sympathetic fashion and allies himself with the customer in a scheme to "cut down on the Governor's share of the deal" by suggesting that the customer might make out a check for less than the actual selling price of the car. In turn, the manager will make out a bill of sale for the lesser amount. The customer then will pay the difference between the *recorded* selling

price and the *actual* selling price in cash. A car which normally costs $2,000 would carry an additional 8 percent (or $160) state sales tax, thus actually costing the customer $2,160. If a bill of sale which records the selling price as $1,500 is made out, however, then at 8 percent the taxes would be $120, for an apparent total of $1,620. Although the customer still pays $2,000 for the car (1,500 by check and $500 in cash), he "saves" $40 in taxes.

Almost as important as saving the $40 is the obvious delight the customer typically takes at finally discovering himself in a situation where he can "even the odds," "give the big guy what for," and "make sure the little guy gets his two cents too." The attitude and mood which washes through the short-sale suggests a welcome, if minor, triumph in the back-stepping of everyday life. As an observer witnessing this "petty" collusion between little Davids against remote Goliath, I had a rather difficult time identifying it pursuant to the criminal code—as a conspiracy to defraud the government through tax evasion. Obviously, the meaning, value, and sentiment attached to the act by at least one of the participants (the customer) is totally incongruous with the meaning, value, and sentiment attached to it by the criminal code. Thus does a minor victory in everyday life co-exist in the same act with a punishable transgression of law. The victory is often more symbolic than material, however, since, if the customer at any future time has an accident or theft, his insurance company, in part, will initiate compensation calculations based on the selling price recorded in the bill of sale—a sum which understates the actual price paid.

But, if the customer derives both a small material savings and a large measure of delight, what does the dealer derive? For one thing, a lot of money; more precisely, a lot of *unrecorded* cash. At the moment the customer "saves" $40 in taxes the dealer gains $500 in cash. The "short-sale" to the customer allows the dealer to "steal-from-the-top." In any given year an accumulation of these short-sales can total to tens of thousands of dollars. In an effort to determine if "stealing from the top"

---

[12]Although my initial research problem situated me so that I luckily tripped over and recognized a new problem, the new problem actually links to the old problem so that my understanding of the dynamics of customer/salesman interaction is enlarged by my understanding of the systemic dynamics of "short-sales." In fact, deliberate—as opposed to accidental—problem transformation may be integral to the methodologic of contextual, vertical analysis.

was anything other than rank venality, I questioned one of the partners in my principal site.

Q: You've just said that it's [stealing-from-the-top] O.K. for the customer but bad for you. I don't understand that. Jeez, look at the money!

A: Yeah, sure, but who the hell wants to live with any of the retail customers. You see what goes on. They don't know shit about a car. They look at the interior, turn on the radio, check the odometer, kick the tire, push the windshield wiper button, turn on the air conditioner, open up the trunk, look at the paint. What the fuck has any of that got to do with the *condition* of the car? I mean, the way the fucker runs. If I put money into all this crap, I can't put it into improving the mechanical condition. Three weeks later the fucking car falls apart and they're on my ass to fix it. Then I got to live with them. They drive me off the wall. Then that broad down the consumer affairs office wants to know why I don't give the customer a fair shake. Shit, why the hell don't she educate the customer? It would make things a lot easier.

Q: Listen, if they're such a pain, why do you put up with them?

A: What do you mean?

Q: I don't know what I mean, but there is usually a bottom line and it's usually money!

A: Well, if you mean that they bail me out every now and then, sure.

Q: What do you mean?

A: Well, you know those creeps [buyers] I got on the road buying for me, you know what their philosophy is? "If you don't buy, you don't earn." They pay big numbers; what do they care; it's my money. If they get in too high on a package [group of cars] or a piece [one car], and I can't blow [wholesale] it out, then I look for a retail shot [sale]. But that means I can't turn over my money quickly, I got to lay with it out on the lot and hope some yo-yo [retail

customer] comes along. Believe me, it's a pain in the ass. This whole business is in and out, in and out. Anything that slows the turnover costs money.

Q: O.K., so retail customers generally are a pain, but you put up with them because they bail you out on bad buys, but that still doesn't get to it. What about those retail sales that are "short" sales, that's where the bread is. That's what I'm trying to get at.

A: All right, listen: A wholesaler runs a big grocery store; if it's not on the shelves, you can't buy it. Without cars to sell, I can't sell cars. Look, we make enough legit, but you can't pay graft by check. Those bums get you coming and going.

Q: What bums?

A: You ever wanta meet a crook, go see a used car manager [of a new car dealership]. They clip a quarter [$25], a half [$50], a yard [$100], maybe more [on each car]. Put a package together and take it out [buy it from them] and they'll zing you for a week's pay. They steal their bosses blind.

Q: So, you have to pay them to get cars. You mean something under the table?

A: Yeah, the "Vig."

Q: The what?

A: The grease, the commission, the kickback. How I'm gonna stay in business with no cars? You tell me.

Q: Incidentally, how many of your retail sales do you figure are "short"?

A: Maybe 70—75 per cent, I can't be sure.[13]

[13]Since the operation in question is primarily a *wholesale* not a retail house, the proportion of retail sales typically does not exceed 25 percent of total sales. Of these, however, about 75 percent are "short" sales. Thus, of 2,124 total sales, 398 are short. At a minimum of $100 stolen from the top per short-sale, approximately $39,000 is generated in unrecorded cash. Used car *wholesalers* may well engage in retail selling for cash and, therefore, are clearly different from used and new car *retailers* who *avoid* cash sales in favor of "credit" or "installment" sales. This latter point was vividly disclosed at a hearing before

Q: Tell me, do you ever wind up with more than you need for the kickbacks?

A: Sure, am I gonna lie to you? So I put a little away [in safety deposit-boxes]. You think I'm the only one? But if it's buried, you can't use it. Better it should be in the business; I could use it—besides, who needs the aggravation?

Q: Are you ever able to get it [buried money] back into the business?

A: Yeah

Q: How?

A: Aw, you know.

Apparently, the dealer's reasons for engaging in "short-sales" include, but are not confined to, rank venality. After all, most, but not all, of the unrecorded money is passed along in the form of "kickbacks"; only the residual excess actually finds its way directly into his own hands, and even

---

California's Corporations Commissioner when Sears, Roebuck and Company requested a license to make low cost automobile loans *directly* to customers, thus by-passing dealers. Direct loans, in effect, would turn consumers into cash customers. This the dealers emphatically did not want as the following testimony reveals:

Q: . . . Do you want to sell cars for cash?

A: I do not want to sell them for cash if I can avoid it.

Q: You would not want to sell the cars you do for a cash price, then?

A: No, sir.

Q: Does this mean that you are not really in the business of selling automobiles?

A: It does not mean that at all.

Q: But you don't want to sell automobiles for cash?

A: It means that I want to sell cars for the most profit that I can per car. Finance reserve (dealer's share of the carrying charges) and insurance commissions are part of the profit derived from selling a car on time.

Moreover, these dealers have no qualms about extending credit to poor risk customers; the car always can be repossessed and resold (Quoted in Macaulay, 1966:186).

---

this excess must be buried or occasionally laundered.[14] The principal reason the dealer engages in short-sales is to come up with kickback cash in order to keep his sources of supply open, and this imperative is more than enough to keep him involved with "short-sales," even though it means he has to deal with retail customers—the very bane of his existence.

The antagonism the dealer holds toward the retail customer is incredibly intense and appears to have two sources. First, it stems from the dealer's apparent inability to sell the customer what the dealer considers to be the *essential* element of a car—namely, the *mechanical condition*. Instead, he is compelled to sell what to him is nonessential—*physical appearance*. If he is to improve the car's physical appearance, then he must skimp on improving its mechanical condition. This, in the long run, works to his own disadvantage since he must "live with the customer" and, in some measure, make good on repairs affecting mechanical condition. Put another way, the wholesaler's *conceptualization* of the car and the retail customer's *conceptualization* of the car do not overlap. Where the wholesaler wishes to sell such *unobservables* as a good transmission, a

---

[14]*"Burying money"* means putting it in a safety deposit box. Ironically, this money becomes a source of long-term anxiety instead of long term security. First, it remains a concrete symbol of criminality and is at odds with the dealer's self-image. Second, it also always is the target of potential investigatory disclosure although known instances of such activity are virtually unheard of. Third, the dealer resents the accumulation of "idle" cash and is frustrated by his inability to "turn it over" easily and make it productive. *Laundering* occurs in tight money situations when capital *must* be made available. It invokes a symbiotic relationship between the dealer and a "bookie." The bookie is hired on as a "commissioned agent" of the dealership. The dealer "pays" him a weekly salary using a legitimate business check; in return, the bookie gives the dealer an equal amount in cash. The dealer provides the bookie with a W2 form and the bookie declares and pays taxes on this "income." The dealer then "declares" the income brought in by the bookie. Since this income derives from nonexistent buying or selling it is subtly apportioned and spread over actual transactions. The dealer also periodically writes a letter to the bookie's probation officer testifying to the bookie's reliable and gainful contributions to the business.

tight front end, a solid chassis, and an engine without knocks in it, the typical retail customer wishes to buy such *observables* as a nice paint job, a clean interior, etc. The wholesaler and the retail customer basically have a hard time "coming-to-terms," that is, abstracting out of the vehicle the same set of concrete elements to invest with meaning and value. The vehicle literally *means* different things to each of them, and the establishment of a shared meaning which is *mutually* valued is extremely problematic.[15]

The second source of the dealer's antagonism stems from his overwhelming dependence heightens ignorant customers. This dependence heightens dramatically when the dealer's own professional "house" buyers make bad buys; that is, pay too high a "number," or price for the car, which makes it impossible for the car to be quickly re-wholesaled. If the car is in basically sound mechanical condition, it will be "shaped" out in hopes of "bailing out" through a "retail shot." Though a bad buy can be redeemed through a retail sale, this route of redemption bodes ill for the house buyer since it reflects on his competence. It bodes ill for the dealer as well since he must tie up money, men, and space waiting for a fickle retail customer to get everyone off the hook. Thus, the dealer's antagonism toward the retail customer stems from his own dependence, for short-sales and bail-outs, on ignorant yo-yo's who don't know anything about cars. The dealer's redemption, then, lies in the hands of "idiot saviors," an unhappy situation at best.

KICKBACKS AND SUPPLY

In any event, based on what I had seen, heard, and been told, I concluded that the wholesale used car dealer engaged in "short-sales" principally to insure his supply of used cars. Since this conclusion was derived exclusively from observation and

interview, I wanted to check it out against the dealer's inventory files. In the following section, I seek evidence of two things: (a) that the predominant source of the wholesaler's inventory, in fact, is the used car department of new car agencies; and (b) that used car managers in new car agencies universally receive kickbacks.

Accordingly, I classified all vehicles in my base site for the years 1971 and 1972 by their source of origin. Table 1 indicates that, of the 1,501 vehicles bought in 1971, 1,134 or 75.5 percent came from used car departments of new car dealers, of the 2,124 bought in 1972, 1,472 or 69.3 percent came from the same source. These figures corroborate the used car wholesaler's overwhelming dependence on the used car department of the new car agency for supply. This also suggests that there may well be a decreasing supply in the number of used cars available on the market altogether. From 1971 to 1972 there was a 6.2 percent decrease (75.5 to 69.3) in the proportion of cars from used car departments of new car dealers, even though the number of new car agencies dealt with increased from 72 to 94.[16]

Given an overall paucity of used cars on the

---

[15]See my already cited forthcoming article for an elaboration of this.

[16]These figures are consistent with national trend figures provided to me by Thomas C. Webb, research assistant, National Automobile Dealers Assocation (personal communication, March 11, 1974). Estimations of the number of used cars sold "on" and "off" the market in 1960 and 1973 indicate that, of the 20.7 million used cars sold in 1960, 14.9 million or 71.6 percent were sold "on" the market, whereas of the 31.4 million used cars sold in 1973, 18.7 million or 59.6 percent were sold "on" the market. Thus, there was a net decrease of 12.0 percent. A possible explanation for the decreasing supply of used cars on the market may be the consequence of an already established social-economic trend toward the multiple car family. Whereas a decade ago only 15 percent of the total population owned more than one car, today 30 percent do. Indeed, one out of every three families, whose head of household is between the ages of 35−44 owns two cars and one out of ten whose head of household is between 45−54 owns three cars (MVMA, 1974:38−39). What this probably means is that cars are *handed down* from husband to wife to children and literally "run-into-the-ground." In other words, we may well be seeing the reemergence of "second-hand" cars. Cars change hands but outside the commercial nexus, i.e., "off-the-market." An additional factor which may be contributing to this trend is declining public confidence in auto dealers. Not too

TABLE 1. Units* within, and Vehicles Generated by, Various Sources of a Supply

| | 1971 | | 1972 | |
Source of Supply	Units	Vehicles	Units	Vehicles
1. Used car depts. of new car agencies	72	1134	94	1472
2. Rental, lease, or fleet companies	9	145	18	104
3. Off-the-street customers	116	116	172	172
4. Dealers auctions	2	38	1	38
5. Body and fender shops	6	35	6	105
6. Retail used car dealers	11	27	17	193
7. Wholesale used car dealers	3	6	4	40
	219	1501	312	2124

SOURCE: Dealer's Police Books

*The generic term "units" encompasses "establishments" as in categories 1-2 and 4-7, and customers as in category 3.

market, it would seem that used car managers of new car agencies are in a perfect position to exact tribute from the independent used car wholesaler whose major source of supply is in their hand. I thus proceeded to check out the universality of kickbacks. I classified all inventory by the *specific* new car agency it came from, and then asked the older partner of my base operation to indicate at which agencies kickbacks were paid. As shown in column 4 of Table 2, kickbacks were paid on 304 (out of 1,134) vehicles in 1971 and on 614 (out of 1,472) vehicles in 1972. Moreover, column 3—much to my surprise—shows that *all* of these cars come from only *seven* (7) agencies in both 1971 and 1972 and each of these agencies carried a Giant Motors franchise. Note, however, that these seven constitute only a small proportion of the total number of G.M. agencies dealt with, which is 35 in 1971 and 51 in 1972. Moreover, only 10 percent

long ago a poster showed a picture of former President Nixon with a caption which asked, "Would you buy a used car from this man?" The credibility of the new and used car dealer apparently has never been lower. Confirmation of this comes from several different polls which seek to determine the public image of new and used car dealers compared to other occupational groups. Auto dealers uniformly trail way behind others in terms of the trust they inspire in the buying public (Leonard and Weber, 1970). Still another compatible and contemporary factor is the deteriorating condition of our national economy where the combination of rising prices and decreasing purchasing power inhibit overall consumer demand and thus retard new car sales and accompanying trade-ins.

of *all* agencies in 1971 and less than 7 percent in 1972 required kickbacks. Nevertheless, in 1971 these agencies did, in fact, provide nearly 27 percent of all supply coming from used car departments of new car agencies and 20 percent of total supply. Similarly, in 1972 they provided 56 percent of supply from used car departments and 31 percent of all supply.

A closer examination of these seven G.M. agencies, however, discloses some common characteristics. First, an inspection of their zip codes and street addresses reveals that all seven are located in the same high density, urban area. Second, a rank ordering of all new car agencies by the number of cars they supply, as shown in Table 3, reveals that these seven are the top supply sources and, by agreement among house buyers, are large agencies. Third, the remaining eight agencies among the top 15 supply sources all are located in suburban areas and are described by house buyers as medium sized.

With this information in hand, I again questioned the older partner of my base operation.

Q: Listen, didn't you know that you only paid kickbacks at large, urban, G.M. agencies? Why did you guys give me the impression that you paid kickbacks to *all* used car managers?

A: Really?

Q: Really, what!?

TABLE 2. Kickbacks by Vehicle, Agency, and Franchise

Franchise	No. of Agencies 1971	1972	No. of Vehicles 1971	1972	Kickback Agencies 1971	1972	No. of Kickback Vehicles 1971	1972
Giant Motors	35	51	571	976	7	7	304	614
Fore	10	16	159	209	—	—	—	—
Crisis	15	16	256	191	—	—	—	—
National	1	2	1	5	—	—	—	—
Foreign	8	6	143	62	—	—	—	—
Unknown	3	3	4	29	—	—	—	—
	72	94	1,134	1,472	7	7	304	614

TABLE 3. Number of Dealerships by Number of Vehicles Supplied: 1972

Number of Dealerships	Number of Vehicles Supplied
2	100+
1	75+
4	50+
8	25+
79	1+

A: Really, you thought we paid off all the managers? Well, I guess these are the big houses for us—it seems like a lot. I'll tell ya, the hicks are O.K. They don't know from conniving. The city is full of crooks.

Q: Really? Don't you think it has anything to do with these particular agencies, maybe the way they're set up or maybe with G.M.? After all, the other manufacturers have agencies there too.

A: No, it's a freak thing! It just means that seven crooks work at these places.

Q: Aw, come on. I don't believe that.

A: Listen, you're barking up the wrong tree if you think it has anything to do with G.M.

Q: But why only at G.M.? and why only at G.M. agencies in the city?

A: Look, there's more G.M. agencies than [Fore] and [Crisis]. G.M. sells more cars, they get more trade-ins, they have solid used cars operations. These crooks go where the action is.

They're good used car men, they get the best jobs. But they're crooks. I'm telling you, believe me!

Q: But if they're crooks, and you know it, why don't their bosses know it?

A: Look, the bosses aren't stupid. They know what's going on. If the used car man pushes the cars out, and turns over capital, and doesn't beat the boss too bad—they're happy.

Q: I guess I must be thick, I'm still not convinced.

A: All right. The boss is busy running the new car operation. He brings in a sharp used car man and bank rolls him. The used car man pays rent to the boss for the premises and splits profits with him depending on the deal they work out. O.K.? The used car man takes the trade-ins, he keeps the good stuff and wholesales the bad. He wholesales me an off-model, say, for two grand. He tells his boss, the car brought $1,875.00. I send a check for $1,875,00, and grease him a buck and a quarter. At $1,875.00, he still made a legitimate fifty or a hundred on the car—the boss gets half of that. As long as the used car man doesn't get too greedy, there's no problem. The boss takes a short profit but frees up his capital. Believe me, that's crucial, especially if he's paying one percent a month interest on his bank roll to begin with.

Q: So, what you're saying, is that the best agencies are in the city, that they're G.M., that G.M. dealers know their used car men are beating them, but that they don't get uptight as long as they make something and can free-up their capital.

A: Yeah.

Q: Listen, you've got a point, but isn't there another way to look at this? Isn't it possible that the boss does more than just tolerate being ripped off a little by his used car man? Isn't it possible that he's working with the used car man and beating his own business. In other words, he's splitting the kickbacks or something like that?

A: Look, anything's possible, but all I know is that the used car managers are a bunch of crooks. The bosses, I can't say; as for [Giant Motors], forget it, they're a legit concern.

Q: Maybe you're right but it sure would make sense if the bosses [G.M. dealers] did both— you know, turn over money and beat their own business. Hell, you do it and you're the boss, why shouldn't they?

A: Well, I have to. I don't know about them. Just don't go off half-cocked. Be careful before you lean on anybody.

This interview material has two intriguing aspects. Despite the dealer's strenuous insistence that kickbacks are the artifact of corrupt and venal individual used car managers, there is also the suggestion that such venality can take place precisely because large, urban G.M. agencies sell a lot of cars and therefore have an abundance of trade-ins, the best of which are recycled back into the agencies' used car retail line while the surplus is wholesaled out. The power to determine how this surplus is dispersed into the wholesale market places the used car managers of the involved agencies in the position to demand and receive "kickbacks." Moreover, the new car dealer himself, who is under pressure to free up capital in order to avoid paying excess interest on money borrowed to purchase new car inventory, may have an incentive to "look-the-other-way," and perhaps even split "kickbacks" as long as his used car manager keeps moving cars and freeing capital.

THE FINANCIAL SQUEEZE

In the section which follows, I seek to check out (a) the existence of a financial squeeze on dealers, and (b) whether this squeeze inclines dealers to tolerate or even participate in kickbacks. By way of checking these points, I contemplated interviewing some people in the "kickback" agencies. The more I thought about how to guide myself in such interviews, the more I realized I was facing an interesting dilemma. I wanted to do the interviews precisely because I had discovered that the agencies were paid kickbacks by the wholesalers. Yet, in each case the kickback was being paid specifically to the manager of the used car department of the agency and I was not sure if the manager was acting on his own or was acting with the knowledge of his principal. If he was acting on his own, and I disclosed this, I might then put him in jeopardy. If he was acting with the knowledge of his principal, it was certain I would have an unreliable interview since in these cases I did not have personal bonds strong enough to insure truthful responses. Since I did not wish to deceive or jeopardize any of the respondents, and since I did not feel I could be truthful—as no doubt I would have had to disclose just how I had discovered the "kickback" arrangement, and thus transgress the trust that I had established with the wholesalers and run the risk of jeopardizing their ongoing business relationships with the new car dealer—I developed another approach. I decided to interview G.M. dealers in "non-kickback" agencies and try to elicit information which would allow me to pinpoint the key differences between kickback and non-kickback agencies, thereby nailing down an interpretation of the "kickback" phenomenon.

I managed to arrange interviews with three different dealers. The following quoted interview lasted five hours, was granted on the basis of a personal tie, and therefore is most reliable and valid. In addition, the elicited material is highly representative of the other interviews. The general thrust of my questioning was first to ask the dealer to talk about issues which are problematic in the running of his own business, and then to comment on the "kickback" phenomenon at the urban agencies. I was interested mainly in knowing if the pressure to turn over capital and avoid interest payments would encourage a dealer to "look-the-other-way" on "kickbacks" or even split them.

Q: How long have you been a dealer?

A: A dealer? About 20 years. About five or six years after [I finished] college, my dad and I went in as partners. It's mine now.

Q: Have you enjoyed it?

A: Well, it's been good to me for a goodly number of years, but frankly, during these past three to four years the business has changed markedly. It's a tougher, tighter business. I'm more tied down to it now than ever before. I can't be as active in the community as I would like. You know, that's important to me.

Q: Why is that the case? Is the business expanding?

A: Not really, well it depends on how you measure it. I work harder, have a larger sales and service staff than ever, I've expanded the facilities twice and refurbished the fixtures and touched up several times, and yes, I'm selling more new cars than before, but is the business expanding? Well, I suppose, yes, but not the way I'd like it to.

Q: Could you elaborate on that?

A: Well, the point is—and I know this will sound anomalous, well, maybe not to you—but I wish I could ease off on the number of new cars and pick up somewhere else, maybe on used cars.

Q: Why is that?

A: It boils down to investment-return ratios. The factory [manufacturer] has us on a very narrow per unit profit margin [on new car sales]. But if I had the money and the cars, I could use my capital more effectively in used cars.[17]

Q: In other words, G.M. establishes how much profit you can make on each new car you sell?

A: Just about. And more than that, they more or less determine how much [new car] inventory I have to carry, and the composition of that inventory.

Q: So, you have to take what they give you—even if you don't want or need it. How do you pay for the inventory?

A: I borrow money at prevailing interest rates to finance the inventory. And, sometimes it gets tight. Believe me, if I am unable to sell off that inventory relatively quickly, I'm pressed. I have got to keep that money turning or that interest begins to pinch.

Q: Is it fair to say that you compensate for narrow margins on new cars by making wider margins on used cars?

A: Not really, not in practice, at least not out here [in the suburbs]. Used cars, good used cars, are hard to come by. I imagine the city dealers have an easier time getting trade-ins. We get a lot of repeat customers, but I don't believe they trade up. They just buy new cars. Actually, we tend to pick up additional revenue from our service repair operation. I'm not particularly

[17]Leonard and Weber (1970:4) estimate that a dealer can make a gross profit margin of $400 on a $2,000 used car but only $150−200 on a $3,200 new car. Indeed, the new car dealers I interviewed all indicated a desire to be able to sell more used cars.

proud about it, but there is a lot of skimping going on. It's quite complicated. The factory has a terrible attitude toward service repair generally, and the [mechanics] union is overly demanding and inflexible. It's rather demoralizing and, frankly, I'm looking out for myself, too.

Q: Could you expand on that?

A: I prefer you not press me on that.

Q: If you had a choice, how would you prefer to set up your operation?

A: Well, if I had a choice—which I don't—I would rather have a low volume, high margin operation. I could get by with smaller facilities, a smaller staff, put less time into the business, and not constantly face the money squeeze.

Q: Do you think the really large city dealers would prefer the same kind of alternative?

A: I guess so, but it's hard to say. Their situation is somewhat different from mine.

Q: In what way?

A: Well, first of all, some of them, especially if they're located in [megalopolis] have even less control over their operation than I do. Some of them really run factory stores. That is, G.M. directly owns or controls the agency. Those outfits are really high-volume houses. I don't see how they can make a go of it. The factory really absorbs the costs.[18]

Q: You did say that they probably had strong used car operations or, at least, had a lot of trade-ins. Do you think that helps?

[18]According to White (1971), Detroit manufacturers generally avoid owning their own retail outlets or "factory" stores since a network of financially independent but exclusively franchised dealers helps to spread the risk of doing business, defrays cost, and provides local mangement with entreprenurial incentive. Edwards (1965) also suggests that a franchise dealer system establishes identity for products as well as provides facilities which handle trade-ins and repairs. Nevertheless, as a matter of prestige and because no individual dealer can afford the extremely high cost of land in this particular megalopolis, manufacturers usually own retail outlets directly.

A: Possibly.

Q: Do you think a really sharp used car man could do well in that kind of operation?

A: Well, he would do well in any operation in which he had used cars to work with.

Q: He could both retail and wholesale?

A: Oh, yes, if he had the cars to work with.

Q: Is it likely, in the wholesale end, he could demand and receive "kickbacks" from wholesalers?

A: Well, it's been known to happen. You know, those wholesalers, they're always willing to accommodate a friend. But it would only pay them to do that in relatively large operations where they could anticipate a fairly steady flow of cars.

Q: So, it would certainly make sense for them to accommodate friends in large, high volume, urban G.M. agencies?

A: Sure.

Q: Do you suppose the used car managers split kickbacks with their bosses?

A: Well, it's possible, but more than likely, the boss is more interested in moving those cars out quickly any way he can, so he can turn over that money and place it back into new car inventory.

Although this material does not permit any educated guess as to whether the dealers might split kickbacks with their used car managers, it does provide some assurance that new car dealers are under pressure to sell off cars relatively quickly in order to turn over capital and thus reduce interest payments. This pressure may be enough of a stimulus to, at least, incline the dealer to "look-the-other-way" if and when his used car man partakes in graft. As long as the used car man doesn't become too greedy and cut into the boss's pocket, his activity will be tolerated. Of course, we may still speculate, but not conclude, that if a "boss" is merely managing or only controlling a minimal share in a new car agency which is principally owned directly by G.M., he may be inclined to collude with his used car manager against "his own" agency. In any event, it is safe to presume that dealers feel under constant pressure to continuously recycle capital back into new car inventory and to get out from under interest payments. Corroboration of this comes from Vanderwicken (1972:128) who did a financial analysis of a medium-sized Fore agency located in a suburb of Cleveland, Ohio, and reported that:

> The average car is in inventory thirty days before it is sold. Quick turnover is important to a dealer, the instant a car leaves the factory he is billed for it and must begin paying interest on it. This interest is one of [the dealer's] biggest single expenses.

Additional support also comes from Fendell (1975:11) who asked a New Jersey [Fore] dealer how he was coping with decreasing consumer demand and received the following response:

> I'm making deals I lose money on just to get the interest costs off my back. Those cars sit out there, costing me money every second. [Fore] has been paid in full for them a long time ago.

The dealer went on to say that his interest rates run between 10.26 percent to 11 percent per year.

MANUFACTURERS' PRICING POLICY

The constant and unremitting emphasis on new car inventory and the capital squeeze it places dealers in apparently is no accident. To the contrary, it is the calculated outcome of the manufacturers' pricing policy. According to Stewart Macaulay (1966:8), manufacturers and dealers enter into relationships for the mutual goal of making profit; however, their strategies for making that profit may differ.

> For example . . . a dealer might be able to make a hundred dollars profit on the sale of one car or a ten dollar profit on each sale of ten cars . . . [it makes a great deal of difference to the manufacturer] because

in one case it sells only one car while in the other it sells ten . . . It must sell many units of all the various models it makes. . . .

This imperative to sell *many* cars stems from the manufacturers' effort to achieve economies of scale, that is, savings in production and other costs as a result of massive, integrated, and coordinated plant organization. George Romney, when President of American Motors, testified before a Senate Judiciary Subcommittee on Antitrust and Monopoly and reported that:

> A company that can build between 180,000 and 220,000 cars a year on a one-shift basis can make a very good profit and not take a back seat to anyone in the industry in production efficiency. On a two-shift basis, annual production of 360,000 to 440,000 cars will achieve additional small economies . . . (quoted in Lanzillotti, 1968:266.)

An economist, Joe S. Bain (quoted in Edwards, 1966:162), estimates that an even higher minimal production volume is needed for savings.

> In general, 300,000 units per annum is a low estimate of what is needed for productive efficiency in any one line.

Thus, in order to cut costs to a minimum, the manufacturer—as in days gone by—must continue to engage in mass production.[19] which leads to mass distribution and the need for a dealer network into which the manufacturer can pump massive doses of new cars in a *controlled* fashion. According to economist Lawrence J. White (1971:139), this translates into a "forcing model," which may be defined as "the requirement that the retailer sell a specific number of units as a condition of holding

---

[19]In principle, much the same strategy was used in the early 1900s when Henry Ford introduced mass production techniques and reduced the price of the Model "T" from $950.00 in 1909 to under $300.00 in the early 1920s and, as a result, boosted sales from 12,000 to two million and captured 50 percent of the market (Lanzillotti, 1968). Rothchild (1973) undoubtedly is correct when she observes that the auto industry continues to rely on ancient and probably obsolete formulas.

his franchise.''[20] In effect, this allows the manufacturer to manipulate dealer inventories in a way that serves the oligopolist interests of an economically concentrated industry. Oligopolist "rivals" recognize their interdependence and avoid direct competition. Placing new dealerships in each others' territory would only call forth counter placements which, rather than expanding total auto sales, would perhaps cut into one's own already established dealerships. Thus,

> It would be better to concentrate on lowering the [profit] margins of existing dealers, which could only be met by equal actions . . . by one's rivals and, which . . . has the effect of expanding the overall demand for the product (White, 1971:142).

All the manufacturer need do then to reduce per unit margins, which increases total net aggregate profit for the manufacturer, is to increase dealer inventory volume. This puts pressure on the dealer to free up capital from alternative investment possibilities such as used cars or to borrow capital at prevailing interest rates. Either way the dealer faces a financial squeeze and has a powerful incentive to sell off his inventory as quickly as possible, which industry trend statistics bear out. Despite the fact that new car dealers can achieve more efficient investment-return ratios from used car inventory—that is, if it is available—the ratio of new to used car sales from 1958 to 1972 per franchised new car dealer reflects an increasing preoccupation with new car sales. Examination of Table 4, column 3, indicates that over the last decade and a half new car dealers have been forced away from used cars and into new cars. In 1958, the ratio of used to new car sales was 1.77, but steadily declined until it reached 1.00 in 1970. And after 1970 it actually reversed itself so that in 1972 it was .81.[21]

This pressure to slant one's operation overwhelmingly in the direction of new car sales places the dealer in a tight margin operation. Vanderwicken (1972:121) observes that "most people have a vastly exaggerated notion of a car dealer's profits . . . the average car dealer earns less than 1 percent on his volume, a miniscule margin far below that of most other retailers." He also provides a breakdown for the Ford agency he studied. Thus, on a car that the customer paid the dealer $3,337.00, the dealer paid the manufacturer $3,025.00. The dealer's gross margin was therefore $312.00 or 9 percent. (Average gross margin for retailers in other industries runs between 20–25 percent.) Nevertheless, of this $312.00 the dealer paid $90.00 in salesman's commission, $43.00 in wages and salaries, $30.00 in advertising, $28.00 in interest, $27.00 miscellaneous, $24.00 in taxes, $22.00 in rent and maintenance, $16.00 in preparation and pre-delivery work, $9.00 in free customer service, and $7.00 in employee benefits—giving him a net profit of $16.00 per unit. As the boss of the Ford agency remarked, "Our low margins reflect the manufacturer's constant clamor for volume . . . the manufacturer sure as hell gets his . . ." (Vanderwicken, 1972:124).[22]

[20]For a further mathematical articulation of this model, see Pashigan (1961:33–34; 52–56) and White (1971:137–145).

[21]Interestingly enough, the decreasing ratio of used to new car sales more or less parallels the increasing market penetration of foreign auto makers. In 1963 foreign auto makers held 6.0 percent of the American market; that percentage increased to 14.6 percent by 1972. And the very year the ratio of used to new car sales declined to 1.00 or parity in 1970, G.M. lost nearly 7.1 percent of its previous market share (NADA, 1973:5). Put another way, increasing market penetration by foreign firms may have placed greater pressure on American auto makers to push harder on new car sales. One plausible way to accomplish this would be to require the dealer distribution network to put still more capital into new car inventory, thus enabling the manufacturer to increase the volume of sales and thereby hold its market share. There is another compatible interpretation for the dramatic and unprecedented 7.1 percent market loss sustained by G.M. in a one year period. This interpretation is held widely by dealers themselves, namely, that G.M. was attempting to prevent rumored anti-trust action by the Justice Department and was inclined to show itself under competitive seige. In the following year, 1971, G.M. recouped all but 1.6 percent of its previous loss and has held subsequently at about 45.4 percent of the total market.

[22]The per unit net of $16.00 does not reflect per unit revenue from financing or insurance which can boost that figure by 200 percent. Little wonder retail dealers want to avoid cash customers.

TABLE 4. Cars Sold per Franchised New Car Dealer: 1958–1972

Year	New	Used	Ratio Used to New
1958	125	221	1.77
1959	168	272	1.62
1960	191	285	1.49
1961	175	271	1.55
1962	208	302	1.45
1963	225	317	1.41
1964	239	311	1.30
1965	283	354	1.25
1966	285	336	1.18
1967	269	328	1.22
1968	302	326	1.08
1969	309	389	1.26
1970	281	292	1.00
1971	331	—	—
1972	354	275	.81

SOURCES: Compiled from *The Franchised New Car and Truck Dealer Story,* Washington, D.C., National Automobile Dealers Association, 1973, p. 32, and *Automobile Facts and Figures,* Detroit: Automobile Manufacturers Association, 1971, p. 33.

Should the dealer seek to protest this situation because it locks his time, effort, and money exclusively into fixed margin new car sales, he finds himself under subtle coercion. Quick delivery from the factory becomes problematic and so does a substantial supply of "hot" models (Macauley, 1966:173). Moreover, unfavorable sales comparison with "factory" stores, which sell cars below average retail price, raises questions of effective management (Leonard and Weber, 1970:416). And should such subtle coercion fail to reach home, there is always the threat of franchise termination—a threat which cannot be dismissed as idle given the elimination of over 3,300 dealerships between 1961 when there were 33,500 and 1970 when there were 30,200.[23] (NADA, 1973:30). If a franchise is cancelled, it is unlikely that another manufacturer will step in and offer a new franchise or that a new dealer will offer to buy one's premises, equipment, stock, and reputation.

[23]It is difficult to know what percentage of these 3,300 was the result of attrition, voluntary termination, bankruptcy, or direct and indirect franchise cancellation. It is probably safe to assume, however, that the existing network of franchises reflects manufacturers' preferences relative to location and pricing strategy.

Consequently, new car dealers apparently accommodate to this "forcing" procedure and avoid direct reaction. Nevertheless, it appears that they do undertake a form of indirect reaction.

DEALER REACTION

An expert witness who testified before the Senate Judiciary Subcommittee on Antitrust and Monopoly in December 1968 reported on a series of "rackets" which dealers perpetrate on the public in order to supplement their short new car profits. These "rackets" include charging for labor time not actually expended, billing for repairs not actually done, replacing parts unnecessarily, and using rebuilt parts but charging for new parts (Leonard and Weber, 1970). In addition to fleecing customers, they also attempt to retaliate against manufacturers whom they accuse of having a hypocritical attitude on service work. Virginia Knauer (Sheppard, 1972:14), special assistant to the President for consumer affairs, reports that complaints about auto service repair lead the list of all complaints. According to Knauer, local car dealers themselves complain that the manufacturers simply do not care about service repairs because if they did, they would adequately compensate dealers for pre-delivery inspection and for warranty work and they certainly would not set up—as one of the Big Three did—a regional competition in which prizes were awarded to regions that *underspent* their warranty budgets (Leonard and Weber, 1970). Indeed, the resentment held by the dealers toward the factory on the issue of service work, as well as the manner and magnitude of retribution engaged in by the dealers against the factory, has been of such proportion that one manufacturer, General Motors, recently fired its entire Chevrolet Eastern Zone office, which has jurisdiction over no less than 60 Chevrolet dealers, for colluding with those dealers against the factory, in the cause of more just compensation for dealer's service work (Farber, 1975).

It would seem, then, that the forcing of fixed margin new car inventory works to the manufacturers' advantage by increasing total net aggregate profit without risking direct competition. This high volume, low per unit profit strategy, however, precipitates a criminogenic market structure. It forces new car dealers to free up money by minimizing their investment in more profitable used car inventory as well as by borrowing capital at prevailing interest rates. The pressure of interest payments provides a powerful incentive for the dealer to move his inventory quickly. The need to turn money over and the comparatively narrow margins available to the dealer on new car sales alone precipitate several lines of illegal activity: First, it forces dealers to compensate for short new car profit margins by submitting fraudulent warrantee statements to the manufacturers, often with the collusion of the manufacturers' own representatives. Second, it forces dealers to engage in service repair rackets which milk the public of untold sums of money.[24] Third, it permits the development of a

kickback system, especially in large volume dealerships, whereby independent used car wholesalers are constrained to pay graft for supply. Fourth, the wholesalers, in turn, in order to generate unrecorded cash, collude with retail customers in "short-sales." Fifth, to the extent that short-sales spawn excess cash, the wholesaler is drawn into burying and laundering money. In sum, a limited number of oligopolist manufacturers who sit at the pinnacle of an economically concentrated industry can establish economic policy which creates a market structure that causes lower level dependent industry participants to engage in patterns of illegal activity. Thus, criminal activity, in this instance, is a direct consequence of legally established market structure.

REFERENCES

Becker, Howard S. 1970. *Sociological Work: Method and Substance*. Chicago: Aldine Publishing Company.

Brown, Joy. 1973. *The Used Car Game: A Sociology of the Bargain*. Lexington, Mass.: Lexington Books.

Edwards, Charles E. 1965. *Dynamics of the United States Automobile Industry*. Columbia: University of Southern Carolina Press.

Farber, M. A. 1975. "Chevrolet, Citing 'Policy Violations,' Ousts Most Zone Aids Here." *The New York Times*, Sunday, January 12, Section L.

Farberman, Harvey A. 1968. A Study of Personalization in Low Income Consumer Interactions and Its Relationship to Identification with Residential Community," unpublished Ph.D. thesis, Department of Sociology, University of Minnesota.

Farberman, H. A., and E. A. Weinstein. 1970. "Personalization in Lower Class Consumer Interaction." *Social Problems* 17 (Spring):449−457.

Fendell, B. 1975. "Dealers Struggle for Survival." *The New York Times*, Sunday, February 2, Section A.

---

[24]San Francisco Chronicle (1978:10) reports that, Joan Claybook, Chief of the National Highway Traffic Safety Administration, estimates that consumers were bilked out of $20 billion in 1977 for car repairs that were either fraudulent, unnecessary, incompetent, or inadequate. This sum is larger than the entire nation's outlay for doctors visits in 1974. Moreover, Claybook contends that, "40¢ of every dollar spent on car repairs is wasted. . . ."

Gouldner, Alvin. 1970. *The Coming Crisis of Western Sociology.* New York: Basic Books, and 1968. "The Sociologist as Partisan: Sociology and the Welfare State." *American Sociologist:* 3 (May):103−116.

Huber, Joan. 1973. "Symbolic Interaction as a Pragmatic Perspective: The Bias of Emergent Theory." *American Sociological Review* 38 (April): 274−284.

Lanzillotti, Robert F. 1971. "The Automobile Industry." Pp. 256−301 in W. Adams (ed.), *The Structure of American Industry,* 4th edition. New York: The MacMillan Company.

Leonard, W. N. and N. G. Weber. 1970. "Automakers and Dealers: A Study of Criminogenic Market Forces." *Law and Society* 4 (February):407−424.

Levine, L. 1968. "Jerome Avenue." *Motor Trend* 20 (December):26−29.

Liazos, A. 1972. "The Poverty of the Sociology of Deviance: Nuts, Sluts, and Perverts." *Social Problems* 20 (Summer):103−120.

Macaulay, Stewart. 1966. *Law and the Balance of Power: The Automobile Manufacturers and Their Dealers.* New York: Russell Sage Foundation.

Motor Vehicle Manufacturing Association. 1972. *1972 Automobile Facts and Figures.* Detroit: MVMA.

National Automobile Dealers Association. 1973. *The Franchised New Car and Truck Dealer Story.* Washington, D.C.: NADA, Table 6, p. 30.

Pashigan, Bedros P. 1961. *The Distribution of Automobiles, An Economic Analysis of the Franchise System.* Englewood Cliffs, N.J.: Prentice Hall.

Quinney, Richard. 1970. *The Social Reality of Crime.* Boston: Little, Brown and Company.

Robbins, Harold. 1971. *The Betsy.* New York: Trident Press.

Rothchild, Emma. 1973. *Paradise Lose: The Decline of the Auto-Industrial Age.* New York: Random House.

Schervish, P. G. 1973. "The Labeling Perspective: Its Bias and Potential in the Study of Political Deviance." *The American Sociologist* 8 (May):47−57.

Sheppard, Jeffrey M. 1972. *The New York Times,* Sunday, November 5, Section A.

Smith, R. A. 1961. "The Incredible Electrical Conspiracy." Parts I and II. *Fortune* (April−May).

Stone, G. P., D. Maines, H. A. Farberman, G. I. Stone, and N. K. Denzin. 1974. "On Methodology and Craftsmanship in the Criticism of Sociological Perspectives." *American Sociological Review* 39 (June):456−463.

Taylor, I., P. Walton, and J. Young. 1974. "Advances Towards a Critical Criminology." *Theory and Society* 1 (Winter):441−476.

Thio, A. 1973. "Class Bias in the Sociology of Deviance." *The American Sociologist* 8 (February):1−12.

Vanderwicken, Peter. 1972. "How Sam Marshall Makes out with His 'Deal.'" *Fortune* 86 (December):121−130.

White, Lawrence J. 1971. *The Automobile Industry Since 1945.* Cambridge: Harvard University Press.

PART TWO

INTERACTION

Obviously, interaction is the central thrust of this book. We view interaction as the core process of communication in which meanings and selves are established, maintained, altered, and rearranged. In placing interaction at the center of our inquiry, we are not alone. Particularly, we find no little resonance with our view among current Nobel Laureates in divergent disciplines such as economics and medicine.

At the end of 1976, controversy arose over the discovery that the work of the British psychologist, Cyril Burt, on the I.Q. of identical twins was suspect. First, a statistician noted that correlation coefficients reported in Burt's studies were so remarkably consistent that they could not be explained by chance. Something was up! Second, the collaborators working with Burt, Ms. Howard and Ms. Conway, could not be located. Margaret Howard was apparently known by one other professor, John Cohen of the University of Manchester, though no other person has seen or consulted with her. Ms. Conway was never located or found in any registry of psychologists in Britain. There seems to be little doubt that Burt "fudged" his data.[1] This is unfortunate, since his data, indicating that about 80 percent of I. Q. is based on heredity, had much to do with fashioning the educational system in Britain. Tragic as that is, that is not the point.

P. B. Medawar, a Nobel Laureate in medicine, points out the folly of summarizing any complex event with a single numerical index: "net reproduction rate" in demography, "gross national product" in economics, or "I.Q." in psychology.[2] Not only do such indices validate the delusions of "unnatural science": (a) the belief that measurement and enumeration are praiseworthy; (b) the "farrago" of inductivism; and (c) faith in the efficacy of statistics; they also conceal the intricate complexity of the events they purport to measure. Within these complex arrangements, moreover, there is much interaction hidden by such measures. Of course, Medawar was concerned primarily with the controversy aroused by the revelations of Cyril Burt's questionable "truths," but he took the argument a giant step past the issue, pointing out that there is no way to

---

[1] See D. D. Dorfman, "The Cyril Burt Question: New Findings," *Science,* CCI (September 29, 1978), pp. 1177–1186. The editors of the journal insert a caption: "The eminent Briton is shown, beyond reasonable doubt, to have fabricated data on I.Q. and social class," *ibid.*, p. 1177.

[2] P. B. Medawar, "Unnatural Science," *New York Review of Books,* XXIV (February 3, 1977), pp. 13–18.

determine what percentage of anything viable may be attributed to heredity or to environment. (Up to the point of the Burt scandal, most psychologists assumed that I.Q. was determined 80 percent by heredity and 20 percent by environment.) Medawar singles out the *interaction*.

In a particularly lucid example, Medawar cites the case of the "little brackish water shrimp *Gammarus chevreuxi*." This creature comes from the brood with red eyes, but usually ends up with black eyes. The coloration of the eye is affected by a number of environmental factors, and temperature is important,

> for it is possible to choose a genetic makeup such that the coloration of the eye will appear to be wholly under environmental control: black at relatively high temperatures . . . and reddish . . . at lower temperatures. Thus to make any pronouncement about the determination of eye color it is necessary to specify both the genetic makeup and the conditions of upbringing: neither alone will do, for the effect of one is a function of the effect of the other. It would . . . make no . . . sense to ask what percentage the coloration of the eye was due to heredity and what percentage was due to environment.[3]

Medawar goes on to say, in his brilliant discussion, that human beings owe their biological supremacy to communication:

> . . . it was not the making of a wheel that represented a characteristically human activity, but rather the communication from one person to another and therefore from one generation to the next of the know-how to make a wheel. In this view, Man is not so much a tool-making as a communicating animal.[4]

More than is usually the case in discussions of symbolic interaction, this part of the book emphasizes the affective components of communication, although the preliminary statement by Ernest Becker is somewhat more formal and, in the tradition of symbolic interaction which we are trying to extend, a bit more cognitive. The point is that he concludes with the cogent observation that "Two heads are needed for one." Mind emerges out of interaction, and two heads are usually brought together in conventional ways. In short, human beings are born into ongoing societies, and they are, therefore, brought together in diverse ways even before they are "minded."

Probing questions about society have been raised perhaps as long as human beings have been "minded," and answers have been adduced over the centuries. In the dialogue that has pitted this against that set of answers—one theory against another—the basic questions have been lost. Many early sociological answers to important questions, as that posed by Georg Simmel—"What makes society possible?"—established dialectic alternatives. Simmel's proposal of sociation and individuation as fundamental social processes; Hobbes' contrast between "Leviathan," or the highly organized state, and the *bellum omnium in omnes*, or chaos; and Ferdinand Tönnies' *Gemeinschaft* and

[3]*Ibid.*, p. 14.
[4]*Ibid.*, p. 14.

Gesellschaft, built on the psychological antinomy between *Wesenswille* (existential will), or passion and *Kürwille* (optative will), or reason, serve as examples. At any rate, dialectic conceptions do not permit mutually exclusive distinctions. At the height of furious passion, pressures for sweet reasonableness arise; and the coldest calculating reason cries out for the comforting warmth of passion. Cooley pointed out long ago that one's individuality can only be realized in contrast. Individuality demands the presence of others, or society, just as society can never exist without individuals. At one time, Carl Sandburg asked the question, "What did the last man on earth say?" He answered his own question, "The last man on earth said, 'Where is everybody?' " Sociology has ignored the mutual determinativeness of the varieties of personal conduct and has probed, for example, matters of conformity *or* deviance. Why is it, sociologists have asked, that so many conform, while so few deviate? Their answers, for the most part, have extensively searched the matter of conforming behavior, often treating deviance as residual, usually to be explained in terms of aberrations of individual experience.

Yet, in delimiting the perspective of symbolic interaction, it is not enough to confine the alternatives within the walls of sociology. Social psychology inhabits a ground contested by psychology and sociology, and the contest has continued since the nearly simultaneous publications (in 1908) of William McDougall's *Social Psychology* (on the psychological side) and Edward A. Ross's *Social Psychology* (on the sociological side). Much of psychology today is a special area of physiology, and the relation between neurological findings and variations in personal conduct has yet to be established except in very extreme instances. "Mentally retarded" persons, for example, comprise a numerically small, nevertheless socially significant proportion of the population, but, of these, the most generous estimate is that 15 percent can be accounted for on physiological grounds. Moreover, some "retardates" once thought to have been physiologically doomed, for example, hydrocephalics, have shown a remarkable capacity for rational human conduct. As a matter of fact, a whole new horizon is opening up for social psychology. It centers on the question of how retardates become so labeled when the vast majority have no physiological incapacities capable of being diagnosed. Even so, the species traits that qualify us as human beings have little relevance (as opposed to validity) in accounting for the varieties of meaningful human interaction.

Nor are human beings inert objects that must be pushed this way or that to set them into motion. Consequently, we reject psychological behaviorism and its usual explanation of conduct, conditioning. (We might observe, at this juncture, that Pavlov's dog never ate the bell!!) But some branches of psychology continue apace in this vein. For example, Guthrie, in his attempts to formulate "contiguity theory," complains that the poor record of predictability established by S-R theory might well be due to the fact that the "slices" of examined human conduct have not been cut thin enough. "Operant conditioning theory" is currently enjoying some vogue in mental therapy.

Gestalt psychologists claim, however, that the basic tenets of psychological behaviorism are empirically indefensible. People, they say, do not respond to discrete stimuli, but to their configurations of the world. Their argument carries no little weight. Suppose we were confronted with the following five items:

a ⎯⎯⎯

b ⎯⎯⎯⎯

c ⎯⎯⎯

d ⎯⎯⎯

e ⎯⎯⎯⎯⎯⎯⎯

FIGURE 1.

Their arrangement certainly affects our conceptions of item "e," and we would undoubtedly act differently toward "e" in the first Gestalt than we would toward that same item in the second, as in Figure 2.

Gestalt psychology comes close to the symbolic interactionist concept "definition of the situation," but places the mechanisms of definition "in the head." Quite obviously, one can arrange the components of a situation, as we have done in Figure 2, so that the "mental Gestalt" is emphatically altered. Indeed, the clever definer of the situation manipulates and arranges symbols in such a way that the meaning of the "same" space may be *established* in different ways. Yet, most psychologistic schemes that have been formulated for the study of human conduct study meaningless behavior—from the learning of nonsense syllables to the presumably insignificant meanderings of psychotics. They seem studiously to ignore the communicative matrix of human conduct. This studied ignorance we call *the psychologistic fallacy*. The emergence of pragmatism in American thought constitutes a revolutionary mode of interpreting human conduct. It has carried social psychology away from the psychologistic fallacy.

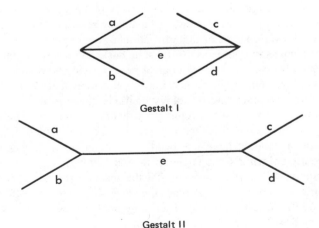

Gestalt I

Gestalt II

FIGURE 2.

John Dewey and George H. Mead undoubtedly made the most outstanding contributions to the development of pragmatism in American thought. For Dewey, constancy in human conduct is not rooted in physiology, but in customs and institutions. So-called instinctual responses are altered easily in contrast to the inertia of custom. This inertia is due to intellect, the individual phase of mind; yet mind is preeminently social. The minded person is one who participates in the communicative processes of the larger society and can propose alternative lines of action for himself, when habits have been blocked and impulses, consequently, released. Thus, education is of overriding importance. It brings man into communication or mind, permitting the possibility of continued growth—the persistent sensitivity to and ability to act upon alternative lines of action. Both Mead and Dewey were very much concerned with education as a source of social change. And, if one views the development of Mead's writings chronologically, it is clear that his participation in educational programs (quite probably because of Dewey's influence when they were together at the University of Chicago at the turn of the century) accounts for his progressively lessened interest in the philosophy of science and his increasing concern with the problems of social psychology.[5]

Mead and Dewey were quite positively influenced by Darwin. For Mead, the attraction was Darwin's emphasis upon process. Indeed, he ignored the *laissez-faire* implications of Darwinism and seized the basic theoretical import: *the same process gives rise to different forms*. Social psychology must focus its inquiries on process, specifically the process of communication. Different selves (forms) emerge from differential participation in the general and universal process of communication.

Mead, therefore, turned his attention to significant communication. This process transforms those who are caught up in it, as well as the world within which their communication takes place. There is, then, no demarcation between mind and body, nor is there any meaningful demarcation between body and environment. Such conventional distinctions disappear in the process of communication. At the same time, those engaged in communication can transform the quality of the process, either as individuals or in concerted conduct. There is a fundamental distinction between the "nonsignificant" gestures of dogs engaged in the "conversation" of a dog fight and the "significant" gestures of socialized persons engaged in mutual talk. The latter envision futures and take one another's future conduct into account in their present actions. One regulates what he is doing at the time in terms of his anticipations of the other's proposed actions and vice versa. Here is the nexus of significance or meaning. The guarantee of such mutually anticipated and proposed acts is language—common symbols or universals. (Mead pays little attention to the matter of rules of syntax or grammar.) One's use of language requires that he take two roles at once—his own and that of the other. *No socialized person ever does one thing at a time* (he smokes a cigarette and talks, he talks and paces, he appears and talks)—another aspect of conduct that most of the metaphors of psychology fail to take into account.

One cannot engage in symbolic communication until he has formed a conception of

---

[5]This transition in Mead's intellectual concerns has been ably documented in a paper, presented to a seminar on the Principles of Sociology by Penelope Baron at the University of Minnesota, 1967.

self. He must conceive that he is different from but related to others. This conception emerges as one takes over others' reactions toward himself in the form of a "me." The "me" is given full expression when one takes over the attitude of the "generalized other," the community, or a social world, and regulates his own conduct in terms of such organized expectations. One becomes something. Yet, there is always process. One acts against, or in dialogue with, these other attitudes. Because these attitudes have been incorporated, the "I" is engaged in constant conversation with the "me"—the internalized attitudes of others. One *thinks,* and thought is an internalized forum—an ongoing conversation between the "I" and the "me"—between experience and conceptualization.

We have seen that interpretation is the core process of human interaction. As Blumer so often has noted, we do not respond automatically to stimuli, but rather cogitate, analyze, judge, and then react. The stimulus can be an idea, thing, or individual; no matter what, we come to some kind of decision regarding its possible meaning for us before we assume a posture toward it. Given our language and the crudity of our research techniques, the phenomenon of process is terribly difficult to apprehend or designate. This is particularly the case when we consider affective dimensions.

Lest we imagine, however, that interpretation is an abstract, detached process, we should remember that it occurs within particular joint acts. Interpretation is as much embedded in acts of mutual aggression, sarcasm, and hatred, as in acts of agreement, friendship, and love. Moreover, each kind of joint act probably affects the process and outcome of interpretation differently; exactly how is in question. Any answer presupposes the ability to identify the properties of the different forms of action.

There is little doubt that different forms of action contain different recognizable dispositional qualities that are invariant and convey the actors' intention or purpose. For example, hardly anyone would confuse very hostile from very friendly communicative acts. But what is it about these types of acts that allows us to interpret them and respond to them appropriately? Is it possible that hostile and friendly communicative acts are based on completely different vocabularies, vocal intonations, rhythmic patterns, breathing phrases, body gestures, eye movements, or whatever?

How do we know, for example, when to take someone seriously or humorously? When do pejorative epithets indicate friendship, as opposed to antagonism? Successful analysis of this sort may well allow us to generate a typology of acts based on their formal invariant properties. To insure the relevance of such a classificatory scheme, it probably should be based on action forms recognized in everyday interaction and related to particular social settings, so that inferences concerning their function would be easier to make.

To be sure, we react to *how* something is presented to us. Moreover, our reaction probably occurs along both cognitive and affective lines. None will deny, for example, Simmel's contention that there is a discernible relationship between the sound of a voice and the meaning of an utterance. We feel ripples of excitation or rubbery limbs as we react to the tone of someone's voice. Or again, who can describe adequately those moments of transcendent ecstasy, when time and place fall away, as one looks deeply and searchingly into the eyes of his love? We reach into the soul of the other as we give up our own in the exchange of glances. But who among us would rush in to describe as cognitive the meaning, value, and sentiment of such ecstasy?

But there is more that meets one's eye than the other's glance. Stone sets forth the notion that all discourse is built on appearance or apparent symbolism which permits personifications of one another, establishing who one another is so that appropriate roles may be taken in the guarantee of discursive meaning. Gender and age are cited as examples of significant appearances in the building of those universal identities.

In Stone's work, the data were generated by interviews on dress, but more than clothing is needed in the building of a role. Embarrassment is examined in the effort to extract from wreckage of interaction the elements of the roles that were destroyed. To build a role comprises quite a complex juggling act. Besides dress, bodies, equipment, props, and spaces must be assembled, arranged, and controlled, and these represent only five of more than fifty "elements" that are drawn upon to stage an interaction. Moreover, poise and confidence in one another must be established. Perhaps it is precisely the visual interaction Simmel speaks of that goes a long way toward the silent establishment of confidence or trust and distrust. "Me thinks he has a lean and hungry look!"

The interpretation going on among the participants surely is influenced by mood and emotion. We have also shown that verbal, nonverbal, or contextual elements establish such dimensions. Consideration of affect, which may qualify or even establish the substantive or cognitive aspects of interaction, leads to the fair assumption that, in many situations, our own *personal* purposes or intentions incline us to present our community in the most dramatic and compelling form possible in order to realize our own ends.

Indeed, the area of fellow-feeling, which bridges both affective and cognitive dimensions, cross-cuts the process of interpretation. As another example, consider Scheler's typology of fellow-feeling, which describes the different ways individuals resonate in terms of emotions and moods. For example, *feeling in common*—a mother and father come together and share the anguish of burying their dead child; *feeling about something*—a close friend of the aggrieved parents commiserates with them; *mere emotional infection*—one enters a situation that is overcast with solemnity and tears and finds himself becoming depressed; and, finally, in the case of true *emotional identification*—we become one with the other and feel his feelings as our own. Love may be considered a form of dramatic presentation aimed at including another over a long period of time without violating his autonomy. According to Foote, love may be defined as that relationship between one person and another that is conducive to the optimal development of both. Optimal development means ever-increasing competence in interpersonal relations or the ability to respect and understand the other person enough to allow him to become what he can be. For the loved one to realize his potential, a critical but appreciative audience, comparatively equal in status and open for reciprocity, is ideal. The audience should be able to view the loved one as *ultimately incommensurable with any other,* thus able to take him on his own terms.

Finally, we may wish to exclude others from our conversation. For example, if our intention is to shut someone out of a circle of conversation, we might employ a sarcastic form of presentation. Although, as Ball contends, no communications are inherently sarcastic, most can be made to be sarcastic. A statement, joke, gesture, or allusion can be transformed from a mere communication into a sarcastic transaction by the parties involved, namely, the producer, the target, and the audience. The actual use of sarcasm is restricted to higher status levels, where verbal facility is well developed and symbolic aggression replaces physical assault; it is always used to control others through isolation, and the person isolated is not left in doubt as to how the interaction should be interpreted.

Whether our form of dramatic presentation be cutting with sarcasm or tender with love, the purpose is to let the other know just how he should interpret our communication. In large measure, just as our interpretation of the meaning, value, and sentiment brought into the interaction by the other will take into account the dramatic form in which it is presented, our definition for the other of the meaning, value, and sentiment brought by us will be conveyed, in part, by appearance and form of our presentation.

SUGGESTED READINGS

Blumer, Herbert. *Symbolic Interactionism*. Englewood Cliffs, N.J.: Prentice-Hall, Inc., 1969.

Brittan, Arthur. *Meanings and Situations*. London and Boston: Routledge and Kegan Paul, 1973.

Burke, Kenneth. *Language as Symbolic Action*. Berkeley: University of California Press, 1966, Parts I and III.

Cardwell, J. D. *Social Psychology: A Symbolic Interaction Perspective*. Philadelphia: F. A. Davis Co., 1971.

Cassirer, Ernst. *An Essay on Man*. New York: Doubleday Anchor Books, 1953.

Dewey, John. *Philosophy and Civilization*. Gloucester, Mass.: Peter Smith, 1968.

Duncan, Hugh D. *Symbols in Society*. New York: Oxford University Press, 1968.

Field, David. *Social Psychology for Sociologists*. London: Thomas Nelson and Sons Ltd., 1974.

Ichheiser, Gustav. *Appearances and Realities*. San Francisco: Jossey-Bass, Inc., 1970.

Kando, Thomas M. *Social Interaction*. St. Louis: C. V. Mosby Co., 1977.

Langer, Suzanne. *Philosophy in a New Key*. New York: Penguin Books, Inc., 1948.

Lauer, Robert H. and Warren H. Handel. *Social Psychology: The Theory and Application of Symbolic Interactionism*. Boston: Houghton Mifflin Co., 1977.

Lewis, M. M. *Language in Society*. New York: Social Sciences Publishers, 1948.

Lindesmith, Alfred R., Anselm L. Strauss, and Norman K. Denzin. *Social Psychology,* Fifth Edition. Hinsdale, Ill.: Dryden Press, 1977.

Manis, Jerome G. and Bernard N. Meltzer. *Symbolic Interaction*. Second Edition. Boston: Allyn and Bacon, Inc., 1972.

Rose, Arnold M. (ed.). *Human Behavior and Social Processes*. Boston: Houghton Mifflin Co., 1962.

Thayer, H. S. *Meaning and Action*. Indianapolis: Bobbs-Merril Co., Inc., 1973.

Vernon, Glenn M. *Symbolic Aspects of Interaction*. Washington, D.C.: University Press of America, 1978.

Whorf, Benjamin Lee. *Language, Thought and Reality*. Cambridge, Mass.: M.I.T. Press, 1956.

EIGHT

FROM ANIMAL TO HUMAN REACTIVITY

ERNEST BECKER

The development of the brain to its present size and complexity in man is a prodigious evolutionary feat. It represents a sensitivity to the environment unique in the animal kingdom. But this sensitivity was once the simple irritability that is characteristic of all of life: when an organism ceases to respond to stimuli we usually judge it dead.

The type of response that can be made to a stimulus varies considerably between organisms. The style of reaction to a given range of stimuli creates the world of experience of a given form. From a behaviorist point of view, "mind" is merely the style of reaction of an organism to the environment. Sherrington observed on the reactivity of the amoeba that if it were the size of a dog we should have to grant it a mind; it does act purposively in relation to various stimuli. The world of meaning is created for an animal out of the range and subtlety of its reactivity; Leslie White used the apt term "reactivity meaning" to describe the emergence of types of sensitivity in evolution.

SOURCE: Ernest Becker. "From Animal to Human Reactivity." Copyright by the Free Press of Glencoe, 1962. From Ernest Becker, *The Birth and Death of Meaning* (Glencoe: The Free Press, 1962), pp. 15–22. Reprinted by permission of The Free Press, A Divison of Macmillan Publishing Company, Inc.

Paying attention to the world with a capacity to react to it in a certain way is "mind" on its most direct level: "minding." Jakob von Uexküll used "Umwelt" to refer to the world an animal is equipped to pay attention to. The "Umwelt" of a fly, for example, would hardly contain a distinction between a rug and slippers; that of a dog would. And Madison Avenue is sensitized to subtle differences in cigarette filters beyond the reactivity of most consumers.

The progressive development of animal reactivity is easy to trace. Let us employ a simplified concept of stimulus, and follow the changes by means of the four diagrams in the text. On its simplest level (Figure 1),* the organism responds

O ——————— S

FIGURE 1. Type 1 reactivity. Simplest type of reactivity: Organism (O) responds directly to stimulus (S).

*The figures in this article are taken from Leslie A. White, "Four Stages in the Evolution of Minding," in *The Evolution of Man: Man, Culture, and Society*, Vol. 2 of *Evolution After Darwin*, edited by Sol Tax (Chicago: University of Chicago Press, 1960). The explanatory text also is adapted from this source.

to a stimulus by a direct reflex. If the stimulus emanates from something edible, the organism ingests the particle it encounters; if inedible, it recoils or ignores the particle. The relationship between the organism and the thing in its field seems to be determined by intrinsic properties. In this kind of direct stimulus-response relationship, the organism is then a slave, so to speak, to the properties of the object itself.

A real liberation took place when the conditioned reflex made its appearance (Figure 2). Remember Pavlov's classic experiment with the salivating dog. At first, the dog salivates in response to food. Then, food and another stimulus, a bell, are presented simultaneously, so that the animal grows accustomed to associating one with the other. Finally, the food is omitted and only the bell presented, but the animal, having associated his gratification with the bell, salivates when it is rung.

The liberation here is ˙fundamental: the animal reacts to a stimulus *whose intrinsic property is of no immediate interest to him*. The dog has little interest in the bell, but since it has now become a sign of something else, it becomes part of his reactive world. Consider how fortunate an animal is to be able to make chance associations and become easily conditioned to them. It is then free from abject dependence upon the stimulus itself. For example, an animal who can associate the sound of a gun with the death of one of the herd can flee immediately at the sound of the gun,

knowing what is inevitably to follow. (But this example is not the best: animals don't usually make this correlation; the intelligent elephant remains unconcerned as members of his herd are shot down around him.) On the human level, the conditioning of the individual to the equation smoke = fire can lead to an instant mobilization of energy, with only the faintest stimulus to the nostrils.

A third type of reactivity (Figure 3) is even more advanced than the conditioned reflex. The best example of it is the chimp who uses a stick to knock down a banana, suspended out of reach. He sees a relationship between two objects in his visual field, and swings the stick to bring down the banana. The crucial difference between this behavior and that of Pavlov's dog is that, for the chimp, the relationship between banana and stick is something he establishes himself. It results from an alertness to a problem situation. The equation is not built into the chimp by an experimenter, in step-by-step fashion. There is some masterful autonomy here that is absent in the simple conditioned reflex. It is not easy for an animal to relate itself to two or more things in the environment. A dog, for example, seeing food through a picket fence, will detour to a gate twenty feet down the fence to get to the food on the other side. He has seen a relationship between the open gate and getting the food. But a hen, seeing the same food and the gate as well, does not establish any relationship, and runs helplessly back and forth

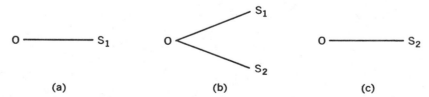

(a)   **(b)**   **(c)**

FIGURE 2. Type 2 reactivity. The conditioned response. In (a), organism responds to food. In (b), food and another stimulus are presented simultaneously, and animal learns to associate the two. So that, in (c), the animal can make the same response to the substitute stimulus that he had previously made to the food.

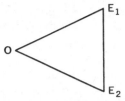

FIGURE 3. Type 3 reactivity. The chimpanzee is O; E_1 is a banana; E_2 is a stick. Unlike the conditioned response, both stimuli are present in the field from start to finish of the problem. Also, the organism, and not an experimenter or a chance association, determines the relationship between the stick and the banana.

directly in front of the food, watching it through the pickets.

The final type of reactivity-meaning is what we are accustomed to calling symbolic behavior. It is given only to man, the symbolic animal, to enjoy the freedom and powerful mastery of this type of reaction potential. In symbol behavior, the human animal responds to an arbitrary designation for an object, a designation coined by him alone, that stands for the object. The word "house," for example, has no intrinsic qualities within itself that would connect it with an object, since someone else may use "casa" or "maison" or "dom." Unlike Pavlov's dog, man *creates* the relationship

between stimuli. But unlike the chimp reaching with a firm pole for a banana, the shadowy word "house" has nothing intrinsic in it that would connect it with the object it stands for. Symbolic behavior depends, of course, upon the ability to create identifiable word sounds that become object representations of infinite degrees of subtlety— from "minnow hook" to "minestrone."

These four types of behavior are curious from one point of view: while they are evolutionary, they do not seem to be *degrees* of difference in minding the environment, but rather actually *kinds* of behavior. An organism can either be conditioned or it cannot; it can correlate two or more objects in its environment or it cannot. Figure 5 is striking. There seems to be a series which is cumulative: Man can respond to all four types of stimulus, but the lowest forms can respond to the simple stimulus or tropism only. Furthermore, at the top of the pyramid, man is by himself in an exclusive club, not only looking down at the lower animals but also, by arbitrarily coining words, assigning the very meaning to the universe.

The development of mind, then, is a progres-

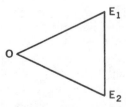

FIGURE 4. Type 4 reactivity. The human organism is O; E_1 is a house; E_2 is the word "house." Again, as in Figure 3, there is a continuous relationship between the organism and both objects in his visual field. The crucial difference in this type of reactivity is that the word "house" is fabricated by the organism itself. The organism not only perceives the relationship between two objects in its field but also creates the relationship by coining the word "house." The symbol creates a world of reference that may or may not be present originally in the perceptual field.

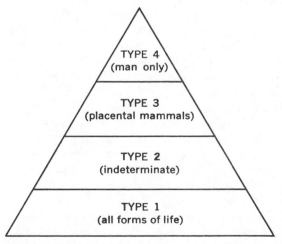

FIGURE 5. As we progress up the pyramid, the number of species capable of a given type of behavior diminishes. Also, those at the top can exercise the entire range of reactivity.

sive freedom of reactivity. The reactive process which is inherent in the organism not only gradually arrives at freedom from the intrinsic properties of things but also proceeds from there to assign *its own stimulus meanings*. Mind culminates in the organism's ability to *choose* what it will react to. White calls this a "traffic in non-sensory meanings." Nature provided all of life with H₂O, but only man could create a world in which "holy" water generates a special stimulus.

There has always been some confusion in distinguishing a sign from a pure symbol. A sign is characterized by the fact that its meaning is identified with its physical form, and may be grasped via the senses. Dark clouds, for example, are a sign of rain; a yellow flag signals quarantine. But the matter is not quite that simple. Actually, the phonetic form of a word symbol, like "holy water," enters our reactivity consciousness through our ears and is grasped by the senses. As soon as we react to the immediate stimulus property of a thing, we are reacting in a conditioned-reflex manner, and sign and symbol become confused. Even though we *assign* meaning to a thing via symbols, once the reaction becomes a habit we may respond unhesitatingly, as though the meaning were inherent in the thing itself. Thus, symbolism represents a form of flexible power over things that is lost when our response to them becomes habitually binding. We may react involuntarily to "holy water" long after we've been converted to another religion, for example. The body remains, in W. H. Gantt's beautiful phrase, "a museum of conditioned reflex antiquities." This is one reason why psychotherapy, for instance, is a long and wearisome, frustrating experience: the individual must patiently unlearn old unquestioning habitual responses, and come to assign new meanings of his own. To control the symbolic meaning of a stimulus is a power that not everyone enjoys to the same degree. An object may obtrude its concrete immediateness despite our best efforts to maintain a symbolic distance. This is one explanation for the unusual feeling of

power and delight that comes with manipulating "four-letter words." We seem to be transacting with the stark objects themselves rather than with their shadowy word representations. The confusion of the concrete and the symbolic can have a less fortunate issue: one patient in a mental hospital could not look at numbers without seeing copulating figures.

A word, of course, is a social object. We learn all our symbols from others in the long, patient acquisition of language. Then, if we wish, we can spend the rest of our lives talking to ourselves. But initially, at least two people had to agree on a word before it became a social symbol. Something had to be expressed *to* someone in order to be communicated. Some schizophrenics are irritating only because so much of their language is not comprehensible to their interlocutor. That they seem to know what they mean is not enough. The private experience has to be conveyed with word signs that are intelligible to others.

Keenly aware of our powers of speech, we look with pity upon our friends, "the dumb animals." Often they seem to have something to say but have not learned words for it. The reader may object that animals can't have thoughts unless they have words in which to formulate them; therefore it would be idle to assume that they have anything to say. But the matter is not that simple. Hallowell thinks there is good evidence for what he calls "intrinsic symbolic processes" on the subhuman level. An animal may privately produce memory representations of objects that are not present in the immediate visual field. After all, an ape's, dog's, or cat's senses are highly developed, and there is no reason to assume that images of remembered striking events do not pop into consciousness. An ape's 450-cubic-centimeter brain is of considerable size, and could conceivably permit imaginary picturing of past or even of potential events. Meredith Crawford observed that chimps were able to learn a gestural form of communication, gentle taps on the shoulder by means of which they could summon one another. Viki the chimpanzee seems to have played sometimes with an imaginary toy on an imaginary string, which she pulled around behind her.

But intrinsic symbolization is not enough. In order to become a social act, the symbol must be joined to some extrinsic mode; there must exist an external graphic mode to convey what the individual has to express. The chimp's gentle taps on the shoulder were already a cue which anticipated a social response. If the response did not come, he would pull forcibly to involve the other chimp in his laboratory task, or continue at it alone. This is a striking example of the developed mammalian intersensitivity, of which we spoke earlier. But it also shows how separate are the worlds we live in, unless we join our inner apprehensions to those of others by means of socially agreed symbols.

Thus, freedom to react to the environment is in its highest degree a social affair. No matter how acute, an animal's capacity to react to stimuli cannot reach a symbolic form until this reaction becomes a mutually shared venture. The helpless postnatal dependence of the mammals laid the basis for a heightened consciousness of an organic environment inhabited by creatures similar in form and function to oneself. But the meaning that man assigns to his world via symbols, as well as the consequent power that he has over it, is not due to his mammalian heritage alone. Helpless young in need of suck came upon the evolutionary scene over seventy million years ago. Paleolithic cave art is only forty thousand years old—the first evidence we have of true extrinsic symbolization. Reactive power over the immediate sensory bondage to the environment had to wait until one animal could intricately link his reaction sensitivity to that of another, by means of extrinsic symbolic modes. The popular "Two heads are better than one," might better be changed: "Two heads are needed for one."

NINE

ON VISUAL INTERACTION

GEORG SIMMEL

It is through the medium of the senses that we perceive our fellow-men. This fact has two aspects of fundamental sociological significance: *(a)* that of appreciation, and *(b)* that of comprehension.

(a) Appreciation—Sense-impressions may induce in us affective responses of pleasure or pain, of excitement or calm, of tension or relaxation, produced by the features of a person, or by the tone of his voice, or by his mere physical presence in the same room. These affective responses, however, do not enable us to understand or to define the other person. Our emotional response to the sense-image of the other leaves his real self outside.

(b) Comprehension—The sense-impression of the other person may develop in the opposite direction when it becomes the medium for understanding the other. What I see, hear, feel of him is only the bridge over which I reach his real self. The sound of the voice and its meaning, perhaps,

SOURCE: Georg Simmel. "On Visual Interaction." Copyright by the University of Chicago Press, 1924. Georg Simmel, "Sociology of the Senses: Visual Interaction," in Robert E. Park and Ernest W. Burgess, *Introduction to the Science of Sociology*, (Chicago: University of Chicago Press, 1924), pp. 356–365. Reprinted by permission of the University of Chicago Press. Translated and adapted from Georg Simmel, *Soziologie*, pp. 646–665.

present the clearest illustration. The speech, quite as much as the appearance of a person, may be immediately either attractive or repulsive. On the other hand, what he says enables us to understand not only his momentary thoughts but also his inner self. The same principle applies to all sense-impressions.

The sense-impressions of any object produce in us not only emotional and aesthetic attitudes toward it but also an understanding of it. In the case of reaction to non-human objects, these two responses are, in general, widely separated. We may appreciate the emotional value of any sense-impression of an object. The fragrance of a rose, the charm of a tone, the grace of a bough swaying the wind, is experienced as a joy engendered within the soul. On the other hand, we may desire to understand and to comprehend the rose, or the tone, or the bough. In the latter case we respond in an entirely different way, often with conscious endeavor. These two diverse reactions which are independent of each other are with human beings generally integrated into a unified response. Theoretically, our sense-impressions of a person may be directed on the one hand to an appreciation of his emotional value, or on the other to an impulsive or deliberate understanding of him. Actually, these two reactions are coexistent and inextricably interwoven as the basis of our relation to him. Of course, appreciation and comprehension develop in quite different degrees. These two diverse responses—to the tone of voice and to the meaning of the utterance; to the appearance of a person and to his individuality, to the attraction or repulsion of his personality and to the impulsive judgment upon his character as well as many times upon his grade of culture—are present in any perception in very different degrees and combinations.

Of the special sense-organs, the eye has a uniquely sociological function. The union and interaction of individuals is based upon mutual glances. This is perhaps the most direct and purest reciprocity which exists anywhere. The highest psychic reaction, however, in which the glances of eye to eye unite men, crystallizes into an objective structure; the unity which momentarily arises between two persons is present in the occasion and is dissolved in the function. So tenacious and subtle is this union that it can only be maintained by the shortest and straightest line between the eyes, and the smallest deviation from it, the slightest glance aside, completely destroys the unique character of this union. No objective trace of this relationship is left behind, as is universally found, directly or indirectly in all other types of associations between men, as, for example, in interchange of words. The interaction of eye and eye dies in the moment in which the directness of the function is lost. But the totality of social relations of human beings, their self-assertion and self-abnegation, their intimacies and estrangements, would be changed in unpredictable ways if there occurred no glance of eye to eye. This mutual glance between persons, in distinction from the simple sight or observation of the other, signifies a wholly new and unique union between them.

The limits of this relation are to be determined by the significant fact that the glance by which the one seeks to perceive the other is itself expressive. By the glance which reveals the other, one discloses himself. By the same act in which the observer seeks to know the observed, he surrenders himself to be understood by the observer. The eye cannot take unless at the same time it gives. The eye of a person discloses his own soul when he seeks to uncover that of another. What occurs in this direct mutual glance represents the most perfect reciprocity in the entire field of human relationships.

Shame causes a person to look at the ground to avoid the glance of the other. The reason for this is certainly not only because he is thus spared the visible evidence of the way in which the other regards his painful situation, but the deeper reason is that the lowering of his glance to a certain degree prevents the other from comprehending the extent of his confusion. The glance in the eye of the other serves not only for me to know the other but also enables him to know me. Upon the line which unites the two eyes, it conveys to the other the real personality, the real attitude, and the real impulse. The "ostrich policy" has in this explanation a real justification: who does not see the other actually conceals himself in part from the observer. A person is not at all completely present to another, when the latter sees him, but only when he also sees the other.

The sociological significance of the eye has special reference to the expression of the face as the first object of vision between man and man. It is seldom clearly understood to what an extent even our practical relations depend upon mutual recognition, not only in the sense of all external characteristics, as the momentary appearance and attitude of the other, but what we know or intuitively perceive of his life, of his inner nature, of the immutability of his being, all of which colors unavoidably both our transient and our permanent relations with him. The face is the geometric chart of all these experiences. It is the symbol of all that which the individual has brought with him as the pre-condition of his life. In the face is deposited what has been precipitated from past experience as the substratum of his life, which has become crystallized into the permanent features of his face.

To the extent to which we thus perceive the face of a person, there enters into social relations, in so far as it serves practical purposes, a super-practical element. It follows that a man is first known by his countenance, not by his acts. The face as a medium of expression is entirely a theoretical organ; it does not act, as the hand, the foot, the whole body; it transacts none of the internal or practical relations of the man, it only tells about him. The peculiar and important sociological art of "knowing" transmitted by the eye is determined by the fact that the countenance is the essential object of the inter-individual sight. This knowing is still somewhat different from understanding. To a certain extent, and in a highly variable degree, we know at first glance with whom we have to do. Our unconsciousness of this knowledge and its fundamental significance lies in the fact that we direct our attention from this self-evident intuition to an understanding of special features which determine our practical relations to a particular individual. But if we become conscious of this self-evident fact, then we are amazed how much we know about a person in the first glance at him. We do not obtain meaning from his expression, susceptible to analysis into individual traits. We cannot unqualifiedly say whether he is clever or stupid, good- or ill-natured, temperamental or phlegmatic. All these traits are general characteristics which he shares with unnumbered others. But what this first glance at him transmits to us cannot be analyzed or appraised into any such conceptual and expressive elements. Yet our initial impression remains ever the keynote of all later knowledge of him; it is the direct perception of his individuality which his appearance and especially his face, discloses to our glance.

The sociological attitude of the blind is entirely different from that of the deaf-mute. For the blind, the other person is actually present only in the alternating periods of his utterance. The expression of the anxiety and unrest, the traces of all past events, exposed to view in the faces of men, escape the blind, and that may be the reason for the peaceful and calm disposition, and the unconcern toward their surroundings, which is so often observed in the blind. Indeed, the majority of the stimuli which the face presents are often puzzling; in general, what we see of a man will be interpreted by what we hear from him, while the opposite is more unusual. Therefore the one who sees, without hearing, is much more perplexed, puzzled, and worried, than the one who hears without seeing. This principle is of great importance in understanding the sociology of the modern city.

Social life in the large city as compared with the towns shows a great preponderance of occasions to *see* rather than to *hear* people. One explanation lies in the fact that the person in the town is acquainted with nearly all the people he meets. With these he exchanges a word or a glance, and their countenance represents to him not merely the visible but indeed the entire personality. Another reason of especial significance is the development of public means of transportation. Before the appearance of omnibuses, railroads, and street cars in the nineteenth century, men were not in a situation where for periods of minutes or hours they could or must look at each other without talking to one another. Modern social life increases in ever growing degree the role of mere visual impression which always characterizes the preponderant part of all sense relationships between man and man, and must place social attitudes and feelings upon an entirely changed basis. The greater perplexity which characterizes the person who only sees, as contrasted with the one who only hears, brings us to the problems of the emotions of modern life: the lack of orientation in the collective life, the sense of utter lonesomeness, and the feeling that the individual is surrounded on all sides by closed doors.

TEN

APPEARANCE

GREGORY P. STONE

A primary tenet of all symbolic interaction theory holds that the self is established, maintained, and altered in and through communication. Seeking to probe this tenet, most investigations have emphasized discourse—or, somewhat inexactly, verbal communication—and have shown that language exerts a very great influence indeed upon the structure and process of the self. The present essay attempts to widen the perspective of symbolic interaction studies by isolating a dimension of communication that has received relatively little attention by sociologists and social psychologists—appearance. Not too long ago, except for psychoanalysts, some psychiatrists, and a few anthropologists, one could find almost no scholars willing to bend their efforts to the study of appearance.[1]

SOURCE: Gregory P. Stone. "Appearance." Copyright by Houghton Mifflin Company, 1962. A revised and expanded version of part of Gregory P. Stone, "Appearance and the Self," in Arnold M. Rose (ed.), *Human Behavior and Social Processes* (Boston: Houghton Mifflin Company, 1962), pp 86–118. Prepared especially for this volume, and reprinted by permission of the author and Houghton Mifflin Company.

[1]Erving Goffman (6) must be exempted from the indictment. He has pushed sociological or social psychological analysis far beyond the conventional limits of a perspective that has restricted the study of social transactions to their linguistic characteristics, conditions, and consequences. Since his groundbreaking effort, the literature on Proxemics (distance), Kinesics, (Body Language), Dress, and Territories (locations), as they bear on interaction, has burgeoned.

Here we demonstrate that the perspective of symbolic interaction, as it has been formulated by George H. Mead, requires (indeed, *demands*) a consideration of appearance for the adequate interpretation of social transactions as well as the careers of selves in such transactions. Mead's analysis of communication, it is suggested, suffers from what might be called a "discursive bias."[2] Consequently, there are crucial unanswered questions posed by his analysis of communication that can only be answered by extending and refining his perspective. This requires a demonstration that: (1) every social transaction must be broken down into at least two analytic components or processes— appearance and discourse; and (2) appearance is at least as important for the establishment and maintenance of the self as is discourse.

[2]Of course, the gesture is considered at length, and gestures may often be employed to establish appearances. However, Mead views the gesture as incipient discourse, more typical of communication in its rudimentary phases. The aptness of the vocal gesture for explaining the emergence of meaning in sub-social communication may be an important source of Mead's discursive bias. Even more than discourse, appearance presupposes an ongoing social process for its meaning. Apparent symbols are often silent and are best intercepted by mirrors, while one's own ear always intercepts one's own vocal gesture about as it is intercepted by others. But mirrors are not always handy; so it happens that the silent appearance, even more than the vocal utterance, comes to require an audience which can serve as a mirror reflecting one's appearance back upon himself.

APPEARANCE, DISCOURSE, AND MEANING

According to Mead, meaning is established only when the response elicited by some symbol is the "same" for the one who produces the symbol as for the one who receives it.[3] "Same" appears here in quotation marks because the responses are *really* never the "same." This is an integral feature of Mead's perspective and calls for some elaboration. The fundamental implication is that *meaning is always a variable*.

We can trace this variable nature of meaning to Mead's conception of the self as process and structure, subject and object, or "I" and "me." The "I" imbues the self with a certain tentativeness—a "certain uncertainty." As a consequence, any future line of action (for example, one's response to one's own symbolism) can never be fully anticipated. Mead put it this way:

> So the "I" really appears experientially as a part of the "me." But on the basis of this experience we distinguish that individual who is doing something from the "me" who puts the problem up to him. The response enters into his experience only when it takes place. If he says he knows what he is going to do, even there he may be mistaken. He starts out to do something and something happens to interfere. The resulting action is always a little different from anything which he could anticipate. . . . The action of the "I" is something the nature of which we cannot tell in advance (19, p. 177).

But the meaning of a symbol, as we have said, is premised upon the notion that the response called out in the other is the *same* as the response called out in the one who produces the symbol— *always a little different from anything which he could anticipate*. Moreover, the other's response has the same characteristically unanticipatable quality.

Meaning, then, is always a variable, ranging between non-sense, on the one hand—the total

absence of coincident responses—and what might be called boredom on the other—the total coincidence of such responses. Neither of these terminals can be approached very often in the duration of a transaction, for either can mean its end. It is seldom that we continue to talk non-sense with others, and, if we know *exactly* what has and will be said, we are encouraged to depart from the other's presence. Thus, meaning is present in communication when the responses that are symbolically mobilized only *more or less* coincide.

This raises the question of *guarantees* for the meaningfulness of social transactions. How can the transaction be prevented from spilling over into non-sense or atrophying into boredom? Because the self is in part an "I"—unpredictable—the risks of boredom are minimized; but, for Mead, the guarantee against non-sense in the transaction is "role-taking," or, more accurately, placing one's self in the attitude of the other. By placing one's self in the attitude or incipient action of the other and representing one's own symbolic production to oneself from that attitude, one guarantees that one's own response will be rather more than less coincident with the response of the other, since the other's incipient actions have become incorporated in the actions of the one producing the symbol. It is here, however, that a gap in Mead's analysis occurs, for a further question arises, and that question was not systematically considered by Mead: if role-taking is the guarantee of meaning, how then is role-taking possible? Obviously, one must apprehend the other's role, the other's attitude—indeed, the other's self—before one can take the other's role or incorporate the other's attitude.

At this point a shift in terminology is required to expedite the analysis of meaning and to provide initial answers to the questions that have been raised. Let us suggest that the guarantee against non-sense in the social transaction is heuristically better conceptualized as *identification*,[4] not role-

---

[3] "Response" is usually the production of other symbolism. The term is distinguished from "symbol" merely to permit the observer to shift his view as he analyzes what is going on in the social transaction. Actually, all that distinguishes a "response" from any symbol in question is its occurrence later in time.

[4] The precedent has been incisively established by Nelson N. Foote (4).

taking or taking the other's attitude—at best a very partial explanation of how meaning is established in social transactions. The term *identification* subsumes at least two processes: *identification of* and *identification with*. Role-taking is but one variant of the latter process, which must also include sympathy,[5] and there may well be other variants.[6] Nevertheless, the point to be made is this: identification *with* one another, in whatever mode, cannot be made without identifications or personifications *of* one another. Above all, personifications or identifications of one another are ordinarily facilitated by appearance and are often accomplished silently or non-verbally. This can be made crystal clear by observing the necessity for and process of establishing gender in social transactions. Everywhere we find vocabularies sexually distinguished: there are languages for males only, languages for females only, and languages employed to communicate across the barriers of gender. Obviously, identifications of the other's gender must be established before the appropriate language can be selected for the upcoming discourse. Seldom, upon encountering another, do we inquire concerning the other's gender. Indeed, to do so would be to impugn the very gender that must be established. The knowing of the other's gender is known silently, established by appearances.

Appearance, then, is that phase of the social transaction which establishes identifications or personifications of the participants. As such, it may be distinguished from *discourse*, which we conceptualize as the text of the transaction—*what* the parties are discussing. Appearance and discourse are two distinct dimensions of the social transaction. The former seems the more basic. It sets the stage for, permits, sustains, and delimits the possibilities of discourse by underwriting the possibilities of meaningful discussion.

Ordinarily, appearance is communicated by such non-verbal symbols as gestures, grooming, clothing, location, and the like; discourse, by verbal symbolism. Yet the relationship between the kinds of symbolism and the dimensions of the transaction is not at all invariant. Gestures and other non-verbal symbols may be used to talk about things and events, and words may have purely apparent significance. In fact, appearances are often discussed, while discussions often "appear"—that is, serve only to establish the identities of the discussants. In the latter case, the person may seem to be talking about matters other than personifications of self or other, but may actually be speaking only about himself. "Name-dropping" serves as an example. In the former case, which we will term *apparent discourse*, whole transactions may be given over to the discussion of appearances, and this occurs most often when some new turn has been taken by the transaction requiring reidentifications of the parties. Indeed, apparent discourse is often *news* and vice versa.

Appearance and discourse are in fact dialectic processes going on whenever people converse or correspond. They work back and forth on one another, at times shifting, at other times maintaining the direction of the transaction. When the direction of the transaction shifts, appearance is likely to emerge into the discursive phases of the transaction; when the direction is maintained over a relatively long period of time and is uninterrupted, discourse is likely to be submerged in appearances. In all cases, however, discourse is impossible without appearance which permits the requisite identification with one another by the discussants. One may, nevertheless, appear without entering the discourse. As Veblen (15), suggested, we may escape our discursive obligations, but not our clothed appearances. As Mead construed those continuing social relations mobilized by verbal symbolism to be universes of discourse, so shall this article establish those continuing social relations mobilized by apparent or

---

[5]Mead himself distinguishes sympathy as a particular mode of "attitude-taking" in a seldom cited article (8); but for the empirical utility of the distinction, see Sheldon Stryker (14).

[6]An imposing taxonomy has been erected by Howard Becker (1).

visible symbolism (except writing) as universes of appearance. Sex and age relations, in particular, will be examined.

As the world changes, so does one's apparel, and, as has been so often ignored in the literature, a change of dress may change one's very world. George Orwell, that meticulous student of appearance, noted in his *Homage to Catalonia* (12), the details of his wardrobe as he arrived in Spain to offer his personal support to the Loyalists—a heroic gesture that seems pitifully quaint in these times. After the failure of his cause, the disappointment of his hope, and the betrayal of his convictions, Orwell fled Spain with the others—frightened, sick at heart, bewildered. The world had changed, and, to guarantee the empty success of his flight—indeed, to insure his very life—Orwell adopted a different dress, rhetorically inducing the enemy, who was everywhere, to ignore his passage.[7]

Earlier, in London, Orwell's world had also collapsed about him (11). At that time, the collapse was temporary, but the reconstruction was fully visible in an imagined future. Unable to continue his work as a *plongeur* in a Paris restaurant, he secured the promise of a job from a friend in London. On his arrival there he learned that his prospective employer was out of the country and would not return for a month. Orwell was without money and without the "indecency" to ask his friend for a loan at that time. He decided to live in "some hole-and-corner way" for as much of the month's time as he could endure. His world had changed. He exchanged his second-best suit for some rags and a shilling:

> The clothes were a coat, once dark brown, a pair of black dungaree trousers, a scarf and a cloth cap. I had kept my own shirt, socks and boots, and I had a comb and razor in my pocket. It gives one a very strange feeling to be wearing such clothes. I had worn bad enough things before, but nothing at all like

these, they were not merely dirty and shapeless, they had—how is one to express it—a patina of antique filth, quite different from mere shabbiness. They were the sort of clothes you see on a bootlace seller, or a tramp. An hour later, in Lambeth, I saw a hand-dog man, obviously a tramp, coming towards me, and when I looked again it was myself, reflected in a shop window. The dirt was plastering my face already. Dirt is a great respecter of persons, it lets you alone when you are well dressed, but as soon as your collar is gone it flies toward you from all directions.

> I stayed in the streets till late at night, keeping on the move all the time. Dressed as I was, I was half afraid that the police might arrest me as a vagabond, and I dared not speak to anyone, imagining that they must notice a disparity between my accent and my clothes. (Later I discovered that this never happened.) *My new clothes had put me instantly into a new world.* Everyone's demeanour seemed to have changed abruptly. I helped a hawker pick up a barrow that he had upset. "Thanks, mate," he said with a grin. No one had called me mate before in my life—it was the clothes that had done it. For the first time I noticed, too, how the attitude of women varies with a man's clothes. When a badly dressed man passes them they shudder away from him with a quite frank movement of disgust, as though he were a dead cat. Clothes are powerful things. Dressed in a tramp's clothes, it is very difficult, at any rate the first day, not to feel that you are genuinely degraded. You might feel the same shame, irrational but very real, your first night in prison.[8]

If we look upon meaning as response, we note that dressing may itself be viewed as meaning. The defeat of the Loyalists *meant* a change of dress for Orwell as did his temporary poverty in London. There is also the meaning of dress that is provided by the responses made to it. In response to his altered appearance in the flight from Spain, the enemy ignored his passage. In response to the ragged appearance in London, Orwell *expressed* his strange feeling and his fear of the police; the

---

[7]George Orwell, *Homage to Catalonia* (London: Secker and Warburg, 1938), pp. 4, 8–9, 306, and especially 309.

[8]George Orwell, *Down and Out in Paris and London* (New York: Avon Publications, Inc., no date), pp. 114–15. Italics mine.

hawker *placed* him as a "mate," *appreciating* his assistance with a grin; and women *appreciated* his appearance with shudders, *expressing* their disgust. The strange mood, thè fear, the grin, the shuddering, and the disgust, involving him as a "mate" of the hawker, in fact, defined Orwell's *new world*. We will regard a *universe of appearance* in this behavioral sense. Such behaviors or acts may be either the appearance mobilized by events or the events mobilized by appearances. The universe of appearance, then, is not some ill-defined *Gestalt* or "field." It is a very *real* behavioral matrix of meaning—a social world.[9]

Within such worlds, because of common apparent meanings, discourse is more readily accomplished than among such worlds. As Orwell said in effect, differences in discourse are lost among those who belong to a common universe of appearance. The accent went unnoticed by the members of Orwell's new world.

> Moreover, without symbols, social sentiments could have only a precarious existence. Though very strong as long as men are together and influence each other reciprocally, they exist only in the form of recollections after the assembly has ended, and when left to themselves, these become feebler and feebler, for since the group is now no longer present and active, individual temperaments easily regain the upper hand. The violent passions which may have been released in the heart of a crowd fall away and are extinguished when this is dissolved, and men ask themselves with astonishment how they could ever have been so carried away from their normal character. But if the movements by which these sentiments are expressed are connected with something that endures, the sentiments themselves become more durable. These other things are constantly bringing them to mind and arousing them, it is as though the causes which excited them in the first place continued to act. Thus these systems of emblems, which are necessary if society is to become conscious of itself,

are no less indispensable for assuring the continuation of this consciousness.

> *So we must refrain from regarding these symbols as simple artifices, as sorts of labels attached to representations already made, in order to make them more manageable: they are an integral part of them.* Even the fact that collective sentiments are thus attached to things completely foreign to them is not purely conventional; it illustrates under a conventional form a real characteristic of social facts, that is, their transcendence over individual minds. In fact, it is known that social phenomena are born, not in individuals, but in the group. Whatever part we may take in their origin, each of us receives them from without. So when we represent them to ourselves as emanating from a material object, we do not completely misunderstand their nature. Of course, they do not come from the specific thing to which we connect them, but nevertheless, it is true that their origin is outside of us. If the moral force sustaining the believer does not come from the idol he adores or the emblem he venerates, still it is from outside of him, as he is well aware. The objectivity of its symbol only translates its externalness.

> Thus social life, in all its aspects and in every period of its history, is made possible only by a vast symbolism. The material emblems and figurative representatives with which we are more especially concerned in our present study, are one form of this; but there are many others.[10]

Durkheim (3) put dress as an "integral part" of the symbolism that we are examining. Sex and age are conceived as mobilizing the dress behavior of the sexes and age groupings, and dress is conceived as mobilizing the placements of those who *review* the sex and age of the wearers. Moreover, dress facilitates the formulation and maintenance of the *programs* of the wearers.[11] By dressing, they are themselves reminded of their sex and age. The mobilization of all these responses may be thought of as a universe of appearance, *visá-vis* the worlds

---

[9]For specification of such terms as "placed," "appreciation," and "expression," see Gregory P. Stone, "Appearance and the Self." (13). Revised in Part Three of this volume.

[10]Emile Durkheim, *The Elementary Forms of the Religious Life* (Glencoe: The Free Press, 1947), pp. 231–32. Italics mine.

[11]For the meaning of "program" and "review," see Gregory P. Stone, *op. cit.*

of sex and age, giving to dress a universal character, as the universality of the word depends upon the responses it elicits in its production.

THE CONCEPT: UNIVERSE OF APPEARANCE

In a review of C. Willet Cunnington's *English Women's Clothing in the Nineteenth Century,* Elizabeth Bowen (2) insisted that:

> To present an appearance, a whole, that shall be not only pleasing but significant (which is, after all, the aim, however imperfectly realized, of the woman buying a hat or a man buying a tie) is at least as difficult technically, requires as close a grip by the imagination, as disabused an attitude, as the writing of a book that should be fit to be published, or the painting of a picture that is to be seen.[12]

Although I would not make a similar distinction between significance and pleasure (which can, of course, be significant), Miss Bowen's insistence upon the matter of making a *significant* or *meaningful* appearance captures the core of my main line of argument. Moreover, the analogy of appearance and writing a book or painting a picture is apt. Writing a book, a discursive production, poses precisely the problem of meaningful communication with some audience, and the meaning of the book lies in the coincident lines of response called out in the writer and his audience. It is, as Mead put it, in the universe of discourse of the writer and the readers.

I shall fashion the concept, universe of appearance, on the leads provided by Mead in his discussions of universal discourse (9). Thus, I would remind the reader:

> The significant gesture or symbol always presupposes for its significance the social process of experience and behavior in which it arises; or, as the logicians say, a universe of discourse is always

implied as the context in terms of which, or as the field within which, significant gestures or symbols do in fact have significance. This universe of discourse is constituted by a group of individuals carrying on and participating in a common social process of experience and behavior, within which these gestures or symbols have the same or common meanings for all members of that group, whether they make them or address them to other individuals, or whether they overtly respond to them as made or addressed to them by other individuals. A universe of discourse is simply a system of common or social meanings.[13]

In its most extensive sense, the universe of discourse was held by Mead to be the community, but the community, in turn, is viewed as a set of continuing differentiated relations or less extensive and more specialized "sub-universes" of discourse. The political party is one example:

> In politics, for example, the individual identifies himself with an entire political party and takes the organized attitudes of that entire party toward the rest of the given social community and toward the problems which confront the party within the given social situation, and he consequently reacts or responds in terms of the organized attitudes of the party as a whole. He thus enters into a special set of social relations with all the other individuals who belong to that political party; and, in the same way, he enters into various other special sets of social relations with various other classes of individuals respectively; the individuals of each of these classes being the other members of some one of the particular organized subgroups (determined in socially functional terms) of which he himself is a member within the entire given society or social community.[14]

From the standpoint of the individual participating in the ongoing communication, he is at once brought together with the other members of the community and set apart from them. Consequently, the behavior of the individual is never a simple reproduction of community response.

---

[12]Elizabeth Bowen, *Collected Impressions* (New York: Knopf, 1950), p. 112. I am grateful to Erving Goffman for recommending this particular discussion of dress.

[13]George Herbert Mead, *Mind, Self, and Society* (Chicago: University of Chicago Press, 1934), pp. 89–90.
[14]*Ibid.,* pp. 156–57.

In other words, the organized structure of every individual self within the human social process of experience and behavior reflects, and is constituted by, the organized relational pattern of that process as a whole; but each individual self-structure reflects, and is constituted by, a different aspect or perspective of this relational pattern, because each reflects this relational pattern from its own unique standpoint, so that the common social origin and constitution of individual selves and their structure does not preclude wide individual differences and variations among them, or contradict the peculiar and more or less distinctive individuality which each of them in fact possesses. Every individual self within a given society or social community, reflects in its organized structure the whole relational pattern of organized social behavior which that society or community exhibits or is carrying on, and its organized structure is constituted by this pattern; but since each of these individual selves reflects a uniquely different aspect or perspective of this pattern in its structure, from its own particular and unique place or standpoint within the whole process of organized social behavior which exhibits this pattern—since, that is, each is differently or uniquely related to that whole process, and occupies its own essentially unique focus of relations therein—the structure of each is differently constituted by this pattern from the way in which the structure of any other is so constituted.[15]

Now, although the members of different political parties may dress differently and respond to dress differently as the members of some religious sects—the Amish, the Quakers, the brothers of the House of David, or the "Moonies"—most certainly do, I do not wish to single out these aspects of social organization, for the communicative lives of everyone are not caught up in such distinctions or subgroups. With sex and age it is a different matter. These are sets of social relations that seem persistently to differentiate the conduct of all members of whatever community within which significant discourse is indeed different.

However, the difference in the discourse among members of different social relations rests upon the

[15]*Ibid.*, pp. 201–02.

universal acknowledgment of their membership in those different social relations. This is a point which Mead did not systematically explore, perhaps thinking (rightly enough) that the style of discourse—the discursive appearance—provided an adequate enough basis for the identification of the different social relations in which the members of the community were engaged. Yet, there seems to be an order of symbolism or a phase of symbolism—apparent symbolism—to which clothing belongs that has its significance precisely in the identification of the relations in which the members of any community are engaged. Clothing has its significance in the recognition, differentiation, and *rapprochement* of people. Coincident lines of identification-of-one-another mobilized by apparent symbols are what we subsume under the concept of universe of appearance. The universe of appearance may, in fact, be regarded as the guarantee, foundation, or substrate of the universe of discourse.

SEX

On January 28, 1955, the following AP news dispatch, datelined Ann Arbor, Michigan, appeared in the Lansing *State Journal:*

> A 34-year-old man, disguised as a woman, was thrown out of the Washtenaw county circuit court Thursday when he appeared for sentencing with long curly hair and tight fitting dress.
>
> Circuit Judge R. Breakey told Dale Upton, alias Dale Sexton, to return at 3:30 p.m. with his hair shorn and in men's clothes.
>
> Upton pleaded guilty to a charge of uttering and publishing after he was arrested by Texas police and returned to Ann Arbor.
>
> Texas authorities arrested Upton in female attire at his job as a waitress in a drive-in restaurant. Returning to Ann Arbor, Upton told police he had worked as a waitress in South Lyon and Whitmore Lake and that his female dress made it easier to pass bad checks.

The motives of transvestitism are diverse and fascinating (the subject begs extensive exploration by sociologists), but the consequences seem always in this country, except in certain circumstances, to be dire. As naive as our transvestite's rationalization may appear to the uninformed there can be little doubt that the donning of female apparel by a man *in the course of daily work* is more acceptably explained to most police authorities in this country as a means of facilitating a "con game" (asexual) than by the frank acknowledgment that it represents a repudiation of one's sexual identity. The law guarantees that men will appear as men (especially at work). With women, the law is less exacting.[16] I have attempted to explore these matters with interviews of over 200 married men and women living in a Midwestern community of 10,000 population. I shall call this community "Vansburg."

Such guarantees of the distinctive dress of the sexes were discovered by some of our respondents as inhering in obedience to the will of God, or at least, as a matter of genetic destiny. Thus, the wife of the foreman of a local manufacturing plant said she didn't like to see men in shorts, adding, "I think the same thing is true of men as women. God gave them clothing and intended them to be clothed." The wife of a molder agreed that she didn't like to see men in shorts, and explained:

> Shorts are disgraceful. Women were born to wear dresses. They banned slacks and shorts at the lodges here in town. I feel women should wear what they are supposed to. Of course, for fishing and hunting, a woman should wear slacks so that she can move around. That's different.

The roots of sexually distinctive dress lie deep in the sentiments of many people. Others did not, however, appeal to the will of God, or the destiny of birth in insisting that the sexes maintain a distinctive dress. For a clothing salesman, it was a matter of liking and disliking: "It's just the difference between the masculine and the feminine. In my opinion, a woman should look feminine. A man doesn't like to have a woman dress as a man." For the wife of a custodial supervisor in a State Training School, the idea of a man in a woman's dress was a surprise so incongruous as to provoke laughter and start a humorous, somewhat irrelevant fantasy. When asked what kind of clothes men should not wear, she replied:

> Dresses, I don't know what to say. Women wear pants. Men ought to start wearing dresses. (Laughter and giggling). I'd like to see that! Oh! Did you put that down? (Gales of laughter.) (Persistently, the interviewer asks whether the informant has any particular reason in mind for suggesting that men should not wear dresses.) Oh, it don't look very masculine. Women can get away with it.

There is considerable evidence that such differences get established early. Among some people they are established in an atmosphere of suspicion and distrust. A cook in a local restaurant maintained that women should not wear "some of these shorts and halters." When asked why, she replied:

> On the little young girls, they're O.K., but, for young married women who have children, you feel as though they should really know better—to set a good example to little young girls. There's a waitress I know who has a girl thirteen or fourteen and a son eight or nine. The little son notices too many things. When she and the little girl sit in a chair, they're careful to pull down their dress. When you have children, you have to set a good example, if you want 'em to grow up to be good. 'Course, you shouldn't go to extremes either.

These differences in the dress of the genders are undoubtedly becoming less evident, as women become more involved with "male activities"—work, and play. There is some evidence, too, to show that the differences in dress are not as sharply

---

[16]The changing nature of sex relations over the last twenty-five years is graphically demonstrated by the honor now mobilized by "Klinger's" dress in the popular TV series, M*A*S*H*. On September 14, 1978, U.P.I. reported that "A gay soldier seeking discharge reportedly wore a dress in a mess hall." No legal sanctions were mentioned. See the Minneapolis *Tribune*, September 4, 1978, p. 4–13.

maintained among younger people. Although there are efforts to encourage men to adopt more "feminine" styles (fashion designers are relentless in their attempts to catch men up in the fashion cycle), the breakdown in apparent differentiation seems, even among the young, to be accomplished more by the girls who are adopting the dress of the boys.[17] A teacher in junior high school digressed in the interview to observe:

> My impression is that the girls are more particular than the boys. (Interviewer: Boys?) Jackets and overall pants and blue jeans. Perhaps the most luxurious things they wear are their shoes. They spend more for their shoes than the rest of their outfit. (Interviewer: What about the girls?) Some of them wear dresses, and some of them I don't think I've ever seen in a dress. They wear blue jeans. They don't wear silk hose. They all wear pretty nice coats—fluffy, wool type coats. They don't take care of their clothes—leave them all around. The clothing—boys' clothing—the likeness is so alike that they get their jackets mixed up. The confusion is great because of the similarities in pattern.

The wife of an "old retailer" has accepted the adolescent adoption of male dress by girls:

> Jeans, slacks, and shorts are all right on young girls, but they better leave them off when they get to be women. They'd be monstrosities. (Interviewer: What would others do, if you went shopping dressed like that?) They would probably gasp.

Despite the exception, the differences in the dress of the sexes are maintained, but the universe of sexual appearance has contracted somewhat. When women enter the occupations and preoccupations of men, they undoubtedly lose something of their femininity—an identity now acquired somewhat later in life than it was at an earlier time. Russell Lynes (7), wondering what has happened to the popular conception of a lady, concluded that a woman is a lady when she makes a man behave like a gentleman.[18] In the work place and on the sporting fields, she is losing that quality.

In spite of the penetrations women are making of the apparent sexual barriers, people generally assign to women a distinctive interest in clothing. The resignation on the part of men to this interest and the appropriation on the part of women of this interest serves as a further guarantee of sexual differentiations. When asked whether he thought the people he worked with noticed his way of dressing on the job, an accountant replied:

> If they did, I'd be unhappy about it. (Interviewer: Why is that?) Well, maybe it's because I feel if a man dresses so it's noticeable, it's wrong. . . . Every six months we have a service rating. We're rated on appearance. If it wasn't all right, I'd have heard about it.

Later, when he said that he thought about his wife's clothes more than about the clothes of any other member of his family, he explained:

> It is more of a catastrophe if the woman isn't dressed just right. A woman is judged much more severely by her clothes. If a woman wears a suit a few times in a row, there are comments.

A weighmaster estimated that his daughter was more interested in clothes than any other member of his family, elucidating:

> My daughter—she's fifteen year old. You know what public school is. You don't send your daughter to school with a gingham gown on. That's one instance where you have to keep up with the Jones's. The children of the banker go to school, and he thinks nothing of peeling off one hundred and fifty bucks for a dress, where fifty bucks to me is a lot of money. Then, she's inherited a desire for out of the ordinary clothes from her mother.

He believed that his son was least interested in clothing:

---

[17]In January 1979, I witnessed an ecdysiast begin her performance in a "feminized" sport shirt and slacks, complete with zipper fly.

[18]Russell Lynes, *A Surfeit of Honey* (New York: Harper and Brothers, 1957), p. 104, but see the entire discussion, pp. 88–104.

My son at Michigan State—he's a two-fisted individual. He doesn't want to call attention to himself as a panty-waist. He doesn't care about a white shirt. Then, there's the younger son—he's the outdoor type—wears overalls a lot of the time. Occasionally, he's the sheik—there's a young woman in his life—but that's under protest. He's a characteristic American boy.

The wife of a local printer echoed some of the sentiments of the weighmaster, when she also acknowledged that her teen-age daughter was the most interested member of the family as far as clothing was concerned:

Girls have to have so many more things, because they are in high school—the boys—and the style standards at high school are high. I've known girls who quit school because they couldn't get the clothes.

The wife of a custodial supervisor asserted:

Women need more clothes than men. A man can wear a suit all the time, but, if a woman tries to wear the same dress all the time, people say that's all you have . . . I guess it's just instinct in a woman that she wants nice clothes, if she can have them.

Her husband had learned the vocabulary of motives well, replying *independently* in response to the same question, "Women need more clothes than men." Our conception of meaning was captured nicely, in this respect, by the wife of a foundry laborer who said, "I think clothes mean more to a girl than a boy. They're noticed more."

The knowing of the other's gender is known silently. Seldom, upon meeting a stranger, do we inquire concerning the stranger's sex, although we may ask age and initiate some circumlocutions in the effort to place and appraise his social status.

A few excerpts from interview materials bear on the point. Various aspects of dress may be viewed as sexual representations. A furniture salesman reminded us of the traditional color distinctions:

When I was selling furniture, I had to know what colors would go with the rest of the room. I do the same with my clothes. I always say that the color of the clothes you wear fits the personality. Know what I mean? Like the color, blue, for a boy and otherwise for a girl.

A doctor's wife seemed to be having difficulty representing her sex to herself, and, perhaps significantly, was being conspicuously shunned by her husband. Her remarks are pertinent:

I'd love to wear frilly and very feminine things . . . I thought I'd like to wear ruffles and organdy, and more feminine things. I tried to, but I swing back . . . My husband likes earrings, and I have to force myself to wear them.

An oil salesman, when asked whose opinion about clothing mattered most to him, said:

The women. (Interviewer: Any particular ones?) All of 'em—old and young. (Interviewer: Any particular reason?) Aw, hell! I don't know. I dress for 'em in the first place.

Selection of the opposite sex as a significant audience for his dress reminds him, perhaps of his maleness. *Vive la difference!*

These materials suggest, then, that sex is, in fact, a universe of appearance. Adopting sexually distinctive dress commits one to a social world, and the commitment is enforced by law, God, birth, and social expectations. However, men and women seem to be involved differently in that world.

AGE

One day it may be well for sociologists—as the anthropologist Linton has distinguished among universals, particulars, and specialties—to propose distinctions along the dimension of, let us say, *circumstance* and *situation*. The circumstance may be said to envelop the act. For whatever reason, escape from or a redefinition of the circumstance lies outside the range of possibility. From the standpoint of the observer, the acting one is trapped, ensnared, fated. On this view, sex is a circumstance for most people, although there are rare and occasional possibilities of escape or redefinition.[19] Play is one of the more common. Serious redefinitions provide headlines for the tabloids. In some societies, age is also a circumstance, but, in our own, it increasingly becomes a situation, eminently capable of redefinition, a situation from which escape is encouraged on a large scale. Not only the ad men—Veblen's "creative psychiatrists"—lure us away from the situation of age, but also most of the columnists in the mass media, popular counselors, and the high priests of physique—the doctors. Thus, age categories, as universes of appearance, are even more riddled than sex categories, as youth spills over into old age, and old age takes on the appearance of youth.

For some, like Judge Hancock in our sample, the scene is viewed with ill-disguised disdain. Aware that people dress in different ways for different reasons, Judge Hancock singled out "old cougars or duffers trying to look young." For others, like the wife of the teacher in a State Training School, the possibilities are examined with a studied concern:

> I have to watch what I wear. I have a square figure and not everything looks well on me. Since I'm prematurely gray, people think that I'm a lot older than I am. I don't want to look older, or I'll feel older. If I feel older, I'll act older! I have to watch what I wear.

For still others, like the wife of a local theater manager, a part-time nurse, the situational character of age was reported matter-of-factly. Asked in what respects she dressed differently from other people in town, the woman replied:

> I don't know as I dress differently from my friends. However I do dress a little younger than many of them. I have daughters in school and often interchange with them.

[19]For an account of such an escape, see Harold Garfinkel, *Studies in Ethnomethodology* (Englewood Cliffs: Prentice-Hall, 1967), pp. 116–185.

She was forty-three years old at the time of the interview; her children in their early teens. For her, this "homogenization of the age grades" seems almost circumstantial. Explaining why she used to dress up in her mother's clothes as a child, she said, "Children like to look older and appear grown up. Then, when they get older, they want to look younger."

Although age undoubtedly lends itself more to manipulation through the rhetorical possibilities of appearance than does sex, age differences have not been completely lost in some large formless sartorial olio. People of different ages still dress differently in Vansburg. There is still a broad distinction between the very young and the old. The manager of a state operated store, maintaining that he seldom thought about his young son's clothing, explained, "His clothing is a regulation children's clothing." Moreover, he expressed a wish for "better quality" clothing, saying, "They can be made to fit better a person of my age." The wife of a gas station owner averred, "If you were a young gal, you might wear an extra supply of jewelry." A telephone repairman, identifying shorts with the knee-pants of his childhood, opined, "Men shouldn't wear knee pants. They look too much like a little boy." Later, asked what kind of clothes should not be worn by a person of his age, he replied, "You shouldn't look too young." Queried about the kind of clothes proscribed by his body build, he said, "Knee pants. Too much like a boy." The wife of the grocery store owner explained that her wardrobe did not include formal gowns. "There are no formal gowns. We don't go out too much any more. We're getting in the older class." Differences in the dress of the age groups persist, but are not enforced by law, the will of God, or the teleology of birth.

Instead, the enforcement of age distinctions in dress is a matter of informal social control not too firmly anchored in institutionalized vocabularies of motive. Such controls may be barely perceptible, exercised by mere *notice* and subtly indicating to the noticed one that the dress is out of place. The wife of a policeman for example, "notices" manipulations of the age situation, ". . . sometimes, when I see an older woman who is dressing in clothes a younger woman should wear." As an "interest" in clothing is generally ascribed to and appropriated by women, so may such "interests" be ascribed to people of a particular age, often adolescents. An elementary school teacher thought most about the clothing of her children, as compared to other family members: "I like to see them dressed as well as we can afford to dress them, because they're at an age when clothes are important." At some unascertainable earlier age, the importance of clothing is denied the child. A gas station owner felt that his children were least interested in clothing among the members of his family, saying, "They are too young to comprehend the meaning of clothes." The wife of a foreman in a local manufacturing plant provided a nice contrast between the expectations of the young and the expectations of the old with respect to dress. Asked whose clothes, among the members of her family, she thought about most, she singled out her daughter:

> She's young, and I feel she's more the center of attraction. She's young and it means more to her than an older person.

She acknowledged that she, herself, was the family member whose clothing was considered least often:

> I think that they [her daughter] are in the limelight more than we who are older. They are more dependent upon clothes. They feel left out, if they have no clothes. I used to feel that way. When you get old, you lose that perspective.

These remarks, made by a woman forty-four years old, might well be compared with the remarks made by the wife of the theater manager, cited earlier, at the age of forty-three.

Occasionally, the controls exerted may take a more positive turn and be more rigorously applied

than has been indicated by the exercise of noticing or the assignment of interest and meaning to those of particular age grades. This is suggested by the imaginative reconstructions of the wife of an assistant cashier in the local bank. She reported that shorts should not be worn by women while shopping:

> It's all right for young girls, but I can't stand heavyset women in shorts. (Interviewer: What would happen if you were to wear shorts shopping?) I can imagine! They would tell me to go home and get a dress on, and I wouldn't blame them. I wouldn't do it anyway.

A retired machine operator in a cement factory recounted an even more positive mode of reenforcing age norms with respect to dress. Asked, "If you could have worn any kind of clothes that you wanted on the job, what would you suggest?", he replied:

> I would have liked to have worn something different than overalls. (Interviewer: What did you have in mind?) Work pants—gabardine —and a matching shirt. (Interviewer: How would the others you worked with feel about that?) I think they would have gone along. (Interviewer: What others do you have in mind?) The younger men. There was older men there who didn't care at all. They had no pride, you'd say. You meet them anywhere. There was one old fellow—I won't mention his name —we got together and bought him an outfit. There's a saying "You dress 'em in silk, and they wouldn't look dressed." He was one of those.

But this man is undoubtedly speaking of a time thirty or forty years before the interview took place. The guarantees of age-distinctive dress, while present, seem no longer so effective.

While the age of the stranger is a more fitting subject of inquiry in establishing an acquaintance than is the stranger's sex (which would only be impugned, if questioned), it is a topic that must be approached with circumspection. Indeed, women have recently been given some legal assistance in carrying off the subterfuge of disguising their age. They need not betray their age to certain official enumerators.

On the basis of these illustrative materials, then, it seems reasonable to assert that sex, and age constitute universes of appearance. However, the limitations upon the representations of age by dress are not so stringent as those placed upon the representation of sex. Age provides, in fact, a more permeable world. Thus, age differences in the meaning assigned to dress are not so consistent, nor so clear-cut, as sex differences. Whatever the case, social relations are clearly mobilized by appearances. Such appearances are crucial for personifications, and personifications make role-taking possible so that meaning can be established in social interaction.

REFERENCES

Becker, Howard. "Empathy, Sympathy, and Scheler," *International Journal of Sociometry,* I (September, 1956), pp. 15−22.

Bowen, Elizabeth. *Collected Impressions,* New York: Knopf, 1950.

Durkheim, Emile. *The Elementary Forms of the Religious Life.* Glencoe Ill.: The Free Press, 1947.

Foote, Nelson N. "Identification as a Basis for a Theory of Motivation," *American Sociological Review,* XVI (February, 1951), pp. 14−21. Included in Part Five of this book.

Garfinkel, Harold. *Studies in Ethnomethodology.* Englewood Cliffs, N.J.: Prentice-Hall, 1967.

Goffman, Erving. *The Presentation of Self in Everyday Life.* Edinburgh: University of Edinburgh Social Science Research Centre, Monograph No. 2, 1956.

Lynes, Russell. *A Surfeit of Honey.* New York: Harper and Brothers, 1957.

Mead, George H. "Philanthropy from the Standpoint of Ethics," in Ellsworth Faris, Ferris Laune, and Arthur J. Todd (eds.), *Intelligent Philanthropy.* Chicago: University of Chicago Press, 1930, pp. 133−148.

Mead, George H. *Mind, Self, and Society.* Chicago: University of Chicago Press, 1934.

Minneapolis Tribune, September 4, 1978.

Orwell, George. *Down and Out in Paris and London.* New York: Avon Publications, Inc., no date.

Orwell, George, *Homage to Catalonia.* London: Secker and Warburg, 1938.

Stone, Gregory P. "Appearance and the Self," in Arnold M. Rose (ed.), *Human Behavior and Social Processes.* Boston: Houghton Mifflin Co., 1962, pp. 86−118. Included in a somewhat revised form in Part Three of this book.

Stryker, Sheldon. "Relationships of Married Offspring and Parent: A Test of Mead's Theory," *American Journal of Sociology.* LXII (November, 1956), pp. 308−319.

Veblen, Thorstein. *The Theory of the Leisure Class.* New York: Modern Library, Inc., 1934.

ELEVEN

EMBARRASSMENT AND THE ANALYSIS OF ROLE REQUIREMENTS

EDWARD GROSS AND GREGORY P. STONE

Attidues, in the view of George Herbert Mead, are incipient acts. Meaningful discourse requires that discussants take one another's attitudes— incorporate one another's incipient activities—in their conversation. Since all social transactions are marked by meaningful communication, discursive or not, whenever people come together, they bring futures into one another's presence. They are ready, balanced, *poised* for the upcoming discussion. The discussion, of course, remands futures to a momentary present, where they are always somewhat inexactly realized, and relegates them in their altered form to the collective past we call memory. New futures are constantly built up in discussions. Indeed, they must be, else the discus-

SOURCE: Edward Gross and Gregory P. Stone. "Embarrassment and the Analysis of Role Requirements." Copyright by the University of Chicago Press, 1964. Edward Gross and Gregory P. Stone. "Embarrassment and the Analysis of Role Requirements," *The American Journal of Sociology,* LXX (July, 1964), pp. 1–15. Reprinted by permission of the University of Chicago Press.

sion is over and the transaction is ended. Without a future, there is nothing else to be done, nothing left to say. Every social transaction, therefore, requires that the participants be poised at the outset and that poise be maintained as the transaction unfolds, until there is an accord that each can turn to other things and carry other futures away to other circles.

Poise is not enough. The futures that are presented, imperfectly realized, and re-established must be relevant. Relevance is achieved by establishing the *identities* of those who are caught up in the transaction. Futures or attitudes are anchored in identities. We speak of *role* as consensual attitudes mobilized by an announced and ratified identity in a specified social situation. In social transactions, then, persons must announce who they are to enable each one to ready himself with reference to appropriate futures, providing attitudes which others may take or assume. Often announced identities are complementary, establishing the transaction as a social relationship, for many identities presuppose counteridentities. Whether or not this is the case, the maintenance of one's identity assists the maintenance of the other.[1]

Furthermore, all transactions are transactions through time. It is not enough that identity and poise be established. They must be continuously reaffirmed, maintained, and provisions made for their repair in case of breakdown. Role performers count on this. We attempt here to limn the structure of transactions by examining instances where identities have been misplaced or forgotten, where poise has been lost or destroyed, or where, for any reason, confidence that identities and poise will be maintained has been undermined. We have in mind instances of embarrassment, whether or not deliberately perpetrated.

EMBARRASSMENT AND THE ANALYSIS OF ROLE REQUIREMENTS

Embarrassment exaggerates the core dimensions of social transactions, bringing them in the eye of the observer in an almost naked state. Embarrassment occurs whenever some *central* assumption in a transaction has been *unexpectedly* and unqualifiedly discredited for at least one participant. The result is that he is incapacitated for continued role performance.[2] Moreover, embarrassment is infectious. It may spread out, incapacitating others not previously incapacitated. It is destructive dis-ease. In the wreckage left by embarrassment lie the broken foundations of social transactions. By examining such ruins, the investigator can reconstruct the architecture they represent.

To explore this idea, recollections of embarrassment were expressly solicited from two groups of subjects: (1) approximately 800 students enrolled in introductory sociology courses; and (2) about 80 students enrolled in an evening extension class. Not solicited, but gratefully received, were many examples volunteered by colleagues and friends who had heard of our interest in the subject. Finally, we drew upon many recollections of embarrassment we had experienced ourselves. Through these means at least one thousand specimens of embarrassment were secured.

We found that embarrassments frequently occured in situations requiring continuous and coordinated role performance—speeches, ceremonies, processions, or working concerts. In such situations, embarrassment is particularly noticeable because it is so devastating. Forgetting one's lines, forgetting the wedding ring, stumbling in a cafeteria line, or handing a colleague the wrong tool, when these things occur without qualification, bring the performance to an obviously premature and unexpected halt. At the same time, manifestations of the embarrassment—blushing, fumbling, stuttering, sweating[3]—coerce awareness of the social damage and the need for immediate repair. In some instances, the damage may be potentially so great that embarrassment cannot be allowed to spread among the role performers. The incapacity may be qualified, totally ignored, or pretended out of existence.[4] For example, a minister, noting the best man's frantic search for an absent wedding ring, whispers to him to ignore it, and all conspire to continue the drama with an imaginary ring. Such rescues are not always possi-

---

[1]Alfred R. Lindesmith and Anselm L. Strauss assert that *every* role presupposes a counter-role. There is a sense of which the assertion is correct, as in Kenneth Burke's "paradox of substance," but it may also be somewhat misleading in sociological analysis. Specifically, there is a role of cigarette smoker, but the role is not really dependent for its establishment on the counter-role of non-smoker in the sense that the parental role is dependent upon child roles and vice versa. Thus, in some social transactions the establishment and maintenance of one identity may be very helpful for the establishment and maintenance of a counter-identity, in other transactions, this may not be the case of all (see Lindesmith and Straus, *Social Psychology* [New York: Dryden Press, 1956], pp. 379–80, and Kenneth Burke, *A Grammar of Motives* [New York: Prentice-Hall, 1945], pp. 21–58).

[2]Not all incapacitated persons are always embarrassed or embarrassing, because others have come to expect their *incapacities* and are consequently prepared for them.

[3]Erving Goffman, in "Embarrassment and Social Organization," *American Journal of Sociology,* LXII (November, 1956), 264–71, describes these manifestations vividly.

[4]A more general discussion of this phenomenon, under the rubric civil inattention, is provided in Erving Goffman, *Behavior in Public Places* (New York: Free Press of Glencoe, 1963), pp. 83–88 and *passim*.

ble. Hence, we suggest that every enduring social relation will provide means of preventing embarrassment, so that the entire transaction will not collapse when embarrassment occurs. A second general observation would take into account that some stages in the life cycle, for example, adolescence in our society, generate more frequent embarrassments than others. These are points to which we shall return.

To get at the content of embarrassment, we classified the instances in categories that remained as close to the specimens as possible. A total of seventy-four such categories were developed, some of which were forced choices between friends, public mistakes, exposure of false front, being caught in a cover story, misnaming, forgetting names, slips of the tongue, body exposure, invasions of others' back regions, uncontrollable laughter, drunkenness in the presence of sobriety (or vice versa), loss of visceral control, and the sudden recognition of wounds or other stigmata. Further inspection of these categories disclosed that most could be included in three general areas: (1) inappropriate identity; (2) loss of poise; (3) disturbance of the assumptions persons make about one another in social transactions.

Since embarrassment always incapacitates persons for role performance (to embarrass is, literally, to bar or stop), a close analysis of the conditions under which it occurs is especially fruitful in the revelation of the requirements *necessary* for role-playing, role-taking, role-making, and role performance in general. These role requirements are thus seen to include the establishment of identity, poise, and valid assumptions about one another among all the parties of a social transaction. We turn now to the analysis of those role requirements.

IDENTITY AND POISE

In every social transaction, selves must be established, defined, and accepted by the parties. Every person in the company of others is, in a sense, obligated to bring his best self forward to meet the selves of others also presumably best fitted to the occasion. When one is "not himself" in the presence of others who expect him to be just that, as in cases where his mood carries him away either by spontaneous seizure (uncontrollable laughter or tears) or by induced seizure (drunkenness), embarrassment ensues. Similarly, when one is "shown up" to other parties to the transaction by the exposure of unacceptable moral qualifications or inappropriate motives, embarrassment sets in all around. However, the concept, self, is a rather gross concept, and we wish to single out two places that frequently provided focal points for embarrassment—identity and poise.[5]

IDENTITY

Identity is the substantive dimension of the self.[6]

> Almost all writers using the term imply that identity establishes what and where the person is in social terms. It is not a substitute word for "self." Instead, when one has identity, he is *situated*—that is, cast in the shape of a social object by the acknowledgement of his participation or membership in social relations. One's identity is established when others *place* him as a social object by assigning the same words of identity that he appropriates for himself or *announces*. It is in the coincidence of placements and announcements that identity becomes a meaning of the self.

Moreover, as we have already pointed out, identity stands at the base of role. When inappropriate identities are established or appropriate identities are lost, role performance is impossible.

If identity *locates* the person in social terms, it follows that locations or spaces emerge as symbols of identity, since social relations are spatially

[5]Other dimensions of the self—value and mood—will be taken up in subsequent publications.

[6]Gregory P. Stone, "Appearance and the Self," in Arnold Rose (ed.), *Human Behavior and Social Processes* (Boston: Houghton Mifflin, 1962), p. 93. A revised version of this article is included in Part Three of this volume.

distributed. Moreover, as Goffman has remarked,[7] there must be a certain coherence between one's personal appearance and the setting in which he appears. Otherwise embarrassment may ensue with the resulting incapacitation for role performance. Sexual identity is pervasively established by personal appearance, and a frequent source of embarrassment among our subjects was the presence of one sex in a setting reserved for the other. Both men and women reported inadvertent invasions of spaces set aside for the other sex with consequent embarrassment and humiliation. The implication of such inadvertent invasions is, of course, that one literally does not know where one is, that one literally has no identity in the situation, or that the identity one is putting forward is so absurd as to render the proposed role performance totally irrelevant. Everyone is embarrassed, and such manifestations as, for example, cries and screams, heighten the dis-ease. In such situations, laughter cannot be enjoined to reduce the seriousness of the unexpected collapse of the encounter, and only flight can insure that one will not be buried in the wreckage.

To establish *what* he is in social terms, each person assembles a set of apparent[8] symbols which he carries about as he moves from transaction to transaction. Such symbols include the shaping of the hair, painting of the face, clothing, cards of identity, other contents of wallets and purses, and sundry additional marks and ornaments. The items in the set must cohere, and the set must be complete. Taken together, these apparent symbols have been called *identity documents*,[9] in that they

---

[7]Erving Goffman, *The Presentation of Self in Everyday Life* (New York: Doubleday Anchor Books, 1959), p. 25.

[8]We use the term ''appearance'' to designate the dimension of a social transaction given over to identification of the participant. Apparent symbols are those symbols used to communicate such identification. They are often non-verbal. Appearance seems, to us, a more useful term than Goffman's ''front'' (*ibid.*), which in everyday speech connotes misrepresentation.

[9]Erving Goffman, *Stigma* (Englewood Cliffs, N.J.: Prentice-Hall, 1963), pp. 59—62. Goffman confines the concept to personal identity, but his own discussion extends it to include matters of social identity.

enable others to validate announced identities. Embarrassment often resulted when our subjects made personal appearances with either invalid or incomplete identity documents. It was embarrassing for many, for example, to announce their identities as customers at restaurants or stores, perform the customer role and then, when the crucial validation of this identity was requested— the payoff—to discover that the wallet had been left at home.

Because the social participation of men in American society is relatively more frequently caught up in the central structures for example, the structure of work, than is the social participation of women who are relatively more immersed in interpersonal relations, the identities put forward by men are often *titles;* by women, often *names.* Except for very unusual titles[10] such identities are shared, and their presentation has the consequence of bringing people together. Names, on the other hand, mark people off from one another. So it is that a frequent source of embarrassment for women in our society occurs when they appear together in precisely the same dress. Then identity documents are invalidated. The embarrassment may be minimized, however, if the space in which they make their personal appearance is large enough. In one instance, both women met the situation by spending an entire evening on different sides of the ballroom in which their embarrassing confrontation occurred, attempting to secure validation from social circles with minimal intersection, or, at least, where intersection was temporarily attenuated. Men, on the other hand, will be embarrassed if their clothing does not resemble the dress of the other men present in public and official encounters. Except for ''the old school tie,'' their neckties seem to serve as numbers on a uniform, marking each man off from every other. Out of uniform, their structural membership cannot be

---

[10]For example, the title, ''honorary citizen of the United States,'' which was conferred on Winston Churchill, served the function of a name, since Churchill was the only living recipient of the title. Compare the titles, ''professor,'' ''manager,'' ''punch-press operator,'' and the like.

visibly established, and role performance is rendered extremely difficult, if not impossible.[11]

Not only are identities undocumented, they are also misplaced, as in misnaming or forgetting, or other incomplete placements. One relatively frequent source of embarrassment we categorized as "damaging someone's personal representation." This included cases of ethnically colored sneers in the presence of one who, in fact, belonged to the deprecated ethnic group but did not put that identity forward, or behind-the-back slurs about a woman who turned out to be the listener's wife. The victim of such misplacement, however inadvertent, will find it difficult to continue the transaction or to present the relevant identity to the perpetrators of the embarrassment in the future. The awkwardness is reflexive. Those who are responsible for the misplacement will experience the same difficulties and dis-ease.

Other sources of embarrassment anchored in identity suggest a basis characteristic of all human transactions, which, as Strauss puts it, are "carried on in thickly peopled and comply imaged contexts."[12] One always brings to transactions more identities than are necessary for his role performance. As a consequence, two or more roles are usually performed at once by each participant.[13]

If we designate the relevant roles in transactions as *dominant roles,*[14] then we may note that *adjunct roles*—a type of side involvement, as Goffman would have it[15]—or better, a type of side *activity*—are usually performed in parallel with dominant role performances. Specifically, a lecturer may smoke cigarettes or a pipe while carrying out the dominant performance, or one may carry on a heated conversation with a passenger while operating a motor vehicle. Moreover, symbols of *reserve identities* are often carried into social transactions. Ordinarily, they are concealed, as when a court judge wears his golfing clothes beneath his robes. Finally, symbols of abandoned or *relict identities* may persist in settings where they have no relevance for dominant role performances.[16] For example, photographs of the performer as an infant may be thrust into a transaction by a doting mother or wife, or one's newly constituted household may still contain the symbols of a previous marriage.

In these respects, the probability of avoiding embarrassment is a function of at least two factors: (1) the extent to which adjunct roles, reserve

---

[11]The implication of the discussion is that structural activities are uniformed, while interpersonal activities emphasize individuation in dress. Erving Goffman suggests, in correspondence, that what may be reflected here is the company people keep in their transactions. The work of men in our society is ordinarily teamwork, and teams are uniformed, but housework performed by a wife, is solitary work and does not require a uniformed appearance, though the "housedress" might be so regarded.

[12]Anselm L. Strauss, *Mirrors and Masks* (Glencoe, Ill.: Free Press, 1959), p. 57.

[13]This observation and the ensuing discussion constitute a contribution to and extension of present perspectives on role conflict. Most discussions conceive of such conflict as internalized contradictory obligations. They do not consider simultaneous, multiple-role performances. An exception is Everett C. Hughes' discussion of the Negro physician innocently summoned to attend a prejudiced emergency case in "Dilemmas and Contradictions in Status," *American Journal of Sociology* I. (March, 1945), pp. 353–59.

[14]We have rewritten this discussion to relate to Goffman's classification which came to our attention after we had prepared an earlier version of this article. Goffman distinguishes between what people do in transactions and what the situation calls for. He recognizes that people do many things at once in their encounters and distinguishes those activities that command most of their attention and energies from those which are less demanding of energy and time. Here, the distinction is made between *main* and *side involvements*. On the other hand, situations often call for multiple activities. Those which are central to the situation, Goffman speaks of as *dominant involvements;* others are called *subordinate involvements*. Dominant roles, therefore, are those that are central to the transactional situation—what the participants have come together to do (see Goffman, *Behavior in Public Places,* pp. 43–59).

[15]Adjunct roles are one type of side involvement or activity. We focus on them because we are concerned here with identity difficulties. There are other side *activities* which are *not* necessarily adjunct *roles*, namely, sporadic nosepicking, scratching, coughing, sneezing or stomach growling, which are relevant to matters of embarrassment, but not to the conceptualization of the problem in these terms. Of course, such activities, insofar as they are constantly proposed and anticipated may become incorporated in the *personal role* (always an adjunct in official transactions), as in the case of Billy Gilbert, the fabulous sneezer.

[16]This phenomenon provides the main theme and source of horror and mystery in Daphne du Maurier's now classic *Rebecca*.

identities, and relict identities are not incongruent with the dominant role performance;[17] and (2) the allocation of prime attention to the dominant role performance so that less attention is directed toward adjunct role performance, reserve identities, and relict identities. Thus the professor risks embarrassment should the performance of his sex role appear to be the main activity in transactions with female students where the professorial role is dominant—for example, if the student pulls her skirt over her knees with clearly more force than necessary. The judge may not enter the courtroom in a golf cap, nor may the husband dwell on the symbols of a past marriage in the presence of a new wife while entertaining guests in his home. Similarly, should adjunct role performance prove inept as when the smoking lecturer ignites the contents of a wastebasket or the argumentative driver fails to observe the car in front in time to avert a collision, attention is diverted from the dominant role performance. Even without the golf cap, should the judge's robe be caught so that his golfing attire is suddenly revealed in the courtroom, the transactions of the court will be disturbed. Fetishistic devotion to the symbols of relict identities by bereaved persons is embarrassing even to well-meaning visitors.

However, the matter of avoiding incongruence and allocating attention appropriately among the several identities a performer brings to a transaction verges very closely on matters of poise, as we shall see. Matters of poise converge on the necessity of controlling representations of the self, and identity-symbols are important self-representations.

PERSONAL POISE

Presentation of the self in social transactions extends considerably beyond making the appropriate personal appearance. It includes the presentation of an entire situation. Components of situations, however, are often representations of self, and in this sense self and situation are two sides of the same coin. Personal poise refers to the performer's control over self and situation, and whatever disturbs that control, depriving the transaction, as we have said before, of any relevant future, is incapacitating and consequently embarrassing.

Loss of poise was a major dimension in our scrutiny of embarrassment, and its analysis can do much to shed light on the components of social situations—a necessary task because the concept, "situation," is quite difficult to specify and operationalize. Working from the outside in, so to speak, we wish to single out five[18] elements of self and situation with reference to which loss of control gave rise to considerable embarrassment.

First, *spaces* must be so arranged and maintained that they are role-enabling. This is sometimes difficult to control, since people appear in spaces that belong to others, over which they exercise no authority and for which they are not responsible. Students, invited to faculty parties where faculty members behave like faculty members will "tighten up" to the extent that the students' role performance is seriously impeded. To avoid embarrassment, people will go to great lengths to insure their appearance in appropriate places, and to some to be deprived of access to a particular setting is to limit performance drastically.

Spaces are often fixed in location and have boundaries. As such they may partake of the character of territories or domains: a particular person (or persons) is "in command" (it is "his" domain) and most familiar with it, and the territory is in continual danger of being invaded (deliberately or inadvertently). Embarrassments were reported for both of these features of space. Being "in command" and familiar with an area means

---

[17]Adjunct roles reserve identities, and relict identities need not cohere with the dominant role; they simply must not clash so that the attention of participants in a transaction is not completely diverted from the dominant role performances.

[18]The five components to be discussed—spaces, props, equipment, clothing, and the body—are not offered as an exhaustive list. We have been able to distinguish close to forty such elements.

knowing where the back regions are and having the right of access to them. The host of a party in his own home, however much he may be vanishing,[19] is at least the person in whose territory the gathering takes place. Should a guest spill food on his clothes, he has no choice but to suffer embarrassment for the remainder of the party. The host, in contrast, can retire to his bedroom and change his clothes quickly, often before the momentary loss of poise becomes known. A striking case of the man "in command" of a territory is the person delivering a speech to a fixed audience in a closed room. In being presented to the audience, he may even be told, "The floor is yours." To underline the exclusive domain, the speaker may wait until waiters clear the last table of cups and saucers and the doors are closed. In such a setting, where the audience is not free to leave, the speaker is now in great danger of embarrassing his audience unless his speech is such that the audience is not let down. Should he show lack of poise, the audience will feel embarrassed for him, yet be unable to escape for that would further embarrass him. Hence they will suffer silently, hoping for a short speech.

In a situation reported to us, the discussant at a professional meeting was able to save the situation. The speaker was a man of national reputation—one of the pillars of his discipline. To everyone's dismay and embarrassment, he proceeded to give a pedestrian address of the caliber of an undergraduate term essay. Everyone hoped the discussant would save them, and he did. His tactic was to make clear to the audience that the identity presented by the speaker was not his real identity. This result he accomplished by reminding the audience of the major contributions of the speaker, by claiming the paper presented must be interpreted as evidence that the speaker was still productive, and that all could expect even more important contributions in the future. When the

audience thundered applause, they were not simply expressing their agreement with the discussant's appraisal of the speaker, they were also thanking him for saving them all from embarrassment by putting the speaker back in command of the territory.

We have already touched upon problems presented by invasions of spaces, and little more need be said. Persons lose poise when they discover they are in places forbidden to them, for the proscription itself means they have no identity there and hence cannot act. They can do little, except withdraw quickly. It is interesting that children are continually invading the territories of others—who can control the course of a sharply hit baseball?—and part of the process of socialization consists of indications of the importance of boundaries. Whether territories are crescive or contrived affects the possibility of invasion. When they are contrived and boundaries are marked, the invader knows he has crossed the boundary and is embarrassed if caught. With crescive territories inadvertent invasions occur, as when a tourist reports discovery of a "quaint" area of the city only to be met with the sly smiles of those who know that the area is the local prostitution region.

Such considerations raise questions concerning both how boundaries are defined and how boundary violations may be prevented. Walls provide physical limits, but do not necessarily prevent communications from passing through.[20] Hence walls work best when there is also tacit agreement to ignore audible communications on the other side of the wall. Embarrassment frequently occurs when persons on one side of the wall learn that intimate matters have been communicated to persons on the other side. A common protective device is for the captive listeners to become very quiet so that their receipt of the communication will not be discovered by the unsuspecting intimates. When no physical boundaries are present, a

---

[19]David Riesman, Robert J. Potter, and Jeanne Watson. "The Vanishing Host," *Human Organization,* XIX (Spring, 1960), 17–21.

[20]See Erving Goffman, *Behavior in Public Places,* pp 151–52.

group gathered in one section of a room may have developed a common mood which is bounded by a certain space that defines the limits of their engagement with one another. The entry of someone new may be followed by an embarrassed hush. It is not necessary that the group should have been talking about that person. Rather, since moods take time to build up, it will take time for the newcomer to "get with it" and it may not be worth the group's trouble to "fill him in." However unintentionally, he has destroyed a mood that took some effort to build up and he will suffer for it, if only by being stared at or by an obvious change of subject. In some cases, when the mood is partially sustained by alcohol, one can prepare the newcomer immediately for the mood by loud shouts that the group is "three drinks ahead" of him and by thrusting a drink into his hand without delay. So, too, a function of foyers, halls, anterooms, and other buffer zones or decompression chambers around settings is to prepare such newcomers and hence reduce the likelihood of their embarrassing both themselves and those inside.

Spaces, then, include bounded areas within which transactions go on. The boundaries may be more or less sharply defined, that is, walled in or marked off by the distances that separate one encounter from another. Overstepping the bounds is a source of embarrassment, signaling a loss of poise. Consequently, the boundaries are usually controlled and patrolled and come to represent the selves of those who are authorized to cross them.

A second component of self and situation that must be controlled to maintain poise is here designated *props*. Props are arranged around settings in an orderly manner commonly called décor. Ordinarily, they are not moved about during a transaction, except as emergencies arise, to facilitate the movement of people about the setting and to protect the group from damage. In some cases, their adherence to settings is guaranteed by law. Wall-to-wall carpeting, mirrors attached to walls, and curtain fixtures, for example, may not be removed from houses, even though ownership of

such domestic settings may change hands. The arrangement of less adhesive props within a setting may mark off or suggest (as in the case of "room dividers") smaller subsettings facilitating the division of large assemblies into more intimate circles. Moreover, although props are ordinarily not moved about *during* transactions, they are typically rearranged or replaced between major changes of scene, marking off changes in life situations.[21]

Perhaps just because of their intimate connections with the life situations of those who control them,[22] loss of control over props is a more frequent (though usually milder) source of embarrassment than the violation of boundaries. When one stumbles over his own furniture or slips on his own throw rug, doubt may be cast on the extent to which such props represent, in fact, the self and situation of the person or team members who have arranged them. Gifts of props are frequently embarrassing to the recipients. Thus, an artist (or would-be artist) may foist a painting on a friend without recognizing that the painting is contrary to the recipient's aesthetic taste. Moreover, the artist may expect that the work will be given a prominent display commensurate with his investment. A conflict is immediately established between loyalty to the artist-friend and loyalty to the recipient's self. A way out is to include the prop in question only in those situations where the donor is present, but this

---

[21]David Riesman and Howard Rosenborough, in a discussion of family careers, indicate the linkage between the rearrangement of props and the rearrangement of life situations: "One of our Kansas City respondents, whose existence had been wrapped up in her daughters' social life, when asked what she did when the daughter married and moved away, said that she slept more—and redecorated the living room. Still another became more active in church work—and redecorated the vestry" ("Careers and Consumer Behavior" in Lincoln Clark (ed.), *Consumer Behavior,* Vol. II: *The Life Cycle and Consumer Behavior* (New York: New York University Press, 1955), p. 14).

[22]Striking examples are provided by Harvey W. Zorbaugh in Ernest W. Burgess (ed.). *The Urban Community* (Chicago: University of Chicago Press, 1920), pp. 103-4, and in Anonymous, *Street-Walker,* (New York: Gramercy Publishing Co., 1962), pp. 46-48.

may become tedious, depending on the frequency and scheduling of visiting. A classic case is the wealthy relative's gift of a self-photograph, which must be dragged out of the closet for display when the relative visits.

Clashing differences in domestic décor will usually terminate or restrict house-to-house visiting. Because of this, many wartime friendships have been abruptly ended shortly after the cessation of hostilities and demobilization. In a common military setting servicemen would meet and become close friends, sometimes building up life-and-death obligations to one another. They would eagerly anticipate extending their hard-won intimacy into the workaday world of peacetime. Then, when they met in one or the other's home, the glaring incompatibility in décor would silently signal an incompatibility in life situation. Such embarrassing confrontations would be covered over with empty promises and futile vows to meet again, and the former friends would part as embarrassed strangers. If incompatabilities in décor can bring about the estrangement of friends who owe their lives to one another, we can see how props and their arrangement become powerful guaranties of the exclusiveness of social circles and status strata.

Much of our earlier discussion of adjunct roles, reserve identities, and relict identities applies to props. The porcelain dinnerware may always be kept visibly in reserve for special guests, and this very fact may be embarrassing to some dinner guests who are reminded that they are not so special after all, while, for other guests, anything but the everyday props would be embarrassing. Relict props also present a potential for embarrassment, persisting as they do when one's new life-situation has made them obsolete. The table at which a woman used to sit while dining with a former husband is obviously still quite serviceable, but it is probably best to buy another.

Third, every social transaction requires the manipulation of *equipment*. If props are ordinarily stationary during encounters, equipment is typi-

cally moved about, handled, or touched.[23] Equipment can range from words to physical objects, and a loss of control over such equipment is a frequent source of embarrassment. Here are included slips of the tongue, sudden dumbness when speech is called for, stalling cars in traffic, dropping bowling balls, spilling food, and tool failures. Equipment appearances that cast doubt on the adequacy of control are illustrated by the clanking motor, the match burning down to the fingers, tarnished silverware, or rusty work tools. Equipment sometimes extends beyond what is actually handled in the transaction to include the stage props. Indeed, items of equipment in disuse, reserve equipment, often become props—the Cadillac in the driveway or the silver service on the shelf—and there is a point at which the objects used or scheduled for use in a situation are both equipment and props. At one instant, the items of a table setting lie immobile as props; at the next, they are taken up and transformed into equipment. The close linkage of equipment and props may be responsible for the fact that *embarrassment* at times not only *infects* the participants in the transaction but the *objects* as well. For example, at a formal dinner, a speaker was discovered with his fly zipper undone. On being informed of this embarrassing oversight after he was reseated, he proceeded to make the requisite adjustment, un-

[23] Whether objects in a situation are meant to be moved, manipulated, or taken up provides an important differentiating dimension between equipment on the one hand and props (as well as clothing, to be discussed shortly) on the other. Equipment is meant to be moved, manipulated, or taken up, *during* a social transaction whereas clothing and props are expected to remain unchanged during a social transaction but will be moved, manipulated, or taken up *between* social transactions. To change props, as in burning the portrait of an old girl friend (or, to change clothes, or in taking off a necktie), signals a change in the situation. The special case of the strip-tease dancer is an exception, for her act transforms clothes into equipment. The reference above to the ''stickiness'' of props may now be seen as another way of describing the fact that they are not moved, manipulated, or taken up during transactions, but remain unchanged for the course of the transaction. Clothing is equally sticky but the object to which it sticks differs. Clothing sticks to the body; props stick to the settings.

knowingly catching the table cloth in his trousers. When obliged to rise again at the close of the proceedings, he took the stage props with him and of course scattered the dinner tools about the setting in such a way that others were forced to doubt his control. His poise was lost in the situation.

Just as props may be adjunct to the dominant role performance, held in reserve, or relict, so may equipment. Indeed, as we have said, reserve equipment is often an important part of décor.

Fourth, *clothing,* must be maintained, controlled, and coherently arranged. Its very appearance must communicate this. Torn clothing, frayed cuffs, stained neckties, and unpolished shoes are felt as embarrassing in situations where they are expected to be untorn, neat, clean, and polished. Clothing is of special importance since, as William James observed,[24] it is as much a part of the self as the body—a part of what he called the "material me." Moreover, since it is so close to the body, it conveys the impression of body maintenance, paradoxically, by concealing body-maintenance activities.[25] Hence, the double wrap—outer clothes and underclothes. Underclothes bear the marks of body maintenance and tonic state, and their unexpected exposure is a frequent source of embarrassment. The broken brassière strap sometimes produces a shift in appearance that few women (or men, for that matter) will fail to perceive as embarrassing.

Fifth, the *body* must always be in a state of readiness to act, and its appearance must make this clear. Hence any evidence of unreadiness or clumsiness is embarrassing. Examples include loss of whole body control (stumbling, trembling, or fainting), loss of visceral control (flatulence, involuntary urination, or drooling), and the communication of other "signs of the animal." The actress who is photographed from her "bad side" loses poise, for it shakes the foundation on which her fame rests. So does the person who is embarrassed about pimples, warts, or missing limbs, as well as those embarrassed in his presence.

Ordinarily, persons will avoid recognizing such stigmata, turn their eyes away, and pretend them out of existence, but on occasion stigmata will obtrude upon the situation causing embarrassment all around. A case in point was a minor flirtation reported by one of our students. Seated in a library a short distance from a beautiful girl, the student began the requisite gestural invitation to a more intimate conversation. The girl turned, smiling, to acknowledge the bid, revealing an amputated left arm. Our student's gestural line was brought to a crashing halt. Embarrassed, he abandoned the role he was building even before the foundation was laid, pretending that his inviting gestures were directed toward some imaginary audience suggested by his reading. Such stigmata publicize body-maintenance activities, and, when they are established in social transactions, interfere with role performances. The pimples on the face of the job applicant cast doubt on his maturity, and, consequently, on his qualifications for any job requiring such maturity.

All this is to say that self and situation must be in a perpetual condition of poise or readiness, adequately maintained, and in good repair. Such maintenance and the keeping of self in a state of good repair obviously require energy and time. While engaged in maintenance or repair, the person is, for that time, unable to play the role. Hence, we may expect that persons will, in order to avoid casting doubt on their ability to play a role, deliberately play down or conceal maintenance and repair activity. Speakers know that spontaneity cannot be left to chance but must be prepared for, even rehearsed. Yet obviously information on the amount of preparation it took to be spontaneous would destroy the audience's belief

---

[24] William James, *Psychology* (New York: Henry Holt & Co., 1892), pp. 177–78.

[25] A complete exposition of the body-maintenance function of clothing is set forth in an advertisement for Jockey briefs, entitled: "A Frank Discussion: What Wives Should Know about Male Support," *Good Housekeeping,* May, 1963, p. 237.

in the spontaneity. Outer clothes require underclothes, as social life requires an underlife (which is, of course, also social).[26]

MAINTENANCE OF CONFIDENCE

When identities have been validated and persons poised, interaction may begin. Its continuation, however, requires that a scaffolding be erected and that attention be given to preventing this scaffolding from collapsing. The scaffold develops as the relationship becomes stabilized. In time persons come to expect that the way they place the other is the way the other announces himself, and that poise will continue to be maintained. Persons now begin to count on these expectations and to have confidence in them. But at any time they may be violated. It was such violations of confidence that made up the greatest single source of embarrassment in our examples. Perhaps this is only an acknowledgement that the parties to every transaction must always maintain themselves *in role* to permit the requisite role-taking, or that identity-switching ought not be accomplished so abruptly that others are left floundering in the encounter as they grope for the new futures that the new identity implies.

This is all the more important in situations where roles are tightly linked together as in situations involving a division of labor. In one instance, a group of social scientists was presenting a progress report of research to a representative of the client subsidizing the research. The principal investigator's presentation was filled out by comments from the other researchers, his professional peers. Negatively critical comments were held to a bare minimum. Suddenly the principal investigator overstepped the bounds. He made a claim that they were well on the road to confirming a hypothesis which, if confirmed, would represent a major contribution. Actually, his colleagues (our informant was one of them) knew that they were very far indeed from confirming the hypothesis. They first sought to catch the leader's eye to look for a hidden message. Receiving none, they lowered their eyes to the table, bit their lips, and fell silent. In the presence of the client's representative, they felt they could not "call" their leader for that would be embarrassing, but they did seek him out immediately afterward for an explanation. The leader agreed that they were right, but said his claim was politic, that new data might well turn up and that it was clearly too late to remedy the situation.

Careful examination of this case reveals a more basic reason for the researchers' hesitance to embarrass the leader before the client's representative. If their leader were revealed to be the kind of person who goes beyond the data (or to be a plain liar), serious questions could have been raised about the kind of men who willingly work with such a person. Thus they found themselves coerced into unwilling collusion. It was not simply that their jobs depended on continued satisfaction of the client. Rather they were unwilling to say to themselves and to the client's representative that they were the kind of researchers who would be party to a fraud. To embarrass the leader, then, would have meant embarrassing themselves by casting serious question upon their identities as researchers. Indeed, it was their desire to cling to their identities that led, not long afterward (and after several other similar experiences) to the breakup of the research team.

Just as, in time, an identity may be discredited, so too may poise be upset. Should this occur, each must be able to assume that the other will render

[26]Consider the fact that the physician often needs time and opportunity to consult medical books and colleagues before he can render an authoritative medical diagnosis. A structural assurance is provided by his having been taught to make diagnoses slowly. Through time thus gained, he takes advantage of informal encounters with colleagues and spare moments between patients when he can consult medical books. A direct revelation of his need for such aids and his rather unsystematic way of getting them would be embarrassing. Yet it is in the patient's best interest that they be kept secret from him, otherwise the patient would be in the position of having to pass judgment on a professional practice when he is, in fact, too involved to render an objective judgment.

assistance if he gets into such control trouble, and each must be secure in the knowledge that the assumption is tenable. Persons will be alert for incipient signs of such trouble—irrelevant attitudes—and attempt to avert the consequences. Goffman has provided many examples in his discussion of dramaturgical loyalty, discipline, and circumspection in the presentation of the self, pointing out protective practices that are employed, such as clearing one's throat before interrupting a conversation, knocking on doors before entering an occupied room, or begging the other's pardon before an intrusion.[27]

The danger that one's confidence in the other's continued identity or his ability to maintain his poise may be destroyed leads to the generation of a set of *performance norms*. These are social protections against embarrassment.[28] If persons adhere to them, the probability of embarrassment is reduced. We discovered two major performance norms.

First, *standards of role performance almost always allow for flexibility and tolerance*. One is rarely if ever, totally in role (an exception might be highly ritualized performances, where to acknowledge breaches of expectation is devastatingly embarrassing).[29] To illustrate, we expect one another to give attention to what is going on in our transactions, but the attention we anticipate is always *optimal*, never total. To lock the other person completely in one's glance and refuse to let go is very embarrassing. A rigid attention is coerced, eventuating in a loss of poise. One is rapt in the other's future and deprived of control almost like the hypnotist's subject. Similarly, never to give one's attention to the other is role-incapacitating. If one focuses his gaze not on the other's eyes, but on his forehead, let us say, the

encounter is visibly disturbed.[30] Norms allowing for flexibility and tolerance permit the parties to social transactions ordinarily to assume that they will not be held to rigid standards of conduct and that temporary lapses will be overlooked. The norm is respected by drinking companions who both understand how it is to have had a drop too much and who can also be counted on not to hold another to everything he says, does, or suggests. So, too, colleagues are persons who know enough to embarrass one another but can ordinarily be trusted not to do so. The exclusiveness of colleague groups can be seen, therefore, as a collective defense against embarrassment.

The second performance norm was that of *giving the other fellow the benefit of the doubt*. For the transaction to go on at all, one has at least to give the other fellow a *chance* to play the role he seeks to play. Clearly, if everyone went around watching for chances to embarrass others, so many would be incapacitated for role performance that society would collapse. Such considerate behavior is probably characteristic of all human society, because of the dependence of social relations on role performance. A part of socialization, therefore, must deal with the prevention of embarrassment by the teaching of tact. People must learn not only not to embarrass others, but to ignore the lapses that can be embarrassing whenever they occur. In addition, people must learn to *cope* with embarrassment. Consequently, embarrassment will occasionally be deliberately perpetrated to ready people for role incapacitation when it occurs.

DELIBERATE EMBARRASSMENT

Although we have emphasized up to this point instances of embarrassment which arise from wholly unexpected acts and revelations, the unex-

---

[27]Goffman, *The Presentation of Self in Everyday Life,* pp. 212–33.

[28]Implicit in Georg Simmel, *The Sociology of Georg Simmel,* trans. Kurt H. Wolff (Glencoe, Ill.: Free Press, 1950), p. 308.

[29]See the discussion of "role distance" in Erving Goffman, *Encounters* (Indianapolis, Ind.: Bobbs-Merrill Co, 1961), pp. 105–52.

[30]Here we are speaking of what Edward T. Hall calls the "gaze line." He points out there are cultural variations in this phenomenon. See his "A System for the Notation of Proxemic Behavior." *American Anthropologist,* LXV (October, 1963), 1012–14.

pected is often deliberately perpetrated. Examples are practical jokes, teasing, initiation into secret societies, puncturing false fronts, and public degradation. Since embarrassment appears to represent social damage that is not at all easily repaired, we might well ask why the condition may be deliberately established. The embarrassed person stands exposed as incapable of continued role performance—a person who cannot be depended upon. In his presence, all must pause and review their assessments and expectations. Whatever they decide, the transaction is halted, and those dependent upon it are deprived of the realization of the futures that they have entrusted to others.

Embarrassments, therefore, always have careers. One person embarrasses others whose hurried attempts to salvage the situation merely call further attention to the embarrassment. A point may be reached where no repair is possible—the embarrassed person breaks into tears, flees, or, in the classic case, commits suicide—not to save face, but because face has been destroyed beyond repair.[31] Other terminations are possible as we have shown. The embarrassing situation may be transformed by humor—laughed off—to define it as unserious and to invite others to symbolize their solidarity with the embarrassed person by joining in the laughter.[32] Blame may be diverted away from the transaction and placed on others on the outside. The embarrassed one may fall sick. There are numerous outcomes, and, while some are less drastic than others, none is completely devoid of risk. Why is it, then, that embarrassment may be deliberately perpetrated? There are at least three reasons or social functions that may be attributed to deliberate embarrassment.

First, since embarrassing situations are inevitable in social life, persons must be schooled to maintain poise when poise is threatened, to maintain the identities they have established in social situations in the face of discreditation, and to sustain the confidence others have built up about such matters. Deliberate embarrassment acts to socialize young people with these skills. Consequently, all young children trip one another, push, disarrange one another's clothing and other items of personal appearance. Besides being fun, such play[33] socializes the child in the maintenance of poise despite direct physical attacks on his "balance." Indeed, young children will spin about, inducing dizziness as they unknowingly test their ability to handle the imbalance in the play that Roger Caillois speaks of as *ilinx* or *vertigo*.[34] But socialization continues throughout life, and adult men, for example, test who can maintain poise in the face of the other's loss by playing at "drinking the other under the table." The roller coaster and tilt-a-whirl and less upsetting machines, like the merry-go-round and ferris wheel, can be interpreted as a technology available to test poise.[35] Almost by definition, every game is a test of poise, but some sports place particular emphasis upon such tests— ski-jumping and gymnastics.[36] Announced identities are also challenged and impugned in play as in "name-calling," and such teasing often reaches out to call into question everything one seeks to establish about himself in social encounters:

Shame! Shame! Double shame!
Everybody knows your name!

The child, of course, learns the institutionalized replies to such tests of identity and self-confidence which throw the challenge back.

---

[31]Goffman, "On Face Work," *Psychiatry* XVIII (August, 1955), 213–31.

[32]See Ruth Laub Coser, "Some Social Functions of Laughter: A Study of Humor in a Hospital Setting," *Human Relations,* XII (May, 1959), 171–82.

[33]Careful attention must be given to all phases of children's play, which includes very much more than the anticipatory and fantastic dramas emphasized by George H. Mead.

[34]"The Structure and Classification of Games," *Diogenes,* No. 12 (Winter, 1955), pp. 62–75.

[35]A definite age-grading of the technology may be noticed in our society. The mildest test of poise is provided for the very young—the merry-go-round—and the devilish devices seem to be reserved for the middle and late teen-agers.

[36]Poise is an essential part of the commercialized tumbling exhibitions we call wrestling. Interviews with professional wrestlers by one of the writers establish that the most feared "opponent" is not at all the most fierce, but the neophyte, upon whose poise the established professional cannot rely.

My name, my name is Puddin' Tame.
Ask me again and I'll tell you the same!

As others have noted, the challenges and responses inherent in such tests of poise, identity, and self-confidence often assume a pattern of interactive insult. The classic case is "playing the dozens."[37]

If one function of deliberate embarrassment is socialization, we would guess that such tests would be concentrated in the formative years and in other periods of major status passage. Our survey of adults in the evening extension class showed this to be true. When we asked them to recall the time of their lives when they were frequently embarrassed, the adolescent years were most commonly mentioned. Instances of deliberate embarrassment also included hazings and the humiliation which accompanied socialization into the armed forces. It may well be that every move into an established social world—every major *rite de passage*—is facilitated by the deliberate perpetration of embarrassing tests of poise, identity, and self-knowledge.[38]

Second, embarrassment is deliberately perpetrated as a negative sanction as in "calling" the one who is giving an undesirable performance. Since

embarrassment does incapacitate the person from performing his role, it can clearly be used to stop someone from playing a role that might descredit a collectivity. Empirical categories include public reprimands, exposure of false fronts, open gossip and cattiness, or embarrassment perpetrated as a retaliation for an earlier embarrassment. In some of these cases, a person is exposed to having no right to play the role he has had claim to, because the identity in which his role is anchored is invalid. In others, the person is punished by terminating his role performance so that he can no longer enjoy its perquisites.

A third function of deliberate embarrassment is the establishment and maintenance of power. The technique here is rather more subtle than those we have discussed. Specifically, the scene may be laid for embarrassment so that only by following the line established by the one who sets the scene may embarrassment be avoided. In this case, one assures himself that his decision will carry the day by guaranteeing that any alternative will result in irreparable damage to the whole collectivity. Organizational policy changes, for example, may be accomplished by cloaking them in a cover story impregnated with the organizational ideology. To resist the proposed changes, consequently, risks the discreditation of the entire organization. Another example is to be found in "kicking an official upstairs." The decision will be reached in a policy-making discussion where the official in question may be present. In the discussion, emphasis will be given to the official's qualifications for the new post so that the "stage manager" leads a new self forward to replace the old self of the official in question. Discreditation of the new self, particularly in the official's presence, would wreak such damage on the transaction that it must be foregone and the "manager's" decisions conceded.[39]

---

[37]This game, found most commonly among American Negroes, is never carried on between two isolated antagonists, but requires the physical presence of peers who evaluate each insult and goad the players to heightened performances. The antagonists and their peers are usually members of the same in-group, again emphasizing the socializing function of the play. As the insults become more and more acrid, one antagonist may "break down" (lose poise) and suggest fighting. That person is perceived as having failed the test and the group then moves to prevent a fight from actually occurring. For Negroes, the ability to take insults without breaking down is clearly functional for survival in Negro-white interaction (see John Dollard, "The Dozens: Dialectic of Insult," *The American Image,* I [November, 1939], 3–25; Ralph E. Berdie, " 'Playing the Dozens,' " *Journal of Abnormal and Social Psychology,* XLII [January, 1947], 120–21; and Cornelius L. Golightly and Israel Scheffler, " 'Playing the Dozens,' " A Research Note," *Journal of Abnormal and Social Psychology,* XLIII, [January, 1948], 104–5).

[38]An interesting comment on this point was made by Erving Goffman in a personal communication: "Since the theater is *the* place for the issue of poise, could our extensive high-school theatrical movement then be part of the socialization you speak off?"

[39]Erving Goffman describes a similar process by which persons are channeled through a "betrayal funnel" into a mental hospital (see "The Moral Career of the Mental Patient," *Psychiatry,* XXII [May, 1959], 123–142. Reprinted in Part Six of this volume.

CONCLUSION

In this paper, we have inquired into the conditions necessary for role performance. Embarrassment has been employed as a sensitive indicator of those conditions, for that which embarrasses incapacitates role performance. Our data have led us to describe the conditions for role performance in terms of identity, poise, and sustained confidence in one another. When these become disturbed and discredited, role performance cannot continue. Consequently, provisions for the avoidance or prevention of embarrassment, or quick recovery from embarrassment when it does occur, are of key importance to any society or social transaction, and devices to insure the avoidance and minimization of embarrassment will be part of every persisting social relationship. Specifically, tests of identity, poise, and self-knowledge will be institutionalized in every society. Such devices, like all mechanisms of social control, are capable of manipulation and may well be exploited to establish and maintain power in social transactions. Yet, deliberate or not, embarrassment is as general a sociological concept as is role.

TWELVE

CLASSIFICATION OF THE PHENOMENA OF FELLOW-FEELING

MAX SCHELER

We must first distinguish from true fellow-feeling all such attitudes as merely contribute to our *apprehending understanding,* and in general, *re-producing* (emotionally) the experience of others, including their states of feeling. Such acts have often, and quite mistakenly, been assimilated to fellow-feeling. This has come about chiefly through the theory of projective "empathy" which attempted to explain both at the same time.

But it should be clear (before we even begin to consider this class of acts) that any kind of rejoicing or pity *presupposes,* in principle, some sort of *knowledge* of the fact, nature and quality of experience in other people, just as the possibility of such knowledge presupposes, as its condition, the existence of other conscious beings. It is not *through* pity in the first place that I learn of someone's being in pain, for the latter must already *be given*

in some form, if I am to notice and then *share* it. One may look at the face of a yelling child as a merely physical object, or one may look at it (in the normal way) as an expression of pain, hunger, etc., though without therefore pitying the child; the two things are utterly different. Thus, experiences of pity, and fellow-feeling are always additional to an experience in the other which is already grasped and understood. The giveness of these experiences (and naturally, their value) is not based, in the first instance, on sympathy or fellow-feeling—still less in the existence of other selves as established (as W. K. Clifford held).[1] Nor does this apply merely to the knowledge given in the proposition. "X is in pain" (for I can also be informed of this), nor to the factual judgment "that X is suffering"—the other person's experience *without* any sort of fellow-feeling being entailed thereby. It is perfectly meaningful to say: "I can quite visualize

SOURCE: Max Scheler. "Classification of the Phenomena of Fellow-Feeling." Copyright by Routledge and Kegan Paul, Ltd., 1954. From Max Scheler, *The Nature of Sympathy* (London: Routledge and Kegan Paul, Ltd., 1954), pp. 8–36. Reprinted by permission of Routledge and Kegan Paul, Ltd. and reprinted from *The Nature of Sympathy* by Max Scheler, translated by Peter Heath (1970). With permission from the publisher, Archon Books, Hamden, Connecticut.

[1]A. Riehl has followed him in this. *Vide Principles of Critical Philosophy* (tr. by Arthur Fairbanks, 1894). Part II, pp. 160. W. K. Clifford, *Seeing and Thinking* London, Macmillan, 1879; O. Külpe's criticism of Clifford's and Riehl's assertions, partly pertinent and partly beside the mark, in his book, *Die Realisierung,* Leipzig, 1920; and also the last chapter of this book.

your feelings, but I have no pity for you.'' Such ''visualized'' feeling remains within the cognitive sphere and is not a morally relevant act. The historian of motives, the novelist, the exponent of the dramatic arts, must all possess in high degree the gift of visualizing the feelings of others, but there is not the slightest need for them to share the feelings of their subjects and personages.

The reproduction of feeling or experience must therefore be sharply distinguished from fellow-feeling. It is indeed a case of feeling the other's feeling, not just knowing of it, nor judging that the other has it, but it is not the same as going through the experience itself. In reproduced feeling we sense the *quality* of the other's feeling, without it being transmitted to us, or evoking a similar real emotion in us.[2] The other's feeling is given exactly like a landscape which we ''see'' subjectively in memory, or a melody which we ''hear'' in similar fashion—a state of affairs quite different from the fact that we remember the landscape or the melody (possibly with an accompanying recollection of the fact ''that it was seen, or heard''). In the present case there is a real seeing or hearing, yet without the object seen or heard being perceived and accepted as really present, the past is simply ''represented.'' Equally little does the reproduction of feeling or experience imply any sort of ''participation'' in the other's experience. Throughout our visualizing of the experience we can remain quite indifferent to whatever has evoked it.

We shall not, at present, give any very detailed account of those acts which serve to establish the existence of other people and their experiences.[3] It only needs to be emphasized that this acceptance and understanding does not come about as the conclusion to an ''argument from analogy,'' nor by any protective *''empathy''* or ''mimetic im-pulse'' (Lipps).[4] That we cannot be aware of an experience without being aware of a self is something which is directly based upon the intuitable intrinsic connection between individual and experience; there is no need of empathy on the part of the percipient. That is why we can also have it given to us that the other has an individual self distinct from our own and that we can never fully comprehend this individual self, steeped as it is in its own psychic experience, but only our own view of it as an individual, conditioned as this is by our own individual nature. It is a corollary of this that the other person has—like ourselves—a sphere of absolute personal privacy, which can never be given to us. But that ''experiences'' occur there is given for us *in* expressive phenomena—again, not by inference, but directly, as a sort of primary ''perception.'' It is *in* the blush that we perceive shame, *in* the laughter joy. To say that ''our only initial datum is the body,'' is completely errone-ous. This is true only for the doctor or the scientist, i.e., for man in so far as he abstracts *artificially* from the expressive phenomena, which have an altogether primary givenness. It is rather that the same basic sense-data which go to make up the body for outward perception, can also construe, for the act of insight, the expressive phenomena which then appear, so to speak, as the ''outcome'' of experience within. For the relation here referred to is a *symbolic,* not a causal, one.[5] We can thus have insight into others, in so far as we treat their bodies as a *field of expression* for their experiences. In the sight of clasped hands, for example, the ''please'' is given exactly as the physical object is—for the latter is assuredly *given* as an object (including the fact that it has a back and an inside), in the visual phenomenon. However, the qualities (i.e., the character) of expressive phenomena and those of

---

[2] We feel the quality of the other's sorrow without suffering with him, the quality of his joy without ourselves rejoicing with him. On this, cf. Edith Stein: ''Neues zum Problem der Einfühlung'; Dissertation, Frieburg, 1917.

[3] Cf. Part III, *The Nature of Sympathy.*

[4] Cf. Theodor Lipps: 'Das Wissen von fremden Ichen,' in *Psychologische Untersuchungen,* Bd, I, Heft 4, 1905.

[5] We might also say that it is not the mere relation of a 'sign' to the presence of 'something,' whereby the latter is sub-sequently inferred, it refers to a genuine, irreducible property of the sign itself.

experiences exhibit connections of a unique kind, which do not depend at all on previous acquaintance with real experience of our own, plus the other's expressive phenomena, such that a tendency to *imitate* the movements of the gesture seen would first have to reproduce our own earlier experiences. On the contrary, imitation, even as a mere "tendency," already presupposes some kind of acquaintance with the other's experience, and therefore cannot explain what it is here supposed to do. For instance, if we (involuntarily) imitate a gesture of fear or joy, the imitation is never called forth simply by the visual image of the gesture, the impulse to imitate only arises when we have already apprehended the gesture *as* an expression of fear or joy. If this apprehension itself were only made possible (as Theodor Lipps believes) by a tendency to imitate and by the *reproduction,* thus evoked, of a previously experienced joy or fear (*plus* an empathic projection of what is reproduced into the other person), we should obviously be moving in a circle. And this applies also to the "involuntary" imitation of gestures. It already presupposes an imitation of the inner intention of action, which could be realized by quite different bodily movements.[6] We do not imitate the same or similar bodily movements in observed connections of the inorganic, e.g., in inanimate nature, where they cannot be phenomena expressive of psychic experience. Further evidence against Lipps' theory of imitation lies in the fact that we can understand the experience of animals, though even in "tendency" we cannot imitate their manner of expression; for instance, when a dog expresses its joy by barking and wagging its tail or a bird by twittering. The relationships between expression and experience have a *fundamental* basis of connection, which is independent of our specifically human gestures of expression. We have here, as it were, a *universal grammar,* valid for all languages of expression, and the ultimate basis of understanding

[6]On the distinction between imitation of action and imitation of movement, cf. K. Koffka: *The Growth of the Mind* (tr. by R. M. Ogden), Kegan Paul, 1924.

for all forms of mime and pantomime among living creatures. Only so are we able to perceive the *inadequacy* of a person's gesture to his experience, and even the contradiction between what the gesture expresses and what it is meant to express. But apart from all this, the imitation of another person's expressive gestures certainly cannot explain the act of *understanding* the inner life. The only way of explaining imitation, and the reproduction of a personal experience similar to that underlying a perceived expressive gesture, is that through this a genuine experience takes place in me, objectively, *similar* to that which occurs in the other person whose expression I imitate. For such objective similarity of experience, however, there need be no present consciousness of the similarity, still less an intentionally directed act of "understanding" or a reproduction of feeling or experience. For my having an experience *similar* to someone else's has nothing whatever to do with understanding him. Besides, such a reproduction in one's experience would require the "understanding" of another's experience in one's experience to be preceded in the participant by a similar *real* experience (however brief), i.e., in the case of feelings, a reproduction of feeling, which would always be itself an actual feeling. But one who "understands" the mortal terror of a drowning man has no need at all to *undergo* such terror, in a real, if weakened, form. This theory therefore contradicts the observable fact that, in the process of understanding, the thing understood is in no way experienced as real.

It also seems clear that what this theory could explain for us is the very opposite of genuine "understanding." This opposite is that *infection* by others' emotions which occurs in its most elementary form in the behavior of herds and crowds. Here there is actually a common making of expressive gestures in the first instance, which has the secondary effect of producing similar emotions, efforts and purposes among the people or animals concerned, thus, for instance, a herd takes fright on seeing signs of alarm in its leader, and so too in human affairs. But it is characteristic of the situation that there is a complete lack of mutual "understanding." Indeed, the purer the case, inasmuch as a rudimentary act of understanding plays little or no part in it, the more clearly do its peculiar features emerge, namely, that the participant takes the experience arising in him owing to his participation to be his *own* original experience, so that he is quite unconscious of the contagion to which he succumbs. This resembles those posthypnotically suggested acts of will which are carried out without awareness of suggestion (unlike the obeying of commands, where one remains consciously aware that the other's will is not one's own), such acts, indeed, are characteristically regarded by the agent as being his *own* and so too the experiences arising through participation in a common gesture of expression are ascribed, not to others, but to *oneself*. For this reason, even in daily life, we distinguish between merely aping someone ("taking him off," for instance) and really understanding him, and point the contrast between them.

Thus, neither "projective empathy" nor "imitation" is necessary in order to explain the primary component of fellow-feeling, viz., understanding, and the vicarious reproduction of feeling or experience. Indeed, so far as the first-mentioned acts come into it, it is not understanding they produce, but the possibility of *delusive* understanding.

Let us now turn to *fellow-feeling* which is primarily based upon . . . "vicarious" understanding . . . .Here there are *four* quite different relationships to be distinguished. I call them:

1. Immediate community of feeling, e.g., of one and the same sorrow, "with someone."

2. Fellow-feeling "about something," rejoicing in his joy and commiseration with his sorrow.

3. Mere emotional infection.

4. True emotional identification.

(1) COMMUNITY OF FEELING

Two parents stand beside the dead body of a beloved child. They feel in common the "same" sorrow, the "same" anguish. It is not that A feels this sorrow and B feels it also, and moreover that they both know they are feeling it. No, it is a *feeling-in-common*. A's sorrow is in no way an "external" matter for B here, as it is, e.g., for their friend C, who joins them, and commiserates "with them" or "upon their sorrow." On the contrary, they feel it together, in the sense that they feel and experience in common, not only the self-same value-situation, but also the same keenness of emotion in regard to it. The sorrow, as value-content, and the grief as characterizing the functional relation thereto, are here *one and identical*. It will be evident that we can only feel mental suffering in this fashion, not physical pain or sensory feelings. There is no such thing as a "common pain." Sensory types of feeling ("feeling-sensations" as Stumpf calls them) are by nature not susceptible of this highest form of fellow-feeling. They are inevitably "external," to us in some respect, inspiring only commiseration "with" and "upon" the suffering of pain by the other person. By the same token, there is certainly such a thing as rejoicing *at* another's sensory pleasure, but never mutual enjoyment of it (as a common feeling-sensation). It may, however, be the case that A first feels sorrow by himself and is then joined by B in a common feeling. But this, as will be seen presupposes the higher emotion of love.

(2) FELLOW-FEELING

The second case is quite different. Here also, the one person's sorrow is not simply the motivating cause of the other's. *All* fellow-feeling involves *intentional reference* of the feeling of joy or sorrow to the other person's experience. It points the way simply *qua* feeling—there is no need of any prior judgment or intimation "that the other person is in trouble," nor does it arise only upon sight of this other's grief, for it can also "envisage" such grief, and does so, indeed, in its very capacity *as* a feeling.[7]But here A's suffering is first presented *as* A's in an act of understanding or "vicarious" feeling experienced as such, and it is to this material that B's primary commiseration is directed. That is *my* commiseration and *his* suffering are phenomenologically *two different facts* not *one* fact, as in the first case. While in the first case the functions of vicarious experience and feeling are so interwoven with the very fellow-feeling itself as to be indistinguishable from it, in the second case the two functions are plainly distinguished even *while* experiencing them. Fellow-feeling proper, actual "participation" presents itself in the very phenomenon as a *re-action* to the state and value of the other's feelings—as these are "visualized" in vicarious feeling. Thus, in this case the two functions of *vicariously visualized* feeling, and *participation* in feeling are separately given and must be sharply distinguished. Very many descriptions of fellow-feeling suffer from failure to make this distinction.[8]

Nothing shows the fundamental diversity of the two functions more plainly than the fact that the first of them cannot only be given without the second, but is also present as a basis for the very *opposite* of an (associated) act of fellow-feeling. This happens, for instance, where there is specific pleasure in cruelty, and to a lesser extent in brutality. The *cruel* man owes his awareness of the pain or sorrow he causes entirely to a capacity for visualizing feeling! His joy lies in "torturing" and

in the agony of his victim. As he feels, vicariously, the increasing pain or suffering of his victim, so his own primary pleasure and enjoyment at the other's pain also increase. Cruelty consists not at all in the cruel man's being simply "insensitive" to other peoples' suffering. Such "insensitivity" is therefore a quite different defect in man to lack of fellow-feeling. It is chiefly found in pathological cases[9] (e.g., in melancholia), where it arises as a result of the patient's exclusive preoccupation in his own feelings, which altogether prevents him from giving emotional acceptance to the experience of other people. In contrast to cruelty, *"brutality"* is merely a disregard of other peoples' experience, despite the apprehension of it in feeling. Thus, to regard a human being as a mere log of wood and to treat the object accordingly, is not to be "brutal" towards him. On the other hand, it is characteristic of brutality, that, given merely a sense of life, undifferentiated, as yet, into separate experiences, given even the fact of an enhanced appearance of life, or a tendency towards it, any violent interruption of this tendency (as in vandalism towards plants and trees, to which one cannot be "cruel") is enough to mark it as brutal.

(3) EMOTIONAL INFECTION

Quite different again from these is the case where there is no true appearance of fellow-feeling at all, although it is very frequently confused with this. Such confusion has given rise to the mistaken theories of positivism concerning the evolution of fellow-feeling (Herbert Spencer) and, moreover, to a quite false appreciation of values, particularly in connection with pity. I have in mind the case of

[7]In *Zur psychologischen Analyse der ästhetischen Anschauung,* Witasek defends the view that what we have called "understanding" and "vicarious feeling," is only an "intuitive presentation of the experience in question." This contention is decisively refuted by Edith Stein, op. cit., § 4: "Der Streit zwischen Vorstellungs und Qualitätsansicht," p. 19.

[8]In particular the theory of projective empathy, developed by Theodor Lipps.

[9]From the psychopathological side, Kurt Schneider's valuable work, *Pathopsychologische Beiträge zur psychologischen Phänomenologie von Liebe und Hass* is in part a verification, in other respects an elaboration and extension, of the phenomenology of sympathetic experience set out in the text (Cologne, Dissertation, 1921). Also in *Zeitschrift für die ges. Neurol. u. Psychiatrie,* Bd. 65, 1921.

mere *emotional infection*. We all know how the cheerful atmosphere in a 'pub' or at a party may "infect" the newcomers, who may even have been depressed beforehand, so that they are "swept up" into the prevailing gaiety. Of course, such people are equally remote from a rejoicing of either the first or the second type. It is the same when laughter proves "catching," as can happen especially with children, and to a still greater extent among girls, who have less sensitivity, but react more readily. The same thing occurs when a group is infected by the mournful tone of one of its members, as so often happens among old women, where one recounts her woes, while the others grow more and more tearful. Naturally, this has nothing whatever to do with pity. Here there is neither a *directing* of feeling towards the other's joy or suffering, nor any participation in her experience. On the contrary, it is characteristic of emotional infection that it occurs only as a transference of the *state* of feeling, and does *not* presuppose any sort of *knowledge* of the joy which others feel. Thus, one may only notice afterwards that a mournful feeling, encountered in oneself, is traceable to infection from a group one has visited some hours before. There is nothing in the mournful feeling itself to point to the origin, only by inference from causal considerations does it become clear where it came from. For such contagion it is by no means necessary that any *emotional* experiences should have occurred in the other person. Even the *objective* aspects of such feelings, which attach to natural objects, or are discerned in an "atmosphere"—such as the serenity of a spring landscape, the melancholy of a rainy day, the wretchedness of a room—can work infectiously in this way on the state of our emotions.[10]

The process of infection is an involuntary one. Especially characteristic is its tendency to return to its point of departure so that the feelings concerned gather momentum like an avalanche. The emotion caused by infection reproduces itself again by means of expression and imitation, so that the infectious emotion increases, again reproduces itself, and so on. In all mass-excitement, even in the formation of 'public opinion,' it is above all this reciprocal effect of a self-generating infection which leads to the uprush of a common surge of emotion, and to the characteristic feature of a crowd in action, that it is so easily carried beyond the intentions of every one of its members, and does things for which no one acknowledges either the will or the responsibility. It is, in fact, the infective process itself, which generates purposes beyond the designs of any single individual.[11]

[10]This shows that the process of infection does *not* lie in the imitation of others' expressed experiences, even though these may actually bring it about, where it is a case of infection through experiences undergone by animals or other human beings.

[11]I refrain here from describing the immense part which infection plays in the historical evolution of whole systems of morality, in the genesis of psychopathic group-movements (from *folie à deux* to the emergence of enduring pathological customs and usages on a national scale), in the onset of panics, and particularly within all revolutionary mass-movements. Cf. Gustave Le Bon, *The Crowd: a Study of the Popular Mind*, Unwin, 1896, and *L'Ame Révolutionaire;* see also Tarde: *Les lois de l'imitation;* and Sigmund Freud, *Group Psychology and the Analysis of the Ego,* who there observes:

"Psycho-analytic research, which has already occasionally attacked the more difficult problems of the psychoses, has also been able to show identification as present in some other cases which are not immediately comprehensible. I shall treat two of these cases in detail as material for our further considerations.

"The genesis of male homosexuality in a large class of cases is as follows: A young man has been unusually long and intensely fixated upon his mother in the sense of the Œdipus complex. But at last, after the end of his puberty, the time comes for exchanging his mother for some other sexual object. Things take a sudden turn: the young man does not abandon his mother: he transforms himself into her, and now looks about for objects which can replace his ego for him, and on which he can bestow such love and care as he has experienced from his mother. This is a frequent process, which can be confirmed as often as one likes, and which is naturally quite independent of any hypothesis which may be made as to the organic driving force and motives of the sudden transformation. A striking thing about this identification is its ample scale; it remoulds the ego in one of its important features—in its sexual character—upon the model of what has hitherto been the object. In this process the object itself is renounced—whether entirely or in the sense of being preserved only in the unconscious is a question outside the present discussion. Identification with an object that is renounced or lost as a substitute for it, introjection of this object into the ego, is indeed no novelty to us. A process

Although these processes of infection are not merely involuntary but operate ''unconsciously,'' (however conspicuous they may be), in the sense that we ''get into'' these states without realizing that this is how it comes about, the process itself can again become an instrument of conscious volition. This occurs, for instance, in the search for ''distraction,'' when we go into gay company, or attend a party, not because we are in festive mood, but simply in order to find distraction; here we anticipate that we shall be infected and ''caught up'' in the prevailing gaiety. When someone says that he wants ''to see cheerful faces around him,'' it is perfectly clear that he does not mean to rejoice with them, but is simply hoping for infection as a means to his *own* pleasure. Conversely, an awareness of possible infection can also create a peculiar *dread* of it, as is found wherever a person shuns melancholy places or avoids the *appearance* of suffering (not the suffering itself) by trying to banish this image from the field of his experience.

That this form of emotional infection also has nothing whatever to do with genuine fellow-feeling should be too obvious for any need of emphasis. And yet the aberration of some most weighty authors make this emphasis necessary. Thus, virtually the whole extent of Herbert Spencer's treat-

ment of the emergence of fellow-feeling (and Darwin's also, to some extent) is no more than a persistent *confusion* of fellow-feeling with emotional infection. This confusion is dominant, especially in the ever-recurring error of these writers, whereby they seek to derive fellow-feeling from the herd-consciousness and herd-behavior of the higher animals. An entire trend of thought having thus gone astray, it is no wonder that, in presupposing this false conception of fellow-feeling, Friedrich Nietzsche, for his part, should have arrived at a completely *misguided evaluation* of fellow-feeling, and especially of pity. I select one passage—among many—from his outbursts against pity: ''Through pity, suffering itself becomes infectious, in certain circumstances it may lead to a total loss of life and vital energy which is absurdly out of proportion to the magnitude of the cause (—the case of the death of the Nazarene). This depressing and infectious instinct thwarts those instincts which aim at the preservation and enhancement of the value of life, by *multiplying* misery quite as much as by preserving all that is miserable, it is the principal agent in promoting decadence'' (*Anti-Christ*, pp. 131 and 134).[12] It is obvious that here, as in all similar passages, pity is confused with emotional infection. Suffering itself does *not* become infectious through pity. Indeed, it is just where suffering is infectious that pity is completely excluded, for to that extent I no longer view it as the *other's* suffering, but as my *own*, which I try to get rid of, by putting the notion of suffering out of mind. Indeed it is just where infection *does* occur via suffering, that pity for the other person's suffering, as being *his*, can stay the infection itself, just as the emotional reliving of an earlier painful experience, which still weighs heavy upon the present, can take this weight off one's mind.[13] Pity would be a ''multiplier of

---

of the kind may sometimes be directly observed in small children. A short time ago an observation of this sort was published in the *Internationale Zeitschrift für Psychoanalyse*. A child who was unhappy over the loss of a kitten declared straight out that now he himself was the kitten, and accordingly crawled about on all fours, would not eat at table, etc. (Marcuszewicz: ''Beitrag zum autistischen Denken bei Kindern,'' *Internationale Zeitschrift für Psychoanalyse*, 1920, Bd. VI).

''Another such instance of introjection of the object has been provided by the analysis of melancholia, an affection which counts among the most noteworthy of its exciting causes the real or emotional loss of a loved object. A leading characteristic of these cases is a cruel self-depreciation of the ego combined with relentless self-criticism and bitter self-reproaches. Analyses have shown that the disparagement and these reproaches apply at bottom to the object and represent the ego's revenge upon it. The shadow of the object has fallen upon the ego, as I have said elsewhere. The introjection of the object is here unmistakably clear,'' p. 66 (tr. by James Strachey, International Psycho-analytical Library, No. 6, 1922).

[12][Translated by A. M. Ludovici, London, T. N. Foulis, 1911].

[13]It is not the mere reconstruction of repressed memories, nor yet the abreaction from them, but this *reliving* of them, that underlies whatever therapeutic efficacy psycho-analysis may possess.

misery'' only if it were identical with emotional infection. For only the latter—as we have seen—can produce in others a real suffering, a state of feeling akin to the infectious one. But such real suffering does not occur, however, in *true* fellow-feeling.

(4) EMOTIONAL IDENTIFICATION

The true *sense of emotional unity*, the act of identifying one's own self with that of another, is only a heightened form, a limiting case as it were, of infection. It represents a limit in that here it is not only the separate process of feeling to any other that is unconsciously taken as one's own, but his self (in all basic attitudes) that is identified with one's own self. Here too, the identification is as involuntary as it is unconscious. Lipps has wrongly sought to construe this as a case of aesthetic empathy. Thus, according to him, the absorbed spectator of an acrobat in a circus turn identifies himself with the performer, whose movements he reproduces within himself, in the character of an acrobat. Lipps believes that only the spectator's real self remains distinct here, his conscious self having sunk itself completely to that of the acrobat. Edith Stein has interposed a just criticism on this point.[14] ''I am not,'' she says, ''one with,'' the acrobat; I am only ''with'' him. The correlated motor-impulses and tendencies are carried out here by a fictional ''I,'' which remains recognizably distinct as a phenomenon from my individual self; it is simply that my attention is passively fixed throughout on the fictional ''I,'' and by way of this, on the acrobat.''

There are other cases, however, insufficiently recognized either by Theodor Lipps or Edith Stein, in which such identification is undoubtedly complete; which do not merely exemplify a moment of true ''ecstasy,'' but may be of long duration, and can even become habitual throughout whole phases of life. They are of two opposite kinds: the *idiopathic* and the *heteropathic*. Thus, identification can come about in *one* way through the total eclipse and absorption of another self by one's own, it being thus, as it were, completely dispossessed and deprived of all rights in its conscious existence and character. It can also come about the other way, where ''I'' (the formal subject) am so overwhelmed and hypnotically bound and fettered by the other ''I'' (the concrete individual) that my formal status as a subject is usurped by the other's personality, with all *its* characteristic aspects in such a case, I live, not in ''myself,'' but entirely in ''him''—the other person—(in and through him, as it were).

Such paradigm-cases of identification, either by way of an all-inclusive propensity to infect, or as a state of complete and total infection of the very roots of individuality, I find exemplifed in very different kinds of experience. . . .

[14]Op. cit.

THIRTEEN

LOVE

NELSON N. FOOTE

The title of this paper has provoked comments from friends and acquaintances ever since it was publicly announced. If those comments are classified according to the attitudes they express, they appear to fall into four rough categories: *cynical, joking, sentimental,* and *matter-of-fact*. Comments falling into the fourth category were least frequent, totaling three cases out of perhaps twenty. Of these three persons, two pointed out to me that love is not considered a proper subject for academic discourse: one claimed that the title would draw only a group of moralistic or sentimental listeners, lacking in scientific motive; the other claimed that the regular academics would be scornful unless I devised a more pompous and wordy title. The third merely made the cryptic remark that it takes courage to speak on this subject. This paper is aimed at drawing scientific attention to a matter-of-fact attitude toward love. Serious matter-of-factness toward love is a minority point of view even among professed social scientists. Indeed, one gains some introductory illuminations of the subject from recognizing that the first three categories of comments are far more representative of the common approach to love.

AMBIVALENCE

Cynicism, joking, and sentimentality alike bespeak a fundamental ambivalence toward love. Cynicism is the attitude of a person who is afraid that he will become the victim of illusions—illusions which he believes exist, entrap others, and are dangerous to himself. He hungers and thirsts for beliefs he can trust, but he never finds any that he can trust. Joking is the classical symptom by which the field ethnologist identifies status relationships that evoke conflicting emotions. And sentimentality is of course the lavish counterfeiting of genuine emotion that occurs when genuine emotion is deemed appropriate in a particular social situation but is not forthcoming spontaneously.

Freud believed that ambivalence was characteristic of all human love, and he also appeared to believe that the characteristic complement of love was hate. There is much truth to what he says, but at the present time some refinement and qualifications are required. In general, the appearance of ambivalence in love relationships is probably peculiar to our own highly competitive society and may not be characteristic of other times and places. To

SOURCE: Nelson N. Foote, "Love." Copyright by The William Alanson White Psychiatric Foundation, Inc., 1953. Nelson N. Foote, "Love," *Psychiatry,* XVI (1953), pp. 245–251. Reprinted by special permission of The William Alanson White Psychiatric Foundation, Inc., copyright owners.

suggest that it may happily be made to disappear in our own time is the only preachment I would proffer in this paper.

To understand how ambivalence toward love may diminish and disappear requires more precise analysis than is implied by the simple concept of ambivalence as the concurrence of love and hate. In a competitive society as Bacon long ago pointed out, "he that hath wife and children hath given hostages to fortune." One who entrusts himself fully to another may find his credulity and kindness exploited. His love may be rejected or betrayed. To expose oneself to another is to run the risk of getting hurt. It may take only foolhardiness, among specialists in human development, to talk about love, but it does take courage to love in a society like our own. Many dare not try; they fear involvement. In short, fear rather than hate appears to be the original rival of love in the ambivalent situation that one encounters daily.

To be sure, when the fear seems justified by some act of the other, then the sense of betrayal is keen, and hostility is at once engendered. Several years ago I formed a habit of collecting clippings about domestic crimes in which wives, husbands, and children burned, poisoned, shot, and butchered each other. These clippings mounted so fast that I soon had a manila folder full of them. I was very glad to terminate the habit by donating the whole batch to Robert Hess of the Committee on Human Development, who has been doing a study of aggression in families for the United States Public Health Service. Aggression against the other is always potential in love relationships, but it forms a secondary and conditional phase, the fear of being hurt oneself is primary and continuous. Yet, to the extent that one is withheld from entering into love relationships by fear of being hurt, he is deprived of love and may crave it all the more.

This unrequited craving for love, in a society which demands the seal of love upon most interpersonal relations, leads not only to the characteristic expressions of cynicism, joking, and sentimen-

tality, but also to a kind of self-renewing vicious circle. The signs of love are demanded, disbelieved, and demanded again. The oftener they are required, the oftener they are simulated; the more often they are distrusted, the more often further reassurance is demanded—until it is a wonder that any sound currency for conducting valid exchanges remains in use at all. The inflation of amatory declaration in the country has regularly puzzled foreign visitors. Fortunately, some Americans do develop a keen and insistent ear for the real article, whereby they can detect it beneath the babble of spurious affirmations. The honored heroes of our best fiction are those who can with relentless accuracy distinguish true from false in this shadowy realm; they are sparing in terms of endearment to the point of taciturnity.

COMPETENCE

A matter-of-fact approach to the study of love requires a redefinition and even some reconceptualization of its nature. Some would doubt that anything new could be said on a subject that has been popular for so many thousands of years. Can contemporary social scientists, for instance, improve upon the old Greek distinction between *eros* and *agape,* the sexual and nonsexual types of love? Did Freud really add something to modern knowledge and insight by his many assertions that *eros* really underlies the expressions of *agape?* In attempting to answer these challenges, it may be helpful strategy to pick out the most basic innovation of modern social science and proceed from that to an appropriately contemporary redefinition of love.

The most basic finding of recent social science is undoubtedly the novel proposition that human nature, conceived in terms of personality, is a cultural product, subject to a continuous process of re-creation and development. This concept is not to be found in the Greeks or the Scholastics or even, in its present form, in the philosophers of the Enlightenment, though these last certainly turned scientific attention to processes of history, change, and progress. As late as Darwin, the notion that personality is biologically given still had sway. The evolutionary model of thought, however, with its emphasis upon continuous creation, eventually became the basis for overthrowing so-called Social Darwinism (approximately in the 1930's in this country if we count in terms of majority sentiment). Even so, we still have with us those who fear that national intelligence is declining because the Ph.D.'s have so few children.

There is a growing number of scholars nowadays who conceive that not only personality in general but intelligence in particular are modifiable and develop differently in both kind and degree as social and cultural conditions are varied. In fact, it seems possible that purposive development of personality along optional lines may soon become an objective of public policy. The recent report of the Midcentury White House Conference on Children and Youth carries a title, *Personality in the Making*,[1] which almost any previous decade would have found revolutionary.

In a recent article entitled "The Role of Love in Human Development," Daniel Prescott attempted to arrive at a satisfactory definition of love in order to explore its implications for human development.[2] He reviewed critically the conceptions of love mentioned by the standard writers of the standard textbooks on child development, and also those set forth by such psychiatric thinkers as James Plant, Erich Fromm, and Harry Stack Sullivan.[3] The results of his library search are interesting, but it seems more illuminating to pursue his

quest in the opposite direction. That is, it may be better to define love in terms of human development, as follows: *Love is that relationship between one person and another which is most conducive to the optimal development of both*. This optimal development is to be measured practically in the growth of competence in interpersonal relations.

Sullivan's definition is a helpful beginning: "When the satisfaction or the security of another person becomes as significant to one as is one's own satisfaction or security, then the state of love exists."[4] But his approximation is static, unilateral, and still tinged with the Christian morality which honors sacrifices of oneself to another as an ultimate good, though it may thwart the development of both. Erich Fromm's notion of productive love, and his insistence upon the legitimacy of self-love, appear more analytically precise and valid: ". . . love is an activity and not a passion . . . the essence of love is to "labor" for something and 'to make something grow.' . . . To love a person productively implies to care and to feel responsible for his life, not only for his physical existence but for the growth and development of all his human powers . . . without *respect* for and *knowledge* of the beloved person, love deteriorates into domination and possessiveness."[5]

Fromm might well have gone further than he did to exclude other kinds of behavior as not coming within a definition of love which emphasizes mutual development—for example, dependency, conceit, and mere tribal identification with kindred. The director of a child care agency told me recently that her agency had come to recognize that the best mother for a child was not the one who regarded the child as an extension of the parent, but the one who could regard the child as *another person,* to be respected, responded to, and understood for his own sake.

If by definition we love most those to whose development we contribute most, whether wit-

[1]Helen Leland Witmer and Ruth Kotinsky (eds.), *Personality in the Making: The Fact-finding Report of the Midcentury White House Conference on Children and Youth;* New York, Harper, 1952.

[2]Daniel A. Prescott, "The Role of Love in Human Development," *J. Home Economics,* (1952) 44:173–176.

[3]James Plant, *The Envelope;* New York: Commonwealth Fund, 1950. Erich Fromm, *Man for Himself: An Inquiry into the Psychology of Ethics;* New York, Rinehart, 1947. Harry Stack Sullivan, *Conceptions of Modern Psychiatry;* Washington, D.C. William Alanson White Psychiatric Foundation, 1947.

[4]Sullivan, reference footnote 3: p. 20.

[5]Fromm, reference footnote 3: pp. 98–101.

tingly or unwittingly, such a definition has specific virtues over the popular conception of love as a fluctuating emotion which can only to a degree be stabilized by ritual or pretense. Rather, love is to be known by its works. The familiar emotions may be evoked intermittently by the works of love; there is nothing drab about the joys of receiving the actual evidence of love as against merely its verbal affirmation; but the more important point is that the growth of love can thus be charted as a developing process, progressive fruition of which is more to be desired than attainment and fixation of a particular state of emotional response. From this viewpoint, one values another not only for what he is at the moment but for his potentialities of development, and these are necessarily assessed longitudinally and not by comparison shopping. One commits himself to another not on the basis of romantic, forced illusions, but of real possibilities which can emerge with proper cultivation. Trust and appreciation accumulate through proven results as indexed in mutual personal development.

AUDIENCE

I want to turn now to the question of the precise delineation of the relationship of lover to loved one—parent and child, husband and wife, friend and friend—which is most conducive to the optimal development of each. A beginning toward the precise characterization of the ideal form of this relationship can be made by likening it to the relationship of artist and audience. There are of course all kinds of artists and all kinds of audiences. But almost every artist is acutely conscious of the bearing of his audience upon his performance and development as an artist. To attain an audience that is critical but appreciative, objective but hopeful, and neither patronizing nor condemnatory nor sentimentally adulatory, is the ideal his experience leads him toward. This ideal audience expects from him a performance as good or better than he has given before; it expects him to work hard for it. But it is identified with the artist, and

sympathetic in an informed, understanding way. Thus it never unrealistically demands that he exceed his powers, achieve a result he never aimed for, or be something he is not. Best of all is the audience that clearly differentiates between the artist and the work of art, judging the latter as a finished product but the former as a never-fully-disclosed realm of potential productivity. Such an audience is only disappointed when its favored artist does less than his best.

Everyone knows the prodigies of creativity which are occasionally unleashed when a person discovers and is discovered by the perfect critic. Many a person can look back upon an incident in his school career when a sensitive teacher recognized at the critical moment an emerging talent and thereby permanently exalted his conception of himself and his capabilities. These are the moments of love in its sublime power to move. Such incidents are the imputed reference when a husband speaks of his wife as his ''best friend and critic,'' although the phrase has become shopworn through sentimental usage. To be critical is thus to be neither hypercritical nor hypocritical. To achieve the delicate adjustment which is required means that criticism itself must become almost an art. Many a great artist has been intimately associated with a great critic.

The ideal audience, however, is often found among those with whom the artist tends to compare himself in measuring his own worth, as in the case of his fellow students. For it is never quite as positive a stimulus for the artist to have his creative productions praised by a teacher or master, as it is for him to have them praised by those who are themselves his potential emulators and who know intimately what these creative productions cost the artist.

Thus, the relationship most conducive to development may be further described as one of social equality and of reciprocity. It cannot be a relationship of superiority and subordination. Nor can it even be the relationship of counselor and client, contrary to some present-day currents of thought, for even the most non-directive counselor-client relationship is unequal and unilateral. It is worth while to glance still more closely at what social equality and reciprocity means between two persons.

Somewhere Durkheim contends that equality is indispensable if genuine discussion is to occur between persons; Simmel has made the same point with reference to the occurrence of sociability.[6] Discussion and sociability are two of the activities indispensable to carrying on the dialectic of creation and criticism from which comes personal development. By equality, however, is not meant sameness; quite the contrary. Let us take parents and children as the most obvious case where the persons involved are never—unless perhaps in the case of twins—of the same age or powers. The practice of equality may be exhibited by sharing alike in certain valued experiences and by such devices as taking turns—things that are familiar to everyone who ever had brothers or sisters. But obviously it would be ruinous for parents to insist that each child reach the same standard of performance. Rather, each is expected by a loving parent to move toward a standard which is reasonable for a person of his capacities. Moreover, the most important expression of the kind of equality I am defining lies in the conception of each child as *ultimately incommensurable with any other*. He may be compared quantitatively to another child in this or that respect, but as a whole person he is unique. Also, as a whole person he is such a pregnant complex, such a rich array of potentialities, that the loving parent can always find some respects in which each child does excel. By developing these special talents or virtues, each child can outshine the others on his own grounds; the competition which is so threatening and destructive when all are judged by a single standard loses its force when each child is judged by his own.

The parent does not have to determine arbitrarily the line of development for which each child is best disposed; he has only to observe attentively the outcome of the child's own search for the notion of his particular talents which is most satisfying and promising, and then to ratify, as only a sympathetic audience can, the correctness of the discovery made. To do otherwise is to be as disruptive of orderly and optimal development as is the patron who tells the artist what he is to create. Wholeness and individuality, integrity and autonomy, are inseparable.

Reciprocity is perhaps a peculiar kind of equality, but so peculiar that it needs careful analysis. Malinowski[7] has analyzed its ubiquitous function in regulating primitive social organization. Someone of equal genius, I hope, will someday set forth in full the way it works throughout interpersonal relations. In the many books and articles on child development, reciprocity rarely gets the attention due it in terms of the scope of its influence. The child who is denied the opportunity to reciprocate according to his powers the favors conferred upon him by his parents is thwarted in the growth of those powers. Many people have no doubt witnessed the crushing effect upon a child of having a parent ignore or disparage a gift which the child has made and tendered him. Conversely, when a child has labored unstintingly to produce some offering and the parent accepts it with honest gratitude and praise, the delight of the child is sometimes almost physically convulsive.

I cannot resist mentioning the first party which my seven-year-old daughter threw for her parents. It consisted only of two pieces of pastry taken secretly from the refrigerator, a small table cloth and napkins spread carefully on her own little table, two cups of milk, and of course two chairs. It was entirely her own idea, and from a realistic point of view it was rather inappropriate, since we had only finished dinner half an hour before. She

---

[6]Kurt H. Wolff (ed.), *The Sociology of Georg Simmel;* Glencoe, Ill., Free Press, 1950; pp. 47–49.

[7]Bronislaw Malinowski, *Argonauts of the Western Pacific,* New York, Dutton, 1950.

did not sit down with us after inviting our presence, but stood there giggling and squirming in ecstasy as we thanked her and praised her cooking. She has already learned the role of hostess and fancies grander successes in the future.

To deny a person opportunities for reciprocating is to forestall his respect for himself, to keep him dependent and inferior. This is one point where resentment of do-gooders arises. A person may garner flattery by surrounding himself with dependents, but flattery can hardly match the satisfaction of contributing to the growth of others by stimulating their achievement of autonomy and equality. In fact, the person who insists upon the expression of affection from dependents whom he cannot let go may not be autonomous himself—as in the case of overprotective parents. On the other hand, the encouragement of reciprocation by those of lesser powers is about as strong a medicine for stimulating their growth as is likely to be found. In competition, as studies on recreation show, stimulation is maximal when rivals are equally matched. Equality and reciprocity are not static concepts; it is hierarchy and unilateralism which are static and which hinder development.

SELF-TRANSCENDENCE

Any present-day scholar would be loath to say that the impulse to explore and develop individuality is natural, in the sense of being an inborn imperative. On the other hand, it is certainly an almost universal discovery that development of one's powers is the primary value of life, since these powers are the instruments which provide access to all other values. If a person is permitted freedom to play and is stimulated by a loving audience, he moves on not merely from one requisite developmental task to another, but toward self-chosen goals which are not requisite but are autonomously affirmed.

No one has quite as well described as has James Mark Baldwin[8]—the father of genetic psy-

chology—the dialectic of personal growth in all its intricacy and cumulative onwardness, whether vicious or benevolent in trend. It is very significant that Baldwin encouraged his wife to translate the two classical treatises on the psychology of play by Karl Groos,[9] for these works stress the importance of play as a kind of practice for the tasks of reality. Some students of human development have lately taken up where Groos left off, and in a few years may go far beyond him. It is nonetheless regrettable for progress in the discipline of human development that there was a fifty-year lapse in serious scientific analysis of the consequences of play.

Art, however, is not play, any more than it is work. It is an activity of intense seriousness and concentration, although it excites joy of a kind and degree which is neither an illusion nor a joking matter nor a hypocrisy. Perhaps art could be called the serious form of play. Both work and play at their best become art. In the best art, the artist performs at the limit of his capacities. By performing at the limit of his capacities, he continually transcends the limits of those capacities. That is, he goes beyond the point he had previously reached in the development of his capacities.

It is at this point that it may be appropriate to mention that at the Family Study Center we are engaged in working out a theory of human development based upon a concept of self-transcendence. I might stick my neck out further and add that this theory in its embryonic form is one of self-transcendence through love. By self-transcendence we have in mind an entirely secular and matter-of-fact approach.

To review briefly some ideas which are by now commonplace: Human beings, as human beings, are among other features distinguished by the acquisition of selves through experience. The self, however, is a symbolic construct postulated for certain kinds of behavior not otherwise explain-

---

[8]James Mark Baldwin, *Social and Ethical Interpretations in Mental Development;* New York, Macmillan, 1809.

[9]Karl Groos: *The Play of Animals;* New York, D. Appleton & Co., 1911. *The Play of Man;* New York, D. Appleton & Co., 1912.

able. This self develops in terms of abilities to perform various kinds of behavior. There are a number of definable abilities, growth in which may properly be taken as the measures of human development. The process by which these abilities increase always occurs and is exhibited within a matrix of interpersonal relations.

The Family Study Center is engaged in a series of studies in the measurement and experimental development of a number of these abilities, which we designate jointly as interpersonal competence. The three we are doing research upon are empathy, autonomy, and creativity, but there are others. In order to generate desired movement in these respects, our staff has been devising a number of very specific hypotheses as to the reproducible conditions under which measurable change in the optimal direction regularly occurs. Once these conditions for the growth of interpersonal competence can be validly stated, we shall have the full description of what I have been speaking of as the relationship of love. Love so defined *is* enough.[10]

This conception of love as [those] interpersonal conditions optimal for self-transcendence is a hard doctrine from which many will shrink, because it puts the claim of love to the test of the results produced. It should have a cauterizing effect upon the sentimentality and falsehood by which a parent can protest that he loves a child while frustrating his development. Likewise it implies a conception of marriage, in which the success of the marriage is judged by the degree to which each partner contributes reciprocally to the continuous development of the other.

The dialectical transactions between artist and audience to which we have referred need not be limited to two persons, though it is convenient to analyze them in this manner. At one time, a child may be considered as a work of art produced by the mother, with the father as audience; at another, by the father, with the mother as audience; and at a third, as himself an aspiring artist engaged in producing some piece of work, with both parents as his audience. Most importantly, as the child increases in interpersonal competence, he becomes a successful artist in evoking desired behavior from his parents—ideally, their delight rather than their dismay.

Professor Frank H. Knight at the University of Chicago has written profoundly about the matter of love. I would particularly recommend his long essay on "Ethics and Economic Reform."[11] He has been heard to declare that if Western civilization succeeds in developing a workable society on a secular basis, it will be for the first time in history. I believe that the effort to advance human development through a matter-of-fact investigation of the relationships most conducive to self-transcendence is a reasonable and even promising experiment. And I would go further to predict that the proven attainment of desired results in this direction will be a more substantial and enduring source of joy than all the pretended ecstasies of those who still put their hope in nonrational wish-fulfillment.

It now seems in order to take another look at Freud's statement that erotic motivation underlies all other expressions of human ties. If one speaks of humans as selves, it is at least equally as plausible that *eros* is the symbol and *agape* the substance. In an age in which the substance is lacking, people in their loneliness grasp feverishly but vainly for the symbol. If by the progressive restoration of trust through proving the consequence of love in action, we are able to diminish the fear of each other which makes our love so ambivalent, then *eros* as the symbol of love becomes no longer counterfeit, and no longer properly regarded with cynicism, joking, or sentimentality.

[10]Cf. Bruno Bettelheim, *Love Is Not Enough: The Treatment of Emotionally Disturbed Children;* Glencoe, Ill., Free Press, 1950.

[11]Frank H. Knight, *Freedom and Reform: Essays in Economics and Social Philosophy;* New York, Harper, 1947, pp. 45–128.

FOURTEEN

SARCASM AS SOCIATION: THE RHETORIC OF INTERACTION

DONALD W. BALL

Like conflict, authority, and many other sociological concepts, sarcasm may profitably be viewed, in Simmel's famous phrase, as a societal form irrespective of content.[1] To use Simmel's terminology again, sarcasm is a sociation,[2] a kind of interaction appearing in the diverse natural settings and situations of face-to-face social behaviour. Social scientists studying interaction have, in general, focused upon rather more abstracted analytical dimensions such as cohesion, differentiation, dominance and subordination, complementarity, and so on. Valuable as their studies are, they ignore the common-sense constructs prevalent in the everyday life of the mundane world where people meet, talk, visit, chat, argue, and so forth.

To the extent that participants implicitly or explicitly analyse the qualities of such sociations, it is not in terms dear to experiment-oriented students of small group interaction, but rather at a different (and not necessarily internally consistent) level: the level of typifications of the everyday world.[3] These common-sense constructs embrace terms of description and evaluation such as strained, friendly, brusque, humorous, pleasant, dull, or sarcastic; assessments of the interaction, or the actors, or both. They constitute what might be called the *rhetoric of interaction,* standing well below the level of abstraction characteristic of the usual dimensions of behavioral analysis.

It is a rhetoric of common-sense constructs, sarcasm and its derivatives among them, which helps to provide vocabularies of motives and

SOURCE: Donald W. Ball. "Sarcasm as Sociation: The Rhetoric of Interaction." Copyright by Canadian Sociology and Anthroplogy Association, 1965. Donald W. Ball, "Sarcasm as Sociation: The Rhetoric of Interaction," *Canadian Review of Sociology and Anthropology,* II (November, 1965), pp. 190–198. Reprinted by permission of the Canadian Sociology and Anthropology Association.

[1]*The Sociology of Georg Simmel,* trans. K. Wolff (Glencoe, 1950), 21–23, 40–43.

[2]*Ibid,* 43–57; also Georg Simmel, "The Sociology of Sociability," trans. E. Hughes, *American Journal of Sociology,* LV, November, 1949, 254–261.

[3]A. Schutz, "Common Sense and Scientific Interpretation of Human Action," *Collected Papers* (The Hague, 1962), I, 3–47; C. Shepherd, *Small Groups* (San Francisco, 1964), 9–14. One exception among social scientists has been Tom Burns. See for instance his consideration of banter and irony in "Friends, Enemies, and the Polite Fiction," *American Sociological Review,* XVIII, December, 1953, 654–63. Like the work of Burns, the following will attempt to view the rhetoric of interaction in other than what are considered socio-linguistic terms.

evaluations for actors involved in the dramas of everyday interaction in natural settings. Of course, this rhetoric may itself be described in more conventional social scientific terms, and should be subjected to such analysis. Such an effort involves creating, in Schutz's terms, typifications of typification, that is, second-order constructs based upon the common-sense categories of everyday experience.[4]

Almost intuitively it can be asserted that, though the rhetoric of interaction is highly evocative, it may be subject to serious methodological problems, especiallly in regard to operationalization. This difficulty will be discussed below; it is argued, however, that the constructs and terminology of the rhetoric of interaction, including sarcasm, are worthy of social scientific consideration.

As a preliminary to such an examination, it may be useful to consider some forms and functions of sarcasm and a few of its possible structural correlates. Such a consideration may shed light upon such questions as: What are typical forms of sarcasm as sociation? What elements or roles or both are involved? What social functions are performed by sarcasm? For or upon whom are these functions performed, or, in other words, where in the social structure is the phenomenon most probable and prevalent? These questions and the following discussion are not meant to be exhaustive. Rather it should be emphasized that the discussion is suggestive and exploratory and highly tentative in speaking to, and about, some of the problems relating to sociological analysis of sarcasm. Perhaps it should also be noted that illustrative examples are deliberately avoided. This is because of the character of sarcasm, as sketched below, and equally important, because of the tendency towards cuteness inherent in such a subject. If the

present treatment seems somewhat ponderous, it is due at least in part to the latter consideration.

FORM

By form is meant a "grammar,"[5] concerned with the generalized social elements of sarcasm, not specific instances of its occurrence, focusing on abstractions rather than particulars.

Sarcasm is, of course, a common everyday linguistic form of biting communication, especially, it would seem, an oral one, with its locus in intimate settings. This follows from the relatively "flat" character of the written as compared to the more readily dramatized spoken word.[6] Most generally, it is probably true that sarcasm requires not only a set of appropriate words, sharply and uniquely relevant to the particular situation, but also a presentation context which allows the use of such other arts of communication as inflection and intonation, gesture, timing, and facial and postural expression.[7]

Ordinarily, it is not enough that the proper potentially sarcastic words and phrases be presented; they must also be accompanied by ancillary elements of communication which summon up a sarcastic totality, that is, by the over- and under-emphasis of key symbols involving not only words, but also tone and expression. In many cases whether or not a given phrase is sarcastic is entirely a function of these other elements; words of commendation may be so presented as to become what is typically considered sarcasm. The meaning of the words "nice job," for instance, remains obscure without additional information; it may be

---

[4]See Schutz, "Common Sense and Scientific Interpretation of Human Action." Although the following is informed by Schutz's methodological perspective, it should not be construed as an attempt systematically to emulate it. Rather, its exploratory nature leads to a method utilizing observation, deduction, and, at times, hopefully well-grounded speculation.

[5]Compare K. Burke, *A Grammar of Motives* (Cleveland, 1962), xviii.

[6]See E. Goffman, *The Presentation of Self in Everyday Life* (Garden City, 1959). Carol Virak has pointed out that sarcasm may occur entirely without words, e.g., in offering a handkerchief as a "crying towel."

[7]*Ibid.* It is this characteristic of sarcasm that allows it to be, in Goffman's words, strategically disattended, i.e., its form may be ignored. For similar reasons, it can also easily be denied by the originator.

high praise or low criticism, depending upon other contextual communicative techniques as they are defined by the interactants' culture. It is in small natural groups with their enlarged private vocabularies, transcending the strictly verbal, that such consensually held definitions, and thus sarcasm, are likely to be highest.

As a form involving a network of roles, sarcasm is analytically at least a triadic relationship, although empirically fewer units may be involved. Minimally, a creator of sarcasm, a *sarcaster,* is necessary, along with an *object* and an *audience* to receive the sarcastic communication. The object is frequently combined with or resides in one of the other two units, so that empirically sarcasm can often be considered as either a self-directed or an other-directed dyad.[8] In self-direction the sarcaster communicates about himself as object to his audience. From a strictly sociological perspective, however, it is the case where audience and object are one and the same which is perhaps most frequently of interest. As an other-directed form, sarcasm is a mechanism frequently used in the application of the informal social controls necessary to give shape and order to interaction in the small groups and encounters of everday social intercourse.[9]

So far no formal definition of sarcasm has been suggested; this has been deliberate. Though sarcasm is often humorous, humour is not a necessary condition and, like humour,[10] sarcasm is difficult, if not impossible, to define precisely and opera-

tionally from an external-observational perspective. Etymologically, sarcasm is derived from the Greek *sarkazein,* to speak bitterly[11]—literally, to tear flesh. This is suggestive of the flavour, but only suggestive. To some literary scholars (to whom social scientists, by default, have left such study) sarcasm is a form of verbal irony,[12] but this definition also is imprecise. Like irony, sarcasm conveys more than its obvious overt meaning. But sarcasm seems, much more than simple irony, to imply a social-purposive, functional use of communication. Where irony has to do with content, the thrust of sarcasm is in terms of social function, that is, the meaning of the early Greek stem refers not so much to what is said as to its consequences. Obviously, this is not to deny the ironic content of much that is deemed sarcastic, nor the sarcastic form of much that is deemed ironic.

None of this seems to lend itself to the operationalization typical of contemporary methodology: a series of words to identify sarcasm having their referents in still other words and intuitions, *ad infinitum.*[13] This is not, however, an insoluble problem for, as may be inferred from the above, that which is crucial to sarcasm is its phenomenology, its existence and apprehension in direct, naïve experience. What is important is that a given message is defined as sarcastic by one or more of the parties involved, the sarcaster, his object, and his audience. The perception and definition of sarcasm as such by at least one of these three are the momentous elements.[14] Sarcasm *per se* is not inherent in a combination of communicative elements, but is relative, existing only

---

[8]Even talking to one's self is dyadic in so far as the actor is playing the two roles of communicator and audience simultaneously. An anonymous reader has suggested that self-directed sarcasm is actually sardonicism.

[9]See E. Goffman, *Behavior in Public Places* (New York, 1963). Note that while the roles of sarcaster and audience are conceived of as social, such a conception vis-à-vis the object is problematic, since this unit may or may not be human, e.g., possibly an element of the physical-spatial-temporal environment. Such an object may have social meaning, but lacks the dynamic *human* interaction potential.

[10]J. Flügel, "Humor and Laughter," in G. Lindzey, ed., *Handbook of Social Psychology* (Reading, 1964), II, 709; M. Eastman, *Enjoyment of Laughter* (New York, 1936).

[11]This root suggests the not always humorous vein in sarcasm.

[12]Thrall and A. Hibbard, *A Handbook to Literature,* (New York, 1960), 435. This is not to suggest sociological poaching, but an alternative and complementary focus.

[13]G. Homans, *The Human Group,* (New York and Burlingame, 1950), 24.

[14]To paraphrase the Thomas dictum: "If things are defined as real, their consequences are real." W. I. Thomas, as quoted in R. Merton, *Social Theory and Social Structure* (Glencoe, 1957), 421. Also Schutz, "Common Sense and the Scientific Interpretation of Human Action."

in the socially structured perceptions and definitions common to the interactants' culture. When such perception and definition take place, sarcasm is seen as rising out of and becoming a sociation—a kind of interaction—not a communication.

Here Simmel's conceptualization of societal forms as sociations independent of their more specific contents may be applied.[15] Regardless of content—the particular words, phrases, expressions, gestures, and emphases—sarcasm ultimately rests upon its apprehension as such by relevant parties. Any given content may or may not be defined as sarcastic depending upon various situational and personal variables. Unless the sarcaster, audience, object, or some combination thereof defines a message as sarcastic, the content is irrelevant. Which party (or parties) makes such a definition will have important functional implications.

Thus, it makes little theoretical sense to think of sarcasm as an always hostile, alienated form of communication. Sarcasm is as much a function of its reception as of its inception.[16] It is a truism of daily interaction that the intent of a given communication does not necessarily equal or even resemble its ultimate perception by the audience. To conceive of sarcasm only in terms of initiations is to over-simplify and even distort empirical reality, to ignore the emergent and reflexive nature of human conduct, especially as it is influenced in the interactions of everyday life.

SOCIAL FUNCTIONS

A major instrumental function of sarcasm, as noted above, is in terms of its utility for social control; what might be termed part of the politics of sarcasm. This is particularly true where the setting is a small, intimate, primary group. In such groups there are few if any legitimized formal sanctions readily available to encourage consistency of interactional behavior. At the same time, the problem exists, whether it is conscious and explicit among the members or not, of maintaining some minimal degree of social order, some base line of conformity to expectations.[17] Given the high degree of mutual awareness among members of such groups, the use of sarcasm becomes particularly appropriate as a mechanism of social control because of the lack of social distance between the members.

It is within intimate natural groups that the desire and regard for the social approval of other members is usually assumed by social scientists to be strongest.[18] To be the sarcaster's object before such an audience is to suffer loss of social approval, and thus be discouraged from future departures from behavioral expectations. Furthermore, in these small groups there is the probability that in the object's mind sarcasm will be imagined as but the first in a series of sanctions of increasing severity, ultimately leading to degradation, ostracism, and expulsion, should deviation persist. In this way the effectiveness of sarcasm, like that of

[15]Simmel, "The Sociology of Sociability." This is, of course, not to deny the possibility of institutionalization, leading to the automatic cognition of a given set of communicative elements as being a case of sarcasm; but again, such a response is based socially, not on inherent characteristics.

[16]Thomas, in Merton, *Social Theory and Social Structure*.

[17]On functional analysis, see Merton, *ibid,* esp. 19—84. On informal social control for much of the recent small group research on cohesion, conformity, etc., see e.g., D. Cartwright and A. Zander, *Group Dynamics,* (Evanston, 1960), 69—341; also M. Sherif, *The Psychology of Social Norms* (New York, 1936).

[18]R. LaPiere, *A Theory of Social Control* (New York, 1954). As a sanction, sarcasm has the functional virtue of having relatively low group disruption potential as compared with many other control techniques involving the manipulation of diminished or denied social approval, without the more unbalancing and sometimes long range effects of these other sanctions, e.g., physical restraint and coercion or violence. Thus the costs are relatively small. See A. R. Radcliffe-Brown on the joking relationship, *Structure and Function in Primitive Society* (Glencoe, 1952), ch. 4. It should also be apparent that to the extent that group stability is valued by its members sarcasm as control functions positively at the individual expressive level. This may even include deviant objects who share the stability value (regardless of whether or not this is to be defined a false-consciousness).

many other informal sanctions, lies in its imagined consequences.

Sarcasm as control is not empirically limited to closed forms of the small group; for example, the object may be external to the sarcaster's immediate audience, but at the same time a "potential" member, whose circumspect receipt of the communication is desired; such a relationship is overtly dyadic but covertly triadic. Other instances of control can be imagined which are overtly triadic and covertly dyadic, as when the object is wholly external to both the sarcaster and the audience. In this situation the control dimensions would come into play only if the object had a contextually meaningful symbolic relationship to the audience.

Conversely, sarcasm may also be utilized as a technique for impairing or destroying control and stability, by deflating or debasing the controller or in some other way encouraging a state of disequilibrium. Thus, sarcasm as control may be a two-edged sword, at the disposal of the controlled as well as the controllers. There the strategies of Potter's gamesmanship seem especially relevant.

Another element in the politics of sarcasm is its utilization in boundary-maintenance. In such cases sarcasm may function to include or exclude, or to do both simultaneously. Fowler's observation, made originally about irony, describes such cases when sarcasm "postulates a double audience" of initiatives and naives, a double circle of knowing "ins" and unaware "outs."[19] For the "ins" such communication serves not only to maintain the boundaries of group exclusiveness, but also promotes or reinforces solidarity in much the same way as a shared joke.

Yet another political function of sarcasm is as a sharpened and pointed form of communication, achieving emphasis through style rather than content, as in sarcastic understatement. Here sarcasm may serve as a functional surrogate for more literal communication such as direct attack upon the object. Thus the sarcaster may select his form as a deliberate political strategy, especially if alternative modes might lead to reprisals or excessive situational disruption. In such instances sarcasm is clearly instrumental. Paradoxically, sarcasm may be chosen as a vehicle of praise if it is desired to inhibit response or put the object at ease or both.[20]

Expressively, sarcasm may function as a means of tension management or release for the sarcaster and his audience, even while operating instrumentally as control or in emphatic communication. Tension control without an instrumental function is probably more frequent than the reverse, however, and is probably the most common function of sarcasm.[21] It should be noted that this function may appear at either the group or the individual level or simultaneously at both.

Finally, a way in which sarcasm may function both instrumentally and expressively at one and the same time may be noted, the explication of which may add to the understanding of a facet of classical sociological theory. In this case persons are subject to the social psychological condition conceptualized by Max Scheler as *ressentiment*.[22] In such situations persons who are the lower members of a status-discrepant relationship are hypothesized to experience feelings of hostility which, because of their positional disadvantage, they are unable to express openly. According to Scheler, their hostility will work itself out through the covert inversion and debasement of the superior's values, even

[19]H. Fowler, *A Dictionary of Modern English Usage* (London, 1927), 295—296.

[20]It should be remembered that not all sarcasm is verbal abuse; such a technique would seem especially likely where the sarcaster and the object are in a superordinate-subordinate relationship respectively, and the dissemination of praise is incongruent with the role definition of the former *vis-à-vis* the latter, and vice-versa. On superordinate-subordinate relationships, see *The Sociology of Georg Simmel*, 181—303. For hierarchical aspects of sarcasm, see structural correlates, below.

[21]This is probably the case even ignoring the biologically oriented tension-reduction theories of behavior.

[22]M. Scheler, *Ressentiment*, ed. L. Coser, trans. H. Holdheim (New York, 1961); D. Ball, "Covert Political Rebellion as *Ressentiment*," *Social Forces*, XLVIII, October, 1964, 93—101.

while they ostensibly confirm these same values. When such a condition is operative, sarcasm becomes particularly appropriate; it seems especially fitted for debasing and inverting the superior object's values, even if the sarcaster alone provides the audience. Such a utilization of sarcasm, if subtle enough in execution, may avoid actual detection if not suspicion by the object or other audience, and thus avoid possible retaliation. In such a situation, sarcasm is instrumental in venting hostility "safely" while the sarcaster at the same time enjoys the release.

Needless to say, the foregoing does not exhaust the functions of sarcasm or the analytic possibilities of sociological examination of it. More specifically, it ignores psychological aspects of sarcasm although they may obviously have social consequences. It does, however, suggest the relevance of some conventional theoretical axes as they relate to the investigation of sarcasm, such as instrumental-expressive and group-individual. The specification of others awaits systematic research and further theorization.

STRUCTURAL CORRELATES

Any discussion of structural correlates must, of course, be highly speculative. Still, given certain rather generally accepted propositions about social structure, some "educated guesses" may be hazarded.

For one thing, it is probable that in terms of class or status, that is, as regards external attributes achieved or ascribed outside the setting (which may of course carry over into the internal situation), sarcasm is a relatively high status phenomenon. This seems probable because of the sheer verbal ability necessary, such ability being to a great extent dependent upon education, in turn closely correlated with status.[23] Also, given the

tendency of people of higher status to express aggression verbally, it would seem logical that such persons would utilize sarcasm;[24] it is an effective weapon in intellectual attack, being at once more subtle, sophisticated, and pointed than the more direct expressions of aggression and hostility.[25]

For internal aspects of stratification, that is, the hierarchical differentiation of those involved, it is probable that sarcasm most frequently involves unequals: either subordinates engaging in a covert aggression which can be denied, or superordinates exercising social power and control in cases where less temperate communication is undesirable. Interestingly, both situations involve techniques whereby the sarcaster utilizes ambiguity to provide a potential strategic withdrawal. Relationally, such cases involve superordinates and subordinates within a division of labour; situationally, the upsmen and downs-men of Potter's manuals;[26] culturally, actors subject to invidious definition and differentiation and their more favorably evaluated colleagues.

Another place in the social structure where sarcasm would seem highly probable is within those groups where the costs of open internal conflict are likely to be excessive but where institutionalized procedures for containing conflict are lacking, as in the family, friendship groups,

[23]This hypothesis deliberately ignores "wit," the measurement of which may be even more culture-bound than intelligence, and thus, like education, related to education and social rank.

[24]A. Cohen, *Delinquent Boys* (Glencoe, 1955); Ball, "Covert Political Rebellion as *Ressentiment*," in D. G. McKinley (ed.), *Social Class and Family Life* (New York, 1964), 51—62.

[25]On this type of hostility and aggression, see E. Goffman, "On Face-Work: An Analysis of Ritual Element and Social Integration," excerpted in W. Bennis, E. Schein, D. Berlew, and F. Steele (eds.), *Interpersonal Dynamics* (Homewood, 1964), 226—249, esp. 240—241. For a more general analysis, derived from Simmel, see L. Coser, *The Function of Social Conflict* (New York, 1964).

[26]The situational inequality does not deny the possibility of a more generalized equality within the relationship, broadly conceived. It seems, in fact, quite probable in equalitarian friendship groups, where activities which temporarily put a participant at a disadvantage, i.e., momentarily declass him, serve to trigger the opportunity for sarcasm by others not so indicted. See S. Potter, *The Theory and Practice of Gamesmanship* and *One-Upmanship* (New York, 1948 and 1952).

gangs,[27] and so on. Whether deliberate or not, sarcasm in these groups would be politically strategic, reducing the possibilities of disruptive cleavage at least temporarily.

Yet another structural correlate, in another context mentioned above, would be those structural relationships characterized by inequality which generate *ressentiment*. Relationships like father and son, powerful or important parishioner and clergyman, daughter-in-law and mother-in-law, are all examples of the types of case referred to by Scheler where the latter partner is constrained against the overt expression of hostility towards the former because of that person's status definition and concommitant rights and power.

Again, the above are merely suggestions and in no way a complete listing of the possibilities. They do, however, suggest starting points for the empirical investigations of sarcasm in terms of locations in behavioral space as they may relate to social structures and processes.[28]

RESEARCH

Given a substantially phenomenological conception of sarcasm, it follows that research must take the common-sense constructs and perceptions of the mundane world as its point of departure. A vital first step, prior to the actual study of sarcasm in social settings, would be to map these common-sense constructs which provide the contextual background for sarcasm-oriented behavior. Here the survey analyst and his techniques of questionnaire and interview can be of much aid. Once preliminary mapping has been accomplished, investigations more directly relevant to the specific social and cultural context in which sarcasm occurs can begin.

Because of sarcasm's presupposition of shared meanings, the purposes of research in this area would seem to be served best by the use of natural, rather than experimentally created groups. Future research should, then, make a genuine effort to relate to theories, constructs, concepts, and research more directly to the natural contexts of interaction in the mundane world. Sarcasm is but one example of the forms of sociation which make up a rhetoric of interaction in everyday life. Existing approaches to the small group are useful, of course, but a broader view, even at the expense of methodological rigour, is desirable. The insidious influence of procedural or technological feasibility upon theory and problem selection is well known. Ultimately, the value of any research must be assessed in terms of its ability to aid in describing and making predictions about life outside its own limited setting.

In brief, then, investigation of sarcasm as a social phenomenon and development of a sociology of sarcasm must bear upon the interrelated structures of personality, group, and culture, examining forms and styles, norms and values,[29] and other factors governing probabilities and establishing qualities of the definition and location of sarcasm within the various social orders of the mundane world of everyday life.

[27]See F. Thrasher, *The Gang,* abridged (Chicago, 1963), 204−205; also Coser, *The Functions of Social Conflict.*

[28]One possibility is shown in Goffman's discussion of how role incumbents attempt to express their lack of total absorption in the role they are playing. See ''Role Distance,'' in *Encounters,* (Indianapolis, 1961).

[29]A pilot study touching upon this and several other areas is currently in progress by the author.

PART THREE

THE SELF

In the preceding section, careful attention was given to interaction processes, and, in their analysis, the centrality of self-indication was established. If self-indication is so central to interaction, meaning, understanding, and realization, we must ask: Just what is this "self" that is indicated and indicates?

There has been a long-standing argument between psychologists and sociologists about the conceptualization of the person. Most psychologists—not all—prefer the term "personality"; most sociologists—not all—prefer the term "self." Obviously, we take the latter position. There are several reasons for this decision.

The meaning of most words or concepts seems to fade[1] over time. As words come into widespread use, their precision ordinarily is blunted. So it is with the term "personality" (and as it may well be for "self" in some ill-defined future). Personality has come to mean all things to all men,[2] and a term that can mean many things at once can come to mean very little indeed.

Yet, it is not for purely semantic reasons that we find the term of relatively little use in our version of social psychology. Usually, in psychology, personality presumes an organized set of persistent and characteristic patterns of individual behavior. Thus situational variations in personal conduct are de-emphasized. We are not suggesting an either-or position here. As a matter of fact, at either extreme we are confronted with personal conduct that usually is labeled pathological.

Total Situational Invariance ⟷ Total Situational Variance
Advanced Psychosis ⟷ Extreme Psychopathy

Rather, we need a conception that can account at once for situational continuity *and* variability—a concept that is rooted in the transforming process of communication.

Furthermore, the concept "personality" often presupposes that behavior is consistent

---

[1]The notion of fading is taken from Suzanne K. Langer, *Philosophy in a New Key* (New York: Penguin Books, Inc., 1948), pp. 114 and 229. Her discussion applies to metaphors.

[2]More than forty years ago, Gordon W. Allport compiled an extensive list of the meanings of the term "personality" employed by psychologists. Even then there were enormous difficulties. See Gordon W. Allport, *Personality: A Psychological Interpretation* (New York: Holt, Rinehart and Winston, Inc., 1937).

and integrated with some presumed "value-attitude system," some "hierarchy of needs," or some differently designated internal system. Quite obviously there is no overriding consistency between what people *want* or *need* to do, and what they actually do. Activities often conflict with goals and needs. We may want very much to give up cigarettes and hold powerful negative attitudes against smoking, but we continue to smoke. Even such tested needs as metabolic requirements may be defied, both in human interaction and by our very biological responses. Thus, we may fast unto death, or decline a well-appointed meal of grasshoppers, ants, or rattlesnakes in the face of starvation (as starving Indian Hindus may decline beef). We are hungry when we do not need food, and "It is reported that after the first few days a person who is starving to death feels little or no hunger."[3] When we find ourselves short of needed oxygen, we enter into a kind of blissful, but ineffectual, dream state—a matter that concerned the United States Air Force in World War II and accounted for strange, apparently untraumatic blackouts by pilots at relatively high altitudes. Thus, inconsistency between wants, needs, and conduct is usual and cannot be adequately explained by invoking some such concept as personality.

The concept "personality" encourages us to look at the individual first and his social relations second in our interpretations of human conduct. Analytical use of this concept has often constrained investigators to look to social relations only when there is something wrong with personal conduct—some breach of expectations—and seldom when there is something right with personal conduct—a meeting of expectations. This mode of analysis is unacceptable to the social psychologist who views conduct from the standpoint of symbolic interaction. *All conduct must be situated in a matrix of communication before analysis and explanation begin.*

Finally, many social psychologists employing the concept "personality" view the *social object* as comprised of "layers" ranging from public to private dimensions, for example, conscious, preconscious, and subconscious or unconscious levels. Often the private or subconscious dimensions are viewed as the "real core" of personality. Now this has considerable rhetorical (and financial) value for the social psychologist, clinical psychologist, psychiatrist, or psychoanalyst. If one can never know who he really is, but the other professes to know, he comes readily under the other's control and becomes, through the process that Kenneth Burke called *secular conversion,*[4] what the other defines him to be—a transaction that often costs him dearly. Our position draws heavily upon that presented by Harry Stack Sullivan in this section. Perhaps there are private meanings that may be construed as personality or individuality, but, once they are communicated, their privacy and individuality are lost. Perhaps there is an unconscious or subconscious, but it is always *known* in another's consciousness! The concept "self" seems less open to the criticism we have made here, but that concept did not make its entry into the field of social psychology without difficulty and controversy.

Although conceptions of the self have been proposed and argued for centuries in the history of Western social thought it is adequate for our discussion to begin with the statement by William James. Contemporary formulations find their fundamental origins in

---

[3] Alfred R. Lindesmith and Anselm L. Strauss, *Social Psychology,* Third Edition (New York: Holt, Rinehart and Winston, 1968), p. 59.
[4] Kenneth Burke, *Permanence and Change* (Los Altos, California: Hermes Publication, 1954), ch. 5.

James' contribution. James immediately establishes the reflexive character of the self—it is apprehended as both Knower and Known, subject and object, "I" and "me." These distinctions are not to be thought of as things or components, but as *discriminated aspects*. Neither aspect can be subjected to fruitful analysis in disregard of the other, and this basic principle persists in the important conceptualizations of the self today. George H. Mead put the point succinctly: ". . . a 'me' . . . is a 'me' which was the 'I' at the earlier time."[5]

A student takes an examination. His answering is his "I." As Mead puts it, "The 'I' is the response of the organism to the attitudes [read "anticipations"—the student's answer is anticipated] of the others."[6] The examination is graded. The student then reflects upon his earlier response in the light of the faculty (or community) response. His conception of self, "me," is altered. Out of the interaction, he views himself as a bit more or less of a student than he was while taking the examination, or he knows a bit more surely that he is the student he thought he was at the time he took the examination. Thus, the "I" pushes into the "me," and the stage is set for further evolving transformations of the self.

But as James points out, *me* is very close to *mine:* "We feel and act about certain things that are ours very much as we feel and act about ourselves." He defines the self-conception, the self as object—the "me"—as ". . . *the sum total of all that he can call his.*" This encompasses a material "me" (which we have not included in this selection)—one's possessions, a social "me," essentially one's reputation, and a spiritual "me" (also deleted from the selection). Central to our discussion is James' version of the social "me," for in that discussion James' oft-quoted statement is made: "A man has as many selves as there are individuals who recognize him and carry an image of him in their minds." In short, the objective self finds its reality in communication—"[one] . . . has as many different social selves as there are distinct groups of persons about whose opinion he cares." Of course this multifaceted character of the self sets up conflicts. Whose opinions do we care about most, and in what situations? How are such decisions made? James singles out the significance of self-esteem and suggests that the maintenance of the *social* self is, in fact, a matter of the maintenance of self-esteem, a ratio between success and aspiration, or what he calls "pretension."

"Me's," then, are sources of the variability of the self as well as its multifaceted character. What, then, is the source of continuity? James turns to the self as Knower, Thinker, or "I." The "I" is the root of identity. Later, George H. Mead echoed the thought of James: The "I" is in a certain sense that with which we do identify ourselves."[7] One is asked, "Who is there?" The proper response is, "It is I." The "I" is formulator; the "me," formulated. Formulations change and proliferate, but the process is continuous and universal over the life cycle. There is, of course, a paradox here—a kind of Simmelesque antimony. The "I" is certainly uncertain, momentary, yet continuing, a source of evolving uncertainly certain objective "me's." We live, as Mead puts it, in a "knife-edge present," conjuring up potential future objective selves, some of which remain in the wake of our lives as the "me's" we were in past time.

Cooley, the profound observer if not the trenchant theorist, was obviously impatient

[5]George Herbert Mead, *Mind, Self, and Society* (Chicago: University of Chicago Press, 1934), p. 174.
[6]*Ibid*, p. 175.
[7]*Ibid.*, pp. 174–175.

with this kind of abstract discussion and attempted to bring the concept of self down to the level of everyday discourse. Observing—but really not incorporating the observation into his explanations—that the ''I'' always must consider others in any adequate conceptualization, Cooley actually built on one of James' definitions of the self. Cooley added the dimension of feeling, mood, or sentiment. Such a self-feeling may be taken as a definitive ''sign and proof'' of the self: ''The social self is simply any idea, or system of ideas, drawn from the communicative life, that the mind *cherishes* as its own.'' The cherishing of ideas is rooted in some sense of appropriation that Cooley thought of as instinctive. Hence, the deficiency as a theorist. The explanation becomes tautological, even though the ''sense of appropriation'' must be developed, refined, and differentiated through communication. One might also query whether such emphasis would be given the appropriative instinct in another world, at a time other than the turn of the century in the United States—a time just beyond the apex of development of industrial capitalism. Nevertheless, the notion of the self as ''mine'' can generate as fruitful a technique of self-study as the notion of self as object. Kuhn's TST, asking ''Who am I?'', might well ask, ''What is mine?''—at least in the context of those societies that place property in the center of their institutional arrangements.

But for Cooley the self is not merely what one appropriates as his own—cherished ideas. It is composed of imagined reflections. It is an outcome of our own imaginations as to how we appear to others, of their judgments of that imagined appearance, and some resultant self-feeling of pride or mortification. James' conception of self-esteem is retained but is charged with the voltage of affect. Mortification is somehow something other than disesteem. Again the observer, Cooley arrives at this conception of self by carefully noting the development of his children. His explanations seem less than adequate. For example, ''The self-feeling had always been there''; the child ''studies'' the movements of others; etc. What in fact must be explained, is presumed, and Cooley's solipsism is laid bare.[8]

Unlike Cooley, George H. Mead was convinced that such human processes as reason and self were phenomena to be explained rather than presumed. There are many discussions of the self by Mead that we might have presented here, but probably because the methodological remonstrance of Cooley—that we attend to what we can observe—still rings in our ears, we have chosen Mead's treatment of the self as object. Such a self can only emerge in the process of communication, for it is only in communication that one can, figuratively, get outside himself, take the attitude of another or organized others, and gain a reflected view of the self as object from these other standpoints. In particular, reason, thought, and intelligence are merely inner forms of this larger social process, but they are not realizable until the self has first emerged out of significant communication with others. As Mead says, ''it is impossible to think of the self arising outside of social experience.'' Once the self is established, however, one can endure long periods of isolation, because one ''has himself as a companion, and is able to think and converse

---

[8]See George H. Mead, ''Cooley's contribution to American Social Thought,'' *American Journal of Sociology,* XXXV (March, 1930), pp. 693–706; and Harvey A. Farberman, ''Mannheim, Cooley, and Mead: Toward a Social Theory of Mentality,'' *Sociological Quarterly* (Winter, 1970), 3–13.

with himself as he had communicated with others.'' Yet, such a process can continue up to some as yet unspecified point in time. Eventually, one must find validation for his inner conversations in direct conversations with others, else one moves perilously near the point of madness or, as Mead so accurately calls it, dissociation. Perhaps this is one important reason why so many successful film actors seek employment in legitimate theater, accepting severe financial penalties—ultimately, they must confront a living audience.

Sullivan begins his analysis of the emergence of the self at a somewhat different point. While Mead begins with gestural conversation, Sullivan begins with babbling and, unlike others—for example, Suzanne K. Langer,[9] who would see in babbling the beginning of symbolization as the expression of a need—he promptly recognizes that the significance of babbling is established by socialized others' responses or intervention. The arousal of significant others' responses by accidental infantile noise may be the origin of a sense of power, consolidated and extended in early socialization as the verbalized ''me'' is succeeded by the verbalized ''I'' in statements of personal action—as self-indication makes possible the formulation of self-initiated acts.

Paradoxically, this very incipience of personal power renders irrelevant the sense of uniqueness or autistic experience. The establishment of a noise as a symbol through *consensual validation* carries one's direct experience into the realm of the understood or the conventional, at least insofar as he can represent that experience to himself or others. In entering an ongoing conversation one's uniqueness is lost, but an entire world or universe is won. Sullivan construes this world as the proper unit of inquiry for psychiatry, the study of interpersonal relations.

But conversation is built on the empathic process. Sullivan singles out empathy as a possible source of disagreeable experience, just as those most often concerned with pathology single out negative aberrant influences on conduct. The empathic processes, notably role-taking and sympathy, of course have their positive consequences for the formulation of the self, as Cooley and Mead so frequently emphasized. Be these things as they may, Sullivan guesses that empathy may be an early source of anxiety for the child, and anxiety is viewed as a powerful ''motivating'' force accounting for the diversities and variations in the formulation of self. Sullivan says elsewhere that the self is comprised of the reflected appraisals of others, but is also viewed as a formulated way of coping with those appraisals, particularly negative ones, in the very early years. Such negative appraisals are *selectively inattended* and are dissociated from the self (as ''not-me''), remaining perhaps as a source of ''autonomous'' anxiety at a later age. At any rate, even such aberrations cannot be construed as individual in character. Their very selectivity, involving both inattention and attention, are formulations. The self is such a formulation, and, since the formulation is accomplished in symbolic or universal terms, the uniqueness of such experiences is not communicable, consequently not capable of study. In this sense, personal individuality is an illusion.

Stone has attempted to draw together the observations and conceptualizations of James, Cooley, Mead, and Sullivan in his conceptualization of self, which emphasizes the dimensions of *identity* (James' and Mead's notions of the self as object), *value* (James'

[9]Suzanne K. Langer, *op. cit.*, pp. 85 ff.

idea of esteem, Cooley's emphasis on judgment, and Sullivan's focus on appraisals), *mood* (Cooley's concern with sentiment and feeling, Sullivan's with anxiety), and *attitude* (a concept taken directly from Mead). He places the analysis of self directly in the matrix of communication and meaning, but stresses the importance of nonverbal or apparent symbols in such an analysis. The establishment of such dimensions in human transactions is accomplished by singling out two foci of the self—the program (''I''?) and the review (the response of others). A third focus—the imagined review (''me''?) is omitted from the discussion in the interest of space and parsimony. Appearance is seen as a fundamental communication of self and other, and an attempt is made to link the significance of appearance to the socialization of the self along the lines sketched out by Cooley, Mead, Piaget, and Sullivan.

Since Stone's contribution, the study of the self has proceeded apace, and it is impossible in a book, such as this, to do full justice to the research of a decade. Yet, the theoretical essentials remain the same. Social psychology has witnessed a considerable refinement of the fundamental concepts presented here. We have already seen, in the Introduction to this volume, that the concepts ''identification with'' and ''identification of,'' although they permit an heuristic play on words, have given way to more general (''empathic processes'') and, at the same time, more precise (drawing on Sullivan, ''personification''—literally ''person-building'') designations. ''Play,'' as used by Mead, has been replaced in some quarters by the more accurate term ''drama''—what Mead was really talking about in his discussions of the early emergence of the self. Play is too general a concept to do the service Mead asked of it, for there are many varieties of play. Such ''tests of poise,'' to offer but one example, as spinning about to induce dizziness or somersaulting are found in the play of children in the most remote and isolated village communities and are important phases of the socialization process.

Another direction taken by research on the self since 1970 points toward the fruitful analysis of what we have called mood—the affective dimensions of the self and symbolic interaction. Contributions the student may wish to pursue in this area have been made by such interactionists as Arlie R. Hochschild, T. D. Kemper, Lillian Rubin and Thomas J. Scheff. These materials are scattered in various journals, compendia, and proceedings. The student will require the instructor's assistance to develop a bibliography.

Nevertheless, such a focus on interaction and emergent selves in whatever dimension leaves the self in interaction. Consequently, there is a tendency to place the study of the self in *interpersonal relations,* as Sullivan would have it, and ignore the larger process of social organization, institutions, and other social arrangements as highly significant contexts for the establishment of self-conceptions—notions of who one is, one's worth, how one feels, what is about to be done. In a mode somewhat reminiscent of the work of David Riesman and his associates twenty-five or thirty years ago,[10] Ralph Turner sets out on this path, but links his endeavor to that of W. I. Thomas (with Florian Znaniecki) and Robert E. Park, preeminent consolidators of the ''Chicago School'' of sociology, with

---

[10]David Riesman, with Nathan Glazer and Reuel Denny, *The Lonely Crowd* (New York: Doubleday Anchor Books, 1955). Turner explicitly repudiates the equation of a self anchored in impulse with ''other-direction.''

which George H. Mead is often identified. Moreover, he casts a different light on the emotional phases of the self from this perspective and provides the opportunity for a debate that will make much sense to most students. It is the old problem of "masks or faces": Is there a "real" self which we all experience, imagine, and try to protect, or are we merely creatures of the scene—players with many parts? The concern with "feelings" as we move from institution to impulse enhances the *phenomenological* reality of the self, but poses problems of order in the larger society.

SUGGESTED READINGS

Baldwin, James Mark. *Social and Ethical Interpretations in Mental Development*. New York: The Macmillan Company, 1897.

Burns, R. B., *The Self Concept in Theory, Measurement, Development and Behavior*. London: Longman Group Ltd., 1979.

Cooley, Charles H. *Human Nature and the Social Order*. New York: Scribner, 1902.

Erikson, Erik H. "The Problem of Ego Identity." *Psychological Issues: Identity and the Life Cycle*. Vol. I, No. I, 1959.

Gergen, Kenneth J. *The Concept of Self*. New York: Holt, Rinehart, and Winston, 1971.

Gordon, Chad and Kenneth J. Gergen (eds.). *The Self in Social Interaction*. New York: John Wiley and Sons, Inc., 1968.

Hewitt, John P. *Self and Society*. Boston: Allyn and Bacon, Inc., 1976.

Lynd, Helen Merrell. *On Shame and the Search for Identity*. New York: Harcourt, Brace, 1958.

McCall, George J. and J. L. Simmons. *Identities and Interaction*. Revised Edition. New York: The Free Press, 1978.

Schwartz, Michael and Sheldon Stryker. *Deviance, Selves, and Others*. Washington, D.C.: American Sociological Association, 1970.

Spitzer, Stephan, Carl Couch, and John Stratton. *The Assessment of the Self*. Iowa City, Iowa: Escort, Sernoll, Inc., no date.

Strauss, Anselm. *Mirrors and Masks*. Glencoe, Ill.: The Free Press, 1959.

Sullivan, Harry Stack. *The Interpersonal Theory of Psychiatry*. New York: W. W. Norton and Co., 1933.

FIFTEEN

THE SOCIAL SELF

WILLIAM JAMES

THE ME AND THE I

Whatever I may be thinking of, I am always at the same time more or less aware of *myself,* of my *personal existence.* At the same time it is *I* who am aware; so that the total self of me, being as it were duplex, partly known and partly knower, partly object and partly subject, must have two aspects discriminated in it, of which for shortness we may call one the *Me* and the other the *I.* I call these "discriminated aspects," and not separate things, because the identity of *I* with *me,* even in the very act of their discrimination, is perhaps the most ineradicable dictum of common-sense, and must not be undermined by our terminology here at the outset, whatever we may come to think of its validity at our inquiry's end.

I shall therefore treat successively of (A) the self as known, or the *me,* the "empirical ego" as it is sometimes called; and of (B) the self as knower, or the I, the "pure ego" of certain authors.

SOURCE: William James, "The Social Self." Copyright unknown. From William James, *Psychology* (New York: Henry Holt and Company, 1892), pp. 189–226.

THE SELF AS KNOWN

THE EMPIRICAL SELF OR ME

Between what a man calls *me* and what he simply calls *mine* the line is difficult to draw. We feel and act about certain things that are ours very much as we feel and act about ourselves. Our fame, our children, the work of our hands, may be as dear to us as our bodies are, and arouse the same feelings and the same acts of reprisal if attacked. And our bodies themselves, are they simply ours, or are they *us?* Certainly men have been ready to disown their very bodies and to regard them as mere vestures, or even as prisons of clay from which they should some day be glad to escape.

We see then that we are dealing with a fluctuating material; the same object being sometimes treated as a part of me, at other times as simply mine, and then again as if I had nothing to do with it at all. *In its widest possible sense,* however, *a man's Me is the sum total of all that he CAN call his,* not only his body and his psychic powers, but his clothes and his house, his wife and children, his ancestors and friends, his reputation and works, his lands and horses, and yacht and bank-account. All these things give him the same emotions. If they wax and prosper, he feels triumphant; if they dwindle and die away, he feels cast down—not necessarily in the same degree for each thing, but in much the same way for all. . . .

THE SOCIAL ME

A man's social me is the recognition which he gets from his mates. We are not only gregarious animals, liking to be in sight of our fellows, but we have an innate propensity to get ourselves noticed, and noticed favorably, by our kind. No more fiendish punishment could be devised, were such a thing physically possible, than that one should be turned loose in society and remain absolutely unnoticed by all the members thereof. If no one turned round when we entered, answered when we spoke, or minded what we did, but if every person we met "cut us dead," and acted as if we were non-existing things, a kind of rage and impotent despair would ere long well up in us, from which the cruellest bodily tortures would be a relief, for these would make us feel that, however bad might be our plight, we had not sunk to such a depth as to be unworthy of attention at all.

Properly speaking, *a man has as many social selves as there are individuals who recognize him* and carry an image of him in their mind. To wound any one of these his images is to wound him. But as the individuals who carry the images fall naturally into two classes, we may practically say that he has as many different social selves as there are distinct *groups* of persons about whose opinion he cares. He generally shows a different side of himself to each of these different groups. Many a youth who is demure enough before his parents and teachers, swears and swaggers like a pirate among his "tough" young friends. We do not show ourselves to our children as to our club-companions, to our customers as to the laborers we employ, to our own masters and employers as to our intimate friends. From this there results what

practically is a division of the man into several selves; and this may be a discordant splitting, as where one is afraid to let one set of his acquaintances know him as he is elsewhere; or it may be a perfectly harmonious division of labor, as where one tender to his children is stern to the soldiers or prisoners under his command.

The most peculiar social self which one is apt to have is in the mind of the person one is in love with. The good or bad fortunes of this self cause the most intense elation and dejection—unreasonable enough as measured by every other standard than that of the organic feeling of the individual. To his own consciousness he *is* not, so long as this particular social self fails to get recognition, and when it is recognized his contentment passes all bounds.

A man's *fame,* good or bad, and his *honor* or dishonor are names for one of his social selves. The particular social self of a man called his honor is usually the result of one of those splittings of which we have spoken. It is his image in the eyes of his own "set," which exalts or condemns him as he conforms or not to certain requirements that may not be made of one in another walk of life. Thus a layman may abandon a city infected with cholera; but a priest or a doctor would think such an act incompatible with his honor. A soldier's honor requires him to fight or to die under circumstances where another man can apologize or run away with no stain upon his social self. A judge, a statesman, are in like manner debarred by the honor of their cloth from entering into pecuniary relations perfectly honorable to persons in private life. Nothing is commoner than to hear people discriminate between their different selves of this sort: "As a man I pity you, but as an official I must show you no mercy"; "As a politican I regard him as an ally, but as a moralist I loathe him"; etc., etc. What may be called "club-opinion" is one of the very strongest forces in life. The thief must not steal from other thieves; the gambler must pay his gambling-debts, though he pay no other debts in the world. The code of honor of fashionable society has throughout history been full of permissions as well as of vetoes, the only reason for following either of which is that so we best serve one of our social selves. You must not lie in general, but you may lie as much as you please if asked about your relations with a lady; you must accept a challenge from an equal, but if challenged by an inferior you may laugh him to scorn: these are examples of what is meant. . . .

RIVALRY AND CONFLICT OF THE DIFFERENT ME'S

With most objects of desire, physical nature restricts our choice to but one of many represented goods, and even so it is here. I am often confronted by the necessity of standing by one of my empirical selves and relinquishing the rest. Not that I would not, if I could, be both handsome and fat and well dressed, and a great athlete, and make a million a year, be a wit, a *bon vivant,* and a lady-killer, as well as a philosopher; a philanthropist, statesman, warrior, and African explorer, as well as a ''tone-poet'' and saint. But the thing is simply impossible. The millionaire's work would run counter to the saint's; the *bon vivant* and the philanthropist would trip each other up; the philosopher and the lady-killer could not well keep house in the same tenement of clay. Such different characters may conceivably at the outset of life be alike *possible* to a man. But to make any one of them actual, the rest must more or less be suppressed. So the seeker of his truest, strongest, deepest self must review the list carefully, and pick out the one on which to stake his salvation. All other selves thereupon become unreal, but the fortunes of this self are real. Its failures are real failures, its triumphs real triumphs, carrying shame and gladness with them. . . . Our thought, incessantly deciding, among many things of a kind, which ones for it shall be realities, here chooses one of many possible selves or characters, and forthwith reckons it no shame to fail in any of those not adopted expressly as its own.

So we have the paradox of a man shamed to death because he is only the second pugilist or the second oarsman in the world. That he is able to beat the whole population of the globe minus one is nothing; he has ''pitted'' himself to beat that one; and as long as he doesn't do that nothing else counts. He is to his own regard as if he were not, indeed he *is* not. Yonder puny fellow, however, whom every one can beat, suffers no chagrin about it, for he has long ago abandoned the attempt to ''carry that line,'' as the merchants say, of self at all. With no attempt there can be no failure; with no failure, no humiliation. So our self-feeling in this world depends entirely on what we *back* ourselves to be and do. It is determined by the ratio of our actualities to our supposed potentialities; a fraction of which our pretensions are the denominator and the numerator our success: thus,

$$\text{Self-esteem} = \frac{\text{Success}}{\text{Pretensions}}$$

Such a fraction may be increased as well by diminishing the denominator as by increasing the numerator. . . .

THE SELF AS KNOWER

The I, or ''pure-ego,'' is a very much more difficult subject of inquiry than the Me. It is that which at any given moment is conscious, whereas the Me is only one of the things which it is conscious *of*. In other words, it is the Thinker; and the question immediately comes up *what* is the thinker? Is it the passing state of consciousness itself, or is it something deeper and less mutable? The passing state . . . [is] the very embodiment of change. . . . Yet each of us spontaneously considers that by ''I,'' he means something always the same. This has led most philosophers to postulate behind the passing state of consciousness a permanent Substance or Agent whose modification or act it is. This Agent is the thinker; the ''state'' is only its instrument or means. ''Soul,'' ''transcendental

Ego,'' ''Spirit,'' are so many names for this more permanent sort of Thinker. . . .

THE SENSE OF PERSONAL IDENTITY

The thoughts which we actually know to exist do not fly about loose, but seem each to belong to some one thinker and not to another. Each thought, out of a multitude of other thoughts of which it may think, is able to distinguish those which belong to it from those which do not. The former have a warmth and intimacy about them of which the latter was completely devoid, and the result is a Me of yesterday, judged to be in some peculiarly subtle sense the *same* with the I who now make the judgment. As a mere subjective phenomena the judgment presents no special mystery. It belongs to the great class of judgments of sameness, and there is nothing more remarkable in making a judgment of sameness in the first person than in the second or the third. The intellectual operations seem essentially alike, whether I say ''I am the same as I was,'' or whether I say ''the pen is the same as it was, yesterday.'' It is as easy to think this as to think the opposite and say ''neither of us is the same.'' The only question which we have to consider is whether it be a right judgment. *Is the sameness predicated really there?*

SAMENESS IN THE SELF AS KNOWN

If in the sentence ''I am the same that I was yesterday,'' we take the ''I'' broadly, it is evident that in many ways I am *not* the same. As a concrete Me, I am somewhat different from what I was: then hungry, now full, then walking, now at rest, then poorer, now richer; then, younger, now older; etc. And yet in other ways I *am* the same, and we may call these the essential ways. My name and profession and relations to the world are identical, my face, my faculties and store of memories, are practically indistinguishable, now and then. Moreover the Me of now and the Me of then are *continuous:* the alterations were gradual and never

affected the whole of me at once. So far, then, my personal identity is just like the sameness predicated on any other aggregate thing. It is a conclusion grounded either on the resemblance in essential respects, or on the continuity of the phenomena compared. And it must not be taken to mean more than these grounds warrant, or treated as a sort of metaphysical or absolute Unity in which all differences are overwhelmed. The past and present selves compared are the same just so far as they *are* the same, and no farther. They are the same in *kind.* But this generic sameness coexists with generic differences just as real; and if from the one point of view I am one self, from another I am quite as truly many. Similarly of the attribute of continuity; it gives to the self the unity of mere connectedness, or unbrokenness, a perfectly definite phenomenal thing—but it gives not a jot or tittle more.

SAMENESS IN THE SELF AS KNOWER

But all this is said only of the Me, or Self as known. In the judgment ''I am the same,'' etc., the ''I'' was taken broadly as the concrete person. Suppose, however, that we take it narrowly, as the *Thinker,* as *''that to which''* all the concrete determinations of the Me belong and are known; does there not then appear an absolute identity at different times? That something which at every moment goes out and knowingly appropriates the *Me* of the past, and discards the non-me as foreign, is it not a permanent abiding principle of spiritual activity identical with itself, wherever found?

That it is such a principle is the reigning doctrine both of philosophy and common-sense, and yet reflection finds it difficult to justify the idea. *If there were no passing states of consciousness,* then indeed we might suppose an abiding principle, absolutely one with itself, to be the ceaseless thinker in each one of us. But if the states of consciousness be accorded as realities, no such ''substantial'' identity in the thinker need be supposed. Yesterday's and today's states of consciousness have no *substantial* identity, for when one is here the other is irrevocably dead and gone. But they have a *functional* identity, for both know the same objects, and so far as the by-gone me is one of those objects, they reach upon it in an identical way, greeting it and calling it *mine,* and opposing it to all the other things they know. This functional identity seems really the only sort of identity in the thinker which the facts require us to suppose. Successive thinkers, numerically distinct, but all aware of the same past in the same way, form an adequate vehicle for all the experience of personal unity and sameness which we actually have. And just such a train of successive thinkers is the stream of mental states (each with its complex object cognized and emotional and selective reaction thereupon) which psychology treated as a natural science has to assume. . . .

The logical conclusion seems then to be that *the states of consciousness are all that psychology needs to do her work with. Metaphysics or theology may prove the Soul to exist; but for psychology the hypothesis of such a substantial principle of unity is superfluous.*

SIXTEEN

SELF AS SENTIMENT AND REFLECTION

CHARLES H. COOLEY

It is well to say at the outset that by the word "self" in this discussion is meant simply that which is designated in common speech by the pronouns of the first person singular, "I," "me," "my," "mine," and "myself." "Self" and "ego" are used by metaphysicians and moralists in many other senses, more or less remote from the "I" of daily speech and thought, and with these I wish to have as little to do as possible. What is here discussed is what psychologists call the empirical self, the self that can be apprehended or verified by ordinary observation. I qualify it by the word social not as implying the existence of a self that is not social—for I think that the "I" of common language always has more or less distinct reference to other people as well as the speaker—but because I wish to emphasize and dwell upon the social aspect of it.

Although the topic of the self is regarded as an abstruse one this abstruseness belongs chiefly, perhaps, to the metaphysical discussion of the "pure ego"—whatever that may be—while the empirical self should not be very much more difficult to get hold of than other facts of the mind. At any rate, it may be assumed that the pronouns of the first person have a substantial, important, and not very recondite meaning, otherwise they would not be in constant and intelligible use by simple people and young children the world over. And since they have such a meaning why should it not be observed and reflected upon like any other matter of fact? . . .

The distinctive thing in the idea for which the pronouns of the first person are names is apparently a characteristic kind of feeling which may be called the my-feeling or sense of appropriation. Almost any sort of ideas may be associated with this feeling, and so come to be named "I" or "mine," but the feeling, and that alone it would seem, is the determining factor in the matter. As Professor James says in his admirable discussion of the self, the words "me" and "self" designate "all the things which have the power to produce in a stream of consciousness excitement of a certain peculiar sort."[1]

[1]*"The words* ME, *then, and* SELF, *so far as they arouse feeling and connote emotional worth, are* OBJECTIVE *designations meaning* ALL THE THINGS *which have the power to produce in a stream of consciousness excitement of a certain peculiar sort." Psychology, i. p. 319. A little earlier, he says: In its widest possible sense,* however, *a man's self is the sum*

SOURCE: Charles H. Cooley, "Self as Sentiment and Reflection." Copyright by Charles Scribner's Sons, 1902. From Charles H. Cooley, *Human Nature and the Social Order* (New York: Charles Scribner's Sons, 1902), pp. 136–167.

I do not mean that the feeling aspect of the self is necessarily more important than any other, but that it is the immediate and decisive sign and proof of what "I" is; there is no appeal from it, if we go behind it it must be to study its history and conditions, not to question its authority. But, of course, the study of history and conditions may be quite as profitable as the direct contemplation of self-feeling. What I would wish to do is to present each aspect in its proper light.

The emotion of feeling of self may be regarded as instinctive, and was doubtless evolved in connection with its important function in stimulating and unifying the special activities of individuals.[2] It is thus very profoundly rooted in the history of the human race and apparently indispensable to any plan of life at all similar to ours. It seems to exist in a vague though vigorous form at the birth of each individual, and, like other instinctive ideas or germs of ideas, to be defined and developed by experience, becoming associated, or rather incorporated, with muscular, visual, and other sensations, with perceptions, apperceptions, and conceptions of every degree of complexity and of infinite variety of content; and, especially, with personal ideas. Meantime the feeling itself does not remain unaltered, but undergoes differentiation and refinement just as does any other sort of crude innate feeling. Thus, while retaining under every phase its characteristic tone or flavor, it breaks up into innumerable self-sentiments. And concrete self-feeling, as it exists in mature persons, is a whole made up of these various sentiments, along with a good deal of primitive emotion not thus broken up. It partakes fully of the general development of the mind, but never loses that peculiar gusto of appropriation that causes us to name a thought with a first-personal pronoun. . . .

The social self is simply any idea, or system of ideas, drawn from the communicative life, that the mind cherishes as its own. Self-feeling has its chief scope *within* the general life, not outside of it; the special endeavor or tendency of which it is the emotional aspect finds its principal field of exercise in a world of personal forces, reflected in the mind by a world of personal impressions. . . .

That the "I" of common speech has a meaning which includes some sort of reference to other persons is involved in the very fact that the word and the ideas it stands for are phenomena of language and the communicative life. It is doubtful whether it is possible to use language at all without thinking more or less distinctly of some one else, and certainly the things to which we give names and which have a large place in reflective thought are almost always those which are impressed upon us by our contact with other people. Where there is no communication there can be no nomenclature and no developed thought. What we call "me," "mine," or "myself" is, then, not something separate from the general life, but the most interesting part of it, a part whose interest arises from the very fact that it is both general and individual. That is, we care for it just because it is that phase of the mind that is living and striving in the common life, trying to impress itself upon the minds of others. "I" is a militant social tendency, working to hold and enlarge its place in the general current of tendencies. So far as it can it waxes, as all life does. To think of it as apart from society is a palpable absurdity of which no one could be guilty who really *saw* it as a fact of life.

> "Der Mensch erkennt sich nur im Menschen, nur
> Das Leben lehret jedem was er sei."[3]

---

total of all he CAN call his, not only his body and his psychic powers, but his clothes and his house, his wife and children, his ancestors, and friends, his reputation and works, his lands and horses and yacht and bank account. All these things give him the same emotions." *Idem,* p. 291.

So Wundt says of "Ich": "Es ist ein *Gefühl,* nicht eine Vorstellung, wie es haüfig genannt wird." *Grundriss der Psychologie,* 4 Auflage, S. 265.

[2] It is, perhaps, to be thought of as a more general instinct, of which anger, etc., are differentiated forms, rather than as standing by itself.

[3] "Only in man does man know himself; life alone teaches each one what he is."—Goethe *Tasso,* act 2, sc. 3.

If a thing has no relations to others of which one is conscious he is unlikely to think of it at all, and if he does think of it he cannot, it seems to me, regard it as emphatically *his*. The appropriative sense is always the shadow, as it were, of the common life, and when we have it we have a sense of the latter in connection with it. Thus, if we think of a secluded part of the woods as "ours," it is because we think, also, that others do not go there. . . .

In a very large and interesting class of cases the social reference takes the form of a somewhat definite imagination of how one's self—that is any idea he appropriates—appears in a particular mind, and the kind of self-feeling one has is determined by the attitude toward this attributed to that other mind. A social self of this sort might be called the reflected or looking-glass self:

"Each to each a looking glass
Reflects the other that doth pass."

As we see our face, figure, and dress in the glass, and are interested in them because they are ours, and pleased or otherwise with them according as they do or do not answer to what we should like them to be, so in imagination we perceive in another's mind some thought of our appearance, manner, aims, deeds, character, friends, and so on, and are variously affected by it.

A self-idea of this sort seems to have three principal elements: the imagination of our appearance to the other person, the imagination of his judgment of that appearance, and some sort of self-feeling, such as pride or mortification. The comparison with a looking-glass hardly suggests the second element, the imagined judgment, which is quite essential. The thing that moves us to pride or shame is not the mere mechanical reflection of ourselves, but an imputed sentiment, the imagined effect of this reflection upon another's mind. This is evident from the fact that the character and weight of that other, in whose mind we see ourselves, makes all the difference with our feeling. We are ashamed to seem evasive in the presence of a straightforward man, cowardly in the presence of a brave one, gross in the eyes of a refined one, and so on. We always imagine, and in imagining share, the judgments of the other mind. . . .

The view that "self" and the pronouns of the first person are names which the race has learned to apply to an instinctive attitude of mind, and which each child in turn learns to apply in a similar way, was impressed upon me by observing my child M. at the time when she was learning to use these pronouns. When she was two years and two weeks old I was surprised to discover that she had a clear notion of the first and second persons when used possessively. When asked, "Where is your nose?" she would put her hand upon it and say "my." She also understood that when someone else said "my" and touched an object it meant something opposite to what was meant when she touched the same object and used the same word. Now, anyone who will exercise his imagination upon the question how this matter must appear to a mind having no means of knowing anything about "I" and "my" except what it learns by hearing them used, will see that it should be very puzzling. Unlike other words, the personal pronouns have, apparently, no uniform meaning, but convey different and even opposite ideas when employed by different persons. It seems remarkable that children should master the problem before they arrive at considerable power of abstract reasoning. How should a little girl of two, not particularly reflective, have discovered that "my" was not the sign of a definite object like other words, but meant something different with each person who used it? And, still more surprising, how should she have achieved the correct use of it with reference to herself which, it would seem, *could not be copied from anyone else,* simply because no one else used it to describe what belonged to her? The meaning of words is learned by associating them with other phenomena. But how is it possible to learn the meaning of one which, as used by others, is never associated with the same phenomenon as when properly used by one's self? Watching her use of the first person, I was at once struck with the fact that she employed it almost wholly in a possessive sense, and that, too, when in an aggressive, self-assertive mood. It was extremely common to see R. tugging at one end of a plaything and M. at the other, screaming, "My, my." "Me" was sometimes nearly equivalent to "my," and was also employed to call attention to herself when she wanted something done for her. Another common use of "my" was to demand something she did not have at all. Thus if R. had something the like of which she wanted, say a cart, she would exclaim, "Where's *my* cart?"

It seemed to me that she might have learned the use of these pronouns about as follows. The self-feeling had always been there. From the first week she had wanted things and cried and fought for them. She had also become familiar by observation and opposition with similar appropriative activities on the part of R. Thus she not only had the feeling herself, but by associating it with its visible expression had probably divined it, sympathized with it, resented it, in others. Grasping, tugging, and screaming would be associated with the feeling in her own case and would recall the feeling when observed in others. They would constitute a language, precedent to the use of first-personal pronouns, to express the self-idea. All was ready, then, for the word to name this experience. She now observed that R., when contentiously appropriating something, frequently exclaimed, *"my!" "mine,"* "give it to *me,"* "*I* want it," and the like. Nothing more natural, then, than that she should adopt these words as names for a frequent and vivid experience with which she was already familiar in her own case and had learned to attribute to others. Accordingly, it appeared to me, as I recorded in my notes at the time, that " 'my' and 'mine,' are simply names for concrete images of appropriateness," embracing both the appropriative feeling and its manifestation. If this is true the child does not at first work out the I-and-you idea in an abstract form. The

first-personal pronoun is a sign of a concrete thing after all, but that thing is not primarily the child's body, or his muscular sensations as such, but the phenomenon of aggressive appropriation, practiced by himself, witnessed in others, and incited and interpreted by a hereditary instinct. This seems to get over the difficulty above mentioned, namely, the seeming lack of a common content between the meaning of "my" when used by another and when used by one's self. This common content is found in the appropriative feeling and the visible and audible signs of that feeling. An element of difference, and strife comes in, of course, in the opposite actions or purposes which the "my" of another and one's own "my" are likely to stand for. When another person says "mine" regarding something which I claim, I sympathize with him enough to understand what he means, but it is a hostile sympathy, overpowered by another and more vivid "mine" connected with the idea of drawing the object my way.

In other words, the meaning of "I" and "mine" is learned in the same way that the meanings of hope, regret, chagrin, disgust, and thousands of other words of emotion and sentiment are learned; that is, by having the feeling, imputing it to others in connection with some kind of expression, and hearing the word along with it. As to its communication and growth the self-idea is in no way peculiar that I see, but essentially like other ideas. In its more complex forms, such as are expressed by "I" in conversation and literature, it is a social sentiment, or type of sentiments, defined and developed by intercourse. . . .[4]

I imagine, then, that as a rule the child associates "I" and "me" at first only with those ideas regarding which his appropriative feeling is aroused and defined by opposition. He appropriates his nose, eye, or foot in very much the same way as a plaything—by antithesis to other noses, eyes, and feet, which he cannot control. It is not

[4]Compare my "Study of the Early Use of Self-Words by a Child," in the *Psychological Review*, vol. 15, p. 339.

uncommon to tease little children by proposing to take away one of these organs, and they behave precisely as if the "mine" threatened were a separable object—which it might be for all they know. And, as I have suggested, even in adult life, "I," "me," and "mine" are applied with a strong sense of their meaning only to things distinguished as peculiar to us by some sort of opposition or contrast. They always imply social life and relation to other persons. That which is most distinctively mine is very private, it is true, but it is the part of the private which I am cherishing in antithesis to the rest of the world, not the separate but the special. The aggressive self is essentially a militant phase of the mind, having for its apparent function the energizing of peculiar activities, and, although the militancy may not go on in an obvious, external manner, it always exists as a mental attitude. . . .

The process by which self-feeling of the looking-glass sort develops in children may be followed without much difficulty. Studying the movements of others as closely as they do they soon see a connection between their own acts and changes in those movements, that is, they perceive their own influence or power over persons. The child appropriates the visible actions of his parent or nurse, over which he finds he has some control, in quite the same way as he appropriates one of his own members or a plaything, and he will try to do things with this new possession, just as he will with his hand or his rattle. . . .

The young performer soon learns to be different things to different people, showing that he begins to apprehend personality and to forsee its operation. If the mother or nurse is more tender than just she will almost certainly be "worked" by systematic weeping. It is a matter of common observation that children often behave worse with their mother than with other and less sympathetic people. Of the new persons that a child sees it is evident that some make a strong impression and awaken a desire to interest and please them, while others are indifferent or repugnant. Sometimes the reason can be perceived or guessed, sometimes not; but the fact

of selective interest, admiration, prestige, is obvious before the end of the second year. By that time a child already cares much for the reflection of himself upon one personality and little for that upon another. Moreover, he soon claims intimate and tractable persons as *mine,* classes them among his other possessions, and maintains his ownership against all comers. M., at three years of age, vigorously resented R.'s claim upon their mother. The latter was "*my* mamma," whenever the point was raised.

Strong joy and grief depend upon the treatment this rudimentary social self receives. In the case of M., I noticed as early as the fourth month a "hurt" way of crying which seemed to indicate a sense of personal slight. It was quite different from the cry of pain or that of anger, but seemed about the same as the cry of fright. The slightest tone of reproof would produce it. On the other hand, if people took notice and laughed and encouraged, she was hilarious. At about fifteen months old she had become "a perfect little actress," seeming to live largely in imagination of her effect upon other people. She constantly and obviously had traps for attention, and looked abashed or wept at any signs of disapproval or indifference. At times it would seem as if she could not get over these repulses, but would cry long in a grieved way, refusing to be comforted. If she hit upon any little trick that made people laugh she would be sure to repeat it, laughing loudly and affectedly in imitation. She had quite a repertory of these small performances which she would display to a sympathetic audience, or even try upon strangers. I have seen her at sixteen months, when R. refused to give her the scissors, sit down and make-believe cry, putting up her under lip and snuffling, meanwhile looking up now and then to see what effect she was producing.

In such phenomena we have plainly enough, it seems to me, the germ of personal ambition of every sort. Imagination co-operating with instinctive self-feeling has already created a social "I," and this has become a principal object of interest and endeavor.

SEVENTEEN

SELF AS SOCIAL OBJECT

GEORGE HERBERT MEAD

It is the characteristic of the self as an object to itself that I want to bring out. This characteristic is represented in the word "self," which is a reflexive, and indicates that which can be both subject and object. This type of object is essentially different from other objects, and in the past it has been distinguished as conscious, a term which indicates an experience with, an experience of, one's self. It was assumed that consciousness in some way carried this capacity of being an object to itself. In giving a behavioristic statement of consciousness we have to look for some sort of experience in which the physical organism can become an object to itself.[1]

. . . How can an individual get outside himself (experientially) in such a way as to become an object to himself? This is the essential psychologi-

[1]Man's behavior is such in his social group that he is able to become an object to himself, a fact which constitutes him a more advanced product of evolutionary development than are the lower animals. Fundamentally it is this social fact—and not his alleged possession of a soul or mind with which he, as an individual, has been mysteriously and supernaturally endowed, and with which the lower animals have not been endowed—that differentiates him from them.

cal problem of selfhood or of self-consciousness; and its solution is to be found by referring to the process of social conduct or activity in which the given person or individual is implicated. The apparatus of reason would not be complete unless it swept itself into its own analysis of the field of experience; or unless the individual brought himself into the same experiential field as that of the other individual selves in relation to whom he acts in any given social situation. Reason cannot become impersonal unless it takes an objective, non-affective attitude toward itself; otherwise, we have just consciousness, not *self*-consciousness. And it is necessary to rational conduct that the individual should thus take an objective, impersonal attitude toward himself, that he should become an object to himself. For the individual organism is obviously an essential and important fact or constituent element of the empirical situation in which it acts; and without taking objective account of itself as such, it cannot act intelligently, or rationally.

The individual experiences himself as such, not directly, but only indirectly, from the particular standpoints of other individual members of the same social group, or from the generalized standpoint of the social group as a whole to which he belongs. For he enters his own experience as a self or individual, not directly or immediately, not by becoming a subject to himself, but only in so far as he first becomes an object to himself just as other individuals are objects to him or in his experience; and he becomes an object to himself only by taking the attitudes of other individuals toward himself within a social environment or context of experience and behavior in which both he and they are involved.

The importance of what we term ''communication'' lies in the fact that it provides a form of behavior in which the organism or the individual may become an object to himself. It is that sort of communication which we have been discussing— not communication in the sense of the cluck of the hen to the chickens, or the bark of a wolf to the pack, or the lowing of a cow, but communication in the sense of significant symbols, communication which is directed not only to others but also to the individual himself. So far as that type of communication is a part of behavior it at least introduces a self. Of course, one may hear without listening; one may see things that he does not realize; do things that he is not really aware of. But it is where one does respond to that which he addresses to another and where that response of his own becomes a part of his conduct, where he not only hears himself but responds to himself, talks and replies to himself as truly as the other person replies to him, that we have behavior in which the individuals become objects to themselves. . . .

The self, as that which can be an object to itself, is essentially a social structure, and it arises in social experience. After a self has arisen, it in a certain sense provides for itself its social experiences, and so we can conceive of an absolutely solitary self. But it is impossible to conceive of a self arising outside of social experience. When it has arisen we can think of a person in solitary confinement for the rest of his life, but who still has himself as a companion, and is able to think and to converse with himself as he had communicated with others. That process to which I have just referred, of responding to one's self as another

responds to it, taking part in one's own conversation with others, being aware of what one is saying and using that awareness of what one is saying to determine what one is going to say thereafter—that is a process with which we are all familiar. We are continually following up our own address to other persons by an understanding of what we are saying, and using that understanding in the direction of our continued speech. We are finding out what we are going to say, what we are going to do, by saying and doing, and in the process we are continually controlling the process itself. In the conversation of gestures what we say calls out a certain response in another and that in turn changes our own action, so that we shift from what we started to do because of the reply the other makes. The conversation of gestures is the beginning of communication. The individual comes to carry on a conversation of gestures with himself. He says something, and that calls out a certain reply in himself which makes him change what he was going to say. One starts to say something, we will presume an unpleasant something, but when he starts to say it he realizes it is cruel. The effect on himself of what he is saying checks him; there is here a conversation of gestures between the individual and himself. We mean by significant speech that the action is one that affects the individual himself, and that the effect upon the individual himself is part of the intelligent carrying-out of the conversation with others. Now we, so to speak, amputate that social phase and dispense with it for the time being, so that one is talking to one's self as one would talk to another person.[2]

[2]It is generally recognized that the specifically social expressions of intelligence, or the exercise of what is often called ''social intelligence,'' depend upon the given individual's ability to take the roles of, or ''put himself in the place of,'' the other individuals implicated with him, in given social situations; and upon his consequent sensitivity to their attitudes toward himself and toward one another. These specifically social expressions of intelligence, of course, acquire unique significance in terms of our view that the whole nature of intelligence is social to the very core—that this putting of one's self in the places of others, this taking of one's self from their roles or attitudes, is not merely one of the various aspects or

This process of abstraction cannot be carried on indefinitely. One inevitably seeks an audience, has to pour himself out to somebody. In reflective intelligence one thinks to act, and to act solely so that this action remains a part of a social process. Thinking becomes preparatory to social action. The very process of thinking is, of course, simply an inner conversation that goes on, but it is a conversation of gestures which in its completion implies the expression of that which one thinks to an audience. One separates the significance of what he is saying to others from the actual speech and gets it ready before saying it. He thinks it out, and perhaps writes it in the form of a book; but it is still a part of social intercourse in which one is addressing other persons and at the same time addressing one's self, and in which one controls the address to other persons by the response made to one's own gesture. That the person should be responding to himself is necessary to the self, and it is this sort of social conduct which provides behavior within which that self appears. I know of no other form of behavior than the linguistic in which the individual is an object to himself, and so far as I can see, the individual is not a self in the reflexive sense unless he is an object to himself. It is this fact that gives a critical importance to communication, since this is a type of behavior in which the individual does so respond to himself.

We realize in everyday conduct and experience that an individual does not mean a great deal of what he is doing and saying. We frequently say that such an individual is not himself. We come away from an interview with a realization that we have left out important things, that there are parts

of the self that did not get into what was said. What determines the amount of the self that gets into communication is the social experience itself. Of course, a good deal of the self does not need to get expression. We carry on a whole series of different relationships to different people. We are one thing to one man and another thing to another. There are parts of the self which exist only for the self in relationship to itself. We divide ourselves up in all sorts of different selves with reference to our acquaintances. We discuss politics with one and religion with another. There are all sorts of different selves answering to all sorts of different social reactions. It is the social process itself that is responsible for the appearance of the self; it is not there as a self apart from this type of experience.

A multiple personality is in a certain sense normal, as I have just pointed out. There is usually an organization of the whole self with reference to the community to which we belong, and the situation in which we find ourselves. What the society is, whether we are living with people of the present, people of our own imaginations, people of the past, varies, of course, with different individuals. Normally, within the sort of community as a whole to which we belong, there is a unified self, but that may be broken up. To a person who is somewhat unstable nervously and in whom there is a line of cleavage, certain activities become impossible, and that set of activities may separate and evolve another self. Two separate "me's" and "I's," two different selves, result, and that is the condition under which there is a tendency to break up the personality. There is an account of a professor of education who disappeared, was lost to the community, and later turned up in a logging camp in the West. He freed himself of his occupation and turned to the woods where he felt, if you like, more at home. The pathological side of it was the forgetting, the leaving out of the rest of the self. This result involved getting rid of certain bodily memories which would identify the individual to himself. We often recognize the lines of cleavage that run through us. We would be glad to

---

expressions of intelligence or of intelligent behavior, but is the very essence of its character. Spearman's "X factor" in intelligence—the unknown factor which, according to him, intelligence contains—is simply (if our social theory of intelligence is correct) this ability of the intelligent individual to take the attitude of the other, or the attitudes of others, thus realizing the significations or grasping the meaning of the symbols or gestures in terms of which thinking proceeds; and thus being able to carry on with himself the internal conversation with these symbols or gestures which thinking involves.

forget certain things, get rid of things the self is bound up with in past experiences. What we have here is a situation in which there can be different selves, and it is dependent upon the set of social reactions that is involved as to which self we are going to be. . . . .

The unity and structure of the complete self reflects the unity and structure of the social process as a whole; and each of the elementary selves of which it is composed reflects the unity and structure of one of the various aspects of that process in which the individual is implicated. In other words, the various elementary selves which constitute, or are organized into, a complete self are the various aspects of the structure of that complete self answering to the various aspects of the structure of the social process as a whole; the structure of the complete self is thus a reflection of the complete social process. The organization and unification of a social group is identical with the organization and unification of any one of the selves arising within the social process in which that group is engaged, or which it is carrying on.

The phenomenon of dissociation of personality is caused by a breaking up of the complete, unitary self into the component selves of which it is composed, and which respectively correspond to different aspects of the social process in which the person is involved, and within which his complete or unitary self has arisen; these aspects being the different social groups to which he belongs within that process.

EIGHTEEN

SELF AS CONCEPT AND ILLUSION

HARRY STACK SULLIVAN

Now, let me run over briefly this . . . general process of becoming a human being, which is manifested in the early years of life: The transfer from the manifestations of potentialities to learn phonemes and words, and even rough grammatical structures, to the capacity to use language to communicate information and misinformation. All children and for that matter, I believe, all the young of all the species on the face of the earth enjoy, whatever that means, playing with their abilities. As the young mature, these abilities become manifest in play activities and are obviously pleasant to manifest in that way. And so, before it is possible for a child to articulate syllables, there is a playing with the phonemal stations which the child has finally been able to hit on in the babbling and cooing business. There follows the picking up of some syllables, and sooner or later every child falls upon the syllable "ma." If there is a slight tendency to perseveration so that it bcomes "ma-ma," then truly the child

SOURCE: Harry Stack Sullivan, "Self as Concept and Illusion," Copyright by The William Alanson White Psychiatric Foundation, 1964. Harry Stack Sullivan, "The Illusion of Personal Individuality," *The Fusion of Psychiatry and Social Science*, with Introduction and Commentaries by Helen Swick Perry (New York: W. W. Norton and Company, Inc., 1964), pp. 211–228. Reprinted by permission of W. W. Norton and Company, Inc.

discovers that there is something that he had not previously suspected: namely, magic in this noise-making apparatus of his, because very significant people begin to rally around and do things, and they don't hurt—quite the contrary, they are pleasant. I suppose that that little experience is the beginning of what to most people seems to be a lifelong feeling that there is nothing about them that is as powerful as the noises they make with their mouths. But anyway, it will not be very long before this child has a whole flock of articulate noises more or less strung together as words, and those words, which will be the delight of grandma and the satisfaction of mama, and perhaps even a source of mild satisfaction to papa, will have very little to do indeed with those words as they will be in that person ten years later. The words as they originally come along are happy accidents of maturation and combination of hearing and motor impulse—and vast bunches of potentialities that I couldn't name if I had time to. Especially we see in the case of "ma-ma"—where almost anything might have been said but that happened to be and it causes commotion among the great significant environment—that this obviously represents some personal power. This is one of the most remarkable performances thus far observed. And so "ma-ma" is of course not the name of a creature that runs around offering breasts and rattles: ''ma-ma'' pertains much more to the general feeling of force, magic, and so on. And I suppose it comes to everyone as a little bit of a letdown to discover that ''ma-ma'' is the thing that this creature [the mother] feels is its proper appellation, and it is only because the creature responds to that name that all this wonderful appearance of magic was called out.

The transfer from the feeling of power in this combination of noise to the realization that it is a pet name for the maternal relative is a transfer from the realm of the autistic or wholly personal, almost animal meaning, to the impersonal, social, conventional, or, as we like to say, *consensually validated* meaning of the word, and to the realm of scientific discourse, and I hope often to the realm of common speech. One's experience in using words has been observed with such care that one has finally learned how to create in the hearer's mind something remotely resembling what one hoped he would think of. Now, that takes a lot of experimenting, a great deal of observation, many corrections, solemn exhortations, rewards and punishments, and, as can be demonstrated in the case of almost everyone, applies only to a large working vocabulary. In addition to that, there is perhaps twice as large a collection of which would come as a mild shock to a lexicographer, and a few words in a very personal vocabulary which are definitely retained in an autistic state—they are a secret language which will be expressed only obscurely in a very intimate relationship. Now, so far as there remain autistic words, those words would be fragments of the culture, torn from it, and kept as magic possessions of, let us say, an animal, and that is not what I am dealing with. In so far as a great deal of consensual validation has gone on and one can make noises which are more or less exactly communicative to a hearer who knows the language, the words have been stripped of as much as possible of the accidents of their personal history in you, and it is by that process that they come to be so peculiarly impersonal, just as if, you see, you

hadn't learned them with the greatest care, having a wealth of meaning to your original words, and gradually sorting out that which was relevant from that which was irrelevant to the purpose of verbal communication.

A great deal of life runs through this process. It starts out defined by the more or less accidental occurrence of something. One experiences, observes, formulates—after perhaps naming, symbolizing—and subsequently thinks about, that is, analyzes, and perhaps finally gets insight into or thoroughly understands the relationship of various parts of this complex experience, has information about it; but it is more or less a unique performance. And then, because of the way we live, the equipment we have, the tendencies we mature, and so on, and perhaps the necessities to which we are subjected by others, we want to talk about this, and as we first discuss anything new in our experience—as you may be able to observe from day to day, however mature you are—we don't make awfully good sense; and now and then we have the unpleasant experience in the act of telling somebody about it of discovering that we don't know what we are talking about, even though it is our experience.

The point is that the process of consensual validation running here before our eyes calls in an illusion, an illusory person, in the sense of a critic, more or less like what we think the hearer is. We observe what goes on in him when we make this string of words or say this sentence, and it isn't satisfactory; and so, we feel that it is an inadequate statement, and therefore, of course, it doesn't communicate, even to us as hearers, what we are trying to say. So we look again at our experience, and we consider, from the standpoint of illusory critics, and so on: How can the thing be made to communicate? How can I tell somebody about this? And we finally, if we are fairly clever, get the answer. Once we have got that, the unique individuality of the experience begins to shrink, it becomes part of the general structure of life, we forget how strikingly novel the experience was and how peculiarly it had fringes which apply only to us—we lose all that in the process of validation.

You might feel that we were impoverished of much of the original richness of life in the process; maybe we are, but we get great richness from social intercourse, the sharing of experience, the growth of understanding, and the benefits of other people's more or less parallel experience, and so on. In fact, the whole richness of civilization is largely due to this very sort of thing. We can't be alone in things and be very clear on what happened *to* us, and we, as I have said already, can't be alone and be very clear even on what is happening *in* us very long—excepting that it gets simpler and simpler, and more primitive and more primitive, and less and less socially acceptable.

In all this process of being socialized and particularly of developing the ability to communicate by verbal behavior, quite a time after little Willie has gotten to talk about "me wanting" bread and jam, little Willie begins to talk about "I"; and when little Willie gets to talking about "I," just the same as when you hear other people talking about "I," you will notice that something is going on that wasn't there when it was "me" that wanted bread; and it is really much more important than when he finally gets around to saying that he is Willie Brown, or something like that. The coming of "I," as a term, is great stuff.

I have now to refer to a type of experience which may or may not exist—I wouldn't know. I believe it exists, but no one seems to have any time to make many observations; and so since it is more or less important from my way of explaining things and since I know that no one can now controvert the idea, I will present it to you for what it is worth. Some way or other—and the less said about that the better—there is a certain direct contagion of disagreeable experiences from significant adults to very young children; in fact this continues in some cases far into life and is part of the paraphernalia that is so puzzling about certain mediumistic and certain hypnotic performances. A simple way

of referring to this is *empathy*.[1] Whether empathy exists or not—as I say, take it or leave it—it is demonstrable that there are feeding difficulties when mother is made apprehensive by a telegram, and that it is not communicated by the tone of her voice; so since it occurs and is often noticed by pediatricians, I guess maybe I am in a moderately defensible position. And, the encouragement of the sublimation by the rote learning of a vast part of the social heritage in the very young is by way of approval and disapproval. Approval, so far as I know, very early in life has almost no effect, but in that case no effect is very welcome. You know that a very young child sleeps as much as possible, and so if there is no disturbance, well, I think it is doing what it wants to do. Disapproval, on the other hand, insofar as there is empathic linkage between the young and significant older people, is unpleasant, lowers the euphoria, the sense of well-being, interferes with the ease of falling asleep, the ease of taking nourishment, and so forth.

All this type of interference is originally profoundly unconscious in that it is in no sense a pure content of consciousness made up of sensations, conceptions, deductions, and inferences; but it does come ultimately to be clearly connected with disapproving attitudes on the part of others, with other people not being pleased with what we are doing, or not being satisfied with our performances. This early experience is the beginning of what goes on through life as a uniquely significant emotional experience, called by the name of a profoundly important concept in social study and psychiatry—the conception of *anxiety*. Anxiety begins that way—it is always that way, the product of a great many people who have disapproved. It

[1Since Sullivan's paper was first presented, empathy has become a field for research. See, for instance, Leonard S. Cottrell, Jr., and Rosalind F. Dymond, "The Empathic Responses: A Neglected Field for Research." *Psychiatry* (1949) 12:355−359. The authors note in this article that Mead accepted empathic reactions as given, which was essentially Sullivan's position; neither of course found a way to "prove" it. H.S.P.]

comes to be represented by abstractions—by imaginary people that one carries around with one, some of them in the shape of ideal statements, some of them actually as almost phenomenologically evident people who disapprove. The disapproval and its effect get to be so subtly effective that a great deal of anxiety which shoos us this way and that, from this and that feeling, emotion, impulse, comes finally to be so smooth-running that very few people have the foggiest notion of what a vast part of their life is influenced by anxiety.

Anxiety is what keeps us from noticing things which would lead us to correct our faults. Anxiety is the thing that makes us hesitate before we spoil our standing with the stranger. Anxiety when it does not work so suavely becomes a psychiatric problem, because then it hashes our most polite utterances to the prospective boss, and causes us to tremble at the most inopportune times. So you see it is only reasonable and very much in keeping with an enormously capable organization, such as the human being, that anxiety becomes a problem only when it doesn't work smoothly, and that the anxiety which has had to be grasped as a fundamental factor in understanding interpersonal relations is by no means an anxiety attack, a hollow feeling to the stomach, and so on. Much, much more frequently it manifests as what I have called *selective inattention,* by which I mean you just miss all sorts of things which would cause you embarrassment, or in many cases great profit to notice. It is the means by which you stay as you are, in spite of the efforts of worthy psychiatrists, clergymen, and others to help you mend your ways. You don't hear, you don't see, you don't feel, you don't observe, you don't think, you don't this, and you don't that, all by the very suave manipulation of the contents of consciousness by anxiety—or, if you must, . . . by the threat of anxiety, which still is anxiety. This very great extent of the effects of disapproval and the disturbance of euphoria by the significant people in early life—the people who are tremendously interested in getting you socialized—is what makes the concept of anxiety so crucially important to understanding all sorts of things.

The part of the personality[2] which is central in the experience of anxiety we call the "self." It is concerned with avoiding the supposedly distressing—which is often illuminating—with the exclusion from awareness of certain types of very humiliating recollections, and correspondingly the failure of the development of insight from experience. It maintains selective inattention.

Now the "self" is not coterminous with the ego of the old ego-psychologist, or the ego of Freud, or the superego of Freud, or anything except what I will say it is—which incidentally I believe is a very simple statement of practically universal experience. *The self is the content of consciousness at all times when one is thoroughly comfortable about one's self-respect, the prestige that one enjoys among one's fellows, and the respect and deference which they pay one.* Under those estimable circumstances there is no anxiety; the self is the whole works; everything else in life runs smoothly without disturbing us the least bit. And it is when any of these things begin to go a little haywire, when we tend to remember a humiliating experience which would disturb our self-esteem, when somebody says something derogatory about us in our hearing or to our face, when somebody snubs us, showing the very antithesis of deference, and when somebody shows up our stupidities, thereby impairing our prestige—it is at those times that anxiety is very apt to manifest itself, but, again, it is apt to be overlooked because it is so generally followed by anger. Anger is much more comfortable to experience than anxiety and, in fact, has

[2]When I speak of "parts of personality," it must be understood that "personality" is a hypothesis, so this is a hypothetical part of a hypothesis.
[The importance of the explicit recognition of the pyramiding of hypotheses was continually emphasized by Sullivan. In writing about personality, it is particularly easy—and common—to conceal the pyramiding of hypotheses by the facile use of terms of common speech, the ambiguity or hypothetical nature of which is not obvious because of their familiarity. H.S.P.]

much the relation of ''I'' to ''me''; anger is much more powerful and reassuring than anxiety, which is the antithesis of power, which is threat and danger. Anger, however, is supposed to intimidate the other fellow, and at least it obscures the damage to our self-esteem, at least temporarily. And so we say that the self is a system within a personality, built up from innumerable experiences from early life; the central notion of which is that we satisfy the people that matter to us and therefore satisfy ourselves and are spared the experience of anxiety.

We can say that the operations by which all these things are done—in contradiction to taking food, getting sexual satisfaction, and sleep, and other delightful things—the operations which maintain our prestige and self-respect, which are dependent upon the respect of others for us and the deference they pay us, are *security operations*. Security operations are things which we might say are herded down a narrow path by selective inattention. In other words, we don't learn them as fast as we might; we never seem to learn how unimportant they are in many circumstances and where they get in our way. They are the things that always have the inside track with denizens of the best of possible variants on the Western culture, the most insecure culture I know—our American people. Well, security operations are the things that don't change much, that have the focus of attention, in and out of season, if there is the least chance of feeling anxious. And the security operations are in many cases assertive, starting out with ''I''— and ''I'' in its most powerful fashion. Sometimes the security operations are more subtle—in fact there are always quite subtle security operations in a person of [at least] ordinary abilities—but they interfere with all sorts of grasps on the universe, grasps which would in essence show that the regard in which a person holds us is defined by the past experience of that person and his actual capacity to know what we were doing, which in some cases is very low. [We often fail to grasp] that the prestige we did or did not get had little

bearing on the prestige which we might get for this particular act six weeks later; that all this vast to-do which in early childhood and the juvenile era is practically necessary to survive the distress of the parents is mostly ancient baggage that could very well be replaced with a few streamlined pieces that make a great deal of sense in the interpersonal world in which we have our being.

As I say, the self does not ''learn'' very readily because anxiety is just so busy and so effective at choking off inquiries where there is any little risk of loss of face with one's self or others. And the operations to maintain this prestige and feeling of security, freedom from anxiety, are of such crucial importance from the cradle on—I mean actually from the very early months of childhood, somewhere around two months onward—that the context of consciousness pertaining to the pursuit of satisfaction and the enjoyment of life is at best marginal. It is one's prestige, one's status, the importance which people feel one is entitled to, the respect that one can expect from people—and even their envy which becomes precious in that it gives a certain illusion that one has prestige—that dominate awareness. *These things are so focal in interpersonal relations of our day and age that the almost unassailable conviction develops, partly based on the lack of information of our parents and others, that each of us, as defined by the animal organism that we were at birth, are unique, isolated individuals in the human world,* as our bodies are—very figuratively—unique and individual in the biological world.

Now I started out by suggesting that the interrelations, interdependence, interpenetrations and so on, of the biological world are very striking. Yet, no one will quarrel with the separation as an instrument for study, for thought, and so on, of organism and environment. And if you are human biologists, I am perfectly willing for you to talk about individual specimens of man. And in so far as you see material objects, I am perfectly willing to agree that you see people walking around individually, moving from hither to yon in geography, and even persisting from now to then in duration, but that does not explain much of anything about the distinctively human. It doesn't even explain very much about the performance of my thoroughly domesticated cocker spaniels. What the biological organism does is interesting and wonderful. What the personality does, which can be observed and studied only in relations between personalities or among personalities, is truly and terribly marvelous, and is human, and is the function of creatures living in indissoluble contact with the world of culture and of people. In the field it is preposterous to talk about individuals and to go on deceiving oneself with the idea of uniqueness of single entity, of simple, central being.

So it has come about that there has developed this conception of interpersonal relations as the field of study of those parts of the social sciences concerned with the behavior of people and as the field of study of psychiatry. In so far as difficulties in living are the subject of psychiatry, we must study the processes of living in which the difficulties are manifested, since otherwise we can't really sort out what is "difficulty" and what is perhaps novel genius; we really do have to study interpersonal relations to know what we are talking about when we talk about difficulties in living. As I say, the conceptual system has grown up which finds its subject matter not in the study of personality, which is beyond reach, but in the study of that which can be observed, namely, interpersonal relations. And when that viewpoint is applied, then one of the greatest difficulties encountered in bringing about favorable change is this almost inescapable illusion that there is a performing, unique, simple existent self, called variously "me" or "I," and in some strange fashion, the patient's, or the subject person's, private property.

Progress begins, life unfolds, and interpersonal relations improve—life can become simple and delightful only at the expense of this deeply ingrained illusion and the parallel conviction that that which has sensations must under all conceivable circumstances be the "same" as that which has

tenderness and love—tenderness and love being as obviously communal, involving two personalities, as anything known to man can be.

And so let me say very simply that in so far as you will care to check over these various incomplete sketches that I have made on a vast field and will not discuss what you heard me say as a misunderstanding, you will find that it makes no sense to think of ourselves as "individual," "separate," capable of anything like definitive description in isolation, that the notation is just beside the point. No great progress in this field of study can be made until it is realized that the field of observation is what people do with each other, what they can communicate to each other about what they do with each other. When that is done, no such thing as the durable unique, individual personality is ever clearly justified. For all I know every human being has as many personalities as he has interpersonal relations, and as a great many of our interpersonal relations are actual operations with imaginery people—that is, in-no-sense-materially-embodied people—and as they may have the same or greater validity and importance in life as have our operations with many materially-embodied people like the clerks in the corner store, you can see that even though "the illusion of personal individuality" sounds quite lunatic when first heard, there is at least food for thought in it.

Discussion[3]

. . . *(In answer to a question asking, in effect, Can we not say that there is a justifiably characterizable self in each person we deal with, which might be called the "real" self?)*

It is, I believe, a statistically demonstrable fact that the interpersonal relations of any person, even though he feels very full of the conviction of his individuality, are under ordinary circumstances

[3In the recording from which this lecture was taken, there are gaps in which questions from the audience can be faintly heard. I have tried to indicate the nature of these questions. H.S.P.]

rather strikingly restricted in variety, freedom you might say. Such a person is very much more apt to do the same sort of thing with a number of people than to do very different things with each one of that number. Furthermore, even more striking are the observable performances in which he will persistently misfunction with certain people in characterizable ways, despite the most incongruous objective data—of which, of course, *he* is unaware. It is a notorious fact about personality problems that people act *as if* someone else were present when he is not—as the result of interpersonal configurations which are irrelevant to the other person's concern—and do this in a recurrent fashion without any great difference in pattern. These various factors are so striking in interpersonal relations, that it is perfectly easy and for many purposes very practical to speak of the structure of the character of the person.

All these are, I believe, correct statements of observable data. But when it comes to attempting to form a general theory on which to approach explanations of everything that happens to one in one's intercourse with others, and all the variety of things that occur in particularly-purposed interpersonal relations such as the psychotherapeutic situation, then it is just as easy to notice that the person maintains quite as many of what you ordinarily call imaginary relationships as he does of those that have the peculiar virtue of objective reference. A person, for example, may be said with considerable justification, to act towards his wife as he did towards his mother. Now it is true that there are many differences in detail, but the general patterns of emotional relationship of conscious versus unnoticed motivation, of intended versus experienced acts, are very much those that the person first developed in manifest behavior with his mother,

and it is quite useful to think of his experience of that mother as interpenetrating the experience of the wife and, in fact, frequently completely suppressing any individualization of or any attention to the characterization of the wife. That is the more difficult part of this conception, but it is quite useful in the sense that it can be made to . . . make sense in many of the maneuvers of interpersonal relations that have effect; whereas operations on any other set of assumptions that explains the same phenomena raise very considerable theoretical difficulties. In other words, it is a matter of what is most generally useful as a theoretical point of departure.

And now to come to the more specific question: Are we not entirely justified—however much we have respect for the fictions which masquerade as human individuals—in realizing that there is a justifiably characterizable self in each person that we deal with?

I, myself, have come gradually to find that unnecessary, whether that be some serious misunderstanding of mine or an insight remains, of course, for others to determine. You know that is true of the evolution of most hypotheses.

One listens, for example, in psychotherapy to a great number of revealing communications, hoping and generally finding finally that the thing has been reviewed very simply in a very small context; and then you run up the flag of hope, and so on, and go hammer and tongs to seeing what can be made of this very simple series of statements which the other fellow won't forget while you are trying to make your point clear. Now, it is decidedly easier to explain this great difficulty on the, you might say, individual-less type of hypothesis than on any other that I have yet dealt with. . . .

NINETEEN

APPEARANCE AND THE SELF: A SLIGHTLY REVISED VERSION

GREGORY P. STONE

Appearance *means* identification of one another,[1] but the question arises whether such identifications follow any ordered pattern. Mead's perspective insists that we look for the meaning of appearance in the responses that appearances mobilize, and we have examined more than 8,000 such responses supplied by interview materials to discern whether they are consistently patterned. Many responses are, of course, gestural in nature. One's appearance commands the gaze of the audience. An eyebrow is fitted. There is a smile or a frown, an approach or withdrawal. One blushes with shame in the shamelessness of the other's appearance or with embarrassment at one's own. The nature of our data precluded the study of such gestural

SOURCE: Gregory P. Stone, "Appearance and the Self: A Slightly Revised Version." Copyright by Houghton Mifflin Company, 1962. From Gregory P. Stone, "Appearance and the Self," in Arnold M. Rose (ed.), *Human Nature and Social Process* (Boston: Houghton Mifflin Company, 1962), pp. 86–118. Reprinted by permission of Houghton Mifflin Company and the author.

[1]The question of how the meaning of appearance is guaranteed is germane and recognized, but will not be treated here. Aside from the "teamwork" analyzed so carefully by Goffman in his *Presentation of Self in Everyday Life* (5), other guarantees are suggested in his "Symbols of Class Status." (4)

responses unless they were recorded by the interviewer. Consequently, apparent discourse was examined for the most part—talk about appearance aroused, in particular, by clothing. Over 200 married men and women living in a Midwestern community of 10,000 population supplied the talk. Of the many statements these people made about dress, only statements referring to those who wore the clothing in question were scrutinized. These were construed as identifications of the wearer. Here we shall be concerned for simplicity's sake with only two modes of such responses: (1) responses made about the wearer of clothes, by others who, we shall say, *review* his clothing; and (2) responses made about the wearer by the wearer—we shall call these responses *programs*. A third mode of response is relevant, but will not be considered here—the wearer's imagination of other's responses to his dress.

When programs and reviews tend to coincide, the self of the one who appears (the one whose clothing has elicited such responses) is validated or established; when such responses tend toward disparity, the self of the one who appears is challenged, and conduct may be expected to move in the direction of some redefinition of the challenged self. Challenges and validations of the self, therefore, may be regarded as aroused by personal appearance. As a matter of fact, the dimensions of the self emphasized by James, Mead, Cooley, and Sullivan effectively embrace the content of the responses to clothing we examined in our quest for the meaning of appearance. In response to his clothes, the wearer was cast as a social object—a ''me''—or, as we shall say, given some identity. A person's dress also imbued him with attitudes by arousing others' anticipations of his conduct as well as assisting the mobilizations of his own activity. In Mead's terms, then, the self as object and attitude is established by appearance. However, the most frequent response to dress was the assignment of value-words to the wearer. One's clothes impart value to the wearer, both in the wearer's own eyes and in the eyes of others. Both Sullivan and Cooley underscore the relevance of value for any adequate conceptualization of the self; Sullivan, by referring to the self as comprised by the ''reflected *appraisals* of others,'' the ''good'' and ''bad'' me (15, pp. 161–162), Cooley, by emphasizing ''imagined *judgments* of appearance.'' Finally, Cooley's emphasis upon self-*feeling,* or the self, as *sentiment* was provided with empirical support by this analysis. A person's clothing often served to establish a mood for himself capable of eliciting validation in the reviews aroused from others. The meaning of appearance, therefore, is the establishment of identity, value, mood, and attitude for the one who appears by the coincident programs and reviews awakened by his appearance. These terms require further discussion.

IDENTITY

It is almost enough to demonstrate the significance of the concept ''identity'' by referring to the rapidity with which it has caught on in social science. Most compellingly re-introduced to the social sciences by Erik Erikson, the term has provided many social-psychological insights. Specifically, fruitful inquiries into the sociological implications of the ego have been made possible by releasing the investigator from the commitment to argument and partisanship that alternative concepts such as ''personality'' demand. Identity, as a concept, is without any history of polemics. However, the impetus to discovery afforded by the term has been so great that its meaning threatens to spill over the bounds of analytic utility. Before its meaning becomes totally lost by awakening every conceivable response in every conceivable investigator (like the term ''personality''), the concept must be salvaged.

Almost all writers using the term imply that identity establishes *what* and *where* the person is in social terms. It is not a substitute word for ''self.'' Instead, when one has identity, he is *situated*—that is, cast in the shape of a social object by the acknowledgment of his participation or membership in social relations. One's identity is established when others *place* him as a social object by assigning him the same words of identity that he appropriates for himself or *announces*. It is in the coincidence of placements and announcements that identity becomes a meaning of the self, and often such placements and announcements are aroused by apparent symbols such as uniforms. The policeman's uniform, for example, is an announcement of his identity as policeman and validated by others' placements of him as policeman.

Such a conception of identity is, indeed, close to Mead's conception of the ''me,'' the self as object related to and differentiated from others. To situate the person by establishing some identity for him is, in a sense, to give him position, and a pun permits further elucidation of the concept: identity is established as a consequence of two processes, apposition and opposition, a bringing together and setting apart. To situate the person as a social object is to bring him together with other objects so situated, and, at the same time to set him apart from still other objects. *Identity is intrinsically associated with all the joinings and departures of social life*. To have an identity is to join with some and depart from others, to enter and leave social relations at once.

In fact, the varieties of identity are isomorphic with the varieties of social relations. At least four different types of words were used to place and announce the identities communicated by clothing: (1) universal words designating one's humanity, such as age, gender, and community (we call these "universal" identities because people everywhere make such distinctions); (2) names and nicknames; (3) titles, such as occupational and marital titles; (4) "relational categories," such as customer, movie-goer, jazz fan, and the like. Social relations, viewed as ongoing transactions, can be classified according to the identities which must be placed and announced to permit entry into the transaction. Thus, *human relations* are those requiring the placement and announcement of such universal identities as age, gender, or community membership. *Interpersonal relations* are those that may only be entered by an exchange of names or nicknames,[2] while *structural relations* are those that may only be entered by exchanging a name for a title. Finally, we may speak of *masses* as social relations that may be anonymously entered.

The distinction between interpersonal and structural relations seems, at this point, to have the greatest analytical utility. Since one's name ordinarily outlasts one's titles, interpersonal relations probably provide an important social basis for the continuity of identity. Structural relations, on the other hand, are more discontinuous and changing.

We can note how one's name is established by dress if we imagine Teddy Roosevelt without the pince-nez, F. D. R. without the cigarette holder, or Jimmy Carter without his teeth. One of our informants, a small-time real estate operator, was well aware of the significance of clothing in his attempts to personalize his occupational identity. Asked, "What do your fellow workers say and

[2]This characterization of interpersonal relations is not reversible. The exchange of names does not guarantee that an interpersonal relationship will always be established.

think when you wear something new for the first time on the job?" he replied:

> Well, I always have a new hat, and I suppose my clientele talks about it. But, you know, I always buy cheap ones and put my name in them. I leave them around in restaurants and places like that intentionally. It has advertising value.

The interviewer asked later, "Would you rather wear a greater variety or a smaller variety of clothes on the job?" and the informant replied:

> A small variety so you will look the same everyday. So people will identify you. They look for the same old landmark.

In response to the same question, a working man who had recently opened a small business said:

> A smaller variety for both sales and shop. I think if a person dresses about the same continually, people will get to know you. Even if they don't know your name, you're easier to describe. I knew an insurance man once who used a wheel chair. Everyone knew him because of that chair. It's the same with clothes.

Distinctive persistent dress may replace the name as well as establish it!

On the other hand, one's career within the structural relation is marked by changes of title, and the change of title demands a change of dress. All of the men in this study were presented with the following story:

> John had an excellent record as foreman in an automobile factory. Eventually, he and two other foremen were promoted to the position of division head. John was happy to get the job, because of the increase in pay. However, he continued to wear his old foreman's vest and work clothes to the office. This went on for several months and the division heads he had been promoted with began to avoid him at lunch and various social gatherings. They had dressed from the beginning in business suits and had mingled more and more with older managerial employees. John found himself without friends in the office.

When asked, "What finally happened to John?" about 80 per cent of the men interviewed predicted termination, demotion, or no further promotion. (3, pp. 47–51). One informant, interviewed by the writer, quite seriously suggested that John was a potential suicide.

Appearances, then, are interrupted in social structures as identities are set apart; appearances, so to speak, endure in interpersonal relations where identities are brought into closer proximity. Yet we find that, in the context of structural relations, identities are given a somewhat different cast than in interpersonal relations. In the former, identities are qualified along the axis of value, in the latter, more usually along the axis of mood.

QUALIFICATIONS OF IDENTITY: VALUE AND MOOD

To engage meaningfully in some transactions it is enough to know merely "what" the parties are—to know their identities. This would seem often to be the case in the anonymous transactions of the masses. As Louis Wirth used to tell his students in his elaborations of the "massive" character of urban life, "You go to a bootblack to have your shoes shined, not to save your soul." The implication is, I think, that, when we become concerned with the bootblack's moods or his larger worth in terms of some scheme of value, our relations with him will lose their anonymous character. By so doing, we have perhaps disadvantaged ourselves of the freedom the city offers. Ordinarily, however, if transactions persistently engage the same persons or seem likely to continue into an ill-defined future, it is not enough merely to establish identities in the guarantee of meaningful discourse. Thus, when we are introduced to strangers who may become acquaintances or possibly friends, we *express* our pleasure with the introduction, and such expressions are ordinarily *appreciated* by those we have met. Or, meeting an acquaintance on the street, we inquire how he *feels* before the

discourse is initiated. In a certain sense, interpersonal relations demand that the *moods* of the participants be established (as well as their names or nicknames) prior to the initiation of discursive phases in the transaction: that "Joe" or "Jane" is mad or sad will have definite consequences for the talk with "Jim" or "Joan."

Ordinarily, also, before a title is bestowed upon us or before we are invested with office, our identities must undergo qualifying scrutiny. In such cases, the qualification does not usually get accomplished in terms of our anger or sadness, but in terms of some assessment of our former careers and future prospects with reference to their *worth*. The tendency is to assess worth in terms of a relatively objective set of standards that can transcend the whim of the assessing one and the whimsy of the one assessed. Upon the initiation of what we have called structural relations, the *values* of the participating persons (as well as their titles) must be established.

Value and mood provide two fundamental axes along which the qualifications of identity are accomplished in *appraising* and *appreciative* responses to appearance. This seems obvious on the face of it: that a teacher is competent has different consequences for faculty-student transactions than that a teacher is a teacher; and that a teacher is temperamental or easy-going presents the possibility of a still different set of consequences for upcoming discussions. The differences between value and mood are suggested by the distinction that Park has made between interests and sentiments, that Helen Lynd has made between guilt and shame, or that Kenneth Burke has made between poetry and pathos (*poeima* and *pathema*). It is the difference between virtue and happiness, and, as we know full well, the virtuous man is not necessarily happy, nor the happy man necessarily virtuous. The problem arises when we observe that happiness may be a virtue in some social circles or that one may be happy because he is virtuous (cynics might say "smug"). Value and mood, so patently distinguishable in discourse, merge together inextricably in experience. Can we conceive of feelings of pride without reference to a set of values? I think not, although it does seem possible to conceive of merit without feeling. Yet, in situations that are totally value-relevant, totally given over to matters of appraisal—the courtroom, the examination, the military review—the very constriction of feeling and mood, their suppression, may saturate the situation with a grim somberness that can transform dispassion into passion—as the austerity of the courtroom has provided a curiously fitting context for the impassioned plea, the silence of the examination room is interrupted by nervous laughter; the ordered rhythm of the march engenders song.

As Helen Lynd has written of guilt and shame, so we conceive value and mood:

> They are in no sense polar opposites. Both the guilt axis and the shame axis enter into the attitudes and behavior of most people, and often into the same situation. But there are for different persons different balances and stresses between the two, and it does matter whether one lives more in terms of one or the other (9, p. 208).

And we would add that one differentiating condition is the type of social relation that regularly mobilizes the time and attention of the person. Thus, we have found that value has a greater saliency for most men in their conceptions of self and others while, for most women, mood has a greater saliency. This finding is ascribed in part to the American male's more frequent participation and absorption in the structure of work relations, in comparison with the American woman's more frequent preoccupation with the interpersonal relations she carried on with friends and acquaintances.

It is much more difficult to characterize value and mood than it has been to characterize identity. However, the responses to dress that were classified as words of value manifested the following references: (1) to *consensual goals*, such as wealth, prestige, or power; (2) to *achievement standards*, universalistic criteria applied to the assessment of one's proximity to or remoteness from such goals; (3) *norms* or rules regulating the pursuit of consensual goals; and (4) *moral precepts* stipulating valued behavior often employed in the assessment of character (e.g., cleanliness, politeness, thriftiness, and the like). Responses classified as mood-words were even more difficult to order, including reference to ease and lack of ease in social transactions, liking, disliking, fearing, and dreading. Anxiety, monotony, rapture, and surprise also were included in the category, as were references to that ill-defined state which the informants called morale.

It may be helpful to borrow again from Helen Lynd, using her technique for contrasting guilt and shame to contrast value and mood. Table 1 attempts to state the social relations for which value and mood *ordinarily* have the greatest saliency, the nature of the criteria which are applied in the establishment of value and mood, the processes by which these qualifications of identity are established, and finally the consequences for the social relationship when identities are qualified along one or the other axis. I wish to emphasize that the summary presentation in Table 1 is in no way meant to be definitive, and that the axes which are characterized as value and mood, although they are set down in a contrasting manner, are not meant to be established as polar opposites. In particular, *sentiments* represent a convergence of the two axes in the qualification of identity. Sentiments are valued feelings or felt values, as for example in Cooley's "looking-glass self"—the sentiments of pride or mortification are *expressive* responses to the judgments or *appraisals* of others. Moreover, it may well be the case that values more often qualify identities, while moods are more closely linked to attitudes.[3]

---

[3]See my "Personal Acts," *Symbolic Interaction*, I (Fall, 1977), pp. 2–19, especially pp. 5–7.

TABLE 1.   Value and Mood as Axes Along Which Qualifications of Identity Are Established

Phases	Value Axis	Mood Axis
Relational Basis	*Structural relations*	*Interpersonal relations*
Criteria	Universalistic Abstract Objective Detachment Poetic (Pious) Neutrality Scalar	Particularistic Concrete Subjective Attachment Pathetic Affectivity Absolute
Establishment	Rationalized Investment Conformity-deviation with respect to universal rules or a social code Future reference Legitimated by appeals to the appraisals of others	Spontaneously communicated Preoccupation or rapture Ease-dis-ease with respect to engagement in social transactions Present reference Legitimated by appeals to the expressions of the self
Relational Consequences	Stratification	Rapport

ACTIVATIONS OF IDENTITY: ATTITUDE

In a brilliant discussion, Kenneth Burke has established the essential ambiguity of the term "attitude": an attitude can be looked upon as a substitute for an act—the "truncated act" of John Dewey—or as an incipient act—a "beginning" from the standpoint of George H. Mead (1, pp. 235–247). The establishment of identity, value, and mood by appearances represents the person as *there, stratified* or assigned a particular distance, and *rapt* or engrossed. There remains the matter of his activation, the assessment of the path along which he has traveled, the path he is travelling, and where he is about to go. These aspects of the person—that he has acted, is acting, and will act further—are also established by appearance. We refer to them as *attitudes*.[4] Attitudes are *antici-pated* by the reviewers of an appearance, *proposed* by the one who appears.

Appearance substitutes for past and present action and, at the same time, conveys an *incipience* permitting others to anticipate what is about to occur. Specifically, clothing represents our action, past, present, and future, as it is established by the proposals and anticipations that occur in every social transaction. Without further elaboration, I think that this can be clearly seen in the doffing of dress, signaling that an act is done (and another act about to begin), the donning of dress, signaling the initiation of a new act, and the wearing of dress, signaling that action is going on.

---

[4]Of course, the concept "attitude" is of central significance for the social psychology of George Herbert Mead, but, in some ways, it is the least satisfying of the terms we have characterized here. All the meanings of dress or appearance have an attitudinal or "activated" character. In particular, programs and reviews may be conceived as incipient, truncated, or on-going acts. It may be, in fact, that the concept "attitude" is of a different order from the concepts "identity," "value," and "mood," asking the observer to inquire not into the context or structure of the event under scrutiny, but rather to seize those events in their full-blown capacity as processes.

APPEARANCE AND THE SELF

The meaning of appearance, therefore, can be studied by examining the responses mobilized by clothes. Such responses take on at least four forms: identities are placed, values appraised, moods appreciated, and attitudes anticipated. Appearance provides the identities, values, moods, and attitudes of the person-in-communication, since it arouses in others the assignment of words embodying these dimensions to the one who appears. As we have noted earlier, this is only one part of the total picture.

Cooley, Mead, and Harry Stack Sullivan have reminded us often that such responses are reflexive in character, reverberating back upon the one who produces them and the one toward whom they are directed. In short, identifications of others are always complemented by identifications of the self, in this case, responses to one's own appearance. In a variety of ways, as a matter of fact, reviews of a person's appearance are intricately linked with the responses he makes to his own appearance. We have called the process of making identifications of the one who appears by that one a *program*. Progammatic responses parallel the responses that have been called reviews. One appears, reflects upon that appearance, and appropriates words of identity, value, mood, or attitude for himself in response to that appearance. By appearing, the person *announces* his identity, *shows* his value, *expresses* his mood, or *proposes* his attitude. If the meaning of appearance is "supplied" by the reviews others make of one's appearance, it is established or consensually validated, as Sullivan would have said, by the relative coincidence of such reviews with the program of the one who appears. In other words, when one's dress calls out in others the "same" identifications of the wearer as it calls out in the wearer, we may speak of the appearance as meaningful. It turns out, in fact, that this is the self, and this may be diagrammed as in Table 2.

In appearance, then, selves are established and mobilized. As the self is dressed, it is simultaneously addressed, for, whenever we clothe ourselves, we dress "toward" or address some audience whose validating responses are essential to the establishment of our self. Such responses may, of course, also be challenges, in which case a new program is aroused. This intimate linkage of self and clothing was masterfully caricatured by a forty-year-old carpenter's wife who was herself working in a local factory. Our guess is that a few bottles of beer were conducive to the spontaneous flow of words, but their import is none the less striking. The woman had interpreted a modified TAT scene as a religious depiction, and the interviewer asked her, after the completion of the stories, which card she liked best:

[Interviewer: Of those three, which did you like best? . . . Oh, that is kinda hard for me to do. I like them all. This one here is good, and that one is good, and that one is good. I think, of course, religion should come first, but I still think this is first right here—of

TABLE 2. Schematic Representation of the Meaning of Appearance, Emphasizing the Validation of Personal Appearance and the Establishment of the Self

Program of Appearance	Review of Appearance			
	Placement	*Appraisal*	*Appreciation*	*Anticipation*
Announcement	Identity			
Show		Value		
Expression			Mood	
Proposal				Attitude

her trying to help this girl. [The card depicts a well-dressed woman talking with another woman in rather drab masculine dress.] Looks to me like she is just telling her what she should do and how she should dress. Don't look very nice. I think that has a lot to do with a person's life afterwards. If they can get straightened out on their personal appearance, they can get straightened out in their religion a lot quicker. You take personal appearance; goes with their minds. Their mind has to work to go with that. They get that straightened out, I think they can go back to religion and get that straightened out. I don't go to church now, but I used to be, and I am still, and always will be, regardless of what it is I ever do. I smoke a cigarette, drink a bottle of beer. I'm not Catholic. I'm Protestant. Church is my first thing. But this [informant hits the picture] comes first, before church. I don't care what anybody says. Clothes, our personal appearance, and getting our minds settled is how we should do. Some people don't believe that, but I do, 'cause you can go into a church and worship, but that ain't all that makes a go of the world. You have got to have something beside that. I don't care how much you worship. People can laugh at you. When you go into a church, they laugh at a girl dressed like this girl is or this woman is. They'll think she is not all there. But, if she gets herself fixed up, and looks nice, and goes to church like this picture here, they'll think she knows what she's talking about. I've seen too much of that. In other words, *clothes, personal appearance, can make one's life*. [Said slowly, deliberately, with much emphasis.] There is something about it that gives you courage. Some people would call it false courage, but I wouldn't. . . . I think anyone has to have a certain amount of clothes to give them courage. It ain't false courage either or false pride. It's just it. . . . Suppose it was just like it was when I went to that banquet tonight. Everybody told me how nice I looked, but I didn't think so. I had to feel right . . . when I get the dress I feel right in, I feel like a million dollars. It makes an altogether different person out of me. That's an awful thing to say, but that's true for me.

Similar, but less dramatic, remarks abound in our interview materials. All point to the undeniable and intimate linkage of self and appearance. As a matter of fact, the analysis we have made permits a suggested modification of perhaps the best definition of the self in the social-psychological literature. Lindesmith and Strauss

> . . . think of the self as: (1) a set of more or less consistent and stable responses on a conceptual level, which (2) exercise a regulatory function over other responses of the same organism at lower levels (8, p. 416).

Dispensing with the notion of levels of behavior, which seems unnecessarily misleading (surely the self exercises a regulatory function over discourse—a set of conceptual responses!), we suggest the following definition: *the self is any validated program which exercises a regulatory function over other responses of the same organism, including the formulation of other programs*. What this definition does is spell out the regulatory responses—that is, one's announcements, shows, expressions, or proposals—while linking their consistency to the consensual validations of others. Such selves are established in significant appearances which provide the foundations of significant discourse and which, of course, may be played back upon and altered as the discourse transpires.

APPEARANCE AND THE EARLY EMERGENCE OF THE SELF

In explaining the emergence of the self, George H. Mead discusses at length the two stages of "play" and the "game." Prior to entering the stage of play, however, the child must have acquired a rudimentary language at least. We will call this early stage of rudimentary communication "pre-play." For Mead, the emergence of the self in society is inextricably linked to the expansion and consolidation of personal communication as the child participates in and successively generalizes an ever widening universe of discourse—that set of social relations that is mobilized by the symbols the child acquires. We may infer that the type of discourse changes in the different stages of the emergence of the self and shall suggest some possibilities. We shall demonstrate, however, the changing character of appearance in these stages. In particular, we will note how these changing appearances hinder or facilitate the establishment of sexual identity or gender for the child.

PRE-PLAY, INVESTITURE, AND THE UBIQUITOUS MOTHER

It is very difficult to establish in any verifiable way how the child acquires its earliest significant symbols, whether they be gestures or words, because the investigator cannot enter into the rudimentary "prototaxic" communication of the infant. At best, he can observe, make inferences, and check those inferences out against the inferences of family members.

It seems to be the case, however, that some "initiative" is required from the child in his early learning process. Cooley, for example, observed that parents imitate the noises and sounds of their very young children in greater degree than those children imitate the noises and sounds of parents (2, p. 25). These observations have since received further empirical support (10, p. 41). Apparently this phenomenon of "parental imitation" or, more accurately, parental re-presentation is usually linked with the infant's babbling. Through babbling, the child hits upon a word-like sound (often "ma-ma"). This sound is then re-presented to the child as a word, together with the appropriate behavior that is the meaning of the word. Through repetition, the child takes over the response pattern it calls out in the adult, and the sound consequently becomes a significant symbol within the domestic universe of discourse.[5]

[5]There is further probative support for the hypothesis in the research of Omar K. Moore at Yale University, where he is teaching two-and-a-half year old children to read and write. The child is first encouraged to "play" at an IBM typewriter—akin to babbling. An adult responds to the play by re-presenting the letter sound. Eventually the child takes over this response pattern of the adult and "learns" the letters of the keyboard. On this point, see the preceding article by Harry Stack Sullivan, "The Self as Concept and Illusion," in this volume.

Another hypothesis seeking to explain the infant's earliest entrance into communication has been proposed by I. Latif.[6] Initially, the presumed discomfort of the infant is "communicated" by a gross writhing and wriggling of the whole body, setting up a series of responses in the parental person—feeding, cuddling, diaper-changing, and so on. Over time these parental responses become differentiated out as the gross movement of the child is progressively curtailed. Ultimately, the mere beginning of movement can elicit the appropriate parental response. Significant gestures have been established.

The point to all of this is that the child enters discursive communication by, in a sense, "initiating" activity construed as symbolic by parental persons and established as meaningful by their persistent cooperative response. In contrast, the appearance of the infant is imposed. The diaper folded in front *invests* the child with masculinity; in back, with femininity. Or dressing the child in blue invests the child with masculinity; in pink, with femininity. In this way, the responses of the world toward the child are differentially mobilized. The world handles the pink-clad child and the blue-clad child differently. The pink-clad child is *identified* differently. It is "darling," "beautiful," "sweet," or "graceful"; the blue-clad child is "handsome," "strong," or "agile." At a very early age the investiture of the child provides the materials out of which the reflected sexual identity and its qualifications are formed. And in America the process of investiture is accomplished overwhelmingly by the mother.

One hundred and eighty-five of our informants were asked, "What is the earliest recollection you have of being made to wear particular clothes?" Then we asked, "Who made you wear them?" One hundred and twenty-six provided determinate answers to the question. Of these, 82 per cent named the mother as the "instrument of coercion"; 10 per cent named both parents. For more

[6]Discussed in Lindesmith and Strauss (8, p. 166).

than 90 per cent of those recalling coercive investiture, the mother was recalled as the agent, usually the sole agent. There were no sex differences in these recollections. She was the sole agent for 83 per cent of the men and for 81 per cent of the women. She acted in conjunction with the father for 13 percent of the men and for 8 per cent of the women.

It is sociologically significant, of course, that the prime agent of investiture for the men of this Midwestern community was a woman, and no matter how much we might be inclined to disparage Geoffrey Gorer's study of "the American people," these data do suggest that Gorer's "encapsulated mother hypothesis" has some basis in fact (6, pp. 55−68, 124−132).

Because of the ubiquity of the American mother as the prime agent of socialization for the child, it will be recalled, Gorer maintained that the "superego" of the American male was characterized by a significant feminine component manifested in extraordinary anxiety about and fear of homosexuality. We need not accept the entire line of analysis when we recognize, first, that the "significant other" for the male child in our sample has been almost unanimously recalled as the "significant mother," and, second, that the adequate early formulation of a sexual identity may have been impeded among men. Indeed, it may not be a "homosexual anxiety" that typifies American men as much as a generalized "sexual anxiety." If he is represented at all by the men of the Midwestern community, the American male may have found it difficult very early in life to establish who he was in sexual terms. Consequently, an adequate basis in which to "ground" subsequent announcements of maleness may not have been provided. As very young children, most of these men were invested with a program of appearance fashioned exclusively by women. This investiture process persisted beyond infancy, even, in some cases, into relatively late childhood. Their first reflected glimpse of themselves was provided by the eyes of a woman—a woman who, in fact, saw

many of those men as girls. Some were dressed as little girls.

A fifty-three year old postal clerk provided a vivid recollection of the early stages in the life cycle as they were represented by dress:

> I can remember back in the South, forty-five years ago, the children—boys—always wore dresses up to the time they were three or four years old. When I was about five, six, seven, or eight, they wore those little Fauntleroy suits. God damn! I hated those. Then knickers came. I wore those until I was about fifteen years old. I was fifteen and a half when I had my first long pants suit.

A sixty-three year old carpenter, born on a Midwestern farm, suggests that the earliest dress of little boys was not restricted to Southern regions:

> Just one thing that always stood out in my mind. I wore dresses until I was six years old, and, as I remember, they were the Mother Hubbard type.

Knee pants, of course, were much more frequently recalled by the men in the sample as early garments in which they were forcibly dressed by the mother, and these were often interpreted as feminine representations. Asked to state his earliest memory of being forced to wear particular clothing, a twenty-seven year old oven-tender replied:

> Knee pants. [Interviewer: Who made you wear them?] Mother.
> [Interviewer: How did you feel about that?] I just felt like a girl in them. They reminded me so much of a dress.

The revulsion against being a "sissy," recalled by many of the male informants in the sample, was generally remembered in the context of investiture in short pants or "fussy" clothing. Again, the investiture was accomplished by the mother, whose decision they could not appeal.

Investiture takes on even greater significance for the interpretation of the meaning that clothing has for men in our society when we recall our earlier remarks about the establishment of identity. Identity, as it has been apprehended here, is only established in the collective or transactive process of announcement and placement. The knowing of gender is, as we have said, known silently. To appear in the dress of either sex is to announce one's gender, and the apparent announcement is seldom questioned. The gender is confirmed by ratifying placements. Dressed as someone he is not, by a ubiquitous mother, in clothing that is employed arbitrarily by his peers (and himself) to establish who he is, the American male may, indeed, have been disadvantaged very early with respect to the formulation of a sense of sexual identity. Advantages, rather, accrued to the female, who from the earliest age was dressed as she was by a mother from whose perspective she was provided with an adequate conception of herself in sexual terms.[7]

PLAY, COSTUME, AND DRESSING OUT

In his discussion of the development of the self (more exactly, the development of the "me"), George H. Mead does not concern himself so much with the establishment of the self *by* others—the phenomenon of investiture—as with the development of a self-conception *reflected* by the attitudes of others. Such attitudes or roles (Mead uses the term interchangeably in his discussion of the self) are at first acted out. By acting out the role of the other, the child develops a conception of his own attitude or role as differentiated from and related to the adopted role. The acting out of the other's role is caricatured by the play of the child in which he amuses himself by acting out the role of the parents, the school-teacher, the policeman, the cowboy, the Indian, the storekeeper, the customer, and various other roles that constitute the institu-

[7]There may be a generational problem involved, but we cannot consider that problem in this place. We are speaking here of those who were adults by 1950, and whose childhoods occurred in the 1930's or earlier.

tional fabric and legendary *personae* of the larger community or society. A mere consideration of these roles, incidentally, betrays the fact that at least two kinds of socialization go on in the stage of play. First, there is a genuine *anticipatory socialization* in which the child acts out roles that might quite realistically be expected to be adopted or encountered in later life, such as parental roles, common occupations, or customer. Second, there is a process of *fantastic socialization* in which the child acts out roles that can seldom, if ever, be expected to be adopted or encountered in later life—cowboy and Indian, for example. This is a point to which we will return.

Now this phase of play in the development of the self cannot be accomplished without costume. Acting out of role implies that one appear out of role. Play demands that the players leave themselves behind so to speak. The players may do this symbolically by doffing their ordinary dress and donning extraordinary dress so that the play may proceed. Playing the role of the other requires that the player *dress out* of the role or roles that are acknowledged to be his own. Costume, therefore, is a kind of magical instrument. It includes all apparent misrepresentations of the wearer. As such its significance or meaning (the collective response that is mobilized—the coincidence of the wearer's program with the review of the other) is built upon the mutual trust of the one who appears and his audience. Collusion is required to carry off the misrepresentation: the parent, for example, cannot "really" insist that his child is, in fact, not a cowboy or a spaceman. Play is easily transformed into a vast conspiratorial secret, if it has not, in fact, begun secretly. As Huizinga has expressed it:

> The exceptional and special position of play is most tellingly illustrated by the fact that it loves to surround itself with an air of secrecy. Even in early childhood, the charm of play is enhanced by making a "secret" out of it. This is for *us*, not for the "others." . . . The "differentness" and secrecy of play are most vividly expressed in "dressing up." Here the "extraordinary" nature of play reaches

perfection. The disguised or masked individual ''plays'' another part, another being. He *is* another being. The terrors of childhood, open-hearted gaiety, mystic fantasy and sacred awe are all inextricably entangled in this strange business of masks and disguises. (7, pp. 12–13).

This element of secrecy would seem to imbue the play of children with sentiment—a nexus of value and mood—establishing for the child *involvements* with the identities that are appropriated in play in addition to the sheer objective *commitments* to such identities, emphasized by Mead. Making the point in another way, it may be that the consequences of childhood play, at least for some children, is not merely the formulation of the self as an object—an identity—differentiated from and related to the objects of play, but the establishment of the self as a sentiment—a base of ''show'' and expression—as Cooley insisted.

All respondents were asked, ''When you were a child, did you ever dress up in anyone else's clothes?'' Of the 180 replying to the question, 35 per cent disavowed dressing up in other people's clothing when they were children. The disavowal was predominantly male. Fifty-nine per cent of the men replying to the question maintained that they had not dressed up in other people's clothing when they were children, and that figure compares to 14 per cent for the women responding to the question. Again, in a sense, the male child seems to have been ''disadvantaged'' in the phase of play. The clothing of the others in his earliest social world is not made available to him.

Indeed, one of the still striking features of childhood costume is the fact that boys' costumes are sold in considerably greater quantities than are girl costumes.''[8] Commercial costumes are generally more fantastic than the costumes available from the cast-off clothing of family members. The disavowals of the men do not mean, of course, that the men did not dress out when they were children,

but that they did not dress out in clothing ordinarily worn by other people. Assuming that the ''dressing out'' of men, at least in the higher ranges of the status order, was facilitated by commercial costume and that the ''dressing out'' of women was facilitated by the ordinary dress of others, it may well be that the early conception of self established by men in the phase of play in this country and among the generations interviewed is, in fact, more fantastic than the early conception of self established by women, who can more often reflect upon their own appearance in the dress of and from the standpoint of others who are the *real* population of their social world. But this is a point for which we have no direct evidence.

Of course, the most striking difference between the sexes with respect to the costume of play is, as we have said, found among those who dressed up in other people's clothing at all when they were children. More than half of the men did not, as Table 3 shows, and more than 85 per cent of the women did. Those who did recall dressing up in other people's clothing when they were children were asked whose clothing was worn, and the responses were coded for the person standing in the most ''objectively'' intimate relationship to the informant. Table 3 shows that the parent of the same sex as the informant was the most frequently mentioned source of childhood costume in play.

Yet the male is again ''disadvantaged.'' Even if we exclude from the analysis those informants who could not recall dressing in other's clothing during childhood, men are still significantly underrepresented among those who dressed in the clothing of the father, and women are significantly overrepresented among those who dressed in the clothing of the mother. Childhood play was accomplished by donning the costume of the relevant adult female model—the mother—among the women of the sample, while many men were denied the costume of the relevant adult male model. Among the men who could recall dressing in other's clothing, brothers and extended kin acted as sources of costume in somewhat greater than expected proportions (as did sisters and

---

[8]The assertion may be verified by telephoning the toy department in any large store. I have not yet found any exceptions to the rule.

TABLE 3. The Most Intimate Sources of Costume Mentioned by Midwestern Men and Women in Their Recollections of Childhood Play

| Most Intimate Sources of Childhood Costume | Sex of Respondents | | | | Totals | |
| | Male | | Female | | | |
	Number	Per Cent	Number	Per Cent	Number	Per Cent
None	50	58.8	13	13.7	63	35.0
Parent, same sex	13	15.3	48	50.5	61	33.9
Parent, opposite sex	2	2.4	—	0.0	2	1.1
Sibling, same sex	6	7.1	10	10.5	16	8.9
Sibling, opposite sex	2	2.4	2	2.1	4	2.2
Extended kin	5	5.9	8	8.4	13	7.2
Unrelated adults and peers	7	8.2	14	14.7	21	11.7
Totals	85	100.1	95	99.9	180	100.0

$\chi^2 = 43.791$ * $\qquad\qquad\qquad\qquad$ $.05 > p < .001$

* The last five rows were combined in the computation of the chi-square, which is for a sixfold table with two degrees of freedom. If the first row is eliminated from the analysis, and the chi-square computed for the second row and the combined remaining rows by sex, then $\chi^2 = 4.432$, and $.05 > p > .02$.

mothers!—but the numbers there are very small), while, among the women making such recollections, the mother was the sole source of childhood costume noticeably overrepresented. Small wonder that we are tempted to generalize that the men of our sample had a difficult time developing an adequate conception of their sexual identity. The adult models were often not available to them.

It may well be that discourse takes on a characteristic form during the stage of play. For one thing, the speech of the child may be what Piaget has called "egocentric." (12). At least, the child enters the stage of play before his egocentric language dwindles to less than 25 per cent of his discursive communication as recorded by Piaget and his associates. At this point the child is capable of socialized speech. Piaget hypothesizes that this occurs around the age of 7 or 8. On the other hand, the discourse of play is highly suggestive of "parataxic" communication. Sullivan, incidentally, did not restrict the concept to the depiction of psychotic behavior:

Now let us notice a feature of all interpersonal relations. . . . This is the parataxic, as I call it, concomitant in life. By this I mean that not only are there quite tangible people involved . . ., but also somewhat fantastic constructs of those people are involved. . . . These psychotic elaborations of imaginary people and imaginary performances are spectacular and seem very strange. But the fact is that in a great many relationships of the most commonplace kind—with neighbors, enemies, acquaintances, and even such statistically determined people as the collector and the mailman—variants of such distortions often exist. The characteristics of a person that would be agreed to by a large number of competent observers may not appear to you to be the characteristics of the person toward whom you are making adjustive or maladjustive movements. The *real* characteristics of the other fellow at that time may be of negligible importance to the interpersonal situation. This we call *parataxic distortion* (14, pp. 25–26).

Consider a typical instance of play. The father returns home from work, is ambushed at the door, and "shot" by the young cowboy. The transaction has no "meaning" within the *real* father-son relationship—some psychoanalysts to the contrary notwithstanding! Instead, father and son are "of negligible importance to the interpersonal situation." The "fantastic constructs" of cowboy and Indian or "good guy" and "bad guy" are the relevant personifications or identifications with reference to which the discursive meaning is established. Of course, *as father,* the adult enables the young actor to carry off the performance, imbuing the play, as we have said, with a secrecy shared by *father and son,* charging the play with affect or mood.

THE GAME, THE UNIFORM, AND DRESSING IN

While the costume of play may be construed as any apparent misrepresentation of the self, permitting the wearer to become another, the uniform is precisely any apparent representation of the self, at once reminding the wearer and others of an *appropriate* identity, a *real* identity. The team-player is uniformed; the play-actor is costumed. When we asked our informants their earliest recollections of wanting to wear any particular item of clothing, they responded almost unanimously by recalling their earliest self-conscious appropriations of the dress of their peer groups. In a sense, the earliest items of clothing they wanted comprised the *uniforms* of the peer circle.

Among the men who experienced the wish for particular items of clothing in late childhood, most were concerned with escaping the investitures of the mother. The tenor of their remarks conveyed the undesirability of the clothing they were forced to wear as mother's sons. Thereafter, beginning in early adolescence, their comments focused more and more on the desirability and necessity of conforming to the dress established by their peers or demanded by the dating situation. The women, on the other hand, were concerned from the earliest age with the desirability of conforming to the dress of peers. Rather than rejecting their early identities as mother's daughters, they began generally to enter the "game of life" at an earlier age than men, and this was represented in part by their self-conscious wishes to don the uniform of their peer circles at earlier ages.

I do not regard these findings as surprising. Indeed, they have been discussed widely by sociologists and social psychologists. It is recognized that women "come of age" more rapidly than men in our society. My only intention here is to frame these data in the perspective of socialization as it concerns the early development of a self-concept in the stages proposed by Mead. Growing up is dressing in. It is signaled by the wish to dress like others who are, in turn, like one's self. The earlier representation of the self is formulated in play which is facilitated by costume. In play one does dress like others, but like others who are, in that case, unlike one's self.

In the stage of the "game," discourse undoubtedly takes on the character of developed speech—what Piaget called "socialized speech" or what Sullivan called "syntaxis." As the game is played, the person becomes an integral part of an ongoing universe of discourse in every sense. The early socialization has been effected; a self has emerged. These stages and processes have been summarized in Table 4.

LATER SOCIALIZATIONS

It may well be the uneasiness attending the American's view of play and the game that inclines him to relegate such matters to the social world of children and disinclines him to acknowledge their central importance in adulthood. However, especially when we employ these processes to caricature socialization, we should not ignore the fact that they occur throughout life. Life must be viewed as a continuous socialization, a series of careers, in which old identities are sacrificed as new identities are appropriated, at which old relations are left behind as new relations are joined. Each critical turning point of life is marked by a change of dress, and, ordinarily, the new upcoming "game" is rehearsed prior to the entry upon the appropriate field of play.

Such rehearsals may be looked upon as the play of the adult. Momentarily the self is misrepresented as the adult plays at the roles he expects to enact in a near future. Particularly for American

TABLE 4. Tentative Model for the Investigation of Processes of Discourse and Appearance in the Early Establishment of the Self

Stages of Early Socialization	Discursive Processes	Types of Discourse	Apparent Processes	Types of Appearance
Pre-play	1. Parental repre-senation of infant babbling as verbal symbols (Cooley, Markey) 2. Progressive curtailment of whole body movement by parental intervention (Latif)	Conversation of gestures (Mead) Prototaxis (Sullivan) Signal communication, or designation, as in "ma-ma"	Investiture	Representation as infant, young child, and gender
Play	Identification with discrete differentiated others as in role-playing (Mead) 1. Anticipatory socialization 2. Fantastic socialization	Egocentric speech (Piaget) Parataxis (Sullivan)	Dressing out	Misrepresentation of the self Costume
Game	Generalization and consolidation of other roles Taking the role of the "generalized other" or "team"	Socialized speech (Piaget) Syntaxis (Sullivan)	Dressing in	Representation of peer-group affiliation Uniform

men, these rehearsals differ from the play of children by virtue of their rather more "realistic" appropriatness. They are much more frequently genuine *anticipatory socializations*. The child plays many more roles than he will enact in later life, while the roles playfully rehearsed by the adult are generally those he firmly expects to enact later on. But his *fantastic socializations* are also different. More often than is the case for the child, they occur in private. In the bathroom, behind closed doors and before a secret mirror, the man may become for an instant a boxer, an Adonis, an operatic virtuoso. The fantastic play of the child occurs in public, usually in areas set aside by the adult community precisely for such fantastic performances. The fact that the play of the adult is more realistic or appropriate, or, if not, more private, does not gainsay its significance. The rehearsal is often a dress rehearsal, and the more critical the turning point, the more likely the rehearsal is designed as a full dress affair—leaving school and entering the adult world of work, marriage, baptism, and the institutionalized recognition of death.

More realistic than adult play is the adult game. Indeed, we can conceive of life as a series of games—contests and engagements—that mark the progress of careers, culminating in losses and victories for the participants. Participation in the many "games" of life is, again, always represented by appropriate dress which assists the players in their identifications of one another and helps those on the sidelines—the spectators—to know, in fact, what game they are watching. However, these—the play and games of adults—are matters we must leave for a subsequent analysis in another place.

SUMMARY

In this article, we have attempted to show the importance of appearance for any general theory of self that is developed in the perspective of symbolic interaction. We have attempted to show also that the self is established, maintained, and altered in social transactions as much by the communications of appearance as by discourse. In this regard, by analyzing many statements evoked by clothed appearances, we have suggested a definition of the self that may have greater empirical utility than existing definitions. Finally, we have staked out the significance of appearance in the early socialization processes. In doing these things, our "real" goal will have been realized if we have encouraged one or two of our colleagues or future colleagues to look at the cloth on which, as Carlyle noted long ago, society may, in fact, be founded.

REFERENCES

Burke, Kenneth. *A Grammar of Motives*. Englewood Cliffs, N.J.: Prentice-Hall, Inc., 1945.

Cooley, Charles H. *Human Nature and the Social Order*. New York: Charles Scribner's Sons, 1902.

Form, William H., and Gregory P. Stone. *The Social Significance of Clothing in Occupational Life*. East Lansing, Mich.: Michigan State University Agricultural Experiment Station Technical Bulletin 262 (November 1957).

Goffman, Erving. "Symbols of Class Status." *British Journal of Sociology*, Vol. 2 (December 1951), pp. 294–304.

Goffman, Erving. *The Presentation of Self in Everyday Life*. Edinburgh. University of Edinburgh Social Science Research Centre Monograph, No. 2, 1956.

Gorer, Geoffrey. *The American People*. New York: W. W. Norton & Company, Inc., 1948.

Huizinga, Jan. *Homo Ludens: A Study of the Play-Element in Culture*. London: Routledge & Kegan Paul, Ltd., 1949.

Lindesmith, Alfred R., and Anselm L. Strauss. *Social Psychology*. New York: The Dryden Press, 1956.

Lynd, Helen Merrell. *On Shame and the Search for Identity*. New York: Harcourt, Brace and Co., 1958.

Markey, John F. *The Symbolic Process and Its Integration in Children*. London: Kegan Paul, Trench, Trübner and Co., Ltd., 1928.

Mead, George H. *Mind, Self, and Society*, ed. by Charles W. Morris. Chicago: The University of Chicago Press, 1934.

Piaget, Jean. *The Language and Thought of the Child*. New York: Meridian Books, 1955.

Stone, Gregory P. "Personal Acts," *Symbolic Interaction*, 1 (Fall, 1977), pp. 2–19.

Sullivan, Harry Stack. *The Psychiatric Interview*. New York: W. W. Norton & Company, Inc., 1954.

Sullivan, Harry Stack, *The Interpersonal Theory of Psychiatry*. New York: W. W. Norton and Company, Inc., 1953.

TWENTY

THE REAL SELF: FROM INSTITUTION TO IMPULSE[1]

RALPH H. TURNER

It is proposed that people variously recognize their real selves either in feelings and actions of an institutional and volitional nature, such as ambition, morality, and altruism, or in the experience of impulse, such as undisciplined desire and the wish to make intimate revelations to other people. A shift toward the impulse pole seems to be under way and might be plausibly explained by changing cultural definitions of reality, modified terms of social integration, shifting patterns of deprivation, or new opportunities and consequences. Many standard sociological assumptions about social control are imcompatible with the new pattern of self-identification.

Except at the most macroscopic and demographic levels, there is no way to study dynamics and change in social systems without attending to the attitudes and conceptions held by their members.

SOURCE Ralph H. Turner. "The Real Self: From Institution to Impulse." From the *American Journal of Sociology* 81, 5 (March, 1976), pp. 989–1016. Published by the University of Chicago Press.

[1]Expanded version of a paper delivered at the meeting of the American Sociological Association in Denver, August 1971. The author gratefully acknowledges support from the National Institute of Mental Health, grant USPHS MH 16505, and comments on an earlier draft from Erving Goffman, David Heise, Rosabeth Kanter, Leo Kuper, Jerald Schutte, Melvin Seeman, Norman Shosid, Stephan Spitzer, Samuel Surace, and Cornelis Van Zeyl.

Subjective data are essential, because people are not just miniature reproductions of their societies (Bendix 1952; Wrong 1961; Etzioni 1968).

One important sociological tradition of bringing personal dynamics into the analysis of social structure began with Thomas and Znaniecki's (1918) concept of *life organization,* which Park (1931) translated into *conceptions of self* and Kuhn and McPartland (1954) converted into an easily applied set of empirical operations. The *self-conception* as an object arises in connection with self-process (Mead 1934). From early experience with the distinction between *mine* and *yours,* I learn to distinguish between *myself* and others (Cooley 1902).

The present discussion emphasizes a related point, that the idea of a self-as-object permits me to distinguish among the various feelings and actions that emanate from my person. Some emanations I recognize as expressions of my real self; others seem foreign to the real me. I take little credit and assume little blame for the sensations and actions that are peripheral to my real self (Turner 1968). Others are of great significance, because they embody my true self, good or bad. The articulation of *real selves* with social structure should be a major link in the functioning and change of societies. This approach to linking person and social structure is especially compatible with symbolic interactionist and phenomenological perspectives which stress the ongoing creation of reality by each member of society.

The aim of this paper is to elaborate a dimension of self-conception that may have important implications for sociological theories of social control and other aspects of societal functioning. To varying degrees, people accept as evidence of their real selves either feelings and actions with an *institutional* focus or ones they identify as strictly *impulse*. There are suggestive signs that recent decades have witnessed a shift in the locus of self away from the institutional pole and toward that of impulse. This shift may have altered substantially the world of experience in which people orient themselves, setting it apart from the one that much established sociological theory describes. I describe these types, examine the hypothesized shift, suggest some theories that might explain it, and explore the implications for sociological thought.

In another publication I shall describe a modification of the ''Who am I?'' technique that I have developed specifically to gather data for analysis in these terms.

SELF AS OBJECT

Before presenting the thesis, I must briefly outline my assumptions concerning self-conception. Out of the distinctively human reflexive process emerges a sense or conception of self as an object, which, however, has no existence apart from the conceptions and attitudes by which one constitutes it (Blumer 1966, pp. 539–40). Identifying the self is not the same as identifying one's values, and self-conception is not to be confused with ideal self or ego ideal (Kuhn and McPartland 1954, p. 69). The self-conception identifies a person in qualitative and locational terms, not merely in evaluative ones such as self-esteem. The self is an object in relation to other objects, all of which are constantly modified in dynamic interrelationship (Berger 1966). Self-conception refers to the continuity—however imperfect—of an individual's experience of himself in a variety of situations. It is most usefully viewed as an intervening variable between some aspect of social structure and the working of the same or another aspect.

How the self can be so constituted as not to be coterminous with all the feelings and actions that emanate from a person has been a constant source of puzzlement. I suggest tentatively that the demarcation has three components. First, it relies on a more generalized discrimination between the real and the unreal in experience. We identify some experiences as fantasies, hallucinations, dreams, or other forms of the unreal. Under crisis conditions we sometimes go so far as to deceive ourselves concerning the reality of behavior and feelings that are not in accord with self (Spiegel 1969). More often we merely borrow the language of reality and unreality and employ its connotations. Second, bounding the self incorporates the general distinction between *attributions* to person and those to situation (Jones et al. 1971). Behaviors thought to reveal the true self are also ones whose causes are perceived as residing in the person rather than the situation. This distinction relies on a commonsense psychology held by the persons making attributions. The bases for bounding the self necessarily change whenever folk understandings of psychology change. The distinction also inextricably mixes normative conceptions of responsibility with naturalistic ones of cause.

The emergence of self cannot be separated from the essentially moral process of establishing human accountability (Kilpatrick 1941). Third, the idea of self incorporates a further sense of a realm that is distinctly personal or *propriative* (Allport 1955). This realm has not been effectively defined; yet awareness of it is a crucial and almost irreducible intuition. Attribution theorists' evidence that self-attribution does not follow entirely the same rules as person attribution gives some clues to the proprium. But beyond the attribution of causation for behavior, the realm of self is characterized by possessiveness, privacy, and sacredness.

INSTITUTION AND IMPULSE AS LOCI OF SELF

The self-conception is most frequently described sociologically by naming the roles that are preeminent in it. In a good example of this approach, Wellman (1971) finds that the self-conceptions of both black and white adolescents can be characterized on the basis of the same set of identities— . namely, their age, gender, family, religion, race, and ethnic heritage, and their roles as students, athletes, and friends. Studies comparing the place of occupation and work in the life organizations of various groups of workers (Dubin 1956; Wilensky 1964) likewise relate the self-conception to particular roles in society.

Self-conceptions can also be compared on the basis of distinctions at a more abstract level. The relationship between self and social order is put in more comprehensive terms when we distinguish between self as anchored in *institutions* and self as anchored in *impulse*.

To one person, an angry outburst or the excitement of extramarital desire comes as an alien impetus that superficially beclouds or even dangerously threatens the true self. The experience is real enough and may even be persistent and gratifying, but it is still not felt as signifying the real self. The true self is recognized in acts of volition, in the pursuit of institutionalized goals, and not in the satisfaction of impulses outside institutional frameworks. To another person, the outburst or desire is recognized—fearfully or enthusiastically—as an indication that the real self is breaking through a deceptive crust of institutional behavior. Institutional motivations are external, artificial constraints and superimpositions that bridle manifestations of the real self. One plays the institutional game when he must, but only at the expense of the true self. The true self consists of deep, unsocialized, inner impulses. Mad desire and errant fancy are exquisite expressions of the self.

Again, conscientious acceptance of group obligations and unswerving loyalty can mean that the real self has assumed firm control and overcome the alien forces. But for those who find out who they really are by listening to the voice of impulse, the same behavior is a meaningless submission to institutional regimens and authoritarianism. A mother's self-sacrifice for her child is the measure of her real self when seen through institutional eyes, and it is a senseless betrayal of the parent's true being to those who find personal reality in the world of impulse.

It is no accident that this polarity parallels Freud's classic distinction between id and superego. To Freud, the id was more truly the person and the superego merely an external imposition. As he turned to examinations of society, he expressed the same conviction when he wrote, "Our civilization is entirely based upon the suppression of instincts" (1931, p. 13), and when he proposed a relaxation of social norms and standards as a solution to the discontents of modern civilization (1930). This position sharply contrasts with a view shared by many writers and exemplified in Park's assertion that "the role we are striving to live up to—this mask is our truer self" (1927, p. 739). Although in other writings Park sometimes expressed a different conviction, his statement epitomized the institutional locus of self, while Freud located the self chiefly in the world of impulse—until his belated concessions to ego.

THE KEY DIFFERENCES

Several crucial differences between the two contrasting loci of self can be briefly stated.

1. Under the institution locus, the real self is revealed when an individual adheres to a high standard, especially in the face of serious temptation to fall away. A person shows his true mettle under fire. Under the impulse locus, the real self is revealed when a person does something solely because he wants to—not because it is good or bad or noble or courageous or self-sacrificing, but because he spontaneously wishes to do so.

2. To *impulsives,* the true self is something to be discovered. A young person drops out of school or out of the labor force in order to reflect upon and discover who he really is. To the *institutional,* waiting around for self-discovery to occur is ridiculous. The self is something attained, created, achieved, not something discovered. If vocational counseling to help the individual find his peculiar niche has elements of the impulse conception of self, the idea that a person can make of himself what he will, that one chooses a task and then works at it, is the view of institutionals. The contrast is well stated in a contemporary prescription for effective living, written from the institutional perspective:

> So if we reach a point of insight at which we become disgustedly aware of how we stage ourselves, play games, and ingratiate others, to say nothing of using defense mechanisms and strategies, and if at this point we want to enrich life by finding honest, deeply felt, loving interactions with others, it is tempting to believe that we can change simply by opening a door and letting out our ''true'' unsullied impulses. Change is never so simple. What is really involved is not the releasing of a true self but the making of a new self, one that gradually transcends the limitations and pettiness of the old. [White 1972, p. 387].

3. Under the institution locus, the real self is revealed only when the individual is in full control of his faculties and behaviors. Allport (1955) locates the self in planning and volition, in contrast to impulse. ''When the individual is dominated by segmental drives, by compulsions, or by the winds of circumstances, he has lost the integrity that comes only from maintaining major directions of striving'' (pp. 50–51). When control is impaired by fatigue, stress, alcohol, or drugs, an alien self displaces the true self. The danger of any of these conditions is that after repeated experiences the individual may lose the capacity to distinguish between the true self and the counterfeit and become progressively less able to resume control and reinstate the true self. If use of alcohol is viewed with favor, it is only on condition that the user is able to practice moderation or ''hold his liquor,'' maintaining control in spite of alcohol.

But under the impulse locus, the true self is revealed only when inhibitions are lowered or abandoned. In a significant statement of an institutional perspective, Wordsworth (1807) called upon Duty, ''stern daughter of the voice of God,'' for relief from the ''weight of chance-desires'' and for ''a repose that ever is the same.'' But let the barest suspicion arise that a good deed has been motivated by a sense of duty, and it loses all value as a clue to self in the eyes of the impulsive. For some impulsives drugs and alcohol are aids—often indispensable—to the discovery of self, for without them socially instilled inhibitions irresistibly overpower the true self. A participant in a Los Angeles ''love-in'' in 1971 said: ''It's a place where people can get out, get smashed, get stoned, or whatever. A love-in is a place to get away from the apartment. It's like being out and touching people for a change, rather than working with paper and working with inanimate objects. It's like being out in the real world for a change.''

4. Hypocrisy is a concern of both types, but the word means different things to each. For the institutionals, hypocrisy consists of failing to live up to one's standards. The remedy is not to lower standards but to make amends and adhere to the standards the next time. If one's failings persist, he ceases to represent himself as what he cannot be,

so that he at least escapes the charge of hypocrisy by presenting himself only as what he is. For the impulsives, hypocrisy consists of asserting standards and adhering to them even if the behavior in question is not what the individual wants to do and enjoys doing. One who sets exacting standards for himself and by dint of dedicated effort succeeds in living up to them is still a hypocrite if he must suppress a desire to escape from these strict demands. Altruism, in the traditional sense of responding to duty and setting one's own interests aside, is a penultimate hypocrisy, compounded by the probability that it is a dissimulated self-seeking and manipulation. The institutional goal is correspondence between *prescription and behavior;* the goal of impulsives is correspondence between *impulse and behavior*: hypocrisy in either instance is a lack of the appropriate correspondence.

5. In the light of the foregoing differences, the qualities that make a performance admirable differ. The polished, error-free performance, in which the audience forgets the actor and sees only the role being played, is the most admired by institutionals. Whatever the task, perfection is both the goal and the means by which the real self finds expression. But impulsives find technical perfection repelling and admire instead a performance that reveals the actor's human frailties. They are in harmony with the motion picture star system, in which Gregory Peck, John Wayne, and Gina Lollobrigida, rather than the characters they play in a given picture, are the centers of attention. Ed Sullivan's popular appeal, generally attributed to his very awkwardness and ineptitude, is incomprehensible to the institutionals. Of course, the specific cues for spontaneity have changed, so a younger generation of impulsives no longer responds to these stars as did an older generation.

6. The difference between discovery and achievement also suggests a difference in time perspective. The self as impulse means a present time perspective, while the self as institution means a future time perspective. Institutionals, who build themselves a real world by making commitments, have difficulty retaining a vital sense of self when the future perspective is no longer tenable. The *malaise* of retirement is a common indication of this pattern. In contrast, freedom from past commitments is heralded poetically in the popular song "Gentle on My Mind," by John Hartford.

7. Just as hypocrisy takes on different meanings within the two patterns, individualism is found in both settings with different implications. The individualist is one who rejects some kind of social pressure that threatens his true identity. But there are different kinds of pressure. In one view, social pressures can divert a person from achievement, from adherence to ethical standards, and from other institutional goals. The rugged individualists of 19th-century America thought in these terms. Children were imbued with an individualistic ethic in order to protect them from peer group pressures toward mediocrity or compromise of principle, either of which meant failure to realize the potential that was the true self. But individualism can also be a repudiation of the institutional and interindividual claims that compete with impulse. The individualist may be protecting himself against a conspiracy to force him into institutional molds, to make him do his duty, or to aspire. Both types would agree that one must resist the blandishments of friends and the threats of enemies in order to be true to himself. But the institutional individualist is most attentive to pernicious pressures on the side of mediocrity and abandonment of principle; the impulsive individualist sees clearly the social pressures in league with a system of arbitrary rules and false goals.

Both institution and impulse loci allow for individualistic and nonindividualistic orientations. We have found it useful to employ a cross-cutting distinction between *individual* and *social* anchorages for the self. Institutionals stress either achievement, a relatively individual goal, or altruism, a social aim, as the road to self-discovery. Somewhere between the two lies adherence to an ethical code which will vary according to whether ethics is viewed as applied altruism or a forum for individual achievement. Impulsives may stress the simple disregard of duties and inhibitions in order to gratify spontaneous impulses; this is essentially an individual route to self-discovery. Or they may seek self-discovery through expressing potentially tabooed feelings to other persons and thereby attain a state of interpersonal intimacy that transcends the normal barriers between people.

RELATED AND UNRELATED DISTINCTIONS

It is essential not to confuse these alternative anchorages with the question of whether people are preoccupied with maintaining appearances or conforming instead of "being themselves." Describing a mass gathering of youths, a student wrote, "People tend to forget how they would hope to come across, and instead act as their true selves." This is a terse statement of how participants felt in the situation and expresses the point of view of an impulse self-anchorage. But from an institutional perspective, the same youths appear to be tumbling over one another in their anxiety to comply with the latest youthful fad and to avoid any appearance of being square. The institutional hopes that after passing through this stage the youths will "find themselves," discovering their special niches in the institutional system. The self-anchorage determines which kinds of behavior seem genuine and which are concessions to appearance.

The polarity bears resemblance to several distinctions already advanced by others. McPartland's "Category B" responses and Kuhn and McPartland's consensual responses (Spitzer, Couch, and Stratton 1973) to the Twenty Statements Test (TST) would all be institutional responses, but so would many responses in other categories. Institutionals have much in common with Riesman, Glazer, and Denney's (1950) inner-directed persons, but other-directed persons cannot be equated with impulsives. Sorokin's (1937—41) sensate types resemble the impulsives in their assignment of ultimate reality to the world of the senses. But Sorokin identifies striving for success with the sensate mind and altruism with the ideational, whereas I see these as alternative expressions of an institutional anchorage. Benedict's (1934) interpre-

tation of Nietzsche's Dionysians suggests impulsives, who are unrestrained in acting on impulse and dream, while the Apollonians are more comfortable in an institutionally articulated system. But the dominating Apollonian theme of moderation certainly does not apply to heroic altruism or unrestrained striving for success.

Compared with the well-known dichotomies employed by Benedict, Sorokin, and Riesman et al., the institution-impulse distinction introduces a somewhat different dimension. It allows for the discovery of reality in either excess or moderation within both self-anchorages, and it allows in each orientation for both mystical and naturalistic realities and both individualizing and unifying realities. Goals of achievement, self-control, morality, and altruism lodge the self-conception more and more firmly in some institutional structure. The impulse release attained in encounter groups, expressive movements, and dropping out may in some forms promote a bond of intimacy with other individuals but always distinguishes the true self specifically from institutional values, norms, and goals.

This polarity has much in common with the widely discussed dimension of alienation. However, three important differences of approach make the concepts complementary rather than redundant. First, alienation is an intrinsically evaluative concept, incorporating a negative view of social trends and requiring that the search for explanation be directed toward disorganization in the social structure. Granted that each investigator's own self-locus will lead him to prefer one pole to the other, there are no a priori judgments that one locus is healthier than the other and no reasons to seek explanations for the shift in the pathologies of society. Second, while alienation implies a single continuum, self-locus implies two continua that may be loosely correlated but not identical. One is the continuum I have described. The other ranges from high to low *self-resolution*, according to whether the individual has a clear and stable self-conception or a vague and uncertain identity. Some scholars think of alienation as loss of self-resolution. But alienation from one's work can signify either an impulse locus or low self-resolution. And for some scholars in the Freudian tradition, self-estrangement *means* institutional anchorage.

A third distinction is that such concepts as alienation and anomie tell only where the self is *not*. The result is an effort to infer and explain self-estrangement without first exploring the possibility that the self may be securely lodged somewhere other than where the investigator has looked. Why *should* the self be lodged in work? Why should not work be carried out as a necessary but tolerable evil, its encroachment on the rest of life appropriately curtailed, as Seeman (1967) has suggested? Perhaps a decline of institutional self-anchorage is less a result of institutional failure than a consequence of the discovery of a new vitality in the world of impulse. Shils (1962) calls our attention to the new kinds of experience made possible for us by the mass society. The merit of examining these shifts in terms of self-loci rather than merely alienation is that we are sensitized to the possibility that the self has found new anchorages as well as losing the old.

Concerning this initial statement of the two loci of self, the reader should bear in mind that specifying polar types such as these is merely a way to start thinking about variation in the sense of self. Except on the fringes of society, we are unlikely to find the extremes. Elements of both anchorages probably coexist comfortably in the average person. Yet differences among groups of people in key facets of self may be of sufficient importance than their experience of each other is noncongruent, and little true communication can occur.

A CONTEMPORARY TREND

It is my speculative hypothesis that over the past several decades substantial shifts have occurred away from an institution and toward an impulse emphasis. Accounts of the "new sensibility" in American culture (Bell 1970, p. 59) or of "consciousness III" (Reich 1970) already associate many of the same features with the youthful protest of the 1960s. But it would be shortsighted not to see the shift in a more extended historical context or to overlook the possibility of rural-urban differences, class differences, and differences among national cultures, as well as generational differences. A revolutionary consciousness often unwittingly adopts perspectives that have been growing in established society, frees them from accommodation in other aspects of that society, and applies them to a contemporary crisis.

There is nothing novel in attending to changing values over the last few generations. But I suggest that the changes be viewed as a shift in what are conceived as valid indications of what is real about ourselves and our associates, telling us whether we really know a person or not. Distinguishing the real from the unreal is a matter of intuition, not of logic. Faultless logic that concerns unreal objects falls on deaf ears. A shifting locus of self means that successive generations are talking about different worlds of reality. At the heart of each are the shared and socially produced intuitions through which people identify their true selves.

Literary themes often presage shifts in popular consciousness. Examining the writings of James Frazer, Friedrich Nietzsche, Joseph Conrad, Thomas Mann, and Sigmund Freud, Lionel Trilling (1961) traces the theme that we must accept the reality of those human impulses that were judged unacceptable by an artificial and unreal civilization. He identifies "a certain theme which appears frequently in modern literature—so frequently, indeed, and in so striking a manner, that it may be said to constitute one of the shaping and controlling ideas of our epoch. I can identify it by calling it the disenchantment of our culture with culture itself—it seems to me that the characteristic element of modern literature, or at least of the most highly developed modern literature, is the bitter line of hostility to civilization which runs through it" (p. 26).

I have already noted Freud's penchant for the impulse perspective. Perhaps the greatest impact Freud had on the modern world was to discredit normative behavior and conscience as manifestations of our true selves and to elevate impulses to that position. Under his aegis, guilt has ceased to be the redemptive experience through which the real self reasserts itself and has become an external impediment to personal autonomy. Lynd (1958) exemplifies this newer intuition of reality when she writes, "Living in terms of guilt and righteousness is living in terms of the sanctions and taboos of one immediate culture. To some extent such living is necessary for everyone. Living in terms of the confronting of shame—and allowing shame to become a revelation of oneself and one's society—makes way for living beyond the conventions of a particular culture. It makes possible the discovery of an integrity that is peculiarly one's own and of those characteristically human qualities that are at the same time most individualizing and most universal" (p. 257).

Concern with discovery of the true self, vaguely identified as a set of impulses that have been repressed or dissipated under institutional constraint, turns up as a novel element in the political process of recent years. It became a prominent theme in youth movements, minority movements, and women's movements during the 1960s (Turner, 1969), Miller (1973) traces the "politics of the true self" back to the poet William Blake and shows that violence is conceived of as the ultimate form of self-expression and self-discovery in the writings of Fanon and Sartre.

The term "soul" has often been used in much the same sense as our term "true self." It can be found in the work of poets as different as Richard Lovelace and William Wordsworth. But its meaning has changed to suit prevailing conceptions of personal reality. A century ago the soul was essentially a moral force. As secular psychology brought the term into disrepute, it disappeared, sank into obscurity, reemerging to describe a special quality attributed to blacks. It retains its character as a dynamic force, but a supposed lack of inhibition is a crucial criterion of "soul."

Miller and Swanson (1958) documented chang-

ing conceptions of child rearing as new middle-class parents evinced less concern about internalized controls and more about social adjustment than did parents from the old middle class. In studies of another stage in life, students, as they progressed through college or university, were found to look more favorably on the expressions of impulses (Feldman and Newcomb 1969, p. 34). If the inner-directed person of Riesman et al. (1950) has much in common with our institutionals, the other-directed person may have been a transitional type, clinging to the institutional framework for his identity but finding a way to accept constant change. Perhaps the total repudiation of institutional identities is the product of a growing sense of unreality in *all* roles that comes from the other-directed person's efforts to *be* all his roles. In the world of business, the shift is from the view that human relations take care of themselves when tasks are effectively managed to the position that human-relations engineering is essential to effective production. In education the progressive movement promoted a conception of the child in terms of his impulses, and not merely his learning and conduct. Rieff's (1966) depiction of cultural change as "the shifting balances of controls and releases" (p. 233) and his account of the "triumph of the therapeutic" describe a historical change toward greater impulsiveness.

Recently Lifton (1970) has described a type of personality he believes is becoming much more common throughout the developed world. His "protean man" has no true shape of his own but assumes varied shapes according to circumstance. Except for the fact that Riesman et al. describe other-direction as a mode of conformity, "protean man" may be a new name for the same kind of person. But the idea that rapid social change makes fixed identities unworkable has also inspired Zurcher (1972, 1973) to identify the "mutable self" as a phenomenon unique to the present generation. Zurcher cites as evidence for the "mutable self" his discovery that students no longer answer Kuhn's TST as they used to. Early use of the procedure produced mostly "B mode" responses, meaning that the subject identified himself with various institutionalized roles and statuses. Now students give principally "C mode" responses which specify characteristic modes of acting, feeling, and responding.

"C mode" responses clearly attenuate the linkage between self and institutional anchorage. The real self is marked by characteristic orientations—attitudes, feelings, desires—rather than characteristic placement in social organization. Young people find self-realization in patterns that are viewed apart from their institutional settings. Consistent with this evidence is the contemporary view that, on meeting a stranger, it is inappropriate to ask where he comes from, what he does, and whether he is married, or to categorize him in other ways. Instead, one seeks to know him through his tastes and his feelings.

THEORIES AND EXPLANATIONS

If we are to explain and predict the self-loci of different populations, we must combine insights about individual dynamics with understanding of social structure and culture. The problem of individual dynamics is to identify circumstances under which experiences seem real or unreal in relation to self. Large-scale differences and shifts must then be linked with the exposure of individuals to such experiences.

An acceptable explanation must also address the question of whether impulse and institutional self-anchorages are the poles of a unitary variable, two separate variables, related in a loose but imperfect inverse correlation, or even unrelated variables. If the conditions that weaken one locus intensify the other, a single continuum is indicated. But if, as seems more likely, the conditions that weaken one locus do not necessarily intensify the other, a more complex conception will be required.

My procedure has been inductive rather than deductive, starting with the observation of a difference and an apparent shift and then searching

for explanations. Hence I now offer a set of alternative explanations rather than advance a single theory of self-locus.

CULTURAL DEFINITIONS OF REALITY

The most parsimonious principle is that people experience as real what they are taught is real. Definitions of reality are crucial components in all cultures, and a cultural shift may have occurred in recent times. Conceptions of reality are buttressed by systems of belief, and the decline of religious belief and its replacement by materialistic or naturalistic belief assigns more reality to physiological and allied psychological impulses. Cultural shift can explain the increasing personal reality attached to impulse as well as the declining personal relevance of institutions.

In tracing the historical evolution of public establishments designed to segregate deviants from the community, Rosen (1969) suggests that a new view of human nature came to the fore in the late 17th century, bringing with it the new idea of a personal self: "Today the idea of a personal self appears as an indispensable assumption of existence. Actually, like other views of human nature, it is in large measure a cultural idea, a fact within history, the product of a given era. At any given period certain criteria are employed to establish normal human nature, as well as any deviation from it" (p. 164). If Rosen's evocative suggestion is correct, the locus of self was probably institutional at first. As Soellner (1972) interprets the recurring theme of self-discovery in Shakespeare's plays, the true self is formed in self-mastery. Cultural changes that occurred principally in the 19th and 20th centuries turned attention increasingly toward impulse as the expression of self.

While economical, this explanation is somewhat question-begging, since we can do little with it except ask the revised question, Why has a cultural shift occurred? But as a starting point, the cultural explanation is useful. A related and well-established line of sociological explanation emphasizes uniformity and diversity of culture rather than its specific content. According to this view, certitudes come from unanimity—the vitality and reality of an experience come from the fact that it fits unmistakably into a consensual world view. But the intimate experience of cultural diversity undermines certitudes. Institutional forms are seen in relativistic, rather than absolute terms. No longer the locus of *real* behavior because they cannot be taken for granted, institutional frameworks begin to seem arbitrary and artificial.

While the latter construction escapes the danger of tautology in explanations that rely on the content of culture, it accounts for a decline in the institutional locus of self without indicating the basis for increasing impulse locus. By itself, this explanation suggests a generally weakened sense of identity instead of a shift from one locus to another.

THE TERMS OF SOCIAL INTEGRATION

A second approach redirects our attention from culture to the fundamental terms of interpersonal relations. Early sociologists (Cooley, 1902; Young 1940; Davis 1940) believed that human nature depends upon social interaction. The human meanings of experience come out of the sharing and exchange of experiences. We tend to believe in experiences we share with others and doubt those we cannot share (Blondel 1928; Halbwachs 1952). Events become real and vital when they become elements in the bonding of interpersonal and group relations. The integration of an individual into solidary groups is the ultimate source of any sense of reality concerning experience.

Festinger (1953) proposes that we often comply with group norms without accepting them as our own, but that, when we wish to be part of the group, our compliance is converted into private acceptance. Much earlier, Park's (1928) and Stonequist's (1937) depiction of the marginal man stressed the interplay between adherence to a particular culture and the desire for social incorporation. Social rejection led the marginal man to doubt his commitment to the group's values and

images of reality. Warner (1941) found confirmation of the conclusion that the stratification people experienced as real was the hierarchy of social identities and affiliations their economic assets helped them attain, not economic standing per se. Davie (1947) found that immigrants of relatively high status who came to the United States as refugees from nazism felt they had lost in the move, even while acknowledging that their economic conditions were as good as or better than before. The loss of social recognition was salient in their estimate of overall position.

From this perspective, the self-conception should incorporate those actions and feelings that are involved in exchange with others and, through exchange, contribute materially to the individual's integration into groups. We are led to search for shifts in kinds of social relations that have relatively lasting and significant effects. Our key may be the shift from the organization of group life around production and mutual protection groups to organization around consumption groups. From Veblen (1899), to Riesman et al. (1950), to Miller and Swanson (1958), observers have remarked a trend in the Western world away from production orientation and toward consumption orientation. At an earlier period, the central problems of society revolved about how to produce efficiently and on a massive scale the goods that people wanted. The individual's round of life was concentrated in extended families, neighborhoods, small communities, and other social units, all of them organized about the aims of production. Disciplined work habits, aspirations that motivated work, and adherence to rules that facilitated collaboration for production were valued qualities that enhanced individual integration into stable and comprehensive social units. Since the same units were also vested with responsibility for mutual protection, altruism was the companion to productive contribution in making the individual an essential group member.

As production problems were increasingly resolved and production routinized and transferred to the domain of organizations with strictly segmental functions, the connections between production-related personal qualities and integration into primary groups became more tenuous and indirect. Likewise, protection became the the routinized responsibility of experts who were external to the groups in which people lived. An altruistic act by an amateur could do more harm than good—witness warnings against amateurs moving automobile accident victims or trying to save drowning swimmers instead of waiting for paramedics or life guards! But of even greater significance, altruism toward a stranger has usually no significance for lasting social ties and identities in a highly segmented society. As their significance for interpersonal bonding declined, altruism, achievement, and righteousness became less credible clues to the real person.

As the consumption of goods, expressive activities, and pleasure became the aims about which the anchoring social groups were organized, a different set of qualities provided the interpersonal cement. The cultivation of personal tastes, expressive styles, and distinctive psychological ''needs'' was at a premium in groups whose vitality and continuation depended on collaboration for consumption. The family was increasingly viewed as a contrast, rather than an adjunct, to the world of production. When the links to production could not be totally severed, some relegated the family to the same sphere of unreality. Ogburn (1933) and Burgess and Locke (1950) noted that interpersonal response was becoming more prominent as a source of family cohesion.

This approach is consistent with the hypothesis that the institutional self is less prevalent and the impulsive self more so among segments of the population for whom production activities are aimed at maintenance rather than expansion. Rural and small-town folk are often characterized as bumpkins because they do not seek to play such rituals as initiations and funerals to dramatic perfection and fail to play their vocational and community roles to the hilt. I suggest that these are

groups in which production is routinized and hence constitutes a less salient social bond. Where a genuine spirit of entrepreneurship prevails, the expansive aim makes routinization impossible, and the institutional self seems more real.

DEPRIVATION AND DESIRE

From psychodynamics comes a third principle that might explain varying loci of self. Sustained denial of any goal or impulse causes a preoccupation with the blocked tendency which makes the latter seem more real and important. While this is a cardinal Freudian assumption, it has a venerable history and is entirely consistent with George Mead's conception of impulse and social act. Lee (1959) gives the same process a different slant when she attempts to explain why Americans conceive of psychodynamics in terms of basic human needs instead of values: ''In maintaining our individual integrity and in passing on our value of individualism to the infant, we create needs for food, for security, for emotional response, phrasing these as distinct and separate. . . . We create needs in the infant by withholding affection and then presenting it as a series of approvals for an inventory of achievements or attributes'' (pp. 74–75). By contrast, in Hopi, Tikopia, Kwoma, Arapesh, Ontong-Javanese, and many other societies, value is undivided and positive. There is no separate motive or need for food, security, or social response.

Whether we start from Freud's or Lee's contrasting assumptions about the ultimate character of human motivation, we find agreement that modern urban, industrial civilization requires a great deal of control and suppression of impulse. If these requirements have increased, the result should be enhancement of the sense of reality associated with impulse. If modern civilization has also frustrated mankind's need for interpersonal response (Horney 1937), it is easy to understand that people may experience their longings for intimacy as manifestations of their real selves. We encounter more difficulty in developing a plausible account of lessened frustration in institutional spheres. Perhaps routinized social services and prepackaged solutions to all problems of production have eliminated the anxieties and potential frustrations in these areas and deprived such activities and concerns of their personal vitality.

Experience has shown how difficult it is for scholars to agree on such broad characterizations of societies as impulse repressive. A more plausible view may be that modern society is not so much repressive as it is contradictory, stimulating to an unparalleled degree the impulses whose expression is then inhibited. But if this is true of impulses Freud would have lodged in the id, it is equally true of achievement and service motivations that he would have placed in the superego. To some extent this entire approach may rest on a mythical conception of uninhibited life in preindustrial societies, based on selective reporting and disproportionate attention to premarital sexual play.

OPPORTUNITIES AND CONSEQUENCES

A final principle is pragmatic and in some ways antithetical to the deprivation-enhancement approach. The postulate is that lines of action with plainly perceived and significant consequences are experienced as real, while ones with undependable or unidentifiable consequences seem less real. Consequences cannot be experienced without opportunity, so the reality of particular goals and impulses is enhanced by either augmented consequences or increased opportunities.

The waning vitality of institutional dispositions can be traced to the emasculation of rites of passage and the permeability of role boundaries. Disappointment over rites of passage, leading to a generalized sense of unreality, is poignantly conveyed in the recently popular song "Is That All There Is?" Each of life's milestones turns out to be of little moment. A vital rite of passage initiates the individual into closely guarded secrets and skills and opens up new privileges, conditional upon his successful performance or endurance of the rite.

When secrets, skills, and privileges are readily accessible to those who have not been through the rite, and when passage becomes pro forma, the entire sequence of institutional steps loses its reality. Likewise the potential of any institutional role for self-anchorage depends upon the degree to which it incorporates distinctive privileges, responsibilities, and skills. Such monopolies may have been progressively undermined in recent years.

There may be a key to the changing sense of what is real in the fate of the once-popular belief in self-discovery through self-sacrifice. One side of institutional identity is incorporation into the self of a whole range of socially generated objects that augment the interest, richness, and possibilities of gratification in life. The obverse, however, is the relinquishment of those random sensations and impulses which—like Blondel's (1928) *cénesthésie*—offer a constant threat to the ordered world of the institutional self. From the poet Francis Thompson (1893), writing in religious terms, to the psychoanalyst Fromm (1941), students of human nature have understood the appeal of self-surrender. For Thompson, the errant soul flees the Hound of Heaven in desperation until in abject surrender he discovers the fulfillment of his deepest desires. For Fromm, identification with an omnipotent, charismatic leader and his movement resolves the problems of the troubled self.

But implicit in self-discovery through surrender is the assumption that one has been absorbed into a caring, gratifying entity, both powerful and dependable. When Ruth of the Old Testament found a true self in surrendering her life to Naomi, she did so in the firm knowledge that Naomi would care for her, protect her, and give her a meaningful and rewarding place in her household. Thompson assures us that to those who surrender, God will grant many times more than they have given up. It is this rich return for surrender that vests the institutional self-conception with a vital sense of reality. The discovery of self in love for another is made real by the reciprocated love, the dependability of the relationship, and the new opportunities for gratification that come from the relationship. The discovery of self through immersion in an institutional framework is real when the dependability of that framework makes the world predictable and the rich body of objects opens up a new world of gratifications.

But if reciprocation does not occur, neither does the vital sense of a real self. When the institutional framework is characterized by disorder and undependability, when it fails as an avenue to expanded opportunity for gratification, the true self cannot be found in institutional participation. Because *perceived* consequences are crucial, objective order and dependability may be less important than whether consequences are early or delayed and whether effects are intrinsic or extrinsic. Here the analysis converges with many treatments of alienation in the Marxian tradition. The institutional order may still be relatively efficient and predictable, but the increasing time span between action and consequences and the increasing dependence on extrinsic rewards may contribute to a sense of unreality in institutional activities.

On the other hand, as Shils (1962) has eloquently indicated, mass society opened up opportunities for an augmented range of gratifications. As existence became less precarious, people could afford to act on their impulses. More of society's resources could be applied to creating avenues for the gratification of impulse:

> The individual organism has become a seeker after experience, a repository of experience, an imaginative elaborator of experience. To a greater extent than in the past, the experiences of the ordinary person, at least in youth, is admitted to consciousness and comes to form part of the core of the individual's outlook. There has come about a greater openness to experience, an efflorescence and intensification of sensibility. . . . In a crude, often grotesque way, the mass society has seen the growth, over wide areas of society, of an appreciation of the value of the experience of personal relationships, of the intrinsic value of a personal attachment. . . . [Pp. 58−59]

In accordance with this more positive view of mass society, the sense of unreality attending institutional activity may be a crisis phenomenon, related to a stage in life or restricted to a small but vocal segment of the population. On the other hand, a relative decline in institutional self-anchorage may have occurred just because of the newly discovered vitality in the world of impulse. Instead of alienation from our institutions, we may be witnessing a reestablishment of balance between institutional and impulsive loci of the self.

ALTERNATIVE THEORIES

I have by no means covered all plausible approaches to explaining the hypothesized shift in self-anchorage. For example, the massive amount of literature on patterns of deferred gratification should offer clues. Nor am I prepared to recommend a choice among theories. The major conflict is between deprivation theory, on the one hand, and opportunity theory and social integration theory, on the other. But even here the opposition may not be complete.

Evidence and experience suggest a curvilinear relationship between deprivation and the sense of reality. Severe and continued deprivation probably leads to a lessened sense of reality and sometimes even a complete divorcement between self and desire. "Narcotization" (Koos 1946, p. 48) and "analgesic" (Ball 1968) are terms sociologists have used to designate a pervading sense of unreality that stems from exceptional deprivation.

Furthermore, relative rather than absolute deprivation is probably the key. Hence, stimulation of desire without equivalent increase in gratification should also increase the sense of reality. With this modification, the deprivation approach need not be inconsistent with the others. Changing definitions of reality may be the source of, or bring an end to, relative deprivation. Modest relative deprivation may be the normal consequence when new opportunities for gratification become available. Just as competition may increase the interest in work of both winners and losers (Myers 1962;

Julian, Bishop, and Fiedler 1966) and a healthy anxiety enhance the excitement of love, the combination of accessible gratification and some degree of risk may create the most vital sense of reality. Individuals today may experience their impulses as more vital expressions of self than heretofore, because opportunities to gratify impulse have increased and norms against doing so have weakened, at the same time that lingering inhibitions from the past and contradictory cultural definitions add an increment of risk to the expression and pursuit of impulse.

Application of this approach to institutional activities suggests two phases. An early period of institutional innovation greatly elaborated the scope of potential human gratification, through family, work, community activity, and other institutional spheres; yet the growing and changing nature of the institutions maintained a universal element of risk. This combination of promise and risk led to a more profound personal investment in institutional pursuits than formerly, with the result that more people experienced their true selves as distinctively lodged in these spheres. As institutions came to perform more smoothly and routinely, the risk was reduced and the sense of reality declined. Thereafter ensued the second phase, already amply described.

IMPLICATIONS FOR SOCIAL STRUCTURE

Any massive shift in the focus of identity should have substantial consequences for social structure and may negate the implicit assumptions on which some sociological theories are founded. Theories deeply rooted in the past often take for granted an actor who locates his real self in an institutional setting. Conflict theories are no different from order theories in this respect, since they merely shift the focus of self to a class-bounded institutional framework. It is difficult to find sociological theories that locate bases for order rather than pathology when institutional participation is strictly instrumental and when only those impulses

that seem unrelated to institutions are experienced as genuine and personal. I shall suggest how alternate loci of self bear on a few major concepts in sociology.

ROLE DISTANCE

Few would deny that society exists only when members are enacting roles. Sartre (1956, p. 59) argues that society requires every person to play his roles to the hilt. Role theory assumes that role behavior is monitored and evaluated on scales of role adequacy. Evaluations by the actor and significant others influence subsequent role performances. When role theory is refined in accordance with self theory, evaluations of role adequacy are understood to have the greatest impact for roles that are paramount in the self-conception. Whatever society may expect, the actor usually plays to the hilt only those roles in which his ego is strongly involved (Sherif and Cantril 1947). So long as the roles attached to institutionally *key statuses* (Hiller 1947) are also most salient in personal identities, institutional and personal dynamics are mutually supporting.

But Goffman (1961) has identified a pervasive phenomenon of *role distance*. The role-distancing antics of parents on the merry-go-round with their children plainly ward off identification with a role that does violence to their self-conceptions. But when the surgeon engages in role distancing with nurses and assistants during a difficult operation, he can hardly be guarding against inappropriate institutional placement and identification. The distance is between the real person and *any* formalized role. If role distancing in such situations is as prevalent and important as Goffman suggests, it is difficult to accept Sartre's assertion.

The apparent contradiction between these two sensitive observers may come from their having viewed different cultures at different moments in time. When the self is securely lodged in institutions, the individual will play at least the most crucial roles to the hilt. When he does so, he will appear genuine to his instituional auditors. When he does not, he will seem insincere, because role distancing behavior is inappropriate flippancy, a denial of respect to significant others in the encounter. Indeed, the behavior of Goffman's surgeon would be so regarded in many medical circles. But when the true self is lodged in impulse, role distancing shows that one is not really the uptight, false, or plastic person his conformity with institutional routine might suggest. Role distancing reminds significant others of a real self that is temporarily obscured by compliance with an institutional role.

On the one hand, organizational theories should take account of role distancing as a crucial aspect of the meshing of person and institution. On the other hand, role distancing is probably not a universal feature of social behavior but a distinctive feature of societies like our own, in which the locus of self is widely found in noninstitutional impulses.

VALUES AND NORMS

Sociologists distinguish between norms and values as part of the directing and regulating apparatus of society. Because of their preoccupation with distinguishing between these two components of social structure, sociologists often fail to notice that the difference is principally in the eye of the beholder: values and norms are largely the same phenomenon viewed in different ways. Honesty is a value; "thou shalt not lie" is a norm. But the two are inseparable, and, as Blake and Davis (1964) argue persuasively, neither can be derived from the other. But the object (value) and the rule (norm) are two constructions the individual can place on the same phenomenon. Which construction is foremost in his experience makes important differences in his relationship to social structure.

Honesty is a positively valued object, a goal to be achieved as a matter of self-respect and pride. One who values it does not feel that society is depriving him of the privilege of telling lies when he wishes, nor does he feel frustrated or constrained when he passes up the temptation to lie.

Instead he has a positive sense of accomplishment and well-being from having lived up to his values. But one who thinks in terms of the norm experiences deprivation and frustration. Like a driver adhering to the speed limit on an open highway, he gains no warm sense of worth and satisfaction from adhering to the rule; even when complying he often feels resentful of the restraint imposed upon him. The practice of premarital and marital chastity has been variously experienced as an opportunity for self-development and as an external restraint on a fundamental human need. *Self-as-impulse tends to transform the institutional order into a set of norms, all cramping expression of the true self. Self-as-institution subordinates the normative sense to a set of values, such as integrity, piety, patriotism, considerateness, and many others.*

Sociologists frequently prejudge the constructions people place on the social order and reify them into features of an objective social structure. They emphasize the constraints of society by seeing principally norms, or they emphasize the creation of new opportunities for self-fulfillment by underlining social values. A more adequate sociological understanding can be reached if we stop reifying the value-norm distinction and seek instead to understand what it is in the social structure that fosters anchorage of the self in either institution or impulse, with the resultant predisposition to see either values of norms in the institutional order.

SENTIMENTS

Much of the spontaneous joy that lubricates the functioning of social orders resides in the social sentiments. Love is of paramount importance among the sentiments. Because sentiment seems to express the inner person, in contrast to external behavior that may be contrived, people seek agreement on signs by which to tell genuine from false sentiment. The choice of cues reflects the anchorage of self. Self-as-impulse can feel love as genuine, as a true reflection of self, only when it arises and persists as a spontaneous attachment, untrammeled by promises, covenants, and codes of behavior. Sentiment is not helped along by a facilitative social order: it erupts in spite of the order and threatens it. The less organization and preparation, the more easily can the individual discover his true sentiments. Institutionals, on the other hand, understand love as something that requires effort to attain and preserve. The infatuation that explodes impulsively is undependable and unreal. The institutional seeks to learn how to achieve true love and turns for guidance to such documents as Paul's chapter on love in the New Testament (1 Cor. 13). The contrasting perspectives are represented in the analysis of popular sex manuals by Lewis and Brissett (1967). Manuals popular with married middle-class people in the past two or three decades are institutional in orientation. They offer readers an opportunity to enhance the vitality and mutuality of sexual experience, leading to a deeper union of the two selves. But Lewis and Brissett read the manuals from the impulsive perspective. Stripped of the institutional perspective, the quest for mutual self-attainment becomes sheer, meaningless "work." Thus, they write of "sex as work." To the extent to which the self-locus has moved away from institutions, the correlations found by Burgess and Cottrell (1939), Burgess and Wallin (1953), and Locke (1951) with persistence and love in marriage may become increasingly invalid, and new and different indicators may become relevant.

THE MEANING OF RITUAL

In 1930, an article entitled "Ritual the Conserver" (Cressman) appeared in the *American Journal of Sociology*. It elaborated the crucial part played by ritual in sustaining the Catholic church and its doctrines. To a contemporary reader, the paper seems peculiarly unconvincing. To those who find not only religious ritual but also marriage ceremonies, funerals and memorial services, initiation ceremonies, and graduation exercises devoid of meaning, it is unclear how ritual could add vitality and reality to anything. Yet plainly many people have been, and continue to be, moved deeply by participation in collective ritual, and for many people dedication to institutional goals and forms is strengthened in this way. The locus of self must be closely intertwined with the ability to gain a vital experience from engaging in collective rituals. It would be premature to label one cause and the other effect, but the impulsive's self-fulfilling prophecy that he will not experience his real self through participation in institutional ritual contrasts with the equally self-fulfilling prophecy from the institutional.

But the matter cannot be reduced to a differential receptivity to ritual. Writing on the "collective search for identity," Klapp (1969) describes the contemporary poverty of ritual, then insists that "ritual is the prime symbolic vehicle for experiencing emotions and mystiques together with others—including a sense of oneself as sharing such emotions . . ." (p. 118). In the place of traditional forms, there have arisen new rituals that participants experience as spontaneous outpourings instead of institutional routines. Sitting on the floor in a circle and singing to the accompaniment of guitars takes the place of sitting in rows on pews and listening to an organ. Rock festivals and love-ins are only the more dramatic rituals, for even the conventional partying rituals of middle-class establishmentarians are experienced as a welcome contrast to institutional routine. Here, then, is another set of rituals that have meaning and vitality as opportunities for experiencing a self that contains more impulse than institution.

Ritual is commonly viewed as a support of the institutional order, and Klapp's "poverty of ritual" does indeed characterize many of the forms that have been employed to strengthen a collective sense of institutional commitment. But it is doubtful that there is any poverty of ritual today in those forms that increase the vitality of an impulsive view of self.

GENERAL IMPLICATIONS

Each of the foregoing points bears on the theory of social control. Concern with the prestige of one's role and the esteem that goes with high role adequacy buttresses the institutional structure. A sense of value eases the pathos of conformity with social norms. Social sentiments domesticate potentially disruptive emotions yet preserve their sensed vitality and spontaneity. And through collective ritual, group solidarity and dedication to the institutional structure are continually renewed. But all of this depends upon the individual's feeling that his real self is engaged in these experiences. If he finds that self elsewhere, control can only be instrumental.

One side of what I have described sounds much like a condition of anomie. But if people recognize their real selves in impulse, they become susceptible to social control from that quarter. And if impulses are generated in unrecognized ways by the social order and follow unsensed but consistent patterns, the impulsive self is as much a vehicle for social control as the institutional self. However, the relationship to recognized institutional structures will be complex and indirect. We need a theory of social control that relies more extensively on the creation and manipulation of situations and on symbiosis than on the internalization and enhancement of norms and values.

AFTERTHOUGHTS

My chain of speculation has consisted of five links. First, I have assumed that each person develops at least a vague conception by which he recognizes some of his feelings and actions as more truly indicative of his real self than other feelings and actions. He does so in part on the basis of unique experience and in part in accordance with the guidelines shared by members of his society, subsocieties, and groups. Second, I have identified a distinction between locating the real self in sentiments and activities of an institutional and volitional nature, such as ambition, morality, and altruism, and recognizing the real self in the experience of impulse—for example, in apparently undisciplined desires and fancies and the wish to make ultimate revelations in the presence of others. This appears to be a significant polarity in the contemporary relationship between individual and society. Third, I have assembled a number of suggestive indications to support the intuition that there has been a long-term shift in the direction of impulse, intensified in the last decade or so. Fourth, I have drawn from analyses of contemporary society to suggest four theoretical approaches that might explain the shift in self-loci and differences in self-anchorage among diverse population segments. And fifth, I have assumed that many sociological theories, especially those having to do with social control, take for granted a population with institutional self-anchorages and need revision to allow for the more hidden ways in which societies control members who find their true selves in impulse.

I stress that there is no objectively, but only a subjectively, true self. Likewise institutional versus impulsive self is a subjective distinction and not a statement of psychogenesis. Institutional motivations are effective vehicles for a multitude of private impulses. And few of the instigations and sensations that people experience as impulse are not institutionally conditioned and generated. We are like the Plains Indians who sought purely personal visions to establish the basis of each individual's authority but faithfully replicated their culture in the form and content of their visions (Benedict 1934, p. 84).

One might suppose on the basis of attribution research that the self should necessarily be anchored overwhelmingly in impulse rather than institution. When an external cause is present, "the behavior is discounted, so to speak, as an indicator of personal disposition" (Kelley, in Jones et al. 1971, p. 155). But there are two important differences. First, although we understand achievement, ethical conformity, and altruism as rooted in institutions, the pattern is internalized, so there need be no sense of an external cause. Second, when we ask people to describe circumstances that reveal their true selves, the institutional replies usually involve going beyond requirements of a role or adhering to goals or norms in the face of obstacles that constitute acceptable excuses for failing to do so. Thus the behavior in question is unlikely to be ascribed to external causes.

As we explore the polarity of institution and impulse, we must ask whether choice between the two is of universal significance or peculiar to certain cultures and social structures. Thomas and Znaniecki (1918) discovered philistines and bohemians, but the fact that the society they studied tended to dichotomize people thus and force each person to choose between those polar types was probably more important than the objective typing of individuals. Mannheim ([1928], 1952) described the distinctive socializing experience that sets one historical generation apart from others in terms of the *issues* over which people divide into rival camps rather than the association of a point of view with a generation. We must not, then, assume that a distinction between institutional and impulse self-anchorages found to be significant in contemporary American society should necessarily be significant in other societies.

We may indeed assume that because the polarity is important, most individuals will seek both kinds of anchorages. For much of life, these alternate anchorages will coexist in fairly easy accommodation. But at crucial transitions in the life cycle the coexistence will be interrupted. The latent opposition between institutional and impulsive selves then becomes manifest, figuring strongly in the turmoil of choice. The point of choice may be passed and the conflict recede into dormancy without the individual's self-conception being firmly anchored at one pole to the exclusion of the other.

Perhaps the feature of the distinction that warrants greatest stress and is most heavily freighted with implications for examining social structure is the hypothesized correlation between self-locus and a disposition to perceive either values or norms. Sociologists writing from a structural perspective often reify the distinction and speak as if values and norms existed as separate entities in society. To a large degree, however, it is the nature of the self conception, in the way it identifies the individual's relationship to social structure, that leads one to perceive principally values or norms. Perceiving values and discovering the true self in the achievement of high institutional-role adequacy facilitates the operation of social control systems as they are commonly described in sociological theory. Perceiving norms and recognizing the true self specifically in the experience of impulses that are thought not to have an institutional basis subjects one to quite a different system of social control, one that is much less well described in sociological theory.

REFERENCES

Allport, Gordon W. 1955. *Becoming: Basic Considerations for a Psychology of Personality*. New Haven, Conn.: Yale University Press.

Ball, Richard A. 1968. "A Poverty Case: The Analgesic Subculture of the Southern Appalachians." *American Sociological Review* 33 (December): 885−95.

Bell, Daniel. 1970. "Quo Warranto." *Public Interest* 19 (Spring): 53−68.

Bendix, Reinhard. 1952. "Compliant Behavior and Individual Personality." *American Journal of Sociology* 58 (November): 292−303.

Benedict, Ruth. 1934. *Patterns of Culture*. Boston: Houghton Mifflin.

Berger, Peter L. 1966. "Identity as a Problem in the Sociology of Knowledge." *European Journal of Sociology* 7:105−15.

Blake, Judith, and Kingsley, Davis. 1964. "Norms, Values, and Sanctions." Pp. 456−84 in *Handbook of Modern Sociology,* edited by Robert E. L. Faris. Chicago: Rand-McNally.

Blondel, Charles. 1928. *The Troubled Conscience and the Insane Mind*. London: Kegan Paul, Trench, Trubner.

Blumer, Herbert, 1966. "Sociological Implications of the Thought of George Herbert Mead." *American Journal of Sociology* 71 (March):535−48.

Burgess, Ernest W., and Leonard S. Cottrell, Jr. 1939. *Predicting success or Failure in Marriage*. Englewood Cliffs, N.J.: Prentice-Hall.

Burgess, Ernest W., and Harvey J. Locke. 1950. *The Family: From Institution to Companionship*. New York: American Book.

Burgess, Ernest W., and Paul Wallin. 1953. *Engagement and Marriage*. Chicago: Lippincott.

Cooley, Charles H. 1902. *Human Nature and the Social Order*. New York: Scribner.

Cressman, Luther S. 1930. "Ritual the Conserver." *American Journal of Sociology* 35 (January): 564−72.

Davie, Maurice R. 1947. *Refugees in America*. New York: Harper.

Davis, Kingsley. 1940. "Final Note on a Case of Extreme Isolation of a Child." *American Journal of Sociology* 45 (May): 554−65.

Dubin, Robert. 1956. "Industrial Workers' World." *Social Problems* 3 (January): 131−42.

Etzioni, Amitai. 1968. "Basic Human Needs, Alienation and Inauthenticity." *American Sociological Review* 33 (December): 870−85.

Feldman, Kenneth A., and Theodore M. Newcomb. 1969. *The Impact of College on Students*. Vol. 1. San Francisco: Jossey-Bass.

Festinger, Leon. 1953. "An Analysis of Compliant Behavior." Pp. 232−56 in *Group Relations at the Crossroads*, edited by Muzafer Sherif and M. O. Wilson. New York: Harper.

Freud, Sigmund, 1930. *Civilization and Its Discontents*. London: Hogarth.

―――. 1931. *Modern Sexual Morality and Modern Nervousness*. New York: Eugenics.

Fromm, Erich. 1941. *Escape from Freedom*. New York: Farrar & Rinehart.

Goffman, Erving. 1961. *Encounters*. Indianapolis: Bobbs-Merrill.

Halbwachs, Maurice. 1952. *Les Cadres sociaux de la mémoire*. Paris: Presses Universitaires de France.

Hiller, E. T. 1947. *Social Relations and Structures*. New York: Harper.

Horney, Karen. 1937. *The Neurotic Personality of Our Time*. New York: Norton.

Jones, Edward E., David E. Kanouse, Harold H. Kelley, Richard E. Nisbett, Stuart Valins, and Bernard Weiner. 1971. *Attribution: Perceiving the Causes of Behavior*. Morristown, N.J.: General Learning.

Julian, James W., Doyle W. Bishop, and Fred E. Fiedler. 1966. "Quasi-therapeutic Effects of Intergroup Competition." *Journal of Personality and Social Psychology* 3 (March): 321−27.

Kilpatrick, William H. 1941. *Selfhood and Civilization: A Study of the Self-Other Process*. New York: Macmillan.

Klapp, Orrin E. 1969. *Collective Search for Identity*. New York: Holt, Rinehart & Winston.

Koos, Earl I. 1946. *Families in Trouble*. New York: Kings Crown.

Kuhn, Manford H., and Thomas S. McPartland. 1954. "An Empirical Investigation of Self-Attitudes." *American Sociological Review* 19 (February): 68−76.

Lee, Dorothy D. 1948. "Are Basic Needs Ultimate?" *Journal of Abnormal and Social Psychology* 43 (July): 391−95.

Lewis, Lionel S., and Dennis Brissett. 1967. "Sex as Work: A Study of Avocational Counselling." *Social Problems* 15 (Summer): 8−17.

Lifton, Robert J. 1970. *Boundaries: Psychological Man in Revolution*. New York: Random House.

Locke, Harvey J. 1951. *Predicting Adjustment in Marriage*. New York: Holt.

Lynd, Helen Merrell. 1958. *On Shame and the Search for Identity*. New York: Harcourt, Brace.

Mannheim, Karl. (1928) 1952. "The Problem of Generations." Pp. 276−322 in *Essays on the Sociology of Knowledge,* edited by Paul Kecskemeti. New York: Oxford University Press.

Mead, George H. 1934. *Mind, Self, and Society*. Chicago: University of Chicago Press.

Miller, Daniel R., and Guy E. Swanson. 1958. *The Changing American Parent*. New York: Wiley.

Miller, Stephen. 1973. "The Politics of the 'True Self.' " *Dissent* 20 (Winter): 93−98.

Myers, Albert. 1962. "Team Competition, Success, and the Adjustment of Group Members." *Journal of Abnormal and Social Psychology*. 65 (November): 325–32.

Ogburn, William F. 1933. "The Family and Its Functions." Pp. 661–708 in *Recent Social Trends in the United States,* by President's Research Committee on Social Trends. New York: McGraw-Hill.

Park, Robert E. 1927. "Human Nature and Collective Behavior." *American Journal of Sociology* 32 (March): 733–41.

———. 1928. "Human Migration and the Marginal Man," *American Journal of Sociology* 33 (May): 881–93.

———. 1931. "Human Nature, Attitudes, and the Mores." Pp. 17–45 in *Social Attitudes,* edited by Kimball Young. New York: Holt.

Reich, Charles A. 1970. *The Greening of America.* New York: Random House.

Rieff, Philip. 1966. *The Triumph of the Therapeutic.* New York: Harper & Row.

Riesman, David, Nathan Glazer, and Reuel Denney. 1950. *The Lonely Crowd.* New Haven, Conn.: Yale University Press.

Rosen, George. 1969. *Madness in Society.* New York: Harper & Row, Harper Torchbooks.

Sartre, Jean-Paul. 1956. *Being and Nothingness: An Essay on Phenomenological Ontology.* Translated by Hazel E. Barnes. New York: Philosophical Library.

Seeman, Melvin. 1967. "On the Personal Consequences of Alienation in Work." *American Sociological Review* 32 (April): 273–85.

Sherif, Muzafer, and Hadley Cantril. 1947. *The Psychology of Ego-Involvements.* New York: Wiley.

Shils, Edward. 1962. "The Theory of Mass Society." *Diogenes* 39 (Fall): 45–66.

Soellner, Rolf. 1972. *Shakespeare's Pattern of Self-Knowledge.* Columbus: Ohio University Press.

Sorokin, Pitirim A. 1937–41. *Social and Cultural Dynamics.* Englewood Cliffs, N.J.: Bedminster.

Spiegel, John P. 1969. "Campus Conflict and Professional Egos." *Trans-action* 6 (October): 41–50.

Spitzer, Stephan, Carl Couch, and John Stratton. 1973. *The Assessment of the Self.* Iowa City, Ia.: Sernoll.

Stonequist, Everette V. 1937. *The Marginal Man.* New York: Scribner.

Thomas, William I., and Florian Znaniecki. 1918. *The Polish Peasant in Europe and America.* New York: Dover.

Thompson, Francis. 1893. "The Hound of Heaven."

Trilling, Lionel. 1961. "The Modern Element in Modern Literature." *Partisan Review* 28 (January): 9–25.

Turner, Ralph H. 1968. "The Self in Social Interaction." Pp. 93–106 in *The Self in Social Interaction,* vol. 1, edited by Chad Gordon and Kenneth Gergen. New York: Wiley.

———. 1969. "The Theme of Contemporary Social Movements." *British Journal of Sociology* 20 (December): 390–405.

———. 1975. "Is There a Quest for Identity?" *Sociological Quarterly* 16 (Spring): 148–61.

Veblen, Thorstein. 1899. *The Theory of the Leisure Class.* New York: New American Library.

Warner, W. Lloyd, and Paul S. Lunt, 1941. *The Status System of a Modern Community.* New Haven, Conn.: Yale University Press.

Wellman, Barry, 1971. "Social Identities in Black and White." *Sociological Inquiry* 41 (Winter): 57–66.

White, Robert W. 1972. *The Enterprise of Living: Growth and Organization in Personality.* New York: Holt, Rinehart & Winston.

Wilensky, Harold L. 1964. "Varieties of Work Experiences." Pp. 125–54 in *Man in a World at Work,* edited by Henry Borow. Boston: Houghton Mifflin.

Wordsworth, William. 1807. "Ode to Duty."

Wrong, Dennis H. 1961. "The Oversocialized Conception of Man in Modern Sociology." *American Sociological Review* 26 (April): 183–93.

Young, Kimball. 1940. *Personality and Problems of Adjustment.* New York: Crofts.

Zurcher, Lewis A. 1972. "The Mutable Self: An Adaptation in Accelerated Sociocultural Change." *Et al* 3 (1): 3–15.

———. 1973. "Alternative Institutions and the Mutable Self: An Overview." *Journal of Applied Behavioral Science* 9 (2–3): 369–80.

PART FOUR

SOCIALIZATION AS A LIFE PROCESS

Encompassing, as it does, not only the emergence of selves, their maintenance, change, loss, and reformulation, but also appropriate formulations and transformations of motive in the context of such relationships as family, school, church, work, and government, the literature on socialization is vast. Moreover, one can conceive of the study of the personal life in the perspective of symbolic interaction as a continuing endeavor to explain the socialization process. In this section, we cannot begin to cover the extensive theory and research that falls under this rubric.[1] Rather, we have attempted to open and close the section with important theoretical statements which can inform the intervening empirical studies and surveys presented along what Faulkner refers to as the "contingency" of age.

Above all, *socialization is conceived as a lifelong process.* Symbolic interactionists eschew holistic applications of such folk dicta as "the child is father to the man" or "as the twig is bent, so grows the tree." Psychoanalytic writings have probably most often been called upon to justify or rationalize such gross assertions. Sewell's early attempt to give some empirical precision to these so-called chamber-pot hypotheses accounts, in no small part, for our scepticism in regard to the overriding importance of infantile experience upon the subsequent course of personal careers or biographies.[2] Although various tendentious arguments have been directed at Sewell's research, while other social scientists have simply ignored it, so far as we know the literature is devoid of empirical refutations.

This does not mean that symbolic interactionists may not offer some plausible

---

[1]The best concise review of this literature remains John A. Clausen (ed.), *Socialization and Society* (Boston: Little, Brown, and Co., 1968), but for a grasp of the perspective presented here, see the recent collection of studies in Peter I. Rose (ed.), *Socialization and the Life Cycle* (New York: St. Martin's Press, 1979).

[2]William H. Sewell, "Infant Training and the Personality of the Child," *American Journal of Sociology,* LVIII, (September, 1952), pp. 150–159. Sewell ran 460 Chi-square tests of the association between infant training practices and six tests of personality adjustment among 162 children in the age group five to six. Eighteen tests were significant at the .05 level or less. At that level, 23 would be expected by chance! Of the eighteen significant tests, eleven were in the direction expected from what he called "the psychoanalytic position"; seven were in the opposite direction.

arguments against the uncritical generalization of Sewell's findings and in favor of some consideration for the hypothesis that early childhood experience *may have some consequence* for later self-formulations. Sewell, in fact, admitted this, but his reasoning was more technical (what some call methodological) than theoretical. The argument, for which no direct empirical data are available, would focus on the fact that the concept "personality" is too gross and crude to be implemented in socialization studies. Rather, the social psychologist should focus on *identity* or identities. Now, some identities are "stickier" than others. They are more difficult to shrug off or reformulate in later socialization. One might say they are highly institutionalized. Gender, or sex, is one such identity, and we have already suggested that, because of sex differences in early investitures and childhood drama, boys in our society (at least in that generation whose childhood occurred before World War II) may have a more difficult time becoming men than girls have becoming women. However, once adulthood is established, men have an easier time being men than women do being women.[3] This is because of a relatively distinctive and pervasive characteristic of the larger social organization—namely, in all societies we find sexual differentiations of roles. Consequently, the sexual differentiation of communication matrices within which socialization goes on must be carefully considered along with the formulation of institutionalized dimensions of the self. This argument is directly commensurate with Sewell's recommendations for further research at the end of his study of infant training practices.

More speculatively, we might consider another application of this perspective. Orthodox Freudians have often contrasted the seemingly "underdeveloped" feminine superego with the allegedly "stronger" development of the masculine superego. This difference is traced to presumed sexual differences in the resolution of the Oedipus complex. Castration threats, so the reasoning goes, are simply not as convincing to young girls as they are to young boys. Thus, sex differences in the resolution of the Oedipal situation are construed as a matter of genetic destiny or fate—without a penis, a young girl can scarcely be intimidated by castration threats, her tabooed attraction for her father is difficult to discourage, and superego formation is impeded.

Now, let us acknowledge that these Freudian *observations* may well be correct (particularly those made at the turn of the nineteenth century and in the early years of the twentieth), but that an alternative *explanation* is readily available. We have shown that those engaged in interpersonal relations tend to qualify one another's identities more along the axis of mood than the axis of value, while the opposite seems to be the case for those engaged in structural relations.[4] Up until recently in Western civilization, social structures were built for men,[5] while women had to rely most often on interpersonal relations as

---

[3]See Gregory P. Stone, "Appearance and the Self," reprinted in Part Three of this volume. See also "The Play of Little Children" by the same author in this part of the book.

[4]Stone, "Appearance and the Self," *op. cit.*

[5]By 1940, women had apparently participated in all occupations in the U.S. labor force, including that of garbage collector, but problems of equal sexual opportunity in the central institutional structure of the U.S.—occupations—persisted as of 1960. See Edward Gross, "Plus Ça Change . . .? The Sexual Structure of Occupations over Time," *Social Problems*, XVI (Fall, 1968), pp. 198–208. Gross says that changes in sexual participation in the labor force may well represent the maintenance of male hegemony over male occupations along with a male invasion of presumably female occupations!

accessible sources of self-validation. Notions of superego as well as libidinal excess in personality assessment were, of course, obtained by psychoanalysts through content analysis of verbal statements—free association, the recounting of dreams, reports of personal difficulties, etc. Quite probably male accounts contained more value references than female accounts. Hence, superego differences were inferred, and, because of the medical model employed,[6] explanations focused on physiological differences. Our explanation would merely contrast the exclusion of women from structural participation with the participation of men in the central social structures of society, consequently enhancing the saliency of value for men in their reviews of themselves and one another. Therefore, a sociological or, more specifically, a symbolic interactionist perspective would not view such socialization differences as physiological outcomes, but as conditioned by differential sexual participation in the larger social organization.

Symbolic interactionists, then, in their analyses of socialization have not focused upon the unique, biologically relevant experiences of that process, but upon the creation, learning, and modification of rules that culminate in meaningful human differentiation and the formulation of selves. Games readily lend themselves to such an analysis, for they are, in a sense, miniature models of society. This was understood and acted upon long ago by Jean Piaget, a Swiss psychologist, who devoted his life to the study of early socialization.[7]

Piaget used the game of marbles as an entering wedge into the study of socialization. Marbles, seemingly so simple and trivial in the eyes of adults, proves, upon closer examination, to be a highly complex enterprise. Its usefulness as an analogue of the larger society can be readily seen. First, any system of morality is, in fact, a system of rules, and marbles presents such a system. Second, the system is relatively self-contained, since only children participate in the game, and, unlike the larger society, rules are not passed down and enforced by adults, but by other, older children, ultimately apprehended by Piaget as *formal* parent surrogates.[8] Third, and as a consequence, the game world of marbles can be interpreted as a separate world, a kind of subculture, or distinct universe of discourse. On these points, Piaget observed, Pierre Bovet, the psychologist, and Emile Durkheim, the sociologist, would agree.

Durkheim, in his early work *The Division of Labor in Society*,[9] asserted that society progresses from a condition of relative homogeneity to one of relative heterogeneity, with concomitant increases in size, physical density, and dynamic density. In the former

---

[6]See Erving Goffman, ''The Medical Model and Mental Hospitalization,'' in his *Asylums* (New York: Doubleday Anchor Books, 1961). Of course, this is a basic argument leveled by Thomas S. Szasz against conventional psychiatry. See his *The Myth of Mental Illness* (New York: Paul B. Hoeber, Inc., 1961).

[7]Jean Piaget, *The Moral Judgment of the Child* (Glencoe, Ill.: The Free Press, 1948), first published in 1932.

[8]In 1975, the world singles marbles champion was Alan Smith, thirty years old, of Crawley, England. He has won the title four times, and, since 1956, the only other champion has been his father, fifty years old at the time, who taught him how to play. He plays daily with his father and two brothers, aged twenty and twenty-six. All are marbles professionals and seek to restore the game to the popularity it enjoyed in ''ancient Roman times.'' About 2,000 spectators are expected to watch Smith's title defenses which are televised. (From the *Minneapolis Tribune*, May 4, 1975, p. 5—C.) So much for Piaget's conception of the game!

[9]Emile Durkheim, *The Division of Labor in Society*, translated by George Simpson (Glencoe, Ill.: The Free Press, 1947). Also see the article by Gregory P. Stone and Harvey A. Farberman, ''On the Edge of Rapprochement: Was Durkheim Moving Toward the Perspective of Symbolic Interaction?'' *Sociological Quarterly*, VIII (Spring, 1967), pp. 149—164.

mechanically solidary society, rules automatically constrain the members, and violations are repressively punished as violations against the society itself. Thus, the practice of rules is obligatory, and consciousness of them a kind of sacred affair charged with affect or passion. Such a condition is interpreted by Piaget as a manifestation of *heteronomous morality*—the source of rules is found in others whose expectations are unquestioned, and which therefore make one feel strong obligations to conform. Piaget noted that the child is actually prepared for such obligatory observance of rules by his parents before he enters the world of games: "even before language he becomes conscious of certain obligations." In the world of children's games, however, adult intervention is reduced to a minimum, and older children stand *in loco parentis* as socializing agents and enforcers. In the latter *organically solidary society,* rules emerge to regulate the relations of members to one another (as in the case of contracts) rather than to the society as a whole. Violators of such rules must merely make restitution to the offended parties. At least two consequences are implied. First, persons enter into the formulation of rules, as in the process of legislation. Second, persons are confronted with the objective conditions of choice. Such a state of affairs is interpreted by Piaget as a manifestation of *autonomous morality.*

We have here a kind of social recapitulation theory of socialization. The child's practice and consciousness of rules vary throughout his early development. Among younger children up to about the ages of five to eight years, rules constitute a sort of sacred reality. Thereafter, they are more often based on mutual agreement or cooperation. As societies "progress" from mechanical to organic solidarity, children "progress" from heteronomous to autonomous morality. Age, then, is seen as the fundamental differentiating variable in early socialization. There is a gradual disappearance of uncritical conformity as the child grows older.[10] In our view the presumption of relative social homogeneity within age-grades is now highly questionable, given sex differentiation, socio-economic differences in early socialization, and historical variation.

There remains the matter of the emergence of reason in the socialization of the child, and this is a matter to which Piaget devoted extensive time and effort in later works. However, even in this early effort, he was keenly aware of the problem. The sheer objective confrontation of man with choice does not explain how choices are reasonably made. Here, the initial effort to reconcile sociological and psychological perspectives is undertaken. Piaget drew upon Pierre Bovet's observation that "reason requires cooperation as the proliferation of the division of labor requires cooperative law, insofar as being rational consists in situating oneself so as to submit the individual to the universal." Mutual respect is seen, therefore, as the necessary condition of autonomy. The "norm of reciprocity in sympathy" replaces the norms of authority.

[10]Erving Goffman has provided what seems to us a more convincing explanation of this phenomenon, avoiding as it does the many pitfalls of recapitulation theories. He has shown how and speculated why careers in the enactment of *all roles* (not only those of children) begin woodenly and, over time, are characterized by variations and improvisations on the theme or role. See his "Role Distance," in Erving Goffman, *Encounters* (Indianapolis: Bobbs-Merrill Co., 1961), pp. 105−152. In the article, "Child's Play and the Construction of Social Order," *Quest,* Monograph 26 (Summer, 1976), pp. 48−55, Norman K. Denzin has it the other way around, but attributes this to the intrusion of sibling rivalry on the process of learning the rules of a game. Denzin's observations were of his children at home. Again, the significance of the situation and the communicative matrix is proved crucial for the interpretation of observations.

[11]George H. Mead, *Mind, Self, and Society* (Chicago: University of Chicago Press, 1934), pp. 144−173.

Marbles is not a team game, but a type of game that George H. Mead passed over quickly in his well-known attempt to explain the emergence of the self.[11] Mead focused on team games as analogues, since teams may be construed as models of societies or, better, communities. Prior to his participation in team games, however, the child must develop the capacity to communicate with universal symbols and play at the various roles of his community or social circle. The former is accomplished through the transformation of a conversation of gestures, such as that formed in the fighting and playing of dogs. In this case, although reference is consistently made to the behavior of other organisms, reference to the self is absent.[12] Vocal gestures, particularly as they are elaborated into language, are eminently suited to this self-reference or indication. One receives his own vocal gesture in about the way it is received by the other. This facilitates the arousal of responses in the gesturing organism similar to those in the organism toward which the gesture is directed. All this is implied in language that mobilizes concerted activity and lends it a universal character: "Our symbols are universal. You cannot say anything that is absolutely particular."[13] Language enables the mutual assumption of roles or attitudes.

In play, the young child assumes the roles that are established in his larger social world. By playing at such roles, or playing out the attitudes of separate others, the child can, metaphorically, get outside himself and formulate a reflected view of himself as distinct from but related to these individual others. The culmination of such play, however, is the establishment of aggregated selves diversely related to one another depending upon the relationship of these dramatized roles to one another in the larger social organization. Participation in team games is another matter. Here rules, comprising the logic of organization, define the relationships of team members. Team players must each generalize the organization of the entire team and play the game from the standpoint of this "generalized other," incorporating the attitudes of the team in the formulation of an organized and generalized self. In time the teams of childhood games are replaced by "concrete classes" or subgroups, for example political parties, clubs, and corporations, eventually by "abstract classes" or classifications that function only more or less indirectly as social units. Such abstract classes are rather more inclusive than exclusive,

---

[12]It seems to us that even plausible explanations of the transition from the conversations of gestures found among the other animals to the linguistic conversations found among human beings are not provided in Mead's work. First, it is simply not convincing to contrast nonvocal with vocal gestures. The other animals vocalize. Though ranges of vocal tones may be limited in many species, among some birds, for example, the ranges may approximate or transcend the human range. Moreover, recent research has demonstrated the significance of bird calls and their replication for the "adjustment" of young birds to "adult" flocks. In addition, we have already touched upon the importance of nonverbal symbols or appearance for early human socialization. Second, if one scrutinizes carefully the play of "socialized" dogs and permits himself some anthropomorphic license, he can usually detect what *seems* to be a working consensus on what *seem* to be the rules of play. Specifically, the infliction of injury *seems* "studiously" to be avoided, and, if injury is inflicted, the play will usually end. True, animal communication is severely circumscribed and confined to the spatial and temporal dimensions within which it occurs, while human communication typically transcends such limits because of the transforming character of universal symbolism, but perhaps we ought to give up the explanation of the latter as an evolutionary emergent of the former. It is enough to observe, as Mead does elsewhere, after the fashion of Sullivan and Cooley, that infants are born into ongoing conversations, universes of discourse, social circles, or societies, and that this fact *constrains* the great majority of them eventually to join the conversation in one way or another. In this sense, Helen Keller, in spite of severe trauma—early deafness and blindness—was constrained to join the larger conversation. Of course, not all traumatically affected infants are subjected to the same persevering constraints.

[13]George H. Mead, *op. cit.,* p. 146.

and their generalization widens the horizons of self, the universe of discourse in which the self is situated, and the possibilities of thought or intelligence. Mead, therefore, in explicit contrast to James and Cooley, conceived the self as cognitive, arising out of participation in the communicative organization of society.

That Mead viewed cognition as social, and affective experience as not, reflects, perhaps more than anything else, the intellectual temper of the period in which he was working. Then the tendency was to place emotion in the context of bodily passion or unmediated impulse and oppose it to cerebration or mind. It is ironic that Mead, who contributed so much to resolving the mind-body controversy by placing mind unequivocally in social concert, left the emotions "behind" with the body. Though he failed, Cooley at least made the effort to establish the sociality of affect. Today, one of the leading systematizers of symbolic interaction asserts as an axiom: "Emotions, as well as thought and will, are learned in communication."[14]

In the differentiation of the self as an object, then, it is necessary to account for more than the emergence of morality (values) after the fashion of Piaget and rules (values) and identity after the fashion of Mead, and a beginning can be made. The conception of the self as different from but related to the organized expectations of the community, construed as a team, focuses on organizational (in a certain sense, structural) differentiation. Thus, within the same team (community), selves differ by virtue of the positions occupied. The shortstop is a different self from that of the catcher because the expectations directed toward his performance (community attitudes) are different and are, therefore, generalized differently. The generalized other of the shortstop necessarily differs from that of the catcher, though each belongs to the same team. This is a point of fundamental theoretical difference between Mead's conception and the conception of reference group as it has been implemented in data analysis. At bottom, individuality is insured by the division of roles inherent in any concert or joint action. Beyond that, we are constrained to search for individuality in "experience," in the intersections of diverse social circles, or in the generalization of others who play different games on different teams—in Mead's view, a mark of intelligence. (The diversity of social worlds in early socialization has been grossly oversimplified in the literature.)

Harry Stack Sullivan conceived personality as a persistent hangup. In early socialization, one incorporates or rejects the attitudes of significant others so utterly that those attitudes infect one's expectations of others when such attitudes may not be relevant at all. Cacophony is introduced to communication. Sullivan calls it parataxis, and he sees this as an ordinary occurrence in daily life.[15]

Significant others are conceived here as those we cannot love or hate too much. For to love or hate too much is to be transported, to lose one's differentiation, to enter the trance of hypnosis, and to come under the other's control or lose one's self in or to the other. Significant others ordinarily lend a distinctive cast to the generalization of others. We can envision this by shifting Mead's analogue of the game from baseball to basketball. In the latter, the play is much faster, quickly shifting, perhaps even more spontaneous. If we

---

[14]Hugh Dalziel Duncan, *Symbols in Society* (New York: Oxford University Press, 1968), p. 47.

[15]Harry Stack Sullivan, *The Psychiatric Interview* (New York: W. W. Norton and Co., Inc., 1954), pp. 25–26.

imagine the passing back and forth of the ball as a conversation, it is not difficult to understand how the direction of the conversation is shaped by love and hate among the players. Significant others mediate the generalization of team expectations. In such a way, selves are differentiated along the dimension of affective relations as well as by their location in a division of roles.

It is the self in its capacity as a social object that we speak of as identity. Social nomenclatures exist for differentiating it, and it is particularly important to distinguish titles from nicknames in such nomenclatures. In one sense, titled identities are readily understood in Mead's terms, and nicknamed identities in Sullivan's. Yet, such identities are built of incorporated attitudes. To be an object is to be on the edge of action. Here we can understand the meaning of identity found in most dictionaries—continuity. Continuity suggests a process that implies a sameness—an attitude that implies an object. Indeed, objects call out attitudes in us which lend them their meaning. Their meaning is in such responses, and among selves, these responses institute a concert. So identities are always situated; to press the analogy to the absurd, in a bandstand or concert hall.[16]

Were the socialization process apprehended merely as a journey undertaken between two points of nothingness—birth and death—then identities could be easily construed as milestones. But the corridor of life has many exits and entrances, and they escape the limitations of simple aging that Shakespeare so nicely capsuled as seven stages in *As You Like It*. Moreover, the path through it is ordinarily tortuous, filled with backtracking, exiting into blind-alleys, and entering uncharted passages into unimagined nooks and corners, some easily left behind as we blunder about; others sticking with us—walls made of fly paper. Travisano, though dealing with such twists and turns in what has come to be called "later socialization," offers a sheaf of sharpened concepts to assist our interpretation and ordering of the process. Travisano shows that adult change is not all of a piece. To us, any detailed summary of his effort would be redundant. Insights abound. He distinguishes between *alternations* and *conversions* in adult life by contrasting Jews who become Unitarians with those who become fundamental Christians—Hebrew Christians. His analysis of these changes is generalized to adult socialization in American society. Conversion is the more dramatic change in the eyes of most observers. This involves changes in *informing aspect* (the platform from which one views the world), in allegiances from one source of authority to another, and in universes of discourse. Conversions are ordinarily accompanied by emotional upset in oneself and those others whose universe of discourse is left behind. Indeed, those others may treat the one who converts as a traitor. Most of all, conversion involves a sudden and traumatic rupture in that sequence of identities that may be conceived as a career. In contrast, alternation provides a rather easily explained sequence of identities. Some alternations merely involve a transition from one linked identity to another (from fiancé to husband). Others represent *cumulative identity sequences* (from husband to father)—one does not lose an earlier identity through the assumption of a later one. Now, as we have said, identities may be classified in terms of their "stickiness": basic, general, and independent. Ordinarily, conversion implies a

---

[16]This weaving together of the perspectives set forth by Mead and Sullivan, along with the discussion of identity from each point of view, is taken from Gregory P. Stone, "Personal Acts," *Symbolic Interaction*, I (Fall, 1977), pp. 4–5.

change in general identity—hence the change in informing aspect. Yet, every alternation is incipiently a conversion. One of the crucial problems of contemporary society is the increasing antipathy to converts in all areas. This pressure against total belief and faith may well culminate in a world where, as many wags have put it, the bland lead the bland.

Identities may be more or less "sticky," but some are also repellent. They are taken on to be put off. In a sense, this is true of the markings of every age. The child looks forward to the identity of teenager. Asked how old, comes the reply, "Me? I'm twelve and a half." or "I'm almost thirteen." The teenager, cursed with the identity limbo of youth—worse, adolescence—dreams of the time of legal emancipation: eighteen or, at the worst, twenty-one. But false identity cards are generally available. In our society, of course, adulthood carries with it no clearly desirable future age-identity, whether or not life begins at forty. Nevertheless, the identity of child is crucial, for it is, as a child, that one conceives of one's self as an object, subsequently part of a world of objects. It is in this most general or basic sense that "early socialization" is so important.

Stone views the explanation of early socialization as an enormously complicated enterprise. First, the study of socialization is profoundly affected by historical variations in social definitions of the child. This difficulty has been partially met by cross-cultural studies and by studies of "social class" differences within societies, but these studies feature synchronic contrasts and omit diachronic contrasts or matters of historical change. The tendency in the vast majority of socialization studies is to treat the historical situation in which the study has been conducted as pervasive in time, usually by not treating the historical situation at all. How do we arrive at generalizations about the socialization of the child in eras or places when and where there are no children, as in medieval France, or in the Harlem of the fifties?

> . . . "Man, Sonny, they ain't got no kids in Harlem. I ain't never seen any. I've seen some real small people actin' like kids. They were too small to be grown, and they might've looked like kids, but they don't have any kids in Harlem, because nobody has time for a childhood. Man, do you ever remember bein' a kid? Not me. Shit, kids are happy, kids laugh, kids are secure. They ain't scared-a nothin'. You ever been a kid, Sonny? Damn, you lucky. I ain't never been a kid, man. I don't know what happened, man, but I think I missed out on that childhood thing, because I don't ever recall bein' a kid."[17]

The answer can only be uncovered through more extensive historical research—a desideratum that will be difficult to realize, at a time when sociological technicians are preoccupied with ahistorical techniques in their research and in methods curricula.

Mead's concept of play is viewed as too gross a concept, particularly when it is used to depict a phase of socialization. Mead, of course, distinguished between playing and playing at, and he made observations *en passant* about the child as the mother's plaything. However, he focused on the matter of playing at roles as the relevant play form for the emergence of self. Stone prefers to describe this phase as childhood *drama*, recognizing that other play forms, such as tests of poise, may be distinguished from drama and also importantly enter into the socialization process. A second criticism is made of Mead's

---

[17]Claude Brown, *Manchild in the Promised Land* (New York: Signet Books, 1965), p. 295.

conception of play. Although he recognized that children play at roles that are not directly (although they may be mythically) viable in the child's larger community, Mead made no analytical distinction between such roles and those that are directly and immediately present and being enacted by others. Stone therefore distinguishes *fantastic drama* from *anticipatory drama*. In the former, the child assumes identities he cannot reasonably expect to assume or encounter in later life; in the latter, he assumes identities he can reasonably expect to assume or encounter in later life. The fact that boys in our society may more frequently engage in fantastic drama, while girls more frequently engage in anticipatory drama, may well bear on our earlier speculations about the significance of sex differences in earlier socialization. Yet, even this distinction must be employed with caution: One child's fantasy is often another child's reality.

. Nor do the complications in the application of Mead's model end here. One can apply the concept of *awareness context*, developed by Glaser and Strauss,[18] to matters of play, even though they focus primarily on the question of knowledge of one another in interaction.[19] Stone raises the question of the knowledge the child has of the role he is playing. In the dramas of childhood he may, for various reasons, be ignorant of the role he is enacting, but be completely "open" about his performance—he simply doesn't know any better. This situation is not as much "closed" in terms of knowledge of one another as it is in terms of knowledge of oneself. "Pretense awareness" is a frequent though seldom studied context of childhood drama. Probably each of us can recall playing doctor or nurse for reasons other than the drama itself. The performance of such roles grants a license to the child. Adopting such roles, he is granted access to tabooed areas, in this case, of the body.

It is not enough to account for the emergence of the self as a general object by attending only to the consequences of play, as in tests of poise where the self as object is "spun off" in self-induced vertigo, or drama where the performance of other roles provides the actor with a reflected view of self in the identity that complements that at the base of the role being performed, that is, an identity in the "role-set" of the drama. A game is called for. Mead, we have shown, had in mind a team game—baseball—providing multiple identities as one's community does.

Gary Fine, in his extensive studies of Little League Baseball, points out, however, that concrete involvement and participation in such games carries the players beyond the game itself into friendship patterns which operate to socialize older children into a kind of "peer culture." George Herbert Mead viewed the game as a sociological metaphor of community organization, while, paradoxically, the concrete analysis of any given game is incomplete without specific reference to the larger community in which the game is carried on. Children's games, then, may be conceived as a kind of exit leading children beyond any particular game to a variety of social settings and situations which comprise the organization of their larger "real" community. For older children, roughly from the ages of seven to twelve, opportunities are provided to develop relationships and perform

[18]See Barney G. Glaser and Anselm L. Strauss, "Awareness Contexts and Social Interaction," reprinted in Part One of this volume.

[19]For a fascinating discussion of this question, the student is strongly urged to consult Kurt H. Wolff (ed.), *The Sociology of Georg Simmel* (New York: The Free Press of Glencoe, 1964 edition), pp. 307−316.

roles shielded from the view of adult chaperones and overseers. Chums and gangs, either established in or paralleling organized games, are "arenas for social action." It is in such arenas that children learn how to present themselves in the public of peers, as opposed to the public of adults which frequently demands deception or dissemblance. In other words, they learn how to manage their impressions for their own interests in arenas that count rather than in the interests of adults which can easily be called to silent question or actively impugned. As skills of impression management are developed among their peers, rules are called for, and Fine dramatically depicts the changing orientation to such rules along those lines marked off by Piaget which we have discussed earlier. At closer inspection, we can see that autonomous morality is established by *negotiation*—a concept assuming increasing significance in symbolic interactionist interpretations of social organization.[20]

Much of this socialization is accomplished among friends, and friendship is a highly important "staging area" for the socialization of older children. In particular, young boys, in their social circles of friends, teach one another the meaning of their own sexual identity as it is ordinarily realized in relationships with girls.

Fine demonstrates clearly and excellently the ways in which games may lead to friendship, if only by the provision of time to be filled in and spaces to be entered after a game is done. In such time and spaces, game identities are ordinarily left behind, and the identities of chum or gang member take over. All have an impact on the socialization of young children, but Fine does not provide us with (nor should he be expected to) a consideration of the reverberations that such friendships may have on the playing of the game. What is implied is the significance of "identity freight" in socialization. Undoubtedly these young boys brought their friendships back into the game where Goffman's "rules of irrelevance" say they don't belong.[21]

Among professional athletes, rules of irrelevance seem to be more prevalent. Two of the legendary double-play combination, Tinkers-to-Evers-to-Chance, would not speak to one another off the field. Problems arise when the professional athlete—or any professional, for that matter—flaunts such rules in public. Witness the clashes of Reggie Jackson and Billy Martin during the New York Yankee baseball season of 1978 or the difficulty of inducing one physician to testify against another in a court of law. A crucial question, then, would inquire as to what phases of socialization are characterized by the fact that "identity freight" is likely to cause problems. Conversions, as Travisano reminds us, cannot tolerate such freight; alternations must cope. We would also hypothesize that the likelihood of identity freight disturbing socialization may be greater in the socialization of what Becker, following Goffman, calls "batches" than in the serial socialization of individuals. In any case, however sharply focused, socialization into or the appropriation of *any* identity is freighted. Problematical or not, assuming one identity ordinarily builds passages into others.

In a sense, Stone's secondary analysis of the importance of sport for the socialization of youth carries with it the same message that Fine's treatment of children conveys, but there

[20]See especially, Anselm L. Strauss, *Negotiations* (San Francisco: Jossey-Bass, Inc., 1978).
[21]Erving Goffman, *Encounters* (Indianapolis: Bobbs-Merrill Company, Inc., 1961), pp. 19–26.

is an important difference. While the games of young children may operate to seal them off from adult worlds, the games of older youth serve as important entryways to some areas of adult society. Organized team sports, such as those found in high schools and characterized by both intra- and inter-urban competition, expose the athletes and their circles of admirers to adult activities like drinking and gambling. These, in turn, are often linked to organized crime, politics, or both. Of course, drinking and gambling provide obstacles to the socialization of some young people, and they don't catch up all youth, just as the Little League does not catch up all older children. The socialization of the age grades is, as we have insisted earlier, an overwhelmingly complicated matter, involving a vast range of diverse social circles and social alternatives. The materials provided by Fine and Stone merely follow one strand of the complex web of society within which young people must find their way or, at times, repudiate. The reader is encouraged to consider and examine other strands of the web.

Certainly one of the most searching studies of adult socialization that has come to our attention in the last decade is Faulkner's comparative study of hockey players and symphony musicians. Age is seen as an overriding contingency that affects all careers, as may be seen in the cases explored. Age sets the optimal time for career moves. The hockey player had better move up by age twenty-four or twenty-five; the musician, no later than thirty. Failure to do so sets in motion a whole process of career redefinition and the formulation of different goals. Resignation seems to have been more easily accomplished by musicians than by hockey players, but, then, knees on skating rinks wear out faster than do fingers on piano keys or violin strings. Yet, what is important here is not the details of hockey playing versus playing instruments in concert halls. Rather, it is the generality of the process, and this generality is perceptible in the commensurateness with and use made of Becker's contributions, one of which we use to close this section.

Becker provides us with a general treatment of change and stability in adult life. Situations make for change; commitments, for stability. The implications of these conceptualizations are examined with reference to such institutions as the undergraduate college, the medical school, and prisons. Changing situations require adjustments and readjustments, and it is to the character of such situations that we must look to explain why people change. Roles and role performances are always situated, and others recognize a person by such performances, noting the changes that *seem* to occur ''in'' him. Actually, these observed changes ''in'' the person only require of that person a desire to participate in the situation. Thus, prisoners, premeds, and college students all surrender early models of adjustment to these varied institutional situations toward the end of their careers, as they prepare for release. Such adjustments and readjustments are not only personal affairs, they are often collective, as when persons enter and leave situations in ''batches'' (for example, college classes). In these cases more room for deviation from institutional expectations is permitted than is the case for single recruits. Stability may also be afforded by situations, particularly when they are stabilized in highly stable institutions. Ordinarily, however, commitments to situations provide such stability by ''locking'' people into them. Commitments are often built up over time by a process of accruing ''side bets.'' That is to say, the person may have a stake in so many other situations—his family, his home, neighborhood groups—that his commitment to his work is greatly increased and his mobility potential diminished. Often stable situations themselves conduce to such commitments.

So our discussion of socialization must end, and we find that we haven't covered it all. There is the matter of aging, in Shakespeare's view the sixth stage—the pantaloon. We have omitted material on the "aged," since that area has mushroomed in the last decade, and an entire subdiscipline of social gerontology has emerged and crystallized. It is, in fact, a field in itself. We can see the same movement in the study of death.[22] At first glance, death appears as the ultimate socialization. Yet, 1977 will go down as the year in which Robert E. Lee was pardoned, and George Washington finally made it to the rank of five star general!

SUGGESTED READINGS

Ariès, Philippe. *Centuries of Childhood*. Robert Baldick (trans.). New York: Alfred A. Knopf, Inc., 1962.

Becker, Ernest..*The Denial of Death*. New York: The Free Press, 1973.

Becker, Howard S. *Sociological Work: Method and Substance*. New Brunswick, N.J.: Transaction Books, 1977.

Brim, O. G., Jr., and S. Wheeler. *Socialization after Childhood: Two Essays*. New York: John Wiley & Sons, 1966.

Brown, Claude. *Manchild in the Promised Land*. New York: The Macmillan Co., 1965.

Burr, Wesley, Reuben Hill, Filvan Nye, and Ira L. Reiss (eds.). *Contemporary Theories about the Family*. New York: The Free Press, 1978.

Cain, L. D., Jr. "Life, Course, and Social Structure." R.E.L. Faris, (ed.). *Handbook of Modern Sociology*. Chicago: Rand McNally & Co., 1964, pp. 272—309.

Clausen, John (ed.). *Socialization and Society*. Boston: Little, Brown & Co., 1968.

Coleman, J. S. *The Adolescent Society*. New York: The Free Press, 1961.

Denzin, Norman K., "Child's Play and the Construction of Social Order," *Quest*, Monograph 26 (Summer, 1976), pp. 48—55.

Erickson, Erik H. (ed.). *The Challenge of Youth*. Garden City, N.Y.: Doubleday Anchor Books, 1963.

Glaser, Barney G. and Anselm L. Strauss. *Status Passage: A Formal Theory*. Chicago: Aldine-Atherton, Inc., 1971.

Gottlieb, David and Anne Lienhard Heinsohn, "Sociology and Youth," *The Sociological Quarterly*, XIV (Spring, 1973), pp. 249—270.

Hobman, David (ed.). *The Social Challenge of Aging*. New York: St. Martin's Press, 1978.

Kohn, Melvin. *Class and Conformity: A Study in Values*, second edition. Chicago: University of Chicago Press, 1977.

[22]On the preparation for death, see Barney G. Glaser and Anselm L. Strauss, *Awareness of Dying* (Chicago: Aldine Publishing Co., 1965).

Müller, Walter and Karl Ulrich (eds.). *Social Stratification and Career Mobility*. Paris: Mouton & Cie, 1973.

Riley, Matilda W. "Socialization for the Middle and Later Years." D. A. Goslein and D. C. Glasse (eds.)., *Handbook of Socialization Theory and Research*. New York: Rand McNally & Co., 1968.

Ritchie, Oscar W., and Marvin R. Koller. *Sociology of Childhood*. New York: Appleton-Century-Crofts, 1964.

Rose, Peter I. (ed.). *Socialization and the Life Cycle* (New York: St. Martin's Press, 1979).

Rosenmayer, Leopold and Klaus Allerbeck, "Youth and Society," *Current Sociology*, XXVII, Number 2/3 (1979), pp. 1−335.

Saneza Saleh, "Motives for the Emigration of Egyptian Scientists." *Social Problems*, 25, No. 1 (October, 1977): 40−51.

Thornton, Russell and Peter M. Nardi. "The Dynamics of Role Acquisition." *American Journal of Sociology*, LXXX (January, 1975): 870−885.

Whiting, Beatrice. *Six Cultures: Studies of Child Rearing*. New York: John Wiley & Sons, 1963.

Ziegler, Edward and Irvin L. Child. "Socialization." Gardner Lindzey and Elliot Aronson (eds.), *The Handbook of Social Psychology*, second edition. Reading, Mass.: Addison-Wesley Publishing Co., 1969, Volume III, pp. 450−589.

TWENTY-ONE

ALTERNATION AND CONVERSION AS QUALITATIVELY DIFFERENT TRANSFORMATIONS

RICHARD V. TRAVISANO

Kenneth Burke has suggested that every man is a poet. Peter Berger suggests an artist. Ernest Becker suggests a dramatist. They each are concerned with how the individual rationalizes his life; rationalizes, not in the psychological sense of propaganda to conceal "real" motives, but in Weber's sense of legitimizing behavior. Legitimation socializes behavior, and proceeds by labeling behavior with socially understandable categories. This view of human conduct argues that what a man does often has little meaning, rhyme, or reason, until the individual gets busy making autobiographical use of his already completed actions. As Berger has pointed out, we constantly remake our own biographies, and our interpretations and revisions are rarely integrated and consistent:[1]

> . . . Most of us do not set out deliberately to paint a grand portrait of ourselves. Rather we stumble like drunkards over the sprawling canvas of our self-conception, throwing a little paint here, erasing some lines there, never really stopping to obtain a view of the likeness we have produced. . . .

This perspective, then, sees man as an artist who more or less blunders into his biographical materials and then must work them into his story one way or another. From this perspective we wish to distinguish two different kinds of personal transformation.

SOURCE: Richard V. Travisano. "Alternation and Conversion as Qualitatively Different Transformation." Original paper prepared especially for the first edition of this volume, 1970. Reprinted by permission of the author.

The formulations in this paper are the outcome of a study the writer did for a Master's thesis. This study was concerned with Jews who had become fundamental Christians and Jews who had become members of a Unitarian Society. Through this work the writer became interested in general conceptualizations about identity change. See Richard V. Travisano, "Alternation and Conversion in Jewish Identities" (unpublished M.A. thesis, Department of Sociology, University of Minnesota, 1967).

[1]Peter L. Berger, *Invitation to Sociology* (Garden City, N.Y.: Anchor Doubleday, 1963), p. 61.

CONSTANCY AND CHANGE

Certainly, as Anselm Strauss has said, "The awareness of constancy of identity . . . is in the eye of the beholder rather than 'in' the behavior itself."[2] The corollary of this statement is that *change* in identity is also in the eye of the beholder. But who *is* this beholder? He is the self-reflective actor, the actor's others, the generalized others, the sociological observer. As identities are retained, discarded, transformed, or assumed, one or more of these observers will note that a change has, or is, taking place. It is they who say how great that change is. Strauss, then, is saying that such permanence as our personal histories have is defined through the give and take of interaction within shared universes of discourse.[3] We add that, as permanence is rationalized into the confusion of contrary actions and meaning that make up a life, so also is change. Our task, then, as Nelson Foote has put it, is to apprehend the categories of identity and motive employed by the persons we study.[4]

Peter Berger has succinctly portrayed the flux of life and the ubiquity of personal transformations in it. For him values have become "relativized" in modern society. "Traditional societies assign definite and permanent identities to their members," whereas "In modern society identity itself is uncertain and in flux."[5] He argues that our unprece-

dented rates of geographical mobility and travel, along with the enormous amount of information available through our mass media "imply at least potentially the awareness that one's own culture, including its basic values, is relative in space and time."[6]

To continue in Berger's words:[7]

Social mobility . . . augments this relativizing effect. Wherever industrialism occurs, a new dynamism is injected into the social system. Masses of people begin to change their social position, in groups or as individuals. And usually this change is in an "upward" direction. With this movement an individual's biography often involves a considerable journey not only through a variety of social groups but through the intellectual universes that are, so to speak, attached to these groups. Thus the Baptist mail clerk who used to read the *Reader's Digest* becomes an Episcopalian junior executive who reads *The New Yorker,* or the faculty wife whose husband becomes department chairman may graduate from the best-seller list to Proust or Kafka.

Berger then points out that each viewpoint available to modern man carries with it its own slant on some aspect of reality and that,[8]

. . . the more fully elaborated meaning systems [such as Freudianism or Communism] . . . can provide a total interpretation of reality, within which will be included an interpretation of the alternate systems and of the ways of passing from one system to another.

In reference to these "fully elaborated meaning systems," Berger states:[9]

Instead of speaking of conversion (a term with religiously charged connotations) we would prefer to use the more neutral term of "alternation" to de-

---

[2] Anselm Strauss, *Mirrors and Masks* (Glencoe, Ill.: The Free Press, 1959), p. 147.

[3] "Universe of discourse" is used in Mead's sense of "a system of common or social meanings." It "is constituted by a group of individuals carrying on and participating in a common social process of experience." See George Herbert Mead, *Mind, Self and Society* (Chicago, Ill.: University of Chicago Press, 1934), pp. 89—90. Peter Berger uses the term "meaning system," to denote the same idea. (See Berger, *op. cit.*) We shall use "universe of discourse" for two reasons: first, the word "system" implies integration and universes of discourse contain inconsistencies; second, the term "universe of discourse" emphasizes that meanings are established and exist in symbolic interaction.

[4] Nelson Foote, "Identification as the Basis for a Theory of Motivation," *American Sociological Review,* XVI (1951), p. 18. Reprinted in Part Five of this volume.

[5] Berger, *op. cit.*, p. 48.

[6] *Ibid.*, p. 49.

[7] *Ibid.*, pp. 49—50.

[8] *Ibid.*, p. 51. The writer prefers the term "total (i.e., closed and all explaining) universes of discourse" to Berger's "fully elaborated meaning systems." Also see footnote 3 above.

[9] *Ibid.*, pp. 51—52.

scribe this phenomenon. The intellectual situation just described brings with it the possibility that an individual may alternate back and forth between logically contradictory meaning systems. Each time, the meaning system he enters provides him with an interpretation of his existence and of his world, including in this interpretation an explanation of the meaning system he has abandoned.

It is plain enough that Berger is offering a broad sociological explanation for the prevalence of identity changes in our times (i.e., our society assigns us no definite permanent identity while at the same time exposing us to many alternative universes of discourse). Also, he prefers the term ''alternation'' to the term ''conversion.'' There are, however, certain points to be considered if we are to get at the nature of these transformations.

To begin with, when Berger talks about alternation to ''fully elaborated meaning systems'' he is referring to what is called conversion in the narrowest everyday sense. These are the most radically reorganizing changes of everyday life: Christian college students become atheists; Jews become fundamental Christians; communists become Catholics. Berger claims that ''. . . an individual may alternate back and forth between contradictory meaning systems.'' This does not seem true. There are contradictions throughout our meanings, but it is the socially recognized and sanctioned contradictions that are central in what we recognize as antithetic universes of discourse. In addition, adoption of antithetic universes of discourse involves a complete reinterpretation and reorganization of life or autobiography. Kenneth Burke insists that conversion involves a change in the ''informing aspect'' of character.[10] That a person could change quickly back and forth in this respect seems quite unlikely. Experience does leave its mark. As Strauss writes, ''one . . . misconception about conversion is that when a person becomes partly converted and then is 'lost' he returns to his

previous identity. . . .''[11] Surely the point holds for complete conversion as well as for partial conversion. *One can't go home again.* The black sheep who return to the fold are somehow different from those who never left. Do not the angels rejoice more when one sinner repents? This is not to say that less than totally disruptive transformations do not occur. Middle-class youth, after all, will have their fling before they settle down into the world of meaning in which they were raised. While the break with middle-class respectability may be a conversion for such people, settling back into it is no conversion backwards. It is simply ''learning the ropes.'' The fact is that genuine change back and forth between antithetic total universes of discourse is a rare possibility.

In his definition of alternation, Berger ignores many identity changes which do not involve total universes of discourse. Thus he neglects his own example of the Baptist mail clerk who used to read the *Reader's Digest,* who becomes an Episcopalian junior executive who reads *The New Yorker.* What of this fellow? Do all Baptist organization men undergo total and disruptive reorientations of their lives in becoming Episcopalians? Do they all make the difficult move from one total universe of discourse to another? Certainly not! But surely such a move is a change in perspective, in identity, and in situation. Berger has discussed different kinds of changes, but has grouped them all together under the general term ''alternation.'' We will propose that important and useful distinctions between transformations can and should be made.

ALTERNATION AND CONVERSION AS DIFFERENT IDENTITY CHANGES

IDENTITY

To discuss and distinguish transformations we shall utilize the concept of identity. It seems best, moreover, to limit our notion of identity by a

[10]Kenneth Burke, *Permanence and Change* (rev. ed., Los Altos, Cal.: Hermes Publications, 1954), p. 77.

[11]Strauss, *op. cit.,* p. 123.

concise behaviorally objectified definition. Thus, we may follow Stone, who writes:[12]

> Almost all writers using the term imply that identity establishes *what* and *where* the person is in social terms. It is not a substitute word for "self." Instead, when one has identity, he is *situated*—that is, cast in the shape of a social object by the acknowledgement of his participation or membership in social relations. One's identity is established when others *place* him as a social object by assigning him the same words of identity that he appropriates for himself or *announces*. . . .

Identity, then, is a placed or validated announcement. One announces that he is some particular social object; others read his cue and respond in kind, saying by their behavior, that he indeed is what he claims. This "coincidence of placements and announcements" gives one the feeling that he embodies what he has announced himself as, that is, gives him an experiential sense of felt identity. But note Stone's phrase: "when one has identity, he is situated . . ." This acknowledges the fact that people must establish identities for *both* themselves *and* others if an interaction is to proceed in any meaningful manner.

ROLE

Every social interaction proceeds in terms of some definition of the situation, and placing people in identities is an important part of that definition.[13] The importance of identities in this regard indicates the crucial nature of the concept. "Role" is a conceptualization of social probabilities. It is im-

possible to delineate a role completely because a single role demands many different actions in different situations. But "identity" R *is* a signal *in interaction* for the mobilization of specific role expectations. Identities are, so to speak, the labels or names on the scripts of various situationally specified programs of behavior which make up the abstract totalities we call roles. Identities tell people what to do and expect during a given interaction. We use the plural because the specified behavior that an identity mobilizes usually depends on the identities of the others in the interaction. A sociologist acts like a sociologist. But what this means depends on where he is interacting—in the classroom, in the office, at home, or wherever else the identity might be relevant.[14] This is nothing new, but it is important because it emphasizes the interactional specificity of role as compared to identity, and the experiential reality of being a thing (say a sociologist) in a specific interaction, as compared to the non-experiential contemplation of being the same thing in general. Identities alone, of course, do not define situations. But we shall bypass, perhaps arbitrarily, a full consideration of the elements and process of situation definition, and simply state that the establishment of identities is usually an important part of the process.[15]

All this clearly has implications for our discussion of transformation. In the flux of life, it is the changes which get named that are dwelled upon, and the changes dwelled upon that get named. What, then, is the import of these considerations for an analysis of identity change? To establish a

---

[12]Gregory P. Stone, "Appearance and the Self" in Arnold Rose (ed.), *Human Behavior and Social Processes* (Boston: Houghton Mifflin Co., 1962), p. 93. Also reprinted in Part Three in this volume. We might add that even in the best available study of identity, the author, for some mysterious reason, refuses to define the central concept. See Strauss, *op. cit.*, p. 13.

[13]On this point see Foote, *op. cit.*, p. 18. Also Strauss, *op. cit.*, p. 43; Erving Goffman, *The Presentation of Self in Everyday Life* (Garden City, N.Y.: Doubleday Anchor, 1959), p. 13; and the plays of Luigi Pirandello, especially *Enrico IV* and *Six Characters in Search of an Author*.

[14]Identities vary in relevance. Practically anyone, six years old or older, could validate the identity "President of the United States." But a six-year-old child could not validate the identity, "stock broker," as the child has no notion of what a stock broker is, and, more importantly, because the identity, "stock broker," cannot be a meaningful part of the interaction between the man and the child, who is not the child or a friend of the child of the stock broker.

[15]Although identities usually play an important part in defining situations, situations often indicate identities, or at least severely limit the range of identities, that can be utilized. When one takes the rostrum before an assembly of dutifully registered students, one has to be a professor. [The reader may wish to review Part One of this volume.—eds.]

new identity, a new announcement must be recurrently made and validated.[16] But one does not take on only an abstract property called an identity, one takes on new definitions of situations and new situated behavior. This may be relatively easy (as when a husband becomes a father) or difficult (as when a wife becomes a divorcee). This relative ease or difficulty depends on how far afield one goes; that is, on whether a new identity is irrelevant, related, or opposed to old ones; on whether old relationships are unchanged, transformed, or destroyed. And it is on the interactional contingencies which make for relative ease or difficulty that our distinction between conversion and alternation rests. Complete disruption signals conversion while anything less signals alternation. Summary statements from the research which led to this paper will exemplify the differences in these transformation processes.

HEBREW CHRISTIANS AND JEWISH UNITARIANS: CONVERTS AND ALTERNATORS

The differences between a Jew becoming a fundamental Christian (a process of conversion) and a Jew becoming a member of a Unitarian Society (a process of alternation) are simply enormous. The "average" Hebrew Christian (the subjects' term for themselves) is about 23 years old at the time of his *conversion*. He is likely to be unsettled in occupation and life style. He very likely had a usual Jewish upbringing, religiously and "culturally," but he is quite unlikely to be a synagogue member at the time of his conversion. If he does hold membership, it will be dropped. His conver-

sion causes serious consternation among his relatives and friends. He is viewed as an apostate, a traitor, and heavy pressure is brought to bear against him. His change changes his life as his conversion and new identity become his central concern. He is quite likely to become a missionary worker by vocation or, at least, to adopt proselytizing as a very serious avocation. He loves to tell the story of his salvation and is, by this and other means, constantly trying to weave together the broken threads of his biography. The Hebrew Christian very definitely identifies himself as a Jew. He has not abandoned his Jewish identity but has transformed it into a Hebrew Christian one. This affords continuity from the past to the demanding new role of "born-again-believer," and it also affords an argument to meet the multitude of challenges that such a drastic change elicits. After all, who can argue with the basic logic of a statement made by one of my respondents:

> I was born a Jew, and now I have accepted the promised Messiah of Israel who came in fulfillment of the Scriptures. Christ came to the Jews. The first Christians were Jews. As a Hebrew Christian I am a completed Jew.

But the focus of the Hebrew Christian identity is fundamental Christianity. The Hebrew Christian is, so to speak, more Christian than Jewish. He probably knows, and spends time with, other Hebrew Christians,[17] but he attends a gentile Christian church and has mostly gentile Christian friends and associates. The Hebrew Christian identity is viable enough, but only in the limited circle of fundamental Christianity.[18] The wider world re-

---

[16]Of course, the establishing of identities does not always follow the sequence we have indicated. Sometimes a person will be placed before, or differently, than he announces. He may then acknowledge the placement, or he may deny or ignore it and announce another identity. Such placement before or without announcement sometimes results in identity forcing, i.e., a person is forced to take on an identity which is strange to him or which he would rather avoid. Such identity forcing is much utilized by evangelists of all kinds, from students of Stephen Potter to emulators of Elmer Gantry.

[17]Glick reports a small sect of Hebrew Christians who had organized their own Hebrew Christian Church and who defined themselves as separate and different from gentile Christians. There was no similar phenomenon where the writer conducted his study. See Ira O. Glick, "The Hebrew Christians: A Marginal Religious Group," in Marshall Sklare (ed.), *The Jews* (Glencoe, Ill.: The Free Press, 1958), pp. 415–431.

[18]Gentile fundamental Christians, it should be noted, are very sensitive to a "holier than thou" attitude in the Hebrew Christian's much-voiced claim that the first Christians were Jews. They often complain about it.

jects the Hebrew Christian as logically impossible, or regards him with a suspicious eye. Against the position of this wider world, his old others, and his old self, the Hebrew Christian is always arguing.

The "average" Jewish Unitarian is about 32 years old at the time of his *alternation*. He is settled in occupation and life style. He is likely to have had the usual Jewish upbringing, religiously and "culturally," and there is about a 50 per cent chance that he is a member of a synagogue. If he is a member, he is most likely to retain membership concurrently with Unitarian Society membership. The Jew who joins a Unitarian Society does not feel he has made any significant change. He does not think of himself as a "Jewish Unitarian," and he may not even think of himself as a "Unitarian." One may just be a member of a Unitarian Society, one does not have to accept a new label as definitive of self, and most Jewish Unitarians do not.[19] The Jewish Unitarian usually encounters little or no resistance from family or friends. His change does not change his life but actually can be understood as one of the possibilities in an already established and settled life style or program. Being solid middle- or upper-middle class, "liberal," "humanistic," and usually limited in formal ties to the Jewish community, he finds out about the Unitarian Society from friends or some other source; investigates; and joins. He may attend meetings (they are usually not called "services") regularly, or he may never attend, simply giving monetary support to what he feels is a good organization with good aims. If you ask whether he still considers himself a Jew, he will answer, "Yes, of course," but will consider your question strange and unnecessary. If pressed on this matter, he will suspect you are defining him as an apostate and will greatly resent your labeling his Unitarian Society membership in a way which neither he nor any of his associates, old or new, do. An example

from an interview will serve well here. After a series of questions which began with the phrase, "Since you became a Unitarian," a subject exclaimed:

> One thing that bothers me is your phrases. I would say I'm Jewish, and you keep identifying me as a Unitarian. I'm Jewish. There is a Unitarian Society in [another city] where they have candles and robes and crap like that. If that were the case here, you wouldn't be interviewing me.

Clearly, we have in these examples, very different kinds of change. The Hebrew Christian has broken with his past, the Jewish Unitarian has not. The Hebrew Christian has completely reorganized his life, the Jewish Unitarian has not. In short, the Hebrew Christian has a new principle of organization for his action and autobiography, while the Jewish Unitarian has simply extended his old programs in one of many permissible directions. Symptomatically, the Jewish Unitarian identity is seldom or never central to an interaction, while the Hebrew Christian identity is often central, and, when it is not, it is usually threatening. We propose to call these distinctly different kinds of change *conversion* and *alternation*.

CONVERSION AND ALTERNATION DISTINGUISHED

Conversions are drastic changes in life. Such changes require a change in the "informing aspect" of one's life or biography. Moreover, there must be a negation (often specifically forbidden) of some former identity. Conversion is signaled by a radical reorganization of identity, meaning, and life. The convert is recognizable by his piety. As William James observed, "To say a man is 'converted' means . . . that religious ideas, previously peripheral in his consciousness, now take a central place, and that religious aims form the habitual centre of his energy."[20] James unnecessarily lim-

---

[19]In personal conversation Gladys Stone reports a similar finding among Japanese-Americans. They are Buddhist and Christian concurrently, but don't think of either identity as definitive of self.

[20]William James, *The Varieties of Religious Experiences* (New York: Modern Library, 1929), p. 193. Since James talks about ideas "previously peripheral," we should note that some changes which are called conversions in everyday interaction

ited his statement to religious transformations. Of course it is more widely applicable. Kenneth Burke purposely chose an unusual nonreligious example in discussing piety:

> . . . If a man who is a criminal lets the criminal trait in him serve as the informing aspect of his character, piously taking unto him all other traits and habits that he feels should go with his criminality, the criminal deterioration which the moralist with another point of view might discover in him is the very opposite of deterioration as regards the tests of piety. It is *integration*, guided by a scrupulous sense of the appropriate which, once we dismiss our personal locus of judgment, would seem to bear the marks of great conscientiousness.[21]

Conversion, then, involves a change in *informing aspect*. Given the social basis of meanings, such a change implies a change of allegiance from one source of authority to another.[22] Translating into symbolic interactionist terms, we may say that a conversion involves the adoption of a pervasive identity[23] which rests on a change (at least in emphasis) from one universe of discourse to another. Such universes of discourse are, of course, the properties of social groups or authorities. (After all, what is an authority, if not a legislator and guardian of meanings?) We may also note that conversion often involves a period of

emotional upset and indecision during which the individual may become severely depressed or confused and may experience emotionally induced somatic upsets. As for the convert's former associates, they are usually disturbed by the convert's new identity and allegiances and may well treat him as a traitor.

Finally, we must defend our use of the term "conversion" for this kind of transformation. It is, of course, the traditional term, but Berger suggests "alternation" to escape the religious connotations of "conversion." Yet, given the nature of conversion as distinguished from other changes, the religious connotation is just what is needed. By applying the "religious" word to secular areas (examples are communism, psychoanalysis, and science as an enterprise), social thinkers have gained insight into activities in these areas. Such elucidation through juxtaposition of meanings foreign to each other Kenneth Burke has called "perspective by incongruity." In fact, Burke quite correctly sees conversion itself as a process of perspective by incongruity.[24] "Conversion," then, is an apt word for these changes.

As we saw in our Jewish Unitarian example, there are identity changes which are not so drastic as those we have called conversions. These we propose to call "alternations." These are relatively easily accomplished changes of life which do not involve a radical change in universe of discourse and informing aspect, but which are a part of or grow out of existing programs of behavior. A Baptist mail clerk becomes an Episcopalian junior executive; a high school student becomes a college boy; a husband becomes a father; a professor becomes department chairman. To say such changes are easily accomplished, of course, does not mean that everyone makes them with no trouble whatsoever. Adjustments to college or to fatherhood, for example, are often quite painful and pervasive. But these changes and their attendant problems are provided for in established

---

are not conversions in our sense. Many religious "conversions" do not meet our criterion of a change in universe of discourse. While individuals who "get religion," or "get filled with the Spirit," may experience a period of intense emotional upset and indecision, they are not switching to a new authority or universe of discourse when that "religion" or "Spirit" belongs to their established universe of discourse. Such adoption of the "true believer" identity, whether it is for the first time in an individual's life or is a "regeneration" after a period of "backsliding," is not a conversion in our terminology. On this very point see Kurt and Gladys Engel Lang, *Collective Dynamics* (New York: Thomas Y. Crowell Co., 1961), pp. 154–155.

[21]Burke, *op. cit.,* p. 77.

[22]On the point that conversion involves a change in allegiance, see Lang and Lang, *op. cit.,* p. 157, and Strauss, *op. cit.,* p. 123.

[23]By "pervasive identity" we mean an identity which is made central to many, if not most, interactions.

[24]Burke, *op. cit.,* pp. 69–163, especially pp. 69–70 and p. 154.

universes of discourse. The actor is only learning well a new part of a world he was always committed to, with the help of his established others. In conversion, a whole new world is entered, and the old world is transformed through reinterpretation. The father sees his bachelorhood as youthful fun; the convert sees his as debauchery.

Alternations and conversions, then, are different kinds of identity change. Alternations are transitions to identities which are prescribed or at least permitted within the person's established universes of discourse. Conversions are transitions to identities which are proscribed within the person's established universes of discourse, and which exist in universes of discourse that negate these formerly established ones. The ideal typical conversion can be thought of as the embracing of a negative identity.[25] The person becomes something which was specifically prohibited. Thus we might think of a continuum (but infinite gradations are neither implied nor denied at this point). On one side we have the most easily accomplished alternations. One joins a conversation club or perhaps frequents a different bar. Little change is noticed by most of the person's others.[26] There is no trauma. There is little reflection on the part of the actor either before or after. There is no important change in universe of discourse. On the other side we have the most radical of conversions. The person goes through a period of intense ''inner

struggle.'' There is great trauma. The actor reflects at great length on his change. The actor and all his others see his change as monumental and he is identified by himself and others as a new or different person. The actor has a new universe of discourse which negates the values and meanings of his old ones by exposing the ''fallacies'' of their assumptions and reasoning. The actor has great involvement with his new identity and perspective.[27] This ideal is approached and reached in Jews who become fundamental Christians, in young intellectuals who become communists, in communists who become monks, and in psychoanalysis.[28]

IDENTITIES AND ALTERNATIONS

In this paper we have delimited conversion much more closely than alternation. But since we have designated alternations as the usual changes in life and since we have posited that our lives are riddled with change, the reader might well expect that alternations bear much closer attention than we have given them so far. This indeed is true, and in this final section we shall address some of the problems that will face future thinking and research in what, as shall be seen, is a very difficult area.

We used as examples of alternation: a Baptist mail clerk becoming an Episcopalian junior executive; a high school student becoming a college boy; a husband becoming a father; and a professor becoming a department chairman. Our first two examples involve identities which negate old ones in a fully anticipated way. One identity grows

[25]The concept of negative identity is found in Erik H. Erickson's ''The Problem of Ego Identity,'' *Journal of the American Psychoanalytic Association*, IV, No. 1 (1956), pp. 58–121. Essentially the same idea is expressed in the concept of ''anti-model'' as found in Roy G. Francis, ''The Anti-Model as a Theoretical Concept,'' *The Sociologic̀al Quarterly*, IV (Fall, 1963), pp. 197–205.

[26]We are assuming that the person is already a conversationist, or that the person is not a bar ''regular.'' We say *most* of the person's others notice little change because the breaking of even very casual relationships can stir comment from those involved. A friend reports that ending an eighteen-month absence from a bar he had formerly frequented brought him warm welcomes from old associates and the feeling that he was ''home.'' He adds that his return gives these associates the feeling that things are ''right,'' a conviction which they apparently lacked because of his absence.

[27]Accuracy is sacrificed here for a simple definition. The actor does not always consider what is happening to him. Especially where new identities grow out of old ones (i.e., husband to father), the person may well find himself in a new identity before he knows it, and then may grieve for his former situation and identity.

[28]For a delightful fictional account of a career from intellectual-to-communist-to-monk see Nigel Dennis, *Cards of Identity* (New York: Meridian Books, 1960), pp. 255–285. For an equally excellent explication of psychoanalysis as a conversion process see Burke, *op. cit.*, pp. 125–129.

''naturally'' out of another. Such changes cause little disruption in the lives of those involved. We may call such linked identities *identity sequences*.[29] Such sequences may involve changes which are somewhat compulsory (graduate student to Ph.D. or ''flunkie'') or are a matter of choice or fate (high school student to college boy). Our last two examples, husband to father and professor to department chairman, involve identities which do not replace, but rather are added to, established identities. Again, this happens in an expected way with one identity arising ''naturally'' out of the other. And again such changes are easily accomplished. We may call these related identities *cumulative identity sequences*. As with non-cumulative identity sequences, changes may be somewhat compulsory (expectant father to hus-

band) or open to choice or chance (spouse to parent). We should also note that some identity sequences are more casual and less insistent than these we have considered. ''Liberal,'' ''humanitarian'' Jews become Unitarians; nature lovers become conservationists or birdwatchers. These changes are logical; they are extensions or addenda to formerly established programs; they are cumulative identity sequences. But they *are* casual and almost strictly a matter of choice or chance. Relative insistence in identity sequences seems to be *at least in part* dependent on the fact that some sequences (like husband-to-father) are related to formal structure and thus carry relatively binding commitments. For example, a young man may become a casual or frequent dater, a girl-chaser, or an out-and-out rake. He can maintain such an identity for some time. But, once engaged, he is caught in the fiancé-to-spouse (noncumulative) sequence; and, once married, the spouse-to-parent cumulative sequence begins to press. One senses the difference in commitment between the fiancé-to-spouse and spouse-to-parent sequences; the difference between proposing membership in a legally established structure and actually holding membership. When one is betrothed, one is a long way down a ''betrayal funnel,''[30] yet it clearly is easier to break off an engagement than, once married, to decide against having children.

Having attempted some delineation of the identity linkages that alternation gets people involved in, we may turn to a consideration of the pervasiveness of different identities and identity linkages in interaction.

Identities can be pervasive in two ways: they can be relevant in many situations, and they can be central to interaction. As we have noted, identity is trans-situational while role is situationally specified, and these situationally specific expectations of course mean that the meaning of an identity varies with situation. Some identities are relevant to more situations than others. By relevant

[29] I am indebted to Gregory P. Stone for the concept ''identity sequence.'' Stone also makes some useful distinctions between what he calls ''identity sets,'' categorizing relationships between identities as *formal, modal,* and *contingent.* Formal sets include identities which are formally or legally linked—the president of the United States must be thirty-five years old and must be an American citizen. Modal sets are not formally or legally linked, but if a person has one identity in such a set there is a high probability that he will have others—the president is most probably a man. In contingent sets, given one identity, it is neither probable nor required that a person have the other identities involved; but one must be cognizant of them to understand the person's behavior—John F. Kennedy was a Catholic, Muhammad Ali is a Muslim. The terms, ''identity set'' and ''identity sequence'' will remind the reader of Merton's similar terms, ''status-set'' and ''status-sequence.'' Stone prefers his own terms to Merton's because, while every status is an identity, every identity is not a status (e.g., most nicknames).

We may note that Merton also distinguishes ''role-sets.'' What this term indicates, in Merton's own terms, is that a person has many different roles to play within a given status. His example is the medical student, who is a student to his teachers, but something else to fellow students, nurses, medical technicians, etc. Actually, the student is a student in all these situations. It is the behavior and meaning of the identity ''medical student'' which varies situationally. The identity mobilizes different situationally specified role behavior in different situations. As mentioned earlier in this paper the term ''role'' rests on the conceptualization of all these possible behaviors. Perhaps ''role-set'' might be a useful term to adopt since the word ''set'' reminds one of the situationally specific character of behavior in a way that the word ''role'' does not. See Robert K. Merton, *Social Theory and Social Structure* (Glencoe, Ill.: The Free Press, 1957), pp. 368–371.

[30] On ''betrayal funnels'' see Erving Goffman, *Asylums* (Garden City, N.Y.: Doubleday Anchor, 1961), p. 140.

we mean that the identity is an important part of the situation. One can be a father at home or at a PTA meeting, but one can't be a father at a faculty meeting. One can leave a faculty meeting early because one is a father who must take a child to the dentist, but in this case the identity is invoked as a motive to legitimate the termination of interaction.[31]

The centrality of an identity is a question of how many situations it can be dominant in. What we need, then, is some classification of identities according to how they usually operate in interaction. Banton has suggested a classification of roles, in terms of their currency in interaction, which is useful to our purpose here.[32] In a review of Banton's work, Stone has suggested that identity, not role, was the concept needed, as it is identities, not roles, that persist across situations. Bearing identity in mind, then, let us quote from Stone:[33]

> . . . Banton asks us to distinguish at least three different kinds of role, classified, one might say, in terms of their "stickiness"—the number of situations with reference to which their performance is expected. *Basic roles*, like sex, are usually ascribed and seldom "shaken off." *General roles*, like priest, are not ascribed, but, nevertheless, extend through a variety of situations. *Independent roles*, like golfer, are relatively easy to take up or put down.

We may follow Stone's suggestion and change these concepts to basic, general, and independent identities. Now, as Banton realizes, these distinctions are not hard and fast; but they are at least

modal, and they are based on the way identities function in interaction. Basic identities, like sex and age, function most often to help set the ground rules for interaction in terms of language and demeanor. "Basic," then, is an apt description. They are neither central nor secondary to an interaction; rather they are woven throughout it generally without much ado. General and independent identities are more difficult to distinguish. The identity, golfer, certainly is easier to take up and put down than the identity, priest, but it does extend through a variety of situations. One can be a golfer not only on the course, but in the clubhouse, at business luncheons, at cocktail parties, in sporting goods shops, etc. The difference between golfer and priest, however, is the insistence of the priestly identity. Others expect this identity to inform the whole man—he wears a uniform—and so it takes on the quality of a basic identity, i.e., it determines the language and demeanor trans-situationally. It is not a basic identity, however, because it tends to be central to interaction; it is the identity around which the interaction turns. Still, the distinction between general and independent identities is basically sound, and we can see a connection with our concept of identity sequence. Insistent identity sequences, like fiancé-to-husband-to-father, are usually general identities. More casual identity sequences, like nature-lover-to-conservationist-to-birdwatcher, are usually independent identities. Changes in independent identities cause little disruption and are alternations. Changes in general identities can cause much more disruption (one thinks of divorce or of leaving the priesthood) but these also are usually alternations.[34] Changes in basic identities are, of course, seldom made.[35]

---

[31]Stone has discussed how value and mood are differentially relevant to structural and interpersonal interaction respectively. We can see a similar relationship in the case of identities. A secretary is expected to be a worker first and a woman second. But if, when under fire, she bursts into tears, she is making her womanhood foremost in the interaction. If her boss buys this, he is reduced to being a "man helping a woman in distress" and will sheepishly offer her a tissue. See Stone, *op. cit.*, pp. 96–100.

[32]Michael Banton, *Roles: An Introduction to the Study of Social Relations* (New York: Basic Books, 1965).

[33]Gregory P. Stone, Review of *Roles: An Introduction to the Study of Social Relations,* by Michael Banton, *American Sociological Review,* XXXI (December, 1966), p. 899.

[34]We say changes in general identities are "usually" alternations because such changes can be conversions. Of course, identity alone does ot explain conversion. The keystone of conversion, as we have noted, is a change in "informing aspect." Sometimes (as with monks, nuns, and Black Muslims) converts take a new name to lead their new life with. Just as often, however, converts retain their old identity (as the Hebrew Christian retains the identity "Jew") but build new roles around

Thus far, we have distinguished differences in how identities are linked and differences in how identities pervade interaction, and we have noted that adoptions of the kinds of identities we have been speaking of are usually alternations. More careful delineation of these issues awaits future work and research. But where, finally, do conversions come in?

CONVERSION AND UBIQUITY

Conversion means a change in informing aspect. When a person converts, his new identity has, from his new perspective, fantastic generality. Converts, as is well known, make their new identity central to almost all interactions. Actually, a conversion may not be merely a *change* in informing aspect but a *discovery* of one. This is the lure of a total universe of discourse. In a life of multiple alternations demanding constant autobiographical revision, most of us, as Berger notes, "do not set out deliberately to paint a grand portrait of ourselves."[36] Yet this is precisely what converts do. Total universes of discourse offer nothing less than the possibility of organizing and explaining an entire life on a single principle. Conversion, then, involves the ubiquitous utilization of an identity.[37]

Now, the adoption of even independent identities often looks something like conversion. We all know zealous golfers, fishermen, or whatever. Every alternation has the incipience of conversion,[38] which is to say that identities can be insisted upon in situations where they are irrelevant. But independent identities lack the total universe of discourse which would make them ubiquitous.

it. Any transformation, of course, involves continuity, as the paradox of permanence and change is the key to personal life.

[35]Stone, in his review of Banton, points out that modern society has a whole technology (e.g., cosmetics) for changing age. But there are obvious limits to this technology. Besides, one always knows what his age really is, and others are always trying to find out. Where basic identities are really changed, as in sex change operations, society and social psychology are faced with interesting, but perplexing, problems. For a most informative report on the social psychological issues attending a sex change see Harold Garfinkel, *Studies in Ethnomethodology* (Englewood Cliffs, N.J.: Prentice-Hall, 1967), pp. 116—187.

[36]Berger, *op. cit*, p. 61.

[37]This ubiquity, of course, lies in the total universe of discourse in whose terms the identity is defined. It is the total universe of discourse which enables the convert to define almost every situation in his own terms, make every event part of one grand portrait of life. The identities involved in conversions are usually *general* in Banton's terms.They are sometimes *basic* and this raises some very special problems, as changes are

called for in what are unquestioned and supposedly unchangeable grounds of interaction. Garfinkel has dealt with this issue insightfully (see footnote 35). The aforementioned Hebrew Christians had, in these terms, taken the general identity "Jew" and transformed it by becoming "completed Jews" who accepted the promised Messiah of Israel. Thus they entered an evangelical (total) universe of discourse which enabled them to utilize ubiquitously their now transformed Jewishness. Being Jewish is a problem in this society. One has to come to terms with it as others can never leave it alone. Some Jews will claim that being Jewish makes no difference one way or the other and some gentiles will agree. But this claim is belied by the frequency of the question, "By the way, are you Jewish?" The Hebrew Christians have come to terms in the most logical way possible in this Christian society. The bother for them is that only other fundamental Christians appreciate their position.

[38]I am indebted to Gregory Stone for this insightful observation. We should note here that while every alternation has the incipience of conversion, the reverse is not true. Conversions cannot be played as alternations in interaction. An example will serve well. One of the writer's informants proved to be a case of what might be called "incomplete conversion." Living far from home with a gentile husband, this subject went along with her husband's suggestion that she become a Christian for the sake of their children. She met a Hebrew Christian woman and attended some social meetings at a nearby mission. In less than a year she joined her husband's church and was baptized. Her story is that simple, and because of the simplicity she was caught in the tensions of trying to maintain conflicting identities. Having embraced Christianity without any "soul-searching" she did not feel certain that she was a Christian, or that she wanted to be one. She feels she may have made a mistake. She knows the line, "The Hebrew Christian is the true complete Jew who has accepted the promised Messiah of Israel," but it means nothing to her. Her family berates her displays of Jewishness and so the only identity she really knows goes unvalidated. One of her final statements to the writer was a display of her Jewishness through an explanation of her predicament in terms of fate or chance, which stands in contradistinction to the fundamental Christian belief in God's direction of His peoples' lives. She said, with a sad smile, "I don't know. Nothing seems to be right for me. I guess I haven't got the mahzel, that's luck in Jewish." This is the outcome of making a change with little thought as if it were an alternation, and finding that the change is socially defined as a drastic one and thus demands a conversion to make it workable.

This is why they are independent. They don't threaten to spill into, and flood out every interaction. And this is what our middle-class society prefers. We don't like identity without moderation. We don't like identities to be too general. Outside of ethnic communities, one sees no widow's weeds.

Ours, then, is an age of alternation, but not an age of conversion. Although we complain about the lack of focus and direction in our lives (a lack of informing aspect), we are very suspect of converts, who are people with just such focus and direction. While work (in the face of a consumption society) continues to be our most important focus, we insist that the job be left at the office. We insist that the work identity not be too general. The few people we allow informing aspects and ubiquitous identities to are those closely circumscribed by structure (like priests) or by exclusion (like artists). And we are upset when they are too rabid,[39] like Oral Roberts, or when they aren't devout enough, like the Dutch Catholic hierarchy. The clergy seem to be our official "true believers," and we want no others.[40] We look askance at the many who flock to Oral Roberts, who listen religiously to right wing radio programs, who follow the gospel of Timothy Leary. And we simply do not believe Muhammad Ali. But our dislike for converts does not mean that we don't need them. As Kai Erickson has shown, to know "what one is," one needs examples of "what one isn't" handy for comparison.[41]

[39]We must note the word "rabid." Anyone who is greatly enthused about something, be it God, birds, or baseball, we label a mad dog.

[40]Perhaps symptomatically for an age of alternation, the Catholic clergy seems to be defecting in greater numbers of late, or at least such defections are getting better press.

[41]Kai T. Erikson, *Wayward Puritans* (New York: John Wiley and Sons, 1966).

TWENTY-TWO

THE PLAY OF LITTLE CHILDREN

GREGORY P. STONE

Social psychologists have long recognized the significance of play for preparing young children to participate later on in adult society. But social psychology, when viewed against the backdrop of history, is very young. Furthermore, there is a disquieting tendency for many social science disciplines to lose their sense of history and develop what they conceive to be universal propositions based on observations made in quite spatially and temporally delimited milieux. This article is primarily designed to place the play of children in historical perspective and, then, to set forth some functions of contemporary child's play, reserving judgement about the universality of such functions. It is hoped that the very tentativeness with which such assertions are set forth will inspire the curiosity of others and encourage them to extend the spatial and temporal focus of their studies of childhood. Play, like other collective enterprises, is a collective representation: it *re*-presents the arrangements of the society and historical era in which it is carried on.

SOURCE: Gregory P. Stone. "The Play of Little Children." A revised version of Gregory P. Stone, "The Play of Little Children," *Quest,* IV (April, 1965), pp. 23−31. This version prepared especially for the first edition of this volume, 1970. Reprinted by permission of the author.

HISTORICAL EMERGENCE OF CHILDREN AND CHILD'S PLAY

In an extraordinary work (Ref. 1), Philippe Ariès asks the seemingly naive question: where do children come from? He is not, of course, concerned with the biological origins of infants, but with the historical origins of the social *identity*, "child." Although the classical Greek civilization (and those it influenced directly) had distinguished children socially from babes and adults if only as objects of aesthetic appreciation, children did not emerge as social entities in the subsequent history of Western civilization until the early seventeenth century.

FRANCE AS AN EARLY SOURCE OF CHILDREN

Prior to the seventeenth century there were babes and adults in Western civilization, but no in-betweens. Babes were swaddled; adults attired; children were, in fact, *homunculi*. There was no distinctive dress to differentiate them, and expectations directed toward them were not age-specific. The elaborate record of the life of Louis XIII kept by his doctor, Heroard (1: pp. 62−67, 100), amazes us today. The Dauphin was betrothed by his first birthday. At seventeen months, he was singing and playing the violin. By the age of two years, he was dancing various kinds of dances. At three and a half, he was reading, and he was writing at four. It must be emphasized here that the child, Louis, was not thought of as particularly brilliant. Such activities were merely expected of the little people we call children today. Nor was this seemingly precocious activity necessarily confined to children of royalty and aristocracy, although such intricate play forms were undoubtedly concentrated in that estate. Paintings of the period, as well as earlier paintings, show the children of commoners and peasants freely participating in what we think of today as adult settings, e.g., taverns and wine shops.

It is not as though there were no play at that time. Louis had his hobby horse, tops, and balls. Rather, play permeated all segments of the society. Ariès chides the contemporary historian Van Marle for his amazement upon discovering that the games played by grown-ups were no less childish than those played by children, retorting, ''Of course not: they were the same'' (1: p. 72). Festivals were another matrix of community-wide play in medieval Europe. Despite the fact, however, that play was general in the society, its unanticipated consequences were probably different for children and adults as they are today. Certainly some child's play provided young people with a vehicle for anticipatory socialization, permitting them to rehearse roles they would enact or encounter in later life, as in military play. Then as now, the play of children pulled them into the larger society. Adult play, on the other hand, undoubtedly released the players at times from everyday social demands and obligations. That adults and children played the same games makes such differences difficult to verify.

If play was general in the society of medieval Europe, attitudes toward play were not. In fifteenth and sixteenth century France, the Catholic clergy took a dim view of play, unless it followed the performance of work, and this view was subsequently adopted by police and other authorities.

Yet, play could not be suppressed by such moralizers in a society where play was general in the population, and work did not have the significance it was to acquire with industrialization. The only enforceable suppression of play was accomplished in universities where clergy were recruited and trained, and there is evidence to suggest that this was not very effective. Possibly for this very reason, the Jesuits assimilated the play of the larger society in the seventeenth century. Play was redefined as educational and incorporated in college curricula (1: pp. 88–89). At the end of the eighteenth century, emerging nationalism provided a further legitimation of play. Play was conceived as a way of preparing young people for military service. The inclusion of play forms in military training programs is a frequent mode of legitimation. Thus, boxing or ''prize-fighting'' became legal in the United States in 1917 when it became an integral part of the U.S. Army's physical training program (14: p. 258).

As play acquired the approval of the moral custodians of seventeenth and eighteenth century French society, childhood also became established as a separate social identity in the human biography, and play became rather more of a childish thing. Ariès interprets this emergence of the child in the social morphology as one consequence of the rise of an entrepreneurial stratum in European society. As work moved to the center of social arrangements, play became increasingly relegated to childhood, and, *pari passu,* children were established as identifiable social beings. This may have been the case with France, but play and children were to have a more painful birth in the Protestant nations.

PLAY IN THE HISTORY OF ENGLAND AND AMERICA

Protestantism provided a religious justification for the tremendous expansion of work in the emerging industrial societies. Work was the key to the gates of the Protestant heaven: by your works are ye known. In contrast to the relegation of play to childhood in seventeenth and eighteenth century France, play had been generally suppressed in England by the end of the eighteenth century. In particular, the legislated inclosures of open areas deprived much of the population of play space. Play was further suppressed by legislation in English towns which, for example, forbade children from playing with tops in the streets or running races on the roads (7). When Wesley drew up the rules for his school at Kingswood, no time was set aside for play, because, in his view, "he who plays as a boy will play as a man" (7: p. 123).

In America, the status of play in the seventeenth and eighteenth centuries is less clear. We do know, of course, that child labor persisted in the United States into the twentieth century. Tocqueville thought that the Americans of his time were so wrapped up in work that they could not enjoy play: "Instead of these frivolous delights, they prefer those more serious and silent amusements which are like business and which do not drive business wholly out of their minds" (16: p. 221). On the other hand, Green has observed that play was smuggled into many areas of earlier American life in the guise of work, as in quilting parties and barn-raisings (5: p. 480), and, by the end of the nineteenth century, Bryce was impressed by the "brighter" life afforded the factory workers in New England through their "amusements than that of the clerks and shopkeepers of England" (2: p. 223). The picture is, at best, a confused one. moreover, what seemed "serious and silent" to a Frenchman may well have seemed "bright" to an Englishman.

Probably, however, there was no overall moral consensus on the value of work and play. In a very careful study, Miyakawa has shown that there were sharp regional differences and, within regions, denominational differences (12). In nineteenth century Ohio, Presbyterians led a gayer life than Methodists, and, in Connecticut, the Congregationalists did not hesitate to dance and enjoy musical entertainment (12: p. 143). Even on the frontier, "at least some German, Swedish, and other continental settlers had occasional songfests, plays, dances, and music" (12: p. 143). Miyakawa's observations, given the relatively high social status of Presbyterian and Congregational denominations, permit the inference that play was looked upon with favor in the higher socio-economic strata of nineteenth century America. At this status level, as Veblen has shown (17), we find a leisure class straining to shed the trappings of work, and I would offer the general hypothesis that play is introduced into the bleak ages of any society by high status circles and spread throughout the society as a consequence of the emulation carried on by lower status circles and aggregates. Once this is accomplished, the moral "character" of the society is transformed. Yet, the mere emulation of play styles is not a sufficient explanation for the spread of play in society. It is a necessary condition.

Ariès may well be correct in his assertion that the emergence of an entrepreneurial stratum in France established the identity of child and cloaked that identity with distinctive play forms, but in England and America it is a very different matter. It required a *social movement against the excesses of capitalism,* in the Protestant countries, to release children from the bonds of work and confer the privileges of play. The movement had its inception in the reformist and revolutionary thought of the mid-nineteenth century and persisted until the twentieth. Indeed, Ritchie and Koller maintain that, for the United States, the "institutionalization of children's play and games is largely a twentieth century phenomenon" (13: p. 205). It is even possible that this institutionalization was not formally secured until the formulation of the Children's Charter of the 1930 White House Conference on Child Health and Protection which proclaimed: "With the young child, his work is his play and his play is his work" (13: p. 206).

IMPLICATIONS FOR THE SOCIAL PSYCHOLOGY OF PLAY

Children and child's play, then, emerged much later on the social scene in the Protestant than in the Catholic countries. As I have pointed out elsewhere, this difference persists today in contrasting Protestant and Catholic attitudes toward gaming or gambling (14: p. 257). Nevertheless, the fact remains that children and child's play have not always been with us, particularly as we know them today. Thus, when we speculate upon the social significance of child's play, we may well be developing hypotheses that have relevance only for a particular and relatively recent era of Western civilization. I have often wondered whether or not this is the best any social scientist can do—to dramatize effectively his own socio-historical era. As Marx, Veblen, and Freud effectively dramatized the industrial era, so have Mills, Riesman, and Harry S. Sullivan effectively dramatized the era that Walter Rostow calls high mass consumption. This may well be the case because of the interaction between the social scientist and his subject matter. The very publication of social science theory and research alters the behavior it attempts to explain. For example, the incorporation of Keynesian economics into national fiscal policy introduced a political variable into business cycle theory, and nothing has altered sexual attitudes more than the dissemination of Freudian theory, with the result that contemporary psychoanalysts, such as Allen Wheelis (18), are confounded by the presence of disorders which defy explanation in classical Freudian terms.

DIFFERENTIATION AND INTEGRATION OF THE CHILD'S SELF THROUGH PLAY

It is the task of society to make the lives of its members meaningful. This is accomplished by bringing little children into a meaningful communication with adults and one another, and, at the same time, by establishing their selves as objects so they can refer the other objects of their worlds to such established selves, thereby imbuing those worlds with significance (10). Play has a major part in the accomplishment of these tasks.

THE PLAY OF MOTHER AND CHILD

Meaning only exists in communication, and it is established when one's own symbols call out in the other about the same symbolic responses as they call out in himself. (Thus, this article can only be meaningful if readers respond to these words about the way that I have responded. Failing this, the article is nonsense!) This seems to be accomplished very early by the infant when it takes over the response patterns of the mothering one as its own. It may be that babbling is a kind of playing with noise, but we shall never know, for we cannot ask the babbler. Nevertheless, in the course of babbling, the infant may hit upon a word-like sound which is then *re*-presented by the mothering one as a word, together with an appropriate response pattern. "Baa," for example, may be re-presented as "ball" as the round object is grasped and held up before the babbling baby. In time, the infant takes over the response pattern: "ball" *means* grasping the round object.

Too, in this early stage of the development of meaning, the infant is often a plaything, while the mothering one is the player. In time. both the child and the mothering one are mutually players and playthings:

> As actions become possible for him and as words take on meanings, the child is increasingly able to respond to the play actions of his mother with play actions of his own. Thus, for example, he uses his hands to play "peek-a-boo" and "patty cake." (13: p. 202)

Such commonalty of responses establishes a rudimentary domestic universe of discourse which can serve as a base from which a vast social symbolism can be elaborated.

CHILD'S PLAY AS DRAMA

"Play" has several meanings, among which *drama* must be included, and drama is fundamental for the child's development of a conception of self as an object different from but related to other objects—the development of an *identity*. To establish a separate identity (many identities depend for their establishment and maintenance on counter-identities, e.g., man-woman, parent-child, teacher-student), the child must literally get outside himself and apprehend himself from some other perspective. Drama provides a prime vehicle for this. By taking the role of another, the child gains a reflected view of himself as different from but related to that other.[1] Thus, we find little children playing house, store, or school in which they perform the roles of parent, merchant, or teacher, gaining a reflected view of their own identities from the perspective of those identities whose roles they perform. Indeed, in playing house, it is difficult to recruit a child to play the role of child or baby. Such a role has no implication for the building of his own identity. A doll, therefore, is better suited to the role.

We may note an additional consequence of such drama. In the examples cited, the child prepares himself for the subsequent enactment of such roles in later life or for communication with those who will be performing such roles. Merton speaks of such drama as anticipatory socialization (11: pp. 384−386). However, not all childhood drama is of this anticipatory character. Many of the roles the child performs are fantastic, in the sense that the child cannot reasonably be expected to enact or encounter such role performances in later life. I have in mind such identities as cowboy and Indian, creatures from outer space, or pirate. In much fantastic drama, incidentally, we can detect an additional function of child's play. Fantastic drama often serves to maintain and keep viable the past of the society—its myths, legends, villains, and heroes. This is also true of toys and other items of the technology of child's play. As one example,

---

[1]George H. Mead, from whom many of these ideas have been taken, refers to this phase as "play," but, as we have already shown, there are many varieties of play. Drama is the more precise term. (See 5: pp. 149−151 and 15: pp. 108−113.)

the jousting tournament disappeared in the sixteenth century and was replaced by the quintain and the unhooking of a ring by a galloping horseman. The latter persists today in the merry-go-round. This function of child's play has inspired Ariès to remark that "children form the most conservative of human societies" (1: p. 68). But Ariès seems unnecessarily acerb. An argument can be made that the dramatization of Buck Rogers' space feats by those who were children in the early thirties prepared that generation for the space accomplishments of today. There are certainly many areas of creativity and anticipation of the future that are to be found in children's drama.

Fantastic drama seems more to characterize the play of male children in our society than that of female children (15: pp. 110−112). Thus, the dramatic play of children in our society may function more to prepare little girls for adulthood than little boys (3: p. 333). This observation, however, may not necessarily be confined to contemporary American society and its recent past. In discussing the dress of children in eighteenth century France, Ariès points out: "the attempt to distinguish children was generally confined to boys . . . *as if childhood separated girls from adult life less than it did boys*" (1: p. 58). It may well be that the drama of childhood makes it difficult for boys to establish an early well-founded conception of adult life and, consequently, hinders their assumption of an adult identity. In contrast, such drama may facilitate the transition of female children to adulthood. However, once boys do become men (in the social psychological sense), given the sexual arrangements of our society, they have a relatively easy time of it, while the problems of females begin when girls become women!

Children differ, too, according to their *knowledge* of the roles they perform in childhood drama. Although he was not always consistent, Mead presumed an "open awareness" of the roles performed in drama (4: pp. 673−674). There are at least two reasons why such an assumption cannot be maintained. First, the details of the role performance may not be objectively accessible to the young actor. For example, a colleague, Duane Gibson of Michigan State University, noticed a boy and girl playing house in a front yard. The little girl was very busy sweeping up the play area, rearranging furniture, moving dishes about, and caring for baby dolls. The boy, on the other hand, would leave the play area on his tricycle, disappear to the back of the (real) house, remain for a brief while, reappear in the play area, and lie down in a feigned sleep. The little girl had a rather extensive knowledge of the mother role, but, for the boy, a father was one who disappeared, reappeared, and slept, *ad infinitum!* Second, nuances of the role performance may be deliberately concealed from children. We tend to conceal domestic difficulties from children, e.g., financial troubles. Should a child overhear such a discussion, we play it down, encouraging the child not to worry about it (13: p. 215).

There is an additional matter that any student of child's play ought to consider in his investigations. Not all childhood drama bears directly upon either fantasy or preparation for adult life. It is often employed as a means to satisfy tabooed curiosity. Probably most of us can recall playing "doctor" or "nurse," but such drama had little, if anything, to do with preparing ourselves for encountering or assuming such roles in later life. We have here a variant of what Glaser and Strauss call "pretense awareness . . . a modification of the open one: both interactants are fully aware but pretend not to be." (4: p. 670) This variant of childhood drama has seldom been studied, probably because it conjures up feelings of guilt, shame, or embarrassment in the investigator. However, Oscar Lewis has provided an excellent example:

> I was a devil when I was a kid. I used to play with boys all the time, doing things I shouldn't, see? We would play prostitutes or doctor. I would put a pillow over my belly and they would examine me as though I were pregnant. The boys would be my husband and the dolls the babies. We would tie a rag around the doll's waist saying that was its navel. Then the doctor would come and cut the strip of cloth with a piece of glass and say, "All right, the baby is ready. What's missing now is the *mama*." So then they would pull my *panties* all the way down and look at my belly but without touching me, and say that now I was all right.
>
> Then the boys would get hold of me and begin fooling around and dancing dirty with me, rubbing it in, and then I would dance by myself and sing. One day I went under the house, and this boy came along and grabbed me. I asked what he was doing and he said, "You had a child with Guillo González. Now have one of mine. It's easy." We were making believe I was a prostitute, and I would say, "*Ay*, I can't because I'm not well, and when I'm not well I don't go with anybody." My mother was upstairs all the while, watching through a crack and laughing. She came down below, still laughing, and said to me, "So you want to be a whore, do you?" But then she gave me a spanking and I didn't play that any more. (9: p. 576)

Here we have the conversion of what might be called both anticipatory and fantastic dramas into the calculus of children's curiosity. Both dramas have clear implications for socialization, but there is a double *entendre* present in the play.

Finally, in this discussion of childhood drama, we ought to acknowledge that one child's fantasy is another child's reality. The probability that the roles children enact in their dramas will be assumed or encountered in adult life is very much restricted by their position in the various orders of stratification—income, prestige, and accessibility to political office—their rural or urban residence, their "race" or ethnicity, or their sex. It is in short, fantastic for the "children of Sanchez" to play the role of doctor, but not the doctor's children.

We have very few empirical studies of childhood play and, particularly, drama. When we do conduct them, then, we ought to realize the complex nature of drama. Is it anticipatory or fantastic? Is knowledge of the dramatized role accessible to the young performer? What is the meaning of the drama in the child's world? Is it probable that the actor will, in later life, enact or encounter the role performance that he is dramatizing? Above all, how is recruitment into the adult roles that the drama of childhood represents organized by larger social arrangements? When such questions are answered, we will have far better knowledge of precisely how childhood drama provides children with identities, casting them in the character of meaningful objects.

Obviously, as Mead insisted (10: pp. 151–164), drama is not a sufficient source of identity, for it provides the young actor with many parts and scripts, and these are often unrelated. The development of an integrated self requires the playing of team games in which one can generalize the related team positions and adapt his own behavior to the generalized expectations of the entire team. Such games occur later in childhood and are beyond the scope of this article. However, one final form of play found in early childhood will be considered here, namely, tests of poise.

CHILDISH TESTS OF POISE

It is not enough only to establish an identity for one's self; it must be established for others at the same time. Identities are *announced* by those who appropriate them and *placed* by others. Identities must always be validated in this manner to have reality in social interaction. Usually such announcements are silent, accomplished by clothing, the posturing of the body, painting of the face, sculpting of the hair, the manipulation of props, or the physical location of the self on the scene of action. For these reasons, child's play demands costume and body control, and it is facilitated by props and equipment (toys) appropriate to the drama. Moreover, as Huizinga has remarked, play spaces are usually clearly marked off (8), and one's location within them communicates to other players and on-lookers the part he is playing. Thus, child's play demands the assembly, arrangement, and control of spaces, props, equipment, clothing,

and bodies, as well as other elements. If crucial elements are missing, if they become disarranged, or if control over them is lost, the play is spoiled, and the drama cannot be carried off. Loss of control over these elements is literally embarrassing and may be equated to loss of poise (6).

We know that much of the drama of childhood replicates the interaction of the larger society in which it occurs. Indeed, it is almost trite to observe that society *is* drama though the scripts always change. In everyday interaction, we must always announce to others who we are and be poised or prepared for the upcoming communication. This requires the assembly, arrangement, and control of a host of objects and demands considerable skill, for the staging of social interaction is an intricate affair, a highly complex juggling and balancing act.

Much childhood play takes the form of deliberately perpetrating loss of poise with the unintended but highly important consequence of preparing the child for the maintenance of self-control in later life. Thus, everywhere we find little children spinning about inducing dizziness, pushing, and tripping one another, disarranging clothing, teasing, playing pranks, or bringing play to a sudden halt by depriving the players of some crucial item ("I'm going to take my ball and go home"). Indeed, a technology has developed to facilitate such play and is found in playgrounds, amusement parks, and carnivals.

All this is well known, but I have the distinct impression that such play is viewed almost exclusively as contributing to body control or motor efficiency. Playful tests of poise reach out beyond the body to include clothing and grooming. Pranks can be perpetrated by disturbing any element essential to the staging process—furniture, equipment, locations, and a host of other objects and arrangements.[2] The analysis of such play, then,

---

[2]My colleague, Edward Gross, and I have isolated about fifty of these "elements" as we pursue the study of staging prompted by our earlier study of embarrassment (6). The article is reprinted in Part Two of this volume.

ought to take into account the development of body control and coordination, but the emphasis ought to be on its symbolic significance in relation to the other elements of staging essential to the silent definition of situations in everyday life.

CONCLUSIONS

This article has placed the play of little children in the context of social symbolism. It has shown how playing with children, childhood drama, and childish pranks function to prepare little children for their meaningful participation in adult society. Such play, however, is not always functional. Some childhood drama may militate against later social participation because of its relative inappropriateness, and I suppose some pranks may be so severe as to have unforeseen traumatic effects. In any case, the play of little children demands extensive scientific investigation. However, any propositions formulated as a consequence of such research may not have universal validity. Both children and child's play, like all other social phenomena, are creatures of history.

REFERENCES

1. Aries, Philippe. *Centuries of Childhood*. Translated by Robert Baldick, New York: Alfred A. Knopf, Inc., 1962.

2. Bryce, James. *Social Institutions of the United States*. New York: Grosset and Dunlap, 1891.

3. Erikson, Erik H., "Sex Differences in the Play Configurations of American Pre-Adolescents," in Margaret Mead and Martha Wolfenstein (eds.). *Childhood in Contemporary Cultures*. Chicago: The University of Chicago Press, Phoenix Edition, 1963, pp. 324–341.

4. Glaser, Barney G. and Anselm L. Strauss, "Awareness Contexts and Social Interaction," *American Sociological Review*, XXIX (October, 1964), pp. 669–679.

5. Green, Arnold. *Sociology*. New York: McGraw-Hill Book Co., Inc., 1956.

6. Gross, Edward and Gregory P. Stone, "Embarrassment and the Analysis of Role Requirements," *American Journal of Sociology*, LXX (July, 1964), pp. 1–15.

7. Hammond, J. L. and Barbara Hammond. *The Bleak Age*. Middlesex, England: Penguin Books, 1947.

8. Huizinga, Jan. *Homo Ludens: A Study of the Play Element in Culture*. London: Routledge and Kegan Paul, Ltd., 1949.

9. Lewis, Oscar, *La Vida*. New York: Vintage Books, 1968.

10. Mead, George Herbert. *Mind, Self, and Society*. Chicago: University of Chicago Press, 1934.

11. Merton, Robert K. *Social Theory and Social Structure*. Glencoe, Illinois: The Free Press, 1957.

12. Miyakawa, T. Scott. *Protestants and Pioneers*. Chicago: University of Chicago Press, 1964.

13. Ritchie, Oscar W. and Marvin R. Koller. *Sociology of Childhood*. New York: Appleton-Century-Crofts, 1964.

14. Stone, Gregory P., "American Sports: Play and Display," in Eric Larrabee and Rolf Meyersohn (eds.), *Mass Leisure*. Glencoe, Illinois: The Free Press, 1958, pp. 253–264.

15. ———, "Appearance and the Self," in Arnold M. Rose (ed.), *Human Behavior and Social Processes*. Boston: Houghton-Mifflin Co., 1962, pp. 86–118.

16. Tocqueville, Alexis de. *Democracy in America*, II. Translated by Henry Reeves. New York: Alfred A. Knopf, Inc., 1946.

17. Veblen, Thorstein. *The Theory of the Leisure Class*. New York: Modern Library, Inc., 1934.

18. Wheelis, Allen, *The Quest for Identity* (New York: W. W. Norton and Company, Inc., 1958).

TWENTY-THREE

FRIENDS, IMPRESSION MANAGEMENT, AND PREADOLESCENT BEHAVIOR

GARY ALAN FINE

INTRODUCTION

Coexisting with adult society in contemporary America is a subsociety whose members are classified not by race, ethnicity, or religion, but by age. This is the social world of childhood—that stratum of social structure that Glassner (1976) has termed "Kid Society." This children's society possesses a robust culture, significantly different from that of their parents and guardians. Increasingly, folklorists, anthropologists, and sociologists have become interested in exploring the social world of children—an interest which seems to be an extension of research in youth culture and "adolescent society" (Coleman, 1961). This view maintains that children (and adolescents) maintain a social system relatively autonomous from adults. The goal of this paper is to describe this social system, the abilities necessary to interact in it successfully, and the means by which members come to acquire these abilities, that is, how children become socialized to a "peer culture". This will be achieved by the examination of one social world—that of Little League baseball. Observations of Little League baseball players—both in the game and in their free time—suggest that boys by preadolescence have developed considerable impression management skills, and that their socialization to these skills is, in part, a consequence of their friendships.

RESEARCH PERSPECTIVE: SYMBOLIC INTERACTIONISM

My research perspective is symbolic interactionism, an approach to understanding social life developed by Charles Horton Cooley, George Herbert Mead, Herbert Blumer, and Erving Goffman, among others. Blumer (1969) argued that three premises are crucial to this perspective.

SOURCE: Prepared for the Society for Research on Child Development Study Group on the Development of Friendship, University of Illinois, Champaign–Urbana, Illinois. The author wishes to thank David Crist, Jeylan Mortimer, and Zick Rubin for helpful comments on a draft of this paper. This version is an abridged and slightly revised version of the paper which will appear in J. Gottman and S. Asher, *The Development of Children's Friendship* (New York: Cambridge University Press, 1981).

First, human beings act toward things on the basis of the *meanings* that these objects have for them. Thus, actions or objects are said to have no *a priori* stimulus value. Second, the meanings of these stimuli emerge through social interaction. Third, and perhaps most important, these meanings are not static, but can be modified through an interpretive process. Meanings, therefore, are not "reified," but are potentially subject to interpersonal negotiation. Through this assumption the symbolic interactionist perspective orients itself to "change" and "development." Furthermore, the approach argues that social meanings are shaped through communication, and, as such, causes of action are not primarily biological and subconscious, but social and conscious.

The symbolic interactionist approach can be differentiated on two dimensions from the three major approaches to social development: psychoanalysis, learning theory, and cognitive stage theory. It differs from psychoanalysis and learning theory in rejecting the concept of the child as a relatively passive organism whose actions are largely predetermined by environment or biology (or, in sophisticated analyses, by their interaction) but argues that the child is an active interpreter of situations (Faris, 1971, p. 233; orig. 1937). Furthermore, it differs from psychoanalysis and cognitive stage theory in rejecting the existence of an invariant sequence of universal stages of development.

Distinctions between symbolic interactionism and other approaches should not be drawn too firmly. For example, the interactionist approach is congruent with Zigler and Child's (1969) definition of socialization as "the whole process by which an individual develops through transaction with other people, his specific patterns of socially relevant behavior and experiences" (p. 474). The interactionist perspective attempts to give the child (or any actor) more "credit" for his or her actions than deterministic theories allow, and this has led to the criticism that symbolic interactionism is astructural and indeterminate (Zeitlin, 1973), al-though most interactionists admit there are biological and social constraints on behavior. No theory can capture the whole truth of development, and symbolic interactionism is no exception; however, by exploring some of the implications of this approach for social development, childhood behavior can be better understood, and alternative developmental approaches can be better informed about how children act to shape their own social worlds.

ISSUES UNDERLYING THE SYMBOLIC INTERACTIONIST APPROACH

Three important issues underlie the symbolic interactionist approach to development, all of which represent processes which occur early in childhood, and are well developed by preadolescence. These issues are: the development of self through the perception of others, the importance of communication and the use of symbols, and the development of the ability to behave appropriately as a function of the expectations of others.

The relationship between *self* and *other* is seen by symbolic interactionists as crucial to the development of behavior (Wiley, 1979). The *other* is the mirror by which individuals learn of their selves (Mead, 1934, p. 158), and it is the *other* with whom the *self* must negotiate lines of collective action. Cooley (1964; orig. 1902) argues that the child's conception of the *self* is a product of interaction and that, in terms of the acquisition of vocabulary, the child learns to know others before learning to be self-reflective (Cooley, 1908; Bain, 1936). Thus, the self-concept develops through social interaction, and emerges from the child's ability to take the role of the *other*. This role-taking is also seen as crucial by Piaget for the development of the concrete operations stage at which the child learns the basic relational property of objects (e.g., conservation or reversibility). However, contrary to the implications of this and other cognitive approaches, symbolic interactionists argue that the child does not develop a conception of self until after a conception of others has been acquired. Thus, the concept of an "egocentric" stage is not accurate according to the symbolic interactionist perspective. For the young child the most important others typically are the child's parents (or adult guardians), and these individuals are particularly significant in channeling the content of the child's self-concept. The shaping of the child's self by others is expanded with the onset of schooling—at which time the child must learn to deal with multiple others—what Mead has termed the "game stage" (Mead, 1925). This diverse social world shapes the child's self by providing a variety of behavioral options.

Simultaneous with the development of self (and a component of this development) is the growth of communication skills. Mastery of language and gestures is crucial for the preschool child in that it permits an understanding of and participation in interaction. The extent of symbolic universes of discourse varies depending on social factors; for example, the extent to which linguistic codes are elaborated or restricted (Bernstein, 1975). By the time the child is ready for formal schooling, this symbolizing process is well advanced (Denzin, 1977).

The third feature of development emphasized by interactionists is the acquisition of competence to behave properly in a variety of social settings. The young child increasingly acquires the ability to interact with peers and near-peers and spends more time in settings in which adults are not present to enforce their views of mannered interaction (Speier, 1973; MacKay, 1973). Situations in which dominance is not a direct result of age become common, and children must refine their techniques for constructing social meanings consensually; they mutually fit together lines of action, rather than have their situational definitions and courses of action imposed by adults (Elkin and Handel, 1978). Furthermore, children learn, through the response of others, that their behaviors have consequences. While children may define situations as they feel proper and act according to those definitions in the presence of adults, if those

definitions and actions are not congruent with adult prescriptions, children discover that their behaviors may have real (and sometimes painful) consequences. Among peers contrary situational definitions may have negative outcomes as well, but in such situations there is no shared assumption that one party's definition is necessarily legitimate, although peer status influences the exercise of social power.

Once the child recognizes that sets of individuals have different expectations, and that situations may imply different behaviors, the attempt to master a single, consistent set of core behavior patterns is no longer relevant. Symbolic interactionists emphasize the importance of the ability of the child to see him/herself as an object of appropriation (Mead, 1934). By this Mead means that the individual can place himself in relation to an other or set of others (a process Blumer (1969) terms "self-indication") and can shape his behavior in light of their expectations. Stone (1970, p. 399) has conceived of identity as a "coincidence of placements and announcements"—whereby the designation of one's self by others will be similar to the designation of the self that has been presented. By later childhood the key interactional task is to refine one's social identity, and to acquire the skills necessary for the successful positioning of self in multiple social worlds.

PREADOLESCENT SOCIAL DEVELOPMENT

Preadolescence (broadly ages 7 to 12) represents a particularly significant period of early socialization because, in this period, children are expected to develop social lives which are not merely an extension of situations dominated by adults (parents and teachers). While this may occur somewhat earlier or later, in most locales preadolescents are not expected to be under the watchful eye of an adult chaperone. Rather, they may and are expected to develop their own personal relationships. Researchers have noted the importance of friends—either the single chum or the gang—in preadolescent peer relations (see Fine, 1979a; Hartup, 1978 for a summary of this literature). These patterns of chumship and ganging are found in many areas of the globe, although not in every society according to the anthropological reports which are available. It is believed that these relationships have considerable impact in shaping the child's social behavior and attitudes. For example, Sullivan (1953) writes:

> . . . in the company of one's chum, one finds oneself more and more able to talk about things which one had learned, during the juvenile era, not to talk about. . . . [A]bout the last chance troubled children have of favorable change is based on their need for getting along with a chum in preadolescence (p. 227, p. 252).

Whatever the validity of Sullivan's explicit connection between friendship and psychiatric therapy, friendships produce moments of shared fantasy, which Cottle (1971) has argued allow children to escape the boundaries of their troubled existence. Groups also allow children to learn about themselves and society:

> The school-age child spends as much of his time as possible in the company of his peers, from whom he learns at first hand about social structures, about in-groups and out-groups, about leadership and followership, about justice and injustice, about loyalties and heroes and ideals (Stone and Church, 1968, p. 364).

These groups are arenas for social action; they are social locations in which the preadolescent is able to explore available role options and to master methods of impression management in a supportive social environment. Having a set of close friends or a single chum is important to the child because preadolescent interaction is generally not placid (Opie and Opie, 1959), but is filled with the possibilities of sudden denigration. As Stone and Church suggest, "the feeling of inclusion seems to necessitate someone's exclusion" (1957, p. 221). Thus, in this socially tempestuous time, having a friend with whom one can feel secure provides a solid base on which interpersonal confidence can be built, even the notoriously fickle affections of children.

PREADOLESCENT SOCIAL RELATIONS AND LITTLE LEAGUE BASEBALL

For three years I conducted a participant observation study of preadolescent males. During those three years Little League baseball leagues in four American communities were examined by the author: (1) Beanville,[1] an upper-middle class "professional" suburb of Boston, Massachusetts; (2) Hopewell, an exurban township outside of the Providence, Rhode Island metropolitan area, consisting of a string of small towns, beach-front land, farms, and a campus of the state university; (3) Bolton Park, an upper-middle class "professional" suburb of St. Paul, Minnesota, similar to Beanville except for geographical location, and (4) Sanford Heights, a middle-to-lower-middle class suburb of Minneapolis, Minnesota, comprised of a large number of modern mass-produced homes. A research assistant, Harold Pontiff, conducted a parallel investigation of a Little League baseball program in Maple Bluff, an urban, upper-middle class area of St. Paul.

The primary technique employed to collect data about Little Leaguers and their friends was participant observation (see Bogdan and Taylor, 1975). In order to focus our observations, two teams in each league were chosen for intensive study. Detailed records were kept of the players on 10 teams (12 to 15 players per team); less detailed records were kept of 32 other teams, and information was collected on scores of preadolescents who were not involved in the league. At first the intention was to examine the Little League teams, but it soon became apparent that the only way in which preadolescent social behavior could be understood was through observing the larger context of their spring and summer leisure activities. Thus, considerable time was spent with the players and their friends outside of the baseball context. (For a detailed treatment of this research see Fine and Glassner, 1979; Fine, 1979b.) While it would be misleading to claim that the research settings are representative of American children, they do cover a substantial range of environments. Like the Little League organization itself, the basically middle-class sample has fewer rural children, urban children, and poor children than would be expected by chance. While we will speak in terms of generalizations, the reader should always keep in mind the sample from which our analysis derives.

CHILDREN AND PRESENTATION OF SELF

Central to the process of growing up is learning ways of displaying one's social self in public. Adults fear that children will "say the wrong thing in public." For example, they may tell "Aunt Millie" about what they *really* think of her homemade apple pie, or they may tell rich "Uncle Joe" the private conversations their parents have had about him. Such images provide an endless source of jokes and indicate the anxiety that adults feel about the potential "indiscretions" of their offspring. Somewhat facetiously we might suggest the danger is that the child has not mastered the art of being hypocritical. Less facetiously we note that the issue is one of learning situational proprieties and that behavior deemed proper in one situation is often considered grossly improper in another. While etiquette books for children emphasize rules for behavior appropriate in all situations (Cavan, 1970), these rules must be negotiated in their social contexts. The preadolescent does not behave toward his peers in the same way he behaves toward his parents, a point that most parents recognize. While parents may not get upset if their child curses or tells dirty jokes with his friends, this does not mean that the child is given license to behave this way in front of his parents. Conversely, the fact that the child may be willing to admit affection to relatives does not imply that the same child will admit this to peers. Stone and Church

comment: "No ten-year-old boy would be caught dead saying that he 'loved' anything" (1957, p. 220). This evaluation is confirmed by my observation that children who too readily admit to affection become the objects of teasing or scorn by their peers.

By preadolescence a boy normally finds himself in several distinct social worlds, and he discovers that appropriate behavior is dependent upon his interpretation of the nature of these worlds. The popular and socially integrated preadolescent is the one who has mastered techniques of impression management in order to present himself through flexible role performances (see Elkins, 1958) and to cast others into roles that support his role position (Weinstein and Deutschberger, 1963; Weinstein, 1969). In other words, through his actions the child is able to control the behavioral roles of his interaction partners in ways which complement his social position. In his discussion of self-presentation, Goffman (1959) does not consider the development of impression management skills, since his interest is primarily in knowledgeable adults. Goffman's model of man is that of a schemer or actor who must manipulate a world of complex and deceptive meanings (see Goffman, 1974). The acquisition of this competence seems not to be confined to the preadolescent period but develops from birth. However, my research indicates that, by puberty, the child has acquired the basic techniques of impression management, although interactional subtlety is still to be mastered.

Cooley (1964, orig. 1902) notes the importance of the early development of the social self, and he suggests that a very young child attempts to manipulate the impressions that others have of him:

> The young performer soon learns to be different things to different people, showing that he begins to apprehend personality and to foresee its operation. If the mother or nurse is more tender than just she will almost certainly be "worked" by systematic weeping (p. 197).

However, it is unlikely that prior to schooling children are attempting to present different identities, or even to shape the impressions that others have of them. More likely, children are manipulating others to achieve some end, and their impressions are shaped indirectly. Cooley notes:

> A child obviously and simply, at first, does things for effect. Later there is an endeavor to suppress the appearance of doing so; affection, indifference, contempt, etc., *are simulated* to hide the real wish to affect the self-image. It is perceived that an obvious seeking after good opinion is weak and disagreeable (p. 199; emphasis added).

This latter concern involves constructing one's behavior so as to manipulate and constrain others. Corsaro's research with nursery school children (Corsaro, 1981) indicates that some rather young children have considerable ability and finesse in structuring situations to their own advantage, particularly in terms of controlling the access of peers to ongoing play groups. However, in preadolescence and with the preoccupation with peer status, the ability and desire to position oneself in situations consciously and to shape one's presentation of self becomes critical for long-term popularity. In order to manage the impressions of others the preadolescent must expand his or her facility at taking the role of the other (Mead, 1934) and, through this, must role-play to realize the desired impression.[2] By preadolescence the child must deal with a wide range of others, who may expect the child to behave according to several distinct standards of behavior. A four-year-old may use a single behavioral repertoire, but the preteen must learn that several repertoires need to be mastered for different settings. The development of presentation-of-self-ability is exemplified in the child's increasing sophistication in getting along with others and in developing moral and philosophical systems (Selman's stages three and four) by which flexibility of interaction as a function of the needs of one's friend becomes recognized as a part of friendship (Selman, 1981).

RULES AND NEGOTIATION

The growth of social competency can be observed in the child's increasing sophistication in the practice of game rules. Piaget suggests in his analysis of marble playing (1962; orig. 1932) that until the age of three the child has rules only in that there are ritual repetitions that the child performs with play objects. At this stage, rules are not grounded in social interaction, and what regularities exist appear idiosyncratic. Piaget asserts that, until games are played collectively, rules in a meaningful sense do not exist.

The second stage is termed the stage of egocentrism and lasts until approximately the age of six, although Piaget admits these ages are not invariant in all cultures and social classes (p. 46). Marble playing at this age becomes social but, according to Piaget, rules are egocentric; "when they play together they do not watch each other and do not unify their respective rules even for the duration of one game" (p. 40). Piaget's data on two marble players suggest that, while different sets of rules seem to be operating, the children construct a social interaction sequence which is satisfying to both parties and is dependent on the presence of each other (as indicated by the existence of different rules when the child plays alone). While these interactants are not playing a "game" (an adult defined category of activity), they are interacting in a fashion that is meaningful for them.

The two later stages of the development of the practice of rules represent the growth of the preadolescent's ability to deal with his peers. During early preadolescence (ages 7 through 10) the child recognizes the importance of rules as a regulator of others' behavior. Rules are claimed to insure reciprocity in the game world. However, this notion of rules as a model for play does not imply that rules are not used to strategic advantage. For example, Piaget points out that in this stage knowledge of rule content may vary widely. Thus, children construct their game reality (the rule structure) in the course of play:

It is only when they [the marble players] are at play that these same children succeed in understanding each other, either by copying the boy who seems to know most about it or, more frequently, by omitting any usage that might be disputed (p. 42).

Although children claim that rules are absolute, in practice they are negotiated. Furthermore, the rules may be *used* by the knowledgeable player to limit the options of the less familiar (or deliberately naive) player. In this case, Piaget himself:

. . . when I play carelessly, and let the shooter drop out of my hand, Ben exclaims *"Fan-coup"* to prevent me from saying *"coup-passe"* and having another shot." (p. 44).

Rules are conditional, and their use becomes something of a game. A player may get another shot *if* he says *"coup-passe," unless* the opponent first says *"fan-coup."* This requires the ability to place oneself in the opponent's position in order to recognize the appropriate moment for such a challenge, and the decision may be based upon the importance of the game and the relationship between player and challenger. While challenges are legitimate, they may create hard feelings and indicate that the game is "serious" and not "merely" play (Riezler, 1941). Rule-governed games carry with them the potential to be played according to several perspectives. These perspectives imply different social meanings, and, when game meanings are disputed, inferences about the character of the disputants may be drawn by their fellowplayers.

By late preadolescence the negotiation of game rules provides almost as much interest as the game itself (Knapp and Knapp, 1976). Boys acquire techniques for "getting along"—when to use threats of force, when to trade favors, when to use reason, when to back off gracefully, and when angrily to leave the field. Piaget notes that this is a period of "juridical discussions" (p. 43) in which "the dominating interest seems to be interest in the rules themselves." This observation of late preadolescence as a period in which a quasi-legal system operates has been confirmed by Glassner (1976) who notes that children are able to settle interpersonal disputes with a minimum of violence through informal processes of childhood jurisprudence. This process is evident when preadolescents must determine ordering. On one occasion I brought several empty beer cans from Colorado for preadolescent beer can collectors in Minnesota. Since the cans had different values, it was necessary for the children to determine an order for choosing. After discussion, players were able to order themselves in such a way that no player felt publicly humiliated. For example, the high-status boy who chose first claimed that the next time I brought beer cans he would pick sixth. Opie and Opie (1959) speak of children as having a "Code of Oral Legislation" which binds children to allow social relations to take particular forms (e.g., possession typically being *100%* of the law), if ritual declarations, such as those asserting ownership ("finders keepers, losers weepers"), are followed.

Rules as a code of conduct are not crucial during late preadolescence. More important is the social experience that derives from learning to manipulate the social order (the *use* of rules)—the issue is rights and privileges. Despite the supposed inflexibility of the rules (as explained to an interested adult), they are not enforced uniformly; some children are allowed leeway while others are not. Both the legitimacy of rules and the legitimacy of preferential treatment are being acquired in this process. Knapp and Knapp (1976) note:

As they [children] argue about rules, add new ones, agree to exceptions, and censure a playmate who is cheating, they are exploring how necessary rules are, how they are made, and what degree of consensus is needed to make them effective. They are also learning something about the relationship of personality to power, and of fairness to order (p. 17).

Rules provide guidelines for interaction, but do not control the interaction itself; they are topics for negotiation. The sometimes bewildering complex of rules exists not because preadolescents wish every contingency to be considered so that fights are impossible, but because a set of rules provides a store of information which boys can use in their arguments with each other in defining ambiguous situations in the game. It is the process of negotiation that is central to interaction—rather than formal rules.

An example of this negotiation process is depicted by Dennison (1969) in a description of a fight between five troubled boys with severe learning and behavior problems. These preadolescents are supposedly "out of control," and unable to cope with social interaction; they attend a school for delinquent children. In the course of the school year a hostile rivalry has developed between three Puerto Rican friends (Jose, Julio, and Vicente) and two non-Hispanic buddies (Stanley, white and Willard, black). These preadolescents had engaged in a series of violent altercations, and finally the boys decided to fight it out, with Dennison, their teacher, only insisting that they not use weapons. I shall quote from his account at some length, since it indicates the subtlety of preadolescent impression management, and the development of standards for behavior as a result of interaction:

> A great shout went up, a roar, and all five piled into each other . . . and stopped abruptly to let Jose take off his shirt. Stanley and Willard took their shirts off, too. They were about to clash again when Stanley paused and took off his shoes, and so Willard and Jose took their shoes off, too. The roar went up again and they tangled, Stanley and Willard against Jose, Julio, and Vicente. . . . There was much cursing, many shouts of pain—strange shouts, really, for each one had in it a tinge of protest and flattery. It was in these overtones that one could sense the fine changes in their relations. They were saying things for which they had no words, and the refinement of this communication was extraordinary and beautiful. It was apparent immediately that the boys had set some kind of limit to their violence, though they had not spoken of limits. Rules, codes, acknowledgements

popped up spontaneously and changed swiftly. When anyone got hurt, he stepped off the mats . . . and the rule was accepted by all, without having been announced that no one could be attacked when he stepped off the mat. . . . Occasionally as the boys rolled and squirmed, they also punched each other in the ribs. These blows, however, were almost formal and were very subtly adjusted. The loser must prove that he is really struggling, and so in order to ensure himself against the contempt of the victor, he punches him in the ribs. Delivered with just the right force, these punches remain compliments. . . . They are tributes, too, to the reality of the fight. Delivered a bit harder, they are "unfair." Delivered still harder, they precipitate a bloodletting. And so they are very nicely attuned. . . .

> Willard is grinning and trying different holds, but in between the grins he exerts himself to the utmost and still can't pin Jose. And so he shouts again and again, "Give up?" and Jose cries, "You have to kill me!" The decision is in Willard's hands. Soon he lets Jose up, but punches him on the arm so Jose won't think he has been let up. Willard shows great tact in his awareness of victory. He smiles openly at Jose, not a triumphant smile, but a friendly one (Dennison, 1969, pp. 133–137).

These "maladjusted" preadolescents are highly sophisticated in techniques of impression management, and in the staging of social encounters. Even an emotional fight is not a random sequencing of aggressive actions, but is socially ordered, and this structuring occurs not before the event, but during it. While there are certain characteristics that these boys could report about "fighting norms" or rules, the application of these procedures occurs during the fight and is responsive to immediate considerations. This structuring of interaction is equally relevant to games that have rules as part of the oral tradition, but these rules may not be followed or may be altered in the course of the game.

Individuals in these social situations have the power to altercast their fellow interactants. Thus, Willard had the opportunity to defeat his enemy Jose, with a presumably explicit loss of status by

Jose; however, he refrained from doing this—possibly as an attempt to drain the encounter of emotional intensity. This process of constructing social meanings is characteristic of social interaction—even among children.

FRIENDSHIP AND SOCIALIZATION

By preadolescence, the existence and content of peer relationships have become central to the child's social world. This reveals itself in children's self-consciousness of the impressions that others have of them and in the importance they give to their friendships. By incorporating the needs for impression management and friendship, I argue that the friendship bond provides a setting where impression management skills are mastered and in which inadequate displays will typically be ignored or corrected without severe loss of face. Outside of friendship bonds, preadolescents have a critical eye for children's behaviors that are managed inadequately.

Typically, preadolescents name many children as friends. For example, in Sanford Heights, 48 of the 50 12-year-olds in the Little League were asked to evaluate their relationships to the other 12-year-olds in the league. In our sample, 18% of all possible relationships are said to be close friends, 31% are friends, 2% are disliked, and 49% are neither friends nor disliked. It is the boys' rather large network of "friends" that comprises the bulk of the society in which they spend their social leisure time.

Friendship has generally been conceptualized as an affective bond, a relationship charged with positive affect, in some cases approaching "love." While this aspect of the friendship bond exists, other features of friendship should be emphasized as well. In addition to being emotionally involving, friendship is also a staging area for interaction, a cultural institution for the transmission of knowledge and performance techniques, and a crucible for the shaping of selves—in other words,

a primary group. Each of these attributes of the friendship relationship has implications for interaction within and outside of the friendship bond.

FRIENDSHIP AS A STAGING AREA

Friendship is a social relationship, a bond between two individuals. As such it is not a physical entity but a spiritual or ideational one. However, friendships are not continuously activated and, when these relationships are not activated, their effects on social interaction are slight. One's position as a friend can be conceived of as akin to a partial identity that is activated when relevant—with the understanding that multiple friendship identities can be activated simultaneously. Obviously, a friendship identity is likely to be activated when the friend is physically present. Thus, the analysis can be expanded from an emphasis on the ideational aspect of the relationship to include an emphasis on the friendship context. A friendship bond, therefore, can be described as a staging area for action.

The presence of friends produces a social context that allows for the performance of actions which would otherwise be improper. For example, in an earlier paper (Fine, 1979a), I described the social ecology of preadolescent pranks among 12-year-olds in Sanford Heights. Of the 70 prank partners named for four different types of pranks, 89% were close friends of the namer, 9% more were friends, and the remaining 2% were former friends. Close friendships thus can provide a staging area for pranks, which some scholars (Dresser, 1973; Knapp and Knapp, 1976) claim socialize the child by allowing him to explore the boundaries of allowable behavior and to gain social poise in stressful situations.

The friendship bond, in allowing for a wide latitude of behavior, provides a setting in which the child is able to explore modes of expressing sexual attitudes, aggression, and attitudes toward school and work. Even if negatively sanctioned behavior occurs, that sanctioning typically does not imply a derogation of the actor; the disapproved action is not seen as part of the actor's identity. Friends typically have sufficient "idiosyncracy credits" (Hollander, 1958) to allow for a wide range of socially inappropriate actions. The actions of a friend are much less likely to be defined as inappropriate than are the identical behaviors of others.

The friendship group seems of particular importance as a context for action in terms of the developing relationship between boys and girls. Broderick (1966) notes that, at ages twelve and thirteen, 56% of the boys and 76% of the girls in his sample prefer double- or group-dating to single-dating. One group of 12-year-old boys in Hopewell even formalized this to the extent that they formed a "club" with a major function being the support of each other in their dealings with girls. This form of social activity is also evident in private parties of preadolescents (Martinson, 1973). These parties in which the boys are supported by their male friends (and the girls are in the company of their friends) are staging areas for quasi-sexual and quasi-aggressive behaviour. Boys in Sanford Heights informed me that "making out" occurred at these events, and this "making out" apparently consisted of kissing and above the waist petting ("getting to second base"). However, roughhousing may also occur as boys are ignorant of adolescent social norms of chivalrous behavior to girls or ashamed of showing tenderness to girls. One young adult male recalled the way in which male peers are used for social support in situations where social norms are ambiguous, and self-presentation becomes a considerable challenge:

> As I remember there weren't many fellows who were on the dance floor. They were all in a group in the corner, and that is where I ended up too. We told jokes, tested our strength on the bars that stood along the walls, and teased any fellow who dared to ask a girl to dance (Martinson, 1973, pp. 84–85).

On one occasion I went with three preadolescent friends from Sanford Heights to a large amusement park in the Minneapolis-St. Paul area:

> The boys seem very interested in the girls that they see, and there is considerable whispering and teasing about them. Tom had received a small coin bank as a prize which he decides that he no longer wishes to keep. At this time we are standing in line for a roller coaster directly behind three girls—apparently a year or two older than these twelve-year-olds—one of whom is wearing a hooded jacket. Frank tells Tom to take the bank and "stuff it in her hood," which Tom does to the annoyance of his victim. When she turns around, Tom and Hardy tell her that Frank did it and, of course, Frank denies this, blaming Tom. The girls tell the boys to shut up and leave them alone. As things work out, Hardy has to sit with one of these girls on the ride and he clearly appears embarrassed, while Tom and Frank are vastly amused. After the ride Tom and Frank claim that they saw Hardy holding her. Frank said that he saw them holding hands, and Tom said: "He was trying to go up her shirt." Hardy vehemently denies these claims. A short while later we meet these girls again, and Frank turns to Hardy, saying, "Here's your honey." The girl retorts as she walks away, "Oh, stifle it." (Field notes.)

The male friendship group provides a supportive staging area for these boys to practice their impression management skills on each other and on their female contacts, as they are developing a sexualized self. It is attention rather than tenderness that orients the staging of boy-girl encounters in this period:

> A group of boys come across a preadolescent girls' softball team from a different area of town, sitting around a park picnic table. The boys begin teasing them with sexual taunts: "Hey, suck me where the sun never shines," "Pluck my hairs," or "You're innocent like my butthole." The girls are not visibly outraged at this and actually seem to enjoy the attention that the boys are giving them—at one point singing to attract their attention. After whispering

discussion about what they should do to their victims, the boys steal the girls' thermos and pour out the water in it—at which the girls squeal but don't get seriously upset. Later the boys return to the picnic table and throw beer cans at the girls, who giggle and scream. (Field notes.)

The presence of one's friends seems to provide a legitimation for this type of activity, which has important consequences for the sexual socialization of preadolescents. It provides them with a range of experience in dealing with the opposite sex and a testing of their social poise (Stone, 1965). Players are socialized to respond to the demands of a variety of social situations, and their friendships serve to provide access to these situations.

FRIENDSHIP AS A CULTURAL INSTITUTION

Suttles (1970) has described friendship as a social institution and this description certainly applies in terms of the didactic function of friendship. Information transmitted through friendship ties varies in the extent of its diffusion. Some information is highly localized, perhaps shared only by members of a dyad, while other information is widely known among preadolescents or Americans in general. These dyads and groups not only create a private culture (Suttle, 1970; Fine, 1979a), but also transmit cultural information relevant to the problems of growing up. This is of particular significance to socialization, in that it provides the child with a stock of knowledge and repertoire of behavior useful for encounters with other peers. Children acquire information from several sources—the media, schools, churches, and their families—all adult dominated institutions. In contemporary American society, these adults typically share an ideology about what children should and should not know. Thus, there are several topic areas in which children have interest, but which they cannot learn about from adults: the practice of sex, informal rules of institutions (how *really* to suc-

ceed in school), the art of making negative evaluations (insults), and how to have excitement and adventure (pranks, mischief, and illegal behavior).

For example, one 12-year-old boy explains to his friends in clinical detail how to "french" a girl. This first part of the account explains the basic behaviors in "frenching," but of perhaps greater importance is the latter section of the transcript which transmits signals about the structure of sexual relations in contemporary America:

TOM: First of all, you gotta make sure you don't get no more "Ahhhk!" burps in your mouth (Hardy and Frank both laugh). It would be very crude to burp. I mean you make sure you don't have a cold, cause greenies mucus going through there (Tom laughs), going through her mouth would taste awful horseshit (all laugh).

FRANK: And one thing, don't spit while frenching.

TOM: And make sure . . . make sure you don't breathe out of your mouth (all laugh) unless you're doing mouth-to-mouth resuscitation. After all that frenching, you just gotta do mouth-to-mouth to keep your air up. OK, now you take a squirt of your favorite after-shave. You rub it on your hair, and you rub it all around you. And you (Tom giggles "hysterically") and you rub it all around. It sure feels good (more giggling). Frank's choking under pressure. Listen (more "hysterical" laughter), he's got a boner (more laughter). He's got a boner. He's got a boner and he'd like to suck it off.

HARDY: Listen, listen, his lips are on it.

TOM: He's sucking (all laugh).

FRANK: Nuhhh. Nuhhh. Nuhhh (joking, making almost mooing sounds, apparently designed to simulate a sexually excited woman).

. . .

TOM: Hardy, do you like to put anything in my act?

HARDY: No.

TOM: Only that he's got a, Ahhh!, stiff boner (Hardy giggles). Frank. Frank ain't got stiff, uh-uh. Since we're talking about Hardy's girl friend, he's sorta, you know what I mean, doncha?

HARDY: No! (Frank laughs).

TOM: He sorta hit the jack, uh, hit the jack. Hit the jack-off, you know.

HARDY: No, I don't know.

TOM: I do (Tom and Hardy both laugh). Well, anyway, I get to my second lesson. First you walk in, you see a sexy girl in the telephone booth. You don't know who she is, just see the back of her. Gotta make sure she doesn't have a big butt, you know. . . . You just walk into the telephone booth, put your arm around here and say ''Hi.'' And she goes ''Uhhh! Ohhh, hi'' (tone sounds surprised at first, then ''feminine'' and ''willing''). With her tongue around, wrapped around, wrapped around the microphone, her teeth, her teeth are chattering from so much shock. You just take your pants . . . no . . . well.

HARDY: You take her pants.

TOM: Well, you just stick out your tongue, and you say (Tom sings in a mocking romantic fashion): ''Want to, oh baby, you mean it, you let me under your skin.'' (Taped transcript).

This is a fragment of a longer conversation—just one of numerous conversations among one set of close friends—not much different from those of other ''precocious'' preadolescents. These conversations taken together allow for an examination of the dynamics of the acquisition of the male sex role. Through the content of these conversations, boys learn what is expected of them by their peers. The importance of this talk does not derive from the acquisition of sophisticated techniques of french kissing (although specific content learning does occur); rather, boys learn how to present themselves to male peers as ''males.'' This conversation suggests quite dramatically that males are expected by each other to be sexually aggressive

and that females wait for their encounters with undisguised arousal. While we might be reading too much into this short dialogue to suggest that it provides a justification for rape, it does provide a world view which is consistent with masculine dominance and female submission. By this talk, preadolescents are learning skills which will allow them to handle themselves within the context of similar lines of talk and prepares them to act as ''males.''

The same process occurs in other areas as well. Preadolescents in discussing how to evade school-work or cut classes (for example, claim that you have a church confirmation, since teachers never check) acquire rhetoric about schooling. Again, it is less important to learn specific facts and procedures than to learn ways to talk. These tools for interactional negotiation allow the child to deal competently with peers.

Through the support of friends, the child also learns techniques of evaluation, when to use insults and when to avoid them, and the social implications of this process of evaluation. The case of one 10-year-old boy in Sanford Heights who is criticized by several older boys is instructive. The 10-year-old, Tommy, is the son of a Little League manager. During one post-season practice in preparation for a statewide tournament, Tommy and Harmon, a 12-year-old teammate, angrily trade insults. Harmon's temper had caused problems all season, and this episode was the final straw. Tommy's father announced that he was quitting as manager of the team. After the anger subsided he returned, but Harmon's father felt that it was in everyone's best interest if Harmon left the team. The following week some of Harmon's friends met Tommy on a school bus:

Hardy sees Tommy get on the bus and announces loudly, ''Tommy sucks.'' Rod adds: ''Tommy's a wuss.'' In unison Jerry and Rod tell Tommy as he approaches, ''You suck.'' Rod particularly is angry at Tommy, ''Harmon can't play because of you. What a fag!'' Tommy doesn't respond to the abuse from his older tormentors, but looks dejected and perhaps near tears (which is what Rod and Hardy later tell Harmon). The insults build in stridency and anger as Hardy calls Tommy a ''woman,'' Jerry knocks off his hat, and Rod says, ''Give him the faggot award.'' Finally Jerry takes the baseball cap of Tommy's friend and seatmate and tosses it out the window of the moving bus. (Field notes.)

It is a frequent observation that preadolescents can be distressingly cruel to each other, but the social context of this cruelty is not sufficiently emphasized; the cruelty is almost always expressed in the presence of friends. Insults seem to be expressed as much for reasons of self-presentation to one's peers as to attack the target. This point has also been made in studies of ''sounding'' or ''playing the dozens'' by black adolescents (e.g., Kochman, 1972; Abrahams, 1970). The case cited above is representative in that there is an attempt by the insulters to test the boundaries of proper insults, and the insult crescendo typically continues until the target becomes upset, withdraws, or until one of the perpetrators does something that is outside the range of legitimate behavior in that situation. Thus, in this case, tossing the baseball cap out of the bus window ended the insults. Jerry's action was outside the realm of legitimate behavior, and he sullied his social self. Although he was not sanctioned by his friends, he apologized to the victim, claiming that he didn't really intend to get rid of the hat.

To summarize, socialization does not consist of rote learning of behaviors or of an encyclopedia of practical knowledge. Socialization can best be considered instruction in dealing with situations or, as Denzin suggests, learning to fit together lines of action. The child needs to learn the process by which social meanings are constructed, ways of knowing the expectations of others, and methods of determining their likely actions (Mead's notion of the Generalized Other). The friendship group, by placing the child in such situations in a supportive environment, provides the opportunity to ac-

quire and refine skills that are necessary for interaction with others.

FRIENDSHIP AS A SHAPER OF THE SOCIAL SELF

Friendship also contributes to the socialization of the preadolescent through its effects on self-image. Friendship is a crucial factor in the development of the social self—both for popular boys and for boys with few close friends.

Following the symbolic interactionist perspective, individuals can be conceived as having multiple selves, which are a function of setting and audience. The developmental issue from this standpoint is not the traditional psychiatric one of the unitary development of the self, but the interactional issue of acquiring behavioral flexibility to cope with situations and of interpreting the behaviors involved as part of one's larger repertoire of behavior.

In friendship there is less likelihood of any action producing a negative evaluation and a dramatic change in the status of the relationship, as friendships tend to be relatively stable over time, even during preadolescence. Each action has a small incremental effect upon the person's image because of the larger base of previous experiences with that person. It follows that the actor will be freer in terms of self-conscious constraints placed on his behavior in the presence of friends. Furthermore, friends tend to perceive themselves as relatively similar to each other in their preferred activities and, thus, believe that they share patterns of behavior. One of the frequent responses received when I inquired why a boy was friends with another dealt with common interests and activities: ''He likes to do the things I like to do.''

In childhood friendships the child's self (the perceived unitary composite of his multiple selves) develops in situations in which serious threats to the self are not likely to be present, and this argument returns us to the social psychiatric model of friendship proposed by Sullivan (1953). The affective ties between preadolescent chums consist of an interest in and acceptance of the other, and along with this interest is a close attention to role-taking and assuming the perspective of the other. Sullivan (1953) argues:

> . . . your child at preadolescence when he finds a chum begins to develop a real sensitivity to what matters to another person. And this is not in the sense of "what should I do to get what I want," but instead, "what should I do to contribute to the happiness or to support the prestige and feeling of worthwhileness of my chum" (p. 245).

Because the chum has the same orientation, Sullivan suggests that this is the last, best chance for dramatic changes in the child's "self-system"; it is a time for the individual's self to be validated through social interaction. Whether Sullivan is correct about the relative importance of this period is not of concern; more important is the existence of this validation of the self through friendship.

CONCLUSION

I have argued here that children's friendships should be analyzed in terms of their contribution to the development of the child's interactional competence. As in all interaction, participants are able to generate social meanings through such peer relations, and these meanings affect behavior and self-indication. I have argued that preadolescents develop considerable competence at mastering self-presentational skills, and that regular interaction partners are of particular importance in this social learning. These social skills differ from many that the child is acquiring in that they don't consist of a core of knowledge, behavior patterns, or social norms; rather they consist of techniques for negotiating social reality; a *process* that requires an understanding of the social dynamics of peer interaction.

In particular, preadolescent friendships involve three components that are related to the development of interactional skills—components which are generally not considered in developmental

literature on friendship. First, friendships provide a staging arena for behavior. Friendships are situated in social environments, which have implications for the acquisition of interactional competencies. Second, friendships are cultural institutions, and as such they provide didactic training. Third, friendships provide a context for the child's social self to be developed, and for him to learn the appropriate self-image to project in social situations. While these dimensions of friendship are not limited to preadolescence, they seem characteristic of this period because at this age the child is particularly influenced by peers and is simultaneously striving to acquire information and behavior necessary for social competence in adult society.

NOTES

1. All personal and place names used in conjunction with the discussion of the Little League baseball research are pseudonyms.

2. For the distinction between role-taking and role-playing, see Coutu, 1951.

REFERENCES

Abrahams, R. *Deep Down in the Jungle*. Revised Edition. Chicago: Aldine, 1970.

Bain, R. The self-and-other words of a child. *American Journal of Sociology*, 1936, *41*, 767−775.

Bernstein, B. *Class, codes and control*. New York: Schocken, 1975.

Blumer, H. *Symbolic interactionism: Perspective and method*. Englewood Cliffs, New Jersey: Prentice-Hall, 1969.

Bogden, R. and Taylor, S. J. *Introduction to qualitative research methods*. New York: Wiley-Interscience, 1975.

Broderick, C. B. Socio-sexual development in a suburban community. *Journal of Sex Research*, 1966, *2*, 1−24.

Cavan, S. The etiquette of youth. In G. P. Stone and H. A. Farberman (Eds.), *Social psychology through symbolic interaction*. Waltham, Massachusetts: Xerox, 1970.

Coleman, J. *The adolescent society*. New York: Free Press, 1961.

Cooley, C. H. A study of the early use of self-words by a child. *Psychological Review*, 1908, *15*, 339—357.

Cooley, C. H. *Human nature and the social order*. New York: Schocken, 1964 (originally published, 1902).

Corsaro, William A. Friendship in the nursery school: social organization in a peer environment. In S. R. Asher and J. M. Gottman (Eds.), *The development of children's friendships*. New York: Cambridge University Press, 1981.

Cottle, T. J. Prospect Street moon. In T. J. Cottle, *Time's children*. Boston: Little, Brown, 1971.

Coutu, W. Role playing versus role taking: An appeal for clarification. *American Sociological Review*, 1951, *16*, 180—187.

Dennison, G. *The lives of children*. New York: Vintage, 1969.

Denzin, N. K. *Childhood socialization*. San Francisco: Jossey-Bass, 1977.

Dresser, N. Telephone pranks. *New York Folklore Quarterly*, 1973, *29*, 121—130.

Elkin, F. and Handel, G. *The child and society: The process of socialization*. Third edition. New York: Random House, 1978.

Faris, E. *The nature of human nature*. New York: McGraw Hill, 1971 (1937).

Fine, G. A. The natural history of preadolescent male friendship groups. In H. Foot, A. J. Chapman, and J. Smith (Eds.), *Childhood and friendship relations*. Chichester: Wiley, in press, 1979a.

Fine, G. A. Cracking diamonds: The relationship between observer role and observed content in Little League baseball settings. In W. Shaffir, A. Turowetz, and R. Stebbins (Eds.), *The social experience of fieldwork*, in press, 1979b.

Fine, G. A. and Glassner, B. The promise and problems of participant observation with children. *Urban Life*, 1979, *8*, 153—174.

Fine, G. A. and West, C. S. Do Little Leagues work: Player satisfaction with organized preadolescent baseball programs. *Minnesota Journal of Health, Physical Education and Recreation*, 1979, *7*, 4—6.

Glassner, B. Kid society. *Urban Education*, 1976, *11*, 5—22.

Goffman, E. *Presentation of self in everyday life*. Garden City, New York: Anchor, 1959.

Goffman, E. *Frame analysis*. Cambridge, Massachusetts: Harvard University Press, 1974.

Hartup, W. W. Children and their friends. In H. McGurk (Ed.), *Issues in childhood social development*. London: Methuen, 1978.

Hollander, E. P. Conformity, status, and idiosyncrasy credit. *Psychological Review* 1958, *65*, 117—127.

Knapp, M. and Knapp, H. *One potato, two potato . . .: The secret education of American children*. New York: Norton, 1976.

Kochman, T. Toward an ethnography of black American speech behavior. In T. Kochman (Ed.), *Rappin' and stylin' out: Communication in Urban Black America*. Urbana: University of Illinois Press, 1972.

Lever, J. Sex differences in the games children play. *Social Problems*, 1976, *23*, 478—487.

MacKay, R. Conceptions of children and models of socialization. In H. P. Dreizel (Ed.), *Childhood and socialization*. New York: Macmillan, 1973.

Martinson, F. M. *Infant and child sexuality: A sociological perspective*. St. Peter, Maine: Book Mart, 1973.

Mead, G. H. The genesis of the self and social control. *International Journal of Ethics*, 1925, *35*, 251—277.

Mead, G. H. *Mind, self and society*. Chicago, Illinois: University of Chicago Press, 1934.

Opie, I. and Opie, P. *The lore and language of school children*. Oxford: Oxford University Press, 1959.

Piaget, Jean. *The moral judgment of the child*. New York: Collier, 1962 (1932).

Riezler, K. Play and seriousness. *Journal of Philosophy*, 1941, *38*, 505—517.

Selman, R. L. The child as a friendship philosopher in S. R. Asher and J. M. Gottman (Eds.), The development of *children's friendship*. New York: Cambridge University Press, 1981.

Speier, M. *How to observe face-to-face communication*. Pacific Palisades, California: Goodyear, 1973.

Stone, G. P. Appearance and the self. In G. P. Stone and H. A. Farberman (Eds.), *Social psychology through symbolic interaction*. Waltham, Massachusetts: Ginn-Blaisdell, 1970.

Stone, G. P. The play of little children. *Quest*, 1965, *4*, 23−31.

Stone, L. J. and Church, J. *Childhood and Adolescence*. New York: Random House, 1957.

Stone, L. J. and Church, J. *Childhood and Adolescence*. Second edition. New York: Random House, 1968.

Sullivan, H. S. *The interpersonal theory of psychiatry*. New York: Norton, 1953.

Suttles, G. D. Friendship as a social institution. In G. J. McCall, M. McCall, N. K. Denzin, G. D. Suttles and S. B. Kurth (Eds.), *Social relationships*. Chicago: Aldine, 1970.

Waldrop, M. F. and Halverson, C. F. Jr. Intensive and extensive peer behavior: Longitudinal and cross-sectional analysis. *Child Development*, 1975, *46*, 19−26.

Weinstein, E. A. The development of interpersonal competence. In D. A. Goslin (Ed.), *Handbook of socialization theory and research*. Chicago: Rand McNally, 1969.

Weinstein, E. A. and Deutschberger, P. Some dimensions of altercasting. *Sociometry*, 1963, *4*, 454−466.

Wiley, N. The genesis of self: From me to we to I. In N. K. Denzin (Ed.) *Studies in symbolic interaction*. Volume II. Greenwich, Conn.: JAI Press, in press, 1979.

Zeitlin, I. *Rethinking sociology*. Englewood Cliffs, N.J.: Prentice-Hall, 1973.

Zigler, E. and Child, I. L. Socialization. In G. Lindzey and E. Aronson (Eds.), *The handbook of social psychology*. Second Edition, Volume Three. Reading, Massachusetts: Addison-Wesley, 1969.

TWENTY-FOUR

SPORT AND THE SOCIALIZATION OF YOUTH

GREGORY P. STONE

As part of a larger study of the place of sport in community organization, I scanned several major community studies, most carried on in the United States. Because of the general sociological aversion to, disinterest in, or ignorance of sport, little data could be gleaned from such studies and even less on the relationship of sport to the socialization of youth. Nevertheless, there were sufficient data from five such studies[1] to detect a rough pattern for the process. First, the constriction of urban play space has facilitated the appropriation of commu-

SOURCE: This article was especially prepared for this volume. This is a part of a larger manuscript, the main perspective of which has been presented at the meetings of the International Sociological Association in Upsaala, Sweden, 1978.

[1]Four of the studies employ pseudonyms to designate the communities concerned: "Elmtown," Illinois (population about 10,000); "Middletown," Indiana (1925 population—38,628; 1933 population—47,790); "Plainville," Missouri (1940 population—1692; 1950 population—1488); and "Street Corner," Massachusetts (Boston neighborhood study in the early 1940s). Various suburban communities in Westchester County, New York (a part of the greater New York City metropolitan region) studied in the early 1930s are identified by names. Of these studies, "Middletown" and "Plainville" were researched at two different times in the effort to mark out the processes of social change.

nity sport by the school system. Second, sport participation is a major source of self-esteem for the high-school athlete. Third, this esteem has an aura which radiates out to include followings of both sexes. Fourth, esteem must be celebrated, and such celebrations foster teen-age drinking. Fifth, betting on sports facilitates gambling and takes betters into gambling places where games are carried on. Finally, gambling and the rackets are intimately bound up with urban politics, and such activities participated in by youth provide entryways into those adult worlds.

Of course, this is not to say that participation in or a preoccupation with sports inevitably takes young people into politics or the rackets, but it is not unusual to see sports figures in government offices or government officials publicizing high-school or college sport activities. Sport and politics are tightly interwoven in the United States. Presidents, for example, seem almost obligated to show some past or present proficiency in sport, be it bench-warming, softball, jogging, or touch football. Moreover, the rackets can always use muscle, just as business can use images, to push ·its products. So the involvement in sports opens up larger "opportunities" for youth which may or may not be seized as youth "progresses" into adulthood. The important point for the reader to note is that socialization goes on in a changing context, but that there seems to be some permanence in the change. Thus, the references to earlier community studies are instructive.

PLAY-SPACE AND ITS DIMINUTION

Many sociologists tend to think of restrictions on play areas as one of the tolls imposed on human enjoyment by industrialization, and their view is well documented. The Hammonds have observed: "As industry turned country into town in the early nineteenth century, . . . old playgrounds disappeared and new playgrounds were not provided" (Hammond and Hammond, 1947: p. 75). They, then, devote a fascinating chapter to "The Loss of Playgrounds" (ibid: pp. 75—90). Apparently, the consolidation of the Industrial Revolution, at least in the United States, while providing expanding leisure time, has not expanded leisure space. In their revisiting of Middletown, the Lynds were impressed:

> In 1925 . . . youngsters, driven from street play to the sidewalks, were protesting, "Where can I play?" but in 1935 they were retreating even from the sidewalks, and an editorial, headed "Sidewalk Play is Dangerous," said, "It is safe to say that children under the age of eight years should not be permitted to play upon sidewalks" (Lynd and Lynd, 1937: p. 265).

Even so, Middletown, in 1925, cast a wary eye on suburbanization.

> One family, unusually rich in personal resources, has recently built a home a little way out of town, set back from the road almost hidden in trees. So incompatible is such a departure that rumors are afloat as to what secret motive can have prompted such unprecedented action (Lynd and Lynd, 1929: p. 309).

By 1932, at least in the New York metropolitan area, the mystique surrounding the suburban home

had decreased to such an extent that sociologists initiated research on the phenomenon.

Lundberg and his associates, Mirra Komarovsky and Mary Alice McInerny, explored the problem of leisure in Westchester County. No small impetus for suburbanization was furnished by the desire to provide more space and freedom for children. They cite an article by Ethel L. Swift written in 1928:

> We moved so that the children might be near the grass and the trees. . . . My small son builds a hut with packing boxes in the sumac bushes of the vacant lot next door; my daughter wrestles with a cigar box which will presently appear as a bird house meant to lure a bluebird to our garden. The children romp around the neighborhood unsupervised. In the city children cannot be permitted to go far from home alone, a state of affairs which hinders the development of the spirit of independence, so essential to the complete development of the child (Lundberg, et al., 1934: p. 45).

All well and good, but, with the urbanization of suburbia that we have witnessed on such a large scale in the last generation, it is doubtful whether the dreams of the suburban "pioneers" of the middle and late 'twenties are realizeable today. With the exception of the South and the "Sun Belt" in the United States—latecomers to the urbanization process—the decline of central city populations has been continuing. The trend began in the 1940s in the cities of the Northeast, was next manifested in the Midwest, and, by 1970, had reached the Border States. Specifically, 24 of the 153 cities in the United States with populations of 100,000 or more in 1970 showed populations less than those recorded by the Census in 1940. Seventeen (70.8%) of these were located in the northeastern states; five (20.8%) in the midwest; and two (8.3%) in the border states. No cities were characterized by such a decline elsewhere in the United States (U.S. Bureau of the Census, 1974: pp. 23—25). Another way of apprehending the trend is more crude, but simpler. Since 1950, the proportion of the total U.S. population living in "standard metropolitan statistical areas" (SMSAs) has increased from 62.5% to 68.6%, while the central city population for those areas has decreased from 56.8% to 45.8% of the total population residing in SMSAs (U.S. Bureau of the Census, 1974: p. 17). There are two conclusions to be drawn from these data. First, suburban space has become more constricted as population density has increased in the suburbs. Second, the areas most affected have been precisely those in which most of the community studies which we have used in our analysis were conducted.

The implication for socialization into sport and the reflexive influence of sport participation on the larger socialization of sport participants is the increasing importance of organized play and the restriction of play space, particularly to that provided and administered by the school system. It is this context of socialization that has been examined most frequently by students of community life, and for which most of the sparse data are available.

SCHOOLS

Obviously the concentration of community sports in the school system began in the cities of the United States as part of the increase in density, the constriction of play space, and the rationalization of collective life that urbanization establishes, at least in part. Although the interest among the young people is focused on high school activities, in at least one small town, there was some indication of a generation gap in 1955. "Many Plainvillers, including several teachers, lamented that teenagers are expected to show more interest in the high school athletic program than in their studies" (Gallaher, 1961: p. 270, fn. 11). Yet, in 1933, a study was made of 1500 graduates of the Wilkes-Barre, Pennsylvania City schools and reported in the New York *Times*. Sixty percent of those polled said that high school athletics were of great value; 40% considered them unduly stressed (Lundberg, *et al.,* 1934: p. 240). Earlier the Lynds had already observed the concentration of sport interest in the

school system and its subsequent diffusion in the community at large.

> There were no high school teams in 1890. Today, during the height of the basketball season when all the cities and towns of the state are fighting for the state championship amidst the delirious backing of the rival citizens, the dominance of this sport is as all-pervasive as football in a college like Dartmouth or Princeton the week of the "big game." . . . [I]t is the "Bearcats," particularly the basketball team, that dominate the life of the school (Lynd and Lynd, 1929: p. 213).

A mere seven years later, the same pattern was observed in the suburbs of New York City. Lundberg and his associates noted that:

> . . . interscholastic football and basketball games . . . form the real nucleus of student morale and enthusiasm. Nearly all of the senior high schools and a majority of the junior high schools maintain "varsity" basketball squads, a majority have similar teams in baseball, and a third of the senior high schools have varsity football. These teams become the objects of great adulation from the school and the community. . . . The county football championship is a major sport interest. . . . An important game will bring out perhaps 12,000 spectators who will stand or sit for several hours, sometimes in a cold rain, to see the issue decided. These contests tend to dominate in their season the extracurricular activities and school life to a high degree. The members of the team become heroes in the community as well as in the school. The eve of an important game is the occasion for mass "pep" meetings at which organized yelling, martial speeches, and other manifestations of mob spirit are cultivated. There is also much praise on such occasions of "fair play," "loyalty," "team spirit," and other values which are supposed to be represented in such sports. An important victory likewise calls for a triumphal entry of the "gladiators" into their home town behind the school band and all available automobiles bedecked in school colors and filled with noisy supporters of the team. Banquets, parties, and more speeches, as well as editorial encomiums from the school and village papers, are among the rewards of the upholders of the

school's athletic prowess (Lundberg, *et al.,* 1934: p. 236).

Again the emulation by the high schools of the college aura surrounding sport is specified:

> The interscholastic athletic contest is one of the most clearly defined recreational patterns and seems to have been passed down directly from the college to the high school. The high schools of Westchester have also adopted the collegiate scheme of social life, class organization, and ceremonies (Lundberg, *et al.,* 1934: p. 238).

Thus, colleges socialize high schools which socialize junior high schools, and so on down to the elementary grades. The influence on the lower grades has been observed as early as 1925:

> In the elementary grades athletics are still a minor interest, though a school baseball and basketball league have been formed of recent years and the pressure of inter-school leagues is being felt increasingly (Lynd and Lynd, 1929: p. 212 fn. 3).

Moreover, the school system is the major formalized agency of socialization for children in American communities or the society at large.

> Athletic contests afford a relatively harmless, if not beneficial, orgiastic release to both players and spectators and are probably of considerable importance in socialization of an elementary sort. Some of the disciplinary and character-building influences ascribed to these games are undoubtedly operative. There is no doubt either, that they are major recreational pursuits of school children and their families (Lundberg, *et al.,* 1934: p. 237–238).

TEEN-AGE SOCIALIZATION INTO SPORTS

An exception must be entered here to the picture of the socialization process painted by Lundberg and his associates. Athletics as emphasized by the school system performed a more direct socializing function for some boys than for girls and most other boys who experienced this socialization process indirectly or vicariously. The Lynds put it well. Regarding basketball.

> This activity, so enthusiastically supported, is largely vicarious. The press complains that only about forty boys are prominent enough in athletics to win varsity sweaters. In the case of the girls it is almost 100 percent vicarious. Girls play some informal basketball and there is a girls' Athletic Club which has a monogram and social meetings. But the interest of the girls in athletics is an interest in the activities of the young males (Lynd and Lynd, 1929: pp. 213–214).

In Elmtown, direct and vicarious socialization followed the same pattern, though the account is more complete. Baseball, football, field hockey, and basketball were common preadolescent activities carried on by youngsters of all social strata. Such sports were carried over to high school by many entering freshmen and sophomores. Most freshmen, as they grow older, do not necessarily increase in size or athletic skill, and they move to informal play, find part-time work, and develop more interest in girls, as well as in pool, bowling, or extracurricular activities organized by the high school (Hollingshead, 1949: pp. 213–214). After the sophomore year, the pattern is more completely focused on high school athletics.

> The shift from informal team games played in the open to team games . . . inside buildings is part of the maturation process that occurs during the middle years of high school. Since the culture frowns (*sic*) upon the big boy who acts like a youngster, the approved role in the junior and senior years is to watch the highly skilled, carefully trained varsity team play. We believe that the subtle process of identification of self with the team enables the non-player to play the game vicariously and simultaneously to enjoy its thrills through deep ego-involvement. After the game, he experiences the warm glow of glamorizing the players with those who shared the experience with him. This process was evident . . . as we went to the shower rooms with the players after the games, and then to the "coke

spots'' with ''the gang,'' where the players were the center of attention (Hollingshead, 1949: p. 314).

It seems, then, as though the school system, particularly the last two years of high school, emphasizes sport which is employed directly in the socialization of willing and physically qualified boys and indirectly in the socialization of other boys and almost all girls. Such vicarious socialization should not be underemphasized. At least one discussion of sport specifically points out that ''. . . the basis of enjoyment is the same, whether one is taking part or merely watching as spectator'' (*Columbia Encyclopedia,* 1967: p. 2022). Nevertheless, the force of ideology is directed toward direct male participation. Women ought to look elsewhere for their recreation, as the Lynds have shown in their characterization of the ''Middletown Spirit,'' which emphasized ''That 'red-blooded' physical sports are more normal recreations for a man than art, music, or literature. . . .'' and that '''culture and things like that' are more the business of women than of men'' (Lynd and Lynd, 1937: p. 212). This differentiation begins far earlier than the child's entry in the school system:

> In typical American homes the father will take his son to the park or backyard and will teach him the fundamentals of baseball as early as the child can walk. Girls are given no similar encouragement by their parents (Fine, 1977: p. 15).

A professional football player and former All-American told me that his father placed a football in his crib when he was wheeled out of the hospital nursery after his birth, and I believe him!

Sports may also hold young men in high school and, consequently, in that formal socialization process even against their will. Plainville is only one of many communities where this happens.

> When one of the star athletes threatened to quit school in 1954, many people commented on the damage that would result to the basketball team, but few were concerned that the boy should complete

graduation requirements (Gallaher, 1961: pp. 270–271).

In spite of the lack of concern for education evidenced by the public pressure to keep the boy in school, the fact that an athlete must be academically eligible to compete ought not be gainsaid.

Television, today, plays a significant part in the socialization of boys into the world of sport, as the action of the ''big leagues'' is beamed into the small town. Lowell Rasmussen, thirty-five years old, who won twelve letters in high school and ran the local Mobil station in Morristown, Minnesota, observed in 1970:

> I never miss anything that has to do with sports, I've been a fan of everything since I was ten years old, and there's never been anything quite like sports on TV. When I was a kid, I used to dig around for every newspaper clipping and every newspaper story I could find. I'd cut out pictures and keep charts and listen to the radio and I could imagine the whole thing. But the kids now, they get to see it like it really is. And you see them—little rascals in third and fourth grade—out playing football . . . and they'll be fading to pass and pumping their arms like John Unitas. I see them and I can't believe it. They're better at their games than we ever were. They can copy the super-stars because they can see them (Johnson, 1971: p. 220).

Morristown high school had 120 students in 1970—''not exactly a super-star situation . . . things never quite crackle with big-time pressure'' (*ibid*). Still, let's enter the thoughts of Rick Ellingworth, the quarterback for the Morristown ''Comets.'' He is a 15-year-old farm boy who gets up at 5:00 a.m. to milk 50 cows and drives a pick-up truck to and from football practice:

> When I'm doing my chores, . . . I'm always thinking about my roll-outs and sprint-outs the way I seen Roger Staubach do 'em and Fran Tarkenton. Sometimes I think about Bart Starr and I try to think how I'll do my eye-fakes when I'm going to pass. Like Starr. I think about how Joe Namath plays, how great he is. Not the way he *lives*—not that, because Coach

says Namath does things he shouldn't do, and I agree. But I can just see in my mind the stop-action of him dropping back and the way he gets rid of the ball so quick (*ibid.*: p. 221).

But this is not only the substance of the "fantastic" (Stone and Stone, 1976: pp. 37—41) socialization of a 15 year old. Butch LaCanne, a freshman in high school, weighs 97 pounds and is not yet five feet tall. He plays substitute defense for the 'Comets.'

> I never miss a Viking game on TV and I never stop watchin' Carl Eller [an all-pro defensive end, well over six feet tall and 230 pounds, who played for the Minnesota Vikings in the 1970s] when he's in there. I watch how Eller uses his hands to get them guys out of his road. Then I try to t'row guys out of my road just like Eller does. But I'm too little. (*ibid.*).

In such a way the school system selects out physically fit boys and trains them to participate in the world of sports. Most boys are pointed in their direction by the family prior to their school experience and bolstered by the family and the larger community whose members share the experience vicariously. Nor is it only in the United States that this pattern prevails, it has also been reported in Canada (Lucas, 1976: p. 350). Once selected as an athlete, the young player can choose his own role models from the *personae* featured by sports television, and, by fantastic emulation, improve his skills and involvement in the game.

SOCIALIZATION CONTINGENCIES

That males are socialized in this way has a reflexive consequence. The male identity so formed is extended beyond the settings of the sport contest to situations in the wider community. This broader socialization often moves in the direction of establishing a stereotype of the rough, tough, venturesome male both for the player and his admiring associates. Self-esteem at that age, as well as the respect of others, is tightly bound up with such a

"macho" image. Even in Plainville, that image is cultivated among the youth, since ". . . 'teenagers' . . . are expected to be interested in high school athletics, dating, and 'having a big time' " (Gallaher, 1961: p. 111).

DRINKING

A "big time" is frequently Saturday night for teen-agers and characteristically mobilizes the activities of athletes along with their claques and cliques.

> Drinking on Saturday night is more widespread in the athletic crowd both during and after training than in any other group in high school (Hollingshead, 1949: p. 323).

Hollingshead found only two boys on the Elmstown High School football team and one on the basketball team who were total abstainers. The heaviest drinking occurred at the end of the football, basketball, and baseball seasons when practically the whole team went to another town for dinner and an informal drinking bout. The coach knew all this, but felt there was nothing he could do to stop it. He lectured the players, emphasizing the importance of training and performance. Discussion with the superintendent culminated in the decision not to intervene and hope for the best.

The pattern is widespread, but in Hector, Minnesota, the coaches and the superintendent of schools decided to intervene. They placed a tavern in that small town and a ballroom in a town 30 miles away "off limits" to athletes. There has been no little controversy about that decision but the reaction reaffirms the extensive and continuing nature of the practice.

> When the sanctions went on in January, Dugdale [the tavern owner] . . . immediately noticed a sharp drop in his business. "I'd estimate that my gross is down $200 a week, which means a loss (of profit) of $50 to $60 a week. I felt it. You bet, I felt it."
>
> Although only 25 boys were affected by the rule, several students said others involved in athletics also

"got the word" that they should stay out of the tavern. That included the girls' basketball team, the cheerleaders and the pep band.

"It just sort of grew," said Dugdale. "If the athletes can't come in, you know their girl friends aren't coming. And some of the others will stay away, too. . . ." (Minneapolis *Tribune*, February 28, 1977: p. 1—A).

As Hollingshead observed in Elmtown, girls don't drink in cliques, but in couples on dates (Hollingshead, 1949: p. 323). But, "the times—they are a-changing." In January, 1977, again in Minnesota,

> Twenty-five Lakeville High School students . . . [were] . . . suspended from Minnesota State High School League Activities . . . because of . . . violations of the league's rule against consumption of alcoholic beverages.
>
> In addition, . . . the girls gymnastics, volleyball and track coach and a physical education teacher, has resigned, reportedly in connection with one of the incidents.
>
> [The coach] and a group of 23 girl gymnasts were on a trip to Gustavus Adolphus College in St. Peter, Minn., and 13 of the students were involved in one of the drinking incidents. . . . There were 27 students involved, but two are not participating in state league activities . . . The others are involved in girls basketball, cross-country skiing, a one-act play contest and debate. . . . (Minneapolis *Tribune*, February 5, 1977: p. 2—B).

We cannot discuss in this place the matter of women in sport, but we note that high school athletics extends into drinking behavior irrespective of sex and, for the boys, this facilitates the cultivation of a "macho" image.

All socialization includes a dimension of *drama* (Stone and Stone, 1976: pp. 36—37), and this dimension is evident in teen-age drinking.

> To properly impress one's peers, it is good form to overact the part. Sometimes the pseudo-drunk's condition is diagnosed; then the boys belittle him and accuse him of acting drunk. A common reaction. . . .

is to start drinking to prove one's "real" ability (Hollingshead, 1949: p. 322).

In such a way a spiral may be established for those however vulnerable to the chemical. As it escalates, such youngsters may, literally and figuratively, be carried away from the image they are trying to cultivate.

BETTING AND GAMBLING

Betting on sports contests is frequent. In fact, some sports seem deliberately contrived for gambling, as is horse and greyhound racing in the United States. Even so, "the betting experience to end all others" occurred for Michener "on a hurricane Saturday in London." Eight games, figuring in weekly pools on which millions of pounds had been wagered, were cancelled. The wagers were not. Five men "of impeccable reputation" met in a closed room with no telephone, carefully guarded by police, to predict the outcomes of the cancelled games. Those scores were broadcast with the regular scores that evening so the "*betting*" was "not interrupted" (Michener, 1976: p. 408). I use this illustration, not only to establish the linkage between betting and sports, but between betting and gambling. In Elmtown the latter distinction was made. Girls, on special occasions, may bet a sandwich, coke, or soda on a basketball game, but "betting" is different from gambling (Hollingshead, 1949: p. 318). Gambling, Hollingshead observes, is predominantly a male activity among the youngsters. Sixty percent of the boys gambled and only five percent of the girls. As opposed to betting, gambling involves penny-matching, punch boards, playing the numbers, slot machines, pool, bowling, or poker (*ibid.*). Many of these devices and opportunities are provided in pool halls— strictly male territories in Elmtown. If a girl must communicate with a boy in the pool hall, she either sends in a man with a message or telephones (*ibid.*: p. 318). In Plainville as well, the pool hall is seen as a "good loafing place for men . . . where fellers can go and talk—and say what they want to'' (Gallaher, 1961: p. 78).

GAMBLING, POLITICS, AND SPORTS

There is more than euphony in the juxtaposition of pool and politics.

> What one is witnessing in Middletown's gambling is a continuing institutionalized form of leisure closely linked with local politics. The poolrooms and cigar-store card rooms are virtually the political clubs of the city, run by local politicians or by men closely associated with them. The inner business group may meet and make their decisions as regards local politics in quite another setting, but it is here in these shabby smoke-filled rooms and cigar stores, supplemented by the working-class lodges, that the small time political lieutenants maintain their grip on the working-class voters year in and year out (Lynd and Lynd, 1937: p. 334).

The link with sports is also clear, or at least wishfully made clear, as is shown by an excerpt from a handbill distributed in Middletown by ''The People's Friend,'' probably a disgruntled ''out'' in the local underworld. Speaking of a cigar-store, termed a ''joint,'' owned by a member of the ''A'' family,[2] it reads:

> One of his most distinguished customers is Z [a school athletic coach], and [athletic] fans swear and declare that the success or failure of [his teams] is controlled by his success with ponies. . . . A, head of the gambling chain, and [a certain police officer] are bosom friends. They go fishing, hunting, and drinking together, and only recently returned from a big trip out of town, where they spent several days hunting together. There were also other city officials on this trip (Lynd and Lynd, 1937: pp. 335–337).

Lest the reader think that local workingclass politics are exclusively located in pool halls and lodges, and that students of community life have

---

[2]The Lynds designate key persons and families in Middletown by letters of the alphabet.

ignored the bowling alley, he need only review the central place of bowling for the ''street-corner society'' in Boston's North End, its relationship to the organization of the ''corner boys,'' and that connection with the larger political structure (Whyte, 1943: pp. 14–25, *et passim*).

> In the winter and spring of 1937–38 bowling was the most significant social activity for the Nortons. Saturday night's intra-clique and individual matches became the climax of the week's events. During the week the boys discussed what had happened the previous Saturday night and what would happen the coming Saturday night. A man's performance was subject to continual evaluation and criticism. There was, therefore, a close connection between a man's bowling and his position in the group (Whyte, 1943: pp. 17–18).

Leadership was subtly, never blatantly, confirmed in the contests. As Whyte points out, ''. . . his competent performance is a natural consequence of his position. At the same time his performance supports his position'' (Whyte, 1943: p. 259). Thus,

> . . . he is expected to represent the interests of his followers. The politician and the racketeer must deal with the leader to win the support of his followers. The leader's reputation outside the group tends to support his standing within the group, and his position in the group supports his reputation among outsiders (Whyte, 1943: p. 260).

WORK AND SPORT

Finally, the relationship between sport and work other than sport ought to be illustrated. To do this, we return to Middletown, where

> It is not irrelevant . . . that businessmen . . . speak of the ''business game,'' and it is also not by accident that . . . machine operators and laborers do *not* talk of the ''factory game.'' . . . Work in this business-class universe offers to the fortunate . . . something of the exhiliration and adventure associated in our physically unprecarious culture with play . . . .. one's

winnings depend upon one's drive, ingenuity, thrift, and skill, plus a substantial sporting element of luck (Lynd and Lynd, 1937: pp. 243–244).

While businessmen surround their work with the connotative aura of play and sport, the workers set these matters apart, using sport to mark their release from work.

> . . . at the gate of the General Motors plant . . . the men come off the job in the afternoon: Here was a horde of men heavily on the young side, walking rapidly toward the parking space for employees' cars, laughing and talking in groups of twos and threes about baseball, exclaiming, ''Boy! I'm goin' home and have a steak''; or ''What's the weather goin' to do Sunday? We want a drive up to the lakes'' (Lynd and Lynd, 1937: p. 452).

Other examples abound.

CONCLUSIONS

In seeking to explore the strands of socialization into the world of sports and the reverberations of the entrance into that world on the self-image, I have emphasized, as I have elsewhere (Stone, 1976: p. 141), that the world of sport is a man's world and that women are brought into that world vicariously. Currently, that conception must, most probably, be altered. Nevertheless, the community studies dealing with this same problem convey the original impression. Urbanization in general and of the suburbs in particular has constricted the physical space available for sport contests and rigidified the social space available to sport by placing it in the framework of formal organization, especially the school system. Although few youngsters are selected as players by and for the system, many more come to participate vicariously in the world of sports as spectators and idolators. Even players, themselves, may become spectators of highly skilled professionals, translating their spectatorship by selecting models which may serve as living guides who will direct the improvement of their own athletic competence. But sport must be proclaimed, celebrated, and observed to cloak it in respectability or honor (Speier, 1969: pp. 38–39). For the young this means having a ''big time.'' Such occasions incorporate drinking and gambling which may also prove to be obstacles. Those who do not founder on such obstacles are led inexorably into settings where local politics have their place. Moreover, there is an older audience who translates the play of the youngsters into the fabric of their work or who uses sport to escape the web of work. In short the successful confrontation with the ordeal of the ''big time'' generated by high school sport is a *rite de passage* into the adult world of work and politics.

However, sport is usually carried on in the context of neighborhoods and their schools rather than the larger community. ''With the shrinking of the circle, honor is threatened. . . . its extent shrinks in proportion as the knowledge about it diminishes, and if there is complete ignorance of . . . it, there is . . . neither honor or fame'' (Speier, 1969: p. 37). High school sport mobilizes and focuses the attention of a large community of peers—all the peers the player *can* ever know at the time of his play. He is the focus of esteem (or potential esteem) for *everyone* who does or might count at the time. He plays before his entire world in the high school contest, and the consequences for his self-esteem are intensive in their extension.

Finally, the high school offers an annual opportunity for the reunion of those who have left. For some, this may sustain a self-image throughout much of their adult life. Others may merely receive the invitation to reunion and decide to postpone their attendance to some later date (which may never come). Nevertheless, in fondling the invitation and considering the acceptance, old images are called up, and hollow-sounding cheers may bring some reaffirmation of self from the imagined esteem of ghosts. Still others may not open their bids. They have moved to other worlds, and play before other audiences.

REFERENCES

Fine, Gary, "Look at the Monkey Playin' First!: Little League Baseball and the Development of the Male Sex Role," unpublished manuscript. Department of Sociology, University of Minnesota, 1977.

Gallaher, Art Jr., *Plainville Fifteen Years Later* (New York: Columbia University Press, 1961).

Hammond, J. L. and Barbara Hammond, *The Bleak Age* (London: Penguin Books, 1947).

Hollingshead, August B., *Elmtown's Youth: The Impact of Social Classes on Adolescence* (New York: John Wiley, 1949).

Johnson, William O. Jr., *Super-Spectator and the Electric Lilliputians* (Boston: Little, Brown, 1971).

Lucas, Rex, "Sports and Recreation in Communities of Single Industry," in Richard S. Gruneau and John G. Abelson, *Canadian Sport: Sociological Perspectives* (Don Mills, Ontario: Addison-Wesley (Canada) Ltd., 1976), pp. 329–354.

Lundberg, George A., Mirra Komarovsky, and Mary Alice McInerny, *Leisure: A Suburban Study* (New York: Columbia University Press, 1934).

Lynd, Robert S. and Helen Merrell Lynd, *Middletown* (New York: Harcourt, Brace, 1929).

Lynd, Robert S. and Helen Merrell Lynd, *Middletown in Transition* (New York: Harcourt, Brace, 1937).

Michener, James A., *Sports in America* (New York: Random House, Inc., 1976).

Minneapolis *Tribune,* February 5, 28, 1977.

Speier, Hans, *Social Order and the Risks of War* (Cambridge, Mass.: The M.I.T. Press, 1969).

Stone, Gregory P., "Soziale Sinnbezüge des Sports in der Massengesellschaft," in Günther Lüschen and Kurt Weis (Hrsg) *Die Soziologie des Sports* (Darmstad und Neuwied: Hermann Luchterhand Verlag GmbH and Co. KG, 1976), pp. 132–145.

Stone, Gregory P. and Gladys I. Stone, "Ritual as Game: Playing at Becoming a Sanema," *Quest,* Monograph 26 (Summer, 1976), pp. 23–47.

The Columbia Encyclopedia, Third Edition (New York: Columbia University Press, 1967).

U.S. Bureau of the Census, *Statistical Abstract of the United States*: 1974 (95th Edition) (Washington, D.C.: U.S. Government Printing Office, 1974).

Whyte, William F., *Street Corner Society* (Chicago: University of Chicago Press, 1943).

TWENTY-FIVE

COMING OF AGE IN ORGANIZATIONS
A COMPARATIVE STUDY OF CAREER
CONTINGENCIES AND ADULT SOCIALIZATION

ROBERT R. FAULKNER

The processes of promotion and demotion in organizations are of major sociological relevance because the contingencies of status passage (Glaser and Strauss, 1971) are linked to the beliefs and the social organization of success and failure. It is no small irony that work organizations characterized by universalistic-achievement orientations often use ascriptive attributes to determine their members' eligibility for both placement and advancement. The impact of attributes such as age and sex

SOURCE: Robert R. Faulkner. "Coming of Age in Organizations: A Comparative Study of Career Contingencies and Adult Socialization." Copyright by Sage Publications, Inc., 1974. Robert R. Faulkner, "Coming of Age in Organizations: A Comparative Study of Career Contingencies and Adult Socialization," *Sociology of Work and Occupations*, I (May, 1974), pp. 131–173. Reprinted by permission of the publisher, Sage Publications, Inc.

Author's Note: A number of people supplied valuable suggestions and needed encouragement in generous amounts. The author wishes to thank, and absolve from any responsibility, Howard S. Becker, Anselm L. Strauss, Charles H. Page, Anthony R. Harris, and especially Gerald M. Platt. I am deeply indebted to the orchestra musicians and hockey players who freely shared with me their personal reflections and concerns.

upon occupational inclusion or exclusion is not self-evident, however, for as Strauss (1959), Berger (1960), Cain (1964), and Ryder (1965) have suggested, age is a socially constructed and sustained category which may either facilitate or impede access to valued positions and processes. A number of empirical studies (Weinberg and Arond, 1952; Chinoy, 1955; Martin and Strauss, 1956; Wager, 1959; Westby, 1960; Roth, 1963; Reif and Strauss, 1965; Sofer, 1970; Glaser, 1964) have shown that age is a major ascribed attribute by which occupational populations are selected and distributed into career lines. Age can be viewed as a fundamental career contingency, a factor upon which mobility within occupations and work organizations depends. It defines certain roles as available or unavailable and affects individual members' commitments to appropriate lines of collective action. Despite the theoretical importance of age-grading[1] in nonfamilial settings such as occupations, sociological investigations have paid only passing attention to age as a component of selective recruitment policies.

This paper draws on comparative materials to demonstrate the applicability of one specific approach to career mobility and adult socialization: an approach which emphasizes age as a critical variable for understanding both the objective features of career status passage and subjective changes in the mobility motivations and occupational outlooks of individual members. The paper focuses on the meanings imputed by the participants in two occupations to their mobility experiences in the context of age-grading and what this *kind* of change in adult life implies about their attitudes toward their work worlds. Moreover, the relationships between the objective and subjective contingencies of career mobility (Becker and Strauss, 1956; Becker, 1963) take us to some core organizational and practical problems: the schedules for the development and advancement of talent, the management of aging and immobility, and the processes for generating individuals' commitment in the face of possible disappointment and failure (Merton, 1957). Thus, in such diverse contexts as professional sports and the performing arts, and in general where the quick demonstration of performance excellence is required, we can hypothesize that conceptions of age influence the selection of career occupants for mobility. This makes more crucial the organizational problem of maintaining standards of behavior without alienating the demoted, or destroying the motivation of middle-level ''rookies'' and ''veterans.'' This approach explains some thus far implicit assumptions in the sociological study of organizational careers. Five sections are presented. The first develops an overview of current approaches to mobility in work settings and the mechanisms for sustaining the involvement of members. The second describes the study's methods and the settings at issue. The third examines the relation between the structural features of interorganizational careers and the direct impact of ascriptive features on the differential availability and selection of personnel. The personal consequences of these contingencies are discussed in a fourth section, particularly the turning points at which members' expectancies of access to top strata positions undergo transformation. A fifth and concluding section discusses career contingencies in light of the adaptations made by individuals and organizations to these problems. It should be apparent that this paper is an attempt to apply an important, but neglected, sociological perspective to one aspect of organizational structure; it is not to deny the substantive relevance of other aspects of these institutions.

ORGANIZATIONAL CAREERS

The progressive differentiation of work in the direction of age-graded standardization, technical expertise, and ideologies of equal access to valued processes, often lead to an *inconsistency between the promise of success through upward mobility and the reality of failure through immobility*. These inconsistencies underlie various expressions of discontent, the most prevalent, perhaps, being the sense of disaffection that arises from the enforced separation of individuals from valued ongoing courses of action, situations, and objects (including the self) within a given structure. Organizations in which careers unfold thus confront the problem of motivating achievement and mobility aspirations of members toward top-level positions while, at the same time, sustaining the involvement of subordinates to whom access has been denied. The study of these processes has been pursued from two theoretical vantage points.

One approach employs the familiar means-ends theorizing and locates the problem of demotion, immobility, and discharge in terms of hierarchical settings which encourage career occupants to move onward and upward but which simultaneously permit fewer participants to do so at more exclusive and prestigious status levels. This viewpoint offers the distinct advantage of focusing on the functions of stratification in motivating incumbents to fill differentiated positions in a bureaucratic, achievement-oriented social system. Empirical research focuses on the organizational arrangements through which disjunctions can arise between aspirations and avenues as well as the subsequent structural adaptations for promoting the commitment of the stranded, the less able, or the demoted in complex organizations (Levenson, 1961; More, 1962; Smigel, 1964; Goldner, 1965; Goldner and Ritti, 1967; Maniha, 1972). Unless organizations can legitimize failure and promote the identification of the less successful with their work roles, they run the risk of resentment and disengagement among their labor force. Procedures and collective actions for "cooling out" failures become essential for the continuity and integrity of existing social arrangements (Goffman, 1952; Clark, 1960).

A second approach emphasizes that the proper analysis of organizational mobility must include changes in the mobility motivations, purposes, and expectations of the individual. This approach focuses not only on the mobility routes and sequences of personnel circulation through positions, but also on the personal adjustments and shared experiential concerns of actors (Hall, 1948; Becker, 1952; Solomon, 1953; Wilensky, 1956; Wager, 1959; Goffman, 1961; Carlin, 1962; Glaser, 1964; Wood, 1967; Friedman, 1967; Stebbins, 1970; Faulkner, 1973, 1971; Spector, 1973, 1972). In focusing on definitions of success and failure, the term "career" here applies to the sequence of passage through objective statuses and "the moving perspective in which the person sees his life as a whole and interprets the meaning of his various attributes, actions, and the things which happen to him" (Hughes, 1958: 63).

In view of the theoretical importance of careers to the analysis of social psychology, one would expect sociologists to have contributed at both the theoretical and hypothesis-testing levels. Such has not been the case. Despite Chinoy's (1955) study of automobile workers, which examined the process by which workers adapted to limited opportunity in a society that stresses advancement, we have few detailed studies of the chronological demise of mobility aspirations in early adulthood

or the impact of age on the lowering of career sights. That a kind of "coming to terms" does take place has been noted in studies of the meaning of work and work alienation (Morse and Weiss, 1955; Seeman, 1967) as well as in Becker's (1964, 1970) essays on personal change. But the empirical issue—the meanings of such transition phases in the life cycle and how they are managed by personnel in occupations—has been left in question. Adaptations to blocked mobility are usually assumed to have a stable meaning, invariant to the practical exigencies of aging in the work settings under investigation. Although contrasts between "idealistic dreams for success" and "realistic" outlooks are commonplace in the literature, the meanings of the personal mollification of success aspirations appears to be assumed rather than documented. Brim (1968: 204), lamenting this state of affairs in a review of the literature on occupational socialization, states, "It is indeed puzzling that there are so few sociological studies (there are, of course, many plays and novels) of male efforts to adjust aspirations with achievement in their careers." Most efforts beg the sociological question: how do people in highly competitive work structures define and organize their careers so as to handle issues of denial and failure?

In this overview, I must also note the relevance of career socialization for the study of organizational processes. A predominant theme in the literature on socialization presents life as movement from youthful idealism to more or less realistic mobility motivations, more or less contented adjustments which progressively confine behavioral potentialities and imputed identities within an acceptable range and to which an individual becomes committed (Miller and Form, 1951; Becker, 1964; Banton, 1965; Geer, 1966; Faulkner, 1973). Nevertheless, most efforts have been concerned with adaptations to immobility or "coming to terms" as individual processes, and only marginally with the organizational contexts which *facilitate the acquisition of these career outlooks* (for an exception, see Goldner, 1965).

Insofar as "nothing succeeds like success," selection procedures are affected by the way an organization arranges its career lines and personnel circulation, cushions the blows of failure, and structures the temporal processes by which young neophytes become committed to ongoing lines of action. Such contingencies are recognized as fundamental in the allocation of talent. What is less acknowledged is that *inasmuch as youth-intensive organizations are required to structure their career selection procedures around a perishable resource, an aging labor force creates certain specific problems for organizations of high competence.*

METHODS AND SETTING

The material for this paper is drawn from a three-year comparative study of career socialization and mobility patterns of personnel in the occupational worlds of the performing arts and professional sports. Although several work settings are being investigated and several kinds of data gathered (fieldwork observations, analysis of personnel records, informant interrogation, and longitudinal respondent interviewing), those I shall report on here derive mainly from long, unstructured interviews with 60 symphony players in two organizations ranked in the middle strata of the orchestral hierarchy, and from 38 hockey players on two teams in the highest minor league level of professional hockey. The documentation offered is drawn from those sections of the taped interviews which deal with the conditions of interorganizational mobility, definitions of success, and career concerns.

Comparative analysis of orchestra and hockey teams suggests that these two settings have reached a stage of organizational development which seemingly anticipates the growth of other complex, purposely created systems. These formal structures are of theoretical interest because the career lines and allocation of rewards for members are divisible into organizational positions of higher or lower rank in comparison with other such units. In both

settings, the network of institutions in which mobility takes place consists of a top-ranking group of distinguished or elite organizations, a number of second-rank but solidly established organizations below the top, and a third level of marginal quality. The top and middle levels of symphony work and professional hockey can be conceptualized as *organizational sets* (Caplow, 1964: 201−216): stratification systems composed of two or more settings. The higher a given system's prestige and power (a) the more influence it has on the standards of achievement and excellence for the entire array of organizations, (b) the more status and other rewards enjoyed by career incumbents experiencing mobility from the middle levels into the elite ranks, and (c) the more complex the mechanisms for sorting out the promising from the unpromising.

As the terms "major" and "minor" league suggest, organizational arrangements of this type (1) offer the presence of minor league *pipeline organizations* which produce candidates with the requisite skills to meet performance demands in the major leagues, (2) develop a supply of available personnel for whom vertical, interorganizational mobility is a strong career motivation, and (3) generate expectancies of access among colleague competitors throughout the set. A foremost sign of achievement is promotion into the major leagues, and incumbents are encouraged to look forward to reaching the top according to a more or less temporally specific schedule.

The symphony orchestra world is one of the most complex, competitive, and stratified organizational sets in existence. It is comprised of five major symphonies employing a total of about 450 players. In musical excellence, caliber of musicianship, total contract weeks, basic salary, length of season, pension plans, recording guarantees, and paid vacations, the elite set in this country consists of the Boston, Chicago, Cleveland, New York Philharmonic, and Philadelphia orchestras. Below this top rank are 24 established organizations employing about 2,250 total employees; roughly 75% of symphony musicians are situated at the middle echelon level. The sample of performing musicians interviewed is drawn from two orchestras in this middle stratum.[2] One organization is located in the Eastern part of the country, the other on the West Coast. During the years of the study, the number of retirements and voluntary departures ranged from 5% to 8% in each organization. The age of those interviewed ranged from 21 to 61; 11 were between the ages of 21 and 27, 22 were between 28 and 34, and 27 musicians were 35 or older. Interviews were also conducted with players in early career in two major league orchestras. Since the concern here is with interorganizational mobility from the middle levels and the problematic features of immobility, unless otherwise noted my observations shall deal primarily with minor league personnel.

As of the 1970–1972 seasons, the period of my interviewing and fieldwork, the organizational set of hockey was stratified into 14 teams in the National Hockey League (NHL) with a total of approximately 270 players; and 23 teams in the middle-level American, Central, and Western minor leagues totaling around 460 players.[3] Over 60% of the players are situated in this latter stratum in the set. The two organizations studied are in the highest minor league system, the American League (AHL), from which the NHL recruits over 70% of its talent, and to which it sends its fringe players, those in need of experience, or veterans in the twilight of their playing years. The turnover between seasons on these teams ranged from 40% to 80%, for trades, promotions, retirements, and dismissals produce an active system of personnel circulation. The ages of these men ranged from 20 to 33 years; 24 were between the ages of 20 and 24, and 14 interviewed were 25 years of age or older.

CONTINGENCIES OF INTERORGANIZATIONAL CAREERS

The development of a modern organizational structure that facilitates the training and distribution of high-level talent is contingent upon some indispensable mechanisms for the maintenance of interlinking relationships between pipeline and elite strata and for the regulation of the exigencies of aging. While elite or major league organizations may develop their own talent from within, few organizations studied are willing or able to do so. The National Hockey League and top five orchestras must rely on the output of their respective "farm systems" for the socialization and training of aspirants into the occupational culture and its work roles. *The processes by which a population is distributed in these sets stem, at least in part, from institutional arrangements that make certain categories of career incumbents more readily available at certain points of selection for mobility and immobility.* The organizational problem of role placement demands that elite strata select wisely among young aspirants who are in competition for scarce positions at the top, and that middle echelon recruits be prepared and motivated to meet high-level performance demands at these standardized selection points in their careers. Players in the minor leagues are a mixed lot, some needing a few years "seasoning" to "be ready" as it is put in hockey, or a necessary period of "routinization" to orchestral playing, as one personnel committee member phrased it. Other players and performers may indeed be motivated and prepared, but must wait for a vacancy in the major leagues. Also career occupants are at different stages of their careers; some are rookies and others are veterans, and the effective functioning of these organizational sets requires the balancing of the young and older members, keeping the former in anticipation of promotion and the latter motivated in the face of denial.

PROFESSIONAL HOCKEY

There are several conditions inherent in the structure of hockey which necessitate the efficient selection of talent by management as well as the quick demonstration of excellence by players. First, recent expansion from six NHL teams of 20 players each to 12 teams (about 240 players) in

1967, and then to 14 teams (about 280 players) in 1970, has given rise to a personnel market characterized by a scarcity of high-quality performers to fill the number of new positions. Expansion clubs must be stocked with players, and all the organizations compete for promising recruits who are likely to develop rapidly into exemplary performers with several seasons of productive playing ahead of them.[4] All teams must select wisely if they are to build a balanced NHL lineup of first-rate men in the early stages of their careers as well as a core of seasoned veterans. In addition, their continuity and competitive advantage can only be ensured if they develop a backlog of promotable and aspiring minor leaguers for possible future assignment to the parent NHL team.

Second, the paths of movement of personnel through the system of positions in this set are structured by the fact that organizations placing a premium on physical skills can be expected to develop timetables or age-situated schedules for recognition-producing performances. Since it is felt that most athletes in professional hockey are at their peak only for the duration of around four or five years, the pace at which players move through this career line becomes shaped by shared conceptions of physiological attrition. Thus, the meaningfulness of age as a basic status shares an elective affinity with the organizational methods for detecting, processing, and otherwise handling aging in this occupation. The spirit of youth predominates and aging is looked on as a process of steady decline. The gradual "fall from grace" builds upon these socially constructed features of occupational age that render "growing older" meaningful in the first place. Decision makers in the front office are circumspect about discussing the link between age and role placement, but players are candid about their own timetables for promotion, shaping them against what they define as managerial agendas for advancement. The players view getting a chance for promotion and an opportunity to shape and strengthen their capacities through use in the NHL as major career problems which are

contained in a series of *running adjustments with time*. The players interviewed feel that, unless they have been promoted into the NHL parent organization to play a continuous set of games before the age of 25, the occupancy of minor league status for the duration of their careers is heavily ruled in by existing social arrangements. Given a developmental cycle of relatively short duration, superiors prefer to turn to younger and potentially more qualified recruits. As a result, the probability of access to the major leagues declines in the late twenties.

Third, and related, interorganizational mobility from the minors to the majors is precarious by virtue of the power which decision makers (managers, coaches, and scouts) exercise over these players. The term "career precariousness" would seem appropriate where incumbents face the continuous prospect of being displaced by newcomers throughout their work life as well as subject to quick shifts in fortune which are not totally foreseen. Additionally, because these players are the property of the club, they can be moved both vertically and horizontally within this organizational set as management dictates. Not surprisingly, the structure of control over the paths and rates of mobility leads to rather large doses of player anxiety and concern about the impermanence and possible reversibility of status passage.

Critical trial periods are initiated early in the career cycle and involve formidable tests of expertise, patience, and occupational character. Beginning with his early performances in amateur Canadian hockey, or in the college ranks, the player is placed in the midst of a short and fateful testing period. Swift ascent is normatively prescribed as organizations attempt to manage the timing and pacing of their personnel. Starting with the entrance into the professional ranks, it usually takes only two to five years to determine the level of career achievement likely to be attained by the young hockey professional.

Several mobility patterns are generated from these demands for efficient role placement.

Thirty-two percent (86) of those on the active rosters in 1971–1972 were promoted into the elite strata in their first or second year of hockey.[5] At the other extreme, 14% spent seven or more years in the minor leagues before "getting a good shot at the National" or before being promoted for a continued stay that lasted longer than half a season. A handful had been in the minors from ten to fourteen years before becoming aged but eager NHL rookies; the importance of such anomalous cases will be discussed shortly. Despite these variations in entry times into the major league, 60% (163) had arrived in the top strata from the minor leagues before they were 24 years of age. The American Hockey League is the major pipeline for this interleague mobility; three-fourths of the minor leaguers called up by their NHL teams during this season were from the AHL affiliate.[6]

Being called up is a crucial point for getting a leg up on the career ladder, but this foothold is a precarious one indeed. From three to five of the players on each team studied had been promoted but were sent back down to the minors during the course of the season. Only about one or two in twenty stayed in the NHL to become a regular. About one-quarter of the men in the clubs studied were former elite regulars. This indicates that even players who have been promoted for two or more seasons are faced with the prospect of demotion to the farm team. Aggregate data for players in the NHL show that only 22 veterans have sustained a career at the top for 15 or more years and only 30% have been there for six or more seasons. Metaphorically, players step onto a quickly moving career escalator with a prospective ride of short duration ahead of them.

ORCHESTRA WORLD

The processes of personnel succession in orchestras stand in distinct contrast, both in route and timing, to what happens in pro hockey. While a certain structural similarity of interstrata mobility avenues has been noted, the complexes differ in fundamental aspects. First, orchestras have experienced nothing as remarkable as the organizational expansion of professional hockey in the United States during the last decade (see Hart, 1973; Mueller, 1951). Second, professional hockey, much like baseball, tends to be institutionalized around a closely integrated linkage between the minor affiliate and major league organizations. Hockey players are the property of these organizations or clubs. In the symphony world, the individual's possible control over his or her status is much greater because musicians are not formally under contract to a single management at both levels of the set. There are no reserve clauses in orchestra contracts that prohibit musicians from voluntarily moving in order to better their career situation in another organization. Each performing artist is in effect potentially recruitable; consequently, musicians have more opportunities to establish their availability in the labor market through auditions for openings, thereby lessening the exclusive power of any particular employing unit over their career chances.

Third, and related, the range of positions by which a musician can improve his or her standing in the profession is much more diversified than in hockey. Orchestral performers and professional hockey players agree that the elite strata are desirable—it is viewed by most as "the only place to be." Ninety-five percent of the hockey players and about 75% of the musicians acknowledge that their early career aspirations were to play in their respective "major leagues." The actual pattern of mobility, however, is more complex in the orchestral world. Musicians can increase their prestige by moving downward, into a middle-level organization from a major orchestra (from the Chicago Symphony Orchestra to the Los Angeles Philharmonic, for example) while simultaneously increasing their positional status in a particular instrumental section within the orchestra. Fifteen of the musicians interviewed had gone from the major to the minor leagues in order to play principal chair or to be coprincipal of a section (for a similar mechanism in the academic world, see Caplow and McGee, 1958; Caplow, 1964: 210−223, develops this concept of organizational exchange). Moreover, career routes can be either horizontal, as in a move between minor league organizations, or vertical, such as in a move from the middle- to top-level positions. Musicians recognize that patterns such as these are part of a career strategy, for it is important to be on the right promotion time.

The outcome of this diversity of movement and greater degree of control is not so individualistic as the entrepreneurial ethos might suggest. Personnel mobility in this organizational set is an *aggregate phenomenon dependent on the availability of positions into which members seek entry,* as well as on the number of potential recruits for those positions. In the top stratum of the orchestral world, yearly vacancies ranged from about 4 to 35 positions out of the total of around 540. In one of the ''big five'' orchestras investigated, the number of vacancies due to retirements and career moves to other work settings ranged from 2 to 8 players per season over a 7-year period. The average was 3 vacancies per season in each orchestra. As many as 100 applicants—minor-league performers, players fresh out of music conservatories, and others working free-lance in the music world—may apply for one of these openings.[7]

The vacancy rate per se at the top stratum is only one characteristic by which an organizational set is differentiated from its neighbors. The tempo and circulation of movement into the elite level is heavily influenced by how long any one incumbent stays at the top. Duration of occupancy is fundamental to organizational regeneration and change. It is a basis for role allocation and thereby a key indicator of a set's flowchart. Comparisons between professional hockey teams and symphony orchestras at the top strata are instructive in this regard. Table 1 indicates that more than three-fourths of the top-level musicians have been in a major orchestra for six or more years, while only slightly more than 30% of the NHL players have been situated in that stratum for the same length of time. While 1 out of every 3 NHL regulars is a newcomer, in this first or second season, only 1 top-five musicians in 10 has a similar length of service. Moreover, the average stay in the top-five organizations for musicians is around 18 years (a range from 1 to 53 years). In the NHL it is 5 years. Thus, the incorporation of new members and loss of older veterans is exceedingly rapid in hockey but much less so in the orchestral elite.

Table 1 also suggests that hockey players are distributed in a bimodal fashion, indicating a differential recruitment or ''weeding out'' process

TABLE 1.   Length of Time in Elite Organizational Strata: 1971−1972 (in percentages)

Number of Years in Top Strata of Organizational Set	National Hockey League	Elite Orchestra
1 year or less	15	6
2 years	19	3
3 years	10	2
4 years	9	4
5 years	15	4
6 years or more	32	81
Total %	100	100
Number of cases	(270)	(540)

SOURCE: Hockey data are from 1972−1973 Hockey Register (St. Louis: Sporting News, 1972). Orchestra data are from personnel files of the Boston Symphony Orchestra, Chicago Symphony Orchestra, Philadelphia Orchestra, New York Philharmonic, and Cleveland Orchestra.

whereby the "superstars" and "near greats" remain at the top for temporally longer career spans when compared to the modal career pattern. When musicians, however, move into the top stratum, they receive tenure after a one or two-year probationary period, and are then likely to remain at the elite level (if they so choose) for the remainder of their careers. Hockey players, who face the continuous possibility of being displaced by newcomers throughout their careers, are unable to generate such an organizational commitment.

The differentiation of activities gives a distinctive pattern to the recruitment of performing artists seeking entry into top strata positions from pipeline organizations. In two of the top five orchestras studied, the average age of all members is around 45; the average age of new members in their first or second orchestral season is 24 years old (a range of 22 to 44). This suggests that the time of selections is skewed toward younger persons in their mid-to-late twenties who have been seasoned in minor league organizations. While personnel committees typically cite universalistic selection procedures in which "the best player" is always chosen regardless of age and other circumstances, the long-run advantages of hiring youthful but modestly experienced players are not disregarded. Not surprisingly, of those who left the minor league orchestras studied for other orchestras during the period of investigation, nearly 90% were 35 years of age or younger.

As the development of talent and differentiation of recruits by ability and performance comes to be demanded in organizations of high competence, so too *there exist well-defined normative expectations as to the level of excellence deemed appropriate at various age levels*. Starting from the players' entrance into the business of orchestra music, it may take five to eight years to determine where he or she will be situated for the rest of his or her career. The musician, like the hockey player, runs the risk of remaining in a second-rate organization too long and thereby diminishing the chances for selection into the top stratum. Major league orches-

tras are by and large reluctant to hire people in their forties and even late thirties, and because the supply of talent always exceeds the number of top jobs available per season, incumbents can miss opportunities at crucial contingency points. These organizationally shaped agendas for selection may vary because of different local arrangements and rates of personnel circulation; nevertheless, the launching of a successful career appears to be contained by processes that extend over brief spans of career time and that are experienced in different ways by those affected.

SUBJECTIVE CAREERS AND PERSONAL ADAPTATIONS

The theory of occupational socialization suggested here posits that objective and subjective careers develop concurrently in a process of interdependence and mutual transformation. In this framework, rewards are not inherent in the status or organizational arrangement. They must be interpreted and defined as such if they are to motivate behavior toward top-level positions. Since actors need symbols for purposes of interaction, and symbols cannot be shared except in an interactional context, status passage can be conceptualized as a mutually adjusted program of joint behavior that facilitates the acquisition of cognitive beliefs and norms about age. There exists some communication structure by means of which participants acquire the shared meanings of career turning points, signs of promotion, and rules concerning how old candidates for certain positions should be.

Actors view length of time in certain locations as guidelines by which they actively construct benchmarks and understandings about the possibilities and probabilities of receiving major recognition, becoming a "star" performer or "first among equals," and gaining access to processes or situations which are important to them. The import here is that these organizational careers have a prospective contour. Musicians and hockey players can estimate the probabilities of their own mobility into the major leagues by consulting (1) the progress of others and (2) what is taken to be the typical career escalator. In attempting to construct and enact their careers, they assess their own age against the standardized schedules for selection, and then subjectively calculate their personal chances of success—a process which presupposes, of course, determinate and patterned selection points.

The coming of age contains a double viewpoint. Not only do changes take place in the objective chances of interorganizational mobility, but changes also begin to take place within the individual as well. This section examines some of the career concerns expressed, the ways in which performers and players sustain their self-regard in the face of immobility and demotion, and the ways in which they continue as productive members of their respective organizations. I hypothesize that *much of the "coming to terms" that is activitated by the perception of mobility opportunities has to do with the impingement of age-graded criteria for interorganizational advancement.*

CAREER PROBLEMS

The initiation of neophytes into organizational careers involves the transmission of basic sentiments and norms concerning status passage—specifically, the inculcation of attitudes toward time. In characterizing the subjective outlooks of those interviewed, the elements discussed below are or have been present in most respondents' definitions of their career situations.

First, there is general agreement that one is constrained to do something on one's own to improve one's position. One's place in the division of labor stands for where one is situated socially and professionally. Careers are consequential; frequent expressions of frustration and annoyance over blocked mobility and about getting into the right occupational terrain, point to the effects of this hierarchical system. Since positions are assessed in terms of the extent to which they condi-

tion the establishment of footholds or "stepping stones" toward the major leagues, a personal problem centers around being kept waiting at some step in the career process.

Second, and closely related, the ethos of improvement, the more or less continuous competition between colleagues, status rivalry, and subjective effects of this appraisive drama in sports and music, generates a concern over whether a particular position in the set enlarges a person's expertise. Here the concern centers around the conditions for personal development in a given direction and for the chance to be or become a more skilled practitioner.

The following quotations from the interviews suggest that the problem of access to organizational opportunities is in essence the same sort of problem as that of success. These definitions of the situation are an activating and unifying force, precursors of subjective concerns, and forerunners of subsequent adaptations to immobility. These themes are well put by the following respondent.

> Hockey is a race with time. You feel you have to move up a level a year in the minors and make it into the National by 24 or 25, may be 26 at the latest. This axe is always hanging over your head, you've got around four or five years they say to show yourself, to show what you can do. You have to get the ice time to play, you have to get a good shot at it, play steady, get to know the guys on your line, then you can do it. This is a now sport, you can't waste any years. I think I'm ready now, this is my third season, I can play with the guys up there now [in the NHL].

Demands for recognition-producing work, for quick demonstration of talent, and awareness of rapid deterioration of chances, all tend to aggravate personal aging. In both organizational sets, it is clear that one cannot afford to waste any years. Thus, many were concerned about the possibility of getting "boxed into" attitudes and skills that would decrease their chances of improving their situation. One musician offered: "I think you can destroy your chances of going to a top place if you play in a section for too long. It's not a disgrace, but people stereotype you just the same; no one's going to be interested in a player who is too old or has lost that shine in his playing by being buried in a poor orchestra.'' A thirty-year-old colleague summed up a more general feeling:

> Some places will not look at you if you're over a certain age, like 35 or 36, so you have to move fast, audition, and you cannot settle for a lesser job, you have to improve your position with each move. Who wants to get stuck at forty in some situation you can't stand in some nowhere orchestra? This is why I moved here as principal (from a major league setting). My ambition now is to get into one of the big orchestras as a principal, the solos and responsibility I think are important. This is sort of a stepping stone on my way of thinking. I can't spend my life here. . . . A lot of first-rate players are looking for much the same thing I am.

A harder line is taken by hockey players who have been promoted and are under heavy pressure to produce while playing in the major league. They realize that the testing period is of short duration and make invidious comparisons about the career fates of colleague competitors whose own success may, in effect, rule out their own occupancy of desired places. Some become dissatisfied with what they see as low rates of demotion for others and the feeling of denial becomes painfully obvious very rapidly. Related to this is the observation that hockey professionals are exceedingly critical of the chances they are given and the promotion practices of management. This pattern is not as pronounced in the orchestra world. Nearly 80% of the pros interviewed noted some sort of dissatisfaction with the politicking, favoritism, and injustice of selection procedures. Following Stouffer et al. (1949), dissatisfaction with the management of mobility by decision makers can be viewed as the outcome of a system in which opportunities are viewed as relatively plentiful. Specifically, under the conditions of league expansions over the past few seasons, players see a number of their competitors being promoted into the NHL. To be sure, some stay and others are only taken up for a short ''look-see'' and then demoted. Nevertheless, being denied access to these positions—often seen as one's due for dedicated work in the minor league salt mines—comes to be defined as unfair just because so many others throughout the set have received this opportunity. By way of contrast, in the orchestra world where promotion into the top five is comparatively rarer, those who have climbed to the elite strata feel they have done very well while the nonpromoted are less bitter toward their fate because fewer of their competitors have surpassed them.

> My main complaint is that many of the guys up there shouldn't be in the National at all, and guys who are down here ought to be up there. The management's to blame for that. Politics. Many of us don't even get the chance to go up, they've made up their minds already. I was up but didn't get a chance to really play. . . . I'd say my only shot this year or maybe next year too would be if someone gets injured or traded, maybe I'll be traded. I don't think D. or E. [players in his team position on the NHL parent club] will be sent down, so you can't figure it out. I think some guys don't pull their weight, eh? But I have only so many years, you can't play forever. I'd like to get a good shot at it to see if I'm going to play there or not, if I can do it. This is what you look towards, this is it. The problem with hockey is that you don't play long enough to call it a career, a future, you either make it or spend it in the minors and then it's over in, what, ten years? Is that a career? Unless you're a superstar you can't really count on anything.

Q: You never know if you'll go up to stay?

There's one hell of a difference between playing yourself *off* the team and playing yourself *on* the team. If you're on it they will stick with you, give you a chance. If you just go up, if you don't play steady you won't improve, then there's no way. . . .

Any of these events may affect the career, then, in any of several ways, depending on what is happening to the progress of others and the extent to which personal chances of mobility diminish because of the state of a career line at the time the event occurs.

Given the contingencies expressed above, one can hypothesize that mobility assessments will vary according to how long the person has been on the career time track. One concrete aspect of the consequences of age-grading and selection procedures might be seen in the data linking length of service in the organizational set and perceived chances of being promoted. As the phrase "coming of age" indicates, we might predict collisions of expectations with occupational realities to occur at some of the selection points discussed previously. Although the small number of cases compels caution in the use and interpretation of this index, an important feature of adult socialization is nevertheless reflected by a decline with age in the subjective estimates for achieving a position at the top of these organizational sets. Five response alternatives used in the lengthy interviews were subsequently collapsed into three for presentation here: "very likely" and "possible" are termed as indicating "high expectations," and "very un-

likely" and "not likely" as "low expectations." The "undecided" responses are classified as "undecided."

Table 2 indicates that a substantial proportion of those minor leaguers interviewed start their careers in orchestras and hockey organizations with high expectations and that their present positions are for many viewed as a stepping-stone on the way to the top. Almost three-fourths of the musicians under 27 years of age and nearly 60% of the hockey professionals 24 years and younger start with high expectations for making it into the majors. They see a promotion in the prospective future. Many regard it as a strong likelihood or reasonable possibility that they will be among the chosen sooner or later, if indeed they are not already close to the realization of their desired career move.

Few, however, retain these expectations and hopes for achievement throughout their careers. The erosion of subjective assessments is most dramatic among the minor league orchestra players; after about eight to twelve years in the career, more than 50% have either low expectations or are undecided about mobility into the top five. Even though this kind of status passage is still viewed as desirable, the responses strongly suggest that after their mid-thirties it is no longer treated as a very serious prospect. Principal players in the minor leagues may in fact get the chance they look for, and several did experience this mobility during

TABLE 2. Expectations for Achieving Top Strata Position in Organizational Set, By Age and Occupation of Minor League Respondents (in percentages)

	Hockey Players		Orchestra Musicians			
Expectations	20–24 Years	More than 24 Years	21–27 Years	28–34 Years	More Than 34 Years	n
High	58	43	72	46	22	41
Undecided	25	36	10	13	19	23
Low	17	21	18	41	59	34
Total %	100	100	100	100	100	
(n)	(24)	(14)	(11)	(22)	(27)	(98)

the brief years of this study, but most performers find themselves stranded in the middle levels of the orchestral structure. Such experiences change the musicians' attitudes about themselves, and about how far they have progressed toward the dream they had hoped to achieve. This personal change leads many, such as this 37-year-old musician, to redirect their career sights away from their original ambition of being in a major symphony toward their current work reality.

My chances of successfully auditioning as a principal in a major orchestra might not be as great as they should be. I've been asked to play second in C. [top five orchestra], but I prefer first here. There are just not that many openings, a few years ago. . . .Now my aspiration, as I said, isn't as great as it was when I took the job here, not quite as great. I wouldn't turn down something like I had in mind when I came here at first [chair in the section], but my hope isn't as great as it was. My hope isn't any less, it would be nice, but it is just that my goals are now slightly different than they were then.

A string playing colleague was more direct:

Look, let's not kid ourselves, I'm nearly forty years old. I make a good living here, I do some recording work on the side, I'm not going to be first in the New York Philharmonic anyway, not at my age. Maybe at some time we feel this, but face the facts, we've done very well in music, we've done well out here [on the West Coast]. The orchestra has really improved, it's now one of the best in the country, and like they say, things could be worse, like being stuck in some bush league place with little money and no musical satisfaction.

Among the professional hockey players interviewed, the dampening of expectancies for inclusion into the elite strata is not as dramatic as among orchestra musicians. Promotion is for these men almost automatically accepted as desirable, for a career at the top represents what they have wanted throughout their lives. In assessing their promotion chances as well as the amount of difficulty to be

encountered in becoming an elite regular, they recognize that those who stay too long in the middle strata may be penalized. During their first few seasons the young pros are developing their skills, and many at this stage do not consider themselves equipped or "ready" to be promoted. Then there is a period of perhaps three years, starting when the pro is around 23 or 24, after he has had experience in the minors, after some of his colleagues have been promoted, and after he has survived the rituals of status passage accompanying initial entry into the professional ranks. A turning point of immense personal change begins to set in around the age of 25 or 26, when there is a greater degree of uncertainty over success. Table 2 indicates that almost one-half (43%) have high expectations for promotion into the major league, while some 36% can be described as undecided. This latter figure indicates that these players too are not entirely without hope for mobility and getting access to valued activities. Compared to the patterns of mobility and concerns in the orchestral world, the perception of high-level social locations being ruled out is not as clear-cut. The following 28-year-old player was asked a question directed toward each respondent:

Q: What are your chances for being promoted or getting a shot this year?

It can happen I suppose, injuries, or the line might get hot, someone might be sent down, you might get the right break at the right time, and luck and chance are part of this.

A colleague in mid-career was more direct about the gradual erosion of mobility chances and the points of no return in which management and coaches "give up on you." He said:

My chances this year are . . . well, this is a business and they go with youth. I'd say that after 28 the odds are against you. The longer you wait the harder it is, you know? The earlier you get there, the more money you're going to make while you're in the National League. You take a look at what others are doing and you see where you are and with guys who have had as much experience as you've had, the guys in the same position as you are. My wife and I say we'll give it till 26 or 27 maybe, then I'll know if I'll be in the NHL. After that they give up on you. Some have gone up after thirty, look at E. [an older player who just became a NHL rookie during the season]. He is thirty-four I think, a thirty-four year old rookie—he got a shot and then played in the playoffs. It can happen.

Q: Your chances for going up are harder with age? What about your chances next year of getting a promotion?

If I have a good season, we'll get a shot, it's going good. You see the thing is after a while you realize that you're not a big star anymore like maybe you were in Junior A [amateur Canadian hockey]. Now you're just one of the boys, you've got to work, it will pay off I think. But it's a tough transition to make, and each year you don't get any younger, you know?

Players and performers change a great deal from the time they initially enter the career until they reach turning points such as these. We might term the first five or six years of hockey and the first ten or twelve years of an orchestral career as periods of "illusionment" where the person's career is being launched though not securely fulfilled. At this time footholds are being established, occupational ambitions for "arrival" are high, and while access to top organizations is recognized as difficult, such mobility is viewed as a real possibility. What occurs during these early and mid-career years of adult socialization is not so much a stark collision of success dreams with the realities of recruitment and differential promotion by age as much as a construction of new mobility outlooks and motivations.

MAKING DO IN THE MINORS: FACILITATING CONDITIONS

As these performers and players remain in the middle levels, dramatic changes take place in the meanings imputed to mobility. This kind of personal adaptation is rarely consummated in one dramatic moment or turning point. Rather it is contained in a process of self-redefinition that extends over a period of time and is subjectively experienced in different ways by those affected. Throughout the interviews a number of themes describing coming to terms with immobility in the minors appears: (1) members stress the personal benefits of their present position, (2) they comment on the prices to be paid in moving up the career ladder, (3) they strive for average recognition or esteem rather than for outstanding prestige in the set, (4) they shift their life interest away from work to other areas of life, specifically the familial sphere, and (5) they often stress a calculative orientation toward their organizational involvement. These are the components of their emerging realism, and they make it easier to accept a lack of mobility or demotion (compare with Chinoy, 1955; Goldner, 1965; Faulkner, 1973). A 33-year-old minor leaguer with two seasons in the NHL outlined some of these personal changes in a blunt style; when asked if he had once aspired to superstar status, he said:

Sure, you want to be the best, you want to come close to the best, if you don't have any ambition then you're not going to get anywhere, right? I enjoyed playing in the National, I enjoyed the stay very much. I was sent down towards the end of the '68 season. If you got so many that are advanced ahead of you, where's the *room* for *you*? I'd be kidding myself if I'd say I didn't want to be the best but come on, stop daydreaming. This stuff is fine when you're young, but not now, come on. I'm not going to be a superstar, those days are over. Now I'm doing it for the money, for my personal bonus, my own pride. You have qualifications for a certain job, fine, work hard and put yourself in a position where people will need you. You can make a very good living here [in the minors].

A colleague noted that lack of success in the NHL need not be seen as failure but rather as *relative success* (Glaser, 1964). The following suggests that players revise their expectations about the desirability of promotion itself while acquiring a new perspective leading to satisfaction with a smaller accomplishment.

> The National League is *not* the only league to play in. Believe me, I've given it a good shot but the going up and down like a yo yo, the moving of the family, and all that. We've paid the price, but it's a good life here. Even right here in [the minors] where else can you make this kind of money and meet the people you do? I enjoy my friends here, I have no complaints because not everyone gets the chance to have the life we've had. I want to play a few more years, and like I say, it's been good to us.

On this more restricted scale, journeymen players can thus attain a fair measure of recognition, view themselves relative successes because of their material rewards, and prolong their playing careers in the minors where the years of peak productivity are extended. The potential dysfunctions of immobility and demotion for hockey organizations are further minimized by arrangements which facilitate the accumulation of rewards such as esteem and income—rewards which would have to be relinquished if the player chose to start another career at this point in the life cycle. Moreover, in coming to terms with age and occupancy of minor league status, the player often finds that involvements are being deepened for him in other areas as well. During the mid-twenties the process of acquiring familial involvements heightens the attractions of economic rewards which develop as unanticipated offshoots of his work and career involvement.

These crescive commitments are not easily turned aside or undone as players approach the age of thirty and begin facing the possibility of only a few remaining playing years. Taken together, income, personal attachment to the sport itself, and psychic benefits from shared camaraderie sustain the player's affiliation to the middle ranks of the hockey world.

At the same time, the precariousness of the career line still holds out the prospect of interorganizational mobility. Quite consistently, those interviewed display a skepticism toward "not facing the facts" of aging while discussing the problem of "hanging on" past one's playing prime: "I'll give it a few more years, I'll steal a few seasons from the younger kids, but I sure as hell won't hang on. The point is you want to go out with good memories, not bad ones." Somewhat paradoxically the anomalous case itself is a recurrent and integral part of a player's mobility motivations. The older rookie, the promoted veteran who goes up to stay (and there are typically one or two cases every playing season) affects the organizational commitment of other players because they are given hope that the same thing may happen to them. This feature of age-status asynchronization (Cain, 1964) tends to promote staff continuity and individual contribution to the team by providing available recruits in the pipeline strata who never fully give up on the chance of having an exemplary season and then being tapped for the major leagues. The sentiments surrounding this motivation, and the impact of recent league expansion on these, were summed up by a 28-year-old goalie. He said: "Maybe you'll go up, maybe not. You take it a year at a time. With expansion we all have a shot at it. If the legs hold out, who know? You're as good as your last season, that's what they remember. I still might get a shot." While several older men dismiss the most blatant exhortations for success with "be serious, those days are long gone," they nevertheless do not casually dismiss the potent, but statistically remote, possibility of becoming an elite regular. These outlooks suggest that personal adaptations to careers characterized by peak earnings for incumbents, structured uncertainty, and the potential for ''windfalls'' or reversals in career fortune actually enlarge the individual's contribution to collective goals by making it possible for the incumbent to entertain simultaneously the possibility of future success as well as immobility. *The integration of these complex features not only ties the player to a particular minor league situation but sustains as well the illusion and pleasure of viewing oneself if not forever young, then at least forever promising.*

The changing expectancies for inclusion and personal adjustments to immobility appear to be no more stable than the ongoing arrangements to which members adapt. In a comparative sense, professional hockey has the ambience of a series of precarious situations while the orchestra world has the structure of a long ladder with secure rungs or mobility plateaus. For minor league hockey players, their career footholds are shifting and uncertain. Their occupational world is one of contingency, the stay in the minors a provisional one. Ideally their present place is merely one of transit. It is as if they are all at a railroad station. Yet they are constrained to adjust to a highly active structure of personnel circulation and colleague competition. They come to face the prospect of their own eventual demise as players.

Musicians, by way of contrast, remain in an orchestra until they retire. The situation is one of stability. Their stay has a prospective future. They have arrived at their destination. Hockey players are in an occupation which sustains the hope of being among the select; orchestra musicians relinquish career dreams of this sort, scale down their expectations for inclusion, and adjust to what is probable in the long run rather than possible over the short run. *Making a successful personal adaptation lies in the process of personal change and reevaluation of such organizational locations.*

Very often the relinquishing of mobility motiva-

tions occurs in conjunction with efforts to disavow invidious comparisons among organizations at the middle level. It would appear that emphasizing the unstratified features of the organizational set makes it easier to accept one's own lack of mobility. A 38-year-old string player had this to say:

> It's not where you are but how well you're doing. I always felt that the career will take care of itself. Music cannot be thought of as something you can put in some economic formula, how do you know that this place is better than that place, this string section is better than that one? Are we two or three notches better than D. [minor league symphony]? You can play here or there, the important thing is your own progress.

Comments such as this suggest that to the extent that a ranking of minor league organizations is loosely defined, the larger the number of incumbents who can (1) be satisfied with playing in what they consider to be either a top minor league orchestra or one just below the top, (2) remain preoccupied with their chances of moving within the minor leagues rather than into the majors, and (3) move to orchestras at roughly the same level and consider the move a step upward. The interface of positional and organizational mobility noted earlier further facilitates this tradeoff. Unlike the world of professional hockey, the mobility paths in the orchestra are more diversified and the definitions of success decidedly more complex. This very complexity allows for redefinition or modification of career aspirations—an adaptation that may occur in anticipation of immobility.

A related condition of organizational socialization occurs with the development of essential changes in the nature of a musician's minor league involvement. Following Becker (1970; 1964) and Geer (1966), career incumbents become committed whenever they realize that it will cost them more to change their organizational position than it will to remain where they are. The following are some of the valuables whose accumulation restrains career mobility and increases the likelihood of staying at this orchestral level: contributions to pension plan, adjustment to one's way of doing things, rewarding relations with colleagues, a clientele of students, and a measure of local eminence. At about the age of 35, players begin exhibiting intense identification with their particular institutional position and a particular set of predictable and knowable customs; they become increasingly reluctant to face the prospects of, in the words of several, ''starting all over again'' in another organization. A concern centers around losing the accumulated perquisites and privileges of their present work role:

> I suppose part of my situation here is that I've developed a nice reputation for myself, I hope so . . . and going to a major orchestra now would be nice but this is hard to give up. There's a lot of pressure in a big orchestra, take F. [big five symphony], the place is divided into two factions, the one centering around the oboe player, the other around the flute player— you're in one camp or the other. Now we don't have that kind of thing here, it's great here, sort of like a family. The people in my section are my friends, my students have done well, there's not that continual fighting. You see, I'm aware of my ability and I hope I have an understanding of my liabilities, and I just would feel a certain amount of fear about moving someplace else . . . . I admire the players with that confidence and drive to get into the top orchestras, that's great. But for me, at this point, things might not work out and then . . . then were would you be?

Despite the small number of cases, my impression is that comments on the difficulties and personal price to be paid for ''making it'' in the major leagues function as cooling-out mechanisms for these players. Moreover, they facilitate those conditions which allow the abandoning of further aspirations without bitterness while still making it possible for musicians to admire the striver but be perfectly happy not to be one themselves.[8] To repeat, such personal outlooks have concrete con-

sequences for pipeline organizations because they dampen motivations to move onward and upward while calling forth the individual's contribution to institutional efforts.

One of the most potentially important aspects of these careers comes about through the development of unintended involvement deepened for the musician in other areas of life. Unanticipated side-benefits of organizational participation, such as community localization tied to the family, household, and schools are of sufficient value that their loss is subjectively defined as a constraint by the performing artist. The development of investments in the private sphere becomes linked to a more or less permanently given line of occupation action (see Wilensky, 1960; Berger and Kellner, 1964; Friedman, 1967). ''Sinking roots'' and related familial obligations during the late twenties to mid-thirties are in turn made conditional on the musician's continuing to remain in the minor league setting. The prospect of staying in the minor leagues becomes commonplace and even expected, whether they approve or disapprove of it, for these families can produce for themselves a private world in which they can feel secure and at home. Performers may in this way eradicate a sense of inadequacy surrounding their career progress. Asked about his future plans, a 32-year-old brass player has this to say:

> We want to stay here for a bit, I like the teaching and all that goes with this job. We still have plenty of time for the kids. The guys in the brass section . . . we all go skiing, so this is important to me. You asked about my chances for auditioning and getting into a big orchestra like Chicago or Boston, and I don't think I really want that now, not anymore, it's too much work. . . . Maybe at one time, but the family and the leisure, I don't want to lose that, I don't want to be away from them that much.

The solidarity-affirming nature of role reorientation coupled with supportive relationships in other spheres of the life-career can now be briefly enumerated. First, it should be observed that musicians are encouraged to adopt these standpoints, discovering and emphasizing the admirable features of current organizational roles while discounting other possible career lines; they come to reaffirm a multiplicity of collective affiliations, thereby enhancing their current organizational and familial involvement. These arrangements also enhance the shared views of like-situated colleagues who have preceded the person along this adaptive line of action. Second, by eliminating himself or by being eliminated through the operation of occupational expectations and bureaucratic arrangements, any one career fate within a minor league orchestra tends to confirm the views of other immobile colleagues concerning the hazards, injustices, difficulties, and politics of going higher in the organizational ranks. The individual can find, for example, a sympathetic audience of others who have considerable interest in avoiding excessive talk about bootstrap betterment. They will spare him the censure for not having climbed fast or far enough. Finally, in lowering career sights and shifting mobility expectations away from the illustrious slopes toward more probable terrain, many confess relief that their major career speculations and fears are now put to rest. The burning of bridges in this fashion dampens the poignancy of negative self-judgment and allows for appropriate disengagement from intense colleague competition for top strata positions. Considering the length of career time left and the high degree to which the present situation provides valuables out of which commitment grows, a cooling-out process is facilitated in which life in the minors constitutes available alternative achievements. This alleviates the potentially disruptive consequences of striving for success at the top of the organizational set. Personnel circulation is thus achieved, current selection procedures are maintained, and the mollification of the immobile prevents disturbances that can arise from the gap between mobility promises and structured exclusion.

CONCLUSIONS AND IMPLICATIONS

The analysis of career socialization has cogency, insofar as it deals directly with the interplay between members' perspectives and the structural context within which they operate. Referring as it does to directly observable actor-oriented (sometimes called "subjective") constructs and to discernible patterns of personnel turnover and age-grading, "career contingency" is seen as a fundamental concept. I have argued that the way in which a person views himself and colleague competitors in the process of occupational aging affects how one experiences a world of work. Career incumbents develop collective and distinctive ways of looking at the world. The focus and scope of the lenses may be different depending on certain conditions, but the problems of success and access appear to be critical features of this symbolic screen. I have also emphasized that within work organizations persons move through temporally situated opportunities. A comparative approach has been utilized to reveal the arrangements by which certain categories of incumbents are more readily available at certain career points than others for selection into the elite strata. The interdependency between organizational context and career outlook is, so I would argue, a general phenomenon, even if its particular form differs in various occupations.

Research studies of work careers have had no difficulty enumerating the ways in which formal organizations are people-processing institutions. Investigators typically point to the impact of mobility patterns on career concerns. To date however, emphasis has been placed on one or the other, but rarely on both. Moreover, sociologists often produce their understanding of structural conditions from either the generation of ideal types or by directly consulting the accounts given by various personnel within the organization in question—usually those in positions of command authority. As a partial remedy for this state of affairs, I have blended available organizational records and interview interrogations. Some fundamental mobility patterns have thereby been revealed. First, commitment appears to be essentially a segregation, boundary-maintaining mechanism; it promotes the internal cohesion of the pipeline organization and ensures its continuity as a distinctive unit. This is facilitated at the personal level by both cooling out those who do not reach top strata positions as well as by making alternative goals viable. Second, situational adjustment to the exigencies of youth-intensive recruitment can be viewed as an essential feature of the interlinking, associative relations which connect major and minor league units. Thus where age-grading is more intensive, as in professional sports, personal adaptations have their structural consequences in providing the ready availability of recruits. Third, and related, the similarity between these and Goldner's (1965) findings is instructive. Both suggest the importance of managerial control over mobility. The amount of direct and displayed discretion available to top strata managers is much greater in professional hockey than in the orchestra world. This discretion is reinforced by the fact that superiors control the major rewards meaningful to subordinates. High rates of success among colleague competitors should be associated with relatively lower expectancies of anticipatory immobility. Conversely, where managerial decision-making at the elite level is more diffuse and overall organizational metabolism is relatively slower (as in the low turnover patterns per season in the top five orchestras), we should observe increased expectancies of future immobility. Finally, to speculate somewhat, it may well be that both systems are more productive because they utilize their middle-level members efficiently than because they give greater opportunity to the more able. It appears that some proper balance between the mobile and immobile is necessary. As Everett C. Hughes (1949: 219) pointed out years ago, it is essential that occupations ''have a breed known as the 'Thank God' people . . . who can be counted on to stay where they are, and who keep things running while others are busy climbing the mobility ladder from one job to another.''

These data also suggest that occupational culture develops to the degree that members identify, assemble, recognize, and act on the problem of success and failure. In effective interaction with one another, both players and performers turn their concerted attention to discovering what they take to be the ''objective facts'' of their personal mobility. In so doing, they acquire a practiced grasp in discriminating between age-related and ''non-age-related'' problems while learning to act differentially with respect to them. If an occupational culture can be said to be a distinctive set of understandings and ways of acting that arise in response to the problems faced by a group, there is to be found in the materials a dialectic suggesting that age and mobility are to be seen in terms of one another. In both the world of hockey players and that of orchestra musicians, time has its moments and age its crucial objectivity. I have pointed out how age shapes members' conceptions of work reality itself; it defines what is and how to deal with it. Thus the tracking and formulating of career aspirations constitutes an important feature of social organization as well as the very reality in which musicians and athletes are obliged to live.

To follow out the implications of this observation, the making of careers becomes a basic activity through which knowledge of an occupation is detected and displayed. The various practices members employ in sustaining and reporting on their chances for ''making it,'' develop in tandem with their understanding of the recalcitrant features of mobility. The social construction of meaning can be viewed as centering around the conditions of occupational age. Thus fashion models (see Becker and Strauss, 1956), professional fighters (Weinberg and Arond, 1952), lawyers (Smigel, 1964; Spector, 1973), scientists (Reif and Strauss, 1965), industrial executives (Martin and Strauss, 1956), strippers, dancers, actors and actresses, teachers (Becker, 1952; Friedman, 1967), engineers, technical specialists (Sofer, 1970), and astronauts are urged to recognize and face up to the career dilemmas of becoming occupationally and biologically older. All have much in common: looked at in the proper light, their very differences connect them. It is what might be called age-consciousness: an aspect of occupational and organizational life whose centrality has, to borrow a phrase from Alfred Schutz, a paramount reality in experience.

In contrast to some sociological versions of work careers as passage through consensually validated positional structures, the approach advanced here suggests that we view careers as constructions and concerted accomplishments through and by which occupational actors apprehend the objective arrangements in their work lives. I have been principally concerned with analyzing the ways in which coming to terms—as a temporally situated achievement—consists of a set of practical maxims and reigning attitudes for coping with immobility and failure. I have also been concerned with documenting the ways in which these performers and players conceive of their own biographies as subject to, influenced by, and known in terms of the intelligible features of aging and career success. More than a crude set of retrospective reconstructions of the past, coming of occupational age by coming to terms with the work world consists of learning a set of assumptions. These assumptions are known, used, and taken for granted by organizational incumbents. They direct attention to the practical ways in which careers are to be interpreted as well as to the facticity of their design. More than a method of modifying career expectations, the coming of age in adult work life is a way of conceiving what is possible and what is not, what is real and what is not.

It is a sociological commonplace to assert that man actively conceptualizes his work biography and thereby comes to know the working constitution of the setting in which his career is located. Yet the problem of how this is temporally achieved is seldom posed. It seems an obvious matter that personal change occurs during crucial marking points in occupational lives. It seems equally obvious that the selection and sorting processes within organizational sets will affect the manner and degree to which incumbents align success aspirations with actual accomplishments. But the very obviousness of these phenomena should motivate close inspection of them. It is the very special characteristic of occupational socialization that it is the result of a process of social production designed to show the exigencies of age and erosion of mobility chances. To see the social character of career contingencies, therefore, one must see how contingencies are produced. What characterizes organizational membership is not that individuals are merely concerned about their chances of success and access, but that they share these concerns in effective interaction, and produce lines of mutual adjustment under the auspices of their conceptions of occupational reality itself. I have argued that such conceptions of membership are articulated on those occasions when middle-level incumbents review and contemplate the features upon which their personal success depends. Coming up adult in the socially produced world of work is, then, an occasion for us to document the ways in which players and performers display a hard-headed commitment to ''being realistic''—a stance that is the mark of occupational adulthood. An effort should be made to determine whether these formulations (and modifications thereof) apply in a wider variety of organizational sets and occupational worlds.

NOTES

1. The term ''age-grading'' has a very technical meaning in the sociological and anthropological literature (Eisenstadt, 1956); I use it here to refer to socially recognized age-positions or categories defined by work organizations. As such it is one of the social phenomena about which everyone knows, as in the ratified assumptions about ''how old'' candidates for certain positions should be. Relying on participants' knowledge or intuitive understanding of just what occupational age is, the professional social-scientific literature provides little in the way of analytical unity or comparative development of the normative definitions and structural consequences of allocation by age in organizations.

2. The orchestral leagues are composed of organizations in the following urban areas: Atlanta, Baltimore, Buffalo, Cincinnati, Dallas, Denver, Detroit, Houston, Indianapolis, Kansas City, Los Angeles, Milwaukee, Minneapolis, Montreal, New Jersey, New Orleans, Pittsburgh, Rochester, St. Louis, San Antonio, San Francisco, Seattle, Toronto, and the Washington National Symphony. Below these are the bush leagues comprised of semi-pro and amateur symphonies (see Hart, 1973; Caplow, 1964).

3. Over these two seasons the teams were distributed in the following way. American Hockey League—Baltimore, Boston, Cincinnati, Cleveland, Hershey, New Haven, Nova Scotia, Providence, Richmond, Rochester, Springfield, Tidewater. Central Hockey League—Dallas, Forth Worth, Kansas City, Oklahoma City, Omaha, Tulsa. Western Hockey League—Denver, Phoenix, Portland, Salt Lake, San Diego, Seattle.

4. The amateur draft is comprised of Canadian and college performers who are at least 20 years old by December 31. In 1971 the 14 clubs drafted 115 players. Fewer than 15% went directly into the NHL; most were sent to the minor league affiliate. The expansion draft is the next organizational mechanism by which new clubs acquire the bulk of their players. Here the new teams have to be stocked with 18 to 20 players, and they get these men from the already established clubs. The latter want to retain their finest talent so they make out a "protected list," a roster of from 13 to 15 men who the new teams cannot select. The remaining players are available. Whether one is left protected or not, therefore, becomes an important sign of one's standing with managers and coaches. This concern is further intensified as in the 1971–1972 season where each club could dress 17 skaters and 2 goalies for each game. The active roster of 19 is typically comprised of three forward lines and five defensemen, or 14 skaters. In selecting lines some choices are automatic and coaches turn to their proven players, superstars, and talented rookies. Filling out the roster is a managerial procedure of some consequence for the remaining players—those on the low end of the status hierarchy—for it determines how much, or even whether, one is going to have access to the most important activity of all, namely, playing time or "ice-time."

5. These data are drawn from the *1971–1972 Pro and Senior Hockey Guide* (St. Louis: Sporting News, 1971).

6. Of the 379 players who played one or more games in the NHL during the 1971–1972 season, 125 experienced some form of interleague mobility. Of the latter, 92 (75%) were from the American Hockey League, 17 (14%) were from the Central Hockey League, 12 (10%) from the Western Hockey League, and a handful from the International Hockey League. The remaining 254, of course, played every game at the NHL level.

7. Viewed in an a priori fashion, the probability of any musician in the minor orchestral set being hired by a big league orchestra is less than 2% (30/2250). The attractive simplicity of this ratio conceals the processes by which minor league orchestra players remain immobile and unavailable for auditions for any one opening at the level of the "big five." Still, in any one year the active players in the musical marketplace may be as large as 30% (675) raising the chances of any person securing a position at the top to around 4%. This will vary depending upon the status of the opening, orchestral policies concerning hiring from within, and so on. By way of contrast, in professional hockey over the past seasons around 45 jobs have been available in any one year; there are 460 players in the minors, and their chances of being promoted are about one in ten.

8. This insight was suggested by Ralph H. Turner in a personal communication.

REFERENCES

Banton, M. (1955) Roles: An Introduction to the Study of Social Relations. London: Tavistock.

Becker, H. S. (1970) "The self and adult socialization," pp. 289–303 in Sociological Work: Method and Substance. Chicago: Aldine.

——— (1964) "Personal change in adult life." Sociometry 27 (March): 40–53.

——— (1963) Outsiders. New York: Free Press.

——— (1952) "The career of the Chicago public school teacher." Amer. J. of Sociology 57 (March): 470–477.

———— and A. L. Strauss (1956) "Careers, personality, and adult socialization." Amer. J. of Sociology 62 (November): 253—263.

Berger, B. M. (1960) "How long is a generation?" British J. of Sociology 11: 557—568.

Berger, P. and H. Kellner (1964) "Marriage and the construction of reality." Diogenes 4 (Summer): 1—24.

Brim, O. G., Jr. (1968) "Adult socialization," pp. 183—226 in J. A. Clausen (ed.) Socialization and Society. Boston: Little, Brown.

———— (1966) "Socialization through the life cycle," pp. 3—49 in Socialization After Childhood: Two Essays. New York: John Wiley.

Cain, L. D., Jr. (1964) "Life course and social structure," pp. 272—309 in R.E.L. Faris, Handbook of Modern Sociology. Chicago: Rand McNally.

Caplow, T. (1964) Principles of Organization. New York: Harcourt, Brace & World.

———— and R. J. McGee (1958) The Academic Marketplace. New York: Basic Books.

Carlin, J. E. (1962) Lawyers on Their Own: A Study of Individual Practitioners in Chicago. New Brunswick, N.J.: Rutgers Univ. Press.

Chinoy, E. (1955) Automobile Workers and the American Dream. New York: Random House.

Clark, B. R. (1960) "The 'cooling out' function in higher education." Amer. J. of Sociology 65 (May): 569—576.

Eisenstadt, S. N. (1956) From Generation to Generation. New York: Free Press.

Faulkner, R. R. (1973) "Career concerns and mobility motivations of orchestra musicians." Soc. Q. 14 (Summer): 334—349.

———— (1971) Hollywood Studio Musicians: Their Work and Careers in the Recording Industry. Chicago: Aldine-Atherton.

Friedman, N. L. (1967) "Career stages and organizational role decisions of teachers in two public junior colleges." Sociology of Education 40 (Summer): 231—245.

Geer, B. (1966) "Occupational commitment and the teaching profession." School Rev. 74 (Spring): 31—47.

Glaser, B. G. (1964) Organizational Scientists. Indianapolis: Bobbs-Merrill.

———— and A. L. Strauss (1971) Status Passages: A Formal Theory. Chicago: Aldine Atherton.

Goffman, E. (1961) Asylums: Essays on the Social Situation of Mental Patients and Other Inmates. Garden City, N.Y.: Doubleday.

———— (1952) "On cooling the mark out: some aspects of adaptation to failure." Psychiatry 15 (November): 451—463.

Goldner, E. (1965) "Demotion in industrial management." Amer. Soc. Rev. 30 (October): 714—724.

———— and R. R. Ritti (1967) "Professionalization as career immobility." Amer. J. of Sociology 72 (March): 489—502.

Hall, O. (1948) "The stages of a medical career." Amer. J. of Sociology 53 (March): 327—336.

Hart, P. (1973) Orpheus in the New World: The Symphony Orchestra as an American Cultural Institution. New York: W. W. Norton.

Hughes, E. C. (1958) Men and Their Work. New York: Free Press.

———— (1949) "Queries concerning industry and society growing out of study of ethnic relations in industry." Amer. Soc. Rev. 14 (April): 211—220.

Levenson, B. (1961) "Bureaucratic succession," pp. 362—395 in A. Etzioni (ed.) Complex Organizations. New York: Holt, Rinehart & Winston.

Maniha, J. K. (1972) "Organizational demotion and the process of bureaucratization." Social Problems 20 (Fall): 161—173.

Martin, N. H. and A. L. Strauss (1956) "Patterns of mobility within industrial organizations." J. of Business 29 (April): 101—110.

Merton, R. K. (1957) Social Theory and Social Structure. New York: Free Press.

Miller, D. C. and W. H. Form (1951) Industrial Sociology. New York: Harper.

More, D. M. (1962) "Demotion." Social Problems 9 (Winter): 213—221.

Morse, N. C. and R. S. Weiss (1955) "The function and meaning of work and the job." Amer. Soc. Rev. 20 (April): 191—198.

Mueller, J. (1951) The American Symphony Orchestra: A Social History of Musical Taste. Bloomington: Indiana Univ. Press.

Reif, F. and A. L. Strauss (1965) "The impact of rapid discovery upon the scientist's career." Social Problems 12: 297−311.

Roth, J. A. (1963) Timetables. Indianapolis: Bobbs-Merrill.

Ryder, N. B. (1965) "The cohort as a concept in the study of social change." Amer. Soc. Rev. 30 (December): 834−861.

Seeman, M. (1967) "On the personal consequences of alienation in work." Amer. Soc. Rev. 32 (April): 273−285.

Smigel, E. (1964) The Wall Street Lawyer. New York: Free Press.

Sofer, C. (1970) Men in Mid-Career: A Study of British Managers and Technical Specialists. London: Cambridge Univ. Press.

Solomon, D. N. (1953) "Career contingencies of Chicago physicians." Ph.D. dissertation. University of Chicago.

Spector, M. (1973) "Secrecy in job seeking among government attorneys: two contingencies in the theory of subcultures." Urban Life and Culture 2 (July): 211−229.

────── (1972) "The rise and fall of a mobility route." Social Problems 20 (Fall): 173−185.

Stebbins, R. A. (1970) "Career: the subjective approach." Soc. Q. 11 (Winter): 32−49.

Stouffer, S. A., E. A. Suchman, L. C. Devinney, S. A. Star, and R. M. Williams, Jr. (1949) The American Soldier: Adjustment During Army Life. Princeton: Princeton Univ. Press.

Strauss, A. L. (1959) Mirrors and Masks: The Search for Identity. New York: Free Press.

Wager, L. W. (1959) "Career patterns and role problems of airline pilots in a major airline company." Ph.D. dissertation. University of Chicago.

Weinberg, S. K. and H. Arond (1952) "The occupational culture of the boxer." Amer. J. of Sociology 57: 460−469.

Westby, D. L. (1960) "The career experience of the symphony musician." Social Forces 38 (March): 223−230.

Wilensky, H. L. (1960) "Work, careers, and social integration." International Social Science J. 12: 543−560.

────── (1956) Intellectuals in Labor Unions: Organizational Pressures on Professional Roles. New York: Free Press.

Wood, A. L. (1967) Criminal Lawyer. New Haven, Conn.: College & University Press.

TWENTY-SIX

PERSONAL CHANGE IN ADULT LIFE

HOWARD S. BECKER

People often exhibit marked change—in their attitudes, beliefs, behavior and style of interaction—as they move through youth and adulthood. Many social scientists, and others interested in explaining human behavior, think that human beings are governed by deep and relatively unchanging components of the personality or self, so that important changes at late stages in the life cycle are viewed as anomalies that need to be explained away. They may trace the roots of behavior to personality components formed in early childhood—needs, defenses, identifications, and the like—and interpret change in adulthood as simply a variation on an already established theme. Or they may, more sociologically, see the sources of everyday behavior in values established in the society, inculcated in the young during childhood, and maintained thereafter by constraints built into major communal institutions. Like the personality

theorists, those who use values as a major explanatory variable see change in adulthood as essentially superficial, a new expression of an unchanging underlying system of values. In either case, the scientist wishes to concern himself with basic processes that will explain lasting trends in individual behavior.

Both these approaches err by taking for granted that the only way we can arrive at generalized explanations of human behavior is by finding some unchanging components in the self or personality. They err as well in making the prior assumption that human beings are essentially unchanging, that changes which affect only such "superficial" phenomena as behavior without affecting deeper components of the person are trivial and unimportant.

There are good reasons to deny these assumptions. Brim, for instance, has persuasively argued that there are no "deep" personality characteristics, traits of character which persist across any and all situations and social roles.[1] In any case, it is clearly a useful strategy to explore the theoretical possibilities opened up by considering what might

SOURCE: Howard S. Becker. "Personal Change in Adult Life." Copyright by the American Sociological Association, 1964. Howard S. Becker, "Personal Change in Adult Life," *Sociometry*, XXVII (March, 1964), pp. 40—53. Reprinted by permission of the American Sociological Association.

A slightly different version of this paper was presented at the Social Science Research Council Conference on Socialization Through the Life Cycle, New York, May 17, 1963. I wish to thank Orville G. Brim, Jr., Blanche Geer, and Anselm L. Strauss for their comments on an earlier draft.

[1]Orville G. Brim, Jr., "Personality as Role-Learning," in Ira Iscoe and Harold Stevenson, editors, *Personality Development in Children*, Austin: University of Texas Press, 1960, pp. 127—59.

be true if we look in other directions for generalizeable explanations of human behavior.

A good many studies are now available which suggest that an appropriate area in which further explanations might be sought is that of social structure and its patterned effects on human experience. Two of these seem of special importance, and I devote most of what I have to say to them. The process of *situational adjustment,* in which individuals take on the characteristics required by the situations they participate in, provides an entering wedge into the problem of change. It shows us one example of an explanation which can deal with superficial and immediate changes in behavior and at the same time allow us to make generalized theories about the processes involved. The process of *commitment,* in which externally unrelated interests of the person become linked in such a way as to constrain future behavior, suggests an approach to the problem of personal stability in the face of changing situations. Before dealing with these processes, however, I will consider a problem of definition which reveals a further influence of social structure, this time an influence on the very terms in which problems of socialization are cast.

THE EYE OF THE BEHOLDER

Many of the changes alleged to take place in adults do not take place at all. Or, rather, a change occurs but an optical illusion causes the outside observer to see it as a change quite different in kind and magnitude from what it really is. The observer (a layman or a social scientist looking at the phenomenon from a layman's point of view), through a semantic transformation, turns an observable change into something quite different.

Take, for example, the commonly asserted proposition that the professional education of physicians stifles their native idealism and turns it into a profound professional cynicism.[2] Educated

[2]This problem is discussed at greater length in Howard S. Becker and Blanche Geer, "The Fate of Idealism in Medical School," *American Sociological Review,* 23 (Feb., 1958), pp.

laymen believe this, and scientific studies have been carried out to test the proposition.[3] Observed changes in the behavior of fledgling physicians attest to its truth. Doctors are in fact inclined to speak with little reverence of the human body; they appear to be and probably are to a large extent unmoved in the emotional way a layman would be by human death; their standards are not as high as the layman thinks they ought to be, their desire for wealth stronger than it ought to be.

People describe these changes with reference to an unanalyzed conception of idealism and cynicism. It would not be unfair to describe the conception as the perspective of a disgruntled patient, who feels that the doctor he has to deal with is thinking about other things than the patient's welfare. The perspective of the disgruntled patient itself draws on some very general lay conceptions which suggest that those who deal with the unpleasant and the unclean—in this case, with death and disease—must of necessity be cynical, since "normal people" prefer what is pleasant and clean and find the unclean repulsive.

It is typically the case in service occupations, however, that the practitioners who perform the service have a perspective quite different from the clients, patients or customers for whom they perform it.[4] They understand the techniques used by professionals, the reasons for their use in one case and not in another, the contingencies of the work situation and of work careers which affect a man's judgment and behavior, and the occupational ethos and culture which guide him. The client un-

50–56, and in Howard S. Becker, Blanche Geer, Everett C. Hughes, and Anselm L. Strauss, *Boys in White: Student Culture in Medical School,* Chicago: University of Chicago Press, 1961, pp. 419–33.

[3]See Leonard D. Eron, "Effect of Medical Education on Medical Students," *Journal of Medical Education,* 10 (Oct., 1955), pp. 559–66; and Richard Christie and Robert K. Merton, "Procedures for the Sociological Study of the Values Climate of Medical Schools," *ibid.,* 33 (1958), Part II, pp. 125–53.

[4]See, for a discussion of this point, Howard S. Becker, *Outsiders: Studies in the Sociology of Deviance,* New York: The Free Press, 1963, pp. 82 ff.; and Everett C. Hughes, *Men and their Work,* New York: The Free Press, 1958, *passim.*

derstands nothing of this. In an effort to make sense of his experience with those who serve him, he may resort to the folk notions I have already mentioned, reasoning that people who constantly deal with what decent people avoid may be contaminated: some of the dirt rubs off. The client is never sure that the practitioner has his best interests at heart and tends to suspect the worst.

But why should we assess and evaluate the change that takes place in the doctor as he goes through professional school from the point of view of his patient? Suppose we look at it instead from the characteristic perspective of the medical profession. If we do this, we find (as we would find if we studied the views of almost any occupation toward the institutions which train people for entrance into them) that medical schools are typically regarded as too idealistic. They train students to practice in ways that are not "practical," suited to an ideal world but not to the world we live in. They teach students to order more laboratory tests than patients will pay for, to ignore the patient's requests for "new" drugs or "popular" treatments,[5] but do not teach students what to do when the waiting room holds more patients than can be seen during one's office hours. Similarly, people often complain of schools of education that they train prospective teachers in techniques that are not adapted to the situation the teacher will really have to deal with; they idealistically assume that the teacher can accomplish ends which in fact cannot be gained in the situations she will face. They do not tell the teacher how to teach a fifteen-year-old fifth grader, nor do they tell her what to do when she discovers a pupil carrying a switchblade knife.

It is a paradox. In one view, professional training makes physicians less idealistic, in the other, more idealistic. Where does the truth lie? I have already noted that many of the changes seen as signs of increasing cynicism in the young physician do in fact take place. It can equally be demonstrated that the changes which make him

seem too idealistic also take place. The medical students we studied at the University of Kansas expected, when they graduated, to practice in ways that would be regarded as hopelessly idealistic by many, if not most, medical practioners. They proposed to see no more than 20 patients a day; they proposed never to treat a disease without having first made a firm diagnosis. These briefs, inculcated by a demanding faculty, are just the opposite of the cynicism supposed to afflict the new physician.[6]

The lesson we should learn from this is that personality changes are often present only in the eye of the beholder. Changes do take place in people, but the uninformed outsider interprets the change wrongly. Just as doctors acquire new perspectives and ideas as a result of their medical training, any adult may acquire new perspectives and ideas. But it would be a mistake to assume that these changes represent the kind of fundamental changes suggested by such polar terms as "idealism" and "cynicism." We learn less by studying the students who are alleged to have lost their idealism than we do by studying those who claim they have become cynical.

Even so, adults do change. But we must make sure, not only by our own observation but also by careful analysis of the terms we use to describe what we see, that the changes we try to explain do in fact take place. Parenthetically, an interesting possibility of transferring concepts from the study of adults to the study of socialization of children lies in defining the character of the changes that take place as children develop. Is it too farfetched to say that the definitions ordinarily used are excessively parochial in that they are all arrived at from the adult point of view? What would our theories look like if we made a greater effort to capture the child's point of view? What does he think is happening to him? How does his conception of the process differ from that of the adults who bring him up and those who study his growing up?

---

[5]See Eliot Freidson, *Patients' Views of Medical Practice,* New York: Russell Sage Foundation, 1961, pp. 200−202.

[6]Becker, *et al.*, *Boys in White, op. cit.,* pp. 426−428.

SITUATIONAL ADJUSTMENT

One of the most common mechanisms in the development of the person in adulthood is the process of situational adjustment. This is a very gross conception, which requires analytic elaboration it has not yet received. But the major outlines are clear. The person, as he moves in and out of a variety of social situations, learns the requirements of continuing in each situation and of success in it. If he has a strong desire to continue, the ability to assess accurately what is required, and can deliver the required performance, the individual turns himself into the kind of person the situation demands.

Broadly considered, this is much the same as Brim's notion of learning adult roles. One learns to be a doctor or a policeman, learns the definitions of the statuses involved and the appropriate behavior with respect to them. But the notion of situational adjustment is more flexible than that of adult role learning. It allows us to deal with smaller units and make a finer analysis. We construct the process of learning an adult role by analyzing sequences of smaller and more numerous situational adjustments. We should have in our minds the picture of a person trying to meet the expectations he encounters in immediate face-to-face situations: doing well in today's chemistry class, managing to be poised and mature on tonight's date, surmounting the small crises of the moment. Sequences and combinations of small units of adjustment produce the larger units of role learning.

If we view situational adjustment as a major process of personal development, we must look to the character of the situation for the explanation of why people change as they do. We ask what there is in the situation that requires the person to act in a certain way or to hold certain beliefs. We do not ask what there is in him that requires the action or belief. All we need to know of the person is that for some reason or another he desires to continue his participation in the situation or to do well in it. From this we can deduce that he will do what he can to do what is necessary in that situation. Our further analysis must adjust itself to the character of the situation.

Thus, for example, in our present study of college undergraduates,[7] we find that they typically share a strong desire to get high grades. Students work very hard to get grades and consider them very important, both for their immediate consequences and as indicators of their own personal ability and worth. We need not look very deeply into the student to see the reason for his emphasis on grades. The social structure of the campus coerces students to believe that grades are important because, in fact, they are important. You cannot join a fraternity or sorority if your grades do not meet a certain minimum standard. You cannot compete for high office in important campus organizations if your grades are not high enough. As many as one-fourth of the students may not be able to remain in school if they do not raise their grades in the next semester. For those who are failing, low grades do not simply mean blocked access to the highest campus honors. Low grades, for these unfortunates, mean that every available moment must be spent studying, that the time the average student spends dating, playing, drinking beer or generally goofing off must be given over to the constant effort to stay in school. Grades are the currency with which the economy of campus social life operates. Only the well-to-do can afford the luxuries; the poor work as hard as they can to eke out a marginal existence.

The perspectives a person acquires as a result of situational adjustments are no more stable than the situation itself or his participation in it. Situations occur in institutions: stable institutions provide stable situations in which little change takes place. When the institutions themselves change, the situations they provide for their participants shift and

[7]Statements about college students are based on preliminary analysis of the data collected in a study of undergraduates at the University of Kansas, in which I collaborated with Blanche Geer and Everett C. Hughes. A monograph reporting our findings is in preparation. The study was supported by the Carnegie Corporation of New York.

necessitate development of new patterns of belief and action. When, for instance, a university decides to up-grade its academic program and begins to require more and different kinds of work from its students, they must adjust to the new contingencies with which the change confronts them.

Similarly, if an individual moves in and out of given situations, is a transient rather than a long-term participant, his perspectives will shift with his movement. Wheeler has shown that prisoners become more "prisonized" the longer they are in prison; they are more likely to make decisions on the basis of criminal than of law-abiding values. But he has also shown that if you analyze prisoners' responses by time still to be served, they become more law-abiding the nearer they approach release.[8] This may be interpreted as a situational shift. The prisoner is frequently sorry that he has been caught and is in a mood to give up crime; he tends to respect law-abiding values. But when he enters prison he enters an institution which, in its lower reaches, is dominated by men wedded to criminal values. Studies of prisons have shown that the most influential prisoners tend to have stable criminal orientations and that inmate society is dominated by these perspectives.[9] In order to "make out" in the prison, the new inmate discovers that he must make his peace with this criminally oriented social structure, and he does. As he approaches release, however, he realizes that he is going back into a world dominated by people who respect the law and that the criminal values which stand him in such good stead in prison society will not work as well outside. He thereupon begins to shed the criminal values appropriate to the prison and renew his attachment to the law-abiding values of the outside world.

[8]Stanton Wheeler, "Socialization in Correctional Communities," *American Sociological Review,* 26 (Oct., 1961), pp. 697–712.

[9]See Donald R. Cressey, editor, *The Prison: Studies in Institutional Organization and Change,* New York: Holt, Rinehart and Winston, 1961; and Richard A. Cloward, *et al., Theoretical Studies in Social Organization of the Prison,* New York: Social Science Research Council, 1960.

We discovered the same process in the medical school, where students gave up a naive idealistic approach to the problems of medicine for an approach that was specifically oriented toward getting through school. As they approached the end of their schooling, they relinquished their attachment to these school-specific values and once more returned to their concern with problems that would arise in the outer world, albeit with a new and more professional approach than they would have been capable of before.

We find a similar change in college students, when we observe them in the Spring of their last college year. They look back over the four years of school and wonder why they have not spent their time better, wonder if college has been what they wanted. This concern reflects their preoccupation, while in school, with the pursuit of values that are valuable primarily within the confines of the collegiate community: grades, office in campus organizations, and the like. (Even though they justify their pursuit of these ends in part on the basis of their utility in the outside world, students are not sure that the pursuit of other ends, less valued on the campus, might not have even more usefulness for the future.) Now that they are leaving for the adult community, in which other things will be valuable, they find it hard to understand their past concerns as they try, retrospectively, to assess the experience they have just been through.

Situational adjustment is very frequently not an individual process at all, but a collective one. That is, we are not confronted with one person undergoing change, but with an entire cohort, a "class" of people, who enter the institution and go through its socializing program together. This is most clearly the case in those institutions which typically deal with "batches" of people.[10] Schools are perhaps the best example, taking in a class of students each year or semester who typically go through the

[10]See Erving Goffman's use of this idea in *Asylums: Essays on the Social Situation of Mental Patients and Other Inmates,* Garden City: Doubleday and Company, Inc., 1961, pp. 6 and *passim.*

entire training program as a unit, leaving together at the end of their training.

But situational adjustment may have a collective character even where people are not processed in groups. The individual enters the institution alone, or with a small group, but joins a larger group there already, who stand ready to tell him how it is and what he should do, and he will be followed by others for whom he will perform the same good turn.[11] In institutions where people are acted upon in groups by socializing agents, much of the change that takes place—the motivation for it and the perceived desirability of different modes of change—cannot be traced to the predilections of the individual. It is, instead, a function of the interpretive response made by the entire group, the consensus the group reaches with respect to its problems.

The guidelines for our analysis can be found in Sumner's analysis of the development of folkways.[12] A group finds itself sharing a common situation and common problems. Various members of the group experiment with possible solutions to those problems and report their experiences to their fellows. In the course of their collective discussion, the members of the group arrive at a definition of the situation, its problems and possibilities, and develop consensus as to the most appropriate and efficient ways of behaving. This consensus thenceforth constrains the activities of individual members of the group, who will probably act on it, given the opportunity.

The collective character of socialization processes has a profound effect on their consequences. Because the solutions the group reaches have, for the individual being socialized, the character of "what everyone knows to be true," he tends to accept them. Random variation in responses that might arise from differences in prior experiences is drastically reduced. Medical students, for instance, began their training with a variety of perspectives on how one ought to approach academic assignments. The pressure generated by their inability to handle the tremendous amount of work given them in the first year anatomy course forced them to adopt collectively one of the many possible solutions to the problem, that of orienting their studying to learning what the faculty was likely to ask about on examinations. (Where the situation does not coerce a completely collective response, variation due to differences in background and experience remains. Irwin and Cressey[13] argue that the behavior of prisoners, both in prison and after release, varies depending on whether the convict was previously a member of the criminal underworld.)

In addition, where the response to problematic situations is collective, members of the group involved develop group loyalties that become part of the environment they must adjust to. Industrial workers are taught by their colleagues to restrict production in order that an entire work group may not be held to the higher production standard one or two people might be able to manage.[14] Medical students, similarly, find that they will only make it harder for others, and eventually for themselves, if they work too hard and "produce" too much.[15]

One major consequence of the collective character of situational adjustment, a result of the factors just mentioned, is that the group being

---

[11]See Anselm L. Strauss, *Mirrors and Masks: The Search for Identity,* New York: The Free Press, 1959; and Howard S. Becker and Anselm L. Strauss, "Careers, Personality and Adult Socialization," *American Journal of Sociology,* 62 (Nov., 1956), pp. 253—63.

[12]William Graham Sumner, *Folkways,* Boston: Ginn and Co., 1907. See also Albert K. Cohen, *Delinquent Boys: The Culture of a Gang,* New York: The Free Press, 1955; and Richard A. Cloward and Lloyd E. Ohlin, *Delinquency and Opportunity: A Theory of Delinquent Gangs,* New York: The Free Press, 1960.

[13]John Irwin and Donald R. Cressey, "Thieves, Convicts and the Inmate Culture," *Social Problems,* 10 (Fall, 1962), pp. 142—55. See also Howard S. Becker and Blanche Geer, "Latent Culture: A Note on the Theory of Latent Social Roles," *Administrative Science Quarterly,* 5 (Sept., 1960), pp. 304—13.

[14]Donald Roy, "Quota Restriction and Goldbricking in a Machine Shop," *American Journal of Sociology,* 57 (Mar., 1952), pp. 427—42.

[15]Becker, *et al., Boys in White,* pp. 297—312.

socialized is able to deviate much more from the standards set by those doing the socializing than would be possible for an individual. Where an individual might feel that his deviant response was idiosyncratic, and thus be open to persuasion to change it, the member of a group knows that there are many who think and act just as he does and is therefore more resistant to pressure and propaganda. A person being socialized alone, likewise, is freer to change his ways than one who is constrained by his loyalties to fellow trainees.

If we use situational adjustment as an explanation for changes in persons during adulthood, the most interesting cases for analysis are the negative cases, those instances in which people do not adjust appropriately to the norms implicit or explicit in the situation. For not everyone adjusts to the kind of major situational forces I have been discussing. Some prison inmates never take on criminal values; some college students fail to adopt campus values and therefore do not put forth their full effort in the pursuit of grades. In large part, cases in which it appears that people are not adjusting to situational pressures are cases in which closer analysis reveals that the situation is actually not the same for everyone involved in the institution. A job in the library may effectively remove the prisoner from the control of more criminally oriented prisoners; *his* situation does not constrain him to adopt criminal values. The political rewards owed a student's living group may require a campus organization to give him an office his grade point average would otherwise make it difficult for him to attain.

More generally, it is often the case that subgroups in an institution will often have somewhat different life situations. College, for instance, is clearly one thing for men, another for women; one thing for members of fraternities and sororities, another for independents. We only rarely find an institution as monolithic as the medical school, in which the environment is, especially during the first two years, exactly alike for everyone. So we must make sure that we have discovered the effective environment of those whose personal development we want to understand.

Even after removing the variation in personal change due to variation in the situation, we will find a few cases in which people sturdily resist situational pressures. Here we can expect to find a corresponding weakness in the desire to remain in the situation or to do well in it, or a determination to remain in the situation only on one's terms or as long as one can get what one wants out of it. Many institutions have enough leeway built into them for a clever and determined operator to survive without much adjustment.

COMMITMENT

The process of situational adjustment allows us to account for the changes people undergo as they move through various situations in their adult life. But we also know that people exhibit some consistency as they move from situation to situation. Their behavior is not infinitely mutable, they are not infinitely flexible. How can we account for the consistency we observe?

Social scientists have increasingly turned to the concept of commitment for an explanation of personal consistency in situations which offer conflicting directives. The term has been used to describe a great variety of social-psychological mechanisms, such a variety that it has no stable meaning. Nevertheless, I think we can isolate at least one process referred to by the term commitment, a process which will help explain a great deal of behavioral consistency.[16]

Briefly, we say a person is committed when we observe him pursuing a consistent line of activity in a sequence of varied situations. Consistent activity persists over time. Further, even though the actor may engage in a variety of disparate acts, he sees them as essentially consistent; from his point of view they serve him in pursuit of the same

[16]Howard S. Becker, "Notes on the Concept of Commitment," *American Journal of Sociology,* 66 (July, 1960), pp. 32−40.

goal. Finally, it is a distinguishing mark of commitment that the actor rejects other situationally feasible alternatives, choosing from among the available courses of action that which best suits his purpose. In so doing, he often ignores the principle of situational adjustment, pursuing his consistent line of activity in the face of a short-term loss.

The process of commitment consists in the linking of previously extraneous and irrelevant lines of action and sets of rewards to a particular line of action under study. If, for instance, a person refuses to change jobs, even though the new job would offer him a higher salary and better working conditions, we should suspect that his decision is a result of commitment, that other sets of rewards than income and working conditions have become attached to his present job so that it would be too painful for him to change. He may have a large pension at stake, which he will lose if he moves; he may dread the cost of making new friends and learning to get along with new working associates; he may feel that he will get a reputation for being flighty and erratic if he leaves his present job. In each instance, formerly extraneous interests have become linked to keeping his present job. I have elsewhere described this process metaphorically as the making of side-bets.

> The committed person has acted in such a way as to involve other interests of his, originally extraneous to the action he is engaged in, directly in that action. By his own actions . . . he has staked something of value to him, something originally unrelated to his present line of action, on being consistent in his present behavior. The consequences of inconsistency will be so expensive that inconsistency . . . is no longer a feasible alternative.[17]

A person may make side-bets producing commitments consciously and deliberately or he may acquire them or have them made for him almost without his knowledge, becoming aware that he is committed only when he faces a difficult decision. Side-bets and commitments of the latter type,

[17]*Ibid.*, p. 35.

made by default, arise from the operation of generalized cultural expectations, from the operation of impersonal bureaucratic arrangements, from the process of individual adjustment to social positions, and through the need to save face.

One way of looking at the process of becoming an adult is to view it as a process of gradually acquiring, through the operation of all these mechanisms, a variety of commitments which constrain one to follow a consistent pattern of behavior in many areas of life. Choosing an occupation, getting a job, starting a family—all these may be seen as events which produce lasting commitments and constrain the person's behavior. Careful study might show that the operation of the process of commitment accounts for the well-known fact that juvenile delinquents seldom become adult criminals, but rather turn into respectable, conventional, law-abiding lower-class citizens. It may be that the erratic behavior of the juvenile delinquent is erratic precisely because the boy has not yet taken any actions which commit him more or less permanently to a given line of endeavor.

Viewing commitment as a set of side-bets encourages us to inquire into the kind of currency with which bets are made in the situation under analysis. What things are valuable enough to make side-bets that matter with? What kinds of counters are used in the game under analysis? Very little research has been done on this problem, but I suspect that erratic behavior and "random" change in adult life result from situations which do not permit people to become committed because they deny to them the means, the chips with which to make side-bets of any importance.

Members of medical faculties complain, for instance, that students' behavior toward patients is erratic. They do not exhibit the continued interest in or devotion to the patient's welfare supposed to characterize the practicing physician. They leave the hospital at five o'clock, even though a patient assigned to them is in critical condition. Their interest in a surgical patient disappears when the academic schedule sends them to a medical ward and a new set of student duties. The reason for students' lack of interest and devotion becomes clear when we consider their frequent complaint that they are not allowed to exercise medical responsibility, to make crucial decisions or carry out important procedures. Their behavior toward patients can be less constrained than that of a practicing physician precisely because they are never allowed to be in a position where they can make a mistake that matters. No patient's life or welfare depends on them; they need not persist in any particular pattern of activity since deviation costs nothing.[18]

The condition of being unable to make important side-bets and thus commit oneself may be more widespread than we think. Indeed, it may well be that the age at which it becomes possible to make lasting and important side-bets is gradually inching up. People cannot become committed to a consistent line of activity until later in life. As divorce becomes more frequent, for instance, the ability to make a lasting commitment by getting married becomes increasingly rare. In studying the possibilities of commitment afforded by social structures, we discover some of the limits to consistent behavior in adult life.

(It might be useful to apply similar concepts in studies of child socialization. It is likely, for instance, that children can seldom commit themselves. Our society, particularly, does not give them the means with which to make substantial side-bets, nor does it think it appropriate for children to make committing side-bets. We view childhood and youth as a time when a person can make mistakes that do not count. Therefore, we would expect children's behavior to be flexible and changeable, as in fact it seems to be.)

Situational adjustment and commitment are closely related, but by no means identical, processes. Situational adjustment produces change; the person shifts his behavior with each shift in the

situation. Commitment produces stability; the person subordinates immediate situational interests to goals that lie outside the situation. But a stable situation can evoke a well-adjusted pattern of behavior which itself becomes valuable to the person, one of the counters that has meaning in the game he is playing. He can become committed to preserving the adjustment.

We find another such complementary relationship between the two when we consider the length of time one is conventionally expected to spend in a situation, either by oneself or by others, and the degree to which the present situation is seen as having definite connections to important situations anticipated at some later stage of development. If one sees that his present situation is temporary and that later situations will demand something different, the process of adjustment will promote change. If one thinks of the present situation as likely to go on for a long time, he may resist what appear to him temporary situational changes because the strength of the adjustment has committed him to maintaining it. This relationship requires a fuller analysis than I have given it here.

CONCLUSION

The processes we have considered indicate that social structure creates the conditions for both change and stability in adult life. The structural characteristics of institutions and organizations provide the framework of the situations in which experience dictates the expediency of change. Similarly, they provide the counters with which side-bets can be made and the links between lines of activity out of which commitment grows. Together, they enable us to arrive at general explanations of personal development in adult life without requiring us to posit unvarying characteristics of the person, either elements of personality or of "value structure."

A structural explanation of personal change has important implications for attempts to deliberately

[18]Becker, *et al., Boys in White, op. cit.,* pp. 254–73.

mold human behavior. In particular, it suggests that we need not try to develop deep and lasting interests, be they values or personality traits, in order to produce the behavior we want. It is enough to create situations which will coerce people into behaving as we want them to and then to create the conditions under which other rewards will become linked to continuing this behavior. A final medical example will make the point. We can agree, perhaps, that surgeons ought not to operate unless there is a real need to do so; the problem of "unnecessary surgery" has received a great deal of attention both within and outside the medical profession. We might achieve our end by inculcating this rule as a basic value during medical training; or we might use personality tests to select as surgeons only those men whose own needs would lead them to exercise caution. In fact, this problem is approaching solution through a structural innovation: the hospital tissue committee, which examines all tissue removed at surgery and disciplines those surgeons who too frequently remove healthy tissue. Surgeons, whatever their values or personalities, soon learn to be careful when faced with the alternative of exposure or discipline.

PART FIVE

MOTIVES

The sociological approach to motivation begins with an innocuous-looking proposition: *Man is active naturally*. With this stroke, John Dewey relegates to the scrap heap of elegant tautology and/or compelling mystery all attempts to explain action by inside urges and outside attractions. Pushes and pulls are preempted. To some, this unassuming proposition is outrageous, for it discards, out of hand, all attempts to explain *why* man acts in the first place. On the inside, impulsion by instincts, needs, drives, and tension reduction are eliminated, while on the outside, physical, social, cultural, and other such presumed environmental stimuli are neglected. Man simply acts, period!

The sense of Dewey's position, in the selection reprinted here, is that the audience "sees" a given act as displeasing or bad and attempts to get the actor to reassess his action from its point of view. Presumably, the challenging audience (which might be oneself) has some notion of a more acceptable alternative and believes the actor capable of achieving it. If the audience can specify the desirable consequences flowing from the more acceptable alternative, it may well succeed in getting the act redirected. Following Dewey's lead thus shifts the problem of motivation from the strictly psychological to the social psychological by emphasizing the process of interpersonal social control.

For the sociologist, then, motivation is a question of direction, not origination of action. For the sociologist, as with his subjects, the question of motivation arises in those instances where ongoing or anticipated conduct breaches expectation and mobilizes a control reaction from others. This reaction takes the form of a motivational challenge that asks in effect: "Why are you engaging in a deviation from expectation when you might well be doing what is expected of you?"

Probing the function of motives within situated action, C. W. Mills is concerned particularly with how actors use motives to interpret each other's conduct. Rather than explain action from the standpoint of motives, he sets out to explain motives from the standpoint of action. Specifically, he wants to know:

1. Which action situations require a verbalization of motives?
2. Why are some motives verbalized but not others?
3. How, in fact, are motives linked to action?

Mills' answer to the first question is similar to that implied by Dewey. Unexpected conduct occurs and precipitates crisis. The deviant act is usually challenged in the form of a question. In response to the challenge, a motive is verbalized. The function of the motive is to satisfy the challenger by giving him a rationale that makes the disputed act intelligible. This rationale usually consists of a reference to the end toward which the disputed conduct was headed. If the challenger can reinterpret the disputed conduct as a means to an end, and if he deems that end worthy, presumably he will rescind his objection.

The answer to Mills' second question hinges on the legitimacy of the end that is presented. Different social circles typically value different ends. For a motive to be efficacious, it had better verbalize an anticipated consequence that the challenger finds credible. Of course, this means an actor may be quite strategic in his selection of motives. He may pick just the right motive with which to interpret his action. The actor may be aware that certain motives have currency in the social circle of the challenger. The general implication here is that certain social circles may have typical vocabularies of motive that may be invoked in certain typical situations. As Mills sees it, a fruitful line of investigation would be the identification of such social circles and their characteristic vocabularies of motive, keeping in mind that at different historical moments and in different societal circumstances what is characteristic will change.

The question that Mills raises but does not answer, concerning the linkage between motives and action, is faced squarely by Nelson N. Foote. To fill the "unanalyzed hiatus between words and acts," Foote introduces the concept of "identification."

First, he declares that we ought not talk about "motives" in general, but "motivated acts" in particular. Such acts are characterized by choice, control, and an agenda. Activities that are not so characterized, like habitual behavior and physiological functioning, should not be included in a discussion of motivated acts.

Given choices made in terms of preferred ends-in-view, or in anticipation of specific consummations (agenda), how do we insert this abstract calculus into the activity sequences of concrete human actors? Put another way, why should people undertake certain choices and the actions they imply in order to achieve certain ends when they might well make other choices on the basis of other ends? Foote's answer is that the individual chooses means and ends on the basis of his understanding or conception of who he is. If I am so and so, then I will want such and such, and accordingly will do this rather than that.

How, then, do I know who I am? Although Foote does not carry the analysis too far, he does maintain that I can only discover who I am in interaction with other people through the process of mutual categorization or identification. This means that establishing one's own identity as well as that of others is problematic in many situations. If I announce myself to be a Social Democrat, and my radical friends place me as an "establishment lackey," we are going to have identification problems. If I reach the point where I myself am not sure whether I'm the only sane voice left or, indeed, have sold out the cause, my ability to act with determination may be jeopardized.

Who I can be is contingent, in part, on the willingness of others in the situation to accept me for who I say I am. Accordingly, the alternatives available to me in a situation are coordinated with the range of possibilities others allow me. Where alternative identities, in fact, are available, presumably I will appropriate that identity I value most.

The question of value thus presupposes the appropriation of identity, for it is the decision criterion upon which the choice is made. Foote reminds us that meaningful value is experienced or felt value; it is discovered in one's own concrete experience and is not mere conception. Memory of experienced value becomes advisory to but not determinative of the appropriation of identity. Still, it must be remembered that, by and large, an individual's own felt value gains advisory capacity if it resonates with the values of the larger social circle.

Marvin Scott and Stanford Lyman follow this general line of development as they examine more closely the function of motives relative to their currency in particular social circles and in the negotiation of identities. They begin their discussion by introducing the term "account." Accounts presumably supersede the more ambiguous term "motives," but like motives are devices employed to reintegrate disrupted conduct. There are two kinds of accounts: (1) *justifications,* where one assumes responsibility for what he is accused of but sees nothing wrong in what he did and (2) *excuses,* where one refuses to take responsibility.

After adducing a suggestive typology of excuses, which include appeals to accidents, defeasibility, biological drives, and scapegoating, Scott and Lyman contend that certain social circles in dealing with deviation from expectation characteristically invoke certain types of appeal in formulating excuses. For example, blacks and adolescent delinquents formulate excuses that invoke "fatalism" or lack of control over events. "If forces beyond my control determine how I behave, how can I be blamed for my transgressions?"

Unlike excuses, justifications are efforts to interpret the deviation as an act that should be seen as legitimate so that one ought to be able to claim responsibility for it.

Whether or not accounts will be honored depends on their currency in the social circle in which they are offered. In most circles, there is a set of taken-for-granted accounts that are honored invariably. As an example, "I'm having family problems" generally goes undisputed and may be used in a variety of different situations.

Scott and Lyman next consider challenges and accounts vis-à-vis the negotiation of identities. Often, identities must be established as a prerequisite to the exchange of challenges and accounts. Certain identities simply are not open to challenge. Privates do not usually challenge the conduct of generals.

The negotiation of identities can be seen as a power play involving such tactics as mystification, referral, and switching whereby each participant tries to outmaneuver the other—the implication being that the dominant identity controls the flow of motivational challenges and, as such, the establishment of credibility. Generally, who can challenge, who is challenged, and the kind of accounts presented depend upon the distribution of identities.

John Hewitt and Randall Stokes further develop the relationship between motive and identity by introducing the notion of "disclaimers" and by drawing attention to the identity risks which any disclaimer involves. Whereas "accounts" are forthcoming *after* challenges have taken place and aim to reconstruct the past in the present, disclaimers are forthcoming *before* challenges occur and aim to construct the future in the present. In either use, however, the objective is to render acceptable what has been or might be untoward conduct.

There are, at least, five types of disclaimers: (1) hedging, where the individual signals minimal commitment to a forthcoming statement, (2) credentialing, where special expertise is involved, (3) sin licenses, where a general rule that admits of particular violations is mentioned, (4) cognitive disclaimers, where reassurance of accurate understanding is offered, and (5) appeals for the suspension of judgment, where forebearance is requested until the full meaning of what is said is established.

Despite the type of disclaimer offered, the presenter always runs the risk of damaging his own identity in that each disclaimer contains and reveals a meaning, value, or sentiment upon which the audience may well frown. The presenter, therefore, faces the problem of balancing out the risks to identity inherent in the disclaimer against the benefits of having the disclaimer accepted. A totally successful disclaimer would occur, then, if the presenter imposed the substance of the disclaimer without sustaining damage to identity, and a totally unsuccessful disclaimer would occur if the presenter were unable to impose the disclaimer and to prevent identity damage. Thus, Hewitt and Stokes lift into greater relief the relationship between retrospective (and prospective) motives and the dynamics of identity maintenance.

Insofar as a line of cumulative development has emerged within the interactionist orientation to motives, it seems to emphasize the following: (1) the steering or control dimension of joint action, (2) the direction (as opposed to the origination) of action, (3) the explanation of motives in terms of action (as opposed to action in terms of motives), (4) the capacity of the actor strategically to choose situationally efficacious motives, (5) the pivotal role of the actor's identity for selection of a motive, (6) the foundational function of lived-through experience as the source of felt value and thus identity preferences, and (7) the placement of habitual behavior and physiological functioning beyond the domain of motivated action.

Despite the progressive development of this approach, we wish to disclose its continuing *cognitive, discursive,* and *unilateral* bias. The cognitive bias is reflected in the assumption that there is an initial or ultimate awareness on the part of both the initiators and challengers as to the status of the untoward line of conduct. Yet, it frequently is the case that actors with vested interests disguise such conduct precisely to circumvent the awareness (and potential challenge) of co-participants. By shaping the material and ideological context of co-participants, actors with vested interests keep untoward conduct beyond focal concern. This sort of "contextual engineering" invites a broader, more transcendent approach to the study of motives.

The discursive bias assumes that motivational exchanges are always, or even usually, verbal. However, can't motives also be seen, as parts of observable acts, rather than heard, as parts of verbal acts? A uniformed policeman directing traffic is clothed in motive; a plain-clothed policeman directing traffic is in for a challenge. A curl of the lips, an alteration of body posture, a touch, a glance—each of these may devastatingly reflect and thematize a general attitude of intense challenge. To what extent, then, are unspoken challenges the sanctioning framework of everyday life?

The unilateral bias is reflected in the assumption that untoward action is always or even usually challenged. But, if a close friend recurrently breaches expectations, would you challenge and risk losing the friendship; or, would you put up with it? In fact, who challenges whom, when, how, and why? Indeed, are there any conventions for stipulating the appropriateness of both challenges and motives? We can begin to specify the conditions under which challenges and imputations are made or avoided. A simple 2 × 2 table might force the issue:

	Impute	Don't Impute
Challenge	1	2
Don't challenge	3	4

When we impute motives but do not challenge behavior (3), as we might in the case of a uniformed policeman directing traffic, aren't we contributing to social stability by assuming we know why that type of person, in that type of situation, is acting as he is? When we neither impute nor challenge (4), aren't we enacting habitual, routine, taken-for-granted behavior? When we don't impute but do challenge (2), aren't we reacting to someone who has us confused as to who he is? And, when we both challenge and impute, aren't we being typical true believers who offer the "real" reasons behind offensive behavior? Whatever promise these leads hold, the least we can say is that further inquiry into the relationships between identity, motive, situation, and context will be exciting and difficult.

SUGGESTED READINGS

Blum, Alan F. and Peter McHugh. "The Social Ascription of Motives." *American Sociological Review,* XXXVI (36 Spring: 98−109, 1971), pp. 98−109.

Blumstein, P. W., et al. "The Honoring of Accounts." *American Sociological Review,* 39, 4, (August, 1974), pp. 551−566.

Burke, Kenneth. *A Grammar of Motives and a Rhetoric of Motives.* Cleveland and New York: World Publishing Co., 1962.

———. *Permanence and Change.* Los Altos, Calif.: Hermes Publications, 1954.

Cressey, Donald R. "Role Theory, Differential Association, and Compulsive Crimes," in Arnold M. Rose (ed.), *Human Behavior and Social Process.* Boston: Houghton Mifflin Co., 1962, pp. 443−467.

Dewey, John. *Human Nature and Conduct.* New York: Modern Library, 1950.

Gecas, Viktor. "Motives and Aggressive Acts in Popular Fiction: Sex and Class Differences." *American Journal of Sociology,* 77, 4 (January, 1972), pp. 680−696.

Hall, Peter M. and John P. Hewitt. "The Quasi-Theory of Communication and Management of Dissent." *Social Problems,* XVIII (Summer, 1970), pp. 17−27.

Hewitt, John P. and Peter M. Hall. "Social Problems, Problematic Situations, and Quasi-Theories." *American Sociological Review,* XXXVIII (June, 1973), pp. 367−374.

MacIver, Robert M. *Social Causation.* New York: Ginn and Co., 1942, pp. 203−223.

Peters, R. S. *The Concept of Motivation*. London: Routledge and Kegan Paul, 1958.

Schutz, Alfred. "In-Order-To and Because Motive." *Collected Papers I: The Problem of Social Reality*. The Hague: Martinus Nijhoff, 1967, pp. 69−72.

Shibutani, Tamotsu. "A Cybernetics Approach to Motivation," in W. Buckley (ed.), *Modern Systems Research for the Behavioral Scientist*. Chicago: Aldine, 1968, pp. 330−336.

Stone, Gregory P. and Lea Hagoel. "Über den Umgang mit Motiven" ("On Motive Talk"). *Kölner Zeitschrift für Soziologie und Sozialpsychologie,* Sonderheft 20 (1978), pp. 30−66.

Szazs, Thomas. *Law, Liberty and Psychiatry*. New York: Macmillan, 1963.

Zetterberg, Hans. "On Motivation," in Joseph Berger et al., *Sociological Theories in Process I*. Boston: Houghton Mifflin Co., 1966, pp. 124−141.

TWENTY-SEVEN

ON MOTIVE

JOHN DEWEY

Any one who observes children knows that while periods of rest are natural, laziness is an acquired vice—or virtue. While a man is awake he will do something, if only to build castles in the air. If we like the form of words we may say that a man eats only because he is "moved" by hunger. The statement is nevertheless mere tautology. For what does hunger mean except that one of the things which man does naturally, instinctively, is to search for food—that his activity naturally turns that way? Hunger primarily names an act or active process not a motive to an act. It is an act if we take it grossly, like a babe's blind hunt for the mother's breast; it is activity if we take it minutely as a chemico-physiological occurrence.

The whole concept of motives is in truth extra-psychological. It is an outcome of the attempt of men to influence human action, first that of others, then of a man to influence his own behavior. No sensible person thinks of attributing the acts of an animal or an idiot to a motive. We call a biting dog ugly, but we don't look for his motive in biting. If

however we were able to direct the dog's action by inducing him to reflect upon his acts, we should at once become interested in the dog's motives for acting as he does, and should endeavor to get him interested in the same subject. It is absurd to ask what induces a man to activity generally speaking. He is an active being and that is all there is to be said on that score. But when we want to get him to act in this specific way rather than in that, when we want to direct his activity that is to say in a specified channel, then the question of motive is pertinent. A motive is then that element in the total complex of a man's activity which, if it can be sufficiently stimulated, will result in an act having specified consequences. And part of the process of intensifying (or reducing) certain elements in the total activity and thus regulating actual consequence is to impute these elements to a person as his actuating motives.

A child naturally grabs food. But he does it in our presence. His manner is socially displeasing and we attribute to his act, up to this time wholly innocent, the motive of greed or selfishness. Greediness simply means the quality of his act as socially observed and disapproved. But by attributing it to him as his motive for acting in the disapproved way, we induce him to refrain. We analyze his total act and call his attention to an obnoxious element in its outcome. A child with equal spontaneity, or thoughtlessness, gives way to others. We point out to him with approval that he acted considerately, generously. And this quality of action when noted and encouraged becomes a reinforcing stimulus of that factor which will induce similar acts in the future. An element in an act viewed as a tendency to produce such and such consequences is a motive. A motive does not exist prior to an act and produce it. It is an act *plus* a judgment upon some element of it, the judgment being made in the light of the consequences of the act.

TWENTY-EIGHT

SITUATED ACTIONS AND VOCABULARIES OF MOTIVE

C. WRIGHT MILLS

The major reorientation of recent theory and observation in sociology of language emerged with the overthrow of the Wundtian notion that language has as its function the "expression" of prior elements within the individual. The postulate underlying modern study of language is the simple one that we must approach linguistic behavior, not by referring it to private states in individuals, but by observing its social function of coordinating diverse action. Rather than expressing something which is prior and in the person, language is taken by other persons as an indicator of future actions.[1]

Within this perspective there are suggestions concerning problems of motivation. It is the purpose of this paper to outline an analytic model for the explanation of motives which is based on a sociological theory of language and a sociological psychology.[2]

As over against the inferential conception of motives as subjective "springs" of action, motives may be considered as typical vocabularies having ascertainable functions in delimited societal situations. Human actors do vocalize and impute motives to themselves and to others. To explain behavior by referring it to an inferred and abstract "motive" is one thing. To analyze the observable lingual mechanisms of motive imputation and avowal as they function in conduct is quite another. Rather than fixed elements "in" an individual, motives are the terms with which interpretation of conduct *by social actors* proceeds. This imputation and avowal of motives by actors are social phenomena to be explained. The differing reasons men give for their actions are not themselves without reasons.

SOURCE: C. Wright Mills. "Situated Actions and Vocabularies of Motive." Copyright by the American Sociological Association. Copyright renewed 1968 by Yaraslava Mills. C. Wright Mills, "Situated Actions and Vocabularies of Motive," *American Sociological Review*, V (October, 1940), pp. 904–913. Reprinted by permission of Brandt & Brandt.

Revision of a paper read to The Society for Social Research, University of Chicago, August 16–17, 1940.

[1]See C. Wright Mills, "Bibliographical Appendices," Section I, 4: "Sociology of Language" in *Contemporary Social Theory*, ed. by Barnes, Becker & Becker, New York, 1940.

[2]See G. H. Mead, "Social Psychology as Counterpart of Physiological Psychology," *Psychol. Bul.*, VI: 401–408, 1909; Karl Mannheim, *Man and Society in an Age of Reconstruction*, New York, 1940; L. V. Wiese-Howard Becker, *Systematic Sociology*, part I, New York, 1932; J. Dewey, "All psychology is either biological or social psychology," *Psychol. Rev.*, vol. 24:276.

First, we must demarcate the general conditions under which such motive imputation and avowal seem to occur.[3] Next, we must give a characterization of motive in denotable terms and an explanatory paradigm of why certain motives are verbalized rather than others. Then, we must indicate mechanisms of the linkage of vocabularies of motive to systems of action. What we want is an analysis of the integrating, controlling, and specifying function a certain type of speech fulfills in socially situated actions.

The generic situation in which imputation and avowal of motives arise involves, first, the *social* conduct or the (stated) programs of languaged creatures, i.e., programs and actions oriented with reference to the actions and talk of others; second, the avowal and imputation of motives is concomitant with the speech form known as the "question." Situations back of questions typically involve *alternative* or *unexpected* programs or actions which phases analytically denote "crises."[4] The question is distinguished in that it usually elicits another *verbal* action, not a motor response. The question is an element in *conversation*. Conversation may be concerned with the factual features of a situation as they are seen or believed to be or it may seek to integrate and promote a set of diverse social actions with reference to the situation and its normative pattern of expectations. It is in this latter assent and dissent phase of conversation that persuasive and dissuasive speech and vocabulary arise. For men live in immediate acts of experience and their attentions are directed outside themselves until acts are in some way frustrated. It is then that awareness of self and of motive occur.

The "question" is a lingual index of such conditions. The avowal and imputation of motives are features of such conversations as arise in "question" situations.

Motives are imputed or avowed as answers to questions interrupting acts or programs. Motives are words. Generically, to what do they refer? They do not denote any elements "in" individuals. They stand for anticipated situational consequences of questioned conduct. Intention or purpose (stated as a "program") *is* awareness of anticipated consequence; motives are names for consequential situations, and surrogates for actions leading to them. Behind questions are possible alternative actions with their terminal consequences. "Our introspective words for motives are rough, shorthand descriptions for certain typical patterns of discrepant and conflicting stimuli."[5]

The model of purposive conduct associated with Dewey's name may briefly be stated. Individuals confronted with "alternative acts" perform one or the other of them on the basis of the differential consequences which they anticipate. This nakedly utilitarian schema is inadequate because: (a) the "alternative acts" of *social* conduct "appear" most often in lingual form, as a question, stated by one's self or by another; (b) it is more adequate to say that individuals act in terms of anticipation of *named* consequences.

Among such names and in some technologically oriented lines of action there may appear such terms as "useful," "practical," "serviceable," etc., terms so "ultimate" to the pragmatists, and also to certain sectors of the American population in these delimited situations. However, there are other areas of population with different vocabularies of motives. The choice of lines of action is accompanied by representations, and selection among them, of their situational termini. Men discern situations with particular vocabularies, and it is in terms of some delimited vocabulary that

---

[3]The importance of this initial task for research is clear. Most researches on the verbal level merely ask abstract questions of individuals, but if we can tentatively delimit the situations in which certain motives *may* be verbalized, we can use that delimitation in the construction of *situational* questions, and we shall be *testing* deductions from our theory.

[4]On the "question" and "conversation," see G. A. DeLaguna, *Speech: Its Function and Development*, 37 (and index), New Haven, 1927. For motives in crises, see J. M. Williams, *The Foundations of Social Science*, 435 ff., New York, 1920.

[5]K. Burke, *Permanence and Change*, 45, New York, 1936. I am indebted to this book for several leads which are systematized into the present statement.

they anticipate consequences of conduct.[6] Stable vocabularies of motives link anticipated consequences and specific actions. There is no need to invoke ''psychological'' terms like ''desire'' or ''wish'' as explanatory, since they themselves must be explained socially.[7] Anticipation is a subvocal or overt naming of terminal phases and/or social consequences of conduct. When an individual names consequences, he elicits the behaviors for which the name is a red integrative cue. In a *societal* situation, implicit in the names of consequences is the social dimension of motives. Through such vocabularies, types of societal controls operate. Also, the terms in which the question is asked often will contain both alternatives: ''Love or Duty?'', ''Business or Pleasure?'' Institutionally different situations have different *vocabularies of motive* appropriate to their respective behaviors.

This sociological conception of motives as relatively stable lingual phases of delimited situations is quite consistent with Mead's program to approach conduct socially and from the outside. It keeps clearly in mind that ''both motives and actions very often originate not from within but from the situation in which individuals find themselves. . . .''[8] It translates the question of ''why''[9] into a ''how'' that is answerable in terms of a situation and its typal vocabulary of motives, i.e., those which conventionally accompany that type situation and function as cues and justifications for normative actions in it.

It has been indicated that the question is usually an index to the avowal and imputation of motives. Max Weber defines motive as a complex of meaning, which appears to the actor himself or to the observer to be an adequate ground for his con-

duct.[10] The aspect of motive which this conception grasps is its intrinsically social character. A satisfactory or adequate motive is one that satisfies the questioners of an act or program whether it be the other's or the actor's. As a word, *a motive tends to be one which is to the actor and to the other members of a situation an unquestioned answer to questions concerning social and lingual conduct.* A stable motive is an ultimate in justificatory conversation. The words which in a type situation will fulfil this function are circumscribed by the vocabulary of motives acceptable for such situations. Motives are accepted justifications for present, future, or past programs or acts.

To term them justification is *not* to deny their efficacy. Often anticipations of acceptable justifications will control conduct. (''If I did this, what could I say? What would they say?'') Decisions may be, wholly or in part, delimited by answers to such queries.

A man may begin an act for one motive. In the course of it, he may adopt an ancillary motive. This does not mean that the second apologetic motive is inefficacious. The vocalized expectation of an act, its ''reason,'' is not only a mediating condition of the act but it is a proximate and controlling condition for which the term ''cause'' is not inappropriate. It may strengthen the act of the actor. It may win new allies for his act.

When they appeal to others involved in one's act, motives are strategies of action. In many social actions, others must agree, tacitly or explicitly. Thus, acts often will be abandoned if no reason can be found that others will accept. Diplomacy in choice of motive often controls the diplomat. Diplomatic choice of motive is part of the attempt to motivate acts for other members in a situation. Such pronounced motives undo snarls and inte-

[6]See such experiments as C. N. Rexroat's ''Verbalization in Multiple Choice Reactions,'' *Psychol. Rev.*, Vol. 33:458, 1926.

[7]Cf. J. Dewey, ''Theory of Valuation,'' *Int. Ency. of Unified Science*, New York, 1939.

[8]K. Mannheim, *Man and Society*, 249, London, 1940.

[9]Conventionally answerable by reference to ''subjective factors'' within individuals. R. M. MacIver, ''The Modes of the Question Why,'' *J. of Soc. Phil.*, April, 1940. Cf. also his ''The Imputation of Motives,'' *Amer. J. Sociol.*, July, 1940.

[10]*Wirtschaft und Gesellschaft*, 5, Tubingen, 1922, '''Motiv' heisst ein Sinnzusammenhang, welcher dem Handelnden selbst oder dem Beobachtenden als sinnhafter 'Grund' eines Verhaltens in dem Grade heissen, als die Beziehung seiner Bestandteile von uns nach den durchschnittlichen Denk- und Gefühlsgewohnheiten als typischer (wir pflegen in sagen: 'rightiger') Sinnzusammenhang bejaht wird.''

grate social actions. Such diplomacy does not necessarily imply intentional lies. It merely indicates that an appropriate vocabulary of motives will be utilized—that they are conditions for certain lines of conduct.[11]

When an agent vocalizes or imputes motives, he is not trying to *describe* his experienced social action. He is not merely stating "reasons." He is influencing others—and himself. Often he is finding new "reasons" which will mediate action. Thus, we need not treat an action as discrepant from "its" verbalization, for in many cases, the verbalization is a new act. In such cases, there is not a discrepancy between an act and "its" verbalization, but a difference between two disparate actions, motor-social and verbal.[12] This additional (or "*ex post facto*") lingualization may involve appeal to a vocabulary of motives associated with a norm with which both members of the situation are in agreement. As such, it is an integrative factor in *future* phases of the original social action or in other acts. By resolving conflicts, motives are efficacious. Often, if "reasons" were not given, an act would not occur, nor would diverse actions be integrated. Motives are common grounds for mediated behaviors.

Perry summarily states the Freudian view of motives "as the view that the real motives of conduct are those which we are ashamed to admit either to ourselves or to others."[13] One can cover the facts by merely saying that scruples (i.e., *moral* vocabularies of motive) are often efficacious and that men will alter and deter their acts in terms of such motives. One of the components of a "generalized other," as a mechanism of societal control, is vocabularies of acceptable motives. For example, a businessman joins the Rotary Club and proclaims its public-spirited vocabulary.[14] If this

man cannot act out business conduct without so doing, it follows that this vocabulary of motives is an important factor in his behavior.[15] The long acting out of a role, with its appropriate motives, will often induce a man to become what at first he merely sought to appear. Shifts in the vocabularies of motive that are utilized later by an individual disclose an important aspect of various integrations of his actions with concomitantly various groups.

The motives actually used in justifying or criticizing an act definitely link it to situations, integrate one man's action with another's, and line up conduct with norms. The societally sustained motive-surrogates of situations are both constraints and inducements. It is a hypothesis worthy and capable of test that typal vocabularies of motives for different situations are significant determinants of conduct. As lingual segments of social action, motives orient actions by enabling discrimination between their objects. Adjectives such as "good," "pleasant," and "bad" promote action or deter it. When they constitute components of a vocabulary of motives, i.e., are typical and relatively unquestioned accompaniments of typal situations, such words often function as directives and incentives by virtue of their being the judgments of others as anticipated by the actor. In this sense motives are "social instruments, i.e., data by modifying which the agent will be able to influence [himself or others]."[16] The "control" of others is not usually direct but rather through manipulation of a field of objects. We influence a man by naming his acts or imputing motives to them—or to "him." The motives accompanying institutions of war, e.g., are not "the causes" of war, but they do promote continued integrated participation, and they vary from one war to the next. Working vocabularies of

---

[11]Of course, since motives are communicated, they may be lies; but, this must be proved. Verbalizations are not lies merely because they are socially efficacious. I am here concerned more with the social function of pronounced motives, than with the sincerity of those pronouncing them.

[12]See F. Znaniecki, *Social Actions*, 30, New York, 1936.

[13]*General Theory of Value*, 292–93, New York, 1936.

[14]*Ibid.*, 392.

[15]The "profits motive" of classical economics may be treated as an ideal-typical vocabulary of motives for delimited economic situations and behaviors. For late phases of monopolistic and regulated capitalism, this type requires modification; the profit and commercial vocabularies have acquired other ingredients. See N. R. Danielian's *AT & T*, New York, 1940, for a suggestive account of the *noneconomic* behavior and motives of business bureaucrats.

[16]*Social Actions*, 73.

motive have careers that are woven through changing institutional fabrics.

Genetically, motives are imputed by others before they are avowed by self. The mother controls the child: "Do not do that, it is greedy." Not only does the child learn what to do, what not to do, but he is given standardized motives which promote prescribed actions and dissuade those proscribed. Along with rules and norms of action for various situations, we learn vocabularies of motives appropriate to them. These are the motives we shall use, since they are a part of our language and components of our behavior.

The quest for "real motives" supposititiously set over against "mere rationalization" is often informed by a metaphysical view that the "real" motives are in some way biological. Accompanying such quests for something more real and back of rationalization is the view held by many sociologists that language is an external manifestation or concomitant of something prior, more genuine, and "deep" in the individual. "Real attitudes" versus "mere verbalization" or "opinion" implies that at best we only infer from his language what "really" is the individual's attitude or motive.

Now what *could we possibly* so infer? Of precisely *what* is verbalization symptomatic? We cannot *infer* physiological processes from lingual phenomena. All we can infer and empirically check[17] is another verbalization of the agent's which we believe was orienting and controlling behavior at the time the act was performed. The only social items that can "lie deeper" are other lingual forms.[18] The "Real Attitude or Motive" is not something different in kind from the verbalization or the "opinion." They turn out to be only relatively and temporally different.

The phrase "unconscious motive" is also unfortunate. All it can mean is that a motive is not explicitly vocalized, but there is no need to infer unconscious motives from such situations and then posit them in individuals as elements. The phrase is informed by persistence of the unnecessary and unsubstantiated notion that "all action has a motive," and it is promoted by the observation of gaps in the relatively frequent verbalization in everyday situations. The facts to which this phrase is supposedly addressed are covered by the statements that men do not always explicitly articulate motives, and that *all* actions do not pivot around language. I have already indicated the conditions under which motives are typically avowed and imputed.

Within the perspective under consideration, the verbalized motive is not used as an index of something in the individual but *as a basis of inference for a typical vocabulary of motives of a situated action.* When we ask for the "real attitude" rather than the "opinion," for the "real motive" rather than the "rationalization," all we can meaningfully be asking for is the controlling speech form which was incipiently or overtly presented in the performed act or series of acts. There is no way to plumb behind verbalization into an individual and directly check our motive-mongering, but there is an empirical way in which we can guide and limit, in given historical situations, investigations of motives. That is by the construction of typal vocabularies of motives that are extant in types of situations and actions. Imputation of motives may be controlled by reference to the typical constellation of motives which are observed to be societally linked with classes of situated actions. Some of the "real" motives that have been imputed to actors were not even known to them. As I see it, motives are circumscribed by the vocabulary of the actor. The only source for a terminology of motives is the vocabularies of motives actually and usually verbalized by actors in specific situations.

Individualistic, sexual, hedonistic, and pecuniary vocabularies of motives are apparently now dominant in many sectors of twentieth-century urban America. Under such an ethos,

---

[17]Of course, we could infer or interpret constructs posited in the individual, but these are not easily checked and they are not explanatory.

[18]Which is not to say that, physiologically, there may not be cramps in the stomach wall or adrenalin in the blood, etc., but the character of the "relation" of such items to social action is quite moot.

verbalization of alternative conduct in these terms is least likely to be challenged among dominant groups. In this milieu, individuals are skeptical of Rockefeller's avowed religious motives for his business conduct because such motives are not *now* terms of the vocabulary conventionally and prominently accompanying situations of business enterprise. A medieval monk writes that he gave food to a poor but pretty woman because it was "for the glory of God and the eternal salvation of his soul." Why do we tend to question him and impute sexual motives? Because sex is an influential and widespread motive in our society and time. Religious vocabularies of explanation and of motives are now on the wane. In a society in which religious motives have been debunked on a rather wide scale, certain thinkers are skeptical of those who ubiquitously proclaim them. Religious motives have lapsed from selected portions of modern populations and other motives have become "ultimate" and operative. But from the monasteries of medieval Europe we have no evidence that religious vocabularies were not operative in many situations.

A labor leader says he performs a certain act because he wants to get higher standards of living for the workers. A businessman says that this is rationalization, or a lie; that it is really because he wants more money for himself from the workers. A radical says a college professor will not engage in radical movements because he is afraid for his job, and besides, is a "reactionary." The college professor says it is because he just likes to find out how things work. What is reason for one man is rationalization for another. The variable is the accepted vocabulary of motives, the ultimates of discourse, of each man's dominant group about whose opinion he cares. *Determination of such groups, their location and character, would enable delimitation and methodological control of assignment of motives for specific acts.*

Stress on this idea will lead us to investigations of the compartmentalization of operative motives in personalities according to situation and the general types and conditions of vocabularies of motives in various types of societies. The motivational structures of individuals and the patterns of their purposes are relative to societal frames. We might, e.g., study motives along stratified or occupational lines. Max Weber has observed:[19]

> . . . that in a free society the motives which induce people to work vary with . . . different social classes. . . . There is normally a graduated scale of motives by which men from different social classes are driven to work. When a man changes ranks, he switches from one set of motives to another.

The lingual ties which hold them together react on persons to constitute frameworks of disposition and motive. Recently, Talcott Parsons has indicated, by reference to differences in actions in the professions and in business, that one cannot leap from "economic analysis to ultimate motivations; the institutional patterns *always* constitute one crucial element of the problem."[20] It is my suggestion that we may analyze, index, and gauge this element by focusing upon those specific verbal appendages of variant institutionalized actions which have been referred to as vocabularies of motive.

In folk societies, the constellations of motives connected with various sectors of behavior would tend to be typically stable and remain associated only with their sector. In typically primary, sacred, and rural societies, the motives of persons would be regularly compartmentalized. Vocabularies of motives ordered to different situations stabilize and guide behavior and expectation of the reactions of others. In their appropriate situations, verbalized motives are not typically questioned.[21] In second-

---

[19]Paraphrased by K. Mannheim, 316–17.

[20]"The Motivation of Economic Activities," 67, in C. W. M. Hart, *Essays in Sociology,* Toronto, 1940.

[21]Among the ethnologists, Ruth Benedict has come up to the edge of a genuinely sociological view of motivation. Her view remains vague because she has not seen clearly the identity of differing "motivations" in differing cultures with the varied extant and approved vocabularies of motive. "The intelligent understanding of the relation of the individual to his society . . .

ary, secular, and urban structures, varying and competing vocabularies of motives operate coterminously and the situations to which they are appropriate are not clearly demarcated. Motives once unquestioned for defined situations are now questioned. Various motives can release similar acts in a given situation. Hence, variously situated persons are confused and guess which motive "activated" the person. Such questioning has resulted intellectually in such movements as psychoanalysis with its dogma of rationalization and its systematic motive-mongering. Such intellectual phenomena are underlaid by split and conflicting sections of an individuated society which is characterized by the existence of competing vocabularies of motive. Intricate constellations of motives, for example, are components of business enterprise in America. Such patterns have encroached on the old style vocabulary of the virtuous relation of men and women: duty, love, kindness. Among certain classes, the romantic, virtuous, and pecuniary motives are confused. The asking of the question: "Marriage for love or money?" is significant, for the pecuniary is now a constant and almost ubiquitous motive, a common denominator of many others.[22]

Back of "mixed motives" and "motivational conflicts" are competing or discrepant situational patterns and their respective vocabularies of motive. With shifting and interstitial situations, each of several alternatives may belong to disparate systems of action which have differing vocabularies of motives appropriate to them. Such conflicts manifest vocabulary patterns that have overlapped in a marginal individual and are not easily compartmentalized in clear-cut situations.

Besides giving promise of explaining an area of lingual and societal fact, a further advantage of this view of motives is that with it we should be able to give sociological accounts of other theories (terminologies) of motivation. This is a task for sociology of knowledge. Here I can refer only to a few theories. I have already referred to the Freudian terminology of motives. It is apparent that these motives are those of an upper bourgeois patriarchal group with strong sexual and individualistic orientation. When introspecting on the couches of Freud, patients used the only vocabulary of motives they knew; Freud got his hunch and guided further talk. Mittenzwey has dealt with similar points at length.[23] Widely diffused in a postwar epoch, psychoanalysis was never popular in France where control of sexual behavior is not puritanical.[24] To converted individuals who have become accustomed to the psychoanalytic terminology of motives, all others seem self-deceptive.[25]

In like manner, to many believers in Marxism's terminology of power, struggle, and economic motives, all others, including Freud's, are due to hypocrisy or ignorance. An individual who has assimilated thoroughly only business congeries of motives will attempt to apply these motives to all situations, home and wife included. It should be noted that the business terminology of motives has its intellectual articulation, even as psychoanalysis and Marxism have.

It is significant that since the Socratic period

---

involves always the understanding of the types of human motivations and capacities capitalized in his society . . ." "Configurations of Culture in North America," *Amer. Anthrop.*, 25, Jan.–Mar. 1932; see also: *Patterns of Culture,* 242–43, Boston, 1935. She turns this observation into a quest for the unique "genius" of each culture and stops her research by words like "Apollonian." If she would attempt constructively to observe the vocabularies of motives which precipitate acts to perform, implement programs, and furnish approved motives for them in circumscribed situations, she would be better able to state precise problems and to answer them by further observation.

[22]Also motives acceptably imputed and avowed for one system of action may be diffused into other domains and gradually come to be accepted by some as a comprehensive portrait of *the* motive of men. This happened in the case of the economic man and his motives.

[23]Kuno Mittenzwey, "Zur Sociologie der psychoanalystischer Erkenntnis," in Max Scheler, ed. *Versuche zu einer Sociologie des Wissens,* 365–375, Munich, 1924.

[24]This fact is interpreted by some as supporting Freudian theories. Nevertheless, it can be just as adequately grasped in the scheme here outlined.

[25]See K. Burke's acute discussion of Freud, *op. cit.*, Part I.

many "theories of motivation" have been linked with ethical and religious terminologies. Motive is that in man which leads him to do good or evil. Under the aegis of religious institutions, men use vocabularies of moral motives: they call acts and programs "good" and "bad," and impute these qualities to the soul. Such lingual behavior is part of the process of social control. Institutional practices and their vocabularies of motive exercise control over delimited ranges of possible situations. One could make a typal catalog of religious motives from widely read religious texts, and test its explanatory power in various denominations and sects.[26]

In many situations of contemporary America, conduct is controlled and integrated by *hedonistic* language. For large population sectors in certain situations, pleasure and pain are now unquestioned motives. For given periods and societies, these situations should be empirically determined. Pleasure and pain should not be reified and imputed to human nature as underlying principles of all action. Note that hedonism as a psychological and an ethical doctrine gained impetus in the modern world at about the time when older moral-religious motives were being debunked and simply discarded by "middle class" thinkers. Back of the hedonistic terminology lay an emergent social pattern and a new vocabulary of motives. The shift of unchallenged motives which gripped the com-

munities of Europe was climaxed when, in reconciliation, the older religious and the hedonistic terminologies were identified: the "good" is the "pleasant." The conditioning situation was similar in the Hellenistic world with the hedonism of the Cyrenaics and Epicureans.

What is needed is to take all these *terminologies* of motive and locate them as *vocabularies* of motive in historic epochs and specified situations. Motives are of no value apart from the delimited societal situations for which they are the appropriate vocabularies. They must be situated. At best, socially unlocated *terminologies* of motives represent unfinished attempts to block out social areas of motive imputation and avowal. Motives vary in content and character with historical epochs and societal structures.

Rather than interpreting actions and language as external manifestations of subjective and deeper lying elements in individuals, the research task is the locating of particular types of action within typal frames of normative actions and socially situated clusters of motive. There is no explanatory value in subsuming various vocabularies of motives under some terminology or list. Such procedure merely confuses the task of explaining specific cases. The languages of situations as given must be considered a valuable portion of the data to be interpreted and related to their conditions. To simplify these vocabularies of motive into a socially abstracted terminology is to destroy the legitimate use of motive in the explanation of social actions.

[26]Moral vocabularies deserve a special statement. Within the viewpoint herein outlined many snarls concerning "value-judgments," etc., can be cleared up.

TWENTY-NINE

IDENTIFICATION AS THE BASIS FOR A THEORY OF MOTIVATION

NELSON N. FOOTE

Role theory has suffered since inception from lack of a satisfactory account of motivation. It is all very well as far as it goes to state that a person learns to recognize standard situations and to play expected roles in them according to the status defined for him in each. But this is not enough when the person encounters alternatives and must resolve conflicting definitions of his appropriate behavior.[1] Nor is it enough to account for the emergence of new roles in his conduct, nor for his more or less unique variations upon conventional roles. A striking revelation of the need for some theory of motivation to back up situational analysis[2] is disclosed by apathy in the performance of conventional roles, when these are on the verge of abandonment or are accepted only under duress. Roles as such do not provide their own motives.

Most of the recent writers on role theory[3] have recognized this deficiency and have endeavored to make it up through the expedient of eclecticism. Like a Ford car with a Chevrolet motor, each of these "integrators" puts on the road his own model of role theory, one powered by psychic energy, another by a system of tensions or a drive-reduction apparatus, a third by some hierarchy of innate and derived needs. Also, a number of models on the road are said to run through some tendency-to-run established through experiences of the early years, these early years being made to do the work of instincts. Despite the unscientific effort of each writer to achieve uniqueness, their theories all share the postulation of motives as

SOURCE: Nelson N. Foote. "Identification as the Basis for a Theory of Motivation." Copyright by the American Sociological Association, 1951. Nelson N. Foote, "Identification as the Basis for a Theory of Motivation," *American Sociological Review*, XVI (February, 1951), pp. 14–21. Reprinted by permission of the American Sociological Association.

Paper read at the annual meeting of the American Sociological Society held in Denver, September 7–9, 1950.

[1]Leonard S. Cottrell, Jr., "The Adjustment of the Individual to His Age and Sex Roles," *American Sociological Review*, 7 (Dec., 1942).

[2]Leonard S. Cottrell, Jr., "The Analysis of Situational Fields in Social Psychology," *American Sociological Review*, 7 (June, 1942).

[3]Walter Coutu, *Emergent Human Nature*, New York: Knopf, 1949; Gardner Murphy, *Personality*, New York: Harper, 1947; Theodore M. Newcomb, *Social Psychology*, New York: Dryden, 1950; S. S. Sargent, *Social Psychology*, New York: Ronald, 1950.

predispositions, purportedly inferred from behavior. As many critics have contended, this either pushes the problem back into an infinite regress or leads circularly to the pseudo-explanation of behavior by inferences from itself.

Only two or three writers, such as Sherif and Cantril[4] or Lindesmith and Strauss[5] come close to dispensing with the effort to sustain a system of predispositions. After much stretching of "frames of reference," however, Sherif and Cantril emerge with an ego consisting of "ego-attitudes," which unlike some other attitudes are not traceable to basic drives, and they promise another work on motivation. Lindesmith and Strauss are far more daring in describing motives, like Mills,[6] as rationalizations of acts, whereby one relates his acts to previous experience and to the values of the groups to which one feels he must justify his behavior. Their analysis correctly calls attention to the function of language in motivation, but leaves the reader with the uncomfortable feeling of an unanalyzed hiatus between words and acts, of mystery as to just how language does in fact motivate. It is this hiatus which the concept of identification seems adequate to fill.

So that we may ignore non-motivated behavior, motivation or motivated behavior has to be defined. We are inclined to scoff at those medieval souls who ascribed purpose to the shape of stones, the falling of water or the absence of beards among women, although remnants of such thinking are common. It is likewise easy to make jokes about Lundberg's assertion that there is no more justification scientifically to seek out the motives of a man who runs down the street than those of a piece of paper which blows down the street, although Lundberg brings strong arguments to support his extreme position. It is far less easy to specify

where between these extremes a line can be drawn to differentiate motivated from non-motivated human behavior.

The growing of whiskers we take to be non-motivated; the shaving of them off, motivated. Going to bed is motivated, sleeping is not. Physiological functions like growth, digestion, circulation, metabolism, are clearly non-motivated, but there are marginal activities of the organism, like elimination, over which conscious control is only slowly won and may be lost under stress. While we may not gain similar direct control over the former functions, there are almost none which cannot be disrupted by psychic stress or modified by manipulation of their physical conditions.

To approach the dividing line from the opposite side, we go from conscious, rational actions involving choice among alternatives to those which seem compulsive or "unconsciously" motivated, but are not universally so, and thence again to those which seem to be physiologically autonomous.

To generalize, motivated behavior is distinguished by its prospective reference to ends in view, by being more or less subject to conscious control through choice among alternative ends and means. All kinds of human behavior are characterized by direction (or form), intensity, frequency and duration; all literally require expenditure of energy. But only motivated behavior exhibits the fluidity of organization, the paradoxical combinations of phenomenally-experienced choice and compulsion ("I don't want to but I have to because . . ."), the dependence upon learning and the content of previous experience, and, above all, the symbolic structuring which must be taken into account even to begin to understand, for example, the prodigies of effort and self-sacrifice put forth by our representatives in Korea. In a sentence, we take motivation to refer to the degree to which a human being, as a participant in the ongoing social process in which he necessarily finds himself, defines a problematic situation as calling for per-

[4]M. Sherif, and H. Cantril, *The Psychology of Ego-Involvements*, New York: Wiley, 1947, pp. 4—8.

[5]A. R. Lindesmith and A. Strauss, *Social Psychology*, New York: Dryden, 1949.

[6]C. W. Mills, "Situated Actions and Vocabularies of Motive," *American Sociological Review*, 5 (December, 1940). Reprinted in Part Five of this volume.

formance of a particular act, with more or less anticipated consummations and consequences, and *thereby* his organism releases the energy appropriate to performing it. Even the behavior consequent to an irritating organic condition, e.g., heat or hunger, has to be defined according to its meaning in the situation and is so defined, often fallibly. Organic *irritations*, which may or may not be anterior to definition of an act, contrary to some predispositionalists, have no direct and uniform connections with organic *mobilizations*, which are always posterior to definition of an act.

To the extent that we find the term *attitude* useful, it is as a synonym for these mobilizations. Definitions of the situation account for attitudes, not the reverse. And to avoid predispositionalist connotations, we prefer not to speak of particular motives, but only of motivated acts. If we were to speak of motives, it would be as rationalizations of acts, in the sense of Mills and Lindesmith—that is, as symbolic constructs which not only organize these acts in particular situations but make them recognizably recurrent in the life-history of any person or group. This pattern of recurrence constitutes what is often reified as "personality" or "culture." But what is it that makes culture and personality in action different from culture and personality in abstraction? We are back where we began.

Consider the game. For brevity's sake, we must assume reader familiarity with Mead's analysis of play, the game and the generalized "other." Let eighteen strangers, familiar with the rules of baseball and having nothing to do, be told to choose up sides and play a game. At the moment the choosing begins, it makes not the slightest difference to any potential player which side he is on—or which side wins, though if competitively indoctrinated, he might want to be on the winning side. The groups, if such they may be called—the two teams—have no identity. If they could go ahead and play under such conditions—of no identity—the game would be almost pointless. True, people would play the roles appropriate to

their positions on the teams, when at bat or in the field, and any physiological needs defined by them as satisfied through exercise might be met. Here would be role theory in action, as Mead left off in describing it[7]—a sort of empty bottle of behavior and formal relations, without motive or incentive save the undifferentiated physiological necessity to dispense energy and kill time. There would be no more reason to obey the rules than to cheat, but the game might proceed by unimaginative observance of them. Since its progress would offer no more interest or involvement to the players than to a spectator ignorant of the rules, it is inconceivable how the observer could ever get them to play it, unless by offering them a reward, such as money, whose value was extraneous to the game itself. Some jobs are like that, but we do not call them games.

Now by contrast consider a ball game like any World Series, when the Mets played the Orioles in 1969. The roles and the statuses are the same, as are the rules of the game. But what a difference! And what is the nature of the difference? It is in the fact that the empty bottle of role and status suddenly has a content. That content is not drives, tensions, energy or needs; it is *identity*. Yet remember that it is still a game; for all the frenzied involvement of players and spectators, of winners and losers, the gain and loss are purely symbolic. Except for the special identity which gives value to their ensuing activity, the behavior of the players would be mere rote—a perfect example of anomie.

As Mead has shown, one learns many more roles than he ever plays overtly. To interact intelligently with another, he must learn correctly to anticipate the responses of that other—that is, to empathize. But implicit role-taking is no metaphysical transmigration of consciousness. It requires playing sub-overtly the role appropriate to the identity of the other in the situation, as accurately as one can read off that identity. In play or in

[7]G. H. Mead, *Mind, Self and Society*, University of Chicago Press, 1934.

role-playing experiments, a person may disclose the great range of his latent repertoire. The reason he limits his real or realistic behavior to a selected few of all the roles he has learned is that he knows and defines only these certain ones as *his own*. And he can only ascertain which role is his in each situation by knowing *who* he is. Moreover, he must know who he is with considerable conviction and clarity, if his behavior is to exhibit definiteness and force, which is to say, degree of motivation.

All of which thus far may seem so patent as to preclude the raising of more analytical questions about the nature of identity and identification. Is it not altogether obvious that the chairman of this meeting, for instance, is Edward Rose, the one who exists at such and such a time and place and performs largely as others hereabout expect him to? Yet it is just this simple and obvious fact that has to be broken down analytically, like the atom, into its various constituents. And as the analogy suggests, the process of analyzing the self into its parts may go on indefinitely.

Intrusion of the concept of *self* here, however, permits mention of what we take to be the misplaced abstractness of much use of it by social psychologists. Just this wrapping of all the particular constituents of a person's identity into one round bundle and labeling it "the self" have long delayed the analysis of the self and of identity. Too-ready generalization of the identities of any given self into indefinitely extensible statuses has led many social psychologists to feel that they must look "behind" the self for the "underlying" motives of the particular kinds of behavior which spring out of it—even to perpetrate such super-generalities as a "drive for self-actualization."

We mean by *identification* appropriation of and commitment to a particular identity or series of identities. As a process, it proceeds by *naming*; its products are ever-evolving self-conceptions—with the emphasis on the *con-*, that is, upon ratification by significant others. If space permitted, it would be valuable to show in detail how much this

concept of identification owes to Freud[8]—where it differs from his concept, and where it supplements. Being more psychologist than sociologist, Freud tends to ignore the functions of language; for all his discussion of identification, he never speaks of identity or common identity. We are not concerned here to kick the dead horse of Freudian instinct theory, nor to appreciate the leads he gave to the study of empathy, but only to affirm that his concept of identification is inadequate as a basis for a situational theory of motivation. Neither is it the missing link of social psychology—a description of the specific tie which unites individuals with their fellows. Yet expansion and reinterpretation in interactional terms of his concept of identification provides both.

In surveying the multitude of predispositional theories of motivation which have been set forth, one is struck not only by their regular failure. Equally striking and suggestive is the seductive—not to say sinister, as Burke[9] charges—appeal which is exerted by the hope of reducing human behavior to some permanently definitive order through finding certain elemental imperatives to underly it bewildering variety. Criticism has negated every specific naming of "the mainsprings of human action." If we now boldly draw the indicated conclusion and deny wholesale the *scientific* validity of all such attempts, it remains illuminating to ask why their great continuing appeal in the face of repeated collapse or supersession.

Upon close examination it seems predictable that such attempts will continue, for what is involved is the necessary activity of every social being, and not merely of social psychologists. Every man must categorize his fellows in order to interact with them. We never approach another person purely as a human being or purely as an

---

[8] Sigmund Freud, *Group Psychology and the Analysis of the Ego*, London: Hogarth, 1922; *The Ego and the Id*, London: Hogarth, 1927.

[9] Kenneth Burke, *A Grammar of Motives*, New York: Prentice-Hall, 1945.

individual. If a being is human, it shares characteristics with a class of human beings which distinguish them from the non-human. If we ever encountered a creature not identifiable in any other respect than its human-ness, we would be nonplussed. Dewey[10] puts it succinctly:

> We come to know or note not merely this particular which as a particular cannot strictly be known at all (for not being classed it cannot be characterized and identified) but to recognize it as man, tree, stone, leather—an individual of a certain kind, marked by a certain universal form characteristic of a whole species of thing. Along with the development of this common-sense knowledge, there grows up a certain regularity of conduct. The particular incidents fuse, and a *way* of acting which is general, as far as it goes, builds up. . . . This regularity signifies, of course, that the particular case is not treated as an isolated particular, but as one of a kind, which therefore demands a *kind* of action.

Where Dewey's tree, stone or leather is inert and its properties unchanging throughout the known past, his man, however, is not. A rose by any other name may smell as sweet, but a person by another name will act according to that other name. The regularities in our behavior toward him are necessarily based upon our expectation of regularities in his behavior. The regularities in his behavior toward us are in turn based in the same way upon his sharing our conception of his identity and his expectation that we share his conception of our identity. Naturally there is many a slip!

The common man is always classifying thus. And to make things harder for the social psychologist, his classifications vary with time and place, as identities are elaborated and redetermined. Moreover, the common man assumes that categories applied to his fellows immediately indicate the motives to be imputed to them. ''I dislike Communists because I am a Catholic and they are atheistic'' is an example of such common-sense explanation (rationalization) of behavior. It is enough for him when imputation suffices for investigation, and extrapolation for prediction—enough, that is, to make possible a more or less orderly social life. Likewise, his identities give common meaning, stability and predictability to his own behavior as long as he clings to them. Possibly the predictions of social scientists will never excel their apprehension of the categories of identity and motive employed among the groups they study; but predictive power is certainly lost when, in place of these, psychologists substitute simpler and less relevant categories of their own—their lists of predispositions.

If the regularities in human behavior are organized responses to situations which have been classified more or less in common by the actors in them, then names motivate behavior. It is by analysis of the function of language, and especially of names ascribed to categories of people, that we can dispense with predispositions and yet maintain a theory of motivation subject to empirical testing—not throwing out baby with bath, as the postivists do.[11]

Establishment of one's own identity to oneself is as important in interaction as to establish it for the other. One's own identity in a situation is not absolutely given but is more or less problematic. Many expositions of interpersonal behavior omit this point, and describe only the process of ascertaining the position of the other, as if that could be read off like a set of labels. Labels are there, to be sure, but the important fact is what these labels mean in a unified definition of the situation embracing both parties. In abstraction one can consider statuses analytically, as the anthropologists do, but in action it is the unique concatenation of relevant statuses at this one time and place—in this *situation*—which constitutes identity.

[10]John Dewey, *Reconstruction in Philosophy*, New York: Holt, 1920, pp. 79−80.

[11]C. L. Stevenson, *Ethics and Language*, New Haven: Yale University Press, 1944.

Social situations always contain standard elements, and always some unique elements, if only a different position in time and space. When one enters a new situation, he attempts to relate it to old ones by familiar signs, and his response may be automatic. Or the preponderance of new elements may make the situation too problematic for a habitual response to be appropriate. For its definition, nonetheless, he must approach it from some fixed point of reference. He must start from what is most definite, find some *given* elements in it. His capacities are given, but they constitute only inert *limits* to his potential behavior, so they are not definitive enough. Although some pressing organic irritation may be quite definite, again his physical condition helps create the situation he confronts, but does not alone dictate what his response will be. The identity of the others involved is dependent upon his own in the familiar reciprocal manner. So inevitably the elements which have to be ''taken as given'' are his identities or, more exactly, his special pattern of identity.

In most situations our identity is so completely habitual and taken for granted that we virtually ignore its presence or relevance in our reactions, concentrating only upon the stimulating environment. Researchwise, it is strategic to focus observations upon those situations where identity itself is acutely problematic in order to observe its determining effect upon behavior (although study of the opposite type of situation—the teacher who insists she was cut out only for fifth-grade math, the fifth-grader who insists he wàs never cut out for it—is also illuminating).[12] When doubt of identity creeps in, action is paralyzed. Only full commitment to one's identity permits a full picture of motivation. Faith in one's conception of one's self is the key which unlocks the physiological resources of the human organism, releases the energy (or capacity, as Dewey would say) to perform the indicated act. Doubt of identity, or

confusion, where it does not cause complete disorientation, certainly drains action of its meaning, and thus limits mobilization of the organic correlates of emotion, drive and energy which constitute the introspectively-sensed ''push'' of motivated action. We are reminded of James Michener's[13] heroes in the South Pacific who were plagued by the question, ''What am I doing here?'' Also, of William James's contention that only he who has played seriously with the idea of suicide has plumbed the phenomenon of self.

At this moment we can only speculate on how one acquires and gets committed to particular identities. Unless we assume a heaven of unborn souls, the process is obviously a matter of experience. We are limited to the experience available to us from birth, although these limitations become more flexible as we gain in variety of experience. That is, the richer our experience, the more possible it becomes to exercise conscious direction over its further accumulation. Nevertheless, limitations continue, and few persons ever reach the point of considering such a deliberate and drastic shift of identity as to change their names or pass the color line. Primarily then the compulsive effect of identification upon behavior must arise from absence of alternatives, from unquestioned acceptance of the identities cast upon one by circumstances beyond his control (or thought to be). From the point of view of the experiencing individual, however, the process is bound to seem much less like a process of limitation to a few among infinite possibilities than a process of discovery. His accruing conceptions of who he is are usually taken as something verging upon ultimate reality rather than as ultimately arbitrary ascriptions by others. Of course as soon as he encounters alternatives, he is released from such pre-conscious bondage to any particular conception of himself. Thenceforth his identities accrue from more conscious choice and pursuit of the values he has discovered in his experience.

---

[12]Prescott Lecky, *Self-Consistency*, New York: Island Press, 1945.

[13]James Michener, *Tales of the South Pacific*, New York: Pocketbooks, 1948.

Value, we would insist, is discovered in experience, not conferred upon it from without. The concepts by which we may name our various ends-in-view, and through manipulation of which we are enabled to judge among alternatives, should not—in value theory or motivation theory—be allowed to obscure the concrete consummations to which they refer. Once experienced, these appear permanently registered in the organism. If the concepts have no concrete reference for a person, or if through faulty communication the connection between the abstract values and the actual experience is not made, the abstractions are not motivating to *him,* as every parent finds out daily. Our learning is immensely expedited through being directed by means of these names for experienceable values to undergo and acquire them. Also, if through identification with more experienced mentors upon whose judgment we depend, we hold to the expectation of realizing recommended values eventually, experiential confirmation may remain lacking indefinitely. Nevertheless, all signals pointing to where value may be found in experience probably must be corroborated by its actual discovery, at least by some members of any group which shares them, or these signals become empty shibboleths and lingering memorials of an extinct value community.

If we insist that prior experience is necessary to motivation, however, have we not fallen back once more into predispositional thinking? Not if we are correct in assuming that a predisposition denotes more than a mere statistical tendency, some active thrust which constantly presses like a coiled spring to set off a particular line of action. Metaphorically put, the operation of values in the formulation of responses to situations is advisory, not executive. While we can only mobilize for our next act when it or its elements can be construed as similar to acts which have gone before, the determination of the appropriate act is made in the situation, not prior to it. Experience is continually being recombined in new patterns; and even the most habitual act must be defined as appropriate to its immediate context

to be launched overtly. In place of predisposition, therefore, it is necessary and sufficient to put memory (memory plus mobilization equals motivation), by virtue of which we can call up in the present images of past consummations of acts.[14] We set these before us as ideal futures, to be achieved again when we have reconstructed the present situations so as to put us—if this is possible to one of our identity—into an imagined new position where that remembered good will be actually re-experienced. Because we have the capacity through language for conceptualizing these remembered goods as values, and the ingenuity to devise new schemes of relations under which they may be revived in the same or fuller measure, we can invent new roles or deviate from conventional ones. Also, we simultaneously inherit thereby the constant possibility of conflict— both internal and external—which characterizes members of human society.

Because our learning has more often than not been perfected to the point where cognitive judgments in standardized situations are made instantaneously, and the energy for performing the appropriate behavior is released immediately, it has been an easy mistake for many observers to suppose that the organic correlates came first and even account for the definition of the situation, rather than the reverse. Also, it has often led them to ignore or depreciate the long, historical accumulation of experience, organized by our shared conceptual apparatus, which brings our whole past to bear upon our behavior in the momentary present. Yet if past and future did not figure in the determination of the present, would we logically have a phenomenon of motivation or valuation to ponder?

Without the binding thread of identity one could not evaluate the succession of situations. Literally, one could say there would be no value in living, since value only exists or occurs relative to particular identities—at least value as experienced by

[14]G. H. Mead, *The Philosophy of the Act,* University of Chicago Press, 1938, pp. 23—25.

organisms which do not live in the mere present, as animals presumably do, devoid of self and unaware of impending death. Moreover, it is only through identification as the sharing of identity that individual motives become social values and social values, individual motives.

Fuller recognition of these functions of identity should increase the scope, power and precision of situational analysis in social research, while in turn research oriented to identification should contribute to the elaboration and clarification of its working. It is only because one conceives of himself, via a certain identity, as a member of a class which includes certain others, that he can enjoy or suffer the successes and failures of a group. It is only commitment to his identity which makes him subject without physical compulsion to the control of the groups to which he belongs, or arouses his antagonism to members of a category construed as inimical to his category. In fact, we will carry this so far as to say that only full commitment to identities shared with others makes possible the grand human phenomena of love and grief. This is not tautological, because it calls attention to language in general and names in particular as the mediating links among individuals. It enables us to rephrase such imponderable speculations as ''What are the psychological functions of love?'' into definitely researchable form, such as ''How did this person acquire his identity?'' or ''How does he get committed to particular identities which tie him constitutionally as a self to other persons?'' Also, in reverse, ''What kinds of new experience are sufficient to free him from the compulsion of certain old identities?''

This paper must end where it ought to begin. Originally it described some proposals for research on various types of acutely problematic identity, and some suggestions for experimentation with the methods every propagandist—which includes each of us part of the time—uses to motivate others. Space permits only mention of studies of identification among adopted and illegitimate children, the effects of ambiguous identity upon the motiva-

tion of ''marginal men,'' the psychological consequences of name-changing, and problems of self-conception among divorced women who keep their husbands's names. Much understanding is already coming from observation of marked effects upon behavior from identification with Alcoholics Anonymous and other therapeutic groups. Regarding the techniques by which the propagandist succeeds in invoking identification of listener with speaker, Kenneth Burke gives the experimenter many leads in his valuable recent book, *A Rhetoric of Motives*.[15] Would practical successes as a recipe for motivating others be too stringent a test of the validity of a theory of motivation?

We have set forth that (1) role theory needs to be supplemented with an account of motivation consistent with its main premises, (2) a proper definition of motivated and non-motivated behavior makes clear how to avoid both dissolution of the concept of motivation and unchecked imputation of motives, (3) identification is the process whereby individuals are effectively linked with their fellows in groups, (4) predispositional theories, being oblivious to the function of language in motivated behavior, ascribe metaphysical reality to what are actually only the verbal categories whereby human beings regularize their doings, (5) these categorizations of experience motivate behavior through the necessary commitment of individuals to particular concatenations of identity in all situations, (6) commitment to particular identities arises through a limiting and discovering process of acquiring conceptions of self, which are confirmed, revised or elaborated partly by instruction from significant others and partly through direct experience, and (7) the compelling or inhibiting effect of identifications upon the release of varying kinds of behavior can be studied empirically.

In conclusion, let it be emphasized that the title of this paper offered expansion of the concept of

[15]Kenneth Burke, *A Rhetoric of Motives*, New York: Prentice-Hall, 1950.

identification only as the *basis* for a situational theory of motivation, not as a full theory itself, even though it helps dispel certain false theories. By its use are avoided the fallacies of both biological determinism—the person impelled from within—and of cultural determinism—the person driven from without. It also avoids the ingenious pretensions by which some theorists, through the invention of such terms as ''bio-social,'' have resolved a putative opposition between biology and culture which never existed to begin with. When theorists can do no better in explaining conflict and change than to make the environment the enemy of the organism, or give no better explanation of personality organization than as a meeting of protoplasm and society, it is puzzling to note that Cooley was insisting as early as 1902 that individual and social are two sides of the same phenomena.[16] They do not have to be joined together by integration in textbooks. In the concept of identity we can see this clearly: One has no identity apart from society; one has no individuality apart from identity.[17] Only by making use of this concept can we account for motivation in terms consistent with the only social psychology that truly deserves the name ''social.''

[16]C. H. Cooley, *Human Nature and the Social Order,* Scribners, 1902.

[17]Kenneth Burke, *A Grammar of Motives,* New York: Prentice-Hall, 1945, pp. 469–470. A searching criticism of the organism-environment framework.

THIRTY

ACCOUNTS

MARVIN B. SCOTT AND STANFORD M. LYMAN

From time to time sociologists might well pause from their ongoing pursuits to inquire whether their research interests contribute in any way to the fundamental question of sociology, namely, the Hobbesian question: How is society possible? Attempts to answer this question could serve to unite a discipline that may not yet have forgotten its founders, but may still have forgotten why it was founded.

Our purpose here is not to review the various answers to the Hobbesian question,[1] but rather to suggest that an answer to this macro-sociological problem might be fruitfully explored in the analysis of the slightest of interpersonal rituals and the very stuff of which most of those rituals are composed—talk.

Talk, we hold, is the fundamental material of human relations. And though sociologists have not

entirely neglected the subject,[2] the sociology of talk has scarcely been developed. Our concern here is with one feature of talk: Its ability to shore up the timbers of fractured sociation, its ability to throw bridges between the promised and the performed, its ability to repair the broken and restore the estranged. This feature of talk involves the giving and receiving of what we shall call *accounts*.

An account is a linguistic device employed whenever an action is subjected to valuative inquiry.[3] Such devices are a crucial element in the

SOURCE: Marvin B. Scott and Stanford M. Lyman. "Accounts." Copyright by the American Sociological Asssociation. Marvin B. Scott and Stanford M. Lyman, "Accounts," *American Sociological Review*, XXXIII (February, 1968), pp. 46–62. Reprinted by permission of the American Sociological Association.

[1]For a now classic statement and analysis of the Hobbesian question, see the discussion by Talcott Parsons, *The Structure of Social Action*, Glencoe, Ill.: The Free Press, 1949, pp. 89–94.

[2]See, for instance, William Soskin and Vera John, "The Study of Spontaneous Talk," in *The Stream of Behavior*, edited by Roger Barker, N.Y.: Appleton-Century-Crofts, 1963, pp. 228–282. Much suggestive material and a complete bibliography can be found in Joyce O. Hertzler, *A Sociology of Language*, N.Y.: Random House, 1965.

[3]An account has a family resemblance to the verbal component of a "motive" in Weber's sense of the term. Weber defined a motive as "a complex of subjective meaning which seems to the actor himself or to the observer as an adequate ground for the conduct in question." Max Weber, *Theory of Social and Economic Organization*, translated by Talcott Parsons and A. M. Henderson, Glencoe: The Free Press, 1947, pp. 98–99. Following Weber's definition and building on G. H. Mead's social psychology and the work of Kenneth Burke, C. Wright Mills was among the first to employ the notion of accounts in his much neglected essay, "Situated Actions and Vocabularies of Motives," *American Sociological Review*, 5 (December, 1940), pp. 904–913. Reprinted in Part Five of this volume. Contemporary British philosophy, following the leads

social order since they prevent conflicts from arising by verbally bridging the gap between action and expectation.[4] Moreover, accounts are "situated" according to the statuses of the interactants, and are standardized within cultures so that certain accounts are terminologically stabilized and routinely expected when activity falls outside the domain of expectations.

By an account, then, we mean a statement made by a social actor to explain unanticipated or untoward behavior—whether that behavior is his own or that of others, and whether the proximate cause for the statement arises from the actor himself or from someone else.[5] An account is not called for when people engage in routine, common-sense behavior in a cultural environment that recognizes that behavior as such. Thus in American society we do not ordinarily ask why married people engage in sexual intercourse, or why they maintain a home with their children, although the latter question might well be asked if such behavior occurred among the Nayars of Malabar.[6] These questions are not asked because they have been settled in advance in our culture and are indicated by the language itself. We learn the meaning of a "married couple" by indicating that they are two people of opposite sex who have a legitimate right to engage in sexual intercourse and maintain their own children in their own household. When such taken-for-granted phenomena are called into question, the inquirer (if a member of the same culture

group) is regarded as "just fooling around," or perhaps as being sick.[7]

To specify our concerns more sharply we should at this point distinguish accounts from the related phenomenon of "explanations." The latter refers to statements about events where untoward action is not an issue and does not have critical implications for relationship. Much of what is true about accounts will also hold for explanations, but our concern is primarily with linguistic forms that are offered for untoward action. With this qualification to our concern, we may now specify further the nature and types of accounts.

TYPES OF ACCOUNTS

There are in general two types of accounts: *excuses* and *justifications*.[8] Either or both are likely to be invoked when a person is accused of having done something that is "bad, wrong, inept, unwelcome, or in some other of the numerous possible ways, untoward."[9] Justifications are accounts in which one accepts responsibility for the act in question, but denies the pejorative quality associated with it. Thus a soldier in combat may admit that he has killed other men, but deny that he did an immoral act since those he killed were members of an

---

of Ludwig Wittgenstein, has (apparently) independently advanced the idea of a "vocabulary of motives." An exemplary case is R. S. Peters' *The Concept of Motivation*, London: Routledge and Kegan Paul, 1958.

[4]The point is nicely illustrated by Jackson Toby in "Some Variables in Role Conflict Analysis," *Social Forces*, 30 (March, 1952), pp. 323–327.

[5]Thus by an account we include also those non-vocalized but linguistic explanations that arise in an actor's "mind" when he questions his own behavoir. However, our concern is with vocalized accounts and especially those that are given in face-to-face relations.

[6]William J. Goode, *World Revolution and Family Patterns*, New York: The Free Press of Glencoe, 1963, pp. 254–256.

[7]Moreover, common-sense understandings that violate widespread cognitive knowledge, such as are asserted in statements like "The sun rises every morning and sets every night," or avowed in perceptions that a straight stick immersed in water appears bent, are expected to be maintained. Persons who always insist on the astronomically exact statement about the earth's relation to the sun might be considered officious or didactic, while those who "see" a straight stick in a pool might be credited with faulty eyesight. For a relevant discussion of social reactions to inquiries about taken-for-granted phenomena, see Harold Garfinkel, "Studies of the Routine Grounds of Everyday Activities," *Social Problems*, 11 (Winter, 1964), pp. 225–250, and "A Conception of and Experiments with 'Trust' as a Condition of Concerted Action," in *Motivation and Social Interaction*, edited by O. J. Harvey, New York: Ronald Press, 1963, pp. 187–238.

[8]We have taken this formulation from J. L. Austin. See his *Philosophical Papers*, London: Oxford University Press, 1961, pp. 123–152.

[9]*Ibid.*, p. 124.

enemy group and hence "deserved" their fate. Excuses are accounts in which one admits that the act in question is bad, wrong, or inappropriate but denies full responsibility. Thus our combat soldier could admit the wrongfulness of killing but claim that his acts are not entirely undertaken by volition: he is "under orders" and must obey. With these introductory remarks, we now turn our focus to a more detailed examination of types of justifications and excuses.

Excuses are socially approved vocabularies for mitigating or relieving responsibility when conduct is questioned. We may distinguish initially four modal forms by which excuses are typically formulated:[10] *appeal to accidents, appeal to defeasibility, appeal to biological drives, and scapegoating.*

Excuses claiming *accident* as the source of conduct or its consequences mitigate (if not relieve) responsibility by pointing to the generally recognized hazards in the environment, the understandable inefficiency of the body, and the human incapacity to control all motor responses. The excuse of accident is acceptable precisely because of the irregularity and infrequency of accidents occurring to any single actor. Thus while hazards are numerous and ubiquitous, a particular person is not expected ordinarily to experience the same accident often. In other words, social actors employ a lay version of statistical curves whereby they interpret certain acts as occurring or not occurring by chance alone. When a person conducts himself so that the same type of accident befalls him frequently, he is apt to earn a label— such as "clumsy"—which will operate to stigmatize him and to warn others not to put him and themselves or their property in jeopardy by creating the environment in which he regularly has accidents. When the excuse is rooted in an accident that is unobservable or unable to be investigated—such as blaming one's lateness to

work on the heaviness of traffic—frequent pleas of it are likely to be discredited. Excuses based on accidents are thus most likely to be honored precisely because they do not occur all the time or for the most part to the actor in question.[11]

Appeals to *defeasibility*[12] are available as a form of excuse because of the widespread agreement that all actions contain some "mental element." The components of the mental element are "knowledge" and "will." One defense against an accusation is that a person was not fully informed or that his "will" was not completely "free." Thus an individual might excuse himself from responsibility by claiming that certain information was not available to him, which, if it had been, would have altered his behavior. Further, an individual might claim to have acted in a certain way because of misinformation arising from intentional or innocent misrepresentation of the facts by others. An excuse based on interference with the "free will" of an individual might invoke duress or undue influence. Finally both will and knowledge can be impaired under certain conditions, the invocation of which ordinarily constitutes an adequate mitigation of responsibility—intoxication (whether from alcohol or drugs) and lunacy

---

[10]These types of excuses are to be taken as illustrative rather than as an exhaustive listing.

[11]Only where nothing is left to chance—as among the Azande, where particular misfortunes are accounted for by a ubiquitous witchcraft—is the excuse by accident not likely to occur. Azande do not assert witchcraft to be the sole cause of phenomena; they have a "practical" and "realistic" approach to events which would enjoy consensual support from Occidental observers. However, Azande account for what Occidentals would call "chance" or "coincidence" by reference to witchcraft. E. E. Evans-Pritchard writes: "We have no explanation of why the two chains of causation [resulting in a catastrophe] intersected at a certain time and in a certain place, for there is no interdependence between them. Azande philosophy can supply the missing link. . . . It is due to witchcraft. . . . Witchcraft explains the coincidence of these two happenings." *Witchcraft, Oracles and Magic Among the Azande*, London: Oxford University Press, 1937, p. 70.

[12]Defeasibility, or the capacity of being voided, is a concept developed by H. L. A. Hart. This section leans heavily on Hart's essay, "The Ascription of Responsibility and Rights," in *Logic and Language, First Series*, edited by Anthony Flew, Oxford: Basil Blackwell, 1960, pp. 145–166.

(whether temporary or permanent) being examples.

In ordinary affairs and in law a person's actions are usually distinguished according to their intent. Further, a person's intentions are distinguished from the consequences of his actions. Under a situation where an action is questioned an actor may claim a lack of intent or a failure to foresee the consequences of his act, or both. If the action in question involves a motor response—such as knocking over a vase—the situation is not very different from that subsumed under the term accident. When actions going beyond motor responses are at issue, the actor's intentions and foresight can be questioned. "Why did you make her cry?" asks the accuser. The presentational strategies in reply to this question allow several modes of defeating the central claim implied in the question, namely, that the actor intended with full knowledge to make the lady weep. The accused may simply deny any intention on his part to have caused the admittedly unfortunate consequence. However, men ordinarily impute to one another some measure of foresight for their actions so that a simple denial of intent may not be believed if it appears that the consequence of the action in question was indeed what another person might expect and therefore what the actor intended.

In addition to his denial of intent an actor may also deny his knowledge of the consequence. The simplest denial is the cognitive disclaimer, "I did not *know* that I would make her cry by what I did." But this complete denial of cognition is often not honored, especially when the interactants know one another well and are expected to have a more complete imagery of the consequences of their acts to guide them. A more complex denial—the gravity disclaimer—includes admitting to the possibility of the outcome in question but suggesting that its probability was incalculable: "I knew matters were serious, but I did not know that telling her would make her weep."

Still another type of excuse invokes biological drives. This invocation is part of a larger category of "fatalistic" forces which in various cultures are deemed in greater or lesser degree to be controlling of some or all events. Cultures dominated by universalist-achievement orientations[13] tend to give scant and ambiguous support to fatalistic interpretations of events, but rarely disavow them entirely. To account for the whole of one's life in such terms, or to account for events which are conceived by others to be controlled by the actor's conscience, will, and abilities is to lay oneself open to the charge of mental illness or personality disorganization.[14] On the other hand, recent studies have emphasized the situational element in predisposing certain persons and groups in American society to what might be regarded as a "normalized" fatalistic view of their condition. Thus, for example, Negroes[15] and adolescent delinquents[16] are regarded and tend to regard them-

[13]For a general discussion of cultures in terms of their "fatalistic" orientations or universalist-achievement orientations, see Talcott Parsons, "A Revised Analytical Approach to the Theory of Social Stratification," in *Essays in Sociological Theory,* The Free Press of Glencoe, 1954, pp. 386–439. See also Parsons, *The Social System,* Glencoe: The Free Press, 1951.

[14]Thus, in the most famous study of the psychodynamics of prejudice, one of the characteristics of the intolerant or "authoritarian" personality is "externalization," i.e., the attribution of causality of events believed to be within the actor's power or rational comprehension to uncontrollable forces beyond his influence or understanding. See T. W. Adorno, *et al., The Authoritarian Personality,* N. Y.: Harper & Row, 1950, pp. 474–475. See also Gordon W. Allport, *The Nature of Prejudice,* Garden City: Doubleday Anchor, 1958, p. 379. In a recent study an intermittently employed cab driver's insistence that there would inevitably be a revolution after which the world would be taken over by Negroes and Jews is recalled as one of several early warning cues that he is mentally ill. Marion Radke Yarrow, *et al.,* "The Psychological Meaning of Mental Illness in the Family," in Thomas J. Scheff, *Mental Illness and Social Process,* New York: Harper and Row, 1967, p. 35.

[15]See Horace R. Clayton, "The Psychology of the Negro Under Discrimination," in Arnold Rose, editor, *Race Prejudice and Discrimination,* New York: Alfred Knopf, 1953, pp. 276–280; and Bertram P. Karon, *The Negro Personality,* New York: Springer, 1958, pp. 8–53, 140–160.

[16]David Matza, *Delinquency and Drift,* New York: Wiley, 1964, pp. 88–90, 188–191.

selves as less in control of the forces that shape their lives than whites or middle-class adults.

Among the fatalistic items most likely to be invoked as an excuse are the biological drives. Despite the emphasis in Occidental culture since the late nineteenth century on personality and social environment as causal elements in human action, there is still a popular belief in and varied commitment to the efficacy of the body and biological factors in determining human behavior. Such commonplaces as "men are like that" are shorthand phrases invoking belief in sex-linked traits that allegedly govern behavior beyond the will of the actor. Precisely because the body and its biological behavior are always present but not always accounted for in science or society, invocation of the body and its processes is available as an excuse. The body and its inner workings enjoy something of the status of the sociological stranger as conceived by Simmel, namely, they are ever with us but mysterious. Hence, biological drives may be credited with influencing or causing at least some of the behavior for which actors wish to relieve themselves of full responsibility.

The invocation of biological drives is most commonly an appeal to natural but uncontrollable sexual appetite. Among first and second generation Italians in America the recognition and fear of biologically induced sexual intercourse serves men as both an excuse for pre- and extra-marital sexual relations and a justification for not being alone with women ineligible for coitus. Thus one student of Italian-American culture observes:

> What the men fear is their own ability at self-control. This attitude, strongest among young unmarried people, often carries over into adulthood. The traditional Italian belief—that sexual intercourse is unavoidable when a man and a woman are by themselves—is maintained intact among second-generation Italians, and continues even when sexual interest itself is on the wane. For example, I was told of an older woman whose apartment was adjacent to that of an unmarried male relative. Although they had lived in the same building for almost twenty years and saw each other every day, she had never once been in his apartment because of this belief.[17]

Biological drive may be an expected excuse in some cultures, so that the failure to invoke it, and the use of some other excuse, constitutes an improper account when the appropriate one is available. Oscar Lewis provides such an example in his ethnography of a Mexican family. A cuckolded wife angrily rejects her wayward husband's explanation that the red stains on his shirt are due to paint rubbed off during the course of his work. She strongly suggests, in her retelling of the incident, that she would have accepted an excuse appealing to her husband's basic sex drives:[18]

> And he had me almost believing it was red paint! It was not that I am jealous. I realize a man can never be satisfied with just one woman, but I cannot stand being made a fool of.

Homosexuals frequently account for their deviant sexual desires by invoking the principle of basic biological nature. As one homosexual put it:[19]

> It's part of nature. You can't alter it, no matter how many injections and pills they give you.

Another of the biological elements that can be utilized as an excuse is the shape of the body itself. Body types are not only defined in purely anatomical terms, but also, and perhaps more importantly, in terms of their shared social meanings. Hence fat people can excuse their excessive laughter by appealing to the widely accepted proverb that fat

[17]Herbert J. Gans, *The Urban Villagers*, N.Y.: The Free Press, 1962, p. 49. According to another student of Italian-American life, slum-dwelling members of this subculture believe that "a man's health requires sexual intercourse at certain intervals." William F. Whyte, "A Slum Sex Code," *American Journal of Sociology*, 49 (July, 1943), p. 26.

[18]Oscar Lewis, *The Children of Sanchez*, New York: Random House, 1961, p. 475.

[19]Gordon Westwood, *A Minority*, London: Longmans, Green and Co., 1960, p. 46.

men are jolly. Similarly, persons bearing features considered to be stereotypically "criminal"[20] may be exonerated for their impoliteness or small larcenies on the grounds that their looks proved their intentions and thus their victims ought to have been on guard. The phrase, "he looks crooked to me," serves as a warning to others to carefully appraise the character and intentions of the person so designated, since his features bespeak an illegal intent.

The final type of excuse we shall mention is *scapegoating*. Scapegoating is derived from another form of fatalistic reasoning. Using this form a person will allege that his questioned behavior is a response to the behavior or attitudes of another. Certain psychological theory treats this phenomenon as indicative of personality disorder, and, if found in conjunction with certain other characteristic traits, a signal of authoritarian personality.[21] Our treatment bypasses such clinical and pathological concerns in order to deal with the "normal" situation in which individuals slough off the burden of responsibility for their actions and shift it on to another. In Mexican working-class society, for example, women hold a distinctly secondary position relative to men, marriage causes a loss of status to the latter, and sexual intercourse is regarded ambivalently as healthy and natural, but also as a necessary evil.[22] Such a set of orientations predisposes both men and women to attribute many of their shortcomings to women. An example is found in the autobiography of a Mexican girl:[23]

> I was always getting into fights because some girls are vipers; they get jealous, tell lies about each other, and start trouble.

Similarly, a Mexican youth who tried unsuccessfully to meet a girl by showing off on a bicycle explains:[24]

> She got me into trouble with my father by lying about me. She said I tried to run her down with my bike and that all I did was hang around spying on her.

In another instance the same youth attributes his waywardness to the fact that the girl truly loved was his half-sister and thus unavailable to him for coitus or marriage:

> So, because of Antonia, I began to stay away from home. It was one of the main reasons I started to go on the bum, looking for trouble.[25]

Like excuses, *justifications* are socially approved vocabularies that neutralize an act or its consequences when one or both are called into question. But here is the crucial difference: to *justify* an act is to assert its positive value in the face of a claim to the contrary. Justifications recognize a general sense in which the act in question is impermissible, but claim that the particular occasion permits or requires the very act. The laws governing the taking of life are a case in point. American and English jurisprudence are by no means united on definitions or even on the nature of the acts in question, but in general a man may justify taking the life of another by claiming that he acted in self-defense, in defense of others' lives or property, or in action against a declared enemy of the state.

For a tentative list of types of justifications we

---

[20]For an interesting study showing that criminals believe that a fellow criminal's physical attractiveness will vary with type of crime—robbers are the most attractive, murderers the least; rapists are more attractive than pedophiles, etc.—see Raymond J. Corsini, "Appearance and Criminality," *American Journal of Sociology*, 65 (July, 1959), pp. 49–51.

[21]Adorno, *op. cit.*, pp. 233, 485; Allport, *op. cit.*, pp. 235–249, suggests the historicity and uniqueness of each instance of scapegoating.

[22]Arturo de Hoyos and Genevieve de Hoyos, "The Amigo System and Alienation of the Wife in the Conjugal Mexican Family," in Bernard Farber, editor, *Kinship and Family Organization*, New York: Wiley, 1966, pp. 102–115, esp., pp. 103–107.

[23]Lewis, *op. cit.*, p. 143.
[24]*Ibid.*, p. 202.
[25]*Ibid.*, p. 86.

may turn to what has been called "techniques of neutralization."[26] Although these techniques have been discussed with respect to accounts offered by juvenile delinquents for untoward action, their wider use has yet to be explored. Relevant to our discussion of justification are the techniques of "denial of injury," "denial of victim," "condemnation of condemners," and "appeal to loyalties."[27]

In *denial of injury* the actor acknowledges that he did a particular act but asserts that it was permissible to do that act since no one was injured by it, or since no one about whom the community need be concerned with was involved, or finally since the act resulted in consequences that were trifling. Note that this justification device can be invoked with respect to both persons and objects. The denial of injury to *persons* suggests that they be viewed as "deserving" in a special sense: that they are oversupplied with the valued things of the world, or that they are "private" persons ("my friends," "my enemies") who have no standing to claim injury in the public, or to be noticed as injured. Denial of injury to *objects* involves redefining the act as not injurious to it but only using it, e.g., car "borrowing" is not theft.

In *denial of the victim* the actor expresses the position that the action was permissible since the victim deserved the injury. Four categories of persons are frequently perceived as deserving injury. First, there are proximate foes, i.e., those who have directly injured the actor; second, incumbents of normatively discrepant roles, e.g., homosexuals, whores, pimps; third, groups with tribal stigmas, e.g., racial and ethnic minorities; and finally, distant foes, that is, incumbents of roles held to be dubious or hurtful, e.g.,

"Whitey," the "Reds," "politicians." Besides categories of persons, there are categories of objects perceived as deserving of injury. To begin with, the property of any of the above mentioned categories of persons may become a focus of attack, especially if that property is symbolic of the attacked person's status. Thus the clothing of the whore is torn, the gavel of the politician is smashed, and so on. Secondly, there are objects that have a neutral or ambiguous identity with respect to ownership, e.g., a park bench. A final focus of attacked objects are those having a low or polluted value, e.g., junk, or kitsch.

Using the device of *condemnation of the condemners,* the actor admits performing an untoward act but asserts its irrelevancy because others commit these and worse acts, and these others are either not caught, not punished, not condemned, unnoticed, or even praised.

Still another neutralization technique is *appeal to loyalties*. Here the actor asserts that his action was permissible or even right since it served the interests of another to whom he owes an unbreakable allegiance or affection.[28]

Besides these "techniques of neutralization," two other sorts of justification may be mentioned: "sad tales," and "self-fulfillment." The *sad tale* is a selected (often distorted) arrangement of facts that highlight an extremely dismal past, and thus "explain" the individual's present state.[29]

---

[26]Gresham M. Sykes and David Matza, "Techniques of Neutralization," *American Sociological Review,* 22 (December, 1957), pp. 667–669.

[27]One other neutralization technique mentioned by Sykes and Matza, "denial of responsibility," is subsumed in our schema under "appeal to defeasibility."

[28]Note that appeal to loyalties could be an *excuse* if the argument runs that X did to A under the influence of Y's domination or love, or under the coercive influence of Y's injury to him were he not to act, e.g., loss of love, blackmail, etc. In other words, appeal to loyalties is an excuse if X admits it was bad to do A, but refuses to monopolize responsibility for A in himself.

[29]Erving Goffman, *Asylums,* Garden City: Doubleday Anchor, 1961, pp. 150–151. The sad tale involves the most dramatic instance of the general process of reconstructing personal biography whereby—for example—a husband may account for his present divorce by reconstructing the history of earlier events in an ascending scale leading up to the final dissolution. The idea of a reconstruction of biography is a continual theme in the writings of Alfred Schutz. See his *Collected Papers,* Vol. I, edited by Maurice Natanson, The

For example, a mental patient relates:[30]

> I was going to night school to get an M.A. degree, and holding down a job in addition, and the load got too much for me.

And a homosexual accounts for his present deviance with this sad tale:[31]

> I was in a very sophisticated queer circle at the university. It was queer in a sense that we all camped like mad with ''my dear'' at the beginning of every sentence, but there was practically no sex, and in my case there was none at all. The break came when I went to a party and flirted with a merchant seaman who took me seriously and cornered me in a bedroom. There was I, the great sophisticate, who, when it came to the point, was quite raw, completely inexperienced; and I might tell you that seaman gave me quite a shock. I can't say I enjoyed it very much but it wasn't long after before I started to dive into bed with anyone.

Finally we may mention a peculiarly modern type of justification, namely, *self*-fulfillment. Interviewing LSD users and homosexuals in the Haight-Ashbury district of San Francisco, we are struck by the prominence of self-fulfillment as the grounds for these activities. Thus, an ''acid head'' relates:[32]

> The whole purpose in taking the stuff is self-development. Acid expands consciousness. Mine eyes have seen the glory—can you say that? I never knew what capacities I had until I went on acid.

Hague: Martinus Nijhoff, 1962. A short clear summary of Schutz's contribution on the reconstruction of biography is found in Peter L. Berger, *Invitation to Sociology*, Garden City: Doubleday Anchor, 1963, pp. 54−65. Drawing on Schutz, Garfinkel details the concept of reconstruction of biography in a series of experiments on the ''retrospective reading'' of social action. See his ''Common Sense Knowledge of Social Structures,'' in *Theories of the Mind*, edited by Jordon M. Scher, Glencoe: The Free Press, 1962, pp. 689−712. The empirical use of the concept of retrospective reading of action is nicely illustrated by John I. Kitsuse, ''Societal Reaction to Deviant Behavior,'' in *The Other Side*, edited by Howard S. Becker, New York: The Free Press of Glencoe, 1964, pp. 87−102.

[30]Goffman, *op. cit.*, p. 152.
[31]Westwood, *op. cit.*, p. 32.
[32]Tape-recorded interview, May 1967.

And a Lesbian:[33]

> Everyone has the right to happiness and love. I was married once. It was hell. But now I feel I have fulfilled myself as a person and as a woman.

We might also note that the drug users and homosexuals interviewed (in San Francisco) who invoked the justification of self-fulfillment did not appear to find anything ''wrong'' with their behavior. They indicated either a desire to be left alone or to enlighten what they considered to be the unenlightened establishment.

HONORING ACCOUNTS, AND BACKGROUND EXPECTATIONS

Accounts may be honored or not honored. If an account is honored, we may say that it was efficacious and equilibrium is thereby restored in a relationship. The most common situation in which accounts are routinely honored is encounters interrupted by ''incidents''—slips, boners, or gaffes which introduce information deleterious to the otherwise smooth conduct of the interactants.[34] Often a simple excuse will suffice, or the other interactants will employ covering devices to restore the *status quo ante*. A related situation is that in which an individual senses that some incident or event has cast doubt on that image of himself which he seeks to present. ''At such times,'' the authority on impression management writes, ''the individual is likely to try to integrate the incongruous events by means of apologies, little excuses for self, and disclaimers; through the same acts, incidentally, he also tries to save his face.''[35]

One variable governing the honoring of an account is the character of the social circle in which it is introduced. As we pointed out earlier, vocabularies of accounts are likely to be routinized within cultures, subcultures and groups, and some

[33]Tape-recorded interview, June 1967.
[34]Erving Goffman, *Encounters*, Indianapolis: Bobbs-Merrill, 1961, pp. 45−48.
[35]*Ibid.*, p. 51.

are likely to be exclusive to the circle in which they are employed. A drug addict may be able to justify his conduct to a bohemian world, but not to the courts. Similarly kin and friends may accept excuses in situations in which strangers would refuse to do so. Finally, while ignorance of the consequences of an act or of its prohibition may exculpate an individual in many different circles, the law explicitly rejects this notion: "Ignorance of the law excuses no man; not that all men know the law but because 'tis an excuse every man will plead, and no man can tell how to confute him."[36]

Both the account offered by *ego* and the honoring or nonhonoring of the account on the part of *alter* will ultimately depend on the *background expectancies* of the interactants. By background expectancies we refer to those sets of taken-for-granted ideas that permit the interactants to interpret remarks as accounts in the first place.[37] Asked why he is listless and depressed, a person may reply, "I have family troubles." The remark will be taken as an account, and indeed an account that will probably be honored, because "everyone knows" that "family problems" are a cause of depression.

This last illustration suggests that certain accounts can fit a variety of situations. Thus in response to a wide range of questions—Why don't you get married? Why are you in a fit of depression? Why are you drinking so heavily?—the individual can respond with "I'm having family problems." The person offering such an account may not himself regard it as a true one, but invoking it has certain interactional payoffs: since people cannot say they don't understand it—they are accounts that are part of our socially distributed

knowledge of what "everyone knows"—the inquiry can be cut short.

Clearly, then, a single account will stand for a wide collection of events, and the efficacy of such accounts depends upon a set of shared background expectations.

In interacting with others, the socialized person learns a repertoire of background expectations that are appropriate for a variety of others. Hence the "normal" individual will change his account for different role others. A wife may respond sympathetically to her depressed husband because his favorite football team lost a championship game, but such an account for depression will appear bizarre when offered to one's inquiring boss. Thus background expectancies are the means not only for the honoring, but also for the nonhonoring of accounts. When the millionaire accounts for his depression by saying he is a failure, others will be puzzled since "everyone knows" that millionaires are not failures. The incapacity to invoke situationally appropriate accounts, i.e., accounts that are anchored to the background expectations of the situation, will often be taken as a sign of mental illness.[38] There are grounds then for conceptualizing normal individuals as "not stupid" rather than "not ill."[39] The person who is labeled ill has been behaving "stupidly" in terms of his culture and society: he offers accounts not situationally appropriate according to culturally defined background expectations.[40]

[36]John Selden, *Table Talk*, 1696, quoted in Harry Johnson, *Sociology*, New York: Harcourt, Brace and Co., 1960, p. 552n.

[37]The term is borrowed from Harold Garfinkel. Besides the footnote references to Garfinkel already cited, see his *Studies in Ethnomethodology*, Englewood Cliffs, N.J.: Prentice-Hall, 1968. For an original discussion on how the meaning of an account depends upon background expectancies and a methodology for its study, see Harvey Sacks, *The Search for Help*, unpublished doctoral dissertation, University of California, Berkeley, 1966.

[38]On how background expectations are used to determine whether a person is judged criminal or sick see the neglected essay by Vilhelm Aubert and Sheldon L. Messinger, "The Criminal and the Sick," *Inquiry*, 1 (Autumn, 1958), pp. 137–160.

[39]This formulation is persistently (and we believe rightly) argued in the various writings of Ernest Becker. See especially *The Revolution in Psychiatry*, N.Y.: The Free Press of Glencoe, 1964; and his essay "Mills' Social Psychology and the Great Historical Convergence on the Problem of Alienation," in *The New Sociology*, edited by Irving L. Horowitz, N.Y.: Oxford University Press, 1964, pp. 108–133.

[40]In the case of schizophrenics, it has been noted that they are individuals who construct overly elaborate accounts, i.e., accounts that are perceived as being elaborately constructed. These accounts, it appears, take the form of "building up" the

Often an account can be discredited by the appearance of the person offering an account. When a girl accounts for her late return from a date by saying the movie was overlong—that no untoward event occurred and that she still retains virgin status—her mother may discredit the account by noting the daughter's flushed appearance. Since individuals are aware that appearances may serve to credit or discredit accounts, efforts are understandably made to control these appearances through a vast repertoire of "impression management" activities.[41]

When an account is not honored it will be regarded as either *illegitimate* or *unreasonable*. An account is treated as *illegitimate* when the gravity of the event exceeds that of the account or when it is offered in a circle where its vocabulary of motives is unacceptable. As illustration of the former we may note that accidentally allowing a pet turtle to drown may be forgiven, but accidentally allowing the baby to drown with the same degree of oversight may not so easily be excused. As illustration of the latter, male prostitutes may successfully demonstrate their masculinity within the subculture of persons who regularly resort to homosexual acts by insisting that they are never fellators, but such a defense is not likely in heterosexual circles to lift from them the label of "queer."[42]

An account is deemed *unreasonable* when the stated grounds for action cannot be "normalized" in terms of the background expectancies of what "everybody knows." Hence when a secretary explained that she placed her arm in a lighted oven because voices had commanded her to do so in punishment for her evil nature, the account was held to be grounds for commitment to an asylum.[43] In general those who persist in giving unreasonable accounts for questioned actions are likely to be labeled as mentally ill. Or, to put this point another way, unreasonable accounts are one of the sure indices by which the mentally ill are apprehended. Conversely, those persons labeled as mentally ill may relieve themselves of the worst consequences of that label by recognizing before their psychiatrists the truth value of the label, by reconstructing their past to explain how they came to deviate from normal patterns, and by gradually coming to give acceptable accounts for their behavior.[44]

Beyond illegitimacy and unreasonableness are special types of situations in which accounts may not be acceptable. One such type involves the incorrect invocation of "commitment" or "attachment"[45] in account situations where one or the other, but only the correct one, is permitted. By commitment we refer to that role orientation in which one has through investiture become liable and responsible for certain actions. By attachment we refer to the sense of vesting one's feelings and identity in a role. Certain statuses, especially those dealing with distasteful activities or acts that are condemned except when performed by licensed practitioners, are typically expected to invest their incumbents with only commitment and not with attachment. Hangmen who, when questioned about their occupation, profess to be emotionally attracted to killing, are not likely to have their account honored. Indeed, distasteful tasks are often imputed to have a clandestine but impermissible allure, and so those who regularly perform them are often on their guard to assert their commitment, but not their attachment, to the task.

---

possibilities of a situation that others find improbable. Thus the paranoid husband accounts for his frenzied state by relating that his wife went shopping—and, to him, going shopping constitutes the most opportune occasion to rendezvous secretly with a lover. In response to the inquirer, the paranoid asks: "If you wanted to meet a lover, wouldn't you tell your spouse you're going shopping?" For a general discussion, see Becker, *The Revolution in Psychiatry, op. cit.*

[41]Erving Goffman, *Presentation of Self in Everyday Life*, University of Edinburgh, 1956.

[42]Albert J. Reiss, Jr., "The Social Integration of Queers and Peers," in *The Other Side, op. cit.*, pp. 181–210.

[43]Marguerite Sechehaye, *Autobiography of a Schizophrenic Girl*, New York: Grune and Stratton, 1951.

[44]See Thomas Scheff, *Being Mentally Ill*, Chicago: Aldine Press, 1966. See also Erving Goffman, *Asylums, op. cit.*

[45]These terms are adapted from Erving Goffman, *Behavior in Public Places*, New York: The Free Press of Glencoe, 1963, p. 36n, and *Encounters, op. cit.*, pp. 105 ff.

Organizations systematically provide accounts for their members in a variety of situations. The rules of bureaucracy, for instance, make available accounts for actions taken toward clients—actions which, from the viewpoint of the client, are untoward.[46] Again, these accounts "work" because of a set of background expectations. Thus when people say they must perform a particular action because it is a rule of the organization, the account is regarded as at least reasonable, since "everyone knows" that people follow rules. Of course, the gravity of the event may discredit such accounts, as the trials of Nazi war criminals dramatically illustrate.[47]

Under certain situations behavior that would ordinarily require an account is normalized without interruption or any call for an account. Typically such situations are social conversations in which the values to be obtained by the total encounter supersede those which would otherwise require excuses or justifications. Two values that may override the requirement of accounts are *sociability* and *information*.

In the case of *sociability* the desire that the interactional circle be uninterrupted by any event that might break it calls for each interactant to weigh carefully whether or not the calling for an account might disrupt the entire engagement. When the gathering is a convivial one not dedicated to significant matters—that is, matters that have a proactive life beyond the engagement itself—the participants may overlook errors, inept statements, lies, or discrepancies in the statements of others. Parties often call for such behavior but are vulnerable to disruption by one who violates the unwritten rule of not questioning another too closely. In unserious situations in which strangers are privileged to interact as a primary group without future rights of similar interaction—such as in bars—the interactants may construct elaborate and self-contradictory biographies without fear of being called to account.[48]

In some engagements the interactants seek to obtain *information* from the speaker which is incidental to his main point but which might be withheld if any of the speaker's statements were called into account. Among the Japanese, for example, the significant item in a conversation may be circumscribed by a verbal wall of trivia and superfluous speech. To interrupt a speaker by calling for an account might halt the conversation altogether or detour the speaker away from disclosing the particularly valued pieces of information.[49] Among adolescent boys in American society engaged in a "bull session" it is usually inappropriate to challenge a speaker describing his sexual exploits since, no matter how embellished and exaggerated the account might be, it permits the hearers to glean knowledge about sex—ordinarily withheld from them in the regular channels of education—with impunity. Calling for an account in the midst of such disclosures, especially when the account would require a discussion of the speaker's morality, might cut off the hearers from obtaining precisely that kind of information which is in no other way available to them.[50]

So far we have discussed accounts in terms of their content, but it should be pointed out that accounts also differ in form or style. Indeed, as we will now suggest, the style of an account will have bearing on its honoring or dishonoring.

[46]The theme is widely explored in the literature on formal organizations. For an early and perhaps still the clearest statement of the theme, see Robert K. Merton's widely reprinted "Bureaucratic Structure and Personality," available in *Complex Organizations,* edited by Amitai Etzioni, New York: Holt, Rinehart and Winston, 1962, pp. 48−60.

[47]For a literary illustration, see the play by Peter Weiss, *The Investigation,* New York: Atheneum Books, 1967.

[48]See Sherri Cavan, *Liquor License,* Chicago: Aldine Press, 1966, pp. 79−87.

[49]Edward T. Hall, *The Hidden Dimension,* Garden City: Doubleday, 1966, pp. 139−144.

[50]When a boy is interrupted by a call for an account in the midst of his own recounting of sexual exploits he may simply relapse into uncommunicative silence, change the subject, or withdraw from the group. To prevent any of these, and to aid in the continuity of the original story, the other members of the audience may urge the speaker to continue as before, assure him of their interest and support, and sharply reprove or perhaps ostracize from the group the person who called for the account.

LINGUISTIC STYLES AND ACCOUNTS

We may distinguish five linguistic styles that frame the manner in which an account will be given and often indicate the social circle in which it will be most appropriately employed. These five styles, which in practice often shade into one another and are not unambiguously separated in ordinary life, are the *intimate, casual, consultative, formal,* and *frozen* styles.[51] These styles, as we shall see, are ordered on a scale of decreasing social intimacy.[52]

The *intimate* style is the socially sanctioned linguistic form employed among persons who share a deep, intense and personal relationship. The group within which it is employed is usually a dyad—lovers, a married pair, or very close friends. The group can be larger but not much larger, and when it reaches four or five it is strained to its limits. The verbal style employs single sounds or words, and jargon, to communicate whole ideas. An account given in this form may be illustrated by the situation in which a husband, lying beside his wife in bed, caresses her but receives no endearing response. His wife utters the single word, ''pooped.'' By this term the husband understands that the account given in response to his unverbalized question, ''Why don't you make love to me? After all I am your husband. You have wifely duties!'' is ''I realize that under ordinary circumstances I should and indeed would respond to your love making, but tonight I am too exhausted for that kind of activity. Do not take it to mean that I have lost affection for you, or that I take my wifely duties lightly.''

The *casual* style is used among peers, in-group members and insiders. It is a style employed by those for whom the social distance is greater than that among intimates but is still within the boundaries of a primary relationship. Typically it employs ellipses, i.e., omissions, and slang. In casual

[51]We have adapted these styles from Martin Joos, *The Five Clocks,* New York: Harbinger Books, 1961.

[52]Each of these linguistic styles is associated with distinctive physical distances between the interactants. For a discussion of this point see Hall, *op. cit.,* pp. 116—122.

style certain background information is taken for granted among the interactants and may be merely alluded to in order to give an account. Thus among those who are regular users of hallucinogenic drugs, the question ''Why were you running about naked in the park?'' might be answered, ''I was 'on.' '' The hearer will then know that the speaker was under the influence of a familiar drug and was engaged in an activity that is common in response to taking that drug.

While each style differs from that to which it is juxtaposed by degree, the difference between any two styles—skipping an interval on the aforementioned social intimacy scale—is one of kind. Thus intimate and casual styles differ only in degree from one another and suggest a slight but significant difference in social distance among the interactants, but the *consultative* style differs in kind from the intimate. Consultative style is that verbal form ordinarily employed when the amount of knowledge available to one of the interactants is unknown or problematic to the others. Typically in such an interaction the speaker supplies background information which he is unsure the hearer possesses, and the hearer continuously participates by means of linguistic signs and gestures which indicate that he understands what is said or that he requires more background information. In offering accounts in this form there is a definite element of ''objectivity,'' i.e., of non-subjective and technical terms. The individual giving an account relies on reference to things and ideas outside the intimate and personal realm. In response to the question, ''Why are you smoking marijuana? Don't you know that it's dangerous?,'' the individual might reply, ''I smoke marijuana because everybody who's read the LaGuardia Report knows that it's not habit-forming.'' But a casual response might be simply, ''Don't be square.''

Formal style is employed when the group is too large for informal co-participation to be a continuous part of the interaction. Typically it is suited to occasions when an actor addresses an audience greater than six. Listeners must then wait their turn to respond, or, if they interject comments, know that this will be an untoward event, requiring some kind of re-structuring of the situation. Speaker and audience are in an active and a passive role, respectively, and, if the group is large enough, may be obligated to speak or remain silent according to preestablished codes of procedure. Formal style may also be employed when speaker and auditor are in rigidly defined statuses. Such situations occur in bureaucratic organizations between persons in hierarchically differentiated statuses, or in the courtroom, in the interaction between judge and defendant.

Frozen style is an extreme form of formal style employed among those who are simultaneously required to interact and yet remain social strangers. Typically interaction in the frozen style occurs among those between whom an irremovable barrier exists. The barrier may be of a material or a social nature, or both. Thus pilots communicate to air scanners in a control tower in the same lingual style as prisoners of war to their captors or telephone operators to angered clients. Often the frozen accounts offered are tutored, memorized or written down in advance, and they may be applicable to a variety of situations. Thus the prisoner of war reiterates his name, rank and serial number to all questions and refers his interrogators to the Geneva Convention. The pilot replies to questions about his aberrant flight pattern, coming from the anonymous control tower, with a smooth flow of technical jargon quoted from his handbook on flying. The telephone operator refuses to become flustered or angered by the outraged demands and accusations of the caller unable to reach his party, and quotes from memory the rules of telephone conduct required of the situation.

In summary, then, accounts are presented in a variety of idioms. The idiomatic form of an account is expected to be socially suited to the circle into which it is introduced, according to norms of culture, subculture, and situation. The acceptance or refusal of an offered account in part depends on the appropriateness of the idiom employed. Failure to employ the proper linguistic style often results in a dishonoring of the account or calls for further accounts. Sometimes the situation results in requirements of compound accounting wherein an individual, having failed to employ idiomatic propriety in his first account, is required not only to re-account for his original untoward act but also to present an account for the unacceptable language of his first account. Note that idiomatic errors on the part of a person giving an account provide an unusual opportunity for the hearer to dishonor or punish the speaker if he so wishes. Thus even if the content of the tendered account is such as to excuse or justify the act, a hearer who wishes to discredit the speaker may "trip him up" by shifting the subject away from the matter originally at hand and onto the form of the account given. Typical situations of this kind arise when persons of inferior status provide substantially acceptable accounts for their allegedly untoward behavior to their inquiring superiors but employ idiomatically unacceptable or condemnable form. Thus school children who excuse their fighting with others by not only reporting that they were acting in self-defense but also, and in the process, by using profanity may still be punished for linguistic impropriety, even if they are let off for their original defalcation.[53]

STRATEGIES FOR AVOIDING ACCOUNTS

The vulnerability of actors to questions concerning their conduct varies with the situation and the status of the actors. Where hierarchies of authority govern the social situation, the institutionalized office may eliminate the necessity of an account, or even prevent the question from arising. Military officers are thus shielded from accountability to their subordinates. Where culture distance and

---

[53]Besides the five linguistic styles discussed, we may note that accounts may be usefully distinguished in the manner of their *delivery*. For a cogent typology see Robert E. Pittenger, *et al.*, *The First Five Minutes*, Ithaca, New York: Paul Martineau, 1960, p. 255.

hierarchy are combined—as in the case of slaveholders vis-à-vis their new imported slaves—those enjoying the superior status are privileged to leave their subordinates in a perplexed and frightened state.[54]

Besides the invulnerability to giving accounts arising from the status and position of the actors are the strategies that can prevent their announcement. We may refer to these strategies as meta-accounts. Three such strategies are prominent: *mystification, referral,* and *identity switching.*[55]

When the strategy of *mystification* is employed an actor admits that he is not meeting the expectations of another, but follows this by pointing out that, although there are reasons for his unexpected actions, he cannot tell the inquirer what they are. In its simplest sense the actor says "It's a long story," and leaves it at that. Such accounts are most likely to be honored under circumstances which would normally hinder an elaborate account, as when students have a chance meeting while rushing off to scheduled classes.

More complicated versions of mystification are those that suggest that *alter* is not aware of certain facts—facts that are secret—which, if known, would explain the untoward action. Typically this is the response of the charismatic leader to his followers or the expert to his naive assistant. Thus does Jesus sometimes mystify his disciples and Sherlock Holmes his Dr. Watson. Finally, as already mentioned, certain statuses suggest mystification: in addition to charismatic leaders and experts at occult or little-understood arts are all those statuses characterized by specialized information including (but not limited to) doctors, lawyers, and spies.

Using the strategy of *referral,* the individual says, "I know I'm not meeting your expectations but if you wish to know why, please see. . . ." Typically referral is a strategy available to the sick and the subordinate. Illness, especially mental illness, allows the sick person to refer inquiries about his behavior to his doctor or psychiatrist. Subordinates may avoid giving accounts by designating superiors as the appropriate persons to be questioned. A special example of group referral is that which arises when accounts for the behavior of a whole people are avoided by sending the interrogator to the experts. Thus juvenile delinquents can refer inquiries to social workers, Hopi Indians to anthropologists, and unwed Negro mothers to the Moynihan Report.

In *identity switching, ego* indicates to *alter* that he is not playing the role that *alter* believes he is playing. This is a way of saying to *alter,* "You do not know who I am." This technique is readily available since all individuals possess a multiplicity of identities. Consider the following example.[56] A working-class Mexican husband comes home from an evening of philandering. His wife suspects this and says, "Where were you?" He responds with: "None of your business, you're a wife." Here the husband is assuming that it is not the wife's job to pry into the affairs of her husband. She replies, "What kind of a father are you?" What the woman does here is to suggest that she is not a wife, but a mother—who is looking out for the welfare of the children. To this the husband replies: "I'm a man—and you're a woman." In other words, he is suggesting that, in this status of man, there are things that a woman just doesn't understand. We note in this example that the status of persons not only affects the honoring and non-honoring of accounts, but also determines who can call for an account and who can avoid it. Again it should be pointed out that the normal features of

---

[54]Another kind of invulnerability arises in those situations in which physical presence is tantamount to task performance. Students in a classroom, parishioners in a church, and soldiers at a drill may be counted as "present"—their very visibility being all that is required for routine performance—although they might be "away" in the vicarious sense of day-dreaming, musing on other matters, or relaxing into a reverie.

[55]For these terms, in the context of strategies for avoiding accounts, we are indebted to Gregory Stone.

[56]For this illustration we are again indebted to Gregory Stone. The illustration itself is derived from Oscar Lewis' *The Children of Sanchez, op. cit.*

such interaction depend upon the actors sharing a common set of background expectancies.

NEGOTIATING IDENTITIES AND ACCOUNTS

As our discussion of identity-switching emphasizes, accounts always occur between persons in roles—between husband and wife, doctor and patient, teacher and student, and so on. A normative structure governs the nature and types of communication between the interactants, including whether and in what manner accounts may be required and given, honored or discredited.

Accounts, as suggested, presuppose an identifiable speaker and audience. The particular identities of the interactants must often be established as part of the encounter in which the account is presented.[57] In other words, people generate role identities for one another in social situations. In an account-giving situation, to cast *alter* in a particular role is to confer upon him the privilege of honoring a particular kind of account, the kind suitable to the role identity conferred and assumed for at least the period of account. To assume an identity is to don the mantle appropriate to the account to be offered. Identity assumption and "alter-casting"[58] are prerequisites to the presentation of accounts, since the identities thus established interactionally "set" the social stage on which the drama of the account is to be played out.

The identities of speaker and audience will be negotiated as part of the encounter. Each of the interactants has a stake in the negotiations since the outcomes of the engagement will often depend on these pre-established identities. In competitive or bargaining situations[59] the interactants will each seek to maximize gains or minimize losses, and part of the strategy involved will be to assume and accept advantageous identities, refusing those roles that are disadvantageous to the situation. *Every account is a manifestation of the underlying negotiation of identities.*[60]

The most elementary form of identification is that of human and fellow human negotiated by the immediate perceptions of strangers who engage in abrupt and involuntary engagements. Thus once two objects on a street collide with one another and mutually perceive one another to be humans, an apology in the form of an excuse, or mutually paired excuses, will suffice. Those persons not privileged with full or accurate perception—the blind, myopic, or blindfolded—are not in a position to ascertain immediately whether the object with which they have collided is eligible to call for an account and to deserve an apology. In overcompensating for their inability to negotiate immediately such elementary identities, the persons so handicapped may indiscriminately offer apologies to everyone and everything with which they collide—doormen and doors, street-walkers and street signs. On the other hand, their identification errors are forgiven as soon as their handicap is recognized.

Some objects are ambiguously defined with respect to their deserving of accounts. Animals are an example. House pets, especially dogs and cats, are sometimes imputed to possess human attributes and are thus eligible for apologies and excuses when they are trodden upon by their masters. But insects and large beasts—ants and elephants, for example—do not appear to be normally eligible for accounts even when they are trodden upon by unwary (Occidental) humans.

[57]For an excellent discussion of this point as well as an insightful analysis of the concept of identity, see Anselm L. Strauss, *Mirror and Masks,* New York: The Free Press of Glencoe, 1959.

[58]The concept of "alter-casting" is developed by Eugene A. Weinstein and Paul Deutschberger, "Tasks, Bargains, and Identities in Social Interaction," *Social Forces,* V. 42 (May, 1964), pp. 451—456.

[59]See the brilliant discussion by Thomas C. Schelling, *The Strategy of Conflict,* New York: Galaxy Books, 1963, pp. 21—52.

[60]The terms "identities" and "roles" may be used as synonymous in that roles are identities mobilized in a specific situation; whereas role is alway situationally specific, identities are trans-situational.

However, there are instances wherein the anthropomorphosis of the human self is more difficult to negotiate than that of a dog. Racial minorities in caste societies often insist to no avail on the priority of their identity as "human beings" over their identification as members of a racial group.[61] Indeed the "Negro human-being" role choice dilemma is but one instance of a particular form of strategy in the negotiation of identities. The strategy involves the competition between ego and alter over particularistic versus universalistic role identities. In any encounter in which a disagreement is potential or has already occurred, or in any situation in which an account is to be offered, the particularistic or universalistic identity of the interactants might dictate the manner and outcome of the account situation. Each participant will strive for the advantageous identity. A Negro psychoanalyst with considerable experience in Europe and North Africa has shown how the form of address—either consultative or deprecatingly casual—and the tone used, are opening moves in the doctor's designation of his patient as European or Negro:[62]

> Twenty European patients, one after another, came in: "Please sit down . . . Why do you wish to consult me?" Then comes a Negro or an Arab. "Sit here, boy. . . ."

And, as the psychoanalyst points out, the identity imputed to the patient might be accepted or rejected. To reject the particularistic identity in favor of a universalistic one, the Negro patient might reply, "I am in no sense your boy, Monsieur"[63] and the negotiations for identities begin again or get detoured in an argument.

In an account situation there is a further complication. Once identities have been established and an account offered, the individual has committed himself to an identity and thus seemingly assumed the assets and liabilities of that role for the duration of the encounter. If he accepts the identity as permanent and unchangeable, however, he may have limited his range of subsequent accounts. And if he wishes to shift accounts to one appropriate to another identity he may also need to account for the switch in identities. Thus, in the face of a pejorative particularistic identity, a Negro might wish to establish his claim to a positive universalistic one devoid of the pejorative contents of the imputed one. However, once this new universalistic identity has been established, the Negro might wish to shift back to the particularistic one, if there are positive qualities to be gained thereby, qualities utterly lost by an unqualified acceptance of the universalistic identity.[64] But the switch might require an account itself.

Identity switching has retroactive dangers, since it casts doubt on the attachment the claimant had to his prior identity, and his attachment may have been a crucial element in the acceptability of his first account. On the other hand, the hearer of an account may have a vested interest in accepting the entire range of accounts and may thus accommodate or even facilitate the switch in identities. Thus the hearer may "rationalize" the prior commitment, or reinterpret its meaning so that the speaker may carry off subsequent accounts.[65] Another strategy available to a hearer is to engage in alter-casting for purposes of facilitating or frustrating an account. The fact that individuals have

---

[61] "An unconscious desire to be white, coupled with feelings of revulsion toward the Negro masses, may produce an assimilationist pattern of behavior at the purely personal level. Assimilation is in this sense a means of escape, a form of flight from 'the problem.' It involves a denial of one's racial identity which may be disguised by such sentiments as 'I'm not a Negro but a human being'—as if the two were mutually exclusive. This denial is accompanied by a contrived absence of race consciousness and a belittling of caste barriers. By minimizing the color line, the assimilationist loses touch with the realities of Negro life." Robert A. Bone, *The Negro Novel in America*, New Haven: Yale University Press, 1965, p. 4.

[62] Frantz Fanon, *Black Skin, White Masks*, New York: Grove Press, 1967, p. 32.

[63] *Ibid.*, p. 33.

[64] Fanon, *ibid.*, provides one of the most graphic examples of this phenomenon. For a socio-literary treatment, see St. Clair Drake, "Hide My Face—On Pan-Africanism and Negritude," in Herbert Hill, editor, *Soon One Morning*, New York: Alfred Knopf, 1963, pp. 77–105.

[65] Schelling, *op. cit.*, p. 34.

multiple identities makes them both capable of strategic identity change and vulnerable to involuntary identity imputations.

In ordinary life, accounts are usually "phased."[66] One account generates the question which gives rise to another; the new account requires re-negotiation of identities; the identities necessitate excuses or justifications, improvisation and alter-casting; another account is given; another question arises, and so on. The following interview between a Soviet social worker and his client, a young woman, nicely illustrates this phenomenon.[67]

A girl of about nineteen years of age enters the social worker's office and sits down sighing audibly. The interview begins on a note of *mystification* which ends abruptly when the girl establishes her identity—abandoned wife.

"What are you sighing so sadly for?" I asked. "Are you in trouble?" Lyuba raised her prim little head with a jerk, sighed pianissimo and smiled piteously.

"No . . . it's nothing much. I *was* in trouble, but it's all over now. . . ."

"All over, and you are still sighing about it?" I questioned further. Lyuba gave a little shiver and looked at me. A flame of interest had leaped into her earnest brown eyes.

"Would you like me to tell you all about it?"

"Yes, do."

"It's a long story."

"Never mind. . . ."

"My husband has left me."

The interview carries on in what must be regarded as an unsuccessful approach by the social worker. He establishes that Lyuba still loves her wayward husband, has lost faith in men, and is unwilling to take his advice to forget her first husband and remarry. The abandoned wife turns out to be an identity with which the worker has difficulty coping. He, therefore, alter-casts with telling effect in the following manner.

"Tell me, Lyuba, are your parents alive?"

"Yes, they are. Daddy and Mummy! They keep on telling me off for having got married."

"Quite right too."

"No, it's not. What's right about it?"

"Of course, they're right. You're still a child and already married and divorced."

"Well . . . what about it! What's that got to do with them?"

"Aren't you living with them?"

"I have a room of my own. My husband left me and went to live with his . . . and the room is mine now. And I earn two hundred rubles. And I'm not a child! How can you call me a child?"

Note that little bits of information provide the cues for altercasting, so that Lyuba's volunteering the fact of her parents' disapproval of her first marriage, provides the grounds for the social worker's recasting her in the child role. However this new identity is rejected by Lyuba by further evidentiary assertions: she supports herself and maintains her own residence. The child role has been miscast. Even the social worker gives up his attempt at switching Lyuba out from her role as abandoned wife. He writes: "Lyuba looked at me in angry surprise and I saw that she was quite serious about this game she played in life." Thus negotiations for identities—as in financial transactions—usually end with both parties coming to an agreeable settlement.

CONCLUSION

The sociologist has been slow to take as a serious subject of investigation what is perhaps the most distinctive feature of humans—talk. Here we are suggesting a concern with one type of talk: the study of what constitutes "acceptable utterances"[68] for untoward action. The sociological

---

[66]For a discussion on the "phasing" of encounters, see Strauss, *op. cit.*, p. 44 ff.

[67]The following is from A. S. Makarenko, *The Collective Family*, Garden City: Doubleday Anchor, 1967, pp. 230—232.

[68]The term is borrowed from Noam Chomsky, *Aspects of a Theory of Syntax*, Cambridge, Mass.: MIT Press, 1965, p. 10.

study of communications has relegated linguistic utterances to linguists and has generally mapped out non-verbal behavior as its distinctive domain. We are suggesting that a greater effort is needed to formulate theory that will integrate both verbal and non-verbal behavior.[69]

Perhaps the most immediate task for research in this area is to specify the background expectations that determine the range of alternative accounts deemed culturally appropriate to a variety of recurrent situations. We want to know how the actors take bits and pieces of words and appearances and put them together to produce a perceivedly normal (or abnormal) state of affairs. This kind of inquiry crucially involves a study of background expectations.[70] On the basis of such investigations, the analyst should be able to provide a set of instructions on ''how to give an account'' that would be taken by other actors as ''normal.''[71] These instructions would specify how different categories of statuses affect the honoring of an account, and what categories of statuses can use what kinds of accounts.

[69]To our knowledge the most persuasive argument for this need is made by Kenneth L. Pike, *Language in Relation to a Unified Theory of the Structure of Human Behavior*, Glendale: Summer Institute of Linguistics, 1954. A short, clear programmatic statement is found in Dell Hymes' ''The Ethnography of Speaking,'' in Thomas Gladwin and William C. Sturtevant, editors, *Anthropology and Human Behavior*, Washington, D.C.: Anthropological Society of Washington, 1962, pp. 72–85. For an argument that stresses the analytic separation of the content of talk from the forms of talk, see the brief but lucid statement by Erving Goffman, ''The Neglected Situation,'' in The Ethnography of Communications, edited by John Gumperz and Dell Hymes, *American Anthropologist*, 66 (December, 1964), Part 2, pp. 133–136.

[70]For the methodology of such studies sociologists may well investigate the anthropological technique of componential analysis, i.e., the study of contrast sets. The clearest statement of the method of componential analysis is that of Charles O. Frake, ''The Ethnographic Study of Cognitive Systems,'' in *Anthropology and Human Behavior, op. cit.*, pp. 72–85. A related methodology is developed by Sacks in *The Search for Help, op. cit.*

[71]See Charles O. Frake, ''How to Ask for a Drink in Subanun,'' in *The Ethnography of Communications, op. cit.*, pp. 127–132.

Future research on accounts may fruitfully take as a unit of analysis the *speech community*.[72] This unit is composed of human aggregates in frequent and regular interaction. By dint of their association sharers of a distinct body of verbal signs are set off from other speech communities. By speech community we do not refer to language communities, distinguished by being composed of users of formally different languages. Nor do we refer simply to dialect communities, composed of persons who employ a common spoken language which is a verbal variant of a more widely used written language.

Speech communities define for their members the appropriate lingual forms to be used amongst themselves. Such communities are located in the social structure of any society. They mark off segments of society from one another, and also distinguish different kinds of activities. Thus, the everyday language of lower-class teenage gangs differs sharply from that of the social workers who interview them, and the language by which a science teacher demonstrates to his students how to combine hydrogen and oxygen in order to produce water differs from the language employed by the same teacher to tell his inquisitive six-year-old son how babies are created. The types of accounts appropriate to each speech community differ in form and in content. The usage of particular speech norms in giving an account has consequences for the speaker depending upon the relationship between the form used and the speech community into which it is introduced.

A single individual may belong to several speech communities at the same time, or in the course of a lifetime. Some linguistic devices (such as teenage argot) are appropriate only to certain

[72]The idea of a ''speech community'' is usefully developed by John J. Gumperz in ''Speech Variation and the Study of Indian Civilization,'' in *Language in Culture and Society*, edited by Dell Hymes, N.Y.: Harper and Row, 1964, pp. 416–423; and ''Linguistic and Social Interaction in Two Communities,'' in *Ethnography of Communications, op. cit.*, pp. 137–153.

age groups and are discarded as one passes into another age grouping; others, such as the linguistic forms used by lawyers in the presence of judges, are appropriate to certain status sets and are consecutively employed and discarded as the individual moves into and out of interactions with his various status partners. Some individuals are dwellers in but a single speech community; they move in circles in which all employ the same verbal forms. The aged and enfeebled members of class or ethnic ghettos are an obvious example. Others are constant movers through differing speech communities, adeptly employing language forms suitable to the time and place they occupy. Social workers who face teenage delinquents, fellow workers, lawyers, judges, their own wives, and children, all in one day, are an example.

In concluding we may note that, since it is with respect to deviant behavior that we call for accounts, the study of deviance and the study of accounts are intrinsically related, and a clarification of accounts will constitute a clarification of deviant phenomena—to the extent that deviance is considered in an interactional framework.[73]

[73]We refer to the approach to deviance clearly summarized by Howard S. Becker, *The Outsiders*, New York: The Free Press of Glencoe, 1963, esp. pp. 1−18.

THIRTY-ONE

DISCLAIMERS*

JOHN P. HEWITT AND RANDALL STOKES

INTRODUCTION

Problematic events of varying seriousness occur in the concrete situations of everyday life: people are embarrassed by their own and others' *faux pas;* serious and trivial departures from role obligations are noticed; rules are broken (or, more properly, certain actions are treated as rule violations); extraordinary, disturbing, or seemingly inexplicable behavior is observed in self or others.

Such problematic events are important for two reasons. First, they affect the course and outcome of social interaction. People gear their words and deeds to the restoration and maintenance of situated and cherished identities. When the violation of rules fractures the context of interaction, or when the emergent meaning of a situation is disrupted, people endeavor to repair the breaks and restore meaning. Thus, if the direction of social interaction in a given situation is to be well understood, adequate concepts for handling such events are necessary.

Second, a conceptual grasp of the problematic features of identity, social interaction and emergent meaning is crucial to an understanding of the classic problem of social order and cultural continuity. While the sociological treatment of the problem is conventionally anchored in socialization and the internalization of culture, there are several difficulties with such a formulation, most notably that little routine action appears guided by deeply internalized norms. A discussion of problematic events aids in the reformulation of the link between culture and behavior, for it is in relation to such problematic occasions that culture most clearly enters the consciousness of actors, shapes the meaning of their conduct, becomes fundamental to their identities, and is thus made visible and re-affirmed.

Several concepts have been developed to deal with the problem of how actors restore disrupted meaning, repair fractured social interaction, and re-negotiate damaged identities. C. Wright Mills' (1940) conception of "vocabularies of motive"; Marvin Scott and Stanford Lyman's (1968) "accounts"; and John Hewitt and Peter Hall's (1970, 1973) "quasi-theories" each comes to grips with

SOURCE: John P. Hewitt and Randall Stokes. "Disclaimers." Copyright by the American Sociological Association, 1975. John P. Hewitt and Randall Stokes, "Disclaimers," *American Sociological Review*, XL (February, 1975), pp. 1–11. Reprinted by permission of the American Sociological Association.

*We are indebted to Rob Faulkner for his helpful comments on an earlier draft of this paper.

an important aspect of the dual problem of social interaction and culture in problematic situations.

For Mills, the most important feature of motives is that they arise in talk, whether as states of mind the person imputes to others or avows for himself. "As a word, a motive tends to be one which is to the actor and to the other members of a situation an unquestioned answer to questions concerning social and lingual conduct" (Mills, 1940:906). Motive talk is thus important to the ongoing construction of meaning in social interaction, since the continuity of both is sustained (in part) by people's ability to attribute their own and others' acts to "reasons" or "motives." While Mills addresses himself to the issue of how disrupted meaning is restored, his discussion lacks generality, since motive talk, while central to social interaction, is not the only means of dealing with disrupted meaning.

The concepts of accounts and quasi-theories are also addressed, each in a particular way, to problematic meaning. Accounts are the justifications and excuses people offer when the course of interaction has been disrupted by an act or word. Quasi-theories are explanations people construct in social interaction to account for various kinds of problematic situations. Both concepts point to observable features of social interaction in which meaning is restored by efforts undertaken for that purpose. But these concepts are limited because their view of meaning and its reconstruction is largely *retrospective*—they deal with the definition of the past in the present. Neither deals adequately, nor is it intended to do so, with the anticipation of events, with the *prospective* construction of meaning for words and deeds that may be problematic.

This paper introduces, defines and discusses a new concept, the "disclaimer." Its level is that of the account and the quasi-theory: a process that occurs in social interaction in which problematic· events that may disrupt emergent meaning are defined and dealt with. Unlike accounts and quasi-theories, which are retrospective in their effect, disclaimers are prospective, defining the future in the present, creating interpretations of potentially problematic events intended to make them unproblematic when they occur.

THE DISCLAIMER

In order to define the disclaimer and describe its forms we must first attend to some major features of problematic meaning. As individuals in social interaction form their conduct in response to one another, meaning in their situation is created and maintained. The individual organizes meaning thematically: as behavior in the situation emerges he seeks to "fit" events to "theme" (McHugh, 1968). The relationship between the theme that organizes meaning and the specific acts or events that fit the theme is a reflexive one: events take on meaning when pattern is imputed to them; pattern is visible only in the concrete events it is used to interpret. When events or acts no longer seem understandable in terms of the patterns imputed to them, individuals examine discrepant events with some care, seeking to determine what has gone wrong with their understanding of the situation.

Central to the themes used to organize meaning are identities. Whether defined on the basis of conventional, named social roles (father, policeman, teacher) or interpersonal roles established by specific individuals over time in relation to one another (friend, follower, enemy), situated identities are established and known to interactants. Indeed, the thematic organization of meaning by interactants usually depends upon their ability to interpret each others' actions as manifestations of particular identities. It follows that when events fail to fit themes in interaction, identities may come into focus as problematic: if the acts of another fail to appear sensible in light of his identity in the situation, perhaps he is not who he appears to be.

The crucial place of identities in the organization of meaning points more generally to the importance of the process of typifying and the fact of typification in social interaction (Schutz, 1964).

In their relations with one another, people search for and make use of specific cues from others as a means of typifying them, i.e., of treating them as kinds of persons. Socialized individuals carry with them a vast store of information as to how various types of persons will behave, what they are like, their typical motives and values, how to deal with them, etc. In concrete situations they search for cues from others, invoke a typification that appears relevant to those cues and rely upon the store of information organized by the typification in their subsequent interaction with the other, filling in the "gaps" in the other's self-presentation with the typification. Some typifications are essentially identical in content to conventional and interpersonal roles (thus we carry typifications of fathers, enemies, policemen), while others cut across the grain of roles, pointing to other "types" that may, in given cases, be important, even controlling in social interaction (so, for example, we carry typifications of the prejudiced, stupid, incompetent, mentally ill, etc.).

Crucial to the concept of the disclaimer is the fact that individuals *know* their own acts serve as the basis for typifying them; they know that specific acts they undertake will be treated by others as cues for typification. They know this, in the simplest sense, because they do it themselves, seeking in others' acts the "keys" that will unlock the secrets of their behavior. Moreover, with varying degrees of awareness, individuals seek to present others with cues that will lead to desired typifications of them—to present themselves in ways that will lead others to grant their situated identity claims.

This awareness of typification (in general, if not in specific cases) plays an important role in the imaginative preconstructions of conduct that go on continuously in the mental life of the individual. As individuals construct their acts in imagination, they anticipate the responses of others, including the typificatory uses to which their acts will be put. For the individual, any given act is potentially a basis on which others can typify him. Put another

way, as the individual anticipates the response to his conduct, he may see it either as in line with an established identity or as somehow discrepant, in which case it may be taken as a cue for some new typification, possibly a negative one, possibly a more favorable one.

Individuals' anticipation of others' typifications of them are not governed, however, by any simple principle of seeking positive and avoiding negative typifications. Life is filled with occasions on which individuals find it necessary to engage in acts that undermine the emergent meaning of situations and make probable the destruction of their identities in them. Even if they do not feel constrained to act in such ways, individuals may perceive opportunities—even legitimate ones—in lines of action they know others will take exception to. And on some occasions, individuals may sense the possibility of being typified in ways they would like to avoid, but find themselves without any certain way of anticipating the response. Under such circumstances as these and others, disclaimers are invoked.

A disclaimer is a verbal device employed to ward off and defeat in advance doubts and negative typifications which may result from intended conduct. Disclaimers seek to define forthcoming conduct as not relevant to the kind of identity-challenge or re-typification for which it might ordinarily serve as the basis. Examples abound and serve to make the abstract concrete: "I know this sounds stupid, but . . . ."; "I'm not prejudiced, because some of my best friends are Jews, but . . . ."; "This is just off the top of my head, so . . . ."; "What I'm going to do may seem strange, so bear with me." "This may make you unhappy, but . . . ."; "I realize I'm being anthropomorphic. . . . ."

In each of the foregoing examples, individuals display in their speech the expectation of possible responses of others to their impending conduct. In each example, a specific utterance calls the other's attention to a *possible* undesired typification and asks forbearance. Each phrase, in effect, disclaims that the word or deed to follow should be used as a basis for identity challenge and re-typification. the user's clear hope is that his intended act will not disrupt the current relationship, nor undesirably shift the emergent definition of the situation. Each disclaimer is thus a device used to sustain interaction, to manage the flow of meaning in situations, to negotiate a social order in which people can treat one another's acts with discretion, with good judgment, and with deserved good will.

TYPES OF DISCLAIMERS

The examples cited above, as well as others, can best be analyzed by sorting disclaimers into several types, each of which reflects a different set of conditions of use.

Hedging. There are countless situations in which individuals preface statements of fact or opinion, positions in arguments or expressions of belief with disclaimers of the following kind: "I'm no expert, of course, but . . ."; "I could be wrong on my facts, but I think . . ."; "I really haven't thought this through very well, but . . ."; "I'm not sure this is going to work, but let's give it a try"; "Let me play devil's advocate here. . . ."

What does the use of disclaimers of this type indicate about the individual's conduct and his expectations about others' responses? First, each expression is an intentional signal of minimal commitment to the impending line of conduct, an indication of willingness to receive discrepant information, change opinions, be persuaded otherwise or be better informed. Put otherwise, such an expression indicates the tentative nature of forthcoming action. Second, the tentative or negotiable coloration given subsequent conduct indicates a measure of uncertainty about the likely response to the act. From the standpoint of the individual constructing his act, what he is about to say may be taken seriously and importantly by others, thus confirming his identity; or it may be taken by others as damaging to his identity, even as the basis for some new, controlling typification of him. He does not know. Third, the re-typification

that may occur is at least potentially serious. While the individual may suspect that the worst that can happen is that he will be thought ill-informed or wrong-headed, he faces the possibility that his act may fundamentally transform him in the eyes of the other.

Minimal commitment and uncertain response are the defining conditions under which hedging takes place. Where an individual does not know how his act will be received and simultaneously does not think a positive response to his act is essential to his identity or his ends, he will hedge by disclaiming in advance the importance of the act to his identity. "I'm no expert" is a phrase that conveys to others the idea that no expert identity is being claimed; if no expertise is, in fact, shown, no claim needs to be defended. The phrase signals to hearers that they should treat factually faulty statements or deeds that have the wrong effects as the normal prerogative of people who are not and do not claim to be expert in what they are doing.

At the same time, variability in feared seriousness of response makes for variability within the category of hedging. At one extreme, a person may fear his words or deeds will drastically re-cast him in the eyes of others, and thus make attainment of his ends difficult. Persons who *are* expert, therefore, will often appeal to faulty memory, possible misunderstanding or over-specialization if they fear an impending act will lead to their re-typification as incompetent. Persons who occupy central, leadership positions in administrative organizations often adopt the practice of playing devil's advocate of positions they genuinely support, since they fear open and committed advocacy of position might erode their power and authority. At the other extreme, where people feel they have little to fear in the way of drastic re-typification, hedging is more like insurance, and often more like ritual; a way of reminding people that no great emphasis should be put on their success or failure, accuracy or error, in what they are about to say or do.

Credentialing. Expressions of a different sort are employed when the individual *knows* the outcome of his act will be discrediting, but is nevertheless strongly committed to the act. Credentialing encompasses a group of expressions of this kind exemplified by the following: "I know what I'm going to say seems anthropomorphic, but . . ."; "I'm not prejudiced—some of my best friends are Jews, but . . ."; "Don't get me wrong, I like your work, but. . . ."

In credentialing individuals seek to avoid an undesired typification they are certain will follow from an intended act. The expressions of credentialing try to accomplish this by establishing for the actor special qualifications or credentials that, he implies, permit him to engage in the act without having it treated in the usual way as a cue for typification. In the classic "some of my best friends" example, the speaker acknowledges that someone who says what he is about to say might be typified as a prejudiced person, but implies his friendships put him in a protected category of people who cannot be so typified. The man who sees human qualities in his dogs knows that speaking of them in an anthropomorphic way will make him seem foolish, and so seeks to avoid the typification by announcing he knows it could be made.

In this second example, knowledge of the negative aspects of an act is central to the establishment of a right to engage in the act anyway. Knowledge is a credential because it establishes the actor as one who may have *purpose* in what he is doing, so that others cannot easily regard him as an unknowing representative of a particular negative type. One who has purpose may have good purpose, whereas one who acts in blind ignorance of the implications of his act is presumed not to.

Sin Licenses. Another category of expressions is employed when the actor is committed to a line of conduct and is certain of a negative response, but does not fear some specific undesired typification. In some instances of social interaction, actors anticipate that their acts will be treated as rule violations. Instead of a specific typification (e.g., racist, fool), the actor fears destruction of his identity as a "responsible member" of the encounter and the substitution of a "rule breaker" or "irresponsible member" typification of him. The focus of his talk and his concern is upon the rule which he fears will be invoked as a rebuke to his action. Hence the following examples: "I realize you might think this is the wrong thing to do, but . . ."; "I know this is against the rules, but . . ."; "What I'm going to do is contrary to the letter of the law but not its spirit. . . ."

Invoking the sin licensing disclaimer is equivalent to stipulating in advance that an act to follow might ordinarily be deemed a violation of a rule, and thus disruptive of the interaction that is taking place. The disclaimer is an effort to invoke in a specific situation the more general and commonly recognized principle that there are occasions on which rules may legitimately be violated without questioning the status of those who violate them. Just as accounts are invoked retrospectively as a way of placing rule violations in such a category, sin licensing disclaimers are invoked prospectively as a way of defining the conduct in advance. (But clearly there is less flexibility in the disclaimer— some excuses are good retrospectively but not prospectively.)

In many instances the sin licensing disclaimer is invoked seriously; that is, its user genuinely fears typification as a rule breaker. In other cases, however, where rules are routinely broken and participants aware of this fact, licenses to sin are requested and granted on a *pro forma* basis. In either case, the license to sin pays due respect to the rules even while establishing the conditions under which they may be broken.

Cognitive Disclaimers. In routine social interaction, participants seldom have occasion to question one another's empirical grasp of the situation in which they are present. Participants generally assume substantive congruency between their own and others' grasp of the situation. Yet underlying any situation is the possibility that the words or deeds of one participant will be construed by others as lacking sense, as out of touch with empirical reality, as somehow indicating the individual's failure to perceive the situation adequately and correctly. While individuals generally assume that others will assume their acts make empirical sense, they know that some acts may be misconstrued, and that this misconstrual may lead to their own re-typification as lacking sense, as out of touch, as disengaged when they should be engaged, as irrational. Under conditions where they think their acts may be so questioned, individuals use cognitive disclaimers such as the following: "This may seem strange to you. . ."; "Don't react right away to what I'm going to do." "I know this sounds crazy, but I think I saw. . . ."

Cognitive disclaimers anticipate doubts that may be expressed concerning the speaker's capacity to recognize adequately the empirical facts of the situation in which he finds himself. By anticipating doubt, the disclaimer seeks to reassure others that there is no loss of cognitive capacity, that there is still agreement on the facts of the situation. In this form of disclaiming, as in the others, knowledge is a key element: by demonstrating in advance knowledge of a possible basis for re-typification, the individual establishes purpose for acts that might otherwise be taken as having no purpose, as reflecting a loss of cognitive control.

Appeals for the Suspension of Judgment. If much social interaction is pursued in situations in which people have common ends and work to achieve consensus on them and the means of attaining them, still in such interaction individuals recognize that on occasion their acts may offend even their friends. That is, people are aware that what they say and do may be offensive, angering or dismaying to those with whom they interact, unless and until they can place the act in a proper context, give it the "correct" meaning so far as the exchange is concerned. Under such circumstances, individuals appeal to their fellows to suspend judgment until the full meaning of the act can be made known. "I don't want to make you angry by saying this, but. . ."; "Don't get me wrong, but. . ."; "Hear me out before you explode" are illustrative of appeals individuals make for the suspension of judgment.

Frequently, such appeals take the form of appeals for the suspension of affect, in effect asking the other to hold back on what the actor fears will be a powerful affective response until full meaning can be transmitted. In other cases (e.g., "Don't react until I get this all out") the appeal is not to suspend specific affect, but merely to await full meaning. In either case, the disclaiming individual realizes that what he is about to do may disrupt the social situation, partly because the assumption of common purpose may be questioned, partly because it may promote his own re-typification as an "enemy" or "turncoat" and not a comrade, friend or colleague.

RESPONSES TO DISCLAIMERS

The discussion has so far emphasized users' perspectives, grounding its classification in the intentions and expectations of those who disclaim. But the picture is incomplete until we grasp how it is that others respond to disclaimers and how their responses affect the course of social interaction.

From the user's standpoint, the disclaimer is an effort to dissociate his identity from the specific content of his words or deeds. Take, for example, the following use of credentialing: "I'm no racist, because I have a lot of black friends and associates, but I think black people want too much, too soon." In this and similar instances, two fundamental claims are made: first, there is an identity claim—specifically, a negative typification as a racist is disclaimed, and so the opposite, valued identity is claimed; second, there is a substantive claim—specifically, an expressed belief that blacks want improvements more quickly than they can or should be provided. People use disclaimers in order to secure the success of substantive claims, but without the possible negative implications for their identity claims.

By the phrase substantive claim we refer to the fact that every word or deed has implications for the emerging definition of a situation and the joint action it contains. In the above illustration the substantive claim is a factual claim, that is, a statement that certain conditions are true of blacks. In other instances, substantive claims have to do with morality (e.g., ''It is right to do what I am urging we do.''), technical efficiency (e.g., ''This is an appropriate way of doing things.'') and the like. Every word or deed operates, in effect, as a claim that the situation should be defined in a certain way, or that it can be best defined in that way or that for all practical purposes that is the way to define it. While claims are not always (nor, perhaps, often) expressed in so many words, they operate to the same effect.

This distinction is crucial to our discussion of responses, for both uses of and responses to disclaimers proceed on these parallel levels of identity and substance. On one hand, others may either accept or reject the identity portion of the disclaimer, either attributing to the user the identity he seeks to avoid or supporting his existing identity in the situation. On the other hand (and somewhat independently of their response on the issue of identity), others may accept or reject the user's substantive claims, agreeing or disagreeing with his statements, regarding his actions as useful or dangerous, morally acceptable or prohibited.

From the user's point of view, a disclaimer is fully successful if it allows both types of claim to be accepted; the other concedes the substantive import of the user's actions or expressions and makes no undesired re-typification of him. In the example cited above, factual claims about blacks would be granted and no re-typification as a racist would take place. Under such a condition of ''full success,'' we may assume, interaction proceeds on its course—a potential disturbance has been successfully skirted.

Less desirable, but still to be counted a partial success, is the condition where a substantive claim is rejected, but where a possible re-typification is not made. Following the same example, a result such as the following illustrates partial success: ''I think you're wrong about the pace of black progress but, of course, I know you are not a racist.'' In this condition, while the user has failed to define the situation in the hoped-for manner, he has at least succeeded in preserving his identity in the situation and avoiding re-typification.

In either of the above conditions, we can speak of the acceptance of a disclaimer in the sense that the user's identity is preserved intact. A disclaimer is said to be rejected when its user is typified by another in a negative way, whatever his response to the substantive claim. On one hand, it seems likely that most rejected disclaimers involve a rejection of both claims: the use of credentialing, as in the above example, would lead both to a denial of the factual claim being made *and* to the re-typification of the user as a racist. On the other hand, there is at least the logical possibility that a substantive claim will be granted, but that simultaneously the user will be re-typified. ''Being right for the wrong reasons'' is an illustration of a condition where factual claims are granted in the very process of altering a user's identity.

The acceptance or rejection of disclaimers is, however, a more complex and uncertain process than our eliptical discussion indicates. We have glossed over, thus far, the process of inference and signaling that is crucial to the outcome of a given disclaimer. The appropriate questions are the following: How is it that users infer acceptance or rejection of their claims? How is it that others signal acceptance or rejection of users' claims?

The questions of inference and signaling are, in the course of real social interaction, bound closely together; indeed, there is much reflexivity between the two. Whether a signal is, in fact, a signal is not concretely a matter of fact, but depends upon the interplay between the user's inference and the other's intent. What is intended to be a signal may be falsely construed or not construed at all, and what is not intended as a signal may be so construed, either favorably or unfavorably to the user's hopes. And part of the making of an inference involves its being made known to the other that an inference has been made, a linkage that is always subject to possible slippage.

For analytical purposes, however, we must separate inference and signaling. The former can be discussed by paying attention to the rules or procedures invoked by the user, whether inwardly or overtly, in an effort to determine the success of his disclaimer.

In the most elementary sense *prima facie* evidence of a disclaimer's success is to be sought in the other's overt response: if the response the user hoped to avoid is not forthcoming, he has evidence that his tactic has suceeded. If an interactant credentials his prejudical statement, he may infer the success of his credentialing if no charge of prejudice is forthcoming. This will be so at the level of his identity claim, whatever the response given the substance of his action.

The possibility always exists, of course, that others will withhold cues that would enable the interactant to judge the success of his disclaimer. While much of our imagery of role playing and role taking suggests that actors are always forthcoming about their true judgments, there is no reason to assume that awareness contexts are typically open. Closed, pretense or suspicion awareness contexts may characterize the use and response to disclaimers as much as any other form of interaction. Thus, we must observe, inferences about success based on *prima facie* evidence must always be, for the actors who make them, somewhat tentative. Every use of a disclaimer risks the possibility that a user's identity may be damaged without his immediately discovering the damage.

More positively, users may infer acceptance or rejection from cues provided by others. Such cues, insofar as they are meant to signal acceptance, may take a variety of forms. The other may, for example, address himself explicitly to the issue raised by the disclaimer: "I realize you are no expert."; "I know you aren't prejudiced."; "I understand what you mean." These examples suggest responses that more or less explicitly signal the legitimacy of the disclaimer in the situation at hand. Sometimes the positive response may include the sharing of the disclaimer, which entails the other using an expression that indicates that he, also, shares the point of view of the user, that he too might, in similar circumstances, use the same disclaimer. We may assume that when others provide users with positive cues, inferences are made with more confidence and interaction continues on its course. Even here, however, there is slippage between intent and inference, and a nod of the head that signifies to the user the acceptance of his viewpoint may be to the other a means of giving the user more rope with which to hang himself.

The question of inference and signaling also turns on the degree to which those who use disclaimers provide an opportunity for response. Social interaction is not always conducted with full attention to the etiquette of turn-taking; indeed, users of disclaimers may intentionally "rush" their interaction sequences in such a way that others are "left behind" and, having had no opportunity to object, are in the position of having agreed by default. An interaction sequence may be rushed by a refusal to yield the floor to another for a response or a refusal to "see" that the floor is wanted by another. A sequence may also be rushed where deeds follow so quickly upon words that commitments are made that cannot subsequently be escaped.

Opportunities for negative responses to disclaimers may also be limited if users are able to "finesse" interaction sequences. On the one hand, actors can "get away with" words and deeds that are gross threats to their identities if they undertake them in small steps, invoking seemingly minor disclaimers along the way. That is, small disclaimers are honored more readily, we may suggest, than large ones, but a series of small disclaimers may result in a major behavioral cue being treated as irrelevant to the actor's identity. On the other hand, it is not unreasonable to suppose that actors may on occasion make a disclaimer of far greater magnitude than their impending act calls for, knowing the other may thus be more likely to accept it. On any occasion where a disclaimer might be used, the user has some discretion in terms of associating his impending act with a possible negative typification of him. By exaggerating the possibly negative typification, and then proceeding with his word or deed, he hopes to secure acceptance by virtue of contrast.

The net outcome of successful disclaimers, whether the acceptance is voluntary or reflects the user's successful rushing or finessing of the interaction sequence, is that the user's identity in the situation is at least temporarily sustained. No re-typification in negative terms takes place, no disruption in the emergence of meaning occurs. Not only this, acceptance of a disclaimer, and particularly the acceptance of a series of disclaimers, commits both participants to the reciprocal identities being built up. As a situation proceeds and as disclaimers are employed successfully, we can hypothesize that it becomes more difficult for participants to reject subsequent disclaimers—the progressive solidification of identities lays the groundwork for easier disclaiming and, at some stage, makes it possible for actors to assume disclaimers and acceptances of one another rather than having to make each one explicitly.

How, then, are disclaimers rejected? What cues are sought or provided? What procedures are used to make inferences about acceptance? Again, in the simplest sense, *prima facie* evidence of rejection is to be found if the other explicitly avows what the disclaimer had sought to avoid. Rejection is certain if the other affirms that the very re-typification that the user feared is, in fact, to be made of him. ''You should be an expert in this area!'' ''You've had plenty of time to work on a proposal.'' ''If you know it's anthropomorphic, why are you saying it?'' Expressions such as these are used as counters to disclaimers, indicating to the user in direct terms that his tactic has not worked, that he will be re-typified unless he can adduce evidence to show why he should not be.

The failure of a disclaimer makes its user subject to re-typification in the very terms his disclaimer provided to the other. This fact is both a weakness and a strength. It is a weakness, of course, because the use of a given disclaimer provides other interactants with a ready-made issue in terms of which the now-disrupted meaning of the context can be managed. Where hedging has been used, the issue is the identity of the user: thus, for example, a disclaimer of devil's advocacy may be met with a denial that only devil's advocacy is meant, that, in fact, the user is concealing his true purpose or goals, i.e., his true identity. Where credentialing has been employed, the issue becomes one of purpose or intent, specifically of good or bad intent, since the use of credentialing rests largely upon the implication that since the user knows the possibly evil connotations of what he is about to do or say, he may have other than evil intent. Thus charges of evil purpose and identity concealment may also be made. Where sin licensing has been invoked, the issue turns on the applicability of a given rule to the act in question. Where cognitive disclaimers are used, the issue becomes one of fact and its interpretation. Where the appeal is to suspend judgment, the issue is whether, in the end, meaning was in fact clarified during the suspension.

To say that ''the issue'' turns upon this or that point is to say that the focus of interaction itself turns upon the disclaimer, its user's identity and the associated act. Since the user has, via his disclaimer, announced the problematic quality of his words or deeds, he has placed ready-made weapons at the disposal of the other. The question that arises at this point, therefore, is how interaction progresses when it focuses upon the disclaimer.

It is worth noting that up to this point, the user has sought to manage his own identity in the eyes of the other, whatever the outcome with respect to substantive claims. Now the issue is, basically, his identity, and what is important to the user is how that identity may be sustained. While the tactics of identity maintenance in such circumstances is a matter of empirical discovery, it seems likely that altercasting will play an important role in the proceedings.

Altercasting (Weinstein and Deutschberger, 1963) is a process in which actors endeavor to regulate the identities of others: going on the offensive in an argument, treating a particular child as the "baby of the family," creating a "straw man" and identifying an opponent with it are illustrations of the technique of altercasting. In each case, an other's identity is governed, or an effort is made to have it be governed, by an actor's actions. (Altercasting is to be understood in contrast with identity as a phenomenon an actor manages for himself.)

The significance of altercasting in the disclaiming process lies in the fact that an identity established for another has implications for the identity of the altercaster. Identities are reciprocal, which is to say that participants in social interaction establish identities for themselves and each other in a mutually related texture where the position of one has implications for the position of another. In the disclaiming process, altercasting would appear to be significant because it offers the user a "last chance" to salvage his own identity by trying to establish for the rejecting other an identity that will reflect favorably on the rejected user. Having failed to disclaim an identity implied in his actions and utterances, the user may attempt to salvage his identity by more or less forcibly working on the identity of the other, seeking to portray the other in a light that makes his own discredit less serious, or even makes it disappear. Thus, to illustrate, the user may act towards the other as if the latter, too, shared in the discredit: following our example of the credentialing racist, the user may seek to apply the label racist to the other, perhaps by citing or alleging more serious violations on the part of the latter.

In addition to altercasting, the user may turn to various accounts (Scott and Lyman, 1968) as a way of extracting himself from his predicament. As a disclaimer is used and meets a negative response, it passes into the immediate past, and so becomes a proper object of an account. The user may excuse his conduct, thus defusing its relevance to his identity by accepting its undesirable nature by denying responsibility. Or he may attempt a justification, accepting responsibility but arguing for the irrelevance of his act to his identity.

The possible outcomes of rejected disclaimers, in terms of the course of the interaction and the identities of participants, are many, and difficult to summarize or generalize. Underlying all outcomes, however, is the basic fact that issues of substance have become transformed into issues of participants' identities. In effect, when disclaimers are rejected, a situation is transformed, with possibly unpleasant short and long-term consequences for the actor whose identity claims have been destroyed.

That a rejected disclaimer does not inevitably imply the loss of a desirable situated identity, and may in fact be a strength to the user, turns on the fact that a user may under some conditions *seek* to have his disclaimer rejected. If some actors are genuinely concerned with their identities in the eyes of others, others may be cynical in the use of disclaimers. Just as an individual may use a disclaimer that is far out of proportion to the "real" implications of his conduct in the hopes that it will be more easily accepted, he may look ahead, construct alternative scenarios of the conversation on which he is embarked and choose disclaimers in such a way that discussion turns on issues he can best argue. If his disclaimer is accepted, he is able to pursue the line of conduct he had in mind. If it is rejected, he is in a relatively strong position to argue his case, to portray his partner's characterization of him as a "straw man," even though he is himself the source of the characterization.

CONCLUSION: THE DISCLAIMER AND SOCIAL THEORY

The disclaimer and the broader current of thought of which it is a part have significance for a long-standing problem in social theory. This is the question of how culture enters individual action or, more broadly, how social order and continuity are maintained. Culture, in most formulations, is the root of continuity. Parsons (1966: 5—7), for example, visualizes culture as akin to the genetic code of physical organisms. Just as the genetic pool of a species provides the parameters for individual phenotypes, so does culture provide the persisting identity for individual actions and interaction. Yet, the crucial question of how culture enters individual action has not been satisfactorily answered.

The most important link between culture and action is generally seen to be the socialization process. Following Mead's seminal account of the generalized other, and de-emphasizing his concern for emergence, heaviest stress has been placed on *internalization* as the means by which culture is transmitted and becomes influential upon action. From this perspective, internalization constitutes a functional equivalent to instinct in other animal species; the bee's dance is guided by a genetic template and man's by a deeply internalized normative structure. Although the origins of control are different, the consequences are the same. In both cases, the direction and substance of action are provided by a precognitive and involuntary hierarchy of preferences. In those (relatively rare) situations where deviance does occur, the reason is seen to be incomplete or faulty socialization, and the link of culture to behavior is then maintained by mechanisms of external control in the form of sanctions.

The perspective sketched, or perhaps caricatured, above has been seriously questioned in recent years. The fundamental root of such questioning is empirical. While it is clear that certain cultural elements are deeply internalized, particularly language-based logical and inferential canons, primal esthetic preferences and so on, relatively little of routine social action appears to be guided by deeply internalized normative structures. Man does not act like a well-programmed social robot; indeed, in much of everyday social action, variation from normatively prescribed behavior is statistically "normal."

This point has been made from a number of different theoretical perspectives. Dennis Wrong (1961) has argued from a psychoanalytical perspective that sociologists typically err by viewing man as "over-socialized." Sociology, he claims, has historically failed to take account of residual and unsocialized libidinal energy, which continues to exert a dynamic and "unsocial" influence on individual action. David Riesman (1950) and Allen Wheelis (1958), while they don't dispute that traditional views of the link between action and culture may have fitted some earlier time, contend that such models are increasingly inappropriate for contemporary society. Modern man, they argue, is given by his socialization a diffuse capacity to read social cues and to make situationally appropriate responses, rather than any deeply internalized normative set.

A third important critique of internalization as the link between action and culture has emerged from the interactionist and neo-phenomenological traditions. In radical contrast to structural theorists who tend to view culture as given, interactionist and neo-phenomenological theorists are most concerned with the creative and problematic aspects of the relationship between action and culture. Erving Goffman's (1959) vision of the presentation of self as an often laborious and conscious "fitting" of one's line of conduct to cultural norms, Ralph Turner's (1962) substitution of "role-making" for "role-playing," and the ethnomethodological explications of the *et cetera* rule and similar subroutines (cf. Cicourel, 1970) all convey the same essential point: culture is largely exterior to the person and often problematic.

The foregoing questions and reconceptualizations have made the issue of cultural, and thus social, continuity particularly pressing. If indeed there is minimal deep internalization of culture, at least in contemporary society, how do we account for social order? How is it, faced with the ambiguities and contradictions of a complex society, that normative continuity and meaning are sustained in the actions of diverse and individualistic actors?

For a start, it would be well to view culture as learned, and only approximately so, instead of as internalized. Rather than being somehow akin to instinct, culture is best seen as a kind of shifting cognitive map of the social order and largely within the awareness of the actor. From this point of view, culture is environmental to action. It constitutes one of several sets of parameters within which action is framed. Although there is considerable openness to action, culture, meaning here situationally appropriate norms, meanings and judgmental standards, must be taken into account as the actor constructs his line of conduct. The disclaimer, along with accounts and vocabularies of motives, are among the means by which actors "take account" of culture. In the interests of preserving cathected identities, of making situations sensible, and of facilitating interaction, actors explicitly define the relation between their questionable conduct and prevailing norms. Collectively these might be called "aligning actions" in the sense that they are intended to serve as means of bringing problematic conduct into line with cultural constraints. The net consequence of aligning actions is to perpetuate normative order and meaning in the face of lines of conduct which are objectively at variance with situational norms and understandings.

REFERENCES

Cicourel, Aaron. 1970. "Basic and normative rules in the negotiation of status and role." Pp. 4–45 in *Recent Sociology:* II. Hans Peter Dreitzel (ed.), New York: Macmillan.

Goffman, Erving. 1959. *The Presentation of Self in Everyday Life.* Garden City: Anchor.

Hall, Peter M. and John P. Hewitt. 1970. "The quasi-theory of communication and the management of dissent." *Social Problems* 18 (Summer): 17–27.

Hewitt, John P. and Peter M. Hall. 1973. "Social problems, problematic situations, and quasi-theories." *American Sociological Review* 38 (June): 367–74.

McHugh, Peter. 1968. *Defining the Situation.* New York: Bobbs-Merrill.

Mills, C. Wright. 1940. "Situated actions and vocabularies of motive." *American Sociological Review* 5 (October): 904–13.

Parsons, Talcott. 1966. *Societies: Evolutionary and Comparative Perspectives.* Englewood Cliffs, N.J.: Prentice-Hall.

Riesman, David, et al. 1950. *The Lonely Crowd.* Garden City: Anchor.

Schutz, Alfred. 1964. *Collected Papers:* II. Maurice Natanson (ed.), The Hague: Nijhoff.

Scott, Marvin B. and Stanford M. Lyman. 1968. "Accounts." *American Sociological Review* 33 (February): 46–62.

Turner, Ralph. 1962. "Role-taking: process versus conformity" in *Human Behavior and Social Process.* Arnold Rose (ed.), Boston: Houghton-Mifflin.

Weinstein, Eugene and Paul Deutschberger. 1963. "Some dimensions of altercasting." *Sociometry* 26 (December): 454–66.

Wheelis, Allen. 1958. *The Quest for Identity.* New York: Norton.

Wrong, Dennis. 1961. "The oversocialized conception of man in modern sociology." *American Sociological Review* 26 (April): 183–93.

PART SIX

THE POLITICS OF REALITY

From time immemorial, vested interest groups have mobilized sentiment to stigmatize and scapegoat perceived adversaries. Epoch by epoch, such groups have defended cherished beliefs by imputing to adversaries motivational malignancies ranging from demons, to deities, to genetic deformities—and, in retaliation, have brutalized them. The Holy Crusades, the Spanish Inquisition, the Salem witch-hunts, and the Nazi Holocaust are but four scabs on the advance of civilization. Apparently, any group or individual who envisions a moral alternative and willfully implements it is perceived as dangerous to those in power. One technique for rendering such moral opposition politically harmless is to assert that it is not rooted in a consciously chosen alternative at all, but rather in an uncontrollable, compulsive pathology. When ''extremism'' is construed as being grounded in pathology, rather than morality, it is relieved of responsibility and dutifully placed under surveillance. What better way to attempt to neutralize moral-political opposition and the implied power struggle than by reducing it to pathology?

One particularly interesting example of this was played out in the life and times of the Marquis de Sade. From his birth on June 2, 1740, to his death on December 2, 1814, the Marquis was in and out of jails, prisons, and mental institutions no fewer than six times; he was sentenced to death twice and, only by chance, escaped the guillotine. Although the de Sade family was connected to the royal house of Conde, and the Marquis himself held rank in the King's regiment, his penchant for writing erotic literature and his proclivity for sexual encounters of all forms put the Marquis at a decided disadvantage. Neither family, nor rank, nor career could protect the Marquis; he was defined as an incarnate of absolute evil, and, in fact, until the summer of 1977 his philosophical, political, and literary works were officially banned by the French Courts.

Curiously enough, the continual harassment of the Marquis was pursued actively by three successive political regimes of quite dissimilar coloration. Thus, the monarchism of the King of France, the revolutionary terrorism of Robespierre, and the military imperialism of Napoleon were each equally offended by the sexual extremism of de Sade.

In turn, each regime imposed physical bondage, as punishment, on a man who, in part, advocated physical bondage as pleasure. Apparently, the voluntary, unofficial, interpersonal use of pain for pleasure is impermissible—and called sadism—while the involuntary, official, structural use of pain for punishment is permissible—and called justice. We may well wonder if the difference between sadism and justice is power—the power to call the same thing by different names depending on whose interests prevail.

So, was the Marquis a sinner, possessed by the devil, a madman, a lunatic, crazy, insane. . . or was he a pioneer, an adventurer in behavioral and philosophical extremism, a free spirit, one of those creative giants thrown up in the course of species evolution whose mission is to extend the boundaries of human possibility? Perhaps the best we can do is remember that sometimes prophets, in their own country, truly are without honor.

Certainly, there are contemporary events which reinforce the kernel of truth in this adage. One only has to scan recent newspapers and periodicals to understand how pervasive and relentless is the effort by powerful interests to purge those who envision, advocate, and implement "unconventional" alternatives. Indeed, the medicalization of moral, political, and religious alternatives apparently has reached its culmination in the Soviet Union where outspoken dissidents routinely land in psychiatric detention. Although the list is long, the names of Bukovsky, Medvedev, Gluzman, Plyushch, and Fedorenko represent amply documented cases of political dissidents who either have (or are) suffering psychiatric imprisonment for their beliefs.[1] Indeed, Soviet medicine contains some unusual diagnostic categories, including "sluggish schizophrenia" and "reformist delusions."[2] These diagnoses, moreover, have been applied not only to political dissidents, but also to religious dissidents. A. Argentov, of the Orthodox church, participated in an unauthorized seminar on religious philosophy in the summer of 1976 (which was raided by the KGB) and was placed in a mental hospital for observation, where he was declared mentally ill. (After much worldwide protest, eventually he was released.)

But the use of psychiatric stigmatization is not unknown in contemporary American political circles, though seemingly in a milder form. Not too many years ago Senator Goldwater was declared unstable, President Johnson, egomaniacal, and Senator Eagleton, manic-depressive. And, the mere fact that President Nixon was known to have visited some doctor who might have had something to do with psychotherapy led one self-righteous guardian of the public interest to reveal all to the national news media. Again, what better way to attempt to neutralize moral-political opposition—and the implied power struggle—than to reduce it to medical pathology?

Moreover, if we ask who the front line troops are that routinely define, arbitrate, and enforce the permissible and impermissible limits of behavioral extremes, we find a curious coalition of judges, psychiatrists, policemen, social investigators, welfare workers, and secondary school teachers. Together, they are involved in the creation and protection of those meanings, values, sentiments, and rules that constitute and broadly define the bounds of permissible behavior and reality. Moreover, this coalition of reality makers has

[1]"Vladimir Bukovsky: An Interview," *The New York Review of Books*, Vol. XXIV, No. 2, February 17, 1977, pp. 16—17.
[2]Anthony Lewis, "A Challenge to Soviet Psychiatrists," *Minneapolis Tribune*, August 24, 1977, p. 7—A.

power. Although the source of its power derives from social traditions and legal rules, its power, more often than not, results in the restriction of someone's liberty.

From the viewpoint of a behavioral extremist, such as Seymour Krim, the narrow reality legislated and enforced by this coalition works to constrain and condemn anyone who pursues his art and being to the very furthest perimeter of reality. The behavioral pioneer is captured and jailed by the judgments and definitions of people whose conception of normality and sanity is "conditioned by inherited prejudice, fear, questionable middleclass assumptions of the purposes of life, a policeman's narrow idea of freedom, and dollar hard AMA notions of responsibility and expediency."

One may be less than a behavioral pioneer himself, and still pause for thought, as he reads Krim's reaction to a psychiatrist who describes Greenwich Village as a "psychotic community." For one realizes, along with Krim, that "insanity and psychosis can no longer be respected as meaningful definitions—but are used by limited individuals in positions of social power to describe ways of behaving and thinking that are alien, threatening, and obscure to them."

Implicit in Krim's literary excursion is the profound insight that deviance is a matter of judgment, not a matter of fact. Deviance does not inhere in an act but is conferred upon it—and conferred by those who are "incapable of appreciating the rich, subtle and unconventional reality of the independent thinker and artist." Within the past ten years, however, social scientists have come to realize that to continue to speak in literary terms about madness, in legal terms about insanity, or in medical terms about mental illness is to perpetuate a set of beliefs that misses the essentially normative, communicative nature of behavioral extremism.

Indeed, Thomas Szasz opens the assault on the myth of mental illness by distinguishing between the brain and the mind. While the brain may *succumb* to disease, the mind may *develop* problems in living. One is passive, the other active. An individual does not decide to have a disease, but he may decide to have a "mental illness." Moreover, the relationship between the brain and the mind is not reversible. A diseased brain may cause illness which leads to problems in living, but problems in living do not imply a diseased brain. The notion of problems in living, therefore, shifts the focus from organic deterioration to sociological dis-order, from inquiry in medical etiology to inquiry in deviant behavior.

How, then, do we come to the decision that someone's behavior is deviant? If someone were to say he was Napoleon, we would consider this symptomatic of disturbance only if we did not believe him. For example, such a declaration at a masquerade party would hardly upset anyone. The credibility of a piece of behavior stands or falls on whether *we judge* it plausible or not. *Our* judgment, however, implies a set of social, ethical, and legal rules that define, for us, the limits of credible behavior and reality. Statements or behavior that deviate from our standards of credibility are likely to be labeled symptomatic of mental malady. We are, therefore, in the position of defining deviation from social, ethical, and legal rules in medical terms. This inconsistency points again to what may be called the politics of reality, for sooner or later some specialist in psychotherapeutics is retained to confirm our judgment of someone else's deviation.

That this judgment, however, is primarily an exercise of barely disguised power working in the service of a more or less coherent set of legal, moral, political, and economic values is seen most clearly in historical perspective.

Szasz, again, in his article entitled "The Sane Slave," shows how a highly influential member of the medical profession published a report in 1851 in a (then) leading medical journal, which introduced and discussed two new diseases characteristic of Negro slaves—"drapetomania," or the propensity of slaves to run away from their masters, and "dysaesthesia," or the tendency of slaves to refuse to work for their masters. These two diseases were held to be afflictions of the mind which caused runaway and refusal behavior. The medical therapy prescribed for these conditions was whipping, and the cure was achieved when the slave submitted to his master. By definition, then, a sane slave was one who submitted, and an insane slave was one who rebelled. Most contemporary readers can see how this diagnosis and remedy was nothing more than the medical reinforcement of a set of moral, political, and economic doctrines that served the interests of the dominators at the expense of the dominated.

Similarly, today, if a court hires a psychiatrist to determine whether a criminal is insane, it is a sure bet that the psychiatrist will not question the sanity of the men who formulated the social, ethical, and legal rules against which the criminal is being judged.[3] The unstated question is, who has the *power* to legislate reality? People who specialize in the adjudication of reality quite naturally are committed to a particular conception of reality which usually takes into account what they consider to be society's conception. Needless to say, what society's conception of reality may be is open to debate. If the boundaries of reality are somewhat vague, they are not so vague as to prevent us from judging some people as having stepped beyond them. Somewhere, sometime, somehow, all of us have inched beyond the permissible perimeter and have gone off limits—but very few have been caught. (The most frequently cited probability of "being caught" is one in ten.) On the one hand, there are a multiplicity of sources that generate behavior deviant enough to be judged dis-ordered. On the other, there is enough evidence to suggest that not all behavior that breaks rules *is judged* deviant. This leads to the proposition that most rule-breaking is somehow ignored, disguised, rationalized, handled, or denied, and is therefore of transitory significance. The question is, then, how does rule-breaking behavior, most of which is transitory, become stabilized and categorically deviant? The answer is that the rule-breaker is stigmatized by his audience as disturbed and is placed into a deviant status. Thus placed, the deviant proceeds to play out the expected role.[4]

The placement of a person into a deviant status can be seen in Edwin Lemert's brilliant essay on paranoia. The major point can be summed up in the phrase *paranoids have real*

---

[3]See Thomas J. Scheff, *Being Mentally Ill: A Sociological Theory* (Chicago: Aldine Publishing Co., 1966), especially pp. 135—44.

In the 1960's, 22 judicial hearings to determine the "Mental Illness" of persons brought before a midwestern court were observed and timed. The average time taken to determine "sanity" or "insanity" was 1.6 minutes! Psychiatrists took a bit longer. They averaged 10.2 minutes per person for twenty-six cases observed. Obviously, if so little time is spent examining those who are purportedly "mentally ill," little time is given for questioning the assumptions judges and psychiatrists bring to hearings and diagnostic examination. As one psychiatrist put it, "It's not remunerative. I'm taking a hell of a cut. I can't spend forty-five minutes with a patient. I don't have the time, it doesn't pay."

[4]See *Ibid*.

enemies. Lemert places the problem of paranoia squarely within an interactive communications matrix, and he challenges the notion that paranoia is the unfolding of a pathology located in the individual. Paranoia is not a disease or a symptom of a disease. More often than not, it is an individual's behavioral *response* to alternations in norms, values, or attitudes. The onset of stress between an actor and his circle usually is associated with some real status loss for the actor, such as death of a loved one, business failure, or divorce. In *response*, the actor may become gruff, abrupt, and generally offensive. At this initial stage, however, he is not marked as a deviant, but rather as someone who is difficult to get along with. After repeated interaction, or upon receiving additional damaging information about the actor, the circle begins to re-orient its appraisal and sees the actor as someone with whom it is best not to get involved. At this point, the process of excluding the actor begins in earnest. The contention, then, is that the paranoid mobilizes a real, as opposed to a fabricated, social circle that reacts against him in a covert and conspiratorial manner. In sum, paranoia is seen as an *interaction* that implies reciprocal posturing on the part of both actor and audience.

After a person has been labeled mentally ill, the next step usually is to hospitalize and transform him into a patient. In a provocative essay entitled "The Moral Career of the Mental Patient," Erving Goffman analyzes the effect of being tagged mentally ill and treated as such within the institutional setting of a mental hospital. Often, the individual's closest kin or friend brings him to a psychiatrist where the proposed stay at the hospital is described in less than realistic terms. The police escort, which eventually arrives, is chummy and solicitous, and the "admissions suite," where the patient is welcomed, is more hospitable than hospital—in all, it is as though no one were being put away. When the stark reality of it all becomes clear, the patient feels conned, betrayed, and rather skeptical of those around him. Abandoned and confined, he becomes demoralized and withdrawn.

Confronted with isolation, humiliation, stark living circumstances, and the imposition of an unacceptable view of himself, the patient begins to construct a more favorable image of his past, present, and future. Either he proceeds to magnify appealing qualities of himself and his past, or he claims that he is not responsible for his current plight. Presumably, the function of such agreeable image-building is to counter the unacceptable image the patient is compelled to accept. Obviously, the patient cannot legitimate his own preferred image since all staff personnel have access to his case history, which focuses on his aberrant behavior, and thus know what the "real facts" are. Staff generally puncture the altered image of self and situation in accordance with the belief that the patient should be compelled to "face reality." Since information on patients is communicated freely and widely among all echelons of the staff, the patient is faced with a social environment mobilized completely to deny his own more agreeable conception of himself.

Constant moral review of who he is, combined with fairly frequent rises and falls in the hierarchy of living arrangements, eventually convinces the patient that it makes no sense whatever to stake a claim on a particular conception of self, since chances are it will be discredited. The patient, then, becomes rather apathetic and/or cosmopolitan in his commitment to an image of himself. He gives up in the effort to maintain control over the process of self-construction and submits to the environment and those in control of it.

Adoption of the self they present to him becomes a more efficient way of coping with a fundamentally demoralizing situation. Genuine commitment to an agreeable image of self is replaced by a functional, amoral detachment. One begins to give off *impressions* of a self rather than a self that is wholly credible to him.

While the giving off of impressions may satisfy the staff, it presents even greater problems for the patient. The patient does not want to *act* normal; he wants to *be* normal. Moreover, the patient is never quite sure whether the normal act he is putting on is representative of who he actually is. Is the presentation merely a ''constructed object'' or a ''natural self''? Indeed, the connection between the real self and the character presented becomes ambiguous. Furthermore, in the desire to enhance the presentation of his constructed self, the patient develops a manipulative attitude; he uses everything and everybody to make the best presentation possible. Under constant pressure to appear normal, the patient becomes anxious and alienated and never quite establishes a clear-cut commitment to a genuine presentation of self.[5]

But what happens when a ''patient'' *is* normal. Is it actually possible for the patient to convince the staff of that fact? In an interesting field demonstration, D. L. Rosenhan placed eight sane people in various mental institutions. His aim was to see if staff could identify and distinguish sane people in insane contexts. During the admission interview, each pseudopatient alleged that he or she heard voices. All were admitted immediately, whereupon they broke off simulating *any* symptoms and acted normally. In no case did staff detect the sane pseudopatients, even though the pseudopatients spent an average of nineteen days on the wards. However, other patients, in many instances, did identify the pseudopatients as not being crazy and even guessed that the pseudopatients might be participating in some sort of journalistic or academic investigation. When the pseudopatients finally gained release from the hospitals, each of them carried away the initial admission diagnosis. While all but one, upon admission, were diagnosed as schizophrenic (one was diagnosed as manic depressive), upon discharge, all those diagnosed were labeled as schizophrenics ''in remission.'' Thus, perfectly sane people placed in insane contexts were not recognized as such by professional staff. Moreover, each of these sane people left the hospital branded with a label indicating that an illness they had never suffered at all was now in a stage of remission.

With these results in hand, Rosenhan reversed his procedure. He informed a research and teaching hospital that, over the course of three months, one or more pseudopatients would attempt to gain admission to the institution. The staff was asked to rate each patient on the likelihood that that patient was a pseudopatient. Of the 193 patients admitted for treatment, 41 were judged, with great certainty, to be pseudopatients. However, Rosenhan sent *no* pseudopatients to the hospital during that time period. Hence, the staff saw 41 people who had been judged ''insane'' by others, as actually ''sane'' persons. So, sane people are judged insane, and insane people are judged sane in insane places. What then is sanity?—a set of individual attributes, a constellation of environmental features, or a framework of expert expectations? Given such ambiguity, and the documented inability

---

[5]See S. Messinger *et al.,* ''Life as Theatre: Some Notes on the Dramaturgic Approach to Social Reality,'' *Sociometry* XXV (September, 1962), pp. 98–110.

of experts to distinguish the sane from the insane, we can only hope that medical psychiatry will undertake a thoroughgoing self-examination in order to clarify its aims, values, and functions.

SUGGESTED READINGS

Becker, Ernest. *Escape from Evil*. New York: Free Press, 1975.

Becker, Howard S. *Outsiders*. New York: The Free Press of Glencoe, 1963.

Belknap, Ivan, and John G. Steinle. *The Community and Its Hospitals*. New York: Syracuse University Press, 1963.

Brandt, Anthony. *Reality Police: The Experience of Insanity in America*. New York: William Morrow & Co., 1975.

Candland, Douglas K., *et al*. *Emotion*. Monterey, Calif.: Brooks/Cole 1977.

Douglas, Jack D. (ed.). *Deviance and Respectability: The Social Construction of Moral Meanings*. New York: Basic Books, Inc., 1970.

Durkheim, Emile. *Suicide*. John A. Spaulding and George Simpson (trans.). New York: The Free Press of Glencoe, 1951.

Erikson, Kai T. *The Wayward Puritan*. New York: Wiley, 1966.

Foucault, Michael. *Madness and Civilization*. New York: New American Library, 1965.

Freidson, Eliot. *The Hospital in Modern Society*. New York: The Free Press of Glencoe, 1953.

Friedrich, Otto. *Going Crazy: An Inquiry into Madness in Our Time*. New York: Simon & Schuster, 1976.

Gaylin, Willard. *In the Service of Their Country: War Resistors in Prison*. New York: Viking Press, 1970.

————. *Feelings: Our Vital Signs*. New York: Harper & Row, 1979.

Goffman, Erving. *Asylums*. New York: Doubleday Anchor Book, 1961.

————. *Stigma: Notes on the Management of Spoiled Identity*. Englewood Cliffs, N.J.: Prentice-Hall, Inc., 1963.

Goldhamer, Herbert, and A. W. Marshall. *Psychosis and Civilization*. New York: The Free Press of Glencoe, 1953.

Izard, Carroll E. *Human Emotions* New York: Plenum Press, 1977.

Lemert, Edwin. *Human Deviance, Social Problems and Social Control*. 2nd ed. Englewood Cliffs, N.J.: Prentice-Hall, Inc., 1969.

Lofland, John, with Lyn H. Lofland. *Deviance and Identity*. Englewood Cliffs, N.J.: Prentice-Hall, Inc., 1969.

Matza, David. *Becoming Deviant*. Englewood Cliffs, N.J.: Prentice-Hall, Inc., 1969.

Rose, Arnold M. (ed.). *Mental Health and Mental Disorder*. New York: Norton, 1955.

Rosen, George. *Madness in Society*. Chicago: University of Chicago Press, 1968.

Rubington, Earl, and Martin S. Weinberg (eds.). *Deviance: The Interactionist Perspective*. New York: Macmillan Co., 1968.

Scheff, Thomas J. *Being Mentally Ill: A Sociological Theory*. Chicago: Aldine Publishing Co., 1966.

Schur, Edwin M. *Labelling Deviant Behavior*. New York: Harper & Row Publishers, 1971.

Spitzer, Stephan P., and Norman K. Denzin (eds.). *The Mental Patient: Studies in the Sociology of Deviance*. New York: McGraw-Hill Co., 1968.

Szasz, Thomas. *The Manufacture of Madness: A Comparative Study of the Inquisition and the Mental Health Movement*. New York: Harper & Row, 1970.

————. *The Myth of Mental Illness*. New York: Hoeber-Harper, 1964.

————. *Ideology and Insanity*. New York: Anchor Books, 1970.

Thio, Alex. *Deviant Behavior*. Boston: Houghton Mifflin, 1978.

THIRTY-TWO

THE INSANITY BIT

SEYMOUR KRIM

I

Until this time of complete blast-off in seemingly every department of human life, the idea of insanity was thought of as the most dreadful thing that could happen to a person. Little was actually known about it and the mind conjured up pictures of Bedlam, ninnies walking around in a stupor, a living death that lasted until the poor damned soul's body expired and peace tucked him or her away for eternal keeps. But in this era of monumental need to re-think and re-define almost every former presumption about existence—which has inspired a bombing way of looking at what once were considered the most unbudgeable rocks of reality—the locked door of insanity has been shaken loose and shall yet be hurled wide open. Until one day the prisoners of this definition will walk beside us sharing only the insane plight of mortality itself, which makes quiet madmen of us all.

Every American family has its "psychotic" cousin or uncle; every friend has wept, prayed, hoped (and finally slid into indifference) for

another friend sweating it out in insulin or electric-shock behind the grey walls (public institution) or beyond the clipped roses (private sanitarium). Although my brother, Herbert J. Krim, was institutionalized when I was barely in my 20's—and I co-signed the certificate for a pre-frontal lobotomy which ended with his death by hemorrhage on the operating table at Rockland State Hospital—I still had the conventional ideas about insanity that are shared by all "responsible" readers of *The New York Times*. It is true that as a serious writer I had inherited a great tradition of complete independence and honesty to my actual experience, regardless of what I was supposed to feel; but this was sabotaged by my youth, my ignorance, and an inability to separate my own personal life from a responsibility to question the clichés of experience to their ultimate depth. Like most American writers, from would-be's to celebrities, I was intensely preoccupied by my acutely painful and highly exaggerated subjective image—the Jewish cross, looks, sex, masculinity, a swarm of fears and devices for concealment that were secondary to my decent abilities and serious obligations as a writer intent on telling the truth. In other words: I was too narcissistically and masturbatorially stuck on myself to appreciate the horrible waste of my brother Herbert's death; and with

SOURCE: Seymour Krim. "The Insanity Bit." Copyright by Seymour Krim, 1961, 1968. Seymour Krim, "The Insanity Bit," in his *Views of a Nearsighted Cannoneer* (New York: E. P. Dutton & Company, Inc., 1961), pp. 112–129. Reprinted by permission of E. P. Dutton & Company, Inc.

the snotty sense of superiority usually felt by the young American writer, I thought *I* would be forever immune to the judgments of a society which I loftily ignored, or nose-thumbed, without ever coming to grips with on the actual mat of life. Like every creative type of my generation whom I met in my 20's, I was positive I was sanctified, protected by my "genius," my flair, my overwhelming ambition.

I was as wrong as you can be and still live to tell about it. In the summer of 1955, when I was 33, the thousand unacknowledged human (not literary) pressures in my being exploded. I ran barefooted in the streets, spat at members of my family, exposed myself, was almost bodily thrown out of the house of a Nobel Prize-winning author, and believed God had ordained me to act out every conceivable human impulse without an ounce of hypocritical caution. I know today that my instinct was sound, but my reasoning was self-deceptive. It was not God who ordained me, but I who ordained God for my own understandable human purposes. I needed an excuse to force some sort of balance between my bulging inner life and my timid outer behaviour, and I chose the greatest and most comforting symbol of them all. He was my lance and my shield as I tore through the New York streets acting out the bitter rot of a world-full of frustrations that my human nature could no longer lock up. I was finally cornered on the 14th floor of the St. Regis Hotel by two frightened friends and another brother; and with the aid of handcuffs seriously-humorously clipped on by a couple of bobbies I was led off to Bellevue, convinced all along that I was right. I tolerated those who took me away with the kindly condescension of a fake Jesus.

From Bellevue I was soon transferred to a private laughing academy in Westchester and given insulin-shock treatments. No deep attempt was made to diagnose my "case"—except the superficial and inaccurate judgment that I had "hallucinated." Factually, this was not true; I did not have visual images of people or objects which were not there; I merely believed, with the beauti-

ful relief of absolute justice which the soul of man finds when life becomes unbearable, that God had given me the right and the duty to do everything openly that I had secretly fantasied for years. But this distinction was not gone into by my judges and indifferent captors. They did not have the time, the patience, or even the interest because work in a flip-factory is determined by mathematics: you must find a common denominator of categorization and treatment in order to handle the battalions of miscellaneous humanity that are marched past your desk with high trumpets blowing in their minds.

Like all the other patients, I was considered beyond reasoning with and was treated like a child; not brutally, but efficiently, firmly and patronizingly. In the eyes of this enclosed world I had relinquished my rights as an adult human being. The causes for my explosion were not even superficially examined, nor was the cheek-pinching house psychiatrist—with a fresh flower in the button hole of his fresh daily suit—truly equipped to cope with it even if he had tried, which he did not. Private sanitariums and state institutions, I realized much later, were isolation chambers rather than hospitals in the usual sense; mechanical "cures" such as the one I underwent in a setup of unchallenged authority, like the Army or a humanitarian prison, slowly brought 75 percent of the inmates down to a more temporarily modest view of reality. Within nine or ten weeks I too came down, humbled, ashamed, willing to stand up before the class and repeat the middle-class credo of limited expressiveness and the meaning of a dollar in order to get my discharge.

In three months' time I was out, shaken, completely alone, living in a cheap Broadway hotel-room (having been ashamed to go back to Greenwich Village) and going to a conventional Ph.D. psychologist (I had been to three medically trained therapists in the preceding decade) as a sop to both my conscience and family. I had broken beyond the bounds of "reality"—a shorthand word which is used by the average psychiatrist for want of the more truthfully complex approach that must eventually accommodate our beings' increasing flights into higher altitudes—and come back to the position I was in before. But once again the causes that had flung me into my own sky continued to eat me up. Sexually unconfident, I went to whores, ate my meals alone, and forced myself to write a few pieces in that loneliest of places, a tiny blank hotel-room in the middle of nowhere. For the first time in my life the incentive to live, the isolation and frustration of my existence, grew dim; while the psychologist smiled and smoked his pipe—and did the well-adjusted, tweed, urbane act behind his tastefully battered desk as he ladled out platitudes—I was saving up the sleeping bombs, and when I had enough to do the trick I burned the letters I had received through the years from the several men and women I had loved, destroyed my journal of 15 years' standing, and one carefully chosen night went to a hotel in Newark, N.J.

My plan was to take the pills and slowly conk out in the full bathtub, ultimately drowning like Thomas Heggen; if one missed the other would work. I splurged on a beautiful death-room in a modernistic hotel, one that included a bathroom with the biggest tub in the house. But it was too small to fit my long body. The idea of not being able to drown and of surviving the pills afterwards, perhaps to become a burden or an invalid, began to scar what seemed like a paradise of suicide. I went instead to a Polish bar in downtown Newark, vaguely seeking the eternal anodynes of snatch and booze while I mentally played with my fate.

I found the booze and saw a coarse, ignorant Polish girl do such a life-giving, saucy, raucous folk-dance (on the small dance-floor to the right of the bar) that I broke into loving sobs like prayers over my drink. The sun of life blazed from her into my grateful heart. I went back to the beautiful hotel-room, poured the pills down the toilet, and went to sleep. The next morning I returned to Manhattan a chastened man, shaking my head at how close I had come to non-being.

When I told my tale to Mr. Pipe, my psychologist, he speedily hustled me off to a legitimate head-doctor who doped me until a private ambulance came. Very much in my right and one and only mind but too paralyzed by drugs to move, I was once again taken on the long ride—this time to another hedge-trimmed bin in Long Island. I was helpless to protest, mainly because of the shame and guilt I felt for even contemplating suicide. Obviously I was not crazy, mad, psychotic, out of my mind, schizophrenic, paranoiac. I was simply a tormented man-kid who had never steeled himself to face the facts of life—who didn't know what it meant to have principles and live by them come grief or joy—and who thought that human worth and true independence comes as easily as it does in the movies we were all emotionally faked on. As a sputtering fiction-writer and fairly active literary critic, I had had occasional peaks of maturity and illumination; but as a man I was self-deceptive, self-indulgent, crying inwardly for the pleasures of a college-boy even while in my imagination I saw myself as another Ibsen or Dreiser. Ah, the extraordinary mismating of thoughts in the mind of the modern American literary romantic, as fantastic and truly unbelievable a stew of unrelated dreams as have ever been dreamt, believe me!

Once again I was on the human assembly-line: electric shock clubbed my good brain into needless unconsciousness (and I walked to my several executions like a brave little chappie instead of questioning them) and unquestioned Old Testament authority ruled our little club. Good-natured, but mostly cowlike and uneducated male orderlies carried out the orders from above; and apart from the mechanical treatment and the unimaginative grind of occupational therapy, each patient was left completely on his or her bewildered own, a sad and farcical sight when one considered the $125 per week that their frightened families were paying.

I saw now that nine-tenths of the people I was quartered with were not "insane" by any of the standards a normally intelligent person would use: the majority had lost confidence in their own ability to survive in the world outside, or their families were *afraid* of them and had palmed them off on "experts," but positively no serious effort was being made to equip them to become free and independent adults. This was their birthright—beyond country and society, indeed an almost religious obligation—but they were palliated with pills or jolted with shock, their often honest rage echoed back to them as a sign of their "illness." Some of them must have been "sick," you say. I answer: Who can not be conceived as such in a world so complex ("The truth is there is a truth on every side"—Richard Eberhart) that each group has its own method for judging manners, behaviour, ideas, and finally the worth of human values? What was more important was that I, a person from a hip milieu and with a completely opposite set of values, could see their so-called sickness with the human sensibility that an immersion in literature and experience had given me—rather than as a clinical manifestation. When I later recognized the objective provinciality of many psychiatrists in precisely the humanistic areas that could cover the actions of the majority of the inmates without finding it "psychotic," I realized that the independent thinker and artist today must learn to be resolute towards a subtle, socially powerful god-father who often drips paternalism: namely, the newly-enthroned psychiatric minority that has elevated itself to a dangerous position of "authority" in the crucial issues of mind, personality, and sanity.

I now began to fight persistently—but still with shakiness—for my release; my life was my own: it did not belong to the clichés of the salesman-aggressive, well-barbered, Jewish-refugee (my brother, my enemy!) house psychiatrist or to my smiling, betweeded nonentity of a psychologist, who paid me diplomatically inscrutable visits like a Japanese ambassador. Even if I had been or if there were such a reality as a "raving maniac"—which, perhaps childishly, I implore the overimaginative, zeitgeist-vulnerable reader to believe is an impossible conception today—I would and should have fought for my release. What the institution-spared

layman does not realize is that a sensitive and multiple-reacting human being remains the same everywhere, including a sanitarium, and such an environment can duplicate the injustice or vulgarity which drove your person there in the first place. By this I mean that a mental hospital is not an asylum or a sanctuary in the old-fashioned sense: it is just a roped-off side-street of modern existence, rife with as many contradictions, half-truths and lousy architecture as life itself.

Both of the sanitariums I was in were comparable to Grossinger's, in that they took in only financially comfortable, conventionally middle-class, non-intellectual people. By every human standard my being there was life's sarcastic answer to whatever romantic ideas I had about justice. Since the age of 19 I had deliberately led an existence of experimentation, pursuit of truth, bohemianism, and non-commercialism: fate's punishment for my green naivete was for me to recover my supposed mental health in this atmosphere of uncriticizable authority, air-conditioned by just the whiffs of truth that are perfumed and bland, and based on a pillar of middle-class propriety with the cut-throat reality of money underneath. Could I accept my former life, which had produced some good work, as a lie to myself—which the house-psychiatrist wanted me to do (in effect) in his one psychotherapeutic pass at me (he left me alone after this)? I could not and never would: not only for myself but for the great principles and accomplishments of others, both living and dead, which had been my guide throughout my adult life. I might fail—but why go on having an identity at all if in a crisis you will throw away not only your past years, but the moral achievements of rare souls who have shared in your emotional and intellectual experience and whose own contributions to existence are also at stake?

When I heard this second house-psychiatrist literally equate sanity with the current clichés of adjustment and describe Greenwich Village as a "psychotic community," I saw with sudden clarity that *insanity* and *psychosis* can no longer be respected as meaningful definitions—but are used by limited individuals in positions of social power to describe ways of behaving and thinking that are alien, threatening, and *obscure* to them. (A year later when I took a psychiatrist friend of mine to the San Remo, she told me with a straight face that it reminded her of the "admission ward in Bellevue," where she had interned. This was her analogy on the basis of accurate but limited experience, that increasing chasm which separates intelligent people from understanding each other. I realized with a sense of almost incommunicable hopelessness that the gap between her and the well-known poet with whom I had had a beer at the Remo two weeks before was tremendous, and that between these two poles of intelligence the neutral person—who could see the logic of each—was being mashed up with doubt and conflict. The poet was at home, or at least the heat was off, there; while the psychiatrist felt alien and had made a contemptuous psycho-sociological generalization. There was little bond of shared values and therefore genuine communication between both of these intelligent and honest human beings, each of whom contributed to my life.)

To finish with my four months in the sanitarium: I argued and reasoned for the basic right to the insecurity of freedom, and finally a good friend did the dirty in-fighting of getting me out. Had I to do it over again, I believe I would now have the guts to threaten such an institution or psychologist with a law suit, ugly as such a procedure can be to a person already vulnerable with the hash-marks of one legally defined "psychotic episode" and the contemplation of the criminal act of suicide. But I had been—as so many of Jack Kerouac's subterraneans are when faced with the machinery of official society—milk and sawdust when, in such situations, you must be iron and stone in spite of your own frailty. It is not that the present-day authorities of mental life want to railroad anyone, as in your Grade C horror movie; it is merely that as one grows older it

becomes clear that there are almost irremediable differences between people in the total outlook towards life.

Mine had hardened as a result of my experiences, and I realized it was better to die out in the world if need be than be deprived of the necessity to confront existence because of the cheap authority of a lock and key. The majority of people who stay in mental institutions for any length of time do not want to return to the uncertain conditions outside the walls: which in our time spells out to emotionally anarchic, multi-dimensional, brain-trying, anxiety-loaded, and—O hear me mortality, from the Year One!—ultimate and divine life.

II

I returned downtown—to the very Village that I heard the psychiatrist place deep in Freudian Hell, with that pious over-extension of terminology which reveals a limited private morality behind the use of so-called scientific language—and tried to tenderly pick up the threads of my former social life. I saw that my closest and most brilliant friends did not really understand, or were afraid to understand, the contemporary insanity bit. Almost all of them had been soul-whirled by psychotherapy at some time, and each had the particularly contemporary fear of insanity which has become the psychological H-bomb of city life; in theory they may have granted that insanity was no longer the uniform horror it seems to the inexperienced imagination—like a spook in the night—but centuries of inherited fear, plus the daily crises of 1950's living, made them emotionally cautious about seeing my experience as merely an *extension* of their own.

One, a poet-philosopher whom I admire, clapped me on the back and said with some literary awe that I had "returned from the dead, like Lazarus." This struck me as greatly melodramatic, untruthful, and saddening because intellectuals and especially artists should be the very people to understand that insanity today is a matter of definition, not fact; that there can no longer be a fixed criterion, just as there is no longer a reality like that described by Allen Ginsberg in "Howl" (an exciting achievement), where he sees "the best minds of my generation destroyed by madness."

I believe this is lurid sentimentality. Ginsberg may have seen the most gifted people of his generation destroyed by an *interpretation* of madness, which is a much more real threat in a time of such infinite, moon-voyaging extension to experience that the validly felt act is often fearfully jailed in a windowless cell of definition by hard-pressed authorities, whose very moral axis is in danger of toppling. Madness today is a literary word; insanity is a dated legal conception as rigid as an Ibsen play; and "psychosis," the antiseptic modern word that sends chills down the ravines of my friends' minds, has become so weakened (despite its impressive white-jacketed look) by narrow-minded, square, and fast-slipping ideological preconceptions that it must be held at arm's length, like a dead rat, for any cool understanding. When this is done, I believe you will see that the word and the state of mind it tries to fix are subject to the gravest questioning; much of which centers around the amount of freedom either permitted to human expression or, more important, what it must take for itself to live in this time when such *unfamiliar* demands are made on the being. Norms crack when they can no longer fight back the content that spills over cookie-mold conceptions of "sane" behavior—and they must be elasticized to stretch around the new bundle of life.

Two weeks before I was back walking down 8th Street a gratefully free neurotic, I had been thought of in the minds of compassionate but uninformed friends as a fairly wild-eyed psychotic. The mere fact that I had been in a sanitarium had pulled a curtain of emotional blindness down over my friends' vision; and yet I was the same person I had been when I entered the happy-house. The unexamined fear of an "insanity" which no longer exists as a framed picture conventionalizes the very people who should view this now only *symbolic*

word with clear, unafraid, and severely skeptical eyes. I had not been among "the dead"—unless killing time looking at "Gunsmoke" and Jackie Gleason on TV, playing bridge, and reading Tolstoy and Nathanael West is considered death. I had not been "destroyed by madness," Mr. Ginsberg!—in fact, the act of incarceration made me realize how significant (indeed indelible) individual freedom is, and thus helped brick-and-mortar my point of view rather than destroy it. When I was once again semi-knit into a way of life in my new Village home, I discovered that other writers and intellectuals whom I knew had also undergone the sanitarium or mental-hospital holiday, but had kept mum because of indecision as to how frankly one should confess such a stigma.

I understood their practical caution, but discovered that they lived in a sewer-light of guilt, fear and throat-gagging anxiety, instead of openly and articulately coping with the monster of doubt. "Do you think I'm sane?" is the question I ultimately began to hear from these brilliant people (one scarred tribesman to another!) who had been intimidated into denying the worth of their most pregnant ideas, the very ones that create *new concrete standards of sanity* or *sense* in a time that has emotionally, if not yet officially, out-lived the abstractions of the past. For myself—although uncertain as to how expressive I should be, even with the very intellectuals I had always considered my brothers in a completely free inquiry into every nook and cranny of life—the problem was suddenly answered when a gifted young writer told a charming hostess I had just met that I had been in "two insane asylums."

I was pierced and hurt, not because I actually considered my supposed nuttiness a yellow badge of dishonor, but because the writer in question had ducked out from under his own experience (which I instinctively knew included some of the crises which had launched me upon the streets like a human missile) and pretended such melodrama was foreign to him. I was appalled because I thought that of all people my fellow highbrow writers should be the first to understand and concede the universal nature of the blows that had felled me in the eyes of official society. But I was wrong. There are spikes on the truth which are so close to the slashed heart of contemporary mortality that men and women will lie and refuse acknowledgment, even when it is necessary to the survival of others, they forfeit their humanhood and final worth to life by doing this, but even in the small band of the avant-garde the pursuit of the truth is given up with that weak excuse: "a practical sense of reality."

After this turncoat put-down by a member of my own club, so to speak, there was no longer any issue for myself. I could not live with the squirming burden of secretiveness because my personal history had become public gossip in the small Village group I traveled with. After snake-bitten laughter at my own romantically cultivated simple-mindedness in thinking my fall would be taken with the hip sophistication I had truly expected, I was glad I had become a stooge or victim; because I basically knew that I had played a juicy part in a contemporary American morality play that is going to do standing-room nightly until its implications are understood. We live in what for the imaginative person are truly hallucinated times, because there is more life on every side—and the possibility of conceiving this surplus in a dizzying multitude of ways—than our inheritance and equipment enables us to deal with. My type and perhaps your type of person only *acted out* what other less passionate people feel, but do not express. A "breakdown" such as mine can therefore be learned from:

The first thing one can see is that the isolating of a person saves his or her friends and family from being embarrassed (trivial as this seems, it is a nasty factor in institutionalization), perhaps hurt, and theoretically stops the "sick" person from doing something irreparable while in the grip of the furies. Seen this way, the enforced shackling of an individual seems sad but reasonable. But contemporary adults, however disturbed (often with jus-

tice!), are not children; there is doubt in my mind whether we have any right, other than blunt self-interest, to impose our so-called humanitarian wishes on another to the degree where we jail them in order to save them. I must illustrate this with my own case. When I was considered out of my mind during my original upward thrust into the sheer ecstasy of 100 per cent uninhibitedness, I was aware of the "daringness" of my every move; it represented at heart an existential *choice* rather than a mindless discharge. It could not be tolerated by society, and I was punished for it, but my "cure" was ultimately a chastisement, *not a medical healing process*. In my own exhibitionistic and self-dramatizing way, when I flipped, I was nevertheless instinctively rebelling against a fact which I think is objectively true in our society and time: and that is the lack of alignment between an immense inner world and an outer one which has not yet legalized, or officially recognized, the forms that can tolerate the flood of communication from the mind to the stage of action.

Traditionally, it was always taught that the artistic person could work out his or her intense private life by expressing it on the easel or typewriter. In faded theory this seems reasonable, but with the billionaire's wealth of potential human experience both fore, aft, and sideways in the world today, it is abnormal not to want to participate more Elizabethanly in this over-abundant life. The hunchbacked joy the artist once may have had in poring over the objects of his interest, and then putting the extract into his work, can no longer be honestly sufficient to the most human hearts today. There has arisen an overwhelming need for the highly imaginative spirit (based on the recognition that the mere mind of man can no longer lock up the volume of its experience) to forge a bridge so that the bursting galaxy of this inner world can be received in actual public life. But there is such a time-lag between our literally amazing subjective life—which has conceptions of a powerful altitude equal to the heaven-exploring freedom of privacy—and the mummery of outer behavior, that when the contemporary imaginator expresses his genuine thoughts in public he often feels that he has exposed himself beyond redemption. Room has not yet been made by those who dominate social power for the natural outward show of the acrobatic thinking that ceaselessly swings in the surrealistic minds of our most acute contemporaries. Put crudely but simply a bookish notion of what constitutes "normality" in this supremely a-normal age drives the liveliest American sensibilities back into the dungeon of self—creating pressures which must maim the soul one way or another—rather than understanding that the great need today is for imagination to come gloriously out in the open and shrink the light-years that separate the mind from external life. (Trying to fill this need is, hands-down, one of the significant accomplishments of the beats—in my opinion—no matter what defensive moralists say; the raw junk that they have peddled occasionally under a Kotex flag of liberation is a different matter, which doesn't rightly fit in here.)

It was trying to close this distance between Me and Thou, between the mind and externality, that I was instinctively attempting when I cut loose with my natural suffocating self in 1955 upon the taboo grounds of outer life. I could stand unfulfilled desire no longer. Thus it is my conviction today that ideals of social behavior must squat down and broaden to the point where they can both absorb and see the necessity for "aberrations" that were once, squarely and Teddy Rooseveltianly, regarded as pathological. The imagination of living human beings, not dead gods, must be openly embodied if there is to be some rational connection between what people actually are and what they are permitted to show. But as with every significant change in meaning, such acts of expressiveness will cost blood before they will be tolerated and understood by psychiatrists, sociologists, the law, police, and all other instruments of social force. Ironically, it is the very "psychotics" in institutions who have unwittingly done the most to initiate a bigger and more imaginative conception of what constitutes *meaningful* behavior. By deal-

ing with people imprisoned in this category, the most perceptive laymen and psychiatrists are beginning to see symbolic meanings where before they saw flat irrationality, because their approach was literal (as if anyone who had the imagination to go "mad" would be stuffy enough to act in prose!). It is then borne in upon them, out of common sense and humility, that a much more expanded conception of what is "sane" is a prerequisite to doing justice to the real emotional state of human beings today; not the abstract theorems of a clean Euclidian conception, but the real, harsh, multiple, often twisted, on-again, off-again mishmash of the so-called normal mind. One can say without pretense that the pioneering "psychotic" is the human poet of the future; and the most imaginative, least tradition-bound psychiatrists are now playing the role of New Critics, learning to closely read the difficult and unexpected meanings of what formerly were thought of as obscure—in fact, off-limits—warpings of humanity.

III

In my own case I was brought face-to-face because of my trial by shock (both electric and the human aftermath) with a crucial reality which I had long dodged. It can be put approximately this way: A serious artist-type must in the present environment, as always—clichés have a way of becoming profundities when you have to live them!—literally fight for survival if he or she is going to embody the high traditions that originally made the hot pursuit of truth through art the greatest kick in their lives. But to follow this ideal today is tougher than perhaps it has ever been before; and there are specific reasons why. Foremost is the increasing loss of position for the poet (the artist incarnate) as "the unacknowledged legislator of the race" in a period when the terrifying bigness of society makes the average person resort to more immediate and practical oracles (psychiatrists, sociologists, chemists) than to the kind of imaginative truth that the artist can give. Secondly, the artist-type in our mass society is no longer "priveleged" in any way, if indeed he ever was; by this I mean that the laws and shibboleths of the huge democratic tribe judge him as severely as they do the shoemaker next door. Whatever pampering the serious artist once received has become a laugh in our time, when everyone is hustling on approximately the same level for success, lovers, status, money, headlines, thrills, security—for everything.

The emergence of an emotionally mutinous democracy has upset the old categories and cast us all into the boiling sea of naked existence, without the props of class, or profession, or the certainty about one's worth as judged by the seemingly clear-cut hierarchies of the past. While, in my opinion, this should be sizzlingly beautiful to every true artist-type, because it is adventurous in the highest conceivable and most mortally dangerous sense, it is also full of the most sinking fears and doubts. For example: can the intelligent writer, painter or composer—the individual with a view of life all his own, which he believes to be true—be indifferent to the prevailing social climate and risk everything by sticking to a viewpoint which will bring him into conflict with the most *normal* (shared by the most people) human emotions in a mass society? (Tag him with the label of "insanity," estrangement from the tempting pie of regular-guy and regular-gal American experience, bring him the isolating fate of being misunderstood even by the "enlightened," and regarded as a personal challenge by others who have made an uneasy truce.)

This is a very serious problem and entails a bigger threat than in the past. Since the artist-type can no longer be realistically considered as being "outside" our definition of society or human nature—and must in this country above all others be seen within the circle of a mass-democratic humanity, for that is where his final strength probably lies—his defections will be judged by those in positions of social power as fluky aberrations *no different from anyone else's*. He will be judged and penalized by the same standards; and in a majority of cases, from what I have seen, his will

and stamina are broken (or rationalized into loose harness) and his point of view changed. Frankly, for the artist-type in our environment there is no longer any solid ground whatever under his feet— anything solid he possesses must be won from air and shaped by fanatical resoluteness. For all is open to question today, is a gamble, and has none of the "official" security of the acknowledged professions or even any semblance of unity within his own field. It is for such reasons that the genuine artist-thinker is in such an unenviable and peculiar position in America right now. He is of society and yet, by instinct and inheritance, apart from it: therefore he has to clarify his position in his own mind to a menthol-sharp degree if he wants to survive with intactness, because, as I've tried to show, he will be crushed subtly or conclusively unless he separates his eternal role in society from the onrush of personal doubt that every human being worth the name lives with today.

I learned as a result of my far-out public exhibition, and the manhandling that followed, to distrust the definitions of crude social authority as they pertained to myself and my friends, who share a generally akin point of view and are all either professionals or semi-professionals in the arts and intellectual life. We cannot be skimmed off the top and bracketed as thinly as I had been diagnosed at Bellevue; and the psychiatrists who impatiently felt for the bumps within my head, while presumably competent at a human-machine level, are not as a group sensitive, informed or sympathetic enough with my purposes in life to be of help. In fact, in a basic way they must be my defining opposition in history (daily life) while my friends beyond time (the ideal)—if that doesn't read too pretentiously. It was a sharp revelation for me to learn this as a result of my on-your-hands-and-knees, boy! defeat with authority. As I confessed before, like so many confused young Americans puttering around in the arts, I had phonily pumped into my serious intentions the gassiest dreams of what struggle for ideas truly is, of false and sentimentalized views of authority (both bowing before it and blow-hard defiance), and in general acted more like a Hollywood caricature of a ''genius'' than a person with the ballbreaking desire to uphold the immortal flame of art in his smallish hand.

I found after I had been handcuffed, ambulanced, doped, needled, marched in formation and given a leather belt to make as if I were in my dotage rather than the prime of life, that I *had* to disagree basically and deliberately with the cowardly normal notion of what constitutes insanity because it is only by *the assertion of the individual spirit that we can change definitions of reality that are already insecure and losing their hold on the conceptual imagination.* In other words, if a majority of people agree that what was once confidently called insanity no longer exists in its traditional sense, cannot truthfully be a determining measurement in a time like this where each good person in the reaches of his mind is often an amateur lunatic by older slogans of ''rationality,'' then the enslavement of the word and meaning are broken. Not only was I forced to this simple attitude because my human spirit refused the reduction of my total self to only one exaggerated aspect of it—namely the pathological label—I saw in both sanitariums no consistency in what was thought of as ''sick.''

In short, I could no longer afford to think of contemporary insanity as an exact objective phenomenon, like thunder or cancer, but rather as an interpretation of human thought and behavior conditioned by inherited prejudices, fear, questionable middle-class assumptions of the purpose of life, a policeman's narrow idea of freedom, and dollar-hard AMA notions of responsibility and *expediency* (''1. Apt and suitable to the end in view; as, an expedient solution; hence, advantageous. 2. Conducive to special advantage rather than to what is universally right.''—Web. New Colleg. Dict.). No longer could I see any true authority or finality in a conception that could be too conveniently tailored to fit the situation. I knew then that anyone who dares the intellectual conventions of this local time must be prepared to have ''psychotic'' or any of its variants—paranoid, schizo-

phrenic, even the mild psychopathic!—thrown at them. The pathological interpretation of human nature has become a style in our period (overemphasized by the junior science of psychiatry) and has come to mirror the fears, anxieties and values of those currently in positions of social authority more often than the person who is being gutted. Within the iron maiden of this fashion—which undeniably hurts, right down to the roots of the soul—the independent person and the artist-type have no choice but to trust implicitly what they see with their intellect and imagination; for when the climate changes, only the individual vision will stand secure upon its God-given legs of having had faith in actual experience.

I therefore believe that the fear and even the actual living through of much that used to be called ''insanity'' is almost an emotional necessity for every truly feeling, reacting, totally human person in America at this time—*until* he or she passes through the soul-crippling (not healing) judgment of such language and comes out of the fire at the point where other words and hence different conceptions are created from the wounds. The psychiatric vocabulary and definitions, which once seemed such a liberating instrument for modern man, have unwittingly woven a tight and ironically strangling noose around the neck of the brain; contemporary men and women—especially intellectuals—tremblingly judge themselves and others in the black light of psychopathology and shrink human nature to the size of their own fears instead of giving it the liberty of their greatest dreams. But we can be grateful that the human soul is so constructed that it ultimately bursts concepts once held as true out of its terrible need to live and creates the world anew just in order to breathe in it. One final thought: should any readers see this article as an effort at self-justification they are right, as far as they go; but they should remember that it is only out of the self and its experience (even if I have failed here) that new light has ever been cast on the perpetual burden of making life ever more *possible* at its most crucial level.

THIRTY-THREE

INTERVIEW

THOMAS S. SZASZ, MD

THE NEW PHYSICIAN: Dr. Szasz, what do you mean when you say that mental illness is a myth?

SZASZ: Disease means bodily disease. Gould's *Medical Dictionary* defines disease as a disturbance of the function or structure of an organ or a part of the *body*. The mind (whatever *it* is) is not an organ or a part of the body. Hence, it cannot be diseased in the same sense as the body can. When we speak of mental illness, then, we speak *metaphorically*. To say that a person's mind is sick is like saying that the economy is sick or that a joke is sick. When metaphor is mistaken for reality and is then used for social purposes, then we have the makings of myth. I hold that the concepts of mental health and mental illness are mythological concepts, used strategically to advance some social interests and to retard others, much as national and religious myths have been used in the past.

THE NEW PHYSICIAN: But why are people called mentally ill, if, as you say, they are not *really* ill?

SOURCE: Thomas S. Szasz. "Interview: Thomas S. Szasz, M.D." Copyright by the Student American Medical Association, 1969. Thomas S. Szasz, "Interview: Thomas S. Szasz, M.D.," *The New Physician,* XVIII (June, 1969), pp. 453−476. Reprinted by permission of the Student American Medical Association.

SZASZ: Modern psychiatry may be said to have developed from the refinements of three interrelated phenomena: neurological diseases, malingering, and conversion hysteria. Neurological diseases are diseases of the nervous system, like neurosyphilis or multiple sclerosis. They present no conceptual problem. The problem for modern psychiatry really begins with persons who appear to have a neurological disease—seem to be paralyzed or blind—but who, when medically examined, display no abnormal neurological signs. In other words, they are physically normal and only mimic the picture of a neurological illness. Until the second half of the 19th century, persons of this kind were generally categorized as malingerers; that is, not sick. Modern psychiatrists, beginning with Charcot, and then much more actively, with Freud, claimed that these people were sick suffering from an illness called "hysteria," and that they ought to be treated as patients. Two very important things were involved in this process of reclassification. One was the extension of the concept of illness from bodily disorder per se to what only looks like a bodily disorder but is actually a so-called mental disorder. The second was the recognition of the *sick role* as a sufficient criterion of illness (even in persons with healthy bodies), so that hypochondriacs, homosexuals, criminals, and people with all kinds of other deviant conduct could be, and were, classified as ill, mentally ill. With the development of modern psychiatry, the whole concept of illness has expanded; indeed it has become an almost infinitely elastic category capable of including anything psychiatrists want to place in it.

THE NEW PHYSICIAN: Dr. Szasz, could you elaborate on the distinction between illness as a bodily disorder and the sick role, as a social performance?

SZASZ: Yes, I think this is a very important distinction. I believe that much confusion in psychiatry is due to a failure to distinguish between these two elementary concepts and the phenomena they designate.

Strictly speaking, an illness is a biological or physicochemical abnormality of the human body or its functioning. A person is sick if he has diabetes, a stroke, or cancer. Such diseases are physicochemical events, similar to natural events like solar eclipses or typhoons—except that they happen to the human body. It is important to emphasize that medical diseases are things that *happen* to human bodies, rather than things that people *do* with their bodies.

The sick role, on the other hand, is not a biological condition but a social status; it refers to a status of claiming illness by, for example, complaining of pain, fever, or weakness, and/or seeking medical attention. Like other social roles, such as father, husband, soldier, or college student, the sick role denotes a certain kind of relationship to other people in society.

THE NEW PHYSICIAN: Could you give an example?

SZASZ: The example of the person afflicted with cancer is a good starting point. Inasmuch as he suffers from a malignant growth it might be perfectly obvious to himself and others that he *is* sick; that is to say, he has an abnormal biological condition. This is a fact, just as it is a fact that he has brown eyes or blue.

If this man wants medical help he goes to a doctor or a hospital, then he assumes the role of patient, the sick role. This, too, is a fact. It's a social fact—just as real as that he is rich or poor, Christian or Jewish.

Finally, this individual—and note my choice of the word "individual," *not* "patient"—may choose not to go to a doctor or to a hospital. Indeed, let me make the point strongly, if he decides, because he fears physicians or thinks poorly of what medicine could do for him, that he just wants to stay at home, live as long as he can in peace and quiet, and then commit suicide—then this person cannot, and must not, be considered a patient. In other words *he is sick, but he is not a patient.* This may sound strange, at first hearing, because we—and I mean especially physicians, but to a lesser extent everyone—are used to calling everyone who is sick a patient. This is, of course, terribly sloppy thinking and speaking; it's like calling everyone who breaks the law, or is suspected of breaking the law, a criminal—instead of reserving this term only for those convicted of lawbreaking.

THE NEW PHYSICIAN: You mean that a person is a patient only if he volunteers for the role?

SZASZ: No, it's more complicated than that. But first, I must restrict my comments to medical patients. We must clarify our ideas with respect to this group before we can hope to see clearly the problems posed by so-called mental patients.

The concept of "medical patienthood" implies three distinct variables: (a) the individual's actual state of bodily illness or health; (b) his claim to, or rejection of, the status of patient; and (c) the acceptance or rejection by others of his claim to that status. Let me indicate the permutations that this makes possible; these are real, everyday situations.

(1) The person is sick; claims to be sick; and is perceived as sick by others. This is the "ordinary" sick patient.

(2) The person is sick; claims to be sick; but is

perceived as not sick by others (e.g., the diagnosis is missed, as in an early case of cancer of the pancreas).

(3) The person is sick; claims to be not sick; and is perceived as sick by others (e.g., drug-intoxicated individual). This is the sick involuntary patient.

(4) The person is sick; claims to be not sick; and is perceived as not sick by others (e.g., the ill person in the latent or prediagnostic period of his illness).

(5) The person is not sick; claims to be sick; and is perceived as sick by others. This is the person who "malingers" and whose pretended illness and claim to patienthood are accepted by others.

(6) The person is not sick; claims to be sick; and is perceived as not sick by others. This is the person who "malingers" and whose pretended illness and claim to patienthood are rejected by others.

(7) The person is not sick; claims to be not sick; but is nevertheless perceived as sick by others (e.g., the healthy person mistakenly diagnosed as sick).

(8) The person is not sick; claims to be not sick; and is perceived as not sick by others. This is the "ordinary" healthy person.

THE NEW PHYSICIAN: In other words, biological illness and the sick role vary independently.

SZASZ: Yes, exactly. This can be illustrated very simply. A person may be ill, and often is, but may prefer not to assume the sick role. We often do this, for example, when we have a cold but go to the office or theater. Conversely, a person may not be ill, but may prefer to assume the sick role; we often do this, for example, when we offer illness as an excuse for avoiding an unpleasant obligation, like going to a party or meeting. Soldiers, housewives, and other oppressed people have traditionally assumed the sick role, to avoid the dangers of combat or the drudgeries of child-care. Whether this is "malingering," "hysteria,"

or some mysterious disease of the brain caused by a lack of vitamins, enzymes, or God-knows-what, or whether it is best conceptualized as not a disease at all—this is what much of psychiatric theory and controversy is all about.

THE NEW PHYSICIAN: Now, how do you apply these concepts to mental illness? To schizophrenia, for example?

SZASZ: I view all behavior—"well" or "sick"—in the framework of symbolic action, or roles and games (in the serious, not frivolous, sense). This means that we can't talk about the problem as one of "mental illness" or "schizophrenia." Instead, we must identify it in behavioral terms, or, as I like to put it, in plain English. For example, let us assume that when we are talking about schizophrenia we mean a social situation where a person makes a patently false, self-aggrandizing claim. A poor, socially insignificant man may thus claim that he is Jesus; or a poor, socially insignificant woman, that she is the Holy Virgin. If you look at this phenomenon simply, without any complicated psychiatric preconceptions or pretentions, you will notice that, whatever the *reason* for their action, such people make *false claims* about themselves. They impersonate; they pretend to be someone or something they are not. To me this is more like cheating in a game, or like fraudulent advertising—than it is like cancer or pneumonia.

The simple fact, then, is that in such cases we deal with conflicting claims, not with diseases. One man says he is Jesus, and another says he is not. The second half of this sentence—namely, that the psychiatrist says, indeed *insists,* that the person is not Jesus—has been completely overlooked in psychiatry. Why should the psychiatrist do this? The man who says he is Jesus is *not complaining—he is boasting!* Why shouldn't the psychiatrist leave him alone? These questions highlight the psychiatrist's role in such a situation.

But my point here is that a psychiatric problem or diagnosis (or at least one very common type of such problem or diagnosis) does not arise until there is a conflict of claims such as I have sketched earlier. For example, when Fleming made certain claims about penicillin, the claims were verified, and he was acclaimed as a great man. When Ivy made certain claims about Krebiozen—well, you know what happened. But we should not get lost here in the problem of who is right. Sometimes correct claims are contradicted and disallowed—that's what happened to poor Ignaz Semmelweis. Sometimes incorrect claims are accepted and honored—that's how I, at least, view the awarding of a Nobel Prize to Egas Moniz for his great discovery of how to treat schizophrenia: by amputating the frontal lobes of the brain!

In certain cases of interpersonal and social conflict, then, it sometimes happens that one party defines the other as ''mentally sick'' or ''schizophrenic.'' This is one of the ''solutions'' our society provides for resolving such conflicts. In this sense, ''schizophrenia'' is an assigned or ascribed role—like convict or draftee. If we only looked at the ''psychotic'' as an individual cast in a role he does not want to be in—cast in it by his ''loved ones,'' by his employer, by his psychiatrist, by society generally—we would at least be in a position to start to deal honestly with what we now call, quite misleadingly, the problem of ''serious mental disease.''

THE NEW PHYSICIAN: How does your emphasis on the fact that the psychiatrist deals with conflict, rather than disease, relate to your views on what the psychiatrist does?

SZASZ: In the face of conflict, there are three alternatives, and three only: you side with one party, or with the other, or you try to remain neutral and act as an arbitrator. Psychiatric interventions, so-called psychiatric ''treatments,'' are actually a confused and confusing mixture of these kinds of social actions.

THE NEW PHYSICIAN: Can you give examples of each?

SZASZ: Yes. When a person goes, on his own accord, to a psychotherapist, a psychoanalyst, pays

him for his services, and enlists his aid to help him pursue his self-defined interests—for example, to become sexually more potent, or to be able to secure a divorce without feeling excessively guilty—in such cases, if indeed the therapist *contracts* to deliver this kind of service to the patient, we deal with psychiatric interventions on behalf of the patient. On the other hand, when a person is committed to a mental hospital as a schizophrenic—by his mother or wife—the psychiatrist has a contract with the state to do something *against, not for,* the patient's self-defined interests. This should be obvious. In the case of involuntary mental hospitalization, the patient's self-defined interest is, first of all, to be left alone by the psychiatrist. The very fact that the psychiatrist accepts this individual as a ''patient'' defines him as the patient's adversary, not his ally. Finally, when the psychiatrist is paid to ''evaluate'' individuals—for the draft board, the Peace Corps, and so forth—then he acts, or tries to act, as an arbitrator or judge.

THE NEW PHYSICIAN: Which of these psychiatric functions do you consider the most important?

SZASZ: From a psychotherapeutic point of view, the most important intervention is when the psychiatrist acts as the patient's agent. Morally, if not technically, this is similar to what the physician does. He helps, or tries to help, his patient. If the patient does not want help, he leaves the physician. Although what happens technically may be largely under the control of the physician, *the fact that it happens* is entirely under the control of the patient. I refer here to the fundamental civil right, in American society at least, to *reject medical treatment.* The individual in a totalitarian society does not have this right. Ostensibly, he has a ''right to treatment,'' but actually, this means that the doctor, as an employee of the state, is in control of the medical relationship. This same type of control—that is, power over the patient, backed by the coercive apparatus of the state—has characterized the role of the alienist, of the psychiatrist, for the past 300 years. This is why, from a social point of view, I consider the most important psychiatric intervention the commitment, the involuntary mental hospitalization, of the so-called mentally ill.

THE NEW PHYSICIAN: Why do we have commitment?

SZASZ: One of the standard contemporary justifications for commitment is the claim that mental patients do not know they are mentally ill and hence must be confined for their own protection. In my opinion, it's pure rhetoric. Look how similar this contemporary psychiatric claim is to the medieval religious claim that individuals who rejected the beliefs of the religious authorities were "misguided" and had to be converted to the "true faith," for their (that is, the victims's) own benefit. This posture justified the use of unlimited force and fraud by inquisitors against heretics, and now justifies the use of unlimited force by and fraud by institutional psychiatrists against involuntary mental patients.

As I see it, the basic issue in commitment is the need for the control of social relationships and social conduct, and the problem of by whom and how this control should be exercised. As I mentioned, in the past such *social control*—for that's what we are talking about—was exercised under the aegis of religious ideologies and by religious institutions. Since the scientific revolution, there have been two principal methods of exercising such controls: the criminal law and the mental hygiene law. Those who break the law may be controlled by means of the criminal law. Those who do not break the law but annoy or disturb others—or whom others can successfully persecute or make into scapegoats—may be controlled by means of the mental hygiene law; that is, they can be stigmatized as "crazy" and locked up in mental hospitals.

THE NEW PHYSICIAN: Are you saying that the intervention of the medical doctor is for the patient, whereas that of the psychiatrist is for society?

SZASZ: Not quite. As you know, I make a very sharp distinction between at least two kinds of psychiatry. One is to help the patient, even if it harms society; the other is to help society, even if it harms the so-called patient. The two have nothing in common; indeed, they are mutually antagonistic. I analogize these two psychiatric functions to the two typical functions of the law in the criminal trial: prosecution and defense. These are not two similar interventions, they are antagonistic interventions. Most of psychiatry—historically, socially, economically—is prosecutorial psychiatry; it is psychiatry to help society, and harm the "patient." Now, what I can't emphasize too much is that it is a central characteristic of contemporary psychiatry *not* to make this distinction—indeed, not to allow it to be made. To insist on the difference, as I do, is sometimes considered unprofessional conduct. After all, the conventional psychiatrists say that the psychiatric physician always tries to help his "patient." You see, this is why it is so useful to define the "psychotic" as someone crazy, someone who does not know what's wrong with him and what he needs. Once this imagery is accepted, the psychiatrist can define anything he does—no matter how harmful to the patient, no matter how much resisted by the patient—as "therapeutic," serving the "patient's best interests." Look through any textbook on psychiatry, and you will not find this distinction between the two psychiatries. The "diagnosis" and "treatment" of voluntary and involuntary patients is all lumped together, as if it were all the same thing. Well, if that's how you start, how far can you get?

THE NEW PHYSICIAN: This distinction between voluntary and involuntary patients is evidently crucial to your whole thinking about psychiatric problems. Is it because of your view that the psychiatrist deals with human conflicts rather than medical diseases?

SZASZ: Yes. But, actually, my analysis of psychiatric problems rests not only on a distinction between the practice of psychiatry on voluntary and involuntary patients, but also on two related distinctions. The first is that between what constitutes a "psychiatric problem" for the self (the client or patient), and what constitutes such a problem for others (the "patient's" relatives, institutional psychiatrists, etc); and the second is the distinction between the assumption of the role of "mental patient" by the self and its ascription to others.

THE NEW PHYSICIAN: Do the people who work in state mental hospitals make this distinction between voluntary and involuntary patients, and the two corresponding kinds of psychiatric interventions?

SZASZ: Of course, they realize this distinction privately and I think they often suffer from the conflicts and turmoil of their work. But, officially, they do not make such a distinction. How could they? It would render their work, first, nonmedical—and the institutional psychiatrists, perhaps because what they do is so obviously nonmedical, always insist that their work is medical and can be done only by doctors; and second, it would render it non-therapeutic, indeed, anti-therapeutic or noxious. This explains, I think, why institutional psychiatrists—even more than psychoanalysts (though they do it, too)—cast their activities into the idiom and imagery of medicine and therapy. After all, when you control bleeding in an accident victim, you are "treating" the person whether or not he has consented to your intervention. Wouldn't it be just lovely if the same imagery would apply to the maniacal "patient" whose "illness" consists of drinking too much and assaulting his wife, and perhaps also assaulting the policemen who come to take him to the mental hospital? When he is given Thorazine—if necessary, by injection while being held down by burly attendants—is that similar to or different from the accident victim's treatment? And when such a person's imprisonment—for weeks, months, years, often for life—can also be defined as "treatment," as commitment is, obviously we have a professional imagery and rhetoric that's immensely useful for those who deal with involuntary mental patients.

THE NEW PHYSICIAN: You are describing a rhetoric of helpfulness used to conceal interventions which the patient experiences as punitive. Is that your objection to it? If the nature of the services or interventions was made clear as penalties for certain kinds of behavior, I take it you would favor that.

SZASZ: Not quite. Certainly, I would favor making a clear and honest distinction between psychiatrists who are for and those who are against the patient—as we now do between district attorneys and defense attorneys. When someone is in trouble with the income tax authorities or is accused of a criminal offense, he does not go to the district attorney for help. So one really can't speak of "services" as "penalties"—that's a contradiction. A service may be useless, even harmful, but it can't be a penalty. To have a penalty, to impose a penalty on a person—one must use force or fraud on him. In other words, one must either fool him or coerce him or preferably do both. If the distinctions I have outlined were made more openly, and were recognized more generally, several consequences would follow. First, some of the things now considered "services" could not be offered under that rubric; second, some other "services"—like commitment to mental hospitals—might not even be tolerated as criminal sanctions.

Again, the point here is that contemporary psychiatry and what is often, I think euphemistically, called "mental health education," is devoted to confusing, not to clarifying the distinction between voluntary and involuntary psychiatry, or between the psychiatrist as the patient's agent and the agent of the patient's adversaries, or between psychiatric interventions for "therapy" and for "punishment."

THE NEW PHYSICIAN: Dr. Szasz, you seem to be opposed to involuntary mental hospitalization under any circumstances. Are there no situations when commitment, involuntary medication, or shock treatment, and similar psychiatric procedures, are good things, useful interventions?

SZASZ: There are none. I am unqualifiedly opposed to involuntary mental hospitalization and treatment. To me, it's like slavery: the problem is not how to improve it, but how to abolish it.

Now, as to the question of the "usefulness" of commitment and other involuntary psychiatric interventions—to me, this is not a question of *when* such things are useful, but rather *for whom*. To put this sort of thing in terms of "indications" as if it were penicillin or digitalis is quite false. There are *always* indications for commitment, and there are *never* indications for it. It depends on whether you are for it or against it.

From a purely practical point of view, whenever commitment occurs, it *is* indicated or useful. Otherwise it would not occur. Someone has to *want* to commit a person, otherwise that person would not be committed. Now, for the person who wants the commitment, it's useful. It's as simple as that. In other words, commitment is *always* useful for the committers, for the patient's "loved ones," and others who are annoyed or disturbed by him. My analogy between commitment and slavery is not just a dramatic figure of speech. It should be taken quite seriously. When you ask, "When is commitment useful or when is it indicated?" you might as well ask, "When is Negro slavery useful or indicated?" The answer is obvious. Negro slavery is always a good idea for white men, assuming that they prefer not to work and have Negro slaves do the work for them. Similarly, commitment is always a good idea. It's always indicated, for those on the outside, for the "mentally healthy." That's why it's so popular. As long as there are more people outside of mental hospitals than inside, commitment will probably have some appeal. Similarly, so long as there are more white men in a country than black, some kind of discrimination against black men, if not their outright enslavement, will be popular, and vice versa (at least, until human nature changes in some

fundamental way). You see, I believe there is such a thing as evil. Most of my psychiatric colleagues never use that word; they prefer the term "mentally ill."

THE NEW PHYSICIAN: But how about the suicidal person? We prevent his suicide, and the chances are that when he recovers from his depression he will thank us for saving his life.

SZASZ: You are talking medicalese and psychiatrese. Let's speak English. What depression? What recovery? You have raised a complex moral question but are dealing with it as if it were a medical question. I just won't go along with that. I have discussed this problem in detail in my book, *Law, Liberty, and Psychiatry*,[1] and can only give you my conclusions. First, you must ask the question, "Who owns a person's life?" If the person does, then perhaps he has the "right" to destroy it; if he doesn't, then other implications follow. Second, you imply that good ends, namely, the prolongation of life, justify questionable means, namely, locking someone up in an insane asylum and probably stigmatizing him for life. I, for one, don't believe that. Third, you imply that physicians, especially psychiatrists, know when a person is going to kill himself, when he is a "suicidal risk." Well, of course, sometimes they do, and sometimes they don't. But there is obviously nothing easier than to *ascribe* suicidal intent to someone in order to justify controlling him, committing him. You don't say anything about what kinds of safeguards might be necessary to prevent such false ascription, even if one were to grant (as I don't for a minute) that the prevention of suicide by means of force and fraud (that is, involuntary hospitalization and deceptive diagnostic rhetoric) is a legitimate psychiatric activity.

THE NEW PHYSICIAN: Still, what about a person who, having taken an overdose of pills, comes to an emergency room voluntarily thereby putting himself in a position where he can be committed to a mental hospital?

SZASZ: Well, of course, that's the way things are now. But by not succeeding with the suicidal act—that is, by not being dead, but instead by being a chemically poisoned, and hence sick, person—such an individual has, in effect, made himself into a medical patient. The proper place to treat him therefore is a medical hospital. Moreover, since he comes to the hospital voluntarily, there is obviously no need to commit him. It is precisely because such a person runs the risk of commitment that he may not go to a doctor or a hospital. Commitment is antitherapeutic. There are people who want medical and other care for their depression or dissatisfaction with life, and their suicidal ideas, and their case is jeopardized by the present concepts and legal status of psychiatry.

THE NEW PHYSICIAN: How should this be changed?

SZASZ: Involuntary mental hospitalization should be abolished just as Negro slavery was abolished. It is an unqualified moral evil. There should be no such thing. There should be no place called a hospital from which a person cannot walk out without any further ado or by signing a piece of paper—that is, leaving against medical advice.

THE NEW PHYSICIAN: But would it be possible to do away with involuntary mental hospitalization? There are hundreds of thousands of people in mental hospitals, most of them on a committed status. What would happen to them if you just opened the doors and said, "O.K., you can leave"?

SZASZ: Well, of course, it would be possible.

THE NEW PHYSICIAN: What would happen?

SZASZ: What do you think would happen?

THE NEW PHYSICIAN: Many would stay.

SZASZ: Correct. Many would stay because they are poor, disabled, have no other place to go. In this sense, the mental hospital is an asylum. That's a nice, old term for insane asylum—but without the "insane." Civilized people ought to provide such places. The Salvation Army does, for example. Homes for the homeless. Orphanages for adults. But this has nothing to do with medicine. You don't need doctors to run such places. You don't even need psychologists or social workers. Just decent people.

THE NEW PHYSICIAN: That way there would be no need for medicine or psychiatry to feel guilty that there are so few doctors in state mental hospitals.

SZASZ: Right. But it goes further than that. Millions of dollars could be saved that now go to prop up the stage-settings, so to speak, of a fraudulent and wasteful pseudomedical enterprise. This could be spent simply on food and lodging and the kind of help that people who would stay in such places would want and could use, like rehabilitation, job training. Also such a place could be just a haven where people could be left alone, away from annoying relatives.

THE NEW PHYSICIAN: What about those people who, if there were no commitment, would want to leave, but who are considered dangerous or who are criminals?

SZASZ: Here again I should like to refer you to *Law, Liberty, and Psychiatry,* where I answer this question in detail. Briefly, my position is that no one should be deprived of liberty without due process of law and, to me, due process includes the concept that the only justification for loss of liberty is the commission of an illegal act. In other words, if someone is suspected of lawbreaking, he should be accused, tried, and, if convicted, sentenced. If the sentence calls for loss of liberty, he should be confined in an institution that's penal, not medical, in character. I don't think doctors should be jailers. That's what hospital psychiatrists are now. I say, a man who locks up someone is a jailer, even if he has an MD and wears a white coat. If jails are bad, and of course many are, they should be improved. Placing lawbreakers, or suspected law-breakers, in mental hospitals against their will is not a proper substitute for prison reform.

THE NEW PHYSICIAN: Many people who are committed to mental hospitals are diagnosed as schizophrenic, like a person who says he is Jesus Christ. What should be done with them?

SZASZ: It's very important to specify who these people are, what they do and to whom, and so forth. For example, is your hypothetical schizophrenic a clerk in the post office, doing a perfectly acceptable job, not bothering anyone, but who is expressing some peculiar ideas at home to his widowed mother? If so, then the problem, on the first level, at least, is what can she tolerate, how can she handle the son. She could throw him out if it's her house and if she is prepared to live alone; but, of course, it's easier for people in this sort of situation to define their offending relative as crazy and have him committed.

Let's change the situation a little, and assume that the person offends people in society—in stores, bars, at the office. Let's assume that the person goes around and makes some sort of megalomaniacal claim to anyone who will listen. He is a general nuisance. We deal here with socially deviant, obnoxious behavior, but with behavior which does not qualify as lawbreaking, as crime. The correct analogy here is not to disease (like cancer or pneumonia) but to religious deviance in a theological society. In other words, much of what we now call schizophrenia (and mental illness, generally) is similar to being Jewish in 15th-century Spain. In medieval Spain, you were supposed to be a Catholic, not a Jew; in contemporary America, if you are an insignificant clerk or blue-collar worker, you are supposed to be that and not make fraudulent claims about who you are or want to be. The question is how much tolerance does society show toward certain kinds of deviance? What kinds of deviance are permitted, and what kinds prohibited?

THE NEW PHYSICIAN: So some people who somehow or other fall outside of what society allows may end up in mental hospitals labeled as schizophrenic.

SZASZ: That's what the label really means. Still, people are looking for chemical abnormalities in the brain. Of course, some people may have brain diseases which we don't know anything about yet; and some of the people with these, as yet unknown, brain diseases may be "schizophrenics"—and others may not be, they may be "normal" citizens. I do not deny or minimize the importance of the body as a physicochemical machine that may malfunction. On the contrary, it's because I value so highly the basic biological understanding of how the body and brain work that I want to distinguish clearly between biological abnormalities and deviant role performances. Both are important.

THE NEW PHYSICIAN: But how do you know that schizophrenia is a deviant role performance?

SZASZ: I did not say that "schizophrenia" was a deviant role performance. I am not quibbling. I don't know what schizophrenia *is*. Or rather, it's just a word. When I was speaking about role deviance what I meant was that if Dr. Smith considers Mr. Jones's behavior socially deviant in certain ways, then he is likely to call Mr. Jones a schizophrenic. This is a statement about their relationship, not just about Mr. Jones or his "mind."

Another way of putting this would be to say that "schizophrenia" is a strategic label, like "Jew" was in Nazi Germany. If you want to exclude people from the social order you must justify this to others but especially to yourself. So you invent a justificatory rhetoric. That's what the really nasty psychiatric words are all about: they are justificatory rhetoric, legitimizing the removal of the people so labeled from society. It's like labeling a package "garbage"; it means: "take it away," "get it out of my sight," etc. That's what the word "Jew" meant in Nazi Germany; it did not mean a person with a certain kind of religious belief. It meant "vermin," "gas him!" I am afraid that "schizophrenia" and "sociopathic personality" and many other psychiatric diagnostic terms mean exactly the same thing; they mean "human garbage," "take him away!" "get him out of my sight!"

THE NEW PHYSICIAN: This calls into question the whole enterprise of psychiatric diagnosis. Is diagnosis an appropriate task for psychiatry, and if so, what is its purpose?

SZASZ: Well, we are getting back to our starting point here. Unless we define clearly, and keep in mind steadfastly, what kind of psychiatry we are talking about, it is impossible to answer the question you ask. As I have explained in my various writings, there are *at least* five different kinds of psychiatry. First, there is a psychiatry that is the study and treatment of diseases of the brain; second, one that is the study and treatment of "diseases" of the mind; third, one that is the study and influencing of human behavior; and, fourth and fifth, and these are, of course, different kinds of categories, there is a psychiatry that is practiced on voluntary patients, and another that is practiced on involuntary patients. In contemporary "scientific" psychiatry, all this is mixed up. Now, if we think of psychiatry as the diagnosis and treatment of organic brain disease—paresis, toxic psychoses, etc.—then, of course, making diagnosis is just as reasonable, and indeed potentially beneficial to the patient, as it is in general medicine. On the other hand, if we think of psychiatry as the labeling of personal conduct and as a method of social intervention in such conduct, then diagnosis is just using the rhetoric of medicine to conceal the exercise of social power. In short, in the latter case, making psychiatric diagnoses is a kind of socially tolerated name-calling or libeling—like when Senator Goldwater was diagnosed schizophrenic in the newspapers. This kind of labeling is simply an effort to demean someone, to impose a social handicap on him, to destroy him socially.

THE NEW PHYSICIAN: How about the private practice of psychotherapy, where a patient comes for help to the psychiatrist and wants him to be his agent? Is diagnosis important there?

SZASZ: No, not in the traditional, medical, or psychiatric sense. There is no need to diagnose such persons. Indeed, I would say there is nothing "to diagnose." What the psychotherapist needs to establish is whether he wants to take on the individual as his patient, and whether the patient is able and willing to pay his fee. To do this properly and honestly, the therapist must, of course, make clear to his would-be client what he is "selling" and for how much. Otherwise, the potential patient cannot make an informed choice.

THE NEW PHYSICIAN: Can the diagnosis be useful to see what type of approach should be made and how long therapy will take?

SZASZ: No, I believe it can only be detrimental to these tasks.

THE NEW PHYSICIAN: Why detrimental?

SZASZ: Because a psychiatric diagnosis creates the impression in the mind of both the client and the therapist that there is some kind of disease entity or process that is being attended to, rather than some kind of simply personal, social—human—sort of thing, the same sort of thing that Shakespeare or Goethe or Arthur Miller talks about. Again, you have raised an important and complex issue, and my answer here must of necessity seem too simple or at least too brief. I have dealt with the role of diagnosis in psychotherapy in my book *The Ethics of Psychoanalysis.*[2]

THE NEW PHYSICIAN: In other words, it's not even useful to distinguish between neurosis and psychosis?

SZASZ: If you mean in psychoanalysis, or what I like to call (though it's not synonymous) private, contractual psychotherapy, then certainly it's not useful. Not only is it not useful, it's nonsense. Useful for whom? For what? If, as a therapist, you are offering to sell psychotherapy, then what you want to know is whether the patient wishes to buy it or not. If he doesn't, you may want to call him "psychotic," but if you do that, you are simply maligning him, though you may sincerely believe that you have made some sort of highly scientific diagnosis.

THE NEW PHYSICIAN: How would you sum up your work in psychiatry?

SZASZ: I would sum it up by saying that I have tried to develop concepts and methods appropriate to a psychiatry whose problems are not medical diseases but human conflicts; whose criteria of value are not conformity to social norms or "mental health," but self-determination and responsible liberty; and which is dedicated to diminishing man's coerecive control over his fellowman and increasing his control over himself.

THE NEW PHYSICIAN: It sounds like the changes you wish to see are so great, so profound, that if they were to occur it would have to be in the distant future. I wonder what you would like to see in the near future. What goals could be worked for by physicians, psychiatrists, medical students, people interested in this whole question?

SZASZ: I should like to say, and I think this is obvious from my writings, that although the changes which I should like to see are quite major, I am firmly opposed to sudden, revolutionary changes in social affairs. Meaningful, significant, and lasting changes in human affairs can come only in a slow, gradual fashion. The problems we have been talking about pertain to human nature and to the organization of society. How does man achieve personal significance and self-esteem? Is it by creative work or by robbing others of their self-esteem? The latter alternative has always been frightfully popular, and it still is. Yet, there have been significant moral and social changes over the years. Whether mankind is "improving" or "deteriorating" morally I am certainly not prepared to discuss here and now. But the fact is that we used to have slavery, and slavery was abolished. Women, especially married women, used to be a kind of domestic chattel, and they no longer are. The criminal law used to be unbelievably harsh, prescribing the chopping off of hands for picking pockets; it has become more tame. So that insofar

as psychiatry, that is, institutional psychiatry, is a repressive social institution, there is no reason to believe that it too will not be altered so that its power to oppress and victimize will be reduced.

Those who are interested in working in this direction—that is, toward reducing the coercive power of psychiatry and increasing its ability to help those, and only those, who want and seek such help—such persons could best do so, I think, by demythologizing the medical and coercive ideology of contemporary psychiatry and by putting it on a solidly humanistic, legal, and communicational foundation. I can't say more about this, it's too complex. May I refer you in this connection to *The Myth of Mental Illness*.[3]

THE NEW PHYSICIAN: You might consider yourself in a position like that of an abolitionist of the 1850's. Does this sum up your conclusion on this subject?

SZASZ: Yes, I do like to think of myself, as far as this aspect of my work is concerned, as a kind of abolitionist. Emerson has always been one of my heroes.

The logic of the situation demands either expansion or restriction—whether in slavery or involuntary mental hospitalization. If slavery is a good thing, a noble institution, beneficial both for master and slave—then why indeed not to extend its scope? Why not have more slave territories and more slaves? Similarly, if involuntary mental hospitalization is a noble medical enterprise, beneficial for both doctor and patient—then why indeed should we not extend this "service" to more and more people? That's precisely what has been happening.

THE NEW PHYSICIAN: One last question, Dr. Szasz. I know you have some ideas about why the idea of mental illness is so popular in our day. Could you conclude with a few words about this?

SZASZ: As I see it, there are tremendously powerful ideological and economic interests in Western society—especially in American society—which demand that ever-greater numbers of people in the population be mentally disabled, or that they be regarded and treated as mentally disabled. This has to do in part with the fact that in the industrially advanced nations people are becoming increasingly superfluous and unnecessary as producers. So they must be consumers of goods and services, and what better service to consume than "mental health care"? When people consume *that,* they elevate the dignity and self-esteem of those who are doing the "servicing." How people love to volunteer nowadays for "mental health work"! In this way, people are slowly being transformed into a product on whom other people can work. We thus live in an age characterized by a tremendous need for vast numbers of "madmen" upon whom, as products or things, a large part of the rest of the population can work, and which the non-mad part can proudly support. The result is what I call "The Therapeutic State"—a state whose aim is not to provide favorable conditions for the pursuit of life, liberty, and happiness, but to repair the defective mental health of its citizens. The officials of such a state parody the role of physician and psychotherapist. It's a neat arrangement: it gives life-meaning to the therapists by robbing the "patients" of their life-meaning. Truly, this is the new frontier. We can persecute millions of people, all the while telling ourselves that we are great healers, curing them of mental illness. We have managed to repackage the Inquisition and are selling it as a new, scientific cure-all. How right Santayana was when he said that "Those who do not remember the past are condemned to relive it."

REFERENCES

1. Szasz, Thomas: *Law, Liberty, and Psychiatry.* New York: Macmillan, 1963; paperback edition, New York: Collier, 1968.

2. Szasz, Thomas: *The Ethics of Psychoanalysis.* New York: Basic Books, 1965; paperback edition, New York: Dell, 1969.

3. Szasz, Thomas: *The Myth of Mental Illness.* New York: Hoeber-Harper, 1961; paperback edition, New York: Dell, 1967.

THIRTY-FOUR

THE SANE SLAVE
AN HISTORICAL NOTE ON THE USE OF MEDICAL DIAGNOSIS AS JUSTIFICATORY RHETORIC

THOMAS S. SZASZ

I

The passion to dehumanize and diminish man, as well as to superhumanize and glorify him, appears to be a characteristic of human nature. For millennia, the dialectic of vilification and deification and, more generally, of invalidation and validation—excluding the individual from the group as an evil outsider or including him in it as a member in good standing—was cast in the imagery and rhetoric of magic and religion. Thus, at the height of Christianity in Europe, only the faithful were considered human: the faithless—heretics, witches, and Jews—were considered subhuman or nonhuman and were so treated. At the same time, the popes were thought to be infallible and kings ruled by divine decree.

SOURCE: Thomas S. Szasz. "The Sane Slave: An Historical Note on the Use of Medical Diagnosis as Justificatory Rhetoric." Copyright by the American Journal of Psychotherapy, 1971. Thomas S. Szasz, "The Sane Slave: An Historical Note on the Use of Medical Diagnosis as Justificatory Rhetoric," *American Journal of Psychotherapy*, xxv (April, 1971), pp. 228–239. Reprinted by permission of the American Psychotherapy Association.

With the decline of the religious world view, and the ascendancy of the scientific, during the Renaissance and the Enlightenment, the religious rhetoric of validation and invalidation was gradually replaced by the scientific. I have described and documented this transformation in *The Manufacture of Madness* (1), showing, in particular, the birth, development, and flowering of the lexicon of medical diagnosis as a rhetoric of rejection.

In this essay, my aim is to offer an additional illustration of the foregoing thesis. In May, 1851, an essay entitled "Report on the Diseases and Physical Peculiarities of the Negro Race," written by Samuel A. Cartwright, M.D., was published in the then prestigious *New Orleans Medical and Surgical Journal* (2). In this remarkable document, Dr. Cartwright asserted—not only in his own name but also in his capacity as chairman of a committee appointment by the Medical Association of Louisiana to report on the "diseases and peculiarities of the Negro race"—that Negroes are biologically inferior to whites, and sought to justify their enslavement as a therapeutic necessity for the slaves and a medical responsibility for the masters. In support of this thesis, Dr. Cartwright claimed to identify two new diseases peculiar to Negroes: one, which he called "drapetomania," was manifested by the escape of the Negro slave from his white master; the other, which he called "dysaesthesia Aethiopis," was manifested by the Negro's neglecting his work or refusing to work altogether.

II

I consider Cartwright's "Report," and especially the two diseases afflicting the Negro that he discovered, of special interest and importance to us today for the following reasons: first, because Cartwright invoked the authority and vocabulary of medical science to dehumanize the Negro and justify his enslavement by the white man; second, because the language and reasoning he used to justify the coercive control of the Negro are identical to those used today by mental health propagandists to justify the coercive control of the madman (that is, the so-called "psychotic," "addict," "sexual psychopath," and so forth); and third, because Cartwright's "Report" is the sort of medical document that has, for obvious reasons, been systematically ignored or suppressed in standard texts on medical and psychiatric history.

One such omission, discussed in detail in *The Manufacture of Madness,* is Benjamin Rush's theory of Negritude, according to which the black skin and other physical "peculiarities" of the Negro are due to his suffering from congenital leprosy (1, pp. 153–159). This grotesquely self-serving explanation—which postulated white as the only "healthy" human skin color, and defined the normal physiologic state of the Negro as a dreadful disease, justifying his segregation for reasons of alleged ill health rather than imputed racial inferiority—was, moreover, merely a part of Rush's medical world-view in which all types of undesired human characteristics and conduct were considered diseases—usually of the mind. Thus by the time the "Report on the Diseases and Physical

Peculiarities of the Negro Race" appeared, the habit, especially among medical men, of passionately degrading their adversaries as sick, while pretending to be impartially "diagnosing" them, was well established. It is against this general background, and the steadily increasing influence of the abolitionist forces in the United States at that time, that we must consider the Cartwright "Report."

I shall reproduce below excerpts from the "Report" describing drapetomania and dysaesthesia Aethiopis, and shall then offer some comments on them.

III. DRAPETOMANIA, OR THE DISEASE CAUSING SLAVES TO RUN AWAY

Drapetomania is from *"drapetes,"* a runaway slave, and *"mania," mad or crazy.* It is unknown to our medical authorities, although its diagnostic symptom, the absconding from service, is well known to our planters and overseers, as it was to the ancient Greeks, who expressed by the single word *"drapetes"* the fact of the absconding, and the relation that the fugitive held to the person he fled from. I have added to the word meaning runaway slave, another Greek term, to express the disease of the mind causing him to abscond. In noticing a disease not heretofore classed among the long list of maladies that man is subject to, it was necessary to have a new term to express it. The cause, in the most of cases, that induces the negro to run away from service, is as much a disease of the mind as any other species of mental alienation, and much more curable, as a general rule. With the advantages of proper medical advice, strictly followed, this troublesome practice that many negroes have of running away, can be almost entirely prevented, although the slaves be located on the borders of a free State, within a stone's throw of the abolitionists. . . .

To ascertain the true method of governing negroes, so as to cure and prevent the disease under consideration, we must go back to the Pentateuch, and learn the true meaning of the untranslated term that represents the negro race. In the name there given to that race, is locked up the true art of governing negroes in such a manner that they cannot run away. The correct translation of that term declares the Creator's will in regard to the negro; it declares him to be the submissive knee-bender. In the anatomical conformation of his knees, we see *"genu flexit"* written in the physical structure of his knees, being more flexed or bent, than any other kind of man. If the white man attempts to oppose the Deity's will, by trying to make the negro anything else than *"the submissive knee-bender,"* (which the Almighty declared he should be) by trying to raise him to a level with himself, or by putting himself on an equality with the negro; or if he abuses the power which God has given him over his fellow man, by being cruel to him or punishing him in anger, or by neglecting to protect him from the wanton abuses of his fellow-servants and all others, or by denying him the usual comforts and necessities of life, the negro will run away, but if he keeps him in the position that we learn from the Scriptures he was intended to occupy, that is, the position of submission, and if his master or overseer be kind and gracious in his bearing towards him, without condescension, and at the same time ministers to his physical wants and protects him from abuses, the negro is spell-bound, and cannot run away. . . .

Before negroes run away, unless they are frightened or panic-struck, they become sulky and dissatisfied. The cause of this sulkiness and dissatisfaction should be inquired into and removed, or they are apt to run away or fall into the negro consumption. When sulky and dissatisfied without cause, the experience of those on the line and elsewhere was decidedly in favor of whipping them out of it, as a preventive measure against absconding or other bad conduct. It was called whipping the devil out of them.

If treated kindly, well fed and clothed, with fuel enough to keep a small fire burning all night, separated into families, each family having its own house—not permitted to run about at night, or to visit their neighbors, or to receive visits, or to use intoxicating liquors, and not overworked or exposed too much to the weather, they are very easily governed—more so than any other people in the world. When all this is done, if any one or more of them, at any time, are inclined to raise their heads to a level with their master or overseer, humanity and

their own good require that they should be punished until they fall into that submissive state which it was intended for them to occupy in all after time, when their progenitor received the name of Canaan, or "submissive knee-bender." They have only to be kept in that state, and treated like children with care, kindness, attention and humanity, to prevent and cure them from running away.

IV. DYSAESTHESIA AETHIOPIS, OR HEBETUDE OF MIND AND OBTUSE SENSIBILITY OF BODY—A DISEASE PECULIAR TO NEGROES—CALLED BY OVERSEERS, "RASCALITY"

Dyaesthesia Aethiopis is a disease peculiar to negroes, affecting both mind and body, in a manner as well expressed by dysaesthesia, the name I have given it, as could be by a single term. There is both mind and sensibility, but both seem to be difficult to reach by impressions from without. There is partial insensibility of the skin, and so great a hebetude of the intellectual faculties as to be like a person half asleep, that is with difficulty aroused and kept awake. It differs from every other species of mental disease, as it is accompanied with physical signs or lesions of the body, discoverable to the medical observer, which are always present and sufficient to account for the symptoms. It is much more prevalent among free negroes living in clusters by themselves, than among slaves on our plantations, and attacks only such slaves as live like free negroes in regard to diet, drinks, exercise, etc. It is not my purpose to treat of the complaint as it prevails among free negroes, nearly all of whom are more or less afflicted with it, that have not got some white person to direct and to take care of them. To narrate its symptoms and effects among them would be to write a history of the ruins and dilapidation of Hayti and every spot of earth they have ever had uncontrolled possession over for any length of time. I propose only to describe its symptoms among slaves.

From the careless movements of the individuals affected with the complaint, they are apt to do much mischief, which appears as if intentional, but is mostly owing to the stupidity of mind and insensibility of the nerves induced by the disease. Thus, they break, waste and destroy everything they handle—abuse horses and cattle—tear, burn or rend their own clothing, and paying no attention to the rights of property, they steal other's to replace what they have destroyed. They wander about at night, and keep in a half-nodding sleep during the day. They slight their work—cut up corn, cane, cotton or tobacco when hoeing it, as if for pure mischief. They raise disturbances with their overseers and fellow servants without cause or motive, and seem to be insensible to pain when subjected to punishment.

The fact of the existence of such a complaint, making man like an automaton or senseless machine, having the above or similar symptoms, can be clearly established by the most direct and positive testimony. That it should have escaped the attention of the medical profession, can only be accounted for because its attention has not been sufficiently directed to the maladies of the negro race. Otherwise, a complaint of so common occurrence on badly-governed plantations, and so universal among free negroes, or those who are not governed at all—a disease radicated in physical lesions and having its peculiar and well-marked symptoms, and its curative indications, would not have escaped the notice of the profession. The northern physicians and people have noticed the symptoms, but not the disease from which they spring. They ignorantly attribute the symptoms to the debasing influence of slavery on the mind, without considering that those who have never been in slavery, or their fathers before them, are the most afflicted and the latest from the slave-holding South the least. The disease is the natural offspring of negro liberty—the liberty to be idle, to wallow in filth, and to indulge in improper food and drinks.

In treating of the anatomy and physiology of the negro, I showed that his respiratory system was under the same physiological laws as that of an infant child of the white race; that a warm atmosphere, loaded with carbonic acid and aqueous vapor, was the most congenial to his lungs during sleep, as it is to the infant; that, to insure the respiration of such an atmosphere, he invariably, as if moved by instinct, shrouds his head and face in a blanket or some other covering, when disposing himself to sleep; that if sleeping by the fire in cold weather, he turns his head to it, instead of his feet, evidently to inhale warm air; that when not in active exercise, he always hovers over a fire in comparatively warm weather, as if he

took a positive pleasure in inhaling hot air and smoke when his body is quiescent. The natural effect of this practice, it was shown, caused imperfect atmospherization or vitalization of the blood in the lungs, as occurs in infancy, and a hebetude or torpor of intellect—from blood not sufficiently vitalized being distributed to the brain; also, a slothfulness, torpor and disinclination to exercise, from the same cause—the want of blood sufficiently areated or vitalized in the circulating system.

When left to himself, the negro indulges in his natural disposition to idleness and sloth, and does not take exercise enough to expand his lungs and to vitalize his blood, but dozes out a miserable existence in the midst of filth and uncleanliness, being too indolent and having too little energy of mind to provide for himself proper food and comfortable lodging and clothing. The consequence is, that the blood becomes so highly carbonized and deprived of oxygen, that it not only becomes unfit to stimulate the brain to energy, but unfit to stimulate the nerves of sensation distributed to the body. A torpor and insensibility pervades the system; the sentient nerves distributed to the skin lose their feeling to so great a degree, that he often burns his skin by the fire he hovers over, without knowing it, and frequently has large holes in his clothes, and the shoes on his feet burnt to a crisp, without having been conscious of when it was done. This is the disease called dysaesthesia—a Greek term expressing the dull or obtuse sensation that always attends the complaint.

When aroused from his sloth by the stimulus of hunger, he takes anything he can lay his hands on, and tramples on the rights, as well as on the property of others, with perfect indifference as to consequences. When driven to labor by the compulsive power of the white man, he performs the task assigned him in a headlong, careless manner, treading down with his feet, or cutting with his hoe the plants he is put to cultivate—breaking the tools he works with, and spoiling everything he touches that can be injured by careless handling. Hence the overseers call it "rascality," supposing that the mischief is intentionally done. But there is no premeditated mischief in the case—the mind is too torpid to meditate mischief, or even to be aroused by the angry passions to deeds of daring. Dysaesthesia, or hebetude of sensation of both mind and body, prevails to so great an extent, that when the unfortunate individual is subjected to punishment, he neither feels pain of any consequence, or shows any unusual resentment, more than by a stupid sulkiness. In some cases, anaesthesiac would be a more suitable name for it, as there appears to be an almost total loss of feeling. The term ''rascality,'' given to this disease by overseers, is founded on an erroneous hypothesis and leads to an incorrect empirical treatment, which seldom or ever cures it.

The complaint is easily curable, if treated on sound physiological principles. The skin is dry, thick and harsh to the touch, and the' liver inactive. The liver, skin and kidneys should be stimulated to activity, and be made assist in decarbonising the blood. The best means to stimulate the skin is, first, to have the patient well washed with warm water and soap; then to anoint it all over with oil, and to slap the oil in with a broad leather strap; then to put the patient to some hard kind of work in the open air and sunshine, that will compel him to expand his lungs, as chopping wood, splitting rails or sawing with the cross-cut or whip saw. Any kind of labor will do that will cause full and free respiration in its performance, as lifting or carrying heavy weights, or brisk walking; the object being to expand the lungs by full and deep inspirations and expirations, thereby to vitalize the impure circulating blood by introducing oxygen and expelling carbon. . . .

Such treatment will, in a short time, effect a cure in all cases which are complicated with chronic visceral derangements. The effect of this or a like course of treatment is often like enchantment. No sooner does the blood feel the vivifying influences derived from its full and perfect atmospherization by exercise in the open air and in the sun, than the negro seems to be awakened to a new existence, and to look grateful and thankful to the white man whose compulsory power, by making him inhale vital air, has restored his sensation and dispelled the mist that clouded his intellect. His intelligence restored and his sensations awakened, he is no longer the *bipedum neqquissimus,* or arrant rascal, he was supposed to be, but a good negro that can hoe or plow, and handle things with as much care as his other fellow-servants. . . .

Although idleness is the most prolific cause of dysaesthesia, yet there are other ways that the blood gets deteriorated. I said before that negroes are like children, requiring government in everything. . . .

According to unalterable physiological laws, negroes, as a general rule, to which there are but few exceptions, can only have their intellectual faculties awakened in a sufficient degree to receive moral culture, and to profit by religious or other instruction, when under the compulsatory authority of the white man; because, as a general rule, to which there are but few exceptions, they will not take sufficient exercise, when removed from the white man's authority, to vitalize and decarbonize their blood by the process of full and free respiration, that active exercise of some kind alone can effect. A northern climate remedies, in a considerable degree, their naturally indolent disposition; but the dense atmosphere of Boston or Canada can scarcely produce sufficient hematosis and vigor of mind to induce them to labor. From their natural indolence, unless under the stimulus of compulsion, they doze away their lives with the capacity of their lungs for atmospheric air only half expanded, from the want of exercise to superinduce full and deep respiration. The inevitable effect is, to prevent a sufficient atmospherization or vitalization of the blood, so essential to the expansion and the freedom of action of the intellectual faculties. The black blood distributed to the brain chains the mind to ignorance, superstition and barbarism, and bolts the door against civilization, moral culture and religious truth. The compulsory power of the white man, by making the slothful negro take active exercise, puts into active play the lungs, through whose agency the vitalized blood is sent to the brain to give liberty to the mind, and to open the door to intellectual improvement. The very exercise, so beneficial to the negro, is expended in cultivating those burning fields in cotton, sugar, rice and tobacco, which, but for his labor, would, from the heat of the climate, go uncultivated, and their products lost to the world. Both parties are benefitted—the negro as well as his master—even more. But there is a third party benefitted—the world at large. The three millions of bales of cotton, made by negro labor, afford a cheap clothing for the civilized world. The laboring classes of all mankind, having less to pay for clothing, have more money to spend in educating their children, and in intellectual, moral and religious progress.

The wisdom, mercy and justice of the decree, that Canaan shall serve Japheth, is proved by the disease we have been considering, because it proves that his physical organization, and the laws of his nature, are in perfect unison with slavery, and in entire discordance with liberty—a discordance so great as to produce the loathsome disease that we have been considering, as one of its inevitable effects—a disease that locks up the understanding, blunts the sensations and chains the mind to superstition, ignorance and barbarism. Slaves are not subject to this disease, unless they are permitted to live like free negroes, in idleness and filth—to eat improper food, or to indulge in spirituous liquors. . . .

Our Declaration of Independence, which was drawn up at a time when negroes were scarcely considered as human beings, *"That all men are by nature free and equal,"* and only intended to apply to white men, is often quoted in support of the false dogma that all mankind possess the same mental, physiological and anatomical organization, and that the liberty, free institutions, and whatever else would be a blessing to one portion, would, under the same external circumstances, be to all, without regard to any original or internal differences inherent in the organization. . . .

The dysaesthesia Aethiopis adds another to the many ten thousand evidences of the fallacy of the dogma that abolitionism is built on; for here, in a country where two races of men dwell together, both born on the same soil, breathing the same air, and surrounded by the same external agents—liberty, which is elevating the one race of people above all other nations, sinks the other into beastly sloth and torpidity; and the slavery, which the one would prefer death rather than endure, improves the other in body, mind and morals; thus proving the dogma false, and establishing the truth that there is a radical, internal, or physical difference between the two races, so great in kind, as to make what is wholesome and beneficial for the white man, as liberty, republican or free institutions, etc., not only unsuitable to the negro race, but actually poisonous to its happiness.

V

The content of the Cartwright "Report" hardly requires comment. Its form however, which closely resembles contemporary forms of psychiatric denigration, deserves further attention. I shall list my observations in the order in which the statements to which they refer occur in the text—first on "drapetomania," then on "dysaesthesia Aethiopis."

1. Although "running away," or escaping from captivity, is ordinarily thought of as a human act, a deliberate or willed performance, Cartwright refers to it as an occurrence or happening, an event "caused" by certain antecedent events: thus drapetomania "causes" slaves to run away.

2. The "cause . . . that induces the negro to run away from service" is, moreover, identified as a "disease of the mind."

3. Premonitory symptoms of drapetomania are said to be "sulkiness" and "dissatisfaction." When displayed by whites, such emotions were then viewed as the normal expressions of unhappiness with one's lot in life; but when displayed by Negro slaves, they signaled the onset of a dread mental disease.

4. To prevent the full-blown development of drapetomania, exhibited by the actual running away of the slave, whipping is recommended as medical therapy. This treatment, in a revealing allusion to its historical origins, is called "whipping the devil out of them."

5. Finally, the cure of drapetomania, and the restoration of the slave to sanity, is said to require the submission of the Negro slave to his white master. "They have only to be kept in that [submissive]state," concludes Cartwright, "and treated like children, with care, kindness, attention and humanity [sic], to prevent and cure them from running away."

Since Cartwright's foregoing observations, Lincoln has emancipated the Negro slaves and the medical profession has negritized the free whites. Thus, what had been drapetomania became depression. The Negro slave ran away from slavery. Modern man runs away from a life that seems to him a kind of slavery. In trying to escape, he may abandon his family, his job, his very life. Since such behavior is socially disruptive, and in the case of suicidal propensities is life-threatening, it is now generally regarded as a medical problem justifying the involuntary hospitalization and treatment of the alleged patient.

In short, the sane slave is the Negro who accepts his role as the natural and proper order of things. The Negro who rejects this role is defined as insane. In this view, formed more than a century ago, we recognize the current criteria of mental health and mental illness—that is, the acceptance of the social roles imposed upon us by birth, fate, law, or our superiors in life, or their rejection (3, 4).

6. "Dysaesthesia Aethiopis" is an illness which Cartwright identifies as "a disease peculiar to negroes—called by overseers 'rascality.'" It is thus clearly a product of relabeling, pure and simple (4).

7. As with drapetomania, Cartwright further identifies dysaesthesia Aethiopis specifically as a "mental disease . . . accompanied with physical signs or lesions of the body, discoverable to the medical observer. . . ."

8. Although Cartwright mentions not a single free Negro who has consulted him as a patient, for this or any other illness, he refers to "the complaint [sic] as it prevails among free negroes. . . ." Actually, dysaethesia Aethiopis points to certain types of behavior on the part of Negroes deemed offensive to whites—by the whites, not the blacks. It is Cartwright who "complains," not his alleged "patients." This linguistic form—the oppressor labeling the undesired behavior of his victim a "complaint" or a "symptom"—continues to remain basic to, and indispensable for, the theory and practice of institutional psychiatry (1).

9. "Nearly all" free Negroes "that have not got some white person to direct and to take care of them" are said to be afflicted with dysaesthesia Aethiopsis. This alleged finding re-affirms the equation between sanity and subjection for the black—and sanity and domination for the white. Today, we equate sanity with psychiatric subjection for the patient—and sanity with psychiatric domination for the physician. Since nowadays everyone is considered more or less mentally ill, the measure of mental health is "insight" into, and acceptance of, the role of mental patient by the layman—and the role of mental healer by the physician. The drama of mental illness is thus merely a new version of the drama of Negritude: the cast is new, but the play is the same.

10. The chief symptoms—"complaints," as Cartwright calls them—of dysaesthesia Aethiopis are the doing of "much mischief": the individuals afflicted with the malady "break, waste, and destroy everything they handle . . . slight their work—cut up corn, cane, cotton or tobacco when hoeing it, as if for pure mischief." These acts speak for themselves. Their meaning, and the human dignity of those whose protest they express and signify, are medically redefined as the meaningless manifestations of a mental disorder. And so it is today—except that we now dehumanize black and white equally. From insane "rascalities" in Louisiana to insane murders in Dallas and Los Angeles, it is only a short step.

11. Cartwright not only describes the signs and symptoms of the disease he calls "dysaesthesia Aethiopis," he also identifies its etiology and prescribes its cure. "The disease," he asserts, "is the natural offspring of negro liberty. . . ."

12. "The complaint [sic] is easily curable." To cure the "patient," the doctor is exhorted "to anoint it [the skin] all over with oil, and to slap the oil in with a broad leather strap; then to put the patient [sic] to some hard kind of work in the open air and sunshine, that will compel him to expand his lungs, as chopping wood, splitting rails or sawing with the cross-cut or whip saw." This posture is indistinguishable from the "therapeutic attitude" of our "liberal" psychiatric criminologist (5, 6). The basic formula is here in its entirety: call the victim "patient" and the punishment "treatment," and he will surely be "cured" of his "affliction"—provided, of course, that the physician is left in full charge not only of the patient and his treatment but of the evaluation of the therapeutic results as well.

13. Although Cartwright attributes the destructive behavior of Negroes to dysaesthesia Aethiopis and claims that the disease is curable, even complete recovery from this affliction fails to restore the blacks to a physiologic state comparable to that of the whites. ''Although idleness is the most prolific cause of dysaesthesia, yet there are other ways that the blood gets deteriorated. I said before that the negroes are like children, requiring government in everything.''

14. Lastly, Cartwright provides us with an exceptionally clear and unqualified statement regarding the subhuman character of Negroes which, though rarely put so badly nowadays, applies equally to the modern view of all men—black *and* white—stigmatized as mentally ill. ''Our Declaration of Independence,'' Cartwright writes, ''which was drawn up at a time when negroes were scarcely considered as human beings, 'That all men are by nature free and equal,' and only intended to apply to white men, is often quoted in support of the false dogma that all mankind possesses the same mental, physiological, and anatomical organization. . . . The dysaesthesia Aethiopis adds another to the many ten thousand [sic] evidences of the fallacy of the dogma that abolitionism is built on. . . .'' Liberty, Cartwright concludes, is beneficial for the white man, but is ''actually poisonous to the happiness'' of his black brother. No more fitting epitaph could be written for involuntary mental hospitalization, a practice that enshrines the identical proposition: Liberty, beneficial for the sane (psychiatrist), is actually poisonous to the happiness of the insane (patient).

VI

It would be misleading to leave off here, implying that our forebears accepted Cartwright's claims without the skepticism that is as characteristic of man as is his gullibility. In the September, 1851 issue of the *New Orleans Medical and Surgical Journal,* there appeared a devastating criticism of Cartwright's paper. Written by James T. Smith,

Surgeon, Louisiana, it is titled: ''Review of Dr. Cartwright's Report on the Diseases and Physical Peculiarities of the Negro Race'' (7). I shall quote from it only those passages that are relevant to our contemporary infatuation with the rhetoric of mental health and mental illness.

Commenting on ''drapetomania,'' Smith writes: ''This may well be called a new disease, discovered by Dr. Cartwright. . . . It is calculated to marshal the way to the pathology of a very numerous class of diseases hitherto never dreamed of as being anything but vices; for if a strong desire to do what is wrong be a disease, the violation of any one of the ten commandments will furnish us with a new one so that with a long Greek word for the commencement, and the addition of the magic 'mania,' we shall have a disease for coveting your neighbor's money (a disease common to both the white and black races), or a disease of bearing false witness, or a disease for cutting your neighbor's throat, commonly called 'murder'; all of which shall no longer be treated by the penitentiary, but by calomel, capsicum, etc. This we consider as the greatest step in the progress of philanthropy made in modern times'' (7).

Smith was no less astute in his remarks on Cartwright's treatment of dysaesthesia Aethiopis. For this disease, he writes, Cartwright ''suggests a species of remedy which, with some modifications, the Greek master applied to his drapetes and the Roman to his fugitivus—it is, the 'strapping-in' recommended by the doctor. 'The best means,' says he, 'of stimulating the skin is to have the patient well washed with warm water and soap, then to anoint it all over with oil, and to slap it in with a broad leather strap.' Now they, the Romans and the Greeks, used the strapping in without the anointment; and with a much narrower strap than the one rocommended'' (7).

And one final comment on drapetomania: It may be of some interest to note that standard medical dictionaries (such as *Gould's* and *Stedman's*) continue to list this term, defining it as ''a morbid desire to wander or run away.''

VII

It would be misleading still, to stop here, implying that Cartwright's vicious paternalism toward the Negro is safely behind us. In 1851, Samuel A. Cartwright, M.D. asserted that the Negro was a child who must be governed by the white man. In 1969, Graham B. Blaine, Jr., M.D., chief of Psychiatric Service of the Harvard University Health Services, asserts that the Negro is an adolescent whose ''symptoms'' must be borne with ''patience'' and ''tolerance'' by the white man (8). From the ''drapetomania'' and ''dysaesthesia Aethiopis'' of the black slave, to the ''adolesence of the black race'' and its ''identity conflict,'' the road is direct and the passage swift: The way is through the land of medicine and is marked clearly, all the way, by diagnostic labels.

As to the Negro's present medical condition—couched in the vocabulary of the most up-to-date and ''humanistic'' terms of psychiatry—I shall let Blaine speak about it for himself. ''In addition to helping black students cope with the problems of their individual adolescence,'' he writes, ''they must also be helped to deal with the conflicts that arise from the adolescence of the black race. It is in this country, at this time, a group which is struggling to define its identity. After such definition occurs, the race can take its place harmoniously within the larger culture. Rebellion and group distinctiveness are symptoms of this identity conflict. The rest of society must be patient and tolerant about these symptoms much as parents must deal with the paradoxical, provocative behavior of their adolescent children'' (8).

VIII

I have tried to call attention, by means of an article published in the *New Orleans Medical and Surgi-*cal *Journal* for 1851, to some of the historical origins of the modern psychiatric rhetoric. In the article cited, conduct on the part of the Negro slave displeasing or offensive to his white master is defined as the manifestation of mental disease, and subjection and punishment are prescribed as treatments. By substituting involuntary mental patients for Negro slaves, institutional psychiatrists for white slave owners, and the rhetoric of mental health for that of white supremacy, we may learn a fresh lesson about the changing verbal patterns man uses to justify exploiting and oppressing his fellow man, in the name of helping him.

Perhaps Shaw—and Hegel whom he was paraphrasing—were right: ''We learn from history, that we learn nothing from history.''

REFERENCES

1. Szasz, T. S. *The Manufacture of Madness: A Comparative Study of the Inquisition and the Mental Health Movement.* Harper & Row, New York, 1970

2. Cartwright, S. A. Report on the diseases and physical peculiarities of the negro race. *New Orleans Medical and Surgical Journal,* 7:691–715, 1851.

3. Szasz, T. S. *The Myth of Mental Illness.* Hoeber-Harper, New York, 1961.

4. ———. *Ideology and Insanity.* Doubleday-Anchor, Garden City, N.Y., 1970.

5. Halleck, S. L. *Psychiatry and the Dilemmas of Crime.* Hoeber-Harper, New York, 1967.

6. Menninger, K. *The Crime of Punishment.* Viking Press, New York, 1968.

7. Smith, J. T. Review of Dr. Cartwright's Report on the diseases and physical peculiarities of the negro race. *New Orleans Medical and Surgical Journal,* 8:228–237, 1851.

8. Blaine, G. B., Jr. What's Behind the Youth Rebellion? *Sunday Herald Traveler* (Boston) November 16, 1969, pp. 22–23.

THIRTY-FIVE

PARANOIA AND THE DYNAMICS OF EXCLUSION

EDWIN M. LEMERT

One of the few generalizations about psychotic behavior which sociologists have been able to make with a modicum of agreement and assurance is that such behavior is a result or manifestation of a disorder in communication between the individual and society. The generalization, of course, is a large one, and, while it can be illustrated easily with case history materials, the need for its conceptual refinement and detailing of the process by which disruption of communication occurs in the dynamics of mental disorder has for some time been apparent. Among the more carefully reasoned attacks upon this problem is Cameron's formulation of the paranoid pseudocommunity (1).

In essence, the conception of the paranoid pseudocommunity can be stated as follows:

Paranoid persons are those whose inadequate social learning leads them in situations of unusual stress to incompetent social reactions. Out of the fragments of the social behavior of others the paranoid person symbolically organizes a pseudocommunity whose functions he perceives as focused on him. His reactions to this *supposed community* of response which he sees loaded with threat to himself bring him into open conflict with the actual community and lead to his temporary or permanent isolation from its affairs. The "real" community, which is unable to share in his attitudes and reactions, takes action through forcible restraint or retaliation *after* the paranoid person "bursts into defensive or vengeful activity."[1]

That the community to which the paranoid reacts is "pseudo" or without existential reality is made unequivocal by Cameron when he says:

> As he (the paranoid person) begins attributing to others the attitudes which he has towards himself, he unintentionally organizes these others into a functional community, a group unified in their supposed reactions, attitudes and plans with respect to him. He in this way organizes individuals, some of whom are actual persons and some only inferred or imagined, into a whole which satisfies for the time being his

SOURCE: Edwin M. Lemert. "Paranoia and the Dynamics of Exclusion." Copyright by the American Sociological Association, 1962. Edwin M. Lemert, "Paranoia and the Dynamics of Exclusion," *Sociometry*, XXV (March, 1962), pp. 2—20. Reprinted by permission of the American Sociological Association.

[1] In a subsequent article Cameron (2) modified his original conception, but not of the social aspects of paranoia, which mainly concern us.

immediate need for explanation but which brings no assurance with it, and usually serves to increase his tensions. The community he forms not only fails to correspond to any organization shared by others but actually contradicts this consensus. More than this, the actions ascribed by him to its personnel are not actually performed or maintained by them; *they are united in no common undertaking against him* (1). (Italics ours.)

The general insightfulness of Cameron's analysis cannot be gainsaid and the usefulness of some of his concepts is easily granted. Yet a serious question must be raised, based upon empirical inquiry, as to whether in actuality the insidious qualities of the community to which the paranoid reacts are pseudo or a symbolic fabrication. There is an alternative point of view, which is the burden of this paper, namely that, while the paranoid person reacts differentially to his social environment, it is also true that "others" react differentially to him and this reaction commonly if not typically involves covertly organized action and conspiratorial behavior in a very real sense. A further extension of our thesis is that these differential reactions are reciprocals of one another, being interwoven and concatenated at each and all phases of a process of exclusion which arises in a special kind of relationship. Delusions and associated behavior must be understood in a context of exclusion which attenuates this relationship and disrupts communication.

By thus shifting the clinical spotlight away from the individual to a relationship and a process, we make an explicit break with the conception of paranoia as a disease, a state, a condition, or a syndrome of symptoms. Furthermore, we find it unnecessary to postulate trauma of early childhood or arrested psychosexual development to account for the main features of paranoia—although we grant that these and other factors may condition its expression.

This conception of paranoia is neither simple *a priori* theory nor is it a proprietary product of sociology. There is a substantial body of writings and empirical researches in psychiatry and psychology which question the sufficiency of the individual as primary datum for the study of paranoia. Tyhurst, for example, concludes from his survey of this literature that reliance upon intrapsychic mechanisms and the "isolated organism" have been among the chief obstacles to fruitful discoveries about this disorder (18). Significantly, as Milner points out, the more complete the investigation of the cases the more frequently do unendurable external circumstance make their appearance (13). More precisely, a number of studies have ended with the conclusions that external circumstances—changes in norms and values, displacement, strange environments, isolation, and linguistic separation—may create a paranoid disposition in the absence of any special character structure (15). The recognition of paranoid reactions in elderly persons, alcoholics, and the deaf adds to the data generally consistent with our thesis. The finding that displaced persons who withstood a high degree of stress during war and captivity subsequently developed paranoid reactions when they were isolated in a foreign environment commands special attention among data requiring explanation in other than organic or psychodynamic terms (7, 10).

From what has been said thus far, it should be clear that our formulation and analysis will deal primarily with what Tyhurst (18) calls paranoid patterns of behavior rather than with a clinical entity in the classical Kraepelinian sense. Paranoid reactions, paranoid states, paranoid personality disturbances, as well as the seldom-diagnosed "true paranoia," which are found superimposed or associated with a wide variety of individual behavior or "symptoms," all provide a body of data for study so long as they assume priority over other behavior in meaningful social interaction. The elements of behavior upon which paranoid diagnoses are based—delusions, hostility, aggressiveness, suspicion, envy, stubbornness, jealousy, and ideas of reference—are readily comprehended and to some extent empathized by others as social reactions, in contrast to the bizarre, manneristic behavior of schizophrenia or the tempo and affect changes stressed in manic-depressive diagnoses. It is for this reason that paranoia suggests, more than any other forms of mental disorder, the possibility of fruitful sociological analysis.

DATA AND PROCEDURE

The first tentative conclusions which are presented here were drawn from a study of factors influencing decisions to commit mentally disordered persons to hospitals, undertaken with the cooperation of the Los Angeles County Department of Health in 1952. This included interviews by means of schedules with members of 44 families in Los Angeles County who were active petitioners in commitment proceedings and the study of 35 case records of public health officer commitments. In 16 of the former cases and in 7 of the latter, paranoid symptoms were conspicuously present. In these cases family members and others had plainly accepted or "normalized" paranoid behavior, in some instances longstanding, until other kinds of behavior or exigencies led to critical judgments that "there was something wrong" with the person in question, and, later, that hospitalization was necessary. Furthermore, these critical judgments seemed to signal changes in the family attitudes and behavior towards the affected persons which could be interpreted as contributing in different ways to the form and intensity of the paranoid symptoms.

In 1958 a more refined and hypothesis-directed study was made of eight cases of persons with prominent paranoid characteristics. Four of these had been admitted to the state hospital at Napa, California, where they were diagnosed as paranoid schizophrenic. Two other cases were located and investigated with the assistance of the district attorney in Martinez, California. One of the persons had previously been committed to a California state hospital, and the other had been held on an insanity petition but was freed after a jury trial. Added to these was one so-called "White House case," which had involved threats to a President of the United States, resulting in the person's commitment to St. Elizabeth's Hospital in Washington, D.C. A final case was that of a professional person with a history of chronic job difficulties, who was designated and regarded by his associates as "brash," "queer," "irritating," "hypercritical," and "thoroughly unlikeable."

In a very rough way the cases made up a continuum ranging from one with very elaborate delusions, through those in which fact and misinterpretation were difficult to separate, down to the last case, which comes closer to what some would call paranoid personality disturbance. A requirement for the selection of the cases was that there be no history or evidence of hallucinations and also that the persons be intellectually unimpaired. Seven of the cases were of males, five of whom were over 40 years of age. Three of the persons had been involved in repeated litigations. One man published a small, independent paper devoted to exposures of psychiatry and mental hospitals. Five of the men had been or were associated with organizations, as follows: a small-town high school, a government research bureau, an association of agricultural producers, a university, and a contracting business.

The investigations of the cases were as exhaustive as it was possible to make them, reaching relatives, work associates, employers, attorneys, police, physicians, public officials and any others who played significant roles in the lives of the persons involved. As many as 200 hours each were given to collecting data on some of the cases. Written materials, legal documents, publications and psychiatric histories were studied in addition to the interview data. Our procedure in the large was to adopt an interactional perspective which sensitized us to sociologically relevant behavior underlying or associated with the more apparent and formal contexts of mental disorder. In particular we were concerned to establish the order in which delusions and social exclusion occur and to determine whether exclusion takes conspiratorial form.

THE RELEVANT BEHAVIOR

In another paper (8) we have shown that psychotic symptoms as described in formal psychiatry are not relevant bases for predictions about changes in social status and social participation of persons in whom they appear. Apathy, hallucinations, hyperactivity, mood swings, tics, tremors, functional paralysis or tachychardias have no intrinsic social meanings. By the same token, neither do such imputed attributes as "lack of insight," "social incompetence," or "defective role-taking ability" favored by some sociologists as generic starting points for the analysis of mental disorders. Rather, it is behavior which puts strain on social relationships that leads to status changes: informal or formal exclusion from groups, definition as a "crank," or adjudication as insane and commitment to a mental hospital (8). This is true even where the grandiose and highly bizarre delusions of paranoia are present. Definition of the socially stressful aspects of this disorder is a minimum essential, if we are to account for its frequent occurrence in partially compensated or benign form in society, as well as account for its more familiar presence as an official psychiatric problem in a hospital setting.

It is necessary, however, to go beyond these elementary observations to make it pre-eminently clear that strain is an emergent product of a relationship in which the behaviors of two or more persons are relevant factors, and in which the strain is felt both by ego and *alter* or *alters*. The paranoid relationship includes reciprocating behaviors with attached emotions and meanings which, to be fully understood, must be described cubistically from at least two of its perspectives. On one hand the behavior of the individual must be seen from the

perspective of others or that of a group, and conversely the behavior of others must be seen from the perspective of the involved individual.

From the vantage of others the individual in the paranoid relationship shows:

1. A disregard for the values and norms of the primary group, revealed by giving priority to verbally definable values over those which are implicit, a lack of loyalty in return for confidences, and victimizing and intimidating persons in positions of weakness.

2. A disregard for the implicit structure of groups, revealed by presuming to privileges not accorded him, and the threat or actual resort to formal means for achieving his goals.

The second items have a higher degree of relevancy than the first in an analysis of exclusion. Stated more simply, they mean that, to the group, the individual is an ambiguous figure whose behavior is uncertain, whose loyalty can't be counted on. In short, he is a person who can't be trusted because he threatens to expose informal power structures. This, we believe, is the essential reason for the frequently encountered idea that the paranoid person is "dangerous" (4).

If we adopt the perceptual set of ego and see others or groups through his eyes, the following aspects of their behavior become relevant:

1. the spurious quality of the interaction between others and himself or between others interacting in his presence;

2. the overt avoidance of himself by others;

3. the structured exclusion of himself from interaction.

The items we have described thus far—playing fast and loose with the primary group values by the individual, and his exclusion from interaction—do not alone generate and maintain paranoia. It is additionally necessary that they emerge in an interdependent relationship which requires trust for its fulfillment. The relationship is a type in which the goals of the individual can be reached only through cooperation from particular others, and in which the ends held by others are realizable if cooperation is forthcoming from ego. This is deduced from the general proposition that cooperation rests upon perceived trust, which in turn is a function of communication (11). When communication is disrupted by exclusion, there is a lack of mutually perceived trust and the relationship becomes dilapidated or paranoid. We will now consider the process of exclusion by which this kind of relationship develops.

THE GENERIC PROCESS OF EXCLUSION

The paranoid process begins with persistent interpersonal difficulties between the individual and his family, or his work associates and superiors, or neighbors, or other persons in the community. These frequently or even typically arise out of bona fide or recognizable issues centering upon some actual or threatened loss of status for the individual. This is related to such things as the death of relatives, loss of a position, loss of professional certification, failure to be promoted, age and physiological life cycle changes, mutilations, and changes in family and marital relationships. The status changes are distinguished by the fact that they leave no alternative acceptable to the individual, from whence comes their "intolerable" or "unendurable" quality. For example: the man trained to be a teacher who loses his certificate, which means he can never teach; or the man of 50 years of age who is faced with loss of a promotion which is a regular order of upward mobility in an organization, who knows that he can't "start over"; or the wife undergoing hysterectomy, which mutilates her image as a woman.

In cases where no dramatic status loss can be discovered, a series of failures often is present, failures which may have been accepted or adjusted to, but with progressive tension as each new status situation is entered. The unendurability of the current status loss, which may appear unimportant to others, is a function of an intensified commitment, in some cases born of an awareness that there is a quota placed on failures in our society. Under some such circumstances, failures have followed the person, and his reputation as a "difficult person" has preceded him. This means that he often has the status of a stranger on trial in each new group he enters, and that the groups or organizations willing to take a chance on him are marginal from the standpoint of their probable tolerance for his actions.

The behavior of the individual—arrogance, insults, presumption of privilege and exploitation of weaknesses in others—initially has a segmented or checkered pattern in that it is confined to status-committing interactions. Outside of these, the person's behavior may be quite acceptable—courteous, considerate, kind, even indulgent. Likewise, other persons and members of groups vary considerably in their tolerance for the relevant behavior, depending on the extent to which it threatens individual and organizational values, impedes functions, or sets in motion embarrassing sequences of social actions. In the early generic period, tolerance by others for the individual's aggressive behavior generally speaking is broad, and it is very likely to be interpreted as a variation of normal behavior, particularly in the absence of biographical knowledge of the person. At most, people observe that "there is something odd about him," or "he must be upset," or "he is just ornery," or "I don't quite understand him" (3).

At some point in the chain of interactions, a new configuration takes place in perceptions others have of the individual, with shifts in figure-ground relations. The individual, as we have already indicated, is an ambiguous figure, comparable to textbook figures of stairs or outlined cubes which reverse themselves when studied intently. From a normal variant the person becomes "unreliable," "untrustworthy," "dangerous," or someone with whom others "do not wish to be involved." An illustration nicely apropos of this came out in the reaction of the head of a music department in a university when he granted an interview to a man who had worked for years on a theory to compose music mathematically:

> When he asked to be placed on the staff so that he could use the electronic computers of the University *I shifted my ground* . . . when I offered an objection to his theory, he became disturbed, so I changed my reaction to "yes and no."

As is clear from this, once the perceptual reorientation takes place, either as the outcome of continuous interaction or through the receipt of biographical information, interaction changes qualitatively. In our words, it becomes *spurious,* distinguished by patronizing, evasion, "humoring," guiding conversation onto selected topics, underreaction, and silence, all calculated either to prevent intense interaction or to protect individual and group values by restricting access to them. When the interaction is between two or more persons in the individual's presence it is cued by a whole repertoire of subtle expressive signs which are meaningful only to them.

The net effects of spurious interaction are to:

1. stop the flow of information to ego;

2. create a discrepancy between expressed ideas and affect among those with whom he interacts;

3. make the situation or the group image an ambiguous one for ego, much as he is for others.

Needless to say this kind of spurious interaction is one of the most difficult for an adult in our society to cope with, because it complicates or makes decisions impossible for him and also because it is morally invidious.[2]

The process from inclusion to exclusion is by no

---

[2]The interaction in some ways is similar to that used with children, particularly the *"enfant terrible."* The function of language in such interaction was studied by Sapir (16) years ago.

---

means an even one. Both individuals and members of groups change their perceptions and reactions, and vacillation is common, depending upon the interplay of values, anxieties and guilt on both sides. Members of an excluding group may decide they have been unfair and seek to bring the individual back into their confidence. This overture may be rejected or used by ego as a means of further attack. We have also found that ego may capitulate, sometimes abjectly, to others and seek group re-entry, only to be rejected. In some cases compromises are struck and a partial reintegration of ego into informal social relations is achieved. The direction which informal exclusion takes depends upon ego's reactions, the degree of communication between his interactors, the composition and structure of the informal groups, and the perceptions of "key others" at points of interaction which directly affect ego's status.

ORGANIZATIONAL CRISIS AND FORMAL EXCLUSION

Thus far we have discussed exclusion as an informal process. Informal exclusion may take place but leave ego's formal status in an organization intact. So long as this status is preserved and rewards are sufficient to validate it on his terms, an uneasy peace between him and others may prevail. Yet ego's social isolation and his strong commitments make him an unpredictable factor; furthermore the rate of change and internal power struggles, especially in large and complex organizations, means that preconditions of stability may be short lived.

Organizational crises involving a paranoid relationship arise in several ways. The individual may act in ways which arouse intolerable anxieties in others, who demand that "something be done." Again, by going to higher authority or making appeals outside the organization, he may set in motion procedures which leave those in power no other choice than to take action. In some situations ego remains relatively quiescent and does not openly attack the organization. Action against him is set off by growing anxieties or calculated motives of associates—in some cases his immediate superiors. Finally, regular organizational procedures incidental to promotion, retirement or reassignment may precipitate the crisis.

Assuming a critical situation in which the conflict between the individual and members of the organization leads to action to formally exclude him, several possibilities exist. One is the transfer of ego from one department, branch or division of the organization to another, a device frequently resorted to in the armed services or in large corporations. This requires that the individual be persuaded to make the change and that some department will accept him. While this may be accomplished in different ways, not infrequently artifice, withholding information, bribery, or thinly disguised threats figure conspicuously among the means by which the transfer is brought about. Needless to say, there is a limit to which transfers can be employed as a solution to the problem, contingent upon the size of the organization and the previous diffusion of knowledge about the transferee.

Solution number two we call encapsulation, which, in brief, is a reorganization and redefinition of ego's status. This has the effect of isolating him from the organization and making him directly responsible to one or two superiors who act as his intermediators. The change is often made palatable to ego by enhancing some of the material rewards of his status. He may be nominally promoted or "kicked upstairs," given a larger office, or a separate secretary, or relieved of onerous duties. Sometimes a special status is created for him.

This type of solution often works because it is a kind of formal recognition by the organization of ego's intense commitment to his status and in part a victory for him over his enemies. It bypasses them and puts him into direct communication with higher authority who may communicate with him in a more direct manner. It also relieves his associates of further need to connive against him.

This solution is sometimes used to dispose of troublesome corporation executives, high-ranking military officers, and academic *personae non gratae* in universities.

A third variety of solutions to the problem of paranoia in an organization is outright discharge, forced resignation or non-renewal of appointment. Finally, there may be an organized move to have the individual in the paranoid relationship placed on sick leave, or to compel him to take psychiatric treatment. The extreme expression of this is pressure (as on the family) or direct action to have the person committed to a mental hospital.

The order of the enumerated solutions to the paranoid problem in a rough way reflects the amount of risk associated with the alternatives, both as to the probabilities of failure and of damaging repercussions to the organization. Generally, organizations seem to show a good deal of resistance to making or carrying out decisions which require expulsion of the individual or forcing hospitalization, regardless of his mental condition. One reason for this is that the person may have power within the organization, based upon his position, or monopolized skills and information,[3] and unless there is a strong coalition against him the general conservatism of administrative judgments will run in his favor. Herman Wouk's novel of *The Caine Mutiny* dramatizes some of the difficulties of cashiering a person from a position of power in an essentially conservative military organization. An extreme of this conservatism is illustrated by one case in which we found a department head retained in his position in an organization even though he was actively hallucinating as well as expressing paranoid delusions.[4] Another factor working on the individual's side is that discharge of a person in a position of power reflects unfavorably upon those who placed him there. In-group solidarity of administrators may be in-

---

[3]For a systematic analysis of the organizational difficulties in removing an "unpromotable" person from a position see (9).
[4]One of the cases in the first study.

volved, and the methods of the opposition may create sympathy for ego at higher levels.

Even when the person is almost totally excluded and informally isolated within an organization, he may have power outside. This weighs heavily when the external power can be invoked in some way, or when it automatically leads to raising questions as to the internal workings of the organization. This touches upon the more salient reason for reluctance to eject an uncooperative and retaliatory person, even when he is relatively unimportant to the organization. We refer to a kind of negative power derived from the vulnerability of organizations to unfavorable publicity and exposure of their private lives that are likely if the crisis proceeds to formal hearings, case review or litigation. This is an imminent possibility where paranoia exists. If hospital commitment is attempted, there is a possibility that a jury trial will be demanded, which will force leaders of the organization to defend their actions. If the crisis turns into a legal contest of this sort, it is not easy to prove insanity, and there may be damage suits. Even if the facts heavily support the petitioners, such contests can only throw unfavorable light upon the organization.

THE CONSPIRATORIAL NATURE OF EXCLUSION

A conclusion from the foregoing is that organizational vulnerability as well as anticipations of retaliations from the paranoid person lay a functional basis for conspiracy among those seeking to contain or oust him. Probabilities are strong that a coalition will appear within the organization, integrated by a common commitment to oppose the paranoid person. This, the exclusionist group, demands loyalty, solidarity and secrecy from its members; it acts in accord with a common scheme and in varying degrees utilizes techniques of manipulation and misrepresentation.

Conspiracy in rudimentary form can be detected in informal exclusion apart from an organizational crisis. This was illustrated in an office research team in which staff members huddled around a water cooler to discuss the unwanted associate. They also used office telephones to arrange coffee breaks without him and employed symbolic cues in his presence, such as humming the Dragnet theme song when he approached the group. An office rule against extraneous conversation was introduced with the collusion of supervisors, ostensibly for everyone, actually to restrict the behavior of the isolated worker. In another case an interview schedule designed by a researcher was changed at a conference arranged without him. When he sought an explanation at a subsequent conference, his associates pretended to have no knowledge of the changes.

Conspiratorial behavior comes into sharpest focus during organizational crises in which the exclusionists who initiate action become an embattled group. There is a concerted effort to gain consensus for this view, to solidify the group and to halt close interaction with those unwilling to completely join the coalition. Efforts are also made to neutralize those who remain uncommitted but who can't be kept ignorant of the plans afoot. Thus an external appearance of unanimity is given even if it doesn't exist.

Much of the behavior of the group at this time is strategic in nature, with determined calculations as to "what we will do if he does this or that." In one of our cases, a member on a board of trustees spoke of the "game being played" with the person in controversy with them. Planned action may be carried to the length of agreeing upon the exact words to be used when confronted or challenged by the paranoid individual. Above all there is continuous, precise communication among exclusionists, exemplified in one case by mutual exchanging of copies of all letters sent and received from ego.

Concern about secrecy in such groups is revealed by such things as carefully closing doors and lowering of voices when ego is brought under discussion. Meeting places and times may be varied from normal procedures; documents may be filed in unusual places and certain telephones may not be used during a paranoid crisis.

The visibility of the individual's behavior is greatly magnified during this period; often he is the main topic of conversation among the esclusionists, while rumors of the difficulties spread to other groups, which in some cases may be drawn into the controversy. At a certain juncture steps are taken to keep the members of the ingroup continually informed of the individual's movements and, if possible, of his plans. In effect, if not in form, this amounts to spying. Members of one embattled group, for example, hired an outside person unknown to their accuser to take notes on a speech he delivered to enlist a community organization on his side. In another case, a person having an office opening onto that of a department head was persuaded to act as an informant for the nucleus of persons working to depose the head from his position of authority. This group also seriously debated placing an all-night watch in front of their perceived malefactor's house.

Concomitant with the magnified visibility of the paranoid individual come distortions of his image, most pronounced in the inner coterie of exclusionists. His size, physical strength, cunning, and anecdotes of his outrages are exaggerated, with a central thematic emphasis on the fact that he is dangerous. Some individuals give cause for such beliefs in that previously they have engaged in violence or threats, others do not. One encounters characteristic contradictions in interviews on this point, such as: "No, he has never struck anyone around here—just fought with the policemen at the State Capitol," or "No, I am not afraid of him, but one of these days he will explode."

It can be said parenthetically that the alleged dangerousness of paranoid persons storied in fiction and drama has never been systematically demonstrated. As a matter of fact, the only substantial data on this, from a study of delayed admissions, largely paranoid, to a mental hospital in Norway, disclosed that "neither the paranoiacs nor the paranoids have been dangerous, and most not particularly troublesome" (14). Our interpretation of this, as suggested earlier, is that the imputed dangerousness of the paranoid individual does not come from physical fear but from the organizational threat he presents and the need to justify collective action against him.

However, this is not entirely tactical behavior—as is demonstrated by anxieties and tensions which mount among those in the coalition during the more critical phases of their interaction. Participants may develop fears quite analogous to those of classic conspirators. One leader in such a group spoke of the period of the paranoid crisis as a "week of terror," during which he was wracked with insomnia and "had to take his stomach pills." Projection was revealed by a trustee who, during a school crisis occasioned by discharge of an aggressive teacher, stated that he "watched his shadows," and "wondered if all would be well when he returned home at night." Such tensional states, working along with a kind of closure of communication within the group, are both a cause and an effect of amplified group interaction which distorts or symbolically rearranges the image of the person against whom they act.

Once the battle is won by the exclusionists, their version of the individual as dangerous becomes a crystallized rationale for official action. At this point misrepresentation becomes part of a more deliberate manipulation of ego. Gross misstatements, most frequently called "pretexts," become justifiable ways of getting his cooperation, for example, to get him to submit to psychiatric examination or detention preliminary to hospital commitment. This aspect of the process has been effectively detailed by Goffman, with his concept of a "betrayal funnel" through which a patient enters a hospital (5). We need not elaborate on this, other than to confirm its occurrence in the exclusion process, complicated in our cases by legal strictures and the ubiquitous risk of litigation.

THE GROWTH OF DELUSION

The general idea that the paranoid person symbolically fabricates the conspiracy against him is in our estimation incorrect or incomplete. Nor can we agree that he lacks insight, as is so frequently claimed. To the contrary, many paranoid persons properly realize that they are being isolated and excluded by conceived interaction, or that they are being manipulated. However, they are at a loss to estimate accurately or realistically the dimensions and form of the coalition arrayed against them.

As channels of communication are closed to the paranoid person, he has no means of getting feedback on consequences of his behavior, which is essential for correcting his interpretations of the social relationships and organization which he must rely on to define his status and give him identity. He can only read overt behavior without the informal context. Although he may properly infer that people are organized against him, he can only use confrontation or formal inquisitorial procedures to try to prove this. The paranoid person must provoke strong feelings in order to receive any kind of meaningful communication from others—hence his accusations, his bluntness, his insults. Ordinarily this is non-deliberate; nevertheless, in one complex case we found the person consciously provoking discussions to get readings from others on his behavior. This man said of himself: 'Some people would describe me as very perceptive, others would describe me as very imperceptive.''

The need for communication and the identity which goes with it does a good deal to explain the preference of paranoid persons for formal, legalistic, written communications, and the care with which many of them preserve records of their contracts with others. In some ways the resort to litigation is best interpreted as the effort of the individual to compel selected others to interact directly with him as equals, to engineer a situation in which evasion is impossible. The fact that the person is seldom satisfied with the outcome of his letters, his petitions, complaints and writs testifies to their function as devices for establishing contact and interaction with others, as well as ''setting the record straight.'' The wide professional tolerance of lawyers for aggressive behavior in court and the nature of Anglo-Saxon legal institutions, which grew out of a revolt against conspiratorial or star-chamber justice, mean that the individual will be heard. Furthermore his charges must be answered; otherwise he wins by default. Sometimes he wins small victories, even if he loses the big ones. He may earn grudging respect as an adversary, and sometimes shares a kind of legal camaraderie with others in the courts. He gains an identity through notoriety.

REINFORCEMENT OF DELUSION

The accepted psychiatric view is that prognosis for paranoia is poor, that recoveries from ''true'' paranoia are rare, with the implication that the individual's delusions more or less express an unalterable pathological condition. Granting that the individual's needs and dispositions and his self-imposed isolation are significant factors in perpetuating his delusional reactions, nevertheless there is an important social context of delusions through which they are reinforced or strengthened. This context is readily identifiable in the ideas and institutionalized procedures of protective, custodial, and treatment organizations in our society. They stand out in sharpest relief where paranoid persons have come into contact with law enforcement agencies or have been hospitalized. The cumulative and interlocking impacts of such agencies work strongly to nurture and sustain the massive sense of injustice and need for identity which underlie the delusions and aggressive behavior of the paranoid individual.

Police in most communities have a well-defined concept of cranks, as they call them, although the exact criteria by which persons are so judged are not clear. Their patience is short with such persons: in some cases they investigate their original complaints and if they conclude that the person in question is a crank they tend to ignore him thereafter. His letters may be thrown away unanswered, or phone calls answered with patronizing reassurance or vague promises to take steps which never materialize.

Like the police, offices of district attorneys are frequently forced to deal with persons they refer to as cranks or soreheads. Some offices delegate a special deputy to handle these cases, quaintly referred to in one office as the "insane deputy." Some deputies say they can spot letters of cranks immediately, which means that they are unanswered or discarded. However, family or neighborhood quarrels offer almost insoluble difficulties in this respect, because often it is impossible to determine which of two parties is delusional. In one office some complainants are called "fifty-fifty," which is jargon meaning that it is impossible to say whether they are mentally stable. If one person seems to be persistently causing trouble, deputies may threaten to have him investigated, which, however, is seldom if ever done.

Both police and district attorney staffs operate continuously in situations in which their actions can have damaging legal or political repercussions. They tend to be tightly ingrouped and their initial reaction to outsiders or strangers is one of suspicion or distrust until they are proved harmless or friendly. Many of their office procedures and general manner reflect this—such as carefully recording in a log book names, time, and reason for calling of those who seek official interviews. In some instances a complainant is actually investigated before any business will be transacted with him.

When the paranoid person goes beyond local police and courts to seek redress through appeals to state or national authorities, he may meet with polite evasion, perfunctory treatment of his case or formalized distrust. Letters to administrative people may beget replies up to a certain point, but thereafter they are ignored. If letters to a highly placed authority carry threats, they may lead to an investigation by security agencies, motivated by the knowledge that assassinations are not unknown in American life. Sometimes redress is sought in legislatures, where private bills may be introduced, bills which by their nature can only be empty gestures.

In general, the contacts which the delusional person makes with formal organizations frequently disclose the same elements of shallow response, evasion, or distrust which played a part in the generic process of exclusion. They become part of a selective or selected pattern of interaction which creates a social environment of uncertainty and ambiguity for the individual. They do little to correct and much to confirm his suspicion, distrust and delusional interpretations. Moreover, even the environment of treatment agencies may contribute to the furtherance of paranoid delusion, as Stanton and Schwartz have shown in their comments on communication within the mental hospital. They speak pointedly of the "pathology of communication" brought about by staff practices of ignoring explicit meanings in statements or actions of patients and reacting to inferred or imputed meanings, thereby creating a type of environment in which "the paranoid feels quite at home" (17).

Some paranoid or paranoid-like persons become well known locally or even throughout larger areas to some organizations. Persons and groups in the community are found to assume a characteristic stance towards such people—a stance of expectancy and preparedness. In one such case, police continually checked the whereabouts of the man and, when the governor came to speak on the courthouse steps, two officers were assigned the special task of watching the man as he stood in the crowd. Later, whenever he went to the state capitol, a number of state police were delegated to accompany him when he attended committee hearings or sought interviews with state officials.[5] The notoriety this man acquired because of his reputed great strength in tossing officers around like tenpins was an obvious source of pleasure to him, despite the implications of distrust conveyed by their presence.

It is arguable that occupying the role of the mistrusted person becomes a way of life for these paranoids, providing them with an identity not otherwise possible. Their volatile contentions with public officials, their issuance of writings, publications, litigations in *persona propria,* their overriding tendency to contest issues which other people dismiss as unimportant or as "too much bother" become a central theme for their lives, without which they would probably deteriorate.

If paranoia becomes a way of life for some people, it is also true that the difficult person with grandiose and persecutory ideas may fulfill certain marginal functions in organizations and communities. One is his scapegoat function, being made the subject of humorous by-play or conjectural gossip as people "wonder what he will be up to next." In his scapegoat role, the person may help integrate primary groups within larger organizations by directing aggressions and blame towards him and thus strengthening feelings of homogeneity and consensus of group members.

There are also instances in which the broad, grapeshot charges and accusations of the paranoid person function to articulate dissatisfactions of those who fear openly to criticize the leadership of the community, organization, or state, or of the informal power structures within these. Sometimes the paranoid person is the only one who openly espouses values of inarticulate and politically unrepresented segments of the population (12). The "plots" which attract the paranoid person's attention—dope rings, international communism,

[5]This technique in even more systematic form is sometimes used in protecting the President of the United States in "White House cases."

monopolistic "interests," popery, Jewry, or "psychopoliticians"—often reflect the vague and ill-formed fears and concerns of peripheral groups, which tend to validate his self-chosen role as a "protector." At times in organizational power plays and community conflicts his role may even be put to canny use by more representative groups as a means of embarrassing their opposition.

THE LARGER SOCIO-CULTURAL CONTEXT

Our comments draw to a close on the same polemic note with which they were begun, namely, that members of communities and organizations do unite in common effort against the paranoid person prior to or apart from any vindictive behavior on his part. The paranoid community is real rather than pseudo in that it is composed of reciprocal relationships and processes whose net results are informal and formal exclusion and attenuated communication.

The dynamics of exclusion of the paranoid person are made understandable in larger perspective by recognizing that decision making in American social organization is carried out in small, informal groups through casual and often subtle male interaction. Entree into such groups is ordinarily treated as a privilege rather than a right, and this privilege tends to be jealously guarded. Crucial decisions, including those to eject persons or to reorganize their status in larger formal organizations, are made secretly. The legal concept of "privileged communication" in part is a formal recognition of the necessity for making secret decisions within organizations.

Added to this is the emphasis placed upon conformity in our organization-oriented society and the growing tendency of organization elites to rely upon direct power for their purposes. This is commonly exercised to isolate and neutralize groups and individuals who oppose their policies both inside and outside of the organization. Formal structures may be manipulated or deliberately reorganized so that resistant groups and individuals are denied or removed from access to power or the available means to promote their deviant goals and values. One of the most readily effective ways of doing this is to interrupt, delay, or stop the flow of information.

It is the necessity to rationalize and justify such procedures on a democratic basis which leads to concealment of certain actions, misrepresentation of their underlying meaning, and even the resort to unethical or illegal means. The difficulty of securing sociological knowledge about these techniques, which we might call the "controls behind the controls," and the denials by those who use them that they exist are logical consequences of the perceived threat such knowledge and admissions become to informal power structures. The epiphenomena of power thus become a kind of shadowy world of our culture, inviting conjecture and condemnation.

CONCLUDING COMMENT

We have been concerned with a process of social exclusion and with the ways in which it contributes to the development of paranoid patterns of behavior. While the data emphasize the organizational forms of exclusion, we nevertheless believe that these are expressions of a generic process whose correlates will emerge from the study of paranoia in the family and other groups. The differential responses of the individual to the exigencies of organized exclusion are significant in the development of paranoid reactions only insofar as they partially determine the "intolerable" or "unendurable" quality of the status changes confronting him. Idiosyncratic life history factors of the sort stressed in more conventional psychiatric analyses may be involved, but equally important in our estimation are those which inhere in the status changes themselves, age being one of the more salient of these. In either case, once situational intolerability appears, the stage is set for the interactional process we have described.

Our cases, it will be noted, were all people who remained undeteriorated, in contact with others and carrying on militant activities oriented towards recognizable social values and institutions. Generalized suspiciousness in public places and unprovoked aggression against strangers were absent from their experiences. These facts, plus the relative absence of "true paranoia" among mental-hospital populations, leads us to conclude that the "pseudo-community" associated with random aggression (in Cameron's sense) is a sequel rather than an integral part of paranoid patterns. They are likely products of deterioration and fragmentation of personality appearing, when and if they do, in the paranoid person after long or intense periods of stress and complete social isolation.

REFERENCES

1. Cameron, N., "The Paranoid Pseudocommunity," *American Journal of Sociology,* 1943, 46, 33–38.

2. Cameron, N., "The Paranoid Pseudocommunity Revisited," *American Journal of Sociology,* 1959, 65, 52–58.

3. Cumming, E., and J. Cumming, *Closed Ranks,* Cambridge, Mass.: Harvard University Press, 1957, Ch. VI.

4. Dentler, R. A., and K. T. Erikson, "The Functions of Deviance in Groups," *Social Problems,* 1959, 7, 102.

5. Goffman, E., "The Moral Career of the Mental Patient," *Psychiatry,* 1959, 22, 127 ff.

6. Jaco, E. G., "Attitudes Toward, and Incidence of Mental Disorder: A Research Note," *Southwestern Social Science Quarterly,* June, 1957, p. 34.

7. Kine, F. F., "Aliens' Paranoid Reaction," *Journal of Mental Science,* 1951, 98, 589–594.

8. Lemert, E., "Legal Commitment and Social Control," *Sociology and Social Research,* 1946, 30, 370–378.

9. Levenson, B., "Bureaucratic Succession," in *Complex Organizations,* A. Etzioni, (ed.), New York: Holt, Rinehart and Winston, 1961, 362–395.

10. Listivan, I., "Paranoid States: Social and Cultural Aspects," *Medical Journal of Australia,* 1956, 776—778.

11. Loomis, J. L., "Communications, The Development of Trust, and Cooperative Behavior," *Human Relations,* 1959, 12, 305—315.

12. Marmor, J., "Science, Health and Group Opposition" (mimeographed paper), 1958.

13. Milner, K. O., "The Environment as a Factor in the Etiology of Criminal Paranoia," *Journal of Mental Science,* 1949, 95, 124—132.

14. Ödegard, Ö., "A Clinical Study of Delayed Admissions to a Mental Hospital," *Mental Hygiene,* 1958, 42, 66—77.

15. Pederson, S., "Psychological Reactions to Extreme Social Displacement (Refugee Neuroses)," *Psychoanalytic Review,* 1946, 36, 344—354.

16. Sapir, E., "Abnormal Types of Speech in Nootka," *Canada Department of Mines, Memoir* 62, 1915, No. 5.

17. Stanton, A. H., and M. S. Schwartz, *The Mental Hospital,* New York: Basic Books, 1954, 200—210.

18. Tyhurst, J. S., "Paranoid Patterns," in A. H. Leighton, J. A. Clausen, and R. Wilson (eds.), *Exploration in Social Psychiatry,* New York: Basic Books, 1957, Ch. II.

THIRTY-SIX

THE MORAL CAREER OF THE MENTAL PATIENT

ERVING GOFFMAN

Traditionally the term *career* has been reserved for those who expect to enjoy the rises laid out within a respectable profession. The term is coming to be used, however, in a broadened sense to refer to any social strand of any person's course through life. The perspective of natural history is taken: unique outcomes are neglected in favor of such changes over time as are basic and common to the members of a social category, although occurring independently to each of them. Such a career is not a thing that can be brilliant or disappointing; it can no more be a success than a failure. In this light, I want to consider the mental patient.

One value of the concept of career is its two-sidedness. One side is linked to internal matters held dearly and closely, such as image of self and felt identity; the other side concerns official position, jural relations, and style of life, and is part of a publicly accessible institutional complex. The

concept of career, then, allows one to move back and forth between the personal and the public, between the self and its significant society, without having to rely overly for data upon what the person says he thinks he imagines himself to be.

This paper, then, is an exercise in the institutional approach to the study of self. The main concern will be with the *moral* aspects of career— that is, the regular sequence of changes that career entails in the person's self and in his framework of imagery for judging himself and others.[1]

The category "mental patient" itself will be understood in one strictly sociological sense. In this perspective, the psychiatric view of a person becomes significant only in so far as this view itself alters his social fate—an alteration which seems to become fundamental in our society when, and only when, the person is put through the

SOURCE: Erving Goffman. "The Moral Career of the Mental Patient." Copyright by The William Alanson White Psychiatric Foundation, Inc., 1959. Erving Goffman, "The Moral Career of the Mental Patient," *Psychiatry*, XXII (1959), pp. 123–142. Reprinted by permission of The William Alanson White Psychiatric Foundation, Inc.

[1]Material on moral career can be found in early social anthropological work on ceremonies of status transition, and in classic social psychological descriptions of those spectacular changes in one's view of self that can accompany participation in social movements and sects. Recently new kinds of relevant data have been suggested by psychiatric interest in the problem of "identity" and sociological studies of work careers and "adult socialization."

process of hospitalization.[2] I therefore exclude certain neighboring categories: the undiscovered candidates who would be judged "sick" by psychiatric standards but who never come to be viewed as such by themselves or others, although they may cause everyone a great deal of trouble;[3] the office patient whom a psychiatrist feels he can handle with drugs or shock on the outside: the mental client who engages in psychotherapeutic relationships. And I include anyone, however robust in temperament, who somehow gets caught up in the heavy machinery of mental-hospital servicing. In this way the effects of being treated as a mental patient can be kept quite distinct from the effects upon a person's life of traits a clinician would view as psychopathological.[4] Persons who become mental-hospital patients vary widely in the kind and degree of illness that a psychiatrist would impute to them, and in the attributes by which laymen would describe them. But once started on the way, they are confronted by some importantly similar

circumstances and respond to these in some importantly similar ways. Since these similarities do not come from mental illness, they would seem to occur in spite of it. It is thus a tribute to the power of social forces that the uniform status of mental patient cannot only assure an aggregate of persons a common fate and eventually, because of this, a common character, but that this social reworking can be done upon what is perhaps the most obstinate diversity of human materials that can be brought together by society. Here there lacks only the frequent forming of a protective group life by ex-patients to illustrate in full the classic cycle of response by which deviant subgroupings are psychodynamically formed in society.

This general sociological perspective is heavily reinforced by one key finding of sociologically oriented students in mental-hospital research. As has been repeatedly shown in the study of nonliterate societies, the awesomeness, distastefulness, and barbarity of a foreign culture can decrease to the degree that the student becomes familiar with the point of view of life that is taken by his subjects. Similarly, the student of mental hospitals can discover that the craziness or "sick behavior" claimed for the mental patient is by and large a product of the claimant's social distance from the situation that the patient is in, and is not primarily a product of mental illness. Whatever the refinements of the various patients' psychiatric diagnoses, and whatever the special ways in which social life on the "inside" is unique, the researcher can find that he is participating in a community not significantly different from any other he has studied. Of course, while restricting himself to the off-ward grounds community of paroled patients, he may feel, as some patients do, that life in the locked wards is bizarre; and while on a locked admissions or convalescent ward, he may feel that chronic "back" wards are socially crazy places. But he need only move his sphere of sympathetic participation to the "worst" ward in the hospital, and this, too, can come into social focus as a place with a livable and continuously meaningful social

[2] This point has recently been made by Elaine and John Cumming, *Closed Ranks* (Cambridge: Commonwealth Fund, Harvard University Press, 1957), pp. 101–2: *"Clinical experience supports the impression that many people define mental illness as 'that condition for which a person is treated in a mental hospital.' . . . Mental illness, it seems, is a condition which afflicts people who must go to a mental institution, but until they go almost anything they do is normal."* Leila Deasy has pointed out to me the correspondence here with the situation in white-collar crime. Of those who are detected in this activity, only the ones who do not manage to avoid going to prison find themselves accorded the social role of the criminal.

[3] Case records in mental hospitals are just now coming to be exploited to show the incredible amount of trouble a person may cause for himself and others before anyone begins to think about him psychiatrically, let alone take psychiatric action against him. See John A. Clausen and Marian Radke Yarrow, "Paths to the Mental Hospital," *Journal of Social Issues,* XI (1955), pp. 25–32; August, B. Hollingshead and Frederick C. Redlich, *Social Class and Mental Illness* (New York: Wiley, 1958), pp. 173–74.

[4] An illustration of how this perspective may be taken to all forms of deviancy may be found in Edwin Lemert, *Social Pathology* (New York: McGraw-Hill, 1951), see especially pp. 74–76. A specific application to mental defectives may be found in Stewart E. Perry, "Some Theoretic Problems of Mental Deficiency and Their Action Implications," *Psychiatry,* XVII (1954), pp. 45–73, see especially pp. 67–68.

world. This in no way denies that he will find a minority in any ward or patient group that continues to seem quite beyond the capacity to follow rules of social organization, or that the orderly fulfillment of normative expectations in patient society is partly made possible by strategic measures that have somehow come to be institutionalized in mental hospitals.

The career of the mental patient falls popularly and naturalistically into three main phases: the period prior to entering the hospital, which I shall call the prepatient phase; the period in the hospital, the inpatient phase; the period after discharge from the hospital, should this occur, namely, the ex-patient phase.[5] This paper will deal only with the first two phases.

THE PREPATIENT PHASE

A relatively small group of prepatients come into the mental hospital willingly, because of their own idea of what will be good for them, or because of wholehearted agreement with the relevant members of their family. Presumably these recruits have found themselves acting in a way which is evidence to them that they are losing their minds or losing control of themselves. This view of oneself would seem to be one of the most pervasively threatening things that can happen to the self in our society, especially since it is likely to occur at a time when the person is in any case sufficiently troubled to exhibit the kind of symptom which he himself can see. As Sullivan described it,[6]

> What we discover in the self-system of a person undergoing schizophrenic change or schizophrenic processes, is then, in its simplest form, an extremely fear-marked puzzlement, consisting of the use of

rather generalized and anything but exquisitely refined referential processes in an attempt to cope with what is essentially a failure at being human—a failure at being anything that one could respect as worth being.

Coupled with the person's disintegrative re-evaluation of himself will be the new, almost equally pervasive circumstance of attempting to conceal from others what he takes to be the new fundamental facts about himself, and attempting to discover whether others, too, have discovered them.[7] Here I want to stress that perception of losing one's mind is based on culturally derived and socially engrained stereotypes as to the significance of symptoms such as hearing voices, losing temporal and spatial orientation, and sensing that one is being followed, and that many of the most spectacular and convincing of these symptoms in some instances psychiatrically signify merely a temporary emotional upset in a stressful situation, however terrifying to the person at the time. Similarly, the anxiety consequent upon this perception of oneself, and the strategies devised to reduce this anxiety, are not a product of abnormal psychology, but would be exhibited by any person socialized into our culture who came to conceive of himself as someone losing his mind. Interestingly, subcultures in American society apparently differ in the amount of ready imagery and encouragement they supply for such self-views, leading to differential rates of *self*-referral; the capacity to take this disintegrative view of oneself without psychiatric prompting seems to be one of the questionable cultural privileges of the upper classes.[8]

---

[5]This simple picture is complicated by the somewhat special experience of roughly a third of ex-patients—namely, readmission to the hospital, this being the recidivist or "repatient" phase.

[6]Harry Stack Sullivan, *Clinical Studies in Psychiatry*, edited by Helen Swick Perry, Mary Ladd Gawel, and Martha Gibbon (New York: Norton, 1956), pp. 184—85.

[7]This moral experience can be contrasted with that of a person learning to become a marihuana addict, whose discovery that he can be "high" and still "op" effectively without being detected apparently leads to a new level of use. See Howard S. Becker, "Marihuana Use and Social Control," *Social Problems*, III (1955), pp. 35—41; see especially pp. 40—41.

[8]See Hollingshead and Redlich, *op. cit.*, p. 187, Table B, where relative frequency is given of self-referral by social class grouping.

For the person who has come to see himself—with whatever justification—as mentally unbalanced, entrance to the mental hospital can sometimes bring relief, perhaps in part because of the sudden transformation in the structure of his basic social situation; instead of being to himself a questionable person trying to maintain a role as a full one, he can become an officially questioned person known to himself to be not so questionable as that. In other cases, hospitalization can make matters worse for the willing patient, confirming by the objective situation what has therefore been a matter of the private experience of self.

Once the willing prepatient enters the hospital, he may go through the same routine of experiences as do those who enter unwillingly. In any case, it is the latter that I mainly want to consider, since in America at present these are by far the more numerous kind.[9] Their approach to the institution takes one of three classic forms: they come because they have been implored by their family or threatened with the abrogation of family ties unless they go ''willingly''; they come by force under police escort; they come under misapprehension purposely induced by others, this last restricted mainly to youthful prepatients.

The prepatient's career may be seen in terms of an extrusory model; he starts out with relationships and rights, and ends up, at the beginning of his hospital stay, with hardly any of either. The moral aspects of his career, then, typically begin with the experience of abandonment, disloyalty, and embitterment. This is the case even though to others it may be obvious that he was in need of treatment, and even though in the hospital he may soon come to agree.

The case histories of most mental patients document offenses against some arrangement for face-to-face living—a domestic establishment, a work place, a semi-public organization such as a church or store, a public region such as a street or park. Often there is also a record of some *complainant,* some figure who takes that action against the offender which eventually leads to his hospitalization. This may not be the person who makes the first move, but it is the person who makes what turns out to be the first effective move. Here is the *social* beginning of the patient's career, regardless of where one might locate the psychological beginning of his mental illness.

The kinds of offenses which lead to hospitalization are felt to differ in nature from those which lead to other extrusory consequences—to imprisonment, divorce, loss of job, disownment, regional exile, non-institutional psychiatric treatment, and so forth. But little seems known about these differentiating factors; and when one studies actual commitments, alternate outcomes frequently appear to have been possible. It seems true, moreover, that for every offense that leads to an effective complaint, there are many psychiatrically similar ones that never do. No action is taken; or action is taken which leads to other extrusory outcomes; or ineffective action is taken, leading to the mere pacifying or putting off of the person who complains. Thus, as Clausen and Yarrow have nicely shown, even offenders who are eventually hospitalized are likely to have had a long series of ineffective actions taken against them.[10]

Separating those offenses which could have been used as grounds for hospitalizing the offender from those that are so used, one finds a vast number of what students of occupation call career contingencies.[11] Some of these contingencies in the mental patient's career have been suggested, if not explored, such as socioeconomic status, visibility of the offense, proximity to a mental hospital, amount of treatment facilities available, com-

---

[9]The distinction employed here between willing and unwilling patients cuts across the legal one of voluntary and committed, since some persons who are glad to come to the mental hospital may be legally committed, and of those who come only because of strong familial pressure, some may sign themselves in as voluntary patients.

[10]Clausen and Yarrow, *op. cit.*

[11]An explicit application of this notion to the field of mental health may be found in Edwin Lemert, ''Legal Commitment and Social Control,'' *Sociology and Social Research,* XXX (1946), pp. 370–78.

munity regard for the type of treatment given in available hospitals, and so on.[12] For information about other contingencies one must rely on atrocity tales: a psychotic man is tolerated by his wife until she finds herself a boy friend, or by his adult children until they move from a house to an apartment; an alcoholic is sent to a mental hospital because the jail is full, and a drug addict because he declines to avail himself of psychiatric treatment on the outside; a rebellious adolescent daughter can no longer be managed at home because she now threatens to have an open affair with an unsuitable companion; and so on. Correspondingly there is an equally important set of contingencies causing the person to by-pass this fate. And should the person enter the hospital, still another set of contingencies will help determine when he is to obtain a discharge—such as the desire of his family for his return, the availability of a "manageable" job, and so on. The society's official view is that inmates of mental hospitals are there primarily because they are suffering from mental illness. However, in the degree that the "mentally ill" outside hospitals numerically approach or surpass those inside hospitals, one could say that mental patients distinctively suffer not from mental illness, but from contingencies.

Career contingencies occur in conjunction with a second feature of the prepatient's career—the circuit of agents—and agencies—that participate fatefully in his passage from civilian to patient status.[13] Here is an instance of that increasingly important class of social system whose elements are agents and agencies which are brought into systemic connection through having to take up and send on the same persons. Some of these agent roles will be cited now, with the understanding that in any concrete circuit a role may be filled more than once, and that the same person may fill more than one of them.

First is the *next-of-relation*—the person whom the prepatient sees as the most available of those upon whom he should be able to depend most in times of trouble, in this instance the last to doubt his sanity and the first to have done everything to save him from the fate which, it transpires, he has been approaching. The patient's next-of-relation is usually his next of kin; the special term is introduced because he need not be. Second is the *complainant,* the person who retrospectively appears to have started the person on his way to the hospital. Third are the *mediators*—the sequence of agents and agencies to which the prepatient is referred and through which he is relayed and processed on his way to the hospital. Here are included police, clergy, general medical practitioners, office psychiatrists, personnel in public clinics, lawyers, social service workers, schoolteachers, and so on. One of these agents will have the legal mandate to sanction commitment and will exercise it, and so those agents who precede him in the process will be involved in something whose outcome is not yet settled. When the mediators retire from the scene, the prepatient has become an inpatient, and the significant agent has become the hospital administrator.

While the complainant usually takes action in a lay capacity as a citizen, an employer, a neighbor, or a kinsman, mediators tend to be specialists and differ from those they serve in significant ways. They have experience in handling trouble, and some professional distance from what they handle. Except in the case of policemen, and perhaps some clergy, they tend to be more psychiatrically oriented than the lay public, and will see the need for treatment at times when the public does not.[14]

An interesting feature of these roles is the

---

[12]For example, Jerome K. Meyers and Leslie Schaffer, "Social Stratification and Psychiatric Practice: A Study of an Outpatient Clinic," *American Sociological Review,* XIX (1954), pp. 307–10; Lemert, *op. cit.,* pp. 402–3; *Patients in Mental Institutions, 1941* (Washington, D.C.: Department of Commerce, Bureau of the Census, 1941), p. 2.

[13]For one circuit of agents and its bearing on career contingencies, see Oswald Hall, "The Stages of a Medical Career," *American Journal of Sociology,* LIII (1948), pp. 327–36.

[14]See Cumming and Cumming, *op. cit.,* p. 92.

functional effects of their interdigitation. For example, the feelings of the patient will be influenced by whether or not the person who fills the role of complainant also has the role of next-of-relation—an embarrassing combination more prevalent, apparently, in the higher classes than in the lower.[15] Some of these emergent effects will be considered now.[16]

In the prepatient's progress from home to the hospital he may participate as a third person in what he may come to experience as a kind of alienative coalition. His next-of-relation presses him into coming to "talk things over" with a medical practitioner, an office psychiatrist, or some other counselor. Disinclination on his part may be met by threatening him with desertion, disownment, or other legal action, or by stressing the joint and exploratory nature of the interview. But typically the next-of-relation will have set the interview up, in the sense of selecting the professional, arranging for time, telling the professional something about the case, and so on. This move effectively tends to establish the next-of-relation as the responsible person to whom pertinent findings can be divulged, while effectively establishing the other as the patient. The prepatient often goes to the interview with the understanding that he is going as an equal of someone who is so bound together with him that a third person could not come between them in fundamental matters; this, after all, is one way in which close relationships are defined in our society. Upon arrival at the office the prepatient suddenly finds that he and his next-of-relation have not been accorded the same roles, and apparently that a prior understanding between the professional and the next-of-relation has been put in operation against him. In the extreme but common case, the professional first sees the prepatient alone, in the role of examiner and diagnostician, and then sees the next-of-relation alone, in the role of adviser, while carefully avoiding talking things over seriously with them both together.[17] And even in those non-consultative cases where public officials must forcibly extract a person from a family that wants to tolerate him, the next-of-relation is likely to be induced to "go along" with the official action, so that even here the prepatient may feel that an alienative coalition has been formed against him.

The moral experience of being third man in such a coalition is likely to embitter the prepatient, especially since his troubles have already probably led to some estrangement from his next-of-relation. After he enters the hospital, continued visits by his next-of-relation can give the patient the "insight" that his own best interests were being served. But the initial visits may temporarily strengthen his feeling of abandonment; he is likely to beg his visitor to get him out or at least to get him more privileges and to sympathize with the monstrousness of his plight—to which the visitor ordinarily can respond only by trying to maintain a hopeful note, by not "hearing" the requests, or by assuring the patient that the medical authorities know about these things and are doing what is medically best. The visitor then nonchalantly goes back into a world that the patient has learned is incredibly thick with freedom and privileges, causing the patient to feel that his next-of-relation is merely adding a pious gloss to a clear case of traitorous desertion.

The depth to which the patient may feel betrayed by his next-of-relation seems to be increased

---

[15]Hollingshead and Redlich, *op. cit.*, p. 187.

[16]For an analysis of some of these circuit implications for the inpatient, see Leila Deasy and Olive W. Quinn, "The Wife of the Mental Patient and the Hospital Psychiatrist," *Journal of Social Issues*, XI (1955), pp. 49–60. An interesting illustration of this kind of analysis may also be found in Alan G. Gowman, "Blindness and the Role of the Companion," *Social Problems*, IV (1956), pp. 68–75. A general statement may be found in Robert Merton, "The Role Set: Problems in Sociological Theory," *British Journal of Sociology*, VIII (1957), pp. 106–20.

[17]I have one case record of a man who claims he thought *he* was taking his wife to see the psychiatrist, not realizing until too late that his wife had made the arrangements.

by the fact that another witnesses his betrayal—a factor which is apparently significant in many three-party situations. An offended person may well act forbearantly and accommodatively toward an offender when the two are alone, choosing peace ahead of justice. The presence of a witness, however, seems to add something to the implication of the offense. For then it is beyond the power of the offended and offender to forget about, erase, or suppress what has happened; the offense has become a public social fact.[18] When the witness is a mental health commission, as is sometimes the case, the witnessed betrayal can verge on a "degradation ceremony."[19] In such circumstances, the offended patient may feel that some kind of extensive reparative action is required before witnesses, if his honor and social weight are to be restored.

Two other aspects of sensed betrayal should be mentioned. First, those who suggest the possibility of another's entering a mental hospital are not likely to provide a realistic picture of how in fact it may strike him when he arrives. Often he is told that he will get required medical treatment and a rest, and may well be out in a few months or so. In some cases they may thus be concealing what they know, but I think, in general, they will be telling what they see as the truth. For here there is quite relevant difference between patients and mediating professionals; mediators, more so than the public at large, may conceive of mental hospitals as short-term medical establishments where required rest and attention can be voluntarily obtained, and not as places of coerced exile. When the prepatient finally arrives he is likely to learn quite quickly, quite differently. He then finds that the information given him about life in the hospital has had the effect of his having put up less resistance to entering than he now sees he would have put up

had he known the facts. Whatever the intentions of those who participated in his transition from person to patient, he may sense they have in effect "conned" him into his present predicament.

I am suggesting that the prepatient starts out with at least a portion of the rights, liberties, and satisfactions of the civilian and ends up on a psychiatric ward stripped of almost everything. The question here is how this stripping is managed. This is the second aspect of betrayal I want to consider.

As the prepatient may see it, the circuit of significant figures can function as a kind of betrayal funnel. Passage from person to patient may be effected through a series of linked stages, each managed by a different agent. While each stage tends to bring a sharp decrease in adult free status, each agent may try to maintain the fiction that no further decrease will occur. He may even manage to turn the prepatient over to the next agent while sustaining this note. Further, through words, cues, and gestures, the prepatient is implicitly asked by the current agent to join with him in sustaining a running line of polite small talk that tactfully avoids the administrative facts of the situation, becoming, with each stage, progressively more at odds with the facts. The spouse would rather not have to cry to get the prepatient to visit a psychiatrist; psychiatrists would rather not have a scene when the prepatient learns that he and his spouse are being seen separately and in different ways; the police infrequently bring a prepatient to the hospital in a strait jacket, finding it much easier all around to give him a cigarette, some kindly words, and freedom to relax in the back seat of the patrol car; and finally, the admitting psychiatrist finds he can do his work better in the relative quiet and luxury of the "admission suite" where, as an incidental consequence, the notion can survive that a mental hospital is indeed a comforting place. If the prepatient heeds all of these implied requests and is reasonably decent about the whole thing, he can travel the whole circuit from home to hospital

---

[18] A paraphrase from Kurt Riezler, "Comment on the Social Psychology of Shame," *American Journal of Sociology*, XLVIII (1943), p. 458.

[19] See Harold Garfinkel, "Conditions of Successful Degradation Ceremonies," *American Journal of Sociology*, LXI (1956), pp. 420–24.

without forcing anyone to look directly at what is happening or to deal with the raw emotion that his situation might well cause him to express. His showing consideration for those who are moving him toward the hospital allows them to show consideration for him, with the joint result that these interactions can be sustained with some of the protective harmony characteristic of ordinary face-to-face dealings. But should the new patient cast his mind back over the sequence of steps leading to hospitalization, he may feel that everyone's current comfort was being busily sustained while his long-range welfare was being undermined. This realization may constitute a moral experience that further separates him for the time from the people on the outside.[20]

I would now like to look at the circuit of career agents from the point of view of the agents themselves. Mediators in the person's transition from civil to patient status—as well as his keepers, once he is in the hospital—have an interest in establishing a responsible next-of-relation as the patient's deputy or guardian; should there be no obvious candidate for the role, someone may be sought out and pressed into it. Thus while a person is gradually being transformed into a patient, a next-of-relation is gradually being transformed into a guardian. With a guardian on the scene, the whole transition process can be kept tidy. He is likely to be familiar with the prepatient's civil involvements and business, and can tie up loose ends that might otherwise be left to entangle the hospital. Some of the prepatient's abrogated civil rights can be transferred to him, thus helping to sustain the legal fiction that while the prepatient does not actually have his rights he somehow actually has not lost them.

Inpatients commonly sense, at least for a time, that hospitalization is a massive unjust deprivation, and sometimes succeed in convincing a few persons on the outside that this is the case. It often turns out to be useful, then, for those identified with inflicting these deprivations, however justifiably, to be able to point to the co-operation and agreement of someone whose relationship to the patient places him above suspicion, firmly defining him as the person most likely to have the patient's personal interest at heart. If the guardian is satisfied with what is happening to the new inpatient, the world ought to be.[21]

Now it would seem that the greater the legitimate personal stake one party has in another, the better he can take the role of guardian to the other. But the structural arrangements in society which lead to the acknowledged merging of two persons' interests lead to additional consequences. For the person to whom the patient turns for help—for protection against such threats as involuntary commitment—is just the person to whom the mediators and hospital administrators logically turn for authorization. It is understandable, then, that some patients will come to sense, at least for a time, that the closeness of a relationship tells nothing of its trustworthiness.

There are still other functional effects emerging from this complement of roles. If and when the next-of-relation appeals to mediators for help in the trouble he is having with the prepatient, hospitalization may not, in fact, be in his mind. He may not

---

[20]Concentration-camp practices provide a good example of the function of the betrayal funnel in inducing co-operation and reducing struggle and fuss, although here the mediators could not be said to be acting in the best interests of the inmates. Police picking up persons from their homes would sometimes joke good-naturedly and offer to wait while coffee was being served. Gas chambers were fitted out like delousing rooms, and victims taking off their clothes were told to note where they were leaving them. The sick, aged, weak, or insane who were selected for extermination were sometimes driven away in Red Cross ambulances to camps referred to by terms such as "observation hospital." See David Boder, *I Did Not Interview the Dead* (Urbana: University of Illinois Press, 1949), p. 81; and Elie A. Cohen, *Human Behavior in the Concentration Camp* (London: Jonathan Cape, 1954), pp. 32, 37, 107.

[21]Interviews collected by the Clausen group at NIMH suggest that when a wife comes to be a guardian, the responsibility may disrupt previous distance from in-laws, leading either to a new supportive coalition with them or to a marked withdrawal from them.

even perceive the prepatient as mentally sick, or, if he does, he may not consistently hold to this view.[22] It is the circuit of mediators, with their greater psychiatric sophistication and their belief in the medical character of mental hospitals, that will often define the situation for the next-of-relation, assuring him that hospitalization is a possible solution and a good one, that it involves no betrayal, but is rather a medical action taken in the best interests of the prepatient. Here the next-of-relation may learn that doing his duty to the prepatient may cause the prepatient to distrust and even hate him for the time. But the fact that this course of action may have had to be pointed out and prescribed by professionals, and be defined by them as a moral duty, relieves the next-of-relation of some of the guilt he may feel.[23] It is a poignant fact that an adult son or daughter may be pressed into the role of mediator, so that the hostility that might otherwise be directed against the spouse is passed on to the child.[24]

Once the prepatient is in the hospital, the same guilt-carrying function may become a significant part of the staff's job in regard to the next-of-relation.[25] These reasons for feeling that he himself has not betrayed the patient, even though the patient may then think so, can later provide the next-of-relation with a defensible line to take when visiting the patient in the hospital and a basis for hoping that the relationship can be re-established after its hospital moratorium. And of course this position, when sensed by the patient, can provide him with excuses for the next-of-relation, when and if he comes to look for them.[26]

Thus while the next-of-relation can perform important functions for the mediators and hospital administrators, they in turn can perform important functions for him. One finds, then, an emergent unintended exchange or reciprocation of functions, these functions themselves being often unintended.

The final point I want to consider about the prepatient's moral career is its peculiarly retroactive character. Until a person actually arrives at the hospital there usually seems no way of knowing for sure that he is destined to do so, given the determinative role of career contingencies. And until the point of hospitalization is reached, he or others may not conceive of him as a person who is becoming a mental patient. However, since he will be held against his will in the hospital, his next-of-relation and the hospital staff will be in great need of a rationale for the hardships they are sponsoring. The medical elements of the staff will also need evidence that they are still in the trade they were trained for. These problems are eased, no doubt unintentionally, by the case-history construction that is placed on the patient's past life, this having the effect of demonstrating that all along he had been becoming sick, that he finally became very sick, and that if he had not been hospitalized much worse things would have happened to him—all of which, of course, may be true. Incidentally, if the patient wants to make sense out of his stay in the

[22]For an analysis of these non-psychiatric kinds of perception, see Marian Radke Yarrow, Charlotte Green Schwartz, Harriet S. Murphy, and Leila Deasy, "The Psychological Meaning of Mental Illness in the Family," *Journal of Social Issues*, XI (1955), pp. 12–24; Charlotte Green Schwartz, "Perspectives on Deviance—Wives' Definitions of Their Husbands' Mental Illness," *Psychiatry*, XX (1957), pp. 275–91.

[23]This guilt-carrying function is found, of course, in other role complexes. Thus, when a middle-class couple engages in the process of legal separation or divorce, each of their lawyers usually takes the position that his job is to acquaint his client with all of the potential claims and rights, pressing his client into demanding these, in spite of any nicety of feelings about the rights and honorableness of the ex-partner. The client, in all good faith, can then say to self and to the ex-partner that the demands are being made only because the lawyer insists it is best to do so.

[24]Recorded in the Clausen data.

[25]This point is made by Cumming and Cumming, *op. cit.*, p. 129.

[26]There is an interesting contrast here with the moral career of the tuberculosis patient. I am told by Julius Roth that tuberculous patients are likely to come to the hospital willingly, agreeing with their next-of-relation about treatment. Later in their hospital career, when they learn how long they yet have to stay and how depriving and irrational some of the hospital rulings are, they may seek to leave, be advised against this by the staff and by relatives, and only then begin to feel betrayed.

hospital, and, as already suggested, keep alive the possibility of once again conceiving of his next-of-relation as a decent, well-meaning person, then he, too, will have reason to believe some of this psychiatric work-up of his past.

Here is a very ticklish point for the sociology of careers. An important aspect of every career is the view the person constructs when he looks backward over his progress; in a sense, however, the whole of the prepatient career derives from this reconstruction. The fact of having had a prepatient career, starting with an effective complaint, becomes an important part of the mental patient's orientation, but this part can begin to be played only after hospitalization proves that what he had been having, but no longer has, is a career as a prepatient.

THE INPATIENT PHASE

The last step in the prepatient's career can involve his realization—justified or not—that he has been deserted by society and turned out of relationships by those closest to him. Interestingly enough, the patient, especially a first admission, may manage to keep himself from coming to the end of this trail, even though in fact he is now in a locked mental-hospital ward. On entering the hospital, he may very strongly feel the desire not to be known to anyone as a person who could possibly be reduced to these present circumstances, or as a person who conducted himself in the way he did prior to commitment. Consequently, he may avoid talking to anyone, may stay by himself when possible, and may even be "out of contact" or "manic" so as to avoid ratifying any interaction that presses a politely reciprocal role upon him and opens him up to what he has become in the eyes of others. When the next-of-relation makes an effort to visit, he may be rejected by mutism, or by the patient's refusal to enter the visiting room, these strategies sometimes suggesting that the patient still clings to a remnant of relatedness to those who made up his past, and is protecting this remnant

from the final destructiveness of dealing with the new people that they have become.[27]

Usually the patient comes to give up this taxing effort at anonymity, at not-hereness, and begins to present himself for conventional social interaction to the hospital community. Thereafter he withdraws only in special ways—by always using his nickname, by signing his contribution to the patient weekly with his initial only, or by using the innocuous "cover" address tactfully provided by some hospitals; or he withdraws only at special times, when, say, a flock of nursing students makes a passing tour of the ward, or when, paroled to the hospital grounds, he suddenly sees he is about to cross the path of a civilian he happens to know from home. Sometimes this making of oneself available is called "settling down" by the attendants. It marks a new stand openly taken and supported by the patient, and resembles the "coming-out" process that occurs in other groupings.[28]

Once the prepatient begins to settle down, the main outlines of his fate tend to follow those of a

---

[27]The inmate's initial strategy of holding himself aloof from ratifying contact may partly account for the relative lack of group formation among inmates in public mental hospitals, a connection that has been suggested to me by William R. Smith. The desire to avoid personal bonds that would give licence to the asking of biographical questions could also be a factor. In mental hospitals, of course, as in prisoner camps, the staff may consciously break up incipient group formation in order to avoid collective rebellious action and other ward disturbances.

[28]A comparable coming out occurs in the homosexual world, when a person finally comes frankly to present himself to a "gay" gathering not as a tourist but as someone who is "available." See Evelyn Hooker, "A Preliminary Analysis of Group Behavior of Homosexuals," *Journal of Psychology*, XLII (1956), pp. 217–25; see especially p. 221. A good fictionalized treatment may be found in James Baldwin's *Giovanni's Room* (New York: Dial, 1956), pp. 41–57. A familiar instance of the coming-out process is no doubt to be found among prepubertal children at the moment one of these actors sidles *back* into a room that had been left in an angered huff and injured *amour propre*. The phrase itself presumably derives from a *rite-de-passage* ceremony once arranged by upper-class mothers for their daughters. Interestingly enough, in large mental hospitals the patient sometimes symbolizes a complete coming out by his first active participation in the hospital-wide patient dance.

whole class of segregated establishments—jails, concentration camps, monasteries, work camps, and so on—in which the inmate spends the whole round of life on the grounds, and marches through his regimented day in the immediate company of a group of persons of his own institutional status.

Like the neophyte in many of these total institutions, the new inpatient finds himself cleanly stripped of many of his accustomed affirmations, satisfactions, and defenses, and is subjected to a rather full set of mortifying experiences: restriction of free movement, communal living, diffuse authority of a whole echelon of people, and so on. Here one begins to learn about the limited extent to which a conception of oneself can be sustained when the usual setting of supports for it are suddenly removed.

While undergoing these humbling moral experiences, the inpatient learns to orient himself in terms of the "ward system."[29] In public mental hospitals this usually consists of a series of graded living arrangements built around wards, administrative units called services, and parole statuses. The "worst" level often involves nothing but wooden benches to sit on, some quite indifferent food, and a small piece of room to sleep in. The "best" level may involve a room of one's own, ground and town privileges, contacts with staff that are relatively undamaging, and what is seen as good food and ample recreational facilities. For disobeying the pervasive house rules, the inmate will receive stringent punishments expressed in terms of loss of privileges; for obedience he will eventually be allowed to reacquire some of the minor satisfactions he took for granted on the outside.

The institutionalization of these radically different levels of living throws light on the implications for self of social settings. And this in turn affirms that the self arises not merely out of its possessor's interactions with significant others, but

also out of the arrangements that are evolved in an organization for its members.

These are some settings that the person easily discounts as an expression or extension of him. When a tourist goes slumming, he may take pleasure in the situation not because it is a reflection of him but because it so assuredly is not. There are other settings, such as living rooms, which the person manages on his own and employs to influence in a favorable direction other persons' views of him. And there are still other settings, such as a work place, which express the employee's occupational status, but over which he has no final control, this being exerted, however tactfully, by his employer. Mental hospitals provide an extreme instance of this latter possibility. And this is due not merely to their uniquely degraded living levels, but also to the unique way in which significance for self is made explicit to the patient, piercingly, persistently, and thoroughly. Once lodged on a given ward, the patient is firmly instructed that the restrictions and deprivations he encounters are not due to such blind forces as tradition or economy—and hence dissociable from self—but are intentional parts of his treatment, part of his need at the time, and therefore an expression of the state that his self has fallen to. Having every reason to initiate requests for better conditions, he is told that when the staff feel he is "able to manage" or will be "comfortable with" a higher ward level, then appropriate action will be taken. In short, assignment to a given ward is presented not as a reward or punishment, but as an expression of his general level of social functioning, his status as a person. Given the fact that the worst ward levels provide a round of life that inpatients with organic brain damage can easily manage, and that these quite limited human beings are present to prove it, one can appreciate some of the mirroring effects of the hospital.[30]

[29]A good description of the ward system may be found in Ivan Belknap, *Human Problems of a State Mental Hospital* (New York: McGraw-Hill, 1956), ch. ix, especially p. 164.

[30]Here is one way in which mental hospitals can be worse than concentration camps and prisons as places in which to "do" time; in the latter, self-insulation from the symbolic implications of the settings may be easier. In fact, self-

The ward system, then, is an extreme instance of how the physical facts of an establishment can be explicitly employed to frame the conception a person takes of himself. In addition, the official psychiatric mandate of mental hospitals gives rise to even more direct, even more blatant, attacks upon the inmate's views of himself. The more ''medical'' and the more progressive a mental hospital is—the more it attempts to be therapeutic and not merely custodial—the more he may be confronted by high-ranking staff arguing that his past has been a failure, that the cause of this has been within himself, that his attitude to life is wrong, and that if he wants to be a person he will have to change his way of dealing with people and his conceptions of himself. Often the moral value of these verbal assaults will be brought home to him by requiring him to practice taking this psychiatric view of himself in arranged confessional periods, whether in private sessions or group psychotherapy.

Now a general point may be made about the moral career of inpatients which has bearing on many moral careers. Given the stage that any person has reached in a career, one typically finds that he constructs an image of his life course—past, present, and future—which selects, abtracts, and distorts in such a way as to provide him with a view of himself that he can usefully expound in current situations. Quite generally, the person's line concerning self defensively brings him into appropriate alignment with the basic values of his society, and so may be called an apologia. If the person can manage to present a view of his current situation which shows the operation of favorable personal qualities in the past and a favorable destiny awaiting him, it may be called a success story. If the facts of a person's past and present are extremely dismal, then about the best he can do is to show that he is not responsible for what has become of him, and the term sad tale is appropri-

ate. Interestingly enough, the more the person's past forces him out of apparent alignment with central moral values, the more often he seems compelled to tell his sad tale in any company in which he finds himself. Perhaps he partly responds to the need he feels in others of not having their sense of proper life courses affronted. In any case, it is among convicts, ''winos,'' and prostitutes that one seems to obtain sad tales the most readily.[31] It is the vicissitudes of the mental patient's sad tale that I want to consider now.

In the mental hospital, the setting and the house rules press home to the patient that he is, after all, a mental case who has suffered some kind of social collapse on the outside, having failed in some over-all way, and that here he is of little social weight, being hardly capable of acting like a full-fledged person at all. These humiliations are likely to be most keenly felt by middle-class patients, since their previous condition of life little immunizes them against such affronts, but all patients feel some downgrading. Just as any normal member of his outside subculture would do, the patient often responds to this situation by

insulation from hospital settings may be so difficult that patients have to employ devices for this which staff interpret as psychotic symptoms.

[31]In regard to convicts, see Anthony Heckstall-Smith, *Eighteen Months* (London: Allan Wingate, 1954), pp. 52–53. For ''winos'' see the discussion in Howard G. Bain, ''A Sociological Analysis of the Chicago Skid-Row Lifeway'' (Unpublished M.A. thesis, Department of Sociology, University of Chicago, September 1950), especially ''The Rationale of the Skid-Row Drinking Group,'' pp. 141–46. Bain's neglected thesis is a useful source of material on moral careers.

Apparently one of the occupational hazards of prostitution is that clients and other professional contacts sometimes persist in expressing sympathy by asking for a defensible dramatic explanation for the fall from grace. In having to bother to have a sad tale ready, perhaps the prostitute is more to be pitied than damned. Good examples of prostitute sad tales may be found in Henry Mayhew, *London Labour and the London Poor*. Vol. IV. *Those That Will Not Work* (London: Charles Griffin and Co., 1862). pp. 210–72. For a contemporary source, see *Women of the Streets*, edited by C. H. Rolph (London: Secker and Warburg, 1955), especially p. 6: ''*Almost always, however, after a few comments on the police, the girl would begin to explain how it was that she was in the life, usually in terms of self-justification. . . .*'' Lately, of course, the psychological expert has helped out the profession in the construction of wholly remarkable sad tales. See, for example, Harold Greenwald, *The Call Girl* (New York: Ballantine Books, 1958).

attempting to assert a sad tale proving that he is not "sick," that the "little trouble" he did get into was really somebody else's fault, that his past life course had some honor and rectitude, and that the hospital is therefore unjust in forcing the status of mental patient upon him. This self-respecting tendency is heavily institutionalized within the patient society where opening social contacts typically involve the participants' volunteering information about their current ward location and length of stay so far, but not the reasons for their stay—such interaction being conducted in the manner of small talk on the outside.[32] With greater familiarity, each patient usually volunteers relatively acceptable reasons for his hospitalization, at the same time accepting without open immediate question the lines offered by other patients. Such stories as the following are given and overtly accepted.

> I was going to night school to get a M.A. degree, and holding down a job in addition, and the load got too much for me.

> The others here are sick mentally but I'm suffering from a bad nervous system and that is what is giving me these phobias.

> I got here by mistake because of a diabetes diagnosis, and I'll leave in a couple of days. [The patient had been in seven weeks.]

> I failed as a child, and later with my wife I reached out for dependency.

> My trouble is that I can't work. That's what I'm in for. I had two jobs with a good home and all the money I wanted.[33]

The patient sometimes reinforces these stories by an optimistic definition of his occupational

status. A man who managed to obtain an audition as a radio announcer styles himself a radio announcer; another who worked for some months as a copy boy and was then given a job as a reporter on a large trade journal, but fired after three weeks, defines himself as a reporter.

A whole social role in the patient community may be constructed on the basis of these reciprocally sustained fictions. For these face-to-face niceties tend to be qualified by behind-the-back gossip that comes only a degree closer to the "objective" facts. Here, of course, one can see a classic social function of informal networks of equals: they serve as one another's audience for self-supporting tales—tales that are somewhat more solid than pure fantasy and somewhat thinner than the facts.

But the patient's apologia is called forth in a unique setting, for few settings could be so destructive of self-stories except, of course, those stories already constructed along psychiatric lines. And this destructiveness rests on more than the official sheet of paper which attests that the patient is of unsound mind, a danger to himself and others—an attestation, incidentally, which seems to cut deeply into the patient's pride, and into the possibility of his having any.

Certainly the degrading conditions of the hospital setting belie many of the self-stories that are presented by patients, and the very fact of being in the mental hospital is evidence against these tales. And of course there is not always sufficient patient solidarity to prevent patient discrediting patient, just as there is not always a sufficient number of "professionalized" attendants to prevent attendant discrediting patient. As one patient informant repeatedly suggested to a fellow patient:

> If you're so smart, how come you got your ass in here?

The mental-hospital setting, however, is more treacherous still. Staff have much to gain through discreditings of the patient's story—whatever the felt reason for such discreditings. If the custodial

---

[32]A similar self-protecting rule has been observed in prisons. Thus, Alfred Hassler, *Diary of a Self-Made Convict* (Chicago: Regnery, 1954), p. 76, in describing a conversation with a fellow prisoner: *"He didn't say much about why he was sentenced, and I didn't ask him, that being the accepted behavior in prison."* A novelistic version for the mental hospital may be found in J. Kerkhoff, *How Thin the Veil: A Newspaperman's Story of His Own Mental Crackup and Recovery* (New York: Greenberg, 1952), p. 27.

[33]From the writer's field notes of informal interaction with patients, transcribed as nearly verbatim as he was able.

faction in the hospital is to succeed in managing his daily round without complaint or trouble from him, then it will prove useful to be able to point out to him that the claims about himself upon which he rationalizes his demands are false, that he is not what he is claiming to be, and that in fact he is a failure as a person. If the psychiatric faction is to impress upon him its views about his personal make-up, then they must be able to show in detail how their version of his past and their version of his character hold up much better than his own.[34] If both the custodial and psychiatric factions are to get him to co-operate in the various psychiatric treatments, then it will prove useful to disabuse him of his views of their purposes, and cause him to appreciate that they know what they are doing, and are doing what is best for him. In brief, the difficulties caused by a patient are closely tied to his version of what has been happening to him, and if co-operation is to be secured, it helps if this version is discredited. The patient must ''insightfully'' come to take, or affect to take, the hospital's view of himself.

The staff also have ideal means—in addition to the mirroring effect of the setting—for denying the inmate's rationalizations. Current psychiatric doctrine defines mental disorder as something that can have its roots in the patient's earliest years, show its signs throughout the course of his life, and invade almost every sector of his current activity. No segment of his past or present need be defined, then, as beyond the jurisdiction and mandate of

psychiatric assessment. Mental hospitals bureaucratically institutionalize this extremely wide mandate by formally basing their treatment of the patient upon his diagnosis and hence upon the psychiatric view of his past.

The case record is an important expression of this mandate. This dossier is apparently not regularly used, however, to record occasions when the patient showed capacity to cope honorably and effectively with difficult life situations. Nor is the case record typically used to provide a rough average or sampling of his past conduct. One of its purposes is to show the ways in which the patient is ''sick'' and the reasons why it was right to commit him and is right currently to keep him committed; and this is done by extracting from his whole life course a list of those incidents that have or might have had ''symptomatic'' significance.[35] The misadventures of his parents or siblings that might suggest a ''taint'' may be cited. Early acts in which the patient appeared to have shown bad judgment or emotional disturbance will be recorded. Occasions when he acted in a way which the layman would consider immoral, sexually perverted, weak-willed, childish, ill-considered, impulsive, and crazy may be described. Misbehaviors which someone saw as the last straw, as cause for immediate action, are likely to be reported in detail. In addition, the record will describe his state on arrival at the hospital—and this is not likely to be a time of tranquillity and ease for him. The record may also report the false line taken by the

---

[34]The process of examining a person psychiatrically and then altering or reducing his status in consequence is known in hospital and prison parlance as bugging, the assumption being that once you come to the attention of the testers you either will automatically be labeled crazy or the process of testing itself will make you crazy. Thus psychiatric staff are sometimes seen not as discovering whether you are sick, but as making you sick; and ''Don't bug me, man'' can mean, ''Don't pester me to the point where I'll get upset.'' Sheldon Messinger has suggested to me that this meaning of bugging is related to the other colloquial meaning, of wiring a room with a secret microphone to collect information usable for discrediting the speaker.

[35]While many kinds of organizations maintain records of their members, in almost all of these some socially significant attributes can only be included indirectly, being officially irrelevant. But since mental hospitals have a legitimate claim to deal with the ''whole'' person, they need officially recognize no limits to what they consider relevant, a sociologically interesting licence. It is an odd historical fact that persons concerned with promoting civil liberties in other areas of life tend to favor giving the psychiatrist complete discretionary power over the patient. Apparently it is felt that the more power possessed by medically qualified administrators and therapists, the better the interests of the patients will be served. Patients, to my knowledge, have not been polled on this matter.

patient in answering embarrassing questions, showing him as someone who makes claims that are obviously contrary to the facts:

> Claims she lives with oldest daughter or with sisters only when sick and in need of care; otherwise with husband, he himself says not for twelve years.

> Contrary to the reports from the personnel, he says he no longer bangs on the floor or cries in the morning.

> . . . conceals fact that she had her organs removed, claims she is still menstruating.

> At first she denied having had premarital sexual experience, but when asked about Jim she said she had forgotten about it 'cause it had been unpleasant.[36]

Where contrary facts are not known by the recorder, their presence is often left scrupulously an open question:

> The patient denied any heterosexual experiences nor could one trick her into admitting that she had ever been pregnant or into any kind of sexual indulgence, denying masturbation as well.

> Even with considerable pressure she was unwilling to engage in any projection of paranoid mechanisms.

> No psychotic content could be elicited at this time.[37]

And if in no more factual way, discrediting statements often appear in descriptions given of the patient's general social manner in the hospital:

> When interviewed, he was bland, apparently self-assured, and sprinkles highsounding generalizations freely throughout his verbal productions.

> Armed with a rather neat appearance and natty little Hitlerian mustache this 45 year old man who has spent the last five or more years of his life in the hospital, is making a very successful hospital adjustment living within the role of a rather gay liver and jim-dandy type of fellow who is not only quite

superior to his fellow patients in intellectual respects but who is also quite a man with women. His speech is sprayed with many multi-syllabled words which he generally uses in good context, but if he talks long enough on any subject it soon becomes apparent that he is so completely lost in this verbal diarrhea as to make what he says almost completely worthless.[38]

The events recorded in the case history are, then, just the sort that a layman would consider scandalous, defamatory, and discrediting. I think it is fair to say that all levels of mental-hospital staff fail, in general, to deal with this material with the moral neutrality claimed for medical statements and psychiatric diagnosis, but instead participate, by intonation and gesture if by no other means, in the lay reaction to these acts. This will occur in staff-patient encounters as well as in staff encounters at which no patient is present.

In some mental hospitals, access to the case record is technically restricted to medical and higher nursing levels, but even here informal access or relayed information is often available to lower staff levels.[39] In addition, ward personnel are felt to have a right to know those aspects of the patient's past conduct which, embedded in the reputation he develops, purportedly make it possible to manage him with greater benefit to himself and less risk to others. Further, all staff levels

---

[36]Verbatim transcriptions of hospital case-record material.
[37]Verbatim transcriptions of hospital case-record material.
[38]Verbatim transcriptions of hospital case-record material.
[39]However, some mental hospitals do have a "hot file" of selected records which can be taken out only by special permission. These may be records of patients who work as administration-office messengers and might otherwise snatch glances at their own files; of inmates who had elite status in the environing community; and of inmates who may take legal action against the hospital and hence have a special reason to maneuver access to their records. Some hospitals even have a "hot-hot file," kept in the superintendent's office. In addition, the patient's professional title, especially if it is a medical one, is sometimes purposely omitted from his file card. All of these exceptions to the general rule for handling information show, of course, the institution's realization of some of the implications of keeping mental-hospital records. For a further example, see Harold Taxel, "Authority Structure in a Mental Hospital Ward" (Unpublished M.A. thesis, Department of Sociology, University of Chicago, 1953), pp. 11–12.

typically have access to the nursing notes kept on the ward, which chart the daily course of each patient's disease, and hence his conduct, providing for the near present the sort of information the case record supplies for his past.

I think that most of the information gathered in case records is quite true, although it might seem also to be true that almost anyone's life course could yield up enough denigrating facts to provide grounds for the record's justification of commitment. In any case, I am not concerned here with questioning the desirability of maintaining case records, or the motives of staff in keeping them. The point is that, these facts about him being true, the patient is certainly not relieved from the normal cultural pressure to conceal them, and is perhaps all the more threatened by knowing that they are neatly available, and that he has no control over who gets to learn them.[40] A manly looking youth who responds to military induction by running away from the barracks and hiding himself in a hotel-room clothes closet, to be found there, crying, by his mother; a woman who travels from Utah to Washington to warn the President of impending doom; a man who disrobes before three young girls; a boy who locks his sister out of the house, striking out two of her teeth when she tries to come back in through the window—each of these persons has done something he will have very obvious reason to conceal from others, and very good reason to tell lies about.

The formal and informal patterns of communication linking staff members tend to amplify the disclosive work done by the case record. A discreditable act that the patient performs during one part of the day's routine in one part of the hospital community is likely to be reported back to those who supervise other areas of his life where he implicitly takes the stand that he is not the sort of person who could act that way.

Of significance here, as in some other social establishments, is the increasingly common practice of all-level staff conferences, where staff air their views of patients and develop collective agreement concerning the line that the patient is trying to take and the line that should be taken to him. A patient who develops a "personal" relation with an attendant, or manages to make an attendant anxious by eloquent and persistent accusations of malpractice, can be put back into his place by means of the staff meeting, where the attendant is given warning or assurance that the patient is "sick." Since the differential image of himself that a person usually meets from those of various levels around him comes here to be unified behind the scenes into a common approach, the patient may find himself faced with a kind of collusion against him—albeit one sincerely thought to be for his own ultimate welfare.

In addition, the formal transfer of the patient from one ward or service to another is likely to be accompanied by an informal description of his characteristics, this being felt to facilitate the work of the employee who is newly responsible for him.

Finally, at the most informal of levels, the lunchtime and coffee-break small talk of staff often turns upon the latest doings of the patient, the gossip level of any social establishment being here

---

[40]This is the problem of "information control" that many groups suffer from in varying degrees. See Goffman, "Discrepant Roles," in *The Presentation of Self in Everyday Life* (New York: Anchor Books, 1959), ch. iv, pp. 141–166. A suggestion of this problem in relation to case records in prisons is given by James Peck in his story, "The Ship that Never Hit Port," in *Prison Etiquette*, edited by Holley Cantine and Dachine Rainer (Bearsville, N.Y.: Retort Press, 1950), p. 66:

The hacks of course hold all the aces in dealing with any prisoner because they can always write him up for inevitable punishment. Every infraction of the rules is noted in the prisoner's jacket, a folder which records all the details of the man's life before and during imprisonment. There are general reports written by the work detail screw, the cell block screw, or some other screw who may have overheard a conversation. Tales pumped from stoolpigeons are also included.

Any letter which interests the authorities goes into the jacket. The mail censor may make a photostatic copy of a prisoner's entire letter, or merely copy a passage. Or he may pass the letter on to the warden. Often an inmate called out by the warden or parole officer is confronted with something he wrote so long ago he had forgot all about it. It might be about his personal life or his political views—a fragment of thought that the prison authorities felt was dangerous and filed for later use.

intensified by the assumption that everything about him is in some way the proper business of the hospital employee. Theoretically there seems to be no reason why such gossip should not build up the subject instead of tear him down, unless one claims that talk about those not present will always tend to be critical in order to maintain the integrity and prestige of the circle in which the talking occurs. And so, even when the impulse of the speakers seems kindly and generous, the implication of their talk is typically that the patient is not a complete person. For example, a conscientious group therapist, sympathetic with patients, once admitted to his coffee companions:

> I've had about three group disrupters, one man in particular—a lawyer [*sotto voce*] James Wilson— very bright—who just made things miserable for me, but I would always tell him to get on the stage and do something. Well, I was getting desperate and then I bumped into his therapist, who said that right now behind the man's bluff and front he needed the group very much and that it probably meant more to him than anything else he was getting out of the hospital—he just needed the support. Well, that made me feel altogether different about him. He's out now.

In general, then, mental hospitals systematically provide for circulation about each patient the kind of information that the patient is likely to try to hide. And in various degrees of detail this information is used daily to puncture his claims. At the admission and diagnostic conferences, he will be asked questions to which he must give wrong answers in order to maintain his self-respect, and then the true answer may be shot back at him. An attendant whom he tells a version of his past and his reason for being in the hospital may smile disbelievingly, or say, "That's not the way I heard it," in line with the practical psychiatry of bringing the patient down to reality. When he accosts a physician or nurse on the ward and presents his claims for more privileges or for discharge, this may be countered by a question which he cannot answer truthfully without calling up a time in his past when he acted disgracefully. When he gives his view of his situation during group psychotherapy, the therapist, taking the role of interrogator, may attempt to disabuse him of his face-saving interpretations and encourage an interpretation suggesting that it is he himself who is to blame and who must change. When he claims to staff or fellow patients that he is well and has never been really sick, someone may give him graphic details of how, only one month ago, he was prancing around like a girl, or claiming that he was God, or declining to talk or eat, or putting gum in his hair.

Each time the staff deflates the patient's claims, his sense of what a person ought to be and the rules of peer-group social intercourse press him to reconstruct his stories; and each time he does this, the custodial and psychiatric interests of the staff may lead them to discredit these tales again.

Behind these verbally instigated ups and downs of the self is an institutional base that rocks just as precariously. Contrary to popular opinion, the "ward system" insures a great amount of internal social mobility in mental hospitals, especially during the inmate's first year. During that time he is likely to have altered his service once, his ward three or four times, and his parole status several times; and he is likely to have experienced moves in bad as well as good directions. Each of these moves involves a very drastic alteration in level of living and in available materials out of which to build a self-confirming round of activities, an alteration equivalent in scope, say, to a move up or down a class in the wider class system. Moreover, fellow inmates with whom he has partially identified himself will similarly be moving, but in different directions and at different rates, thus reflecting feelings of social change to the person even when he does not experience them directly.

As previously implied, the doctrines of psychiatry can reinforce the social fluctuations of the ward system. Thus there is a current psychiatric view that the ward system is a kind of social hothouse in which patients start as social infants and end up, within the year, on convalescent wards as resocialized adults. This view adds considerably to the weight and pride that staff can attach to their work, and necessitates a certain amount of blindness, especially at higher staff levels, to other ways of viewing the ward system, such as a method for disciplining unruly persons through punishment and reward. In any case, this resocialization perspective tends to overstress the extent to which those on the worst wards are incapable of socialized conduct and the extent to which those on the best wards are ready and willing to play the social game. Because the ward system is something more than a resocialization chamber, inmates find many reasons for "messing up" or getting into trouble, and many occasions, then, for demotion to less privileged ward positions. These demotions may be officially interpreted as psychiatric relapses or moral backsliding, thus protecting the resocialization view of the hospital; these interpretations, by implication, translate a mere infraction of rules and consequent demotion into a fundamental expression of the status of the culprit's self. Correspondingly, promotions, which may come about because of ward population pressure, the need for a "working patient," or for other psychiatrically irrelevant reasons, may be built up into something claimed to be profoundly expressive of the patient's whole self. The patient himself may be expected by staff to make a personal effort to "get well," in something less than a year, and hence may be constantly reminded to think in terms of the self's success and failure.[41]

In such contexts inmates can discover that deflations in moral status are not so bad as they had imagined. After all, infractions which lead to these demotions cannot be accompanied by legal sanctions or by reduction to the status of mental patient, since these conditions already prevail. Further, no past or current delict seems to be horrendous enough in itself to excommunicate a patient from the patient community, and hence failures at right living lose some of their stigmatizing meaning.[42] And finally, in accepting the hospital's version of his fall from grace, the patient can set himself up in the business of "straightening up," and make claims of sympathy, privileges, and indulgence from the staff in order to foster this.

Learning to live under conditions of imminent exposure and wide fluctuation in regard, with little control over the granting or withholding of this regard, is an important step in the socialization of the patient, a step that tells something important about what it is like to be an inmate in a mental hospital. Having one's past mistakes and present progress under constant moral review seems to make for a special adaptation consisting of a less than moral attitude to ego ideals. One's shortcomings and successes become too central and fluctuating an issue in life to allow the usual commitment of concern for other persons' views of them. It is not very practicable to try to sustain solid claims about oneself. The inmate tends to learn that degradations and reconstructions of the self need not be given too much weight, at the same time learning that staff and inmates are ready to view an inflation or deflation of a self with some indifference. He learns that a defensible picture of self can be seen as something outside oneself that can be constructed, lost, and rebuilt, all with great speed and some equanimity. He learns about the viability of taking up a standpoint—and hence a self—that is outside the one which the hospital can give and take away from him.

The setting, then, seems to engender a kind of cosmopolitan sophistication, a kind of civic apathy. In this unserious yet oddly exaggerated moral context, building up a self or having it destroyed becomes something of a shameless game, and learning to view this process as a game seems to make for some demoralization, the game being such a fundamental one. In the hospital,

---

[41]For this and other suggestions, I am indebted to Charlotte Green Schwartz.

[42]See "The Underlife of a Public Institution," in Erving Goffman, *Asylums* (New York: Doubleday-Anchor, 1961).

then, the inmate can learn that the self is not a fortress, but rather a small open city; he can become weary of having to show pleasure when held by troops of his own, and weary of having to show displeasure when held by the enemy. Once he learns what it is like to be defined by society as not having a viable self, this threatening definition—the threat that helps attach people to the self society accords them—is weakened. The patient seems to gain a new plateau when he learns that he can survive while acting in a way that society sees as destructive of him.

A few illustrations of this moral loosening and moral fatigue might be given. In state mental hospitals currently a kind of ''marriage moratorium'' appears to be accepted by patients and more or less condoned by staff. Some informal peer-group pressure may be brought against a patient who ''plays around'' with more than one hospital partner at a time, but little negative sanction seems to be attached to taking up, in a temporarily steady way, with a member of the opposite sex, even though both partners are known to be married, to have children, and even to be regularly visited by these outsiders. In short, there is licence in mental hospitals to begin courting all over again, with the understanding, however, that nothing very permanent or serious can come of this. Like shipboard or vacation romances, these entanglements attest to the way in which the hospital is cut off from the outside community, becoming a world of its own, operated for the benefit of its own citizens. And certainly this moratorium is an expression of the alienation and hostility that patients feel for those on the outside to whom they were closely related. But, in addition, one has evidence of the loosening effects of living in a world within a world, under conditions which make it difficult to give full seriousness to either of them.

The second illustration concerns the ward system. On the worst ward level, discreditings seem to occur the most frequently, in part because of lack of facilities, in part through the mockery and sarcasm that seem to be the occupational norm of social control for the attendants and nurses who administer these places. At the same time, the paucity of equipment and rights means that not much self can be built up. The patient finds himself constantly toppled, therefore, but with very little distance to fall. A kind of jaunty gallows humor seems to develop in some of these wards, with considerable freedom to stand up to the staff and return insult for insult. While these patients can be punished, they cannot, for example, be easily slighted, for they are accorded as a matter of course few of the niceties that people must enjoy before they can suffer subtle abuse. Like prostitutes in connection with sex, inmates on these wards have very little reputation or rights to lose and can therefore take certain liberties. As the person moves up the ward system, he can manage more and more to avoid incidents which discredit his claim to be a human being, and acquire more and more of the varied ingredients of self-respect; yet when eventually he does get toppled—and he does—there is a much farther distance to fall. For instance, the privileged patient lives in a world wider than the ward, containing recreation workers who, on request, can dole out cake, cards, table-tennis balls, tickets to the movies, and writing materials. But in the absence of the social control of payment which is typically exerted by a recipient on the outside, the patient runs the risk that even a warmhearted functionary may, on occasion, tell him to wait until she has finished an informal chat, or teasingly ask why he wants what he has asked for, or respond with a dead pause and a cold look of appraisal.

Moving up and down the ward system means, then, not only a shift in self-constructive equipment, a shift in reflected status, but also a change in the calculus of risks. Appreciation of risks to his self-conception is part of everyone's moral experience, but an appreciation that a given risk level is itself merely a social arrangement is a rarer kind of experience, and one that seems to help to disenchant the person who undergoes it.

A third instance of moral loosening has to do with the conditions that are often associated with the release of the inpatient. Often he leaves under the supervision and jurisdiction of his next-of-relation or of a specially selected and specially watchful employer. If he misbehaves while under their auspices, they can quickly obtain his readmission. He therefore finds himself under the special power of persons who ordinarily would not have this kind of power over him, and about whom, moreover, he may have had prior cause to feel quite bitter. In order to get out of the hospital, however, he may conceal his displeasure in this arrangement, and, at least until safely off the hospital rolls, act out a willingness to accept this kind of custody. These discharge proceedings, then, provide a built-in lesson in overtly taking a role without the usual covert commitments, and seem further to separate the person from the worlds that others take seriously.

The moral career of a person of a given social category involves a standard sequence of changes in his way of conceiving of selves, including, importantly, his own. These half-buried lines of development can be followed by studying his moral experiences—that is, happenings which mark a turning point in the way in which the person views the world—although the particularities of this view may be difficult to establish. And note can be taken of overt tacks or strategies—that is, stands that he effectively takes before specifiable others, whatever the hidden and variable nature of his inward attachments to these presentations. By taking note of moral experiences and overt personal stands, one can obtain a relatively objective tracing of relatively subjective matters.

Each moral career, and behind this, each self, occurs within the confines of an institutional system, whether a social establishment such as a mental hospital or a complex of personal and professional relationships. The self, then, can be seen as something that resides in the arrangements prevailing in a social system for its members. The self in this sense is not a property of the person to whom it is attributed, but dwells rather in the pattern of social control that is exerted in connection with the person by himself and those around him. This special kind of institutional arrangement does not so much support the self as constitute it.

In this paper, two of these institutional arrangements have been considered, by pointing to what happens to the person when these rulings are weakened. The first concerns the felt loyalty of his next-of-relation. The prepatient's self is described as a function of the way in which three roles are related, arising and declining in the kinds of affiliation that occur between the next-of-relation and the mediators. The second concerns the protection required by the person for the version of himself which he presents to others, and the way in which the withdrawal of this protection can form a systematic, if unintended, aspect of the working of an establishment. I want to stress that these are only two kinds of institutional rulings from which a self emerges for the participant; others, not considered in this paper, are equally important.

In the usual cycle of adult socialization one expects to find alienation and mortification followed by a new set of beliefs about the world and a new way of conceiving of selves. In the case of the mental-hospital patient, this rebirth does sometimes occur, taking the form of a strong belief in the psychiatric perspective, or, briefly at least, a devotion to the social cause of better treatment for mental patients. The moral career of the mental patient has unique interest, however; it can illustrate the possibility that in casting off the raiments of the old self—or in having this cover torn away—the person need not seek a new robe and a new audience before which to cower. Instead he can learn, at least for a time, to practise before all groups the amoral arts of shamelessness.

THIRTY-SEVEN

ON BEING SANE IN INSANE PLACES

D. L. ROSENHAN

If sanity and insanity exist, how shall we know them?

The question is neither capricious nor itself insane. However much we may be personally convinced that we can tell the normal from the abnormal, the evidence is simply not compelling. It is commonplace, for example, to read about murder trials wherein eminent psychiatrists for the defense are contradicted by equally eminent psychiatrists for the prosecution on the matter of the defendant's sanity. More generally, there are a great deal of conflicting data on the reliability, utility, and meaning of such terms as "sanity," "insanity," "mental illness," and "schizophrenia."[1] Finally, as early as 1934, Benedict suggested that normality and abnormality are not universal.[2] What is viewed as normal in one culture may be seen as quite aberrant in another. Thus, notions of normality and abnormality may not be quite as accurate as people believe they are.

To raise questions regarding normality and abnormality is in no way to question the fact that some behaviors are deviant or odd. Murder is deviant. So, too, are hallucinations. Nor does raising such questions deny the existence of the personal anguish that is often associated with "mental illness." Anxiety and depression exist. Psychological suffering exists. But normality and abnormality, sanity and insanity, and the diagnoses that flow from them may be less substantive than many believe them to be.

At its heart, the question of whether the sane can be distinguished from the insane (and whether degrees of insanity can be distinguished from each other) is a simple matter: do the salient characteristics that lead to diagnoses reside in the patients themselves or in the environments and contexts in which observers find them? From Bleuler, through Kretchmer, through the formulators of the recently revised *Diagnostic and Statistical Manual* of the American Psychiatric Association, the belief has been strong that patients present symptoms, that those symptoms can be categorized, and, implicitly, that the sane are distinguishable from the insane. More recently, however, this belief has been questioned. Based in part on theoretical and anthropological considerations, but also on philosophical, legal, and therapeutic ones, the view has grown that psychological categorization of mental illness is useless at best and downright

SOURCE: D. L. Rosenhan. "On Being Sane in Insane Places." Copyright by the American Association for the Advancement of Science, 1973. D. L. Rosenhan, "On Being Sane in Insane Places," *Science*, CLXXIX (January, 1973), pp. 250–258. Reprinted by permission of the Association for the Advancement of Science.

harmful, misleading, and pejorative at worst. Psychiatric diagnoses, in this view, are in the minds of the observers and are not valid summaries of characteristics displayed by the observed.[3,4,5]

Gains can be made in deciding which of these is more nearly accurate by getting normal people (that is, people who do not have, and have never suffered, symptoms of serious psychiatric disorders) admitted to psychiatric hospitals and then determining whether they were discovered to be sane and, if so, how. If the sanity of such pseudopatients were always detected, there would be prima facie evidence that a sane individual can be distinguished from the insane context in which he is found. Normality (and presumably abnormality) is distinct enough that it can be recognized wherever it occurs, for it is carried within the person. If, on the other hand, the sanity of the pseudopatients were never discovered, serious difficulties would arise for those who support traditional modes of psychiatric diagnosis. Given that the hospital staff was not incompetent, that the pseudopatient had been behaving as sanely as he had been outside of the hospital, and that it had never been previously suggested that he belonged in a psychiatric hospital, such an unlikely outcome would support the view that psychiatric diagnosis betrays little about the patient but much about the environment in which an observer finds him.

This article describes such an experiment. Eight sane people gained secret admission to 12 different hospitals.[6] Their diagnostic experiences constitute the data of the first part of this article; the remainder is devoted to a description of their experiences in psychiatric institutions. Too few psychiatrists and psychologists, even those who have worked in such hospitals, know what the experience is like. They rarely talk about it with former patients, perhaps because they distrust information coming from the previously insane. Those who have worked in psychiatric hospitals are likely to have adapted so thoroughly to the settings that they are insensitive to the impact of that experience. And while there have been occasional reports of researchers who submitted themselves to psychiatric hospitalization.[7] These researchers have commonly remained in the hospitals for short periods of time, often with the knowledge of the hospital staff. It is difficult to know the extent to which they were treated like patients or like research colleagues. Nevertheless, their reports about the inside of the psychiatric hospital have been valuable. This article extends those efforts.

PSEUDOPATIENTS AND THEIR SETTINGS

The eight pseudopatients were a varied group. One was a psychology graduate student in his 20's. The remaining seven were older and "established." Among them were three psychologists, a pediatrician, a psychiatrist, a painter, and a housewife. Three pseudopatients were women, five were men. All of them employed pseudonyms, lest their alleged diagnoses embarrass them later. Those who were in mental health professions alleged another occupation in order to avoid the special attentions that might be accorded by staff, as a matter of courtesy or caution, to ailing colleagues.[8] With the exception of myself (I was the first pseudopatient and my presence was known to the hospital administrator and chief psychologist and, so far as I can tell, to them alone), the presence of pseudopatients and the nature of the research program was not known to the hospital staffs.[9]

The settings were similarly varied. In order to generalize the findings, admission into a variety of hospitals was sought. The 12 hospitals in the sample were located in five different states on the East and West coasts. Some were old and shabby, some were quite new. Some were research-oriented, others not. Some had good staff-patient ratios, others were quite understaffed. Only one was a strictly private hospital. All of the others were supported by state or federal funds or, in one instance, by university funds.

After calling the hospital for an appointment, the pseudopatient arrived at the admissions office complaining that he had been hearing voices.

Asked what the voices said, he replied that they were often unclear, but as far as he could tell they said "empty," "hollow," and "thud". The voices were unfamiliar and were of the same sex as the pseudopatient. The choice of these symptoms was occasioned by their apparent similarity to existential symptoms. Such symptoms are alleged to arise from painful concerns about the perceived meaninglessness of one's life. It is as if the hallucinating person were saying, "My life is empty and hollow". The choice of these symptoms was also determined by the *absence* of a single report of existential psychoses in the literature.

Beyond alleging the symptoms and falsifying name, vocation, and employment, no further alterations of person, history, or circumstances were made. The significant events of the pseudopatient's life history were presented as they had actually occurred. Relationships with parents and siblings, with spouse and children, with people at work and in school, consistent with the aforementioned exceptions, were described as they were or had been. Frustrations and upsets were described along with joys and satisfactions. These facts are important to remember. If anything, they strongly biased the subsequent results in favor of detecting sanity, since none of their histories or current behaviors were seriously pathological in any way.

Immediately upon admission to the psychiatric ward, the pseudopatient ceased simulating *any* symptoms of abnormality. In some cases, there was a brief period of mild nervousness and anxiety, since none of the pseudopatients really believed that they would be admitted so easily. Indeed, their shared fear was that they would be immediately exposed as frauds and greatly embarrassed. Moreover, many of them had never visited a psychiatric ward; even those who had, nevertheless had some genuine fears about what might happen to them. Their nervousness, then, was quite appropriate to the novelty of the hospital setting, and it abated rapidly.

Apart from that short-lived nervousness, the pseudopatient behaved on the ward as he "normally" behaved. The pseudopatient spoke to patients and staff as he might ordinarily. Because there is uncommonly little to do on a psychiatric ward, he attempted to engage others in conversation. When asked by staff how he was feeling, he indicated that he was fine, that he no longer experienced symptoms. He responded to instructions from attendants, to calls for medication (which was not swallowed), and to dining-hall instructions. Beyond such activities as were available to him on the admissions ward, he spent his time writing down his observations about the ward, its patients, and the staff. Initially these notes were written "secretly," but as it soon became clear that no one much cared, they were subsequently written on standard tablets of paper in such public places as the dayroom. No secret was made of these activities.

The pseudopatient, very much as a true psychiatric patient, entered a hospital with no foreknowledge of when he would be discharged. Each was told that he would have to get out by his own devices, essentially by convincing the staff that he was sane. The psychological stresses associated with hospitalization were considerable, and all but one of the pseudopatients desired to be discharged almost immediately after being admitted. They were, therefore, motivated not only to behave sanely, but to be paragons of cooperation. That their behavior was in no way disruptive is confirmed by nursing reports, which have been obtained on most of the patients. These reports uniformly indicate that the patients were "friendly", "cooperative," and "exhibited no abnormal indications."

THE NORMAL ARE NOT DETECTABLY SANE

Despite their public "show" of sanity, the pseudopatients were never detected. Admitted, except in one case, with a diagnosis of schizophrenia,[10] each was discharged with a diagnosis of schizophrenia "in remission." The label "in remission'' should in no way be dismissed as a formality, for at no time during any hospitalization had any question been raised about any pseudopatient's simulation. Nor are there any indications in the hospital records that the pseudopatient's status was suspect. Rather, the evidence is strong that, once labeled schizophrenic, the pseudopatient was stuck with that label. If the pseudopatient was to be discharged, he must naturally be ''in remission''; but he was not sane, nor, in the institution's view, had he ever been sane.

The uniform failure to recognize sanity cannot be attributed to the quality of the hospitals, for, although there were considerable variations among them, several are considered excellent. Nor can it be alleged that there was simply not enough time to observe the pseudopatients. Length of hospitalization ranged from 7 to 52 days, with an average of 19 days. The pseudopatients were not, in fact, carefully observed, but this failure clearly speaks more to traditions within psychiatric hospitals than to lack of opportunity.

Finally, it cannot be said that the failure to recognize the pseudopatients' sanity was due to the fact that they were not behaving sanely. While there was clearly some tension present in all of them, their daily visitors could detect no serious behavioral consequences—nor, indeed, could other patients. It was quite common for the patients to ''detect'' the pseudopatients' sanity. During the first three hospitalizations, when accurate counts were kept, 35 of a total of 118 patients on the admissions ward voiced their suspicions, some vigorously. ''You're not crazy. You're a journalist, or a professor [referring to the continual note-taking]. You're checking up on the hospital.'' While most of the patients were reassured by the pseudopatient's insistence that he had been sick before he came in but was fine now, some continued to believe that the pseudopatient was sane throughout his hospitalization.[11] The fact that the patients often recognized normality when staff did not raises important questions.

Failure to detect sanity during the course of hospitalization may be due to the fact that physicians operate with a strong bias toward what statisticians call the type 2 error.[5] This is to say that physicians are more inclined to call a healthy person sick (a false positive, type 2) than a sick person healthy (a false negative, type 1). The reasons for this are not hard to find: it is clearly more dangerous to misdiagnose illness than health. Better to err on the side of caution, to suspect illness even among the healthy.

But what holds for medicine does not hold equally well for psychiatry. Medical illnesses, while unfortunate, are not commonly pejorative. Psychiatric diagnoses, on the contrary, carry with them personal, legal, and social stigmas.[12] It was therefore important to see whether the tendency toward diagnosing the sane insane could be reversed. The following experiment was arranged at a research and teaching hospital whose staff had heard these findings but doubted that such an error could occur in their hospital. The staff was informed that at some time during the following 3 months, one or more pseudopatients would attempt to be admitted into the psychiatric hospital. Each staff member was asked to rate each patient who presented himself at admissions or on the ward according to the likelihood that the patient was a pseudopatient. A 10-point scale was used, with a 1 and 2 reflecting high confidence that the patient was a pseudopatient.

Judgments were obtained on 193 patients who were admitted for psychiatric treatment. All staff who had had sustained contact with or primary responsibility for the patient—attendants, nurses, psychiatrists, physicians, and psychologists—were asked to make judgments. Forty-one patients were alleged, with high confidence, to be pseudopatients by at least one member of the staff. Twenty-three were considered suspect by at least one psychiatrist. Nineteen were suspected by one psychiatrist *and* one other staff member. Actually, no genuine pseudopatient (at least from my group) presented himself during this period.

The experiment is instructive. It indicates that

the tendency to designate sane people as insane can be reversed when the stakes (in this case, prestige and diagnostic acumen) are high. But what can be said of the 19 people who were suspected by being "sane" by one psychiatrist and another staff member? Were these people truly "sane", or was it rather the case that in the course of avoiding the type 2 error the staff tended to make more errors of the first sort—calling the crazy "sane"? There is no way of knowing. But one thing is certain: any diagnostic process that lends itself so readily to massive errors of this sort cannot be a very reliable one.

THE STICKINESS OF PSYCHODIAGNOSTIC LABELS

Beyond the tendency to call the healthy sick—a tendency that accounts better for diagnostic behavior on admission than it does for such behavior after a lengthy period of exposure—the data speak to the massive role of labeling in psychiatric assessment. Having once been labeled schizophrenic, there is nothing the pseudopatient can do to overcome the tag. The tag profoundly colors others' perceptions of him and his behavior.

From one viewpoint, these data are hardly surprising, for it has long been known that elements are given meaning by the context in which they occur. Gestalt psychology made this point vigorously, and Asch[13] demonstrated that there are "central" personality traits (such as "warm" versus "cold") which are so powerful that they markedly color the meaning of other information in forming an impression of a given personality.[14] "Insane," "schizophrenic," "manic-depressive," and "crazy" are probably among the most powerful of such central traits. Once a person is designated abnormal, all of his other behaviors and characteristics are colored by that label. Indeed, that label is so powerful that many of the pseudopatients' normal behaviors were overlooked entirely or profoundly misinterpreted. Some examples may clarify this issue.

Earlier I indicated that there were no changes in the pseudopatient's personal history and current status beyond those of name, employment, and, where necessary, vocation. Otherwise, a veridical description of personal history and circumstances was offered. Those circumstances were not psychotic. How were they made consonant with the diagnosis of psychosis? Or were those diagnoses modified in such a way as to bring them into accord with the circumstances of the pseudopatient's life, as described by him?

As far as I can determine, diagnoses were in no way affected by the relative health of the circumstances of a pseudopatient's life. Rather, the reverse occurred: the perception of his circumstances was shaped entirely by the diagnosis. A clear example of such translation is found in the case of a pseudopatient who had had a close relationship with his mother but was rather remote from his father during his early childhood. During adolescence and beyond, however, his father became a close friend, while his relationship with his mother cooled. His present relationship with his wife was characteristically close and warm. Apart from occasional angry exchanges, friction was minimal. The children had rarely been spanked. Surely there is nothing especially pathological about such a history. Indeed, many readers may see a similar pattern in their own experiences, with no markedly deleterious consequences. Observe, however, how such a history was translated in the psychopathological context, this from the case summary prepared after the patient was discharged.

> This white 39-year-old male . . . manifests a long history of considerable ambivalence in close relationships, which begins in early childhood. A warm relationship with his mother cools during his adolescence. A distant relationship to his father is described as becoming very intense. Affective stability is absent. His attempts to control emotionality with his wife and children are punctuated by angry outbursts and, in the case of the children, spankings. And while he says that he has several good friends, one

senses considerable ambivalence embedded in those relationships also. . . .

The facts of the case were unintentionally distorted by the staff to achieve consistency with a popular theory of the dynamics of a schizophrenic reaction.[15] Nothing of an ambivalent nature had been described in relations with parents, spouse, or friends. To the extent that ambivalence could be inferred, it was probably not greater than is found in all human relationships. It is true the pseudopatient's relationships with his parents changed over time, but in the ordinary context that would hardly be remarkable—indeed, it might very well be expected. Clearly, the meaning ascribed to his verbalizations (that is, ambivalence, affective instability) was determined by the diagnosis: schizophrenia. An entirely different meaning would have been ascribed if it were known that the man was "normal."

All pseudopatients took extensive notes publicly. Under ordinary circumstances, such behavior would have raised questions in the minds of observers, as, in fact, it did among patients. Indeed, it seemed so certain that the notes would elicit suspicion that elaborate precautions were taken to remove them from the ward each day. But the precautions proved needless. The closest any staff member came to questioning these notes occurred when one pseudopatient asked his physician what kind of medication he was receiving and began to write down the response. "You needn't write it," he was told gently. "If you have trouble remembering, just ask me again."

If no questions were asked of the pseudopatients, how was their writing interpreted? Nursing records for three patients indicate that the writing was seen as an aspect of their pathological behavior. "Patient engages in writing behavior" was the daily nursing comment on one of the pseudopatients who was never questioned about his writing. Given that the patient is in the hospital, he must be psychologically disturbed. And given that he is disturbed, continuous writing must be a behavioral

manifestation of that disturbance, perhaps a subset of the compulsive behaviors that are sometimes correlated with schizophrenia.

One tacit characteristic of psychiatric diagnosis is that it locates the sources of aberration within the individual and only rarely within the complex of stimuli that surrounds him. Consequently, behaviors that are stimulated by the environment are commonly misattributed to the patient's disorder. For example, one kindly nurse found a pseudopatient pacing the long hospital corridors. "Nervous, Mr. X?" she asked. "No, bored," he said.

The notes kept by pseudopatients are full of patient behaviors that were misinterpreted by well-intentioned staff. Often enough, a patient would go "berserk" because he had, wittingly or unwittingly, been mistreated by, say, an attendant. A nurse coming upon the scene would rarely inquire even cursorily into the environmental stimuli of the patient's behavior. Rather, she assumed that his upset derived from his pathology, not from his present interactions with other staff members. Occasionally, the staff might assume that the patient's family (especially when they had recently visited) or other patients had stimulated the outburst. But never were the staff found to assume that one of themselves or the structure of the hospital had anything to do with a patient's behavior. One psychiatrist pointed to a group of patients who were sitting outside the cafeteria entrance half an hour before lunchtime. To a group of young residents he indicated that such behavior was characteristic of the oral-acquisitive nature of the syndrome. It seemed not to occur to him that there were very few things to anticipate in a psychiatric hospital besides eating.

A psychiatric label has a life and an influence of its own. Once the impression has been formed that the patient is schizophrenic, the expectation is that he will continue to be schizophrenic. When a sufficient amount of time has passed, during which the patient has done nothing bizarre, he is considered to be in remission and available for discharge. But the label endures beyond discharge, with the unconfirmed expectation that he will behave as a schizophrenic again. Such labels, conferred by mental health professionals, are as influential on the patient as they are on his relatives and friends, and it should not surprise anyone that the diagnosis acts on all of them as a self-fulfilling prophecy. Eventually, the patient himself accepts the diagnosis, with all of its surplus meanings and expectations, and behaves accordingly.

The inferences to be made from these matters are quite simple. Much as Zigler and Phillips have demonstrated that there is enormous overlap in the symptoms presented by patients who have been variously diagnosed,[16] so there is enormous overlap in the behaviors of the sane and the insane. The sane are not "sane" all of the time. We lose our tempers "for no good reason." We are occasionally depressed or anxious, again for no good reason. And we may find it difficult to get along with one or another person—again for no reason that we can specify. Similarly, the insane are not always insane. Indeed, it was the impression of the pseudopatients while living with them that they were sane for long periods of time—that the bizarre behaviors upon which their diagnoses were allegedly predicated constituted only a small fraction of their total behavior. If it makes no sense to label ourselves permanently depressed on the basis of an occasional depression, then it takes better evidence than is presently available to label all patients insane or schizophrenic on the basis of bizarre behaviors or cognitions. It ·seems more useful, as Mischel[17] has pointed out, to limit our discussions to *behaviors*, the stimuli that provoke them, and their correlates.

It is not known why powerful impressions of personality traits, such as "crazy" or "insane," arise. Conceivably, when the origins of and stimuli that give rise to a behavior are remote or unknown, or when the behavior strikes us as immutable, trait labels regarding the *behaver* arise. When, on the other hand, the origins and stimuli are known and available, discourse is limited to the behavior itself. Thus, I may hallucinate because I am

sleeping, or I may hallucinate because I have ingested a peculiar drug. These are termed sleep-induced hallucinations, or dreams, and drug-induced hallucinations, respectively. But when the stimuli to my hallucinations are unknown, that is called craziness, or schizophrenia—as if that inference were somehow as illuminating as the others. . . .

THE CONSEQUENCES OF LABELING AND DEPERSONALIZATION

Whenever the ratio of what is known to what needs to be known approaches zero, we tend to invent "knowledge" and assume that we understand more than we actually do. We seem unable to acknowledge that we simply don't know. The needs for diagnosis and remediation of behavioral and emotional problems are enormous. But rather than acknowledge that we are just embarking on understanding, we continue to label patients "schizophrenic," "manic-depressive," and "insane," as if in those words we had captured the essence of understanding. The facts of the matter are that we have known for a long time that diagnoses are often not useful or reliable, but we have nevertheless continued to use them. We now know that we cannot distinguish insanity from sanity. It is depressing to consider how that information will be used.

Not merely depressing, but frightening. How many people, one wonders, are sane but not recognized as such in our psychiatric institutions? How many have been needlessly stripped of their privileges of citizenship, from the right to vote and drive to that of handling their own accounts? How many have feigned insanity in order to avoid the criminal consequences of their behavior, and, conversely, how many would rather stand trial than live interminably in a psychiatric hospital—but are wrongly thought to be mentally ill? How many have been stigmatized by well-intentioned, but nevertheless erroneous, diagnoses? On the last point, recall again that a "type 2 error" in psychiatric diagnosis does not have the same consequences it does in medical diagnosis. A diagnosis of cancer that has been found to be in error is cause for celebration. But psychiatric diagnoses are rarely found to be in error. The label sticks, a mark of inadequacy forever.

NOTES

1. P. Ash, *J. Abnorm. Soc. Psychol.* 44, 272 (1949); A. T. Beck, *Amer. J. Psychiat.* 119, 210 (1962); A. T. Boisen, *Psychiatry* 2, 233 (1938); N. Kreitman, *J. Ment. Sci.* 107, 876 (1961); N. Kreitman, P. Sainsbury, J. Morrisey, J. Towers, J. Scrivener, *ibid.*, p. 887; H. O. Schmitt and C. P. Fonda, *J. Abnorm. Soc. Psychol.* 52, 262 (1956); W. Seeman, *J. Nerv. Ment. Dis.* 118, 541 (1953). For an analysis of these artifacts and summaries of the disputes, see J. Zubin, *Annu. Rev. Psychol.* 18, 373 (1967); L. Phillips and J. G. Draguns, *ibid.* 22, 447 (1971).

2. R. Benedict, *J. Gen. Psychol.* 10, 59 (1934).

3. See in this regard H. Becker, *Outsiders: Studies in the Sociology of Deviance* (Free Press, New York, 1963); B. M. Braginsky, D. D. Braginsky, K. Ring, *Methods of Madness: The Mental Hospital as a Last Resort* (Holt, Rinehart & Winston, New York, 1969); G. M. Crocetti and P. V. Lemkau, *Amer. Sociol. Rev.* 30, 577 (1965); E. Goffman, *Behavior in Public Places* (Free Press, New York, 1964); R. D. Laing, *The Divided Self: A Study of Sanity and Madness* (Quadrangle, Chicago, 1960); D. L. Phillips, *Amer. Sociol. Rev.* 28, 963 (1963); T. R. Sarbin, *Psychol. Today* 6, 18 (1972); E. Schur, *Amer. J. Sociol.* 75, 309 (1969); T. Szasz, *Law, Liberty and Psychiatry* (Macmillan, New York, 1963); *The Myth of Mental Illness: Foundations of a Theory of Mental Illness* (Hoeber Harper, New York, 1963). For a critique of some of these views, see W. R. Gove. *Amer. Sociol. Rev.* 35, 873 (1970).

4. E. Goffman, *Asylums* (Doubleday, Garden City, N.Y., 1961).

5. T. J. Scheff, *Being Mentally Ill: A Sociological Theory* (Aldine, Chicago, 1966).

6. Data from a ninth pseudopatient are not incorporated in this report because, although his sanity went undetected, he falsified aspects of his personal history, including his marital status and parental relationships.

His experimental behaviors therefore were not identical to those of the other pseudopatients.

7. A. Barry, *Bellevue Is a State of Mind* (Harcourt Brace Jovanovich, New York, 1971); I. Belknap, *Human Problems of a State Mental Hospital* (McGraw Hill, New York, 1956); W. Caudill, F. C. Redlich, H. R. Gilmore, E. B. Brody, *Amer. J. Orthopsychiat.* 22, 314 (1952); A. R. Goldman, R. H. Bohr, T. A. Steinberg, *Prof. Psychol.* 1, 427 (1970); unauthored, *Roche Report* 1 (No. 13), 8 (1971).

8. Beyond the personal difficulties that the pseudopatient is likely to experience in the hospital, there are legal and social ones that, combined, require considerable attention before entry. For example, once admitted to a psychiatric institution, it is difficult, if not impossible, to be discharged on short notice, state law to the contrary notwithstanding. I was not sensitive to these difficulties at the outset of the project, nor to the personal and situational emergencies that can arise, but later a writ of habeas corpus was prepared for each of the entering pseudopatients and an attorney was kept "on call" during every hospitalization. I am grateful to John Kaplan and Robert Bartels for legal advice and assistance in these matters.

9. However distasteful such concealment is, it was a necessary first step to examining these questions. Without concealment, there would have been no way to know how valid these experiences were; nor was there any way of knowing whether whatever detections occurred were a tribute to the diagnostic acumen of the staff or to the hospital's rumor network. Obviously, since my concerns are general ones that cut across individual hospitals and staffs, I have respected their anonymity and have eliminated clues that might lead to their identification.

10. Interestingly, of the 12 admissions, 11 were diagnosed as schizophrenic and one, with the identical symptomatology, as manic-depressive psychosis. This diagnosis has a more favorable prognosis, and it was given by the only private hospital in our sample. On the relations between social class and psychiatric diagnosis, see A. B. Hollingshead and F. C. Redlich, *Social Class and Mental Illness: A Community Study* (Wiley, New York, 1958).

11. It is possible, of course, that patients have quite broad latitudes in diagnosis and therefore are inclined to call many people sane, even those whose behavior is patently aberrant. However, although we have no hard data on this matter, it was our distinct impression that this was not the case. In many instances, patients not only singled us out for attention, but came to imitate our behaviors and styles.

12. J. Cumming and E. Cumming, *Community Ment. Health* 1, 135 (1965); A. Farina and K. Ring, *J. Abnorm. Psychol.* 70, 47 (1965); H. E. Freeman and O. G. Simmons, *The Mental Patient Comes Home* (Wiley, New York, 1963); W. J. Johannsen, *Ment. Hygiene* 53, 218 (1969); A. S. Linsky, *Soc. Psychiat.* 5, 166 (1970).

13. S. E. Asch, *J. Abnorm. Soc. Psychol.* 41, 258 (1946); *Social Psychology* (Prentice-Hall, New York, 1952).

14. See also I. N. Mensh and J. Wishner, *J. Personality* 16, 188 (1947); J. Wishner, *Psychol. Rev.* 67, 96 (1960); J. S. Bruner and R. Tagiuri, in *Handbook of Social Psychology,* G. Lindzey, Ed. (Addison-Wesley, Cambridge, Mass, 1954), vol. 2, pp. 634−654; J. S. Bruner, D. Shapiro. R. Tagiuri, in *Person Perception and Interpersonal Behavior,* R. Tagiuri and L. Petrullo, Eds. (Stanford Univ. Press, Stanford, Calif., 1958), pp. 277−288.

15. For an example of a similar self-fulfilling prophecy, in this instance dealing with the "central" trait of intelligence, see R. Rosenthal and L. Jacobson, *Pygmalion in the Classroom* (Holt, Rinehart & Winston, New York, 1968).

16. E. Zigler and L. Phillips, *J. Abnorm. Soc. Psychol.* 63, 69 (1961). See also R. K. Freudenberg and J. P. Robertson, *A.M.A. Arch. Neurol. Psychiatr.* 76, 14 (1956).

17. W. Mischel, *Personality and Assessment* (Wiley, New York, 1968).

PART SEVEN

DEVELOPMENTS AND DEBATES

Over a decade ago—1964 to be exact—Manford Kuhn published a review of the previous twenty-five years of work in symbolic interaction.[1] Picking up where Kuhn left off, David Maines provides a review of the major developments in the perspective beginning with 1962 and coming up to about 1980. However, where Kuhn thematized his review along the determinancy-indeterminancy continuum, and effectively emphasized what he perceived to be an underlying fissure in the perspective (between those who had a humanistic bent and those who saw man as determined), Maines ignores this (alleged) split and, instead, categorizes recent work by topical area. He organizes his review into three categories: (1) related theoretical areas, (2) social organization, and (3) research techniques.

Under the heading of "related theoretical areas," Maines identifies, distinguishes, and compares the principal features of phenomenology-ethnomethodology, labeling theory, sociolinguistics, interaction processes and strategic interaction. He also gives passing attention to critical theory, and attribution theory. Under the rubric "social organization," he points to the potential interface between symbolic interaction and cybernetics as well as to advances made within the area of "negotiated order" theory. Underlying his review of these two areas, Maines manifests an implicit concern for how well each of these developments deals with the processes of "power" and "structure"—conceptual dimensions of increasing interest to interactionists.

Within the classification "research techniques," Maines reports on (1) the declining use of the "Twenty Statements Test" (which measures self-conception), (2) the increasing use of "videotape" (which enables repeated analysis of emerging behavior), (3) the broader use of "multiple site" qualitative field studies (which enable naturalistic comparisions), and (4) the innovative use of "historical analysis" and "quantitative analysis" as background material for qualitative analysis.

Since one of the areas of ongoing debate has been generated by the interface between

---

[1]. Manford H. Kuhn, "Major Trends in Symbolic Interaction Theory in the Past Twenty-Five Years," *Sociological Quarterly*, V (Winter, 1964), pp. 61–84.

symbolic interaction and phenomenology-ethnomethodology, we have included an article by Robert S. Perinbanayagam entitled "The Significance of Others in the Thought of Alfred Schutz, G. H. Mead and C. H. Cooley." After examining Schutz's formulation of the "general thesis of the alter-ego," "the reciprocity of perspectives," and the "we relationship," Perinbanayagam asserts that, contrary to uncovering an integral view of "other," these notions depict an isolated, discrete subjectivity that merely exists but does not interexist with others. Underlying Schutz's work is a conception of an atomistic, *a priori,* universalistic ego. Perinbanayagam contends that Mead, in his intrinsically social conception of self, and Cooley, in his social-emotional conception of the primary group, provide an integral formulation of self and other. The self develops in, through, against, because of, and, often, despite others. Where there is other, there can be self: other is the interactional, epistemological, and ontological condition of self—an obdurate reality eluded only through death and insanity. Perinbanayagam thus discloses the pitfalls attending orientations that meta-theoretically arise from overly subjectivistic presumptions and he defends an interactional orientation that provides for an objective sphere of experience in which self and other can interexist.

Finally, we include David Rauma's article entitled "Herbert Blumer, the Scientific Attitude, and the Problem of Demarcation," which is a revision of a paper that won the undergraduate student competition prize of the Midwest Sociological Society in 1976. In this paper, Rauma reviews the properties of demonstrative versus nondemonstrative and amplative versus nonamplative forms of inference and notes that, as yet, there is no system of inductive logic that can separate correct from incorrect inferences. The best way to fill the breach is with Blumer's recommendation to adopt an attitude that encourages investigators to develop "sensitizing concepts" calling for continuing refinement through contact with the empirical world. This research attitude invites a perpetual search for the negative or exceptional instance which, in turn, mobilizes a further refinement in the concept. This logic of return and refinement demands respect for the integrity of the empirical world and insures the empirical content of the concept. In a sense, it is another, but differently formulated, call for "grounded theory."[2]

---

[2]Barney G. Glazer and Anselm L. Strauss. *The Discovery of Grounded Theory* (Chicago: Aldine Publishing Co., 1967).

THIRTY-EIGHT

RECENT DEVELOPMENTS IN SYMBOLIC INTERACTION

DAVID R. MAINES

I suspect that essays such as this, which attempt to assess shifts and movements within a definable area of an academic discipline, rest on assumptions and goals lying just beneath the publicly announced objective of the assessment itself. Such was the case with Manford Kuhn's (1964) analysis of trends in symbolic interactionism. He viewed the subtypes of that perspective as spinning off from the determinancy-indeterminancy axis,[1] which by any measure represents a fundamentally central principle in the analysis of human conduct. But that principle merged with Kuhn's faith and hope regarding the transformation of symbolic interactionism into a truly scientific program, and as such he revealed himself as an advocate of traditional science. Kuhn's assessment, as such assessments must be, was thus cast and proferred within a value framework. While objective analyses in this sense are not possible, however, the changes, substantive and conceptual solidifications, and controversies found in areas of sociology can facilitate and perhaps even necessitate

SOURCE: David R. Maines. "Recent Developments in Symbolic Interaction." Original paper prepared especially for this volume, 1980. Used by permission of the author.

their evaluation. Correspondingly, the springboard for this essay rests in the very advances made within symbolic interactionism since Kuhn's paper of well over a decade ago.[2]

I have tried to keep two things in mind in writing this essay. First, I am writing primarily for the student, since most professionals working in the field of social psychology are generally aware of the major developments in the perspective. Second, as a rough temporal benchmark and point of departure, I have used Arnold Rose's *Human Behavior and Social Processes,* although material that predates that volume will be included in those instances where a more encompassing continuity seems warranted. Within this time period of nearly decades, I have sought to place the literature in five categories: (1) theoretical areas closely related to symbolic interactionism, (2) interaction processes, (3) strategic interaction, (4) social organization, and (5) methods. By virtue of the very nature of that literature, of course, these categories cannot be mutually exclusive, and so in the analysis of certain specific cases I have had to be somewhat arbitrary. In the end, they are designed primarily for purposes of presentation and organization rather than as a set of indicators of what ultimately must constitute the structure of the perspective. Because of the breadth of the essay, moreover, I will not be able to give each section the kind of depth it deserves. Thus, my attempt is to highlight the significant developments in symbolic interactionist thought of recent years, and my hope is that students will be sufficiently stimulated to inquire further on their own.[3]

RELATED THEORETICAL AREAS

While it is difficult to isolate the specific elements involved in recent developments in symbolic interactionism, I suspect that among them is the inception of novel and closely related theoretical approaches and the resurgence of others. One such approach is critical sociology, or critical theory. People such as Ropers (1973), Lichtman (1970), and Bandyopathyay (1971) have echoed Bottomore's (1963) insistence of the vitality in a convergence of Marx and Mead, and others (Reynolds, 1973) have outlined the basic root images of critical theory. These images are remarkably similar to those found in symbolic interactionism: man is seen as active and creative, society is constituted of a dialectical process of freedom and constraint, and the problematic aspects of social life are viewed primarily as caught up in processes of social change. However, there are two areas lying at the core of critical theory which are less related to traditional approaches taken by symbolic interactionists. One is the contention, taken largely from C. Wright Mills, that the essential structure of society has a materialistic base which is lodged in massive and powerful social institutions, namely, political, military, and economic institutions. The second is the value commitment of critical theory. Whether expressed in general or particularistic terms, it advocates a praxis (the practical application of theory) orientation to the alleviation of human suffering and the enrichment of social life. It is in this latter sense that this perspective becomes "critical"; it is in

opposition to establishment perspectives and practices that function to perpetuate inequality, alienation, and other forms of institutionalized debasement.[4]

While not underemphasizing the significance of critical theory, I wish to devote more detail to discussions of three other areas that bear on symbolic interactionism. These areas are phenomenological sociology, labeling theory, and sociolinguistics.

PHENOMENOLOGICAL SOCIOLOGY

In considering phenomenological sociology and ethnomethodology, first it is important to note that their relationships to symbolic interactionism are rather unclear at this time. While some see them as quite distinct perspectives (Heap and Roth, 1973; Zimmerman and Wieder, 1970), others regard them as analytically very close (Wallace, 1969; Petras and Meltzer, 1973). In addition, there is some disagreement over which perspective is the more all-encompassing. Psathas (1973), Douglas (1973), and Schearing (1973) regard symbolic interactionism as a variant of phenomenological sociology, and Petras and Meltzer (1973) see the reverse relationship as the more appropriate view. Moreover, one begins to wonder about the utility of such comparisons when reading analyses such as that represented by Dreitzel (1970: viii) who, in the course of only one page of text, places the work of George H. Mead in both the realms of structural functionalism and phenomenology. Thus, the problem of boundary-identification exists, and in the course of the various debates, symbolic interactionism has been subjected to a good deal of status forcing. While functionalists (Coser, 1976) tend to relegate the perspective to just another brand of subjectivism, ethnomethodologists (Zimmerman and Wieder, 1970) tend to equate it with functionalism.[5] Furthermore, ethnomethodologists are prone to assert that symbolic interactionists, or anyone else for that matter, cannot possibly understand such distinctions and similarities unless they have been thoroughly trained in ethnomethodology (see Zimmerman, 1976 and Mehan and Wood, 1976 for an expression of this attitude).[6]

One approach in sorting out the differences between the two perspectives is to examine their domain assumptions. Both are concerned with and take as a major problem the production, transformation, and maintenance of meaning. In this sense, Denzin (1969) is accurate. At the core of these perspectives lies the contention that human activity hinges on matters of meaning, and thus any comparison on this score is bound to be a strategic one. For Mead, meaning arises from the conjoint adjustive responses of interacting persons.

> Meaning is thus not to be conceived fundamantally as a state of consciousness or as a set of organized relations existing or subsiding mentally outside the field of experience into which they enter; on the contrary, it should be conceived objectively as having its existence entirely within the field itself. The response of one organism to the gesture of another in any given social act is the meaning of that gesture (Mead, 1934:78).

Thus, there can be no meaning unless there is an *other*, whether that other is physically present, anticipated, or held in the memory. Meaning for the phenomenologist, however, originates in the stream of consciousness or experiences of the solitary ego. Note the following passage from Schutz.

> It is misleading to say that experiences have meaning. Meaning does not lie in experience. Rather, those experiences are meaningful which are grasped reflectively. The meaning is the way in which Ego regards its experience. The meaning lies in the attitude of the Ego toward that part of its stream of consciousness which has already flowed by, toward its "elapsed duration" (Schutz, 1967:69–70).

Phenomenology thus depends upon transcendental consciousness for its source of reality and meaning rather than interacting persons. Mead probably would conclude that in this respect phenomenology cannot embrace a processual view because the term "transcendental" refers to the "logical preexistence of the form of the object" (Mead, 1936:153). In that sense, it is a non-evolutionary concept. Meaning for the phenomenologist, therefore, lies outside of process and interpersonal transactions.[7]

This point of divergence is readily seen in instances of ethnomethodological research. Zimmerman (1974), for example, identifies the "investigative stance" of caseworkers in public assistance agencies. This stance, which represents the caseworker's organizational perspective, consists of a skepticism regarding an applicant's claim of eligibility for assistance. Zimmerman's analysis reveals how caseworkers handle problematic situations regarding agency documents, and how a sense of organizational order is "artfully accomplished." Caseworkers and applicants, each of whom had different and in some respects incompatible perspectives, however, are not seen as differentially entering into a dialogue and joint process of interaction. In other words, the ethnomethodological position of *the person and his personal experience* is adopted rather than the more fundamentally sociological view of *persons and their jointly constructed situations,* which is a central focus in symbolic interactionism.

Perinbanayagam's (1974, 1975) extensive analyses comparing ethnomethodology and symbolic interactionism lead to very similar conclusions: "In McHugh's and Garfinkel's work, the notion of responsive discourse, of mutuality of actions is absent" (1974:539). Similarly, Maryl concludes that phenomenology holds "an essentially individualistic theory of the self and the genesis of meaning" (1973:27). Together with other analysts (e.g., Farberman, 1970), these authors agree that, although there are "others" for phenomenologists, these others are conceived very differently. Whereas others enter into direct and manifest transactions from the standpoint of symbolic interactionism, such is not the case for phenomenology. There, others remain as basically passive subjects with no capacity for participation in processes through which meaning is constructed, transformed, and maintained. Rather, they become a part of the setting and are relegated to the status of just another feature of that setting. Accordingly, it is this very *asocial* imagery and conceptualization which should rest at the base of any pessimism concerning the compatibility of phenomenology and symbolic interactionism.

LABELING THEORY[8]

Labeling theory has a closer and much more comfortable relationship to symbolic interactionism. Although in the 1930s Tannenbaum and Sutherland attended somewhat to the labeling process and in the 1950s Lemert was working well within the perspective, labeling theory as an acknowledged frame of reference, according to Lindesmith et al. (1975:533–534), arose as a sort of accident in the 1960s. Howard Becker's now famous statement, "The deviant is one to whom that label has been successfully applied. . . ." (1963:9), was for him an application or logical derivative of symbolic interactionism, and was developed as an alternative to the functionalist view of deviance as mere rule-breaking. Becker conceptualized deviance as a defining process. The perspective somehow stuck, was identified as a perspective, and was transformed through the work of others. Therefore, Lindesmith et al. refer to the "labeling myth," and it was only later that Becker learned that he had "fathered" a school of thought.[9]

In the past decade, the labeling perspective has undergone considerable development and seems to have taken on proportions of its own. Trice and Roman (1970), for instance, regard it as a true paradigm, while Schur, who has reservations concerning that characterization, acknowledges "its powerful ability to codify, redirect, and organize analysis" (1971:35). With this insurgence and in

spite of its origins being squarely within symbolic interactionism, it is clear that labeling theory has taken on certain divergent directions, or at least can be thought of as involving emphases in its application which are new.

Even though labeling theory is far from coherent in terms of its advocate views and empirical application (N. Davis, 1972; Gibbs, 1966; Spector, 1976), it has effectively directed questions concerning the nature of deviance into the processes through which people are categorized, stigmatized, and defined. Deviance, in other words, is seen to lie not in the act itself but in the responses of various audiences to acts. In this sense, it seems to me that the newness of labeling theory rests in the fact that it contains an explicitly political perspective on social control. It extends beyond a simple micro-process account of typifications to an inquiry into the relations between and among segments of society and the interstitial mechanisms governing those relations. Central to issues of social control is the analysis of power arrangements that either maintain or alter the distribution of power resources. One such resource is the very rule structure in which conduct takes place. Becker (1963) has argued that deviance is a consequence of the selective application of certain rules and some people's invoking sanctions on others. Moreover, the invokers of rules tend to be "moral entrepreneurs," or those who are instrumental in deciding what conduct is to be regarded as deviant and/or are involved in the enforcement of those rules. A classic example of moral entrepreneurs is the activity of temperance leagues which led to the passing of the prohibition amendment (Gusfield, 1963). The crucial element in the labeling process, therefore, is power. Those who have power are more successful in defining the nature and meaning of activity, in using organizational arrangements and resources to act on those definitions, and in selectively enforcing rules that give form to definitions.

The labeling perspective has been criticized

primarily on three scores. Gibbs (1972) argues that the perspective contains vague concepts and is insufficient as a truly scientific theory; N. Davis (1972) insists that it is shot through with ideological bias; and Gove (1970) argues that the substance of labeling theory is incorrect. Scheff (1974) effectively deals with each of these criticisms, the most important of which is Gove's substantive critique. Scheff evaluates eighteen studies of the labeling of mental illness and shows that thirteen of them support the perspective while five do not. The most significant of these are the experimental study conducted by Temerlin (1968) and the naturalistic study by Rosenhan (1973). Temerlin showed that psychiatric diagnoses are strongly influenced by prior definitions of the state of a person's mental health. Rosenhan's investigation, however, which involved sane persons gaining admittance to mental hospitals as patients, revealed the power dimension of the labeling process. During the initial interview, each person in the study simulated certain psychotic symptoms, but upon admission to the ward, they immediately stopped the simulations. In all twelve hospitals studied, those who had been admitted through this procedure had tremendous difficulty establishing the fact of their sanity. The hospitalizations ranged from one to nearly eight weeks, and, on the basis of the data gathered, Rosenhan concluded that "the evidence is strong that once labeled schizophrenic, the pseudo-patient was stuck with the label" (1973:252). The issue in labeling theory, therefore, is not so much a matter of whether labeling a person as "mentally ill" has any organic relationship to functional disorders, as N. Davis (1972:458) and Gove (1974) argue, but of how the person, once labeled, is treated, processed, and categorized by various communities, organizations, and agencies. The evidence gathered so far demonstrates that labels, as representations and "carriers" of what is taken to be real, are highly instrumental in determining reactions to people once they have been categorized.

SOCIOLINGUISTICS

Unlike ethnomethodology and labeling theory, sociolinguistics refers to a substantive area rather than to a theoretical perspective. It may seem a bit odd to some to include this area in an essay devoted to "recent developments" because from its inception symbolic interactionism has emphasized language and the self, communication, and society. As Deutscher (1969–1970) has commented, however, symbolic interactionists have for the most part taken the importance of language per se for granted. By that assertion, Deutscher means that the analysis of language has been implicit rather than explicit in symbolic interactionist investigations. There are, of course, notable exceptions. Bain (1936), Mills (1939), Bossard (1943, 1945), Schatzman and Strauss (1955), Strauss (1959), and, more recently, Deutscher (1966, 1968, 1972, 1973) have provided explicit analyses of language. The late 1960s, however, witnessed a resurgence of sociolinguistics primarily in comparative analyses (e.g., Anderson, 1967; Cicourel, 1967), ethnomethodology (Garfinkel, 1967; Schegloff, 1968), and intergroup relations (e.g., Tucker and Lambert, 1969; Entwisle, 1968). It is this revitalization which justifies its being mentioned here.[10]

It is not essential that I devote a great deal of space in this essay to sociolinguistics simply because a number of excellent and recent reviews are available. Manning (1973) and Lindesmith et al. (1975), for example, provide good general discussions of the importance of language for understanding human group behavior, Denzin (1975) has reemphasized the role of language in the socialization process, and Grimshaw (1973, 1974) has written excellent reviews of nearly two dozen works in the area. Of particular interest in the Grimshaw essays is his coverage of the work of Basil Bernstein, William Labov, Joshua Fishman, and Dell Hymes. Each has made major contributions to sociolinguistics in the past decade.

Language can be considered from a variety of standpoints: the physiological basis of speech; grammar; form and mechanics; cross-cultural variations; and the like. Social psychologists tend to focus on language as behavior especially as it relates to other forms of behavior. Pavlov's (1927) advice is instructive in this respect. He noted that human language represents a "second signal system" which makes comparisons between human and nonhuman studies problematic. Like Mead, he insisted that human linguistic behavior has special distinguishing features—primarily in the human capacity for symbolization. The Bergers (1975) have carried this notion to its logical sociological conclusion. They imply that language is the fundamental and indispensable process giving rise to social facts by arguing not only that language makes social institutions possible but also that in fact it is itself an institution. In other words, language serves as a mechanism for bringing people together into instances of collective behavior (Whorf, 1956).

But language also sets people apart. Note the prevalence of "special languages" or argots. Not only does each society have its own native tongue, but also any number of subsections or social worlds within a society may develop idiosyncratic terms and modes of speech. Becker and Geer (1957) show how medical students use the term "crock," factory workers distinguish between "stinker" and "gravey" jobs (Roy, 1952), social classes can be differentiated by speech differences (Schatzman and Strauss, 1955; Labov, 1966), and different cultures elaborate linguistic taxonomies on the basis of what is of central significance for them (Lindesmith et al., 1975). Special languages, then, are important for what they indicate concerning self-conceptions, the meanings of events and encounters, and the boundaries of groups (Shibutani, 1961). In this respect, Strauss (1959) has stressed the significance of names and naming. They are "containers," as it were, and "poured into them are the conscious or unwitting evaluations of the namer" (1959:15). Names indicate

meanings, they serve to place people in social situations, and in some cases they convey the history of groups and intergroup relations.

Recent work in sociolinguistics, therefore, is of particular importance for contemporary symbolic interactionism. It reemphasizes one of the central benchmarks of the perspective, and, properly used in analysis, it should aid in comprehending the processes giving rise to human conduct.

INTERACTION PROCESSES

Symbolic interactionists always have maintained a hard and sustained focus on processes of interaction, a focus that has influenced not only their choices of what substantive areas to study but also the methodological techniques to be used. The interactionist approach to interaction contrasts with the more structurally based approaches (Nadel, 1957; Gross et al., 1958; Biddle and Thomas, 1966) by emphasizing the process of interpretation.[11] At the center of the interpretive process is Mead's notion of role-taking, and rather than opting for a deterministic conception of role (e.g., Linton, 1936), stress is placed on role as activity, or as Turner (1962) has put it, on "role-making." Actors not only respond and conform to expectations, but they also are actively engaged in the creation of those expectations. Turner notes that in an attempt "to make aspects of the roles explicit he [the actor] is creating and modifying roles as well as merely bringing them to light; the process is not only role-taking but also role-making" (1962:22). Thus, role-making is a creative process that involves persons defining the anticipations of others and then responding to those definitions. There is an "as if" quality to human associations, as Vahinger (1925) has commented.

This line of thought overlaps with ethnomethodology and psychology in the conceptual framework known as "attribution theory." Stemming primarily from Heider's (1958) contributions to studies of person perception and resembling W. I. Thomas's notion of the "definition of the situation," Blum and McHugh's (1971) "ascription of motives," Scott and Lyman's (1968) "accounts," and Hewitt and Hall's (1973) "quasi-theories," this approach focuses on processes through which meanings are imputed (or "attributed") to the conduct of other people. Two steps are generally regarded as significant in the attribution process: (1) attributing causality ("someone hit me with a stick," or "a branch fell off a tree and hit me") and (2) attributing motive (either the person who hit me did so by accident, or he did it on purpose). Both steps involve a process of interpreting what the social object is which is being encountered and then determining or defining the nature of that object. In this interpretive sense, attribution theory seems reasonably close to Blumer's (1969) discussion of the central premises of symbolic interactionism. One problem with attribution theory, however, is its failure to account for the social organization of the attribution process. In other words, it fails from what Whorf has called the "psychologistic fallacy" insofar as it accepts the "division of person and situation" (Jones, 1976:300). In this respect, symbolic interactionism and the psychological approach to attribution differ. Turner and Shosid (1976), however, have made a preliminary attempt to specify what might be thought of as the social organizational circumstances affecting attribution processes. They point to two contingencies, the degree of role ambiguity and role interchangeability, which shape the attribution process. While these situational variations are important and, indeed, place attribution theory closer to the symbolic interactionist approach, a considerable amount of work needs to be done in this area if the genuine merging of social psychology and social organization envisioned by Strauss (1959) is to be achieved.

Psychologists such as Kelley (1971) argue that one function of attributional processes is the production of a sense of control in the *perceiver*. A more properly symbolic interactionist approach emphasizes the process of communication and self-indication as essential for control in *situations*. This might be seen as one other point of divergence in the two approaches. In this connection, Goffman (1959) has shown that interpersonal control can be based on contrived compliance, and Weinstein and Deutschberger (1963) have documented that we can intentionally create expectations ("altercasting") by placing others in identities where they feel compelled to act as we desire them to act. Rose (1969:476) has generalized the inverse relationship between sensitivity to others and privileges of power, while Thomas et al. (1972) have more specifically shown that role-taking ability and power in family contexts are inversely related. Not having control over situations, in other words, is a circumstance that leads to an increase in alertness of the expectations of those who do have control. Thus, in the hands of symbolic interactionists, Mead's notion of role-taking has led to explicit analyses of social control (Shibutani, 1961:194−201; Strauss, 1978b) while avoiding the psychologistic trap.

The secret to avoiding that trap lies in recognizing the significance of *others* in social conduct, and, indeed, there seems to be an increasing awareness of the importance of identifying the "other." It is perhaps paradoxical, however, that in spite of the major emphasis Mead placed on the other, he failed to specify both the identity of the other and the conditions under which the other appears in the person's experience. In the past decade, however, a number of papers have been devoted to this very question.[12] Everett Hughes (1962) asks "What Other?" and in so asking reminds us of the variety and types of others and that they unevenly enter into and are implicated in our lives. In his very fine but brief discussion of social worlds as communication matrices, Shibutani argues for a processual view of reference groups in which he asks that we remember Simmel's analysis of social circles and that "each individual stands at that point at which a unique combination of his social circles intersect" (1961:139). When these circles are in conflict or when the intersection is problematic, the person becomes increasingly aware of who the other is as well as the differences involved in his various others. In other words, problematic situations, as Dewey told us a half century ago, tend to increase awareness and sharpen identities.

Through their analysis of consensus, Glaser and Strauss (1964) and Scheff (1967, 1970) have more systematically inquired into the circumstances and interactive conditions under which one becomes known to another, and then what, in fact, *is* known about the other. They postulate that we most fruitfully should talk about degrees of sharedness—that not only is complete knowledge of the other impossible but that what is known can be and often is situationally manipulated. Scheff correctly critiques Glaser and Strauss for presuming a "true identity," and then he redirects us to ask what forms of coordinated conduct or agreement are possible and to what extent there can be an interpenetration of perspectives, given the transacted, situated identities of the participants. In this view, the others who enter into social dialogue are always partial persons and what they "are" changes as awareness contexts change. In the face of such flux, admittedly variable in extent and intensity, interpersonal continuity might well be analyzed from the standpoint of the social construction of others and the discounting practices in which persons engage in an effort to maintain others.

Identities and the meaning of others are therefore always variable and always transacted. Stone (1962) identifies two processes involved in such transactions: the *announcements* we make regarding ourselves, and *placements* or the identities in which we are cast by others.[13] Criticizing what he calls Mead's "discursive bias," Stone shows not only that appearances are implicated in this identification process, but also that they are conventionally patterned and staged, and thus are embedded in social structures. More recently, Leichty (1975) and Maines (1977a) have shown how the social definitions and conventional arrangements regarding matters of touching can structure and become implicated in interactive patterns. There are many universes of interaction, then—discursive, appearance, tactile—which give form and direction to interactive relationships. They serve as frameworks in which the interpersonal meaning of the other is established. Such establishment, however, must be seen as a process; it is negotiated. Identity establishment and validation is an ongoing process (see McCall and Simmons, 1966, for an extended discussion of this point), and the exact form of this process is influenced by the awareness context and shifts in contexts surrounding interaction. What identities must be established, may be established, or are sought to be established depend upon what information is available, known, or suspected. Others, that is to say, are specified and come into our experience in contexts of shifting networks of information. Thus, interaction is a process of negotiation, and as meaning is transacted and transformed, so are our "others."[14]

Ethnomethodologists, however, inform us that there are "worlds-taken-for-granted" (Garfinkel, 1967). We are never told exactly what these worlds are, but they seem to refer to norms and expectations that are so embedded and implicit in our routines that they rarely enter consciousness; nor are they discussed unless violated. This is an important consideration because under the conditions of worlds-taken-for-granted, others can enter into a person's experience in such routine and unobtrusive ways that, indeed, they may be "seen but unnoticed." The person's name and even his title, as well as certain observable characteristics such as sex and race, may well serve as a summary of who the other "is." Thus, problems of interaction become circumscribed and segmentalized.[15] Joan Emerson points out one process contributing to the pervasiveness of such worlds.

> Because people so frequently meet a "nothing unusual" stance from others they accept as legitimate socializing agents, they are prepared by analogy to

accede to the stance under less legitimate circumstances (1970:212).

"Nothing unusual" stances, as routine or situationally efficacious definitions of situations, thus tend to circumscribe interaction, to bound it, and to give it direction. These claims may be challenged, however, and so they are always subject to negotiation. Thus, while an inertia is provided by worlds-taken-for-granted, they must be seen as in process insofar as they are sustained and realized in the course of ongoing human conduct.

STRATEGIC INTERACTION

Strategic interaction, which is closely linked to but more general than dramaturgical analysis, might well be emerging as a relatively powerful mini-paradigm in symbolic interactionism (Lofland, 1970:39). With its conceptual origins firmly rooted in Mead's assertion that man actively organizes and constructs his environment and Dewey's sharp focus on problematic situations, and with its empirical origins stemming from certain of the case studies of the early Chicago School, it has served as the underlying imagery and informing perspective for a number of recent inquiries.[16]

The underlying contention in this approach is that "all social situations are problematic" (Lyman and Scott, 1970:6). Indeed, as Darwin showed, all life is composed of individual members or groups in a species encountering problems. Whether on a species or individual basis, problems continually appear and reappear, are episodic or cyclical, but they are always conveyed and dramatized by others. Ultimately, therefore, problematic situations are to be found in the complex social arrangements created by interacting persons.

Marvin Scott's study of the world of horse racing brilliantly illustrates the strategic interaction approach. His investigation was premised on the contention that *"the proper study of social organization is the study of the organization of information"* (emphasis in original) (1968:3). Given this assumption, the study of interaction comes to involve the management of knowledge and ignorance held by the various participants of the horse racing scene: jockeys, officials, owners, trainers, and crowds. Scott effectively demonstrates how the horse race, presumably depicting nature in the raw, is really an outcome of social staging in which each participant has a self-interest in his performance.

> A trainer, wishing to disguise the true ability of his animal, may instruct the jockey to win by the narrowest possible margin (1968:viii).

> The racing secretary . . . is to bring together equally matched horses to ensure close races, and his success is measured in terms of the frequency of close finishes (1968:viii).

> The placing judge also contributes to the illusion of the natural reality of closeness by designating as a "photo finish" any distance less than half a length that may separate the first, second, and third horses (1968:viii).

> . . . the jockey must at least *appear* to be riding energetically and cleanly. To bring off these appearances the jockey has developed certain communication strategies (1968:43).

The horse race, then, must be seen as a process of dramatic presentation and representation in which the person's position in the overall setting establishes a perspective for managing meaning as well as providing the circumstances for what is to be staged.

A similar imagery can be seen in a number of other studies. Glaser and Strauss show that in order to maintain a closed awareness context, medical staff members use "tactics intended to encourage the patient to make his own interpretations inaccurately optimistic" (1964:36). As Julius Roth so well points out, however, patients also are caught up in the process of bargaining. Because tuberculosis patients desire to shorten the extent of their hospitalization, they try to make deals with the physician. Patient tactics include getting "someone outside the hospital to apply pressure for him,'' threatening to leave ''the hospital against advice if they do not get a certain privilege,'' or staging a ''medication strike'' in which the patient refuses to take any more drugs unless his case is reviewed more quickly (1963:50−52). Doctors and patients, then, have within their unique perspectives on one another an array of devices and situated alternatives by which they can selectively define certain of the features of their environment.

A few other studies can be mentioned in which strategic analysis is explicit. Fred Davis's research on the families of polio victims established that these families must cope with the problem of ''how to view, interpret, and respond to the many negative meanings imputed to a visible handicap in our society'' (1963:163). Davis found that such coping revolves around ''two broad strategems of adjustment.'' Olesen and Davis also appraised the problem of identity and change in their analysis of the process of becoming a nurse (1972). Here strategic coping was in response to identity ambivalence in the transition from coed to student nurse. By comparison, the ''problem'' for institutionalized skid row alcoholics is harshly concrete—they must return to society. The steps involved in that return are equally concrete—they must get a job and a room, and maintain sobriety (Wiseman, 1970:217−238). But such middle-class plans are products of a rehabilitation perspective, and they are usually neutralized by the facts of marginal employability and the meanings the alcoholic has built up with other street alcoholics and upon whom he depends for social contact and friendship. Thus, for some, there are rather firm boundaries around the strategies available to them.

In addition to these studies, a few analyses have been carried out on the staging of situations. Gross and Stone (1964) identify five elements of situations that must be properly assembled and controlled if a role performance is to be brought off: spaces, props, equipment, clothing, and the body. They argue that a loss of poise can result from the misalignment or improper staging of any one of these elements. The staging of situations is more

dramatically seen, however, in Ball's (1966) ethnographic analysis of an abortion clinic. In view of the middle-class conception of abortion as deviant, the successful abortionist must devise a set of means whereby the act is neutralized or at least is seen as acceptable.[17] So, he uses the rhetoric of medical practice and stages the clinic to mobilize such imagery and meaning. The waiting room is luxurious, there is certain amount of red tape to go through, the preoperative medical history is taken, surgical gloves are used, and apparently sterilized surgical tools are displayed. All of these arrangements are intended to bring off the scene and the performance, and in this sense it is reality that is being staged.

This point of view has been further expressed, albeit from a slightly different angle, in investigations of space. Robert Sommer (1969) discusses the architecture and geography of hospital wards, and shows that arrangements of furniture, equipment, room size and shape, and the like all have dramatic consequences for patient behavior and treatment progress. In addition, Ball (1973) very cleverly weaves together matters of space and the self. Space, Ball argues, is problematic because ''part of our definitions of 'who we are' depend on answers to the question of 'where we are''' (1973:6). The ecology of space, in other words, becomes the social psychology of space,[18] and Ball puts great stock in its explanatory power. In concluding his examination with the assertion that ''we owe our spatially situated selves to our spatially situated others'' (1973:30), he openly challenges the individualistic psychologies by showing that spatial and interpersonal characteristics combine to explain more of the variation in situations than any personally consistent characteristic of those who happen to be occupying space. The problematic and emergent nature of space and situated conduct thus requires that performances be staged and the meaning of action be monitored.

The voluntaristic assumptions of symbolic interactionism are brought forward and give primary attention in strategic analysis. This is true even in examinations of power and constraint. Rather than opting for the functionalist view of power and order as normative systems, we find the view that "power always matters in social relations, and that the gaining, holding, recognition, exercise, and consequences of power are always problematic" (Lyman and Scott, 1970:213). Power systems with their typical sociological components are fully recognized, but power relations are analytically cast in a game metaphor. The "sociology of the absurd" sees society as essentially meaningless, institutions as inherently self-contradictory, and interaction as fundamentally risky. Actors therefore must calculate the odds in forming their conduct and choosing among alternative lines of action simply because "power is an essential variable in every game" (Lyman and Scott, 1970:217). Thus, strategic interaction is an attempt to develop a perspective on social control in which the processes of constraint and human freedom are seen as aspects of the same communicative and interactive processes. Attention is focused on the bargaining tactics and control moves in which people engage as they attempt to maintain a measure of order in their lives, and on what people can bring to bear on negotiative situations in the way of titles, associations, demeanor, information, expertise, reputation, and the like in an effort to impose their definitions of situations on others. Through these strategic processes, "order somehow emerges from the chaos and conflict" (Lyman and Scott, 1970:9). Thus, strategic interactionists appropriately point to coolness, poise, and style as important dimensions of power and interaction.[19]

SOCIAL ORGANIZATION

Symbolic interactionist approaches to the social organizational phase of society have been one of the primary foci of various critical examinations of the perspective (e.g., Coser, 1976; Reynolds and Reynolds, 1973). One reason for such criticism is substantive in nature insofar as the early interactionists did not devote themselves to working out a detailed conception of social structure. While processes of constraint are to be found in their discussions (Mead, 1934:222–223; Thomas, 1923:42),[20] the imagery of society which is fostered is only at best general. Subsequent scholars such as Park (1916, 1926) and Hughes (1937, 1945) provided a more sharply focused picture of social organization, but the tradition of symbolic interaction never has quite lived up to the expectations of other theoretical positions, especially that of structural functionalism. In my view, however, the early interactionists had no intention of holding society stationary and examining its "structure" per se. Rather, they attempted to bring us all intellectually forward by seeing society as being in process, and as a consequence, they provided a less specifically focused picture of social structure, as any such thrust must. To their credit, they failed brilliantly to freeze society. But while the major tenets of symbolic interactionism lead to a rejection of hard deterministic explanations, they are consistent with "soft determinism" (Matza, 1964). This compatibility can be seen in two lines of thought in contemporary interactionist approaches to social organization.

The first approach lies in the field of communications theory, or cybernetics, which closely resembles Mead's views regarding the ongoing processes in which social objects are constructed (Shibutani, 1968). Hugh Duncan (1968) is properly critical of early versions of communication systems theory as being too "heavily steeped in mechanical imagery" (1968:14), but the perspective is restored by Klapp (1973) who emphasizes its processual potential. Cybernetics involves the transmission of information within and between systems, and as an approach, it attempts to analyze information input and output in terms of system processes and patterns. This includes the possibility for systems to be self-corrective or "purposive" as well as directive or constraining (Stover, 1977). In other words, cybernetics becomes a metaphor for society which envisions a system as simultaneously being structured and transformed through communication processes. Both Dewey and Park advocated this very perspective a half century ago, and in the spirit of their work, Klapp points out that we need not be hampered by the notion of "equilibrium" inherited from Spencer and perpetuated by Parsons, who, at one time, wondered, "who now reads Herbert Spencer?" Klapp does caution against viewing information processing as an internal state, however, and suggests that a mature cybernetics perspective must be able to account for matters of transacted meaning in its vocabulary. The compatibility boils down to whether "information theory must operate with the 'push-pull' concepts of influence and communication, or whether it can handle the subtler aspects of transactions, of constructing and interpreting definitions of situations" (Klapp, 1973:294).

The second approach has been conventionally labeled the "negotiated order." (See Hall, 1972; Day and Day, 1977; and Maines, 1977b and 1978 for recent reviews of this approach.) In the earliest explicit analyses of organizations as negotiated orders (Bucher and Strauss, 1961; Bucher, 1962; Strauss et al., 1963), the imagery fostered stressed the adjustive features of organizations. Professions were seen as segmentalized, and bureaucratic structures were viewed as containing various elements that inevitably led to negotiation between members and segments of organizations.

The more recent literature dealing with this perspective can be heuristically divided into studies of negotiative processes that occur within settings and those that occur between and among settings. Among the former must be included the Glaser and Strauss (1964) study of awareness contexts, which demonstrated not only the transactional nature of organizational identities but also the structural limitations imposed on interpersonal negotiative processes. These processes take the form of a sort of "directed becoming," much in the same sense as those depicted by studies of professional socialization (see Fred Davis, 1972).

This view also bears a resemblance to a number of studies of industrial behavior. Both Roy (1959) and Katz (1968) show how a substantial portion of worker roles are left undefined, which creates the circumstances in which workers can introduce a measure of control over work performances. Additional studies demonstrate that "gaps and ambiguities in the rules are used by people in different ways" (Morgan, 1975:224) and that "organizational knowledge . . . is differentially distributed" (Manning, 1977a:58). Negotiation within organizational and work settings has been further investigated by a number of others, including Blankenship (1973, 1976), Faulkner (1973), and Mukerji (1976). The general sense of the perspective is that bureaucratic structure, when written down, can assume a codified and Weberian appearance. But when that structure is called upon to "act," as it were, it assumes a much looser and less determinative character as it becomes transacted by interacting persons (Freidson, 1976).

An additional collection of studies examines negotiations between and among settings. Freidson's (1975) study of social control in medicine shows that, while administrative structures limit what can potentially occur, they cannot determine the nature of the interaction or variation within structures. This point was earlier noted in more general terms by Bucher and Stelling (1969) who indicate that, while negotiation is an ongoing process, it tends to be more overt in professional organizations and covert in industrial organizations. The imposition of limitations set by policy (Smith, 1958) and various other organizational arrangements require that organizational integration be achieved through a continual political process (Bucher and Stelling, 1969; Bucher, 1970; Daniels, 1975). But the nature of intergroup constraint can vary. Farberman (1975) recently examined the used car industry and found that the relations between its various segments operate in a fairly deterministic manner that results in used car dealers being put in "lower level dependent" positions. Denzin's (1977) study of the American liquor industry, however, reveals an economic market structure that operates in a less deterministic way, in which negotiation among the various "tiers" of the industry is widespread, and Gerson (1976), who examined the market structure of technical work organizations, reveals a "market structure which is inherently extremely fluid" (1976:11).

Along with other studies, these investigations show an appreciation for the linkages between negotiated orders. In general, the perspective is entirely consistent with the assumptions of symbolic interactionism. Negotiations are seen to vary tremendously. They can be explicit or implicit, involve only a few or many participants, be tightly constraining or open-ended, and pertain to issues ranging from the trivial to the highly significant. An important point to make is that negotiations take place within contexts that give them shape and direction, and that each context for negotiation is set in still larger contexts. Viewed this way, both structure and process, stable and unstable relationships can be analyzed within the same interactive framework (Strauss, 1978a).

RESEARCH METHODS

The conceptual apparatus of any theoretical perspective logically leads to certain research questions, implies others, and permits still a wider range of considerations. This point is made either explicitly or implicitly in most texts on research methods. With respect to the relation between theory and method in symbolic interactionism, Glaser and Strauss (1967), Blumer (1969), Bruyn (1966), Habenstein (1970), Schatzman and Strauss (1973), Denzin (1970, 1974), and Lofland (1976) have been the most explicit in recent years. Schatzman and Strauss state the linkage as simply and as concisely as any. They assert that the social psychology of human behavior minimally includes the following elements: humans take perspectives on themselves, they can simultaneously hold multiple perspectives, these perspectives are social in

nature, and they contribute to the setting of conditions on activity (1973:5). These properties are contained in the overall processual approach of symbolic interactionism.

The methodological implications, however, are not as clearly defined as the conceptual premises of the approach. To some, "the choice of method is virtually a logical imperative. The researcher *must* get close to the people whom he studies" (Schatzman and Strauss, 1973:5)—which means field research. But to others, laboratory or field experiments (Birenbaum and Sagarin, 1973; Couch and Hintz, 1975; McPhail, 1979; McPhail and Rexroat, 1979) and surveys (Thomas et al., 1972; Turner, 1975) are also seen as logically consistent with this conceptualization of behavior. One of the dimensions thought to differentiate the Iowa and Chicago Schools of symbolic interactionism (Meltzer and Petras, 1970), for instance, is the selection of method. In addition, Reynolds and Meltzer (1973), who have attempted to describe the range of interactionists' commitments to methodological techniques and epistemological assumptions, have shown that most symbolic interactionists are "middle-of-the-roaders." That is, they see value in a number of techniques and, as Denzin (1970) advocates, are willing to utilize triangulated research designs. Thus, while there is a pervasive sentiment among symbolic interactionists for ethnographic approaches, it is clear that nearly all methods and techniques are represented in one form or another.

One of the notable changes in research methods during the past decade or so is the relative decline in the use of the Twenty Statements Test (TST) made famous by Kuhn in the 1950s. That is not to say that the TST is not currently being used. (See McPhail and Tucker, 1972, for a fairly representative bibliography.) Indeed, it is being used, but not so much in the way that Kuhn and McPartland (1954) envisioned. They viewed the TST as an instrument suitable for measuring the self, particularly the "me" phase. That sort of measurement could be used to correlate or "locate" self-attitudes in various social structural arrangements. However, one of the most recent substantive applications of the TST was Driver's (1969) comparative study. Most of the other recent applications have pertained either to procedure or to the methodological adequacy of the TST (e.g., Tucker, 1966; Spitzer et al., 1970; Franklin and Kohout, 1971; McPhail and Tucker, 1972; Spitzer and Parker, 1976). One reason for this decline in the substantive use pertains to the very issue of the fit between theory and method. Although Kuhn maintained that self-attitudes take on meaning in terms of social contexts (Hickman and Kuhn, 1956), the use of the TST for the most part contradicts that point of view. In other words, TSTs are incapable of handling situational variations in the self. This realization may partially be due to the osmotic influence of ethnomethodology, but more directly I suspect that it is the result of the situational approaches to the self and identity proposed by Erving Goffman, Anselm Strauss, Gregory Stone, and Thomas Scheff. To paraphrase the extensive analysis of Deutscher (1973), selves are significantly the properties of situations rather than exclusively of individuals. Thus, we need instruments designed to measure situations and situational encounters. This sort of interpretation receives indirect support from others as well. Turner (1976) argues that "real selves" are increasingly being defined situationally in terms of feelings and sentiments; Lifton's (1970) notion of "protean man" points to the varying circumstances that shape the self; and, similarly, Zurcher's (1973) identification of the "mutable self" conveys the situational dimension of the self. These views in various ways complement Ball's micro-ecological approach to the self; we need to know not only "where I am" but "who am I with" in order to answer the question "who am I?"

Although Reynolds and Petras (1973) suggest that the Iowa and Chicago Schools are becoming diffused as identifiable entities, it is evident that the Iowa tradition of "hard research" continues. Rather than continuing as applications of TST

instruments, however, the emphasis is almost exclusively on observing behavior that has been recorded on videotape. The work done to date, most of which has been conducted by Carl Couch and his students, is presented in the Couch and Hintz volume (1975) entitled *Constructing Social Life: Readings in Behavioral Sociology from the Iowa School*. Their research covers a range of analytical problems, such as the nature of openings and closings in interpersonal relations, forms of social relations, solidarity and change, the structure of interpersonal formations, and the like. But the central question from which these topics emerge is simply, "How do two people come together in a unified line of action?" The basic justification for the use of video recordings in pursuit of answers to this question is that recorded behavioral acts, episodes, and sequences can be played back again. This introduces a measure of control over observations, and coding, concept formation, and analysis are thereby improved. But, as Saxton and Couch (1975) indicate, these recordings are not the result of merely randomly pointing a camera. Through giving research subjects certain tasks and directions, a measure of analytical control and perspective is introduced. Thus, this strategy, which is based on the contention that very little is systematically known about the structure and formation processes of action, sacrifices the virtues of naturalistic observational procedures in favor of what Couch and his associates regard as the greater virtues of control and systematic observation.

Still, this research orientation and the use of TSTs represent a minority position when compared with the abundance of recent publications concerning ethnographic methods. In fact, field research methods remain the single major source of methodological continuity in symbolic interactionist-informed research. One of the better known and certainly one of the most influential is the Glaser and Strauss (1967) volume on grounded theory. They argue that there is an overemphasis on the verification of theory in sociology and a corresponding neglect of the generation of theory from data. The methods they propose are not totally inductive, however, since they explicitly adopt the position that there must be a systematic working back and forth between theory and data through what they call the "constant comparative method" (1967:101–115). That is, the coding categories used in data gathering and organization should be based on theoretical categories and concepts while those concepts are themselves emergent from data. Intimately involved in this is what Glaser and Strauss term "theoretical sampling"—a procedure discussed earlier but less explicitly by Hughes as "process sampling." Thus, the basic thrust of grounded theory is to bring theory and method into a more equal partnership in the research process rather than making the positivistic assumption that the only function of method is to verify theory.

While this point of view is well expressed in other examinations (e.g., Denzin, 1970), a number of books are devoted more specifically to technique. Lofland (1971), for example, provides many useful suggestions and tried and true techniques concerning sampling, note taking, organizing data and files, as well as coordinating the analytical and data-gathering phases of research. The Schatzman and Strauss (1973) volume is explicitly organized around various field strategies—strategies for entering, watching, listening, recording, analyzing, and communicating the research. Likewise, Habenstein (1970) has compiled over a dozen essays by established ethnographers who attempt to pass on lessons and advice concerning field research strategies learned in a variety of settings. While the strategic aspect of field research is brought out by John Lofland (1976), who has formulated method explicitly based on the dramaturgical perspective, a number of good and recent volumes provide detailed accounts of how to go about conducting field projects (Wax, 1971; Bogdan and Taylor, 1975, Geer, 1972). One thing that is increasingly being made clear is that such techniques need not be confined to the small-scale study. Douglas (1976:195–204)

describes an initial attempt at team field research. This strategy involves "a number of people working together in a flexibly planned and coordinated manner to get at the multi-perspectival realities" (1976:194) of the phenomena being studied. It allows not only for the in-depth analysis of particular settings but also for the attainment of a representative sampling of settings and observations. Douglas's discussion, then, demonstrates what field researchers have long known: although ethnographic techniques have traditionally been used in the intensive case study, by their very nature they are not limited to those studies.[21]

The last topic to be considered in this section is historical analysis. Symbolic interactionism, of course, must by virtue of its conceptual character take the historical perspective into account. However, it has been criticized from time to time for not doing so (e.g., Day and Day, 1977). While this criticism is a fair one, I think that a few analyses can be singled out which have attempted to translate "process" into historical terms. Becker (1967), for instance, has argued that the nature of the personal experience of drug use and the meanings established among drug users are likely to vary according to when they take place historically. He also (1970) has reemphasized the importance of the life history method and has noted that it "more than any other technique except perhaps participant observation, can give meaning to the overworked notion of process" (1970:69). While Denzin (1970:219–259), in addition to Becker, goes to great lengths to point out the virtues of historical analysis, and Lankford (1973) has more generally indicated where and in what respects history can be useful for sociologists,[22] a few substantive studies by symbolic interactionists illustrate that the dimension is not totally ignored or taken for granted. Lyn Lofland (1973) argues that there is historical variation in the criteria people use to identify or establish the identities of strangers. In the pre-industrial city in which there was the heterogeneous use of public space, identities were established on the basis of appearances; in the modern city, however, in which there is specialized use of space, they are established on the basis of location. These, of course, are not suggested as any absolute criteria, but Lofland does argue convincingly that such a trend in urban history exists. The historical dimension of interpersonal and intergroup negotiation processes has also been examined. Albrecht and Levy's (1980) analysis of the process through which osteopathy legitimized itself as a profession emphasizes the interplay between that specialty's attempts to establish itself and the market conditions that shaped the legitimization process. Denzin (1977) analyzes how the "five tier" structure of the American liquor industry came into existence and the effects this process had on transactions in the industry. Fisher (1972a) has examined the historical processes that create career options, as well as (1972b) how educational interest groups use variations of the ideology of failure as one means of establishing and maintaining their positions. Along these same lines must be placed the assertion of Roth et al. (1973) that one of the better ways of studying the professions is through an historical approach in which the nature of the professions is seen in the context of shifting and competing ideologies and power arrangements.

The one thing that is abundantly clear about the use of research methods by symbolic interactionists is that there is a range of commitments to the variety of methods available. Just as there is no credence in the claim that symbolic interactionism is a one-issue perspective, so there is no credence in the claim that it is a one-method perspective. However, some techniques are utilized differently than is usually the case. John Lofland (1971), for instance, argues, and Douglas (1976) demonstrates, that survey data may best be used as sensitizing information for the designing of field studies. That is, "their proper role is that of providing the quantitative backdrop and tests against which qualitative studies move in the foreground" (John Lofland, 1971:5). This approach, of course, reverses the relationship between survey and field data typically advocated by sociologists, and is based on the contention that the determination of *rates* of interaction or events, while important, is not the same thing as the direct inspection of interaction. Not all interactionists use this triangulated approach, but whether it is through the use of survey, experimental, or field research designs, they do have a common focus on interaction processes.

SUMMARY

I have not intended this essay to be encyclopedic in scope, but merely suggestive of some of the more visible developments in symbolic interactionism in about the last two decades. It is evident that along with or perhaps because of the rise of phenomenological sociology, symbolic interactionism has gained greatly in popularity (Klapp, 1973:152). It is equally evident that symbolic interactionism will not fade and disappear as a definable perspective from American sociology, as Mullins (1973:98) has predicted. Mullin's forecast is in error because, unlike predictions of the extinction of nonhuman species, human beings can take themselves and such predictions into account. Thus, the Society for the Study of Symbolic Interaction was established in 1974, which, in addition to its scholarly goals, serves as a mechanism for the encouragement and enrichment of the perspective.

Substantively, it seems that symbolic interactionism has developed a more sophisticated conception of consensus. Through the work of Goffman, Scheff, and Strauss, it is now common to acknowledge the multidimensional nature of consensus, including false consciousness, role distance, situational manipulation, and fictive consensus as well as the traditional components of reciprocity and overt agreement. In addition, most symbolic interactionists feel more comfortable discussing power arrangements and social structure, although their conceptualizations of these phenomena differ from those of, say, functionalists. The work of the negotiated order theorists such as Bucher, Daniels, Freidson, and Strauss as well as the dramaturgical theorists such as Lyman and Scott have made significant inroads into areas of social organization that previously were either ignored or neglected.

The revitalization of sociolingustics is significant because it applies to the very foundations of the symbolic interactionist perspective. This represents the most fundamental area of substantive continuity in the perspective insofar as it links the early interactionists' views on communication and society with contemporary research and scholarly inquiry. It also is the point at which a number of disciplines can come together and can focus not only on interpersonal processes but also on social organizational processes. It is in this same sense that ethnomethodology, although it has certain obvious strengths, is shown to be the weakest. As Douglas (1976) has accurately pointed out, ethnomethodology is ultimately committed to a positivistic position because of its search "for the universal or invariant properties of the mind and thence in all situations at all times for all people" (1976:52). The thrust of sociolinguistics and the basic postulates of symbolic interactionism weave lines of thought away from that viewpoint and toward one in which the conditions under which social phenomena and personal experience must be specified before the nature of human experience can be understood, measured, analyzed, or predicted.

NOTES

1. This distinction pertains to the extent to which people can voluntarily determine their own conduct. Those advocating the determinancy position hold that either social structures or cognitive structures determine conduct; those advocating the indeterminancy position hold that humans actively construct their behavior through processes of interaction. For a brief discussion of this point as it applies to symbolic interactionism, see Petras and Meltzer (1970) and Meltzer et al. (1975).

2. Among the recent texts and monographs using a symbolic interactionist approach are Lindesmith et al. (1975), Brittan (1973), Miller (1975), Field (1974), McCall et al. (1970), Brissett and Edgley (1975), Meltzer et al. (1975), Henslin (1972), Berger and Berger (1975), Schmitt (1972), Morris (1977), Lauer and Handel (1977), Kinch (1973), Hewitt (1976), Robboy et al. (1979), Karp and Yoels (1979), and Karp et al. (1977).

3. For other recent reviews of the symbolic interactionist perspective, see Jones and Day (1977) and Strauss and Fisher (1978).

4. A quick reference to some of the recent literature in critical theory would be Giddens (1977). For a discussion of conflict methodology, see Lundman and McFarlane (1976) and Christie (1976).

5. However, see Scott (1970) for an analysis of the incompatibilities between structural functionalism and symbolic interactionism.

6. It should be noted that it is not only between symbolic interactionism and ethnomethodology, perhaps best exemplified by the Zimmerman-Wieder and Denzin exchange in Douglas (1970), that divergences appear, but also within ethnomethodology. Both Turner (1974) and Cicourel (1974) recognize that ethnomethodology is not a unitary approach, and somewhere Jack Douglas has suggested that it is more accurate to refer to "ethnomethodologies." Lauer and Handel (1977:275), in their introductory remarks about ethnomethodology, speak of the "significant differences among their approaches," and Mehan and Wood (1975:vii) speak of the "many quarreling factions," while Mullins (1973:204) distinguishes "conversation analysis" (e.g., the work of Schegloff) from "language acquisition and rule-using analysis" (e.g., the work of Cicourel) as indicative of variation in ethnomethodological approaches. Mehan and Wood (1975) and Attewell (1974) provide fairly recent general examinations of developments in ethnomethodology since the work done in that area in the 1960s. Wolff (1978) provides a recent and comprehensive review of phenomenology, including a discussion of its relation to ethnomethodology and sociology. He also goes into some detail in specifying the varieties of phenomenological interpretation and debates within phenomenological sociology.

7. Some ethnomethodologists have argued just the opposite of this interpretation. See, for example, Mehan and Wood (1975:95−96).

8. For an excellent review and discussion of the major issues surrounding labeling theory, see Glassner and Corzine (1978).

9. In his "Labeling Theory Reconsidered" (1973), Becker is quite explicit regarding his dislike of the term and in his assertion that labeling theory never was proposed as a theory. He prefers instead to regard the approach as an "interactionist theory of deviance," the utility of which is to be measured by the extent to which it can further systematic understanding in other areas of sociological inquiry as well as in deviance.

10. Perhaps indicative of this trend is the analysis of the boundaries between sociology and linguistics. Labov (1978) notes that the disciplinary boundaries are more sharply drawn between these two than between anthropology and linguistics, but that it is not an insurmountable gulf. He describes two promising areas of research that would be mutually beneficial to sociology and linguistics: the social origins of sound changes and conversational interaction. Grimshaw (1979) sees little to justify the contrivance of those boundaries, and he argues forcefully that language is an inherent dimension of social problems.

11. Not all analysts see the distinction made here. Handel (1979), for example, argues that the structuralist and interactionist approaches to role theory are compatible and complementary.

12. The specification of types of others, of course, is not new in the history of symbolic interactionism. In 1917, W. I. Thomas distinguished the Philistine, the Bohemian, and the Creative Man on the basis of their being differentially sensitive to and selective of others. See pp. 168–181 in *W. I. Thomas: On Social Organization and Social Personality*, edited with an introduction by Morris Janowitz, University of Chicago Press, 1966. The more traditional and social organizational framework for the analysis of others lies in the area of reference group theory. For an extensive review and interpretation of that literature, see Schmitt (1972).

13. The ambiguities created by status inconsistencies function in many cases to dramatize others' placements of us. Charlton (1978) shows that women ministers, who must work in extremely male-dominated work arenas, are quite aware of the various identities and roles in which they are placed, especially when those placements bear little relationship to their life organization.

14. An additional way of analytically dealing with this process is with the use of the concept of social worlds (Strauss, 1978b). Stability and change in social worlds are in part measured by the relative permanence of others who constitute membership. The critical nature of this dimension is shown rather clearly in those investigations of shifting social worlds, as in Levy's (1979) analysis of the problems encountered by middle-aged women who return to college after having been out of school for some time. One of the major problems for them is in redefining friendship circles which to some extent must be left behind, while simultaneously acquiring new circles from a pool of people who are several, and in some cases many, years younger. It is a process at the heart of which rests the realignment of sets of others in terms of the new main involvements of the returning student.

15. Goffman makes a similar point in a recent publication. He states that "True, we personally negotiate aspects of all the arrangements under which we live, but often once these arrangements are negotiated we continue on mechanically as though the matter had always been settled" (1974:2).

16. Even Herbert Blumer, who is not usually associated with the strategic interactionist perspective and who, in fact, has been quite critical of Goffman's work, seems to share at least some of its fundamental views. He states: "Yet the acting individual stands over his scene, viewing it as an arena to be used by him, to be exploited by him at given points, and to be bent by him at other points as he forges his own lines of action" (1970: xi).

17. While I am sure that a decade ago Ball's premise of abortion as deviant was a valid one, it probably would be questionable today. Attitudes have changed markedly, and although it is hard to say how much, it is safe to say that they have at least become polarized into pro- and anti-abortion positions, programs, and organizations. Cf. Zimmerman, Part One.

18. The transformational quality of this process is demonstrated in the research conducted by Maines and Markowitz (1980). They showed that the alteration of the status symbolism conferred on a given spatial arrangement mobilized radically different behavioral patterns among setting participants.

19. Some of the work of Goffman falls quite naturally within the strategic interactionist framework, particularly that bearing on the concept of impression management. Gonos (1977) has recently argued, however, that the fundamental thrust of Goffman's work is

structuralist rather than symbolic interactionist in nature. The reality of the frame, Gonos writes, "poses an apparatus for a kind of structuralism for which Goffman is heavily indebted to Durkheim (1977:855). While Goffman has always been interested in the structure of situations, whether that makes him a "structuralist" in the usual sociological sense of the term is a somewhat more complex matter. The lesson from Stone and Farberman (1967) is *which* Durkheim are we talking about—a question that relates directly to the more generic issue of what is meant by the notion of "structure" (Maines, 1978:494). Some conceptualizations fully allow room for voluntaristic action (e.g., Strauss, 1978a), while others do not. These and related issues are more fully discussed in relation to Durkheim by Deutscher (1979), and useful analyses of Goffman are provided by Manning (1977b) and Jameson (1976). Analyses of substantive areas in which similar issues are discussed include Becker's (1974, 1978) examinations of art worlds, Kling and Gerson's (1977) investigation of computer markets, and Fine and Kleinman's (1979) analysis of subcultures.

20. See Fisher and Strauss (1978, 1979) for a detailed analysis of this point.

21. William F. Whyte (1976) provides an extremely detailed and pointed attack on the notion that qualitative and quantitative methods are inherently incompatible. Through his studies of rural Peru, he shows that ethnographic methods can indeed yield "hard data."

22. See also Heath (1978), who points out the usefulness of historical materials for sociolinguistic analysis, and Mariampalski and Hughes (1978), who present a somewhat more technical analysis on the use of personal documents in historical sociology.

REFERENCES

Albrecht, Gary L. and Judith A. Levy. 1980. "The Professionalization of Osteopathy: Adaption in the Medical Marketplace," in Julius Roth (ed.), *Research in the Sociology of Health Care*. Vol. II, Greenwich, Conn.: JAI Press, in press.

Anderson, R. Bruce. 1967. "On the Comparability of Meaningful Stimuli in Cross-Cultural Research," *Sociometry* 30:124–156.

Attewell, Paul. 1974. "Ethnomethodology Since Garfinkel," *Theory and Society* 1:179–210.

Bain, Read. 1936. "The Self-and-Other Words of a Child," *American Journal of Sociology* 41:767–775.

Ball, Donald. 1966. "An Abortion Clinic Ethnography," *Social Problems* 14:293–301.

———. 1973. *Microecology: Social Situations and Intimate Space*. Indianapolis, Ind.: Bobbs-Merrill.

Bandyopathyay, P. 1971. "One Sociology or Many: Some Issues in Radical Sociology," *Science and Society* 36:1–26.

Becker, Howard S. 1963. *Outsiders*. New York: Free Press.

———. 1967. "History, Culture and Subjective Experience: An Exploration of the Social Bases of Drug-Induced Experiences," *Journal of Health and Social Behavior* 8:163–176.

———. 1970. *Sociological Work*. Chicago: Aldine.

———. 1973. "Labeling Theory Reconsidered," pp. 177–212, in *Outsiders*, Revised Edition, New York: Free Press.

———. 1974. "Art as Collective Action," *American Sociological Review* 39:767–776.

———. 1978. "Arts and Crafts," *American Journal of Sociology* 83:862–889.

Becker, Howard and Blanche Geer. 1957. "Participant Observation and Interviewing: A Comparison," *Human Organization* 16:28–32.

Berger, Peter and Brigitte Berger. 1975. *Sociology: A Biographical Approach*. New York: Basic Books.

Biddle, Bruce and Edwin Thomas. 1966. *Role Theory*. New York: Basic Books.

Birenbaum, Arnold and Edward Sagarin (eds.). 1973. *People in Places*. New York: Praeger.

Blankenship, Ralph. 1973. "Organizational Careers: An Interactionist Approach," *Sociological Quarterly* 14:88–98.

———. 1976. "Collective Behavior in Organizational Settings," *Sociology of Work and Occupations* 3:151–168.

Blum, Alan and Peter McHugh. 1971. "The Social Ascription of Motives," *American Sociological Review* 36:98–109.

Blumer, Herbert. 1969. *Symbolic Interactionism*. Englewood Cliffs, N.J.: Prentice-Hall.

———. 1970. "Foreword," pp. xi–xiv in Jacqueline Wiseman, *Stations of the Lost*, Englewood Cliffs, N.J.: Prentice-Hall.

Bogdan, Robert and Steven Taylor. 1975. *Introduction to Qualitative Research Methods*. New York: Wiley.

Bossard, James. 1943. "Family Table Talk: An Area for Sociological Study," *American Sociological Review* 8:295–301.

———. 1945. "The Bilingual as a Person: Linguistic Identification with Status," *American Sociological Review* 10:699–709.

Bottomore, T. B. (ed.). 1963. *Karl Marx: Early Writings*. New York: McGraw-Hill.

Brissett, Dennis and Charles Edgley (eds.). 1975. *Life as Theater*. Chicago: Aldine.

Brittan, Arthur. 1973. *Meanings and Situations*. London: Routledge and Kegan Paul.

Bruyn, Severyn. 1966. *The Human Perspective in Sociology*. Englewood Cliffs, N.J.: Prentice-Hall.

Bucher, Rue. 1962. "Pathology: A Study of Social Movements Within a Profession," *Social Problems* 10:40–51.

———. 1970. "Social Process and Power in a Medical School," pp. 2–48 in Meyer Zald (ed.), *Power and Organizations*, Nashville, Tenn.: Vanderbilt University Press.

Bucher, Rue and Joan Stelling. 1969. "Characteristics of Professional Organizations," *Journal of Health and Social Behavior* 10:3–15.

Bucher, Rue and Anselm Strauss. 1961. "Professions in Process," *American Journal of Sociology* 66:325–334.

Charlton, Joy. 1978. "Women Entering the Ordained Ministry: Contradictions and Dilemmas of Status," Presented at the Annual Meeting of the Society for the Scientific Study of Religion.

Christie, Robert. 1976. "Comment on Conflict Methodology: A Protagonist Position," *Sociological Quarterly* 17:513–519.

Cicourel, Aaron. 1967. "Kinship, Marriage, and Divorce in Comparative Family Law," *Law and Society Review* 1:103–129.

———. 1974. *Cognitive Sociology*. New York: Free Press.

Coser, Lewis. 1976. "Sociological Theory from the Chicago Dominance to 1965," *Annual Review of Sociology* 2:145–160.

Couch, Carl and Robert Hintz (eds.). 1975. *Constructing Social Life: Readings in Behavioral Sociology from the Iowa School*. Champaign, Ill.: Stipes.

Daniels, Arlene K. 1975. "Advisory and Coercive Functions in Psychiatry," *Sociology of Work and Occupations* 2:55–78.

Davis, Fred. 1963. *Passage Through Crisis*. Indianapolis Ind.: Bobbs-Merrill.

———. 1972. *Illness, Interaction, and the Self*. Belmont, Calif.: Wadsworth.

Davis, Nanette. 1972. "Labeling Theory in Deviance Research," *Sociological Quarterly* 13:447–474.

Day, Robert and JoAnne Day. 1977. "A Review of the Current State of Negotiated Order Theory: An Appreciation and Critique," *Sociological Quarterly* 18:126–142.

Denzin, Norman. 1969. "Symbolic Interactionism and Ethnomethodology: A Proposed Synthesis," *American Sociological Review* 34:922–934.

———. 1970. *The Research Act*. Chicago: Aldine.

———. 1974. "The Methodological Implications of Symbolic Interactionism for the Study of Deviance," *British Journal of Sociology* 25:269–282.

———. 1975. "Play, Games and Interaction: The Contexts of Childhood Socialization," *Sociological Quarterly* 16:458–478.

———. 1977. "A Case Study of the American Liquor Industry: Notes on the Criminogenic Hypothesis," *American Sociological Review* 42:905–920.

Deutscher, Irwin. 1966. "Words and Deeds: Social Science and Social Policy," *Social Problems* 13:235–254.

———. 1968. "Asking Questions Cross-Culturally: Some Problems of Linguistic Comparability," pp. 318–341 in Howard Becker, et al. (eds.), *Institutions and the Person*, Chicago: Aldine.

———. 1969–1970. "Asking Questions (and Listening to Answers): A Review of Some Sociological Precedents and Problems," *Sociological Focus* 3:13–32.

————. 1972. "Public and Private Opinions: Social Situations and Multiple Realities," pp. 323—349 in Saad Nagi and Ronald Corwin (eds.), *Social Context of Research*, New York: Wiley.

————. 1973. *What We Say/What We Do*. Glenview, Ill.: Scott, Foresman.

————. 1979. "Choosing Ancestors: Some Consequences of the Selection from Among Intellectual Traditions," Presented at the Colloquium on Social Representations, Maison des Sciences de l'Home, Paris.

Douglas, Jack. 1973. *Introduction to Sociology: Situations and Structures*. New York: Free Press.

————. 1976. *Investigative Social Research*. Beverly Hills, Calif.: Sage.

Dreitzel, Hans Peter. 1970. "Introduction: Patterns of Communicative Behavior," pp. vii—xxii in Hans Peter Dreitzel (ed.), *Recent Sociology* No. 2, New York: Macmillan.

Driver, Edwin. 1969. "Self-Conceptions in India and the United States: A Cross-Cultural Validation of the Twenty Statement Test," *Sociological Quarterly* 10:341—354.

Duncan, Hugh. 1968. *Symbols in Society*. New York: Oxford University Press.

Emerson, Joan. 1970. "'Nothing Unusual Is Happening,'" pp. 208—222 in Tamotsu Shibutani (ed.), *Human Nature and Collective Behavior*, Englewood Cliffs, N.J.: Prentice-Hall.

Entwisle, Doris. 1968. "Developmental Social Linguistics: Inner City Children," *American Journal of Sociology* 74:37—49.

Farberman, Harvey. 1970. "Mannheim, Cooley, and Mead: Toward a Social Theory of Mentality," *Sociological Quarterly* 11:3—13.

————. 1975. "A Criminogenic Market Structure: The Automobile Industry," *Sociological Quarterly* 16:438—457.

Faulkner, Robert. 1973. "Orchestra Interaction: Some Features of Communication and Authority in an Artistic Organization," *Sociological Quarterly* 14:147—157.

Field, David (ed.). 1974. *Social Psychology for Sociologists*. New York: Halstead Press.

Fine, Gary and Sherryl Kleinman. 1979. "Rethinking Subculture: An Interactionist Analysis," *American Journal of Sociology* 85:1—20.

Fisher, Berenice. 1972a. "The Reconstruction of Failure: Ideologies of Educational Failure in Their Relation to Social Mobility and Social Control," *Social Problems* 19:322—336.

————. 1972b. "Education in the Big Picture," *Sociology of Education* 45:233—257.

Fisher, Berenice and Anselm Strauss. 1978. "The Chicago Tradition and Social Change: Thomas, Park and Their Successors," *Symbolic Interaction* 1:5—23.

————. 1979. "George Herbert Mead and the Chicago Tradition of Sociology (Part One)," *Symbolic Interaction* 2:9—26.

Franklin, B. and F. Kohout. 1971. "Subject-Coded Versus Researcher-Coded TST Protocols," *Sociological Quarterly* 12:82—89.

Freidson, Eliot. 1975. *Doctoring Together: A Study of Professional Social Control*. New York: Elsevier.

————. 1976. "The Division of Labor as Social Interaction," *Social Problems* 23:304—313.

Garfinkel, Harold. 1967. *Studies in Ethnomethodology*. Englewood Cliffs, N.J.: Prentice-Hall.

Geer, Blanche (ed.). 1972. *Learning to Work*. Beverly Hills, Calif.: Sage.

Gerson, Elihu. 1976. "Market Structure and Technical Work Organizations," Presented at the Symposium on Social Structure and Symbolic Interaction, University of Missouri.

Gibbs, Jack. 1966. "Conceptions of Deviant Behavior: The Old and the New," *Pacific Sociological Review* 9:9—14.

————. 1972. "Issues in Defining Deviant Behavior," pp. 36—68 in Robert Scott and Jack Douglas (eds.), *Theoretical Perspectives on Deviance*. New York: Basic Books.

Giddens, Anthony. 1977. "Review Essay: Habermas's Social and Political Theory," *American Journal of Sociology* 83:198—212.

Glaser, Barney and Anselm Strauss. 1964. "Awareness Contexts and Social Interaction," *American Sociological Review* 29:669—679.

————. 1967. *The Discovery of Grounded Theory*. Chicago: Aldine.

Glassner, Barry and Jay Corzine. 1978. "Can Labeling Theory Be Saved?" *Symbolic Interaction* 1:74—89.

Goffman, Erving. 1959. *The Presentation of Self in Everyday Life*. New York: Doubleday Anchor.

———. 1974. *Frame Analysis*. New York: Harper and Row.

Gonos, George. 1977. "'Situation' Versus 'Frame': The 'Interactionist' and the 'Structuralist' Analysis of Everyday Life," *American Sociological Review* 42:854–867.

Gove, Walter. 1970. "Societal Reaction as an Explanation of Mental Illness: An Evaluation," *American Sociological Review* 35:873–884.

———. 1974. "Individual Resources and Mental Hospitalization: A Comparison and Evaluation of the Societal Reaction and Psychiatric Perspectives," *American Sociological Review* 39:86–100.

Grimshaw, Allen. 1973. "On Language in Society: Part I," *Contemporary Sociology* 2:575–585.

———. 1974. "On Language in Society: Part II," *Contemporary Sociology* 3:3–11.

———. 1979. "Social Problems and Social Policies: An Illustration from Sociolinguistics," *Social Problems* 26:582–598.

Gross, Edward and Gregory P. Stone. 1964. "Embarrassment and the Analysis of Role Requirements," *American Journal of Sociology* 70:1–15.

Gross, Neal, Ward Mason, and Alexander McEachern. 1958. *Explorations in Role Analysis*. New York: Wiley.

Gusfield, Joseph. 1963. *Symbolic Crusade*. Urbana, Ill.: University of Illinois Press.

Habenstein, Robert (ed.). 1970. *Pathways to Data*. Chicago: Aldine.

Hall, Peter. 1972. "A Symbolic Interactionist Analysis of Politics," *Sociological Inquiry* 42:35–75.

Handel, Warren. 1979. "Normative Expectations and the Emergence of Meaning as Solutions to Problems: Convergence of Structural and Interactionist Views," *American Journal of Sociology* 84:855–881.

Heap, James and Phillip Roth. 1973. "On Phenomenological Sociology," *American Sociological Review* 38:354–367.

Heath, Shirley Brice. 1978. "Social History and Sociolinguistics," *American Sociologist* 13:84–92.

Heider, Fritz. 1958. *The Psychology of Interpersonal Relations*. New York: Wiley.

Henslin, James (ed.). 1972. *Down to Earth Sociology*. New York: Free Press.

Hewitt, John. 1976. *Self and Society*. Boston: Allyn and Bacon.

Hewitt, John and Peter Hall. 1973. "Social Problems, Problematic Situations, and Quasi-Theories," *American Sociological Review* 38:367–374.

Hickman, C. Addison and Manford Kuhn (eds.). 1956. *Individuals, Groups, and Economic Behavior*. New York: Dryden Press.

Hughes, Everett. 1937. "Institutional Office and the Person," *American Journal of Sociology* 43:404–413.

———. 1945. "Dilemmas and Contradictions of Status," *American Journal of Sociology* 50:353–359.

———. 1962. "What Other?," pp. 119–127 in Arnold Rose (ed.), *Human Behavior and Social Processes*, Boston: Houghton Mifflin.

Jameson, Fredric. 1976. "On Goffman's Frame Analysis," *Theory and Society* 3:119–133.

Jones, Edward. 1976. "How Do People Perceive the Causes of Behavior?" *American Scientist* 64:300–305.

Jones, Russell and Robert Day. 1977. "Social Psychology as Symbolic Interaction," pp. 75–136 in C. Hendrick (ed.), *Perspectives on Social Psychology*, Hillsdale, N.J.: LEA, Inc.

Karp, David and William Yoels. 1979. *Symbols, Selves and Society*. New York: Harper.

Karp, David, Gregory Stone, and William Yoels. 1977. *Being Urban*. Lexington, Mass.: Heath.

Katz, Fred. 1968. *Autonomy and Organization*. New York: Random House.

Kelley, H. H. 1971. *Attribution in Social Interaction*. Morristown, N.J.: General Learning Press.

Kinch, John. 1973. *Social Psychology*. New York: McGraw-Hill.

Klapp, Orrin. 1973. *Models of Social Order*. Palo Alto, Calif.: National Press Books.

Kling, Rob and Elihu Gerson. 1977. "The Social Dynamics of Technical Innovation in the Computing World," *Symbolic Interaction* 1:132–146.

Kuhn, Manford. 1964. "Major Trends in Symbolic Interaction Theory in the Past Twenty-five Years," *Sociological Quarterly* 5:61–84.

Kuhn, Manford and T. S. McPartland. 1954. "An Empirical Investigation of Self Attitudes," *American Sociological Review* 19:68−76.

Labov, William. 1966. "The Effect of Social Mobility on Linguistic Behavior," *Sociological Inquiry* 36:186−203.

———. 1978. "Crossing the Gulf Between Sociology and Linguistics," *American Sociologist* 13:93−103.

Lankford, John. 1973. "The Writing of American History in the 1960's: A Critical Bibliography of Materials of Interest to Sociologists," *Sociological Quarterly* 14:99−126.

Lauer, Robert and Warren Handel. 1977. *Social Psychology: The Theory and Application of Symbolic Interactionism*. Boston: Houghton Mifflin.

Leichty, Marilyn. 1975. "Sensory Modes, Social Activity and the Universe of Touch," pp. 65−79 in Carl Couch and Robert Hinze (eds.), *Constructing Social Life*, Champaign, Ill.: Stipes.

Levy, Judith A. 1979. "Educational Re-entry Processes of Middle Aged Women," Presented at the Annual Meeting of the Midwest Sociological Society, Minneapolis.

Lichtman, R. 1970. "Symbolic Interactionism and Social Reality: Some Marxist Queries," *Berkeley Journal of Sociology* 15:75−94.

Lifton, Robert. 1970. *Boundaries: Psychological Man in Revolution*. New York: Random House.

Lindesmith, Alfred, Anselm Strauss, and Norman Denzin. 1975. *Social Psychology*. Hinsdale, Ill.: Dryden Press.

Linton, Ralph. 1936. *The Study of Man*. New York: Appleton-Century.

Lofland, John. 1970. "Interactionist Imagery and Analytic Interruptus," pp. 35−45 in Tamotsu Shibutani (ed.), *Human Nature and Collective Behavior*. Englewood Cliffs, N.J.: Prentice-Hall.

———. 1971. *Analyzing Social Settings*. Beverly Hills, Calif.: Wadsworth.

———. 1976. *Doing Social Life*. New York: Wiley.

Lofland, Lyn. 1973. *A World of Strangers*. New York: Basic Books.

Lundman, Richard and Paul McFarlane. 1976. "Conflict Methodology: An Introduction and Preliminary Assessment," *Sociological Quarterly* 17:503−512.

Lyman, Stanford and Marvin Scott. 1970. *A Sociology of the Absurd*. New York: Appleton-Century-Crofts.

Maines, David R. 1977a. "Tactile Relationships in the Subway as Affected by Racial, Sexual, and Crowded Seating Situations," *Environmental Psychology and Nonverbal Behavior* 2:100−108.

———. 1977b. "Social Organization and Social Structure in Symbolic Interactionist Thought," *Annual Review of Sociology* 3:235−259.

———. 1978. "Structural Parameters and Negotiated Orders: Comment on Benson, and Day and Day," *Sociological Quarterly* 19:491−496.

Maines, David R. and Marilyn Markowitz. 1980. "Status Symbolism and the Ecology of Participation in Group Counseling Sessions," *International Journal of Social Psychiatry,* in press.

Manning, Peter. 1973. "Language, Meaning, and Action," pp. 278−302 in Jack Douglas, *Introduction to Sociology,* New York: Free Press.

———. 1977a. "Rules in Organizational Context: Narcotics Law Enforcement in Two Settings," *Sociological Quarterly* 18:44−61.

———. 1977b. "The Decline of Civility: A Comment on Erving Goffman's Sociology," *Canadian Review of Sociology and Anthropology* 13:13−25.

Mariampalski, Hyman and Dana Hughes. 1978. "The Use of Personal Documents in Historical Sociology," *America Sociologist* 13:104−113.

Maryl, William. 1973. "Ethnomethodology: Sociology Without Society," *Catalyst* 7:15−28.

Matza, David. 1964. *Delinquency and Drift*. New York: Wiley.

McCall, George, Michael McCall, Norman Denzin, Gerald Suttles, and Suzanne Kurth. 1970. *Social Relationships*. Chicago: Aldine.

McCall, George and J. L. Simmons. 1966. *Identities and Interaction*. New York: Free Press.

McPhail, Clark. 1979. "Experimental Research Is Convergent with Symbolic Interaction," *Symbolic Interaction* 2:89−94.

McPhail, Clark and Cynthia Rexroat. 1979. ''Mead vs. Blumer: The Divergent Methodological Perspectives of Social Behaviorism and Symbolic Interactionism,'' *American Sociological Review* 44:449−467.

McPhail, Clark and Charles Tucker. 1972. ''The Classification and Ordering of Responses to the Question 'Who Am I?''' *Sociological Quarterly* 13:329−347.

Mead, George Herbert. 1934. *Mind, Self and Society*. Chicago: University of Chicago Press.

―――. 1936. *Movements of Thought in the Nineteenth Century*. Chicago: University of Chicago Press.

Mehan, Hugh and Houston Wood. 1975. *The Reality of Ethnomethodology*. New York: Wiley.

―――. 1976. ''De-secting Ethnomethodology,'' *American Sociologist* 11:13−21.

Meltzer, Bernard and John Petras. 1970. ''The Chicago and Iowa Schools of Symbolic Interactionism,'' pp. 3−17 in Tamotsu Shibutani (ed.), *Human Nature and Collective Behavior,* Englewood Cliffs, N.J.: Prentice-Hall.

Meltzer, Bernard, John Petras, and Larry Reynolds. 1975. *Symbolic Interactionism*. Boston: Routledge and Kegan Paul.

Miller, David. 1975. *George Herbert Mead*. Austin, Tex.: University of Texas Press.

Mills, C. Wright. 1939. ''Logic, Language, and Culture,'' *American Sociological Review* 4:187−194.

Morgan, D. 1975. ''Autonomy and Negotiation in an Industrial Setting,'' *Sociology of Work and Occupations* 2:203−226.

Morris, Monica. 1977. *An Excursion into Creative Sociology*. New York: Columbia University Press.

Mukerji, C. 1976. ''Having the Authority to Know: Decision-Making on Student Film Crews,'' *Sociology of Work and Occupations* 3:63−87.

Mullins, Nicholas. 1973. *Theories and Theory Groups in Contemporary American Sociology*. New York: Harper and Row.

Nadel, Siegfried. 1957. *The Theory of Social Structure*. London: Cohen and West.

Olesen, Virginia and Fred Davis. 1972. ''Initiation into a Women's Profession: Identity Problems in the Status Transition of Coed to Student Nurse,'' pp. 8−22 in Fred Davis (ed.), *Illness, Interaction and the Self,* Belmont, Calif.: Wadsworth.

Park, Robert. 1916. ''The City: Suggestions for the Investigation of Human Behavior in the Urban Environment,'' *American Journal of Sociology* 20:577−612.

―――. 1926. ''The Urban Community as a Spatial Pattern and a Moral Order,'' pp. 3−18 in Ernest Burgess (ed.), *The Urban Community*. Chicago: University of Chicago Press.

Pavlov, Ivan. 1927. *Conditioned Reflexes*. London: Oxford University Press.

Perinbanayagam, Robert. 1974. ''The Definition of the Situation: An Analysis of the Ethnomethodological and Dramaturgical View,'' *Sociological Quarterly* 15:521−541.

―――. 1975. ''The Significance of Others in the Thought of Alfred Schutz, G. H. Mead, and C. Cooley,'' *Sociological Quarterly* 16:500−521.

Petras, John and Bernard Meltzer. 1973. ''Theoretical and Ideological Variations in Contemporary Interactionism,'' *Catalyst* 7:1−8.

Psathas, George. 1973. ''Introduction,'' pp. 1−21 in George Psathas (ed.), *Phenomenological Sociology,* New York: Wiley.

Reynolds, Janice and Larry Reynolds. 1973. ''Interactionism, Complicity, and the Astructural Bias,'' *Catalyst* 7:76−85.

Reynolds, Larry. 1973. ''Introduction,'' pp. 1−21 in Larry Reynolds and James Henslin (eds.), *American Society: A Critical Analysis*. New York: David McKay Co.

Reynolds, Larry and Bernard Meltzer. 1973. ''The Origins of Divergent Methodological Stances in Symbolic Interactionism,'' *Sociological Quarterly* 14:189−199.

Robboy, Howard, Sidney Greenblatt, and Candice Clark (eds.). 1979. *Social Interaction*. New York: St. Martin's Press.

Ropers, Richard. 1973. ''Mead, Marx and Social Psychology,'' *Catalyst* 7:42−61.

Rose, Jerry. 1969. ''The Role of the Other in Self-Evaluation,'' *Sociological Quarterly* 10:470−479.

Rosenhan, David. 1973. ''On Being Sane in Insane Places,'' *Science* 179:250−258.

Roth, Julius. 1963. *Timetables*. Indianapolis, Ind.: Bobbs-Merrill.

Roth, Julius, Sheryl Ruzek, and Arlene K. Daniels. 1973. "Current State of the Sociology of Occupations," *Sociological Quarterly* 14:309−333.

Roy, Donald. 1952. "Quota Restriction and Goldbricking in a Machine Shop," *American Journal of Sociology* 57:427−442.

――――. 1959. "Banana Time: Job Satisfaction and Informal Interaction," *Human Organization* 18:156−168.

Saxton, Stanley and Carl Couch. 1975. "Recording Social Interaction," pp. 255−262 in Carl Couch and Robert Hintz (eds.), *Constructing Social Life*, Champaign, Ill.: Stipes.

Schatzman, Leonard and Anselm Strauss. 1955. "Social Class and Modes of Communication," *American Journal of Sociology* 60:329−338.

Schearing, C. D. 1973. "Towards a Phenomenological Sociology," *Catalyst* 7:9−14.

――――. 1973. *Field Research*. Englewood Cliffs, N.J.: Prentice-Hall.

Scheff, Thomas. 1967. "Toward a Sociological Model of Consensus," *American Sociological Review* 32:32−46.

――――. 1970. "On the Concepts of Identity and Social Relationship," pp. 193−207 in Tamotsu Shibutani (ed.), *Human Nature and Collective Behavior*, Englewood Cliffs, N.J.: Prentice-Hall.

――――. 1974. "The Labeling Theory of Mental Illness," *American Sociological Review* 39:444−452.

Schegloff, Emanuel. 1968. Sequencing of Conversational Openings," *American Anthropologist* 70:1075−1095.

Schmitt, Raymond. 1972. *The Reference Other Orientation*. Carbondale, Ill.: Southern Illinois University Press.

Schur, Edwin. 1971. *Labeling Deviant Behavior*. New York: Harper and Row.

Schutz, Alfred. 1967. *The Phenomenology of the Social World*. Translated by George Walsh and Frederick Lehnert. Evanston, Ill.: Northwestern University Press.

Scott, Marvin. 1968. *The Racing Game*. Chicago: Aldine.

――――. 1970. "Functional Analysis: A Statement of Problems," pp. 21−28 in Gregory P. Stone and Harvey A. Farberman (eds.), *Social Psychology Through Symbolic Interaction*, Waltham, Mass.: Xerox.

Scott, Marvin and Stanford Lyman. 1968. "Accounts," *American Sociological Review* 33:46−62.

Shibutani, Tamotsu. 1961. *Society and Personality*. Englewood Cliffs, N.J.: Prentice-Hall.

――――. 1962. "Reference Groups and Social Control" pp. 128−147 in Arnold Rose (ed.) *Human Behavior and Social Processes*. Boston: Houghton Mifflin.

――――. 1968. "A Cybernetics Approach To Motivation," pp. 330−336 in Walter Buckley (ed.), *Modern Systems Research for the Behavioral Scientist*, Chicago: Aldine.

Smith, Harvey. 1958. "Contingencies of Professional Differentiation," *American Journal of Sociology* 63:410−414.

Sommer, Robert. 1969. *Personal Space*. Englewood Cliffs, N.J.: Prentice-Hall.

Spector, Malcolm. 1976. "Labeling Theory in *Social Problems*: A Young Journal Launches a New Theory," *Social Problems* 24:69−75.

Spitzer, Stephan, Carl Couch, and John Stratton. 1970. *The Assessment of the Self*. Iowa City, Iowa: Effective Communications, Inc.

Spitzer, Stephan and Jerry Parker. 1976. "Perceived Validity and Assessment of Self: A Decade Later," *Sociological Quarterly* 17:236−246.

Stone, Gregory P. 1962. "Appearance and the Self," pp. 86−118 in Arnold Rose (ed.), *Human Behavior and Social Processes*. Boston: Houghton Mifflin.

Stone, Gregory P. and Harvey Farberman. 1967. "On the Edge of Rapproachment: Was Durkheim Moving Toward the Perspective of Symbolic Interaction?" *Sociological Quarterly* 8:149−167.

Stover, Stewart. 1977. "Convergences Between Symbolic Interactionism and Systems Theory," *Symbolic Interaction* 1:89−103.

Strauss, Anselm. 1959. *Mirrors and Masks*. New York: Free Press.

――――. 1978a. *Negotiations*. San Fransisco: Jossey-Bass.

――――. 1978b. "A Social World Perspective," pp.

119–128 in Norman K. Denzin (ed.), *Studies in Symbolic Interaction,* Volume 1, Greenwich, Conn.: JAI Press.

Strauss, Anselm and Berenice Fisher. 1978. "Interactionism," pp. 457–498 in Tom Bottomore and Robert Nisbet (eds.), *A History of Sociological Analysis,* New York: Basic Books.

Strauss, Anselm, Leonard Schatzman, Danuta Erlich Rue Bucher, and Melvin Sabshin, "The Hospital and its Negotiated Order." pp. 147–169 in Eliot Freidson (ed.) *The Hospital in Modern Society* NY: Free Press, 1963.

Temerlin, Maurice. 1968. "Suggestion Effects in Psychiatric Diagnosis," *Journal of Nervous and Mental Disease* 147:349–353.

Thomas, Darwin, David Franks, and James Calonico. 1972. "Role-Taking and Power in Social Psychology," *American Sociological Review* 37:605–614.

Thomas, W. I. 1923. *The Unadjusted Girl.* Boston: Little, Brown and Co.

Trice, Harrison and Paul Roman. 1970. "Delabeling, Relabeling, and Alcoholics Anonymous," *Social Problems* 17:538–546.

Tucker, Charles. 1966. "Some Methodological Problems of Kuhn's Self Theory," *Sociological Quarterly* 7:345–358.

Tucker, G. Richard and Wallace Lambert. 1969. "White and Negro Listeners' Reactions to Various American-English Dialects," *Social Forces* 47:463–468.

Turner, Ralph. 1962. "Role-Taking: Process Versus Conformity," pp. 20–40 in Arnold Rose (ed.), *Human Behavior and Social Processes,* Boston: Houghton Mifflin.

———. 1975. "Is There a Quest for Identity?" *Sociological Quarterly* 16:148–161.

———. 1976. "The Real Self: From Institution to Impulse," *American Journal of Sociology* 81:989–1016.

Turner, Ralph and Norma Shosid. 1976. "Ambiguity and Interchangeability in Role Attribution: The Effect of Alter's Response," *American Sociological Review* 41:993–1005.

Vahinger, Hans. 1925. *The Philosophy of the "As If."* London: Routledge and Kegan Paul.

Wallace, Walter (ed.). 1969. *Sociological Theory.* Chicago: Aldine.

Wax, Rosalie. 1971. *Doing Fieldwork.* Chicago: University of Chicago Press.

Weinstein, Eugene and Paul Deutschberger. 1963. "Some Dimensions of Altercasting," *Sociometry* 26:454–466.

Whorf, Benjamin Lee. 1956. *Language, Thought and Reality.* New York: Wiley.

Whyte, William F. 1976. "Research Methods for the Study of Conflict and Cooperation," *American Sociologist* 11:208–216.

Wiseman, Jacqueline. 1970. *Stations of the Lost.* Englewood Cliffs, N.J.: Prentice-Hall.

Wolff, Kurt. 1978. "Phenomenology and Sociology," pp. 499–556 in Tom Bottomore and Robert Nisbet (eds.), *A History of Sociological Analysis,* New York: Basic Books.

Zimmerman, Don. 1974. "Fact as a Practical Accomplishment," pp. 128–143 in Roy Turner (ed.), *Ethnomethodology,* Baltimore: Penguin Books.

———. 1976. "A Reply to Professor Coser," *American Sociologist* 11:4–13.

Zimmerman, Don and D. Lawrence Wieder. 1970. "Ethnomethodology and the Problem of Order: Comment on Denzin," pp. 285–295 in Jack Douglas (ed.), *Understanding Everyday Life,* Chicago: Aldine.

Zurcher, Lewis. 1973. "Alternative Institutions and the Mutable Self: An Overview," *Journal of Applied Behavioral Science* 9:369–380.

THIRTY-NINE

THE SIGNIFICANCE OF OTHERS IN THE THOUGHT OF ALFRED SCHUTZ, G. H. MEAD AND C. H. COOLEY*

R. S. PERINBANAYAGAM

In the early sixties Everett Hughes asked a question that is still pertinent: indeed it has become more relevant with the development of what are claimed to be new ways of doing sociology.[1] The question was "what other?" Herein, Hughes stated:

> . . . systematic attention to the problem of degrees and directions of sensitivity to others turned up rather late among those who study human society in a would-be-scientific way. . . . (However) this theme is almost the central one of that whole school of American sociologists and philosophers which in-

cludes J. Mark Baldwin, Charles Cooley, George Mead, William Thomas, Robert Park, Ellsworth Faris, and their students. Perhaps one should mention Josiah Royce, William James and John Dewey also (1962).

It is necessary to expand Hughes' list and insist that not only the pragmatists and the Chicago school of sociologists, but all sociologists—at least as understood and practiced by the founders and their acknowledged followers—accord a place of importance to the concept of the other in their sociologies.[2] The concept of the other is the path to a social, as opposed to a psychologistic ontology. It is almost axiomatic that the discipline is founded on such an ontology, and the work of the above

SOURCE: R. S. Perinbanayagam. "The Significance of Others in the Thought of Alfred Schutz, G. H. Mead, and C. H. Cooley. Copyright by the Sociological Quarterly, 1975. R. S. Perinbanayagam, "The Significance of Others in the Thought of Alfred Schutz, G. H. Mead, and C. H. Cooley," *The Sociological Quarterly*, XVI (Autumn, 1975), pp. 500−521. Reprinted by permission of the Sociological Quarterly.

*I must express my gratitude to the many readers of an earlier version of this paper who gave me both criticisms and suggestions.
[1]See Zimmerman and Wieder (1970); Douglas (1970).

[2]In fact, in Talcott Parsons' pathfinding analyses of the structure of social action (1937) found in the work of the European social scientists, he missed a great opportunity to examine the continuity of the structures of social action in American social thought by ignoring the works of Cooley, Mead, Thomas, and Dewey.

mentioned sociologists and philosophers as well as that of Marx, Weber, Durkheim and even Simmel, though commonly identified as a phenomenological sociologist, is founded on such an assumption, and insistently separates itself from psychologism in both its epistemological and ontological manifestations.[3]

THE OTHER AND SOCIOLOGY/SOCIAL PSYCHOLOGY

How does sociology accomplish this? It is our argument that the overwhelming importance of the "other," in its various manifestations, is crucial to the understanding of society and the individual. The individual is unknown to social science as Cooley said, because he is defined, created, and sustained by an interaction with the other—known to some sociologists as the primacy of the group, to some others as the importance of institutions and communities, and to some sociologists and anthropologists as the paramountcy of social structure. It is not that the individual has no creativity or voluntariness, but that even such creativity and voluntariness are social and interpersonal activities and, so, are minimally or maximally constrained. All of these latter concerns are best realized by asking what part *the other* plays in any given theory or explanation, and then rejecting theories that have no important part for it as being something less than sociological.

Who or what is the "other"? The "other" is the social psychological form of that abstraction that sociologists and anthropologists call social structure. It is, to paraphrase Levi-Straus, a social psychological means to achieve a sociological result (1967:229)—the result of incorporating society as consisting of separable analytic units which are nevertheless in symbolic interaction with each other (Blumer, 1962:179). The essential relationship between these units, in other words, is not

a mechanical or merely systemic one, but a transactional one. As Levi-Straus puts it, "society consists of individuals and groups which communicate with one another. . . . In any society, communication operates on three different levels: communication of women, communication of goods and services and communication of messages" (1967:289). The notion of social structure is an abstraction, a model built by social scientists as well as by members of the society, based on these patterns of communication. The "other" is the social psychological form in which social structure is articulated and has been given expression in many categories like the generalized other, the primary group, the significant other and reference group, besides the general category of the "other" that is found in the work of many philosophers.

In the works of Mead, Cooley, and Harry Stack Sullivan, as well as in the works of certain philosophers like Martin Buber, Jean Paul Sartre, and Alfred Schutz, the concept of the "other" assumes a great importance. To all of them it became a mechanism for the solution of certain problems in their inquiries. These different solutions and the problems they solve, nevertheless have something in common insofar as they all try to account for the emergence of sociality out of the givenness of individuals. In a universe palpably populated by individual bodies and psyches, it is always possible to discover couples, communities, and societies. How is this possible? It is possible because an "other," a social structure, a society, is incorporated into the individual self, and such a self is always conscious and aware of the "others." The concept of the "other" is the vehicle out of the traps of solipsism or the quagmires of psychologism. In any case, the concept figures prominently in the explanatory and exegetical paradigms of interactionist social psychologists and certain existentialist philosophers. They share many ideas that have an immediate relevance to a theory of self and the "other": for all these thinkers, the encounter with

---

[3]On psychologism see Karl Popper (1963) and Talcott Parsons (1937).

nothingness and a retreat to aloneness is alleviated by an encounter with another, and we would contend that the currency used in these encounters is vocabularies of motives (Mills, 1940).[4]

This relationship between self and "other" is a dialectical, as well as a syntactical one: the "other" forms the self as the self formulates the "other." In all situations of social life, the "other" is manifest, concretely or abstractly. And as the "other" manifests itself, its character and content become causally significant to the emergence of the self and *its* nature and content. Thus, we retrieve the person from solipsism and psychologism while at the same time introducing the notion of power into the conceptualizations about the emergence of the self. The "other" in its capacity as validator and motive-spring, in its capacity as the ground and substance in which the self grows becomes a powerful controller and legislator of the self that in fact emerges. The self emerges in sustained interaction with others; it grows and maintains itself as it receives messages from those it is forced to live with. There is, however, no need to conceive of the "other" in any a priori manner as a neutral, benevolent or indifferent one. The "other" should rather be viewed as exercising power over the emergent self and, to a certain extent, determining the character of that self. From its very beginning, a self emerges in a transaction in which "others" exercise control: infant to child to young adult are stages in which "others" hold power and influence the content of these stages. In adult life, power of the "others" becomes at once more pervasive, as well as institutionalized. It manifests itself in the systems of class, caste, and estate, as they get translated into interpersonal relations; and it is evident in the power of institutions of various sorts

to determine the forms of conduct and character that is acceptable and to reject those that do not conform to them. The "other" is the instrument by which we can talk of power in social psychological inquiries.

In recent years, the work of Alfred Schutz has begun to enjoy a certain eminence. A sociology calling itself phenomenological sociology, as well as another which calls itself ethnomethodology, has emerged; each claims Schutz as the father and, one may add, Edmund Husserl as the grandfather. In addition, the fruitfully eclectic work of Peter Berger and his associates also claims indebtedness to Schutz. All but the last of these scholars disavow any fundamental connection between the thought of Schutz and of the others mentioned earlier, and they imply that Schutz's thought is somehow more powerful and parsimonious as a basis for doing an adequate sociology. Schutz himself, at different points in his writings, refers to Mead's work, at times favorably and at others rather patronizingly, and indeed sees his own work as a continuation of the best elements in that of Mead. One of Schutz's more recent followers, Jack Douglas (1970:3–44), goes to the extent of claiming that Mead was indeed a phenomenologist, and that all his interpreters and followers, with the exception of Natanson and to some extent Blumer, have misunderstood him and/or misinterpreted him.[5] Therefore, it seems important to raise the question whether Schutz and Mead were, in fact, taking similar positions, and examine whether either of them or both of them are more congenial to a social ontology and compatible with the foundations of the sociological argument.[6]

---

[4]There are various discussions and studies in which the concept of the other becomes the focus: Faris (1937); Shibutani (1962). However, Hughes' essay "What Other?" can be taken as a pragmatic statement on the "other" that recognizes the overwhelming importance of the concept for sociology and social psychology. See also Howard Becker's "Selves Emerge When Others Emerge" (1950).

[5]The intriguing question of whether those who interpreted Mead's work as part of a program of a pragmatic philosophy misinterpreted Mead, or those who converted his seminal thought into an effete idealism we will not explore here. However, Bauman's comments seem pertinent (1967).

[6]See Kemper (1972) for a recent statement of this argument. The classic statement, despite many criticisms, still remains that of Talcott Parsons (1937).

THE OTHER IN ALFRED SCHUTZ

Alfred Schutz was the foremost follower of Edmund Husserl in sociology and the figure who introduced European phenomenology into American sociology. Many recent sociologists claim to be either direct intellectual descendants or greatly influenced by his work. But what is the status of the ''other'' in Schutz's work and what function does it perform in establishing a social ontology? Schutz places the ''other,'' ''the alter ego,'' as he calls it, in the center of his work. He describes it as follows:

> The alter-ego therefore is that stream of consciousness whose activities I can seize in their present by my own simultaneous activities. This experience of the other's stream of consciousness in vivid simultaneity I propose to call the *general thesis of the alter-ego's existence*. It implies that this stream of thought which is not mine, shows the same thought through connectedness as mine (1967a:174) (Emphasis in original).

But Schutz does not show what passes between the self and ''other.'' Is there anything else, besides the existence of the ''alter-ego'' whom the self typifies by presumably appealing to its own experience of the world, that is accomplished between the self and the ''alter-ego''? The existence of the ''other'' is granted by Schutz, but its implications in a continued matrix of communication are not fully explicated. In the thesis that is pursued here, the ''other'' is not merely existent, but articulatory—it talks and expresses its intentions, values, judgments, and consolations. The ''other'' is available to me by his acts that he or she dramatizes; even the stream of consciousness of the ''other'' is available to me only in the form of these dramatizations. The ''other,'' usually with care but often carelessly, announces what he wants me to take him to be, and I do the same: this is the manner in which I know him and he knows me. Norman Malcolm has gone to the extent of saying that the knowledge of other minds is not so much inferred from the acts of others by an analogy with

one's own mind, but that these very acts of the ''others'' are, in fact, the *manifestations* of the others (1966).

In any case, the ''other'' is not merely existent, but communicatory, and what it communicates is of immense significance to the lives of the people who accept it as their ''other.'' Schutz does not address himself to the problem of what passes between self and other, except to refer to the general category of communication. The communicative process is said to occur between the ''I'' and the alter-ego, but they do not seem to have any influence on how the *persons* of each of these participants is constituted: they merely observe and understand each other—and sometimes are even said to confront each other. While this position is advanced in various parts of Schutz's work, here is a representative statement:

> . . . in the face-to-face situation, the conscious life of my fellow man becomes accessible to me by a maximum of vivid indications. Since he is confronting me in person, the range of symptoms by which I apprehend his consciousness includes much more than what he is communicating to me purposefully. I observe his movements, gestures and facial expressions, I hear the intonation and the rhythm of his utterances. Each phase of my partner's consciousness is coordinated with a phase of my own . . . (Schutz, 1964:29).

The ''other'' is perceived as an entity, but is not recognized as directing any of his activities toward the self, does not even seem to want to participate in any joint action, in the creation of a social act, in the arrival at a common definition of selves and situations. In fact, the nature of the entity doing the perceiving of the ''other's'' activities is left a total mystery: it is said to be constituting the ''other'' as well as ''the world,'' but who and how it was constituted and sustained is never made clear: it appears to be a kind of Schutzian a priori, thus denying the validity of the processes of socialization and the self as a social and interpersonal emergent.

Further examination of Schutz's work merely confirms this; take for example his notion of reciprocity of perspectives and the we-relation. The former is articulated as follows:

> I take it for granted—and assume my fellowman does the same—that if I change places with him so that his here becomes mine, I shall be at the same distance from things and see them with the same typicality as he actually does; moreover, the same things would be in my reach which are actually his (the reverse is also true) . . . Until counter-evidence, I take it for granted—and assume my fellowman does the same—that the differences in perspectives originating in our unique biographical situation for the purpose at hand of either of us, and that he and I, that we assume that both of us have selected and interpreted the actually or potentially common objects and their features in an identical manner; or at least in an "empirically identical manner", i.e., one sufficient for all practical purposes (1967a:12).

"Intersubjectivity" receives extensive treatment, and in this discussion the subject and the other are allowed to communicate with each other, albeit rather grudgingly. It is said to take place through the language, pictures, and expressive and mimetic signs (Schutz, 1967a:320−322). But, intersubjectivity itself is conceived in a fashion that leaves the other with very little volition, intentionality, or a self that interlocks with those of the subject and jointly creates a meaning:

> Born into a social world, he comes upon his fellowmen and takes their existence for granted without question, just as he takes for granted the existence of the natural objects he encounters. The essence of this assumption about his fellowmen may be put in this short formula: The Thou (or other person) is conscious and his stream of consciousness is temporal in character, exhibiting the same basic form as mine (Schutz, 1967b:98).

Let us take each of these treatments of the importance of the other for further discussion. The reciprocity of perspectives between subject and other is *assumed* by the constituting person, but the other does not participate in any way in the construction of such a perspective of reciprocity. The person doing the constituting or "seeing" is merely aware of the other's perspective, and merely acknowledges his existence. But how he, the subject, becomes aware of the other, and why he assumes that the other has a similar perspective is beyond comprehension. Schutz admits that until counter-evidence is presented, the subject will make this assumption. But the state of affairs until the presentation of *counter-evidence* is not a neutral or passive state: it is on the contrary a state where *evidence is presented* by others, evidence over which they have some control, giving the grounds on which the subject can base his conclusion that the other does, in fact, share a common perspective. The subject makes an *inference* and not an *assumption*, and he does this with the reciprocal intention or cooperation of the other. In fact, if the evidence is not clear on this score, one takes the trouble to find out whether in fact the other would cooperate in creating a reciprocity of perspectives by presenting the evidence necessary to come to even a tentative inference about a shared perspective.

The theory of intersubjectivity falls short of giving substantiality as well as activity to the other. In discussing communication, the other is again given the capacity to relate the "sign" in question to an interpretational scheme, and, when relating is substantially coincidental, intersubjectivity is said to be created. Says Schutz:

> (The subject) . . . is interpreting Objectifications in which the others' subjective experiences manifest themselves. If it is the body of the other that is in question, he concerns himself with act-objectifications, i.e., movements, gestures, or the results of action. If it is artifacts that are in question, these may either be signs in the narrower sense or manufactured external objects, such as tools, monuments, etc. (1967b:132−133).

But the full implications of this position are not examined by Schutz. That a coincidence of responses is necessary is evident, but this leads to the fact that the creation of such "intersubjectivities" (or meanings) is *problematic,* and hence the other who receives communicatory messages has the capacity and the responsibility and the power either to participate cooperatively in the emergence of a meaningful transaction, or to refuse to do so. To the extent that enough people do cooperate, one has a relationship, a group, and a society. But it must be recognized and insisted upon that the other is not a mere recipient of communicatory signs and a source of "appresentations," but an active, interfering, and powerful person, group, or institution who or which interferes, one way or the other, in the ongoing actions of the subject. The fact of interaction, the fact of the joint creation of meaning and reality is not a part of Schutz's reciprocity or intersubjectivity. The other is seen as an analogous "typical" being, but one who does not bear an attitude or a motive or an act directed *toward* the subject. He does not participate with the subjects in constituting the world: he is merely a part of the world that is being constituted by the subject. Notice here the statement on motives that Schutz gives:

> I can apperceive analogically through appresentational references my fellowman's cogitations (for example the motives for his actions) as he can mine (1967a:327).

My fellowman, the other—his attitudes, motives, aims, intentions—however, are not part of the material out of which I constitute myself and my world; they are for Schutz independent and prior to the constitution of myself and my world: I merely apperceive them *analogically.* There is no recognition here that one cannot constitute the world by himself, and that one does it with the help of others, and that the partnership is hardly ever an equal one. For Schutz then, the alter-ego or the other is merely a theoretical possibility for the self and functions in his thought as an intellectual loophole out of the traps of solipsism. Indeed it makes an appearance rather sporadically in his writings at precise moments when his analysis is about to entrap itself into such a state. The rest of the time, the self or the ego, as Schutz calls it, is merrily constituting its world in the Here and Now in a natural attitude, rather than in the There and Then, and not only a world, but a Paramount Reality at that, with no aid or help from others, without benefit of interactions, validation, or socialization.

An examination of another of Schutz's papers, a substantive one rather than an epistemological statement, reveals these shortcomings more clearly. Schutz claims in the opening sentence of this paper, "Choosing Among Projects of Action":

> Our purpose here is the analysis of the processes by which an actor in daily life determines his future conduct after having considered several possible ways of action. The term action shall designate human conduct as an ongoing process which is devised by the actor in advance, that which is based on a preconceived project (1967a:67).

Starting with these premises, Schutz goes on to detail the processes, as he conceives them, by which actors choose among different available projects. The projects exist for Schutz in "a structure of time"—that is, they are assessed in the present, but the assessment takes account of the past and the action in question is contemplated for the future. These actions are "motivated" and these motives are of two types: in-order-to-motives, which refers to the causation of action that is yet to occur, and "because motives," which explain a current action in terms of a past event or experience. Schutz then goes on to distinguish between fancying and projecting, and the differences, it turns out, are that the latter has a "foundation of practicability" which is said to be determined by "the world taken for granted" and the "biographical situation" of the person making the choice. Once this person comes to this stage, he undergoes "doubting and questioning" and confronts face-to, so to speak, Husserl's "Problematic and Open Possibilities,'' and so it goes on finally to an act of choice. This is summed up as:

> We have studied so far the processes of choosing between two objects actually within my reach, both equally obtainable. . . . As such, their constitution is beyond *my* control. I have to take one of them or leave both of them as they are. Projecting, however, is on *my* own making and in this sense within *my* control. Anything that will later on stand to choice in the way of a problematic alternative has to be produced by *me* and in the course of producing it, *I* may modify it at *my* will and within the limits of practicability (1967a:84, our italics).

Besides the conventional plural used in the beginning, this passage reeks with individuality and solipsism: the overused first personal pronoun gives us the clue to an understanding of the problem with phenomenology and why a sociology cannot be built on these foundations without radical modifications. The thesis that Schutz advances about choice is both empirically false and ontologically inadequate. Empirically, choices are made in a social context: others interfere, help, hinder, aid, and assist, asked or unasked, in choosing among projects of action and these others often have a stake in the actual choice. These others who participate in the processes of choice are bearers of role and identity, and they, as the self, become entitled to these attributes only to the extent that they participate in the ongoing acts and projects of choice.

Schutz's position is ontologically inadequate insofar as it does not conceive of all actions as taking place in a nexus of sociality and does not even take his own, admittedly insufficient, theory of intersubjectivity into its framework. How can I anticipate the future in terms of ''my own making,'' ''my control,'' etc.? These events of making and bringing things under my control—do they not occur in an ''intersubjective'' universe? Indeed they occur, in our view, not only in an intersubjective world, but in an *interacting* world of persons. But, in Schutz's world, people do not seem to interact with each other or even seem to talk to each other. Curiously they take action and do not bother to check the responses of other people to find out whether they may have erroneously taken a windmill to be a knight, or have mistaken a peasant girl for a queen! Blithely indifferent to others, they choose among projects of action and presumably carry these actions onward in the Here and Now, without any regard to Thou, Them, They, and Us! It is a splendid view of the human predicament—free and untrammelled and limitless in its powers of constitution—but a false one nevertheless.

One must distinguish between granting man a *capacity* for freedom as against the limitations imposed on him by biologists, instinctivists, ethologists, etc., and the *fact* of freedom in everyday life. Schutzian phenomenology is unable to make this distinction. Our freedom to act is, of course, interrupted by other people's freedom to act against us, and everyone's freedom is circumscribed by the reality of power in everyday life. My constitution of the world is undertaken in these circumscribed fields and any serious sociology must undertake its investigations not only in full awareness of such a circumscription, but is obliged to include these circumscriptions into its investigations and theories.

One of Schutz's students, Zaner, addresses himself to the problem of intersubjectivity and leads us deeper into a further mystery about the nature of this relationship. His essay does not lead to anything but ''overt performances requiring a bodily gearing into the outer world, the transition from inner durée to objective time is accomplished and these working actions thereby partake of both. . . . In the living present, I and my fellowmen simultaneously live through a pluri-dimensionality of time.'' And quoting Schutz: ''we grow older together'' (1962). I am sure they do, and experience pluri-dimensionality as well: but do they say anything of significance to each, do they agree, disagree, struggle, flirt, seduce, insult, cajole, bully, console, comfort each other as they grow older? Indeed, Schutz and Zaner know that these two "copresences" are growing older together; but do they themselves know it and talk about it with each other, and do they get frightened about it? There is no indication that they do anything of this sort: they are merely present to each other. As Zaner puts it: "It is clear that the reciprocal interlocking of *time dimension* is for Schutz, the core phenomenon of intersubjectivity." But, it must be granted that Zaner recognizes the problem with Schutz's notion of intersubjectivity and introduces Gabriel Marcel's thought as a way of rounding out Schutz. This enables Zaner to introduce notions of "concern" for each other, "care," etc., into the argument. But there is really no need to try so hard or travel so far. Zaner's attempt to integrate some of Marcel's ideas into those of Schutz indicates that he himself is conscious of this inadequacy or incompleteness in Schutz's work on the questions of intersubjectivity and the alter-ego.

Phenomenology, it turns out, is nothing more than a descriptive psychology of consciousness, erroneous insofar as it does not accept the facticity of the other, but serviceable as an accounting of that elusive entity that elicited Freud's ire, the Protestant conscience! It tells of the inviolability of the inner man and his ultimate responsibilty for what befalls him, because, after all, he himself constituted it without any help from others, alter-egos, or the mother-church. The monads in Schutz's world indeed have windows, but they are equipped with one-way mirrors: They let us look out but do not let any light in.[7]

G. H. MEAD AND THE "OTHER"

In Mead's work the concept of the "generalized other" occurs in many places, though it is essentially an integral element of his theory of the self. In this context, it appears as the attitude of the community in direct or indirect manifestation, as an instrument of the social control of the self, and as the abstract formulation of the ethos of a community or society. He describes it as follows: "The organized community or social group which gives to the individual his unity of self may be called 'the generalized other'. The attitude of the generalized other is the attitude of the whole community (1932:154). A little later on he avers:

> If a human individual is to develop a self in the fullest sense, it is not sufficient for him to merely take the attitude of other human individuals toward himself and toward one another within the human social process and to bring that social process as a whole into his individual experience merely in these terms (1932:154).

The question that remains in any discussion of the generalized other and its function in the emergence and sustenance of a self is: how do the attitudes of the generalized other manifest themselves? Conversely, how does a self in the process of emerging apprehend the attitudes of the generalized other? Mills gives us a brief answer, but unfortunately does not develop it any further. "One of the components of a 'generalized other' as a mechanism of social control is vocabularies of acceptable motives" (1940). Motives are compo-

---

[7]Interestingly enough, Jean Paul Sartre seems to share the version of the other that Schutz provides, though one can see that in his philosophical career he seems to have had trouble living with his early statement of the issue in his major work. The concept of the other permits him to escape what he himself calls the "reef of solipsism" and describes it thus: "By the mere appearance of the 'other,' I am put in a position of passing judgment on myself as an object for it is as an object that I appear to the other. Yet, this object is not an empty image in the mind of another. . . . I recognize I am, as the 'other' sees me" (1956:222). He then uses shame as an illustration. However, Sartre does not make clear in his discussion how the self and other establish their relationship, how in fact the "other" shows its presence and evaluations to the self. It is indeed true that we feel ashamed *in terms* of the other, but reading Sartre, one gets the impression that one imagines or anticipates the reaction of the other, rather than interacts with him at any time: no physical or material other seems involved, no one would indeed shout "shame on you," or teach what shame was. See also Ortega y Gasset for a diametrically opposite view of the significance of the other. Buber's position is said to be similar to that of Mead (Pfuetze, 1961), and certainly it is different from that of Ortega and Sartre, as well as Schutz. For an excellent analysis of issues relevant to the discussion here, see Barnes (1973).

nents of the generalized other, or conversely, the generalized other is a source of motives. But *who* does the imputation of motives and *when?* It is obvious that they are not imputed and avowed in any random or sporadic manner. They are, on the contrary, given play, in Mills' words, "in delimited situations." The generalized other is constituted of motive-bearing structures and contributes different facets of these structures of the emergence and sustenance of the self.

The "other" is conceived in the work of Mead as an active and attitude-bearing entity which directly influences the self, and in fact the relationship between the one and the other is best described as a dialectical or a syntactical one. Though Mead is careful to point out that the generalized other does not have a necessary relation to "any particular individual," he nevertheless conceives of the relationship as an interactional one: the self "takes" the attitude of the generalized other toward itself, interprets it, understands it, and then incorporates it into his own self-conceptions and universes of meaning; the self and the other, generalized though it may be, *participate* in the construction of self, meaning, and world. The conception of other that Mead develops is of an other that can participate in what he termed the "social act":

> The response of one organism to the gesture of another in any given social act is the meaning of that gesture and is also in a sense responsible for the appearance of, or coming into being of a new object—or new content of an old object—to which that gesture refers through the outcome of the given social act (1932:78).

The substance or content of these "transactions" or interactions by parties to a social act—a self and an other—is attitude and motive-bearing complexes. The process by which these transactions are accomplished, the methodology by which an individual takes account of the generalized other, is provided by Mead's celebrated analogy of the game and the player:

Each one of his own acts is determined by his assumption of the action of the others who are playing the game. What he does is controlled by his being everyone else on that team, at least as far as those attitudes affect his own particular response. We get then an other which is an organization of the attitudes of those involved in the same process (1934:154).

The critical word here once again is that of "attitude," and the individual takes account of these attitudes in organizing his own responses and indeed his own self in terms of these attitudes. Insofar as Mead talks of them as attitudes, there is no reason to suppose that these attitudes, often expressed as a "rhetoric of motives" in Burke's phrase (1950), are in any important sense historically and situationally independent. The attitude that one expects to find expressed by the generalized others will vary from epoch to epoch and situation to situation; generalized others are historical creations and there is really nothing in Mead's work that would lead us to assume the contrary.

If that is the case, what can be said to constitute the generalized other? Religious systems, philosophies, legal systems and ideologies, mythology, literature, and art become the elements out of which the generalized other is constituted. Mead said:

> In abstract thought, the individual takes the attitude of the generalized other toward himself, *without reference to its expression is any particular other individuals;* and in concrete thought he takes that attitude insofar as it is expressed in the attitudes towards his behavior of those other individuals with whom he is involved in the given social situation (1932:156) (Emphasis mine).

In the abstract form, the generalized other is manifest in the symbolic system of the community; in interpersonal situations they are addressed as motives and attitudes by the participants in a social transaction. In these situations, motives drawn from the generalized other are used in everyday interactions; one's experiences are interpreted and accounted for in terms of these motives and attitudes, and thus they constitute the rhetorical instrument by which a self is emerged and sustained. The generalized other is not a cloud hanging over us and exercising control electronically; not is it a sea of customs and conventions in which we wallow. It is materially expressed and enshrined in the documents of the society and articulated in act and speech in everyday life; it cannot be divorced from the normal processes by which a society or community came into being, sustains itself, and in the event ceases to do so. As Mead puts it in another passage:

> It is in the form of the generalized other that the *social process* influences the behavior of the individuals involved in it and carrying it on . . . for it is in this form that the social process or community enters as a determining factor into the individual's thinking (1934:155, our italics).

The generalized other is viewed as a part of the social processes and the individual is said to be influenced determinedly by these same processes: the method by which such an influencing occurs is that of interaction or reciprocal action. Hence, the selves that emerge in a society and the meanings that sustain them are products of a historically derived social process.

THE OTHER IN COOLEY: THE PRIMARY GROUP

Despite its frequent reference in textbooks and introductory statements on sociology, the concept of the primary group has not been fully utilized in sociology and social psychology as a powerful explanatory variable, except in an implicit sense. Everyone recognizes its importance and acknowledges its value, but as a variable in explanatory paradigms it is not very conspicuous. In influential textbooks on social psychology, one hardly finds the concept utilized. Yet, its importance can never be gainsaid—particularly in a discussion of the

crucial experiences of one's life and their relationship to a system of motives. The primary group is Cooley's notion of the "Other," which provides him with a solution to the problem of psychologism and solipsism. But, Cooley proposes a concrete and living set of persons—Other Selves—who support and validate a self and give it the verities and substances of a life. As Cooley defines it:

> By primary groups, I mean those characterized by intimate face-to-face association and cooperation. They are primary in several senses, but chiefly in that they are fundamental in forming the social nature and ideals of the individual. The result of intimate association, psychologically is a certain fusion of individualities in a common whole, so that one's very self, for many purposes at least, is the common life and purposes of the group. Perhaps, the simplest way of describing this wholeness is by saying that it is a "we"; it involves the sort of sympathy and mutual identification for which "we" is the natural expression. One lives in the feeling of the whole and finds the chief aims of his will in that feeling (1962:23).

Cooley goes on to give some examples: the family, the play group of children, and the neighborhood or community group. Faris, making an early stab at clarifying Cooley's notion, argued that one need not insist upon the face-to-face nature of a primary group: that was an accidental feature and not an essential one (1937). The limits of the primary group are the limits of communication: one can communicate face-to-face or communicate by other means—but communicate one must. In the processes of these communications in and from a primary group, a human develops—develops self-feeling, self-pride, and self-assurance. Or, on the contrary, he develops negative feelings about himself—feeling of worthlessness, incapacity, and anxiety.

The primary group is the crucible of the self: the self is carefully or carelessly nurtured in it, tended and attended to in it. One claims rights in these groups and owes responsibilities to its members. What happens, however, when these rights are denied or the responsibilities unfulfilled? In the former case, one has to seek a new primary group; for example, leave one's spouse and find a new companion who will now understand. If the responsibilities are unfulfilled, one gets "expelled" from the primary group; for example, one's spouse is made to leave and goes away. Further complications may arise as well. One may get bored with or outlast a primary group, or become disillusioned with a group; even here, one has to seek another group sooner or later; for example, a Jew may be converted to fundamentalist Christianity and will have to anchor his new faith in primary relationships that share the faith and keep him away from skeptics and unbelievers (Travisano, 1970). Or, one may want to abandon a devotion to sports and the outdoor life and become a scholar and chess champion; commensurate changes have to be made in the organization of one's primary relationships.

The pathos in social mobility is surely found in the incapacity of one who has moved up to be able to relate to those who stayed on (Rose, 1964). One can view a life as a transition from one primary group to another in a series, broken only by insanity or death. In fact, it has been shown that insanity is created by the fact of abandonment—emotionally and legally—by a primary group (Goffman, 1961; Laing et al., 1970). The members of a primary group participate in the definition of the self, in the delineation of what is real and the clarification of what is relevant (Berger and Kellner, 1971). They provide the terms and conditions of one's life and encourage one in the lines of activity they approve of; they dissuade one from lines they disapprove of, and soothe and comfort one when one needs it. All the significant experiences of one's life are felt in terms of the primary group, and those who have no primary groups are the troubled and the emotionally destitute. These people may have people to talk to and occupations to work at and games to play, but they are lonely because they lack trustful and intimate ties with others. Because primary groups retrieve one from the existential loneliness, as far as possible, and

drive home the idea that suicide is infinitely worse than all current anguish. The members of the primary group constitute the basis of what Burkhardt Holzner calls the "epistemic community"—they generate the ontology and the epistemology of the self and world that one takes for granted, of the motives and meanings that constitute one's interactions and consciousness (1968).

It is the group that we create by utilizing all the resources at our command. The family of procreation is, in fact, a primary group that humans create by using their virility and attractiveness, as well as other resources. It is, of course, foolish to think of the family as being created for sex; it is indeed the other way around. One uses sex to create a family. Sexual fulfillment by itself can be obtained by a variety of strategems; but once sexual attractiveness is lost, the chance of creating that *relatively* enduring primary group called the family becomes small. It is the "ensemble" (Marx, 1970:122) that creates and sustains the essential nature of man. The historicity of man does not manifest itself in any mysterious way; rather, it manifests itself in the nature of the social relationship, of the primary group *that is made available to one* in different epochs. The history that is relevant here is: (a) the knowledge of the past that is, in fact, available to the society and its members concerned; and (b) the events, discoveries, and knowledge from the past that has fashioned the social life around him; the pattern and paraphernalia of social relationships, self-images, and self-concepts that the historically derived symbolic system makes available to him. These historical derivatives, however, are mediated by primary relationships. One can be trapped in a primary group that lives by a literal interpretation of the scriptures, and thus be denied the full historicity of the human experience since the time of the scriptures; or else one can be trapped in a group supporting pre-Copernican astronomy and live by that view. The historicity of the human consciousness is not automatic: it is mediated and sustained by the particular history that the particular group in which one is entrapped accepts as *the history*. What are the processes by which this is accomplished? One of the prime—if not the prime—means is by the provision of the appropriate vocabulary of motive—by giving a self in need the necessary rhetoric of motives and validating the motives that the self announces. These motives are naturally drawn from the ones that are socially provided—that the society and culture make available in the form of the generalized other.

When are such motives necessary? When is a self in need of motives? The argument has been—following Kenneth Burke and C. W. Mills—that selves are rhetorically constructed and hence the answer to these questions is that motives are necessary all the time. The primary group, in fact, becomes the intermediary between the generalized other and the self as a transmitter of motives. It is, however, called upon to function at crucial moments in the unfolding of a self, as well as to support, validate, and provide motives. Hence, we can talk of two phases of motive mongering for the primary group: (a) the normal or everyday phase; and (b) the phase of contingencies and crises.

In the normal phase of providing motives to an emerging self, the primary group draws its vocabularies from the generalized other. In the childhood of a person, the family and the peer group constitute the primary group and they become the tutors of vocabularies to the child. The child learns the vocabulary proper to its class, religion, and nation; it learns to delimit its horizons and develop a calculus of probabilities for the conduct of its life in terms of what is available in these early socialization groups. In the absence of alternative structures of rhetoric, to give it alternative probabilities and identities, the child continues into adolescence and adulthood with these vocabularies and the horizons they represent. When alternative vocabularies do become available, we talk of conversion experiences or experiences of alternation (Berger, 1962).

What about the motives at occasions of crisis or contingencies? It is the obligation of the primary group to come to the aid of a member facing a crisis with an appropriate vocabulary of motives. In that general category of experience that we can call "crises," the primary group has many functions to perform—functions that ensure the element of intimacy that is necessary for the self to survive. It is foolhardy, however, to assume that all primary groups fulfill their obligations to their members. Some do and can hence be called friendly groups, and others fail and can be called hostile groups; the latter are groups in which some person is trapped and is unable to escape, and stays to be diminished or destroyed.

The obligations of a primary group (friendly) are fundamentally to validate and support the motives of its members when they face a crisis or contingency. Such responsibilities of the primary group are governed by rules and regulations. Jerry Rose has argued that the other should be conceptualized as a role:

> If we conceive "the other" as a *role*, we can think of just such a normative regulation of responses to the person Role-determined behavior involves the person's orientation toward obligatory actions: he does his "duty" in spite of any personal inclinations in the same socialization process by which he is encumbered with his other social duties. In the context of our problem, he expresses his attitude toward others in a manner which conforms to norms governing the role of "the other" in interactions (1969:474—475) (Emphasis in original).

The attention he calls to the function of rules and norms must be followed through. The others in the primary group, more than the others in other groups, have to fulfill obligations to each other, and they are governed by rules that concern the obligation to feel, or claim to feel, that certain sentiments and rules determine the expression of these sentiments. To violate these rules is also to hurt somebody's feelings, and to hurt somebody is to violate some rule. For example, one can violate the rules concerning fidelity in monogamous marriages, and hurt the feelings of the spouse; one anticipates the feelings of the other and either follows the rules of fidelity or else follows the secondary rule that "What he/she doesn't know can't hurt him/her," and conceals the relevant information. Similarly, members of the primary group cooperate to maintain definitions of self and protect self-esteem by observing the rules of deference and demeanor in the face of defeat, failure, and dishonor experienced by its members. Maintaining social relationships with those who systematically violate these rules and with those who do not have the discipline of primary relationships becomes impossible. In fact, it could be said that these rules forestall the emergence of conflict in primary relationships and ensure their continuance. The argument is considerably broader than the functionalist explanation of incest taboos. It is not only rules forbidding marriage and intercourse between certain types of kin that enable a primary group to sustain itself; it is all the rules of etiquette, decorum, form, and manners that do so. For example, to display glee and ecstasy when a member of one's primary group has been hurt or bereaved is to invite exile from the primary group in question; to challenge one's spouse continuously on his/her manliness/femininity and to be derisive of other significant attributes of the person's cherished "identities" is to be ill-mannered, rude, etc., but it also strains the bonds of the primary group to the breaking point. Nevertheless, it is rather a thin wedge and one can overdo it and create illusions, if not of grandeur at least those that are grander than they should be, which elicit adjectives like quixotic, or worse.

The hostile group, of course, behaves in ways that are contrary to that of the friendly one, and generally it can be said that they violate the rules concerning deference, demeanor, and the expression of sentiments. A member's failures are magnified and his/her negative and self-debasing motives are eagerly accepted and validated, and ready and willing cooperation is provided in defining the other as personally accountable for the failure. The

hostile group may even go to the extent of ensuring that only negative motives and attitudes are available to the person in question, and may eliminate and exclude from contact those who persist in providing supportive vocabularies. While the key function of the friendly group is consolation, the key word here is castigation. Persistent conduct in this fashion leads to the emergence of "negative identities," weakened "self concepts," to depression and other more serious forms of mental illness, depending on how crucial the primary group in question was to the member, and how closely entrapped he was in it (Laing et al., 1970; Rose, 1962).[8] Some people manage to escape their limiting and hostile primary groups and seek friendlier groups, divorce being the more notorious example, with perhaps runaway children coming a close second. If one is not really entrapped, but merely unfortunate enough to be a member of a hostile primary group, one moves away, changes one's friends, joins a new club or starts drinking at a new bar, or joins a new political party, or converts to a different religion.[9]

POWER AND THE CONCEPT OF THE OTHER

There are, however, some unresolved issues in Mead's and Cooley's version of the other. The most critical of these issues is the notion of power

---

[8]The instructive case here is, of course, that of Maya in the Laing et al. (1970) study of the families of children considered insane.

[9]The claim is not being made that Cooley's entire work can be considered to develop a social as opposed to psychological ontology. In fact none other than Mead himself (cf. Farberman, 1970) in an examination of Cooley's work commented on its psychologistic nature (1930). However in his work on social organization (1909) as opposed to his work on human nature (1902), he develops the concept of the primary group as the ultimate feature of such organization as well as its indispensable instrument for the cultivation and maintenance of self and sentiments. It may yet become important to distinguish between Cooley's early and later work. The work on human nature indubitably comes closer to the viewpoint of Schutz, though as Mayrl points out, Cooley's stand "represents an advance over the phenomenologist" (1973:27).

and its consequence, conflict. Is a generalized other arrived at effortlessly, unambiguously, and peacefully? Perhaps it is achieved in many instances in that manner; there must be at least an equal number of occasions when the generalized other is a matter of choice and conflict, instances in which a generalized other had to be fought over. And when generalized others are matters of contention, one must assume that which is eventually selected is the more powerful one. Power in this case, of course, does not refer to physical power alone—it refers primarily to political and moral power. In fact, in social change of many sorts, what is ultimately involved is a change in the generalized other; conflicts of a lesser sort too are conflicts over which generalized other—the official or the unofficial, for example—is to prevail.

Here the best illustration is the entire explanatory paradigm that passes under the rubric of "labeling theory." This particular perspective has all but taken over the field of deviance and there also appears to have developed a reaction to it, with one of the founders, Lemert, suggesting some misgivings (1972). Yet this perspective has provided us with impressive understanding of the processes by which deviance is created: deviance is essentially created, they argue, by the selective reactions of society to certain acts by an agent, and the eventual acceptance of these reactions (articulated in the form of labels) by the agent himself. Needless to say, "society" expresses its reactions through various enforcers of its own—lobbies, legislatures, policemen, juries, judges, psychiatrists, etc., collectively called "moral entrepreneurs" by Becker (1962), which presumably includes also moralistic enforcers.

Yet no one in the labeling school seems to have asked the question, what constitutes this "society" that is reacting to the acts of the agent and labeling it as deviant? What standards and values does it use to arrive at its conclusions? Is it entirely arbitrary and capricious? A recent paper by Schervish argues that the founders and practitioners of the labeling perspective have not been careful to draw

out the full implications of the social psychological aspects of their view (1973). This criticism is quite a valid one, and it is equally valid to claim that they have not explored the societal implications of their perspective fully.

To do this, we have to ask the questions we raised above; the answers to these questions certainly must be in terms of Mead's notion of the generalized other and Marx's theory of ideology and conflict. Ideology is the term that Marx used to refer to that system of ideas that are used by a group/class to defend its privileges and assets in a given historical period; the other half of the concept is false consciousness—the thoughtways of a class that are unsuited to its historical role in the society, and leads to its greater victimization. In any case, both are forms of consciousness—in Burke's phrase, "rhetorics of motives" (1950)—that sustain a community of people. And for our purposes, the emphasis must be placed on the aspects of ideology in its function as a vocabulary of motives.

Hence, in social psychological terms, the generalized other is a relational entity and a historical, cultural, subcultural and situational variable.[10] Historically it changes and is changed in a dialectical process with social structure: it is used to change a social structure, and a changed social structure will sustain an altered generalized other. It is a cultural variable insofar as different cultures have different generalized others and within a culture there are, of course, contending and fractious subdivisions: for example, the law-abiding and law-enforcing sections, as opposed to those who think that laws are instruments of oppression and deprivation with one's task being to disobey them. And situationally, they are variables insofar as when confronted with a situation, humans have the freedom to reject a particular ideology and accept a new one: when apprehended, a lawless citizen can accept his culpability and promise to reform; or a

---

[10]See in this connection an instructive paper by Berger and Pullberg (1965).

law-abiding citizen can begin a life of crime after one or other crucial experience; or a person who has broken the law can successfully reject a label. The "label," or identity as we prefer to call it, that is fixed after an event such as this is subject to the dialectical process between self and other that we indicated earlier: the self does not accept the label willy-nilly. The acceptance itself is problematic and demands investigation. This is an issue for which the labeling theory does not give us any clear answer.

It is, of course, impossible to maintain that the labeling event is a simple one and that the labeling enterprise is always a successful enterprise. Situations and circumstances in which the labeling meets with resistance must be fully examined in order to reveal those circumstances in which labels stick—that is to say the labelers and labelees arrive at a common definition of the identity of the latter.

Clearly, the dimension of power is one circumstance that makes labels stick: the institutional, structural, ideological and interpersonal circumstance of power would compel labelees, or constrain and trap them into the labeled identity. For instance, the state and its institutional manifestations engage in the following processes to label successfully one of its citizens as a deviant: it creates a system of rules, regulations, customs, and conventions that collectively can be called its ideology, and it makes these publicly available; it catches some one who violates one or more of these rules, etc., then it has to prove that such violation occurred, and once such a proof is accepted by certain people, the label is fixed to the subject, and various consequences follow. The labelee at this stage—or at any stage—may reject the label and may defy the labelers and their standards and institutions on his own; yet the subject's destiny is determined by the fact that the label has been successfully fixed on him at the structural level. He will have a hard time sloughing off this label, and the sloughing-off process itself in the future will involve the same or similar institutional elements of the society. What is in-

volved here is the dimension of power—power that enables certain ideologies to be accepted; the labels are based on the ruling ideology of the society in which the labeling takes place.[11]

On the other extreme of this argument are those who willingly—and sometimes even with a great deal of alacrity—accept the label that some one wants to fix on them. Here the most noteworthy example is the relationship between the church and sin: the institutional structure and the hapless labelee have a prior commitment to the same ideology; when the circumstance and situation of one's life come together to make a sinner *confess* his sins and accept the succor of the church, two simultaneous processes are consummated: a label is successfully placed on a subject and his cooperation is elicited, while at the same time the institutional and ideological matrix that accomplished this is *legitimized*. Though we have used religion and sin as examples, they are to be construed as exemplifying a type rather than an instance. Even in criminal courts, political courts, and political parties (e.g., Communist Party), various forms of interpersonal relationships can elicit the "mea culpa" response with varying consequences to the self and its circumstances—including ideologies and institutions.

Finally, one must also consider those who choose labels for themselves, and arrange their lives in order to experience the consequences that certain labels will confer on them. Here we have in mind those who purposively have themselves committed to mental institutions because it gives them a respite from the anxieties and tribulations of daily life. The institution of the mental hospital, as well as the identity of the "mental patient," gives such respite: one does not have to act responsibly anymore; and one does not have to make decisions and engage in the continuous struggle to maintain oneself in the contacts and associations of what is usually called a normal life. The mental hospital

[11]See in this connection John Horton. Also see Laski (1947). The most recent attempt to open up the issue of power in symbolic interactionism is that of Peter Hall (1972).

with its identity becomes a resort—a last resort (Braginsky and King, 1970). There are also, it appears, those who commit various crimes and in effect *invite* the label of a deviant to be placed upon them, so that they can escape from the cares of daily life into a prison—literally, an escape from freedom (Barbara West, 1974).

For the general society too, these considerations apply: historical and structural factors favor the creation of new ideologies and utopias, and the contest between one of these ideologies and another is resolved ultimately by the power of the structures that sustain them. As Berger and Pullberg put it:

> (There is) an overall disintegration of social structures, necessarily entailing a disintegration of their taken-for-granted worlds. History affords a good many examples of how natural or man-caused catastrophes shook to its foundations a particular world, including its hitherto well-functioning unifying apparatus, bring forth doubt and skepticism concerning everything that had previously been taken-for-granted (1965).

In any case, there are contentious generalized others. The process by which these contentions are resolved constitutes the subject matter of a political sociology; an examination of how they are resolved is not necessary to a theory concerned with the emergence and sustenance of the self. It is sufficient to note that an ideology becomes available to the community and to its constituent selves in the form of (a) a clear and unambiguous statement of the general principles, with the receivers developing coherent and self-assured selves, even to the point of smugness, or (b) confused and mutually contradictory statements, causing the receivers to be confused, ambivalent, and excluded. Which form of statement one receives is not merely a matter of one's class position; certain historical periods can create confusion and uncertainty for a substantial section of the overall population.

Within this kind of formulation of the notion of ideology and the generalized other lies a pluralistic concept, with one or the other being dominant in one culture or subculture in any historical period. One or the other will be more powerful in a given social and historical situation, having arrived at that stage in a process of conflict and debate, to be replaced sooner or later by another through a similar process.

CONCLUSION

The contrast between the phenomenological and the interactionist versions of the importance of the "other" is rather striking. In Schutz's world, everyone is a stranger to everyone else and barely escapes being a stranger to himself as well. No other helps one in arriving at a definition of the situation; no other is around to construct a reality, clarify a doubt, express a concern, or introduce a suspicion into the ongoing social process. The person, "the solitary ego," sits by himself, in a strict inner loneliness and phenomenologizes the world. He has no use for an "other" except that he knows that there are "others": He perceives them and presumably understands what they do, but does not invite them in; they do not participate in the creation of consensual validations and most certainly do not engage in any conflict of intentionalities. In fact, conflict, dissensus, differences of opinion, and the nonmerger of intentionalities are unheard of in phenomenological versions. And these instances of consensus or conflict are created by conversation, by the exchange and mutual validation of motives and intentions or by the absence of such validation. In the event such a process of cooperation is achieved, one can talk of consensus, order, stability, etc.; in the event of it not being achieved, we can talk of conflict, disorder, change, etc. The "other" is imbued with his own intentionality, and hence reality is constructed, situations defined, through a process that can be described as a clash of intentionalities or a conflict of selves. After a struggle, mutuality of perspectives is achieved, with varying degrees of completeness and permanence; ecumenism can result only after sectarianism, and the ruling structure of reality is always the construction of who does the ruling in a society, community, or group. The "other" should not be viewed as a convenience by which the self escapes its own lonely plight, but as an insistent, vocal, objectifiable, and often irritating and domineering force. The "other" is not there only when we want it, but is there whether we want it or not—uninvited, omnipresent, and possessing some measure of power, some measure of influence and total intentionality.

The relationship between self and "other" is not best described as an intersubjective one, since there cannot be an interaction between two subjectives. Such a state of affairs is by the nature of the case an absurdity. What is subjective to a self will remain so, and no interaction can hence be created on that basis. The relationship between selves is a relationship between a self and an "other" in which each is subject to himself and an object to the other simultaneously. To achieve this, each person objectifies—dramatizes—his motives, intentions, attitudes, moods, values, with whatever method and instrument is available, so that the other person can *interact* with him on a plausible basis. The relationships between self and others are, in the strict sense of the term, *syntactical ones* rather than intersubjective ones; the self and other are predicated in an interaction, where they are both material objectified and vocal entities.

In the work of Mead and Cooley, the relationship between self and other is conceived as a relationship in which both the nature and the content of the other influence the self, and the self as an "other" reciprocally influences another. The self accomplishes this by taking the role, identity, and attitude of the other as well as by enabling others to take one's own role, identity, and attitude, and each incorporating them into their respective selves. This view enables us to take into account the fact of power and control in social life and permits one to articulate a social psychology in which the fact as well as the power of society,

distributed and expressed in various forms, becomes instrumental in fashioning the nature of the selves that emerge in it—in both the general case and the particular one.

REFERENCES

Barnes, Hazel E. 1973. *Sartre*. New York: Lippincott and Company.

Becker, Ernest. 1964. *The Revolution in Psychiatry*. Glencoe: The Free Press.

Becker, Howard S. 1962. *Outsiders*. Glencoe: The Free Press.

Becker, Howard. 1950. "Selves emerge when others emerge." Pp. 14–17 in *Through Values to Social Interpretation*. Durham, N.C.: Duke University Press.

Berger, Peter. 1964. *Invitation to Sociology*. New York: Doubleday & Co.

Berger, Peter and H. Kellner. 1971. "Marriage and the construction of reality." Pp. 49–72 in Hans Dreitzel (ed.), *Recent Sociology* II, London: The Macmillan Co., 1971.

Berger, Peter and Thomas Luckmann. 1968. *The Social Construction of Reality*. New York: Doubleday & Co.

Berger, Peter and S. Pullberg. 1965. "Reification and the sociological critique of consciousness." *History and Theory* 4:196–211.

Blumer, Herbert. 1969. "Society as symbolic interaction." Pp. 78–89 in *Symbolic Interactionism: Perspective and Method*. New Jersey: Prentice-Hall.

Braginsky, B. M., D. D. Braginsky and R. King. 1970. *Methods of Madness—The Mental Hospital as a Last Resort*. Holt, Rinehart and Winston: New York.

Burke, Kenneth. 1945. *A Rhetoric of Motives*. New Jersey: Prentice-Hall.

Cicourel, Aaron. 1970. "The acquisition of social structures: toward a developmental sociology of language and meaning." Pp. 136–169 in Jack Douglas (ed.), *Understanding Everyday Life*. Chicago: Aldine Publishing Co.

Cooley, C. H. 1962. *Social Organization*. New York: Schocken Books, 1909, republished 1962.

Douglas, Jack. 1970. "Understanding everyday life."

Pp. 3—44 in Jack Douglas (ed.), *Understanding Everyday Life*. Chicago: Aldine Publishing Co.

Farberman, H. 1970. "Mannheim, Cooley and Mead: toward a social theory of mentality." *The Sociological Quarterly* 11 (Winter):3—13.

Faris, Ellsworth. 1937. "The primary group: essence and accident." Pp. 3—24 in *The Nature of Human Nature*. New York: McGraw-Hill Book Co.

Garfinkel, Harold. 1967. "The common sense knowledge of social structures: the documentary method of interpretations in lay and professional fact finding." Pp. 76—103 in *Studies in Ethnomethodology*. Englewood Cliffs: Prentice-Hall.

Goffman, Erving. 1967. "The nature of deference and demeanor." Pp. 47—96 in *Interactional Ritual*. New York: Doubleday & Co.

Hall, P. 1972. "A symbolic interactionist analysis of politics." *Sociological Inquiry,* 42 (3—4):35—75.

Henry, Jules. 1973. *Pathways to Madness*. New York: Random House.

Holzner, Burkhardt. 1968. *Reality Construction in Society*. Cambridge: Schenkman Publishing Co.

Horton, J. 1966. "Order and conflict theories of social problems as competing ideologies." *The American Journal of Sociology* 71 (May):701—713.

Hughes, Everett. 1962. "What other?" Pp. 119—127 in Arnold Rose (ed.), *Human Behavior and Social Process*. Boston: Houghton Mifflin Co.

Kemper, T. 1972. "Division of labor: a post Durkheimian analytical view." *American Sociological Review* 37 (December):739—753.

Laing, R. D. and A. Esterson. 1970. *Sanity, Madness and the Family*. London: Penguin Books, Ltd.

Laski, Harold. 1947. *Crisis in the Modern Theory of the State*. London: Penguin Books, Ltd.

Lemert, Edwin. 1972. *Human Deviance, Social Problems and Social Control*. New Jersey: Prentice-Hall.

Levi-Straus, Claude. 1967. "Social structure." Pp. 269—319 in *Structural Anthropology*. New York: Doubleday & Co.

Lindesmith, Alfred and Anselm Strauss. 1970. *Social Psychology*. New York: Holt, Rinehart and Winston.

Luckmann, T. and P. Berger. 1964. "Social mobility and personal identity." *Archives de Europeane Sociologie* 5:331—343.

Malcolm, Norman. 1966. "Knowledge of other minds." Pp. 371—383 in G. Pitcher (ed.), *Philosophical Investigations—A Collection of Critical Essays*. New York: Doubleday & Co.

Marx, Karl. 1970. "Theses on Feuerbach." In *The German Ideology*. New York: International Publishers.

Mayrl, W. 1973. "Ethnomethodology: sociology without society." *Catalyst* No. 7 (Winter):15—29.

Mead, G. H. 1934. *Mind, Self and Society*. Chicago: University of Chicago Press.

Mills, C. W. 1948. "Situated actions and vocabularies of motives." *American Sociological Review* 5 (December):904—913.

Ortega y Gasset. 1956. "The self and other." In *The Dehumanization of Art and Other Essays*. New York: Doubleday Anchor.

Parsons, Talcott. 1937. *The Structure of Social Action*. Glencoe: The Free Press.

Pfuetze, Paul E. 1962. *Self, Society and Existence*. New York: Harper and Row.

Popper, Karl. 1963. *The Open Society and Its Enemies*. New York: Harper and Row.

Quinney, Richard. 1970. *The Social Reality of Crime*. Boston: Little Brown & Co.

Rose, Arnold. 1964. "Social mobility and social values." *Archives de Europeane Sociologie* 5:324—330.

———. 1962. "A social psychological theory of neuroses." Pp. 537—549 in *Human Behavior and Social Processes*. Boston: Houghton Mifflin.

Rose, J. 1969. "The role of the other in self-evaluation." *Sociological Quarterly* 10 (Fall):470—469.

Sartre, Jean Paul. 1956. *Being and Nothingness*. New York: Philosophical Library.

Schervish, P. G. 1973. "The labeling perspective: its bias and potential in the study of political deviance." *The American Sociologist* 8 (May):47—56.

Schutz, Alfred. 1967a. *Collected Works* Vol. I. The Hague: Martinus Nijhoff.

———. 1967b. *The Phenomenology of the Social World*. Evanston: Northwestern University.

————. 1964. *Collected Works* Vol. II. The Hague: Martinus Nijhoff.

Shibutani, Tamotsu. 1962. *Society and Personality.* Englewood Cliffs: Prentice-Hall.

Stone, Gregory P. and Harvey Farberman. 1970. *Social Psychology Through Symbolic Interaction.* Boston: Ginn-Blaisdel.

Travisano, Richard. 1970. "Alternation and conversion as qualitatively different transformations." In Gregory P. Stone and Harvey Farberman, *Social Psychology Through Symbolic Interaction.* Boston: Ginn-Blaisdel.

West, Barbara. 1974. "Prison as a station between the legs of a journey." Paper read at the Midwest Sociological Society meetings.

Zaner, R. 1961. "The theory of intersubjectivity: Alfred Schutz." *Social Research* 28 (Spring):72–93.

Zimmerman, Don and Lawrence D. Wieder. 1970. "Ethnomethodology and the problem of order: comment on Denzin." Pp. 287–302 in Jack Douglas (ed.), *Understanding Everyday Life.* Chicago: Aldine Publishing Co.

FORTY

HERBERT BLUMER, THE SCIENTIFIC ATTITUDE, AND THE PROBLEM OF DEMARCATION

DAVID RAUMA

It is almost certain that, any time a theoretical stance is taken, answers to key methodological issues are immediately suggested, if not already decided. Such is the case with Herbert Blumer and his symbolic interactionist perspective as, through his writings and criticisms, he attempts to deal with one of the more perplexing problems in the philosophy of science: the controversy over the place of inductive and deductive inference in scientific research. Among logicians and philosophers of science, there is no general agreement as to the exact nature or utility of either type of inference in scientific research. Various attempts have been made to resolve this issue. Logical positivists have attempted to develop an inductive logic, while others have concentrated on deductive logic. Among the points of agreement that are sometimes found between the conflicting viewpoints is the acknowledgment that the

SOURCE: David Rauma. "Herbert Blumer, the Scientific Attitude, and the Problem of Demarcation." Original paper prepared especially for this volume, 1980. Reprinted by permission of the author.

hypothetico-deductive method of inference is the method commonly used in science. Another point of agreement, and, oddly enough, the point at which divergence and controversy begin, is the acknowledgment that the hypothetico-deductive method is not strictly deductive, but that it is also inductive. At least one philosopher of science, Karl Popper, has approached this problem in a different manner. Popper denies that there is such a thing as inductive inference in science; rather, he sees the fundamental problem as one of demarcation between the empirical sciences and the nonempirical fields of logic and mathematics. In response to this problem of demarcation, Popper offers his system of methodological rules called "deductivism." Blumer also recognizes this more fundamental problem, but in relation to the empirical study of the social world. Blumer does not offer an explicit program as does Popper; instead, the solution he presents is an attitude. It is an attitude, derived partially from his symbolic interactionist perspective and partially from the canons of accepted scientific procedure, which, given the nature of the problem, may be quite successful in pointing sociology toward the fruitful scientific inquiry of the natural sciences.

Although philosophers of science cannot agree on the exact nature of inductive or deductive inference for scientific research, there are several points of agreement as to the basic nature of these types of inference. Two significant and interrelated distinctions can be made between them: demonstrative versus nondemonstrative forms of inference and amplative versus nonamplative forms of inference.[1] Demonstrative inferences are such that the conclusion of the inference follows necessarily from its premises. The conclusion cannot be false if the premises are all true. This type of inference is thus truth preserving, but it is also nonamplative. In order for the conclusion to follow necessarily from the premises, its content must be contained entirely within those premises. In other words, nothing new comes from the inference. Demonstrative nonamplative inferences are deductive inferences. Systems of deductive logic, such as propositional logic or Euclidean geometry, have been developed as closed systems of axioms and theorems for making correct deductive inferences. These systems are self-supporting—nothing outside the system is used to justify the inferences. The axioms are accepted as truths and the theorems are deduced from them. In contrast, nondemonstrative inferences may have false conclusions based on true premises because a leap of sorts is made from premises to conclusion. The content of the conclusion exceeds the content of the premises. Consequently, it is both nondemonstrative and amplative. Contained within this category of nondemonstrative amplative inferences are correct inductive inferences and fallacious arguments. To be a correct inductive inference the premises must lend some weight to the conclusion. As yet, no satisfactory system of inductive logic has been developed to separate correct inferences from fallacious arguments. Probability, for example, has been used to develop systems of inductive logic, but there is always some degree of doubt about an inference's validity if its correctness is stated as a matter of degree. The source of much of the debate over inductive and deductive inference in science is the place of the hypothetico-deductive method in relation to these distinctions between the types of inference.

The hypothetico-deductive method used in scientific research involves the deduction, from a theory, of a hypothesis detailing a specific instance of that theory in the empirical world. The hypothesis details the concepts within the theory in such a way as to allow its empirical testing. Through the use of deductive logic, the hypothesis follows necessarily from the theory and is a reformulation of its content in relation to the empirical world. The hypothesis is, in relation to the theory, a demonstrative nonamplative inference, but it is also, in relation to the empirical world, a nondemonstrative amplative inference. That the hypothesis is nondemonstrative and amplative in relation to empirical phenomena can be seen quite clearly by contrasting the nature of the theory it is deduced from with the nature of the test made of it. The theory is intended to apply universally to all empirical instances falling within its scope, but the test is made of a single instance only. Any theory, no matter what its scope or subject matter, is proposed as a universal explanation; otherwise, it is useless for explaining and predicting empirical phenomena. The theory and the hypothesis are inductive inferences because their universal content exceeds the particular cases used to test them. Working forward from theory to hypothesis involves a deductive inference, but working backward testing the theory on the basis of a particular instance involves an inductive inference. The deductive inference is truth preserving, while the inductive inference will remain in doubt. This is the source of the controversy among philosophers of science: how logically to justify the universality of scientific inferences that appear deductive but

[1] Wesley C. Salmon, *The Foundations of Scientific Research* (Pittsburgh: University of Pittsburgh Press, 1967), p. 8.

whose validity is questioned by the inductive nature of the empirical tests. The inductive logic that has been developed has not answered this question. For Herbert Blumer, however, this is not the major problem. The problem is instead to insure the empirical content of scientific theory. This is a more fundamental problem which has received clear formulation by Karl Popper.

Karl Popper attempts to resolve this difficulty of induction by denying that it is used in science. Popper sees the problem of induction as arising from confusion of the psychology of knowledge with the logic of knowledge.[2] The psychology of knowledge deals with empirical phenomena, along with common sense and scientific knowledge of them, but the logic of knowledge deals only with logical relations. The problem of induction has mistakenly been associated with problems of psychology, instead of solely with logical relations, in an attempt to provide psychological justification when deductive-like justification is not possible of inductive inferences. The universal validity of inferences in the empirical world can never be logically and correctly demonstrated on the basis of singular instances. In order for inductive inferences to be deductively valid, all possible empirical instances would have to be known and incorporated into a closed system of demonstrative and nonamplative inferences. Of course, this is based on the assumption that there are no final and absolute empirical truths to be discovered. The problem of inductive inferences is replaced by the more fundamental problem, in the logic of relations, of the demarcation between the empirical sciences on the one hand and metaphysical, logical, and mathematical statements on the other.[3] Despite the fact that they are never to be regarded as final truths, in order to make the empirical world intelligible, scientific theories are always intended to be universal statements from which hypotheses

are deduced as singular instances. There is no logical problem in justifying what is always accepted until proven false. The problem of demarcation is that of distinguishing between the empirical content of universals in scientific theory and the nonempirical content of universals in logic. The aim is not to justify universals statements on the basis of singular ones, for scientific theory, until shown false, is always accepted as universal; otherwise it is useless as an explanation. But the problem is how to determine whether scientific universals are about the world of experience, have empirical content, and are not far removed from experience as are logic and mathematics. This problem properly falls under the logic of relations, not under psychological justification. If theories are to make the world intelligible, there must be some means of determining whether they are actually about that world. Since there can be no correct rules of inductive inference, rules such as exist for deductive inferences, another route must be taken in demarcating logic from the empirical sciences.

For Popper the criterion of demarcation is falsifiability.[4] This criterion, at the center of Popper's deductivism, is based on the simple recognition that, while a single instance is never enough to prove the validity of a theory, a single instance is capable of disproving it. Scientific theories are to be distinguished from logic because of their potential falsifiability when tested against empirical evidence. Logic, as a system of given axioms and theorems, by definition cannot be proven false. Because there can be no logically valid universal empirical truths, Popper states that falsifiability is a matter of degree and not an absolute standard. The degree of falsifiability is to be judged by the content of the theory in question. The greater the empirical content of the theory, that is to say, the more asserted about the empirical world, the greater is its falsifiability. For example, of two competing theories, if one makes a greater number

[2]Karl R. Popper, *The Logic of Scientific Discovery* (New York: Harper & Row, 1968), p. 30.
[3]*Ibid.*, p. 34.
[4]*Ibid.*, p. 40.

of assertions or more specific assertions about the empirical phenomena under study, that theory is more specific about what events can and cannot occur, particularly what cannot occur, and has a greater degree of falsifiability. Making such specific and forbidding assertions greatly facilitates the discovery of falsifying instances. The scientist knows exactly what to look for, what to expect, and what not to expect. The fact that there can be and often are two or more competing theories, each of which has withstood testing, means that there must also be a standard for choosing between them. That standard is their degree of corroboration, which is a function of the number of tests each has survived and their degree of falsifiability as a measure of the severity of those tests. A theory with a greater degree of falsifiability faces a severer test because, by containing more specific assertions, there is a greater possibility of its being shown false.

From this brief outline of Popper's views it is obvious that, by eliminating the problem of induction in science, he has also eliminated the problem of how logically to justify scientific inference. It is now not a question of justifying such inferences, but of justifying their empirical content. Popper's deductivism, however, does raise some other problems. Since Popper states that his deductivism is only a system of methodological rules, not logical rules, there can be no final means of judging its superiority over other systems of rules. Instead, the importance of Popper's system is to show the nature of the problem of demarcation, a problem dealt with implicitly by Blumer in his writings on sociology and symbolic interactionism. While Popper focuses on science generally, Blumer deals with specific problems in social research, but with a firm understanding of the basic nature of science in general. Demarcation is indeed a more fundamental problem in the logic of knowledge, but Blumer has found a more fundamental solution than deductivism. It is a psychological solution— an attitude. However, as will be seen, it is not a

confusion of logic with psychology, but a complement to the logic of relations.

Blumer's general position on science is not, as some critics have contended, a rejection of deductive inference that exclusively favors induction. To cast Blumer's position in these terms is to miss entirely the major thrust of his writings. Actually, Blumer holds the standard view that research is based upon the hypothetico-deductive method in which the scientist approaches his subject matter with a prior theoretical scheme, deduces an hypothesis, tests the hypothesis, and analyzes the test in relation to the theory. In fact, Blumer looks to the natural sciences as the model of scientific inquiry, not for its theories or its techniques, but for the empirical-minded nature of such inquiry and the constant interplay between theory and research.[5] It is this attitude that Blumer finds to be the real nature of scientific inquiry. The attitude Blumer is conveying in his writings is, at its simplest, a respect for empirical phenomena and a need to test scientific theories against them. Natural scientists long ago abandoned philosophical and metaphysical preoccupations, and, by doing so, only then did they begin to make the progress that is the envy of the social sciences. This abandonment was, in turn, an embrace of research, research guided by theory with constant feedback to that theory. Natural scientists propose theories, if none exist already, find a means of testing them, analyze the tests, and refine or discard the theory, depending upon the outcome of the test. This procedure, the epitome of scientific method, is the reason for the progress and success of the natural sciences. That success is not due, as is often believed, to refined techniques and sophisticated theories. Such techniques and theories do not come into being by themselves, nor are they the result of mathematical, logical, or philosophical reasoning. Both are the products of research

[5]Herbert Blumer, *Symbolic Interactionism* (Englewood Cliffs, N.J.: Prentice-Hall, 1969), p. 40.

and more research. Research demarcates the empirical sciences from nonempirical fields. Research has to start somewhere, often with crude techniques, by comparison with later refinements, and very little theory to guide it. Research is the heart of science, guided by theory that is reanalyzed in the face of new evidence. This is the major import of Blumer's writings on social theory and research. It is the research attitude that demarcates science from logic. Only scientists feel the need to test their theories empirically. Logicians need not bother, for empirical evidence is of no matter for them. Of course, it is not quite this simple, as Blumer shows through his elaboration of the attitude to include special problems in studying social phenomena. It is not only that sociologists are not as research minded as they should be, for many, if not most, are, but these special problems make it impossible for sociology to be a carbon copy of the natural sciences. The special nature of social phenomena, along with the special problems they create, is seen clearly in Blumer's symbolic interactionist perspective.

According to Blumer, symbolic interactionism is based on three simple premises: human beings act toward objects, including other human beings, on the basis of the meanings those objects have for them; these meanings are derived from, or arise out of, interaction among human beings; and meanings are handled in, and modified through, a self-conscious interpretive process used by each individual in dealing with the objects he encounters.[6] Important corollaries to these premises are: humans can view themselves as objects and interact with themselves in the interpretive process; and group life consists of individuals in action, either by themselves, collectively, or on behalf of others, but always in relation to other individuals, fitting together their lines of action to achieve individual and group ends. Individual human beings are neither pushed nor pulled about by social and

psychological forces beyond their control; rather, the interpretive process enables them to contribute actively to the construction and continuation of the social world they are involved in. The social world is indeed real. Other individuals and groups, as well as physical objects, have an obdurate quality about them, and the handling of meanings enables individuals to deal with it in order to align their actions with those of others. For the social scientist, this view of social life raises certain questions and problems about the possibilities for its study, especially because of the self-conscious interpretation going on during social interaction. Meanings are not static and may be in an almost constant state of change, depending upon the situation. How then, if meanings and actions can and do change in the course of interaction, can the scientific method be used to study empirical social phenomena? For Blumer the answer is clearly in the research attitude of science, exemplified by his concerns over social theory and social research techniques.

Blumer's concern with social theory centers primarily around the scientific concept. Sociology's concepts are, in his words, "distressingly vague" and can lead to several major problems often associated with social theory. Theory is valuable only when it connects with the empirical world in a manner that is fruitful for research. Concepts are the only means of establishing such a connection. In the natural sciences, concepts such as atom, electron, mass, and acceleration have clear definitions that enable any scientist to move directly from the theory interconnecting the concepts to their empirical instances. Since these concepts clearly identify their empirical instances, the scientist knows what to look for, whether he has found it, and whether the instance corroborates or falsifies the theory. However, in sociology concepts such as norm, institution, role, and social structure have at best vague definitions that depend upon the particular researcher for additional clarity. Three common deficiencies in social theory

---

[6]*Ibid.*, p. 2.

can be traced to this vagueness: social theory is susceptible to schemes and analogies developed outside its own empirical subject matter; social theory is deficient in guiding empirical research; and social theory benefits little from the constantly increasing number of ''facts'' coming from the research carried on with or without its guidance.[7] Without clear and unambiguous concepts to guide research in the development and refinement of its own theory, social theory can easily incorporate organic or mechanistic analogies within its explanations of social phenomena. The difficulty with these analogies is that social phenomena, instead of being studied in their own right, will be molded to fit these handy schemes. Since they do not already contain concepts developed through previous social research, it is likely that social phenomena will be made to fit whatever concepts are already there. As for their guidance of research, to borrow from Popper, ambiguous concepts assert little that is specific. Consequently, the scientist cannot be sure, on the basis of his theory, of what to look for in order to test the theory. The theory cannot be adequately tested and may not be shown false if it is. The ''facts'' that are presently accumulated may either be worthless, possibly due to a lack of theory to guide their systematic collection, or presently unusable because vague concepts deter their being incorporated into existing theory.

These problems with social concepts, and with social theory, are the result not of the immaturity of the social sciences or deficiencies in their methods, but precisely the sensitizing nature of their concepts.[8] In the natural sciences, concepts are ordinarily definitive because they refer precisely to the common features of a class of objects through precise definition in terms of fixed attributes. A definitive concept allows any scientist to move from theory to research through the clear specification of attributes to be found in every

empirical instance. It also makes a theory more testable and more easily falsifiable. This is not the case with concepts that refer to social phenomena inasmuch as there is the ongoing interpretation of meanings by individuals fitting together their lines of action. Every object has some distinctive or unique character about it and lies in the context of the actions of distinct and unique individuals. It is therefore unrealistic, if not impossible, to develop definitive concepts when social phenomena do not have the fixed attributes necessary to anchor these concepts. Definitive concepts cannot possibly represent fully the interpretive process in interaction. Rather, social concepts must be seen as sensitizing and only pointing toward their empirical instances. Recognizing that sociology's concepts are sensitizing does not automatically resolve the problems of social theory; in fact, it would seem to add to them, but this does not have to be the case. Sensitizing concepts do not rule out the deduction of an hypothesis from a theory. Instead, sensitizing concepts mean that both theory and hypothesis will not be definitive in their empirical content. Logically correct deductive inferences are possible, for deductive inference does not depend upon empirical content. It is the necessary feature of deductive inference that it lack empirical content; otherwise it could not be a system of demonstrative and nonamplative inferences. As a demonstrative and nonamplative inference, the hypothesis will contain only what is contained within the theory.

Nor do sensitizing concepts destroy the universality of theory because that universality is accepted as a matter of course. As Popper has pointed out, the universality of theory is accepted until shown to be false. Universality can only be, and in the case of science must be, accepted for the purpose of explanation and prediction, just as the axioms of deductive logic are accepted as truths. The difference is that scientific theories are purported to have empirical content and must be tested against evidence. If the problem of induction is considered, it seems even more impossible to solve from Blumer's perspective: how to justify logically

---

[7]Herbert Blumer, ''What Is Wrong with Social Theory?,'' *American Sociological Review* 19 (February, 1954):4.

[8]*Ibid.*, p. 7.

universal theoretical statements when each empirical instance is admitted to be unique. But this is the unresolvable problem of inductive inference whether the concepts be definitive or sensitizing. No theory, no set of concepts, no methodological procedure can ever logically justify inductive inferences. Definitive concepts are no assurance against their own falsification. Blumer's aim in showing the sensitizing nature of sociology's concepts is not to make sociological research impossible, but to emphasize the even greater need for sociologists to do research, to be ready to modify their theories, and to be ready to reject those theories if necessary. This is the scientific attitude, and only it can assure the empirical content of scientific theory. Sensitizing concepts, although they can never be definitive, can be refined through research. There is, after all, some commonality as individuals fit together their actions. The problem for sociologists is to find it.

Blumer's attitude in relation to sociological research methods is exemplified by his criticisms of variable research.[9] The major problem with this type of research is that it too often lacks respect for the social phenomena it is used to study. In trying to establish clear causal relationships, the use of independent and dependent variables ignores the interpretive process that takes place between the causes of behavior, the independent variables, and the behaviors themselves, the dependent variables. The interpretive process may be set up as an intervening variable or a series of intervening variables, but this turns the process into an almost neutral medium the influence of the independent variable flows through. This self-conscious process is a creative one and must be respected for that quality. This general criticism, lack of respect for empirical social phenomena, can be made of other research techniques used by social scientists. Operational definitions, for example, are not at all suitable for insuring the empirical content of con-

cepts in social theory.[10] Operational definitions in the natural sciences help provide clear definitions of concepts by providing set procedures for measuring empirical instances. Set procedures presuppose the fixed attributes of definitive concepts, but sensitizing concepts, with many diverse instances, cannot be adequately represented by a single operational definition. The intelligence quotient is a ready example since, although it yields clear and replicable data, intelligence manifests itself in many more ways than are measured by the standardized tests used to determine the quotient. Here is an instance in which many tests of a measure have shown its reliability, though never its validity, and such tests have in no way insured its empirical content when it is known and stated that intelligence involves more than the tests measure. Again, the solution Blumer proposes is research into and respect for the nature of social phenomena. Relying solely on high-powered techniques or sophisticated theories is not enough without a respect for the social phenomena they are applied to and their continued test in research. Because sociology's concepts are sensitizing, sociologists must be willing to examine and analyze every empirical instance they can in order to discover their nature and their common features. Research should not be limited because some areas of social interaction seem unyielding to precise quantification or elaborate experimental designs. Again, research has to start somewhere and at some stage of sophistication. If present methods do not seem appropriate, others can be developed. The only truly scientific method has been the procedure of starting with a theory, deducing its implications in relation to empirical phenomena, and analyzing the theory on the basis of an empirical test. All other procedures are refinements of this basic method and are intended to make research easier and the analysis clearer in its implications for the theory.

To return to the problem of demarcation, insur-

[9]Herbert Blumer, "Sociological Analysis and the 'Variable'," *American Sociological Review* 21 (December, 1956):683–689.

[10]Blumer, *Symbolic Interactionism*, p. 30.

ing the empirical content of scientific theories, the scientific attitude seems to be the most fruitful approach for dealing with it. Popper recognizes the problem, but, as he himself states, his deductivism is a set of methodological rules whose validity cannot be proven. Attempts to develop methods, experimental designs, and other techniques are certainly necessary, but none of these can be viewed as ends in themselves. Historically, scientific theories and methods are replaced by new scientific theories and new methods. Since science abandoned philosophy for empirical research, what has survived has been this empirical mindedness. Charles Darwin is one of the exemplars of this attitude. Darwin explored and familiarized himself with the natural world that was his subject matter. Above all else, he analyzed what he found. Can Darwin's procedure be called methodologically unsound because he did not have the benefit of modern experimental designs or statistical techniques, when the results of his exploration and analysis far outweigh any of the particular methods he used? Techniques are like theories. Both are tools for making the world intelligible and must be developed, refined, and especially tested through their application in research. Reduced again to its simplest terms, this is all that Blumer is proposing. What separates science from philosophy, logic, and mathematics is the need for scientists to do research. This empirical mindedness, which includes a respect for the nature of empirical phenomena as worthy and capable of study, is the key to the success of the natural sciences. Sociology, if it intends to be a science, can do no more and be no less.

REFERENCES

Blumer, Herbert. "What Is Wrong with Social Theory?," *American Sociological Review* 19 (February, 1954):3—10.

———. "Sociological Analysis and the 'Variable'," *American Sociological Review* 21 (December, 1956):683—690.

———. *Symbolic Interactionism.* Englewood Cliffs, N.J.: Prentice-Hall, 1969.

Popper, Karl R. *The Logic of Scientific Discovery.* New York: Harper & Row, 1968.

Salmon, Wesley C. *The Foundations of Scientific Inference.* Pittsburgh: University of Pittsburgh Press, 1967.

NAME INDEX

SUBJECT INDEX